THE WALKERTON INQUIRY

The Honourable Dennis R. O'Connor, Commissioner

180 Dundas St. W., 22nd Floor
Toronto, ON M5G 1Z8

Tel:	Toronto Area	(416) 326-4498
	Outside Toronto Area	1-877-543-8598
Fax:	(416) 327-8782	

Ontario

**LA COMMISSION
D'ENQUÊTE WALKERTON**

L'honorable Dennis R. O'Connor, Commissaire

180, rue Dundas Ouest, 22 étage
Toronto, ON M5G 1Z8

Tél:	Région de Toronto	(416) 326-4498
	À l'extérieur de Toronto	1-877-543-8598
Télée:	(416) 327-8782	

January 14, 2002

The Honourable David Young
Ministry of the Attorney General
720 Bay Street, 11th Floor
Toronto, Ontario
M5G 2K1

Dear Mr. Attorney:

With this letter I transmit my Part 1 report of The Walkerton Inquiry.

Yours very truly,

Dennis R. O'Connor
Commissioner

Encl.

Walkerton
220 Trillium Court, P.O. Box 789, Bldg. 3, Unit 4, Walkerton, ON N0G 2V0   (519) 881-3936 (tel.) (519) 881-4706 (fax)
220 Cour Trillium, C.P. 789, édifice 3, pièce 4, Walkerton, ON N0G 2V0   (519) 881-3936 (tél.) (519) 881-4706 (fac.)

Part One

Report of the Walkerton Inquiry:

The Events of May 2000 and Related Issues

The Honourable Dennis R. O'Connor

Published by
Ontario Ministry of the Attorney General

© Queen's Printer for Ontario 2002

Cover Design: Tania Craan Design

ISBN: 0-7794-2559-6

Copies of this and other Ontario Government publications are available from Publications Ontario at 880 Bay St., Toronto. Out-of-town customers may write to Publications Ontario, 50 Grosvenor St., Toronto M7A 1N8. Telephone (416) 326-5300 or toll-free in Ontario 1-800-668-9938. Fax (416) 326-5317. Internet: www.publications.gov.on.ca. The hearing impaired may call toll-free in Ontario 1-800-268-7095. MasterCard and Visa are accepted. Cheques and money orders should be made payable to the Minister of Finance. Prepayment is required.

Contents

Detailed Contents

Chapter 1   Introduction

Chapter 2   The Impact on Walkerton

Chapter 3   The Events in Walkerton in May 2000

Chapter 4   The Physical Causes of the Contamination

Chapter 5   The Role of the Public Utilities Commission Operators

Chapter 6   The Role of the Walkerton Public Utilities Commissioners

Chapter 7   The Roles of the Municipalities and Mayors

Chapter 8   The Role of the Public Health Authorities

Chapter 9   The Role of the Ministry of the Environment

Chapter 10   The Failure to Enact a Notification Regulation

Chapter 11 The Ministry of the Environment Budget Reductions

Chapter 12 Other Government Policies, Practices, and Procedures

Chapter 13 The Legislative, Regulatory, and Policy Framework

Chapter 14   The Process of Part 1 of the Inquiry

Appendices

A   Order in Council

B (i)   List of Parties
B (ii)   List of Witnesses

C (i)   Letter to the Residents of Walkerton
C (ii)   List of Walkerton Presenters

D (i)   Rules of Procedure and Practice
D (ii)   Amendment to Rules of Procedure and Practice
D (iii) Letter Re: Standing
D (iv)   Procedural Guidelines for Part 1A
D (v)   Procedural Guidelines for Part 1B

E (i)   Notice of Standing Hearing
E (ii)   Ruling on Standing and Funding
E (iii) Supplementary Ruling on Standing and Funding

F (i)   Funding Recommendations
F (ii)   Funding Guidelines - Rates

G   Summons to Witness

H (i)   Document Request
H (ii)   Search Warrant

Chapter 1   Introduction

Contents

Chapter 1   Introduction

1.1 Background

Until May 2000, there was little to distinguish Walkerton from dozens of small towns in southern Ontario. It is a pretty town, located at the foot of gently rolling hills, along the banks of the Saugeen River. Walkerton traces its history back to 1850, when Joseph Walker, an Irish settler, built a sawmill on the river, starting a settlement that adopted his name. In time, it became the county seat for Bruce County. The name survived an amalgamation in 1999, when Walkerton was joined with two farming communities to form the Municipality of Brockton. Walkerton has kept its small-town look and feel. Many of its 4,800 residents make their living from businesses that serve the surrounding farms.

In May 2000, Walkerton's drinking water system became contaminated with deadly bacteria, primarily *Escherichia coli* O157:H7.[1] Seven people died, and more than 2,300 became ill. The community was devastated. The losses were enormous. There were widespread feelings of frustration, anger, and insecurity.

The tragedy triggered alarm about the safety of drinking water across the province. Immediately, many important questions arose. What actually happened in Walkerton? What were the causes? Who was responsible? How could this have been prevented? Most importantly, how do we make sure this never happens again?

The government of Ontario responded by calling this Inquiry. I have divided the mandate of the Inquiry into two parts. The first, which I refer to as Part 1, relates only to the events in Walkerton. It directs me to inquire into the circumstances that caused the outbreak – including, very importantly, the effect, if any, of government policies, procedures, and practices. The second, Part 2, goes beyond the events in Walkerton, directing me to look into other matters I consider necessary to ensure the safety of Ontario's drinking water. The overarching purpose of both parts of the Inquiry is to make findings and recommendations to ensure the safety of the water supply system in Ontario.

Because of their importance to the community, the hearings for Part 1 were held in Walkerton. Over the course of nine months, the Inquiry heard from

---

[1] The abbreviation for *Escherichia coli*, *E. coli*, is frequently used in this report.

114 witnesses, including residents of the town, local officials, senior civil servants, two former ministers of the environment, and the Premier. This report outlines my findings and recommendations for Part 1 of the Inquiry.

The Part 2 process has also been completed, and I expect to deliver my report for Part 2 in approximately two months.

I would encourage those who are interested to read the report in full. For convenience, however, I begin this report with a brief summary, in point form, of my most significant conclusions.[2] That is followed by an overview of the entire Part 1 report and then, beginning in Chapter 2, by the full text of the report itself.

1.2 Summary of Conclusions

- Seven people died, and more than 2,300 became ill. Some people, particularly children, may endure lasting effects.

- The contaminants, largely *E. coli* O157:H7 and *Campylobacter jejuni*, entered the Walkerton system through Well 5 on or shortly after May 12, 2000.

- The primary, if not the only, source of the contamination was manure that had been spread on a farm near Well 5. The owner of this farm followed proper practices and should not be faulted.

- The outbreak would have been prevented by the use of continuous chlorine residual and turbidity monitors at Well 5.

- The failure to use continuous monitors at Well 5 resulted from shortcomings in the approvals and inspections programs of the Ministry of the Environment (MOE). The Walkerton Public Utilities Commission (PUC) operators lacked the training and expertise necessary either to identify the vulnerability of Well 5 to surface contamination or to understand the resulting need for continuous chlorine residual and turbidity monitors.

---

[2] Reference should be made to the report itself for the precise wording of my conclusions and for qualifications on those conclusions.

- The scope of the outbreak would very likely have been substantially reduced if the Walkerton PUC operators had measured chlorine residuals at Well 5 daily, as they should have, during the critical period when contamination was entering the system.

- For years, the PUC operators engaged in a host of improper operating practices, including failing to use adequate doses of chlorine, failing to monitor chlorine residuals daily, making false entries about residuals in daily operating records, and misstating the locations at which microbiological samples were taken. The operators knew that these practices were unacceptable and contrary to MOE guidelines and directives.

- The MOE's inspections program should have detected the Walkerton PUC's improper treatment and monitoring practices and ensured that those practices were corrected.

- The PUC commissioners were not aware of the improper treatment and monitoring practices of the PUC operators. However, those who were commissioners in 1998 failed to properly respond to an MOE inspection report that set out significant concerns about water quality and that identified several operating deficiencies at the PUC.

- On Friday, May 19, 2000, and on the days following, the PUC's general manager concealed from the Bruce-Grey-Owen Sound Health Unit and others the adverse test results from water samples taken on May 15 and the fact that Well 7 had operated without a chlorinator during that week and earlier that month. Had he disclosed either of these facts, the health unit would have issued a boil water advisory on May 19, and 300 to 400 illnesses would have been avoided.

- In responding to the outbreak, the health unit acted diligently and should not be faulted for failing to issue the boil water advisory before Sunday, May 21. However, some residents of Walkerton did not become aware of the boil water advisory on May 21. The advisory should have been more broadly disseminated.

- The provincial government's budget reductions led to the discontinuation of government laboratory testing services for municipalities in 1996. In implementing this decision, the government should have enacted a regulation mandating that testing laboratories immediately and directly notify both the MOE and the Medical Officer of Health about adverse results. Had the government done this, the boil water advisory would have been issued by May 19 at the latest, thereby preventing hundreds of illnesses.

- The provincial government's budget reductions made it less likely that the MOE would have identified both the need for continuous monitors at Well 5 and the improper operating practices of the Walkerton PUC.

- This report contains some recommendations directed toward ensuring the safety of drinking water in Ontario. However, the majority of my recommendations in that respect will be in the Part 2 report of this Inquiry.

1.3 An Overview of This Report

1.3.1   The Impact on Walkerton

The first indications of widespread illness began to emerge on Thursday, May 18, 2000. Twenty children were absent from Mother Teresa School, and two children were admitted to the Owen Sound hospital with bloody diarrhea. On Friday, May 19, there was an enteric outbreak among residents of a retirement home. People began to contact the Walkerton hospital, other nearby hospitals, and local physicians to complain of symptoms of enteric illness, including bloody diarrhea, stomach pain, and nausea. More students stayed home from school.

Over the next several days, illness spread quickly in the community. The Walkerton hospital was inundated with telephone calls and with patients visiting the emergency department. Patients were airlifted from Walkerton to London for emergency treatment. The first person died on Monday, May 22.

The story of the outbreak involves much more than a description of the clinical symptoms of the illnesses, the medical treatment, and the numbers of people who became ill and died. Most important are the stories of the suffering endured by those who were infected; the anxiety of their families, friends, and neighbours; the losses experienced by those whose loved ones died; and the uncertainty and worry about why this happened and what the future would bring.

In July 2000, I convened four days of hearings in Walkerton and invited the people of the town to come and talk about the impact of the outbreak on their lives. There were more than 50 presentations: some by individuals, some by groups, and others by families. Some were made in public, and others, when requested, in private. Those stories told a tale of great pain and suffering. They are a vital part of this Inquiry. I have summarized some of these stories in Chapter 2 of this report. Transcripts of all of these stories are part of the public record of the Inquiry and will remain as a lasting account of the hardship endured by the community.

1.3.2   The Bacteria

The vast majority of the deaths and illnesses in Walkerton were caused by two bacteria, *E. coli* O157:H7 and *Campylobacter jejuni*.[3] *E. coli* O157:H7 is a subgroup of *E. coli*. A person infected with *E. coli* O157:H7 experiences intestinal disease lasting on average four days, but sometimes longer. After 24 hours, the person often experiences bloody diarrhea, and in some cases very severe abdominal pain. The illness usually resolves itself without treatment, other than rehydration and electrolyte replacement.

For some people, particularly children under five years of age and the elderly, *E. coli* O157:H7 infection can have more serious consequences. It may cause hemolytic uremic syndrome (HUS) after five to ten days of infection, leading to anemia, low platelet counts, acute kidney failure, and in some cases death.

Campylobacter jejuni, the most common type of *Campylobacter*, was also implicated in the Walkerton outbreak. With *Campylobacter*, diarrhea usually lasts two to seven days, and the fatality rate is much lower than for *E. coli* O157:H7.

Cattle are a common source of *E. coli* O157:H7 and *Campylobacter*. The bacteria can thrive in the gut and intestines of cattle, are commonly found in cattle manure, and can survive in the environment for extended periods. These bacteria may be transmitted to humans in a number of different ways, one of which is through drinking water.

---

[3] Disease-causing agents such as bacteria are referred to as "pathogens," a term generally used elsewhere in this report.

1.3.3 The Events of May 2000

The Walkerton water system is owned by the municipality. For years it was operated by the Walkerton Public Utilities Commission (PUC). Stan Koebel was the PUC's general manager, and his brother Frank Koebel was its foreman.

In May 2000, the water system was supplied by three groundwater sources: Well 5, Well 6, and Well 7. The water pumped from each well was treated with chlorine before entering the distribution system.

I have concluded that the overwhelming majority of the contaminants, if not all of them, entered the water system through Well 5.[4] I have also concluded that the residents became exposed to the contamination on or shortly after May 12.

It rained heavily in Walkerton from May 8 to May 12: 134 mm of rain fell during these five days. The heaviest rainfall occurred on Friday, May 12, when 70 mm fell.

During the period from May 9 to May 15, Well 5 was the primary source pumping water into the distribution system. Well 6 cycled on and off periodically, and Well 7 was not in operation.

On Saturday, May 13, Frank Koebel performed the routine daily check of the operating wells. The purpose of the daily checks was to record data on pumping rate flows and chlorine usage, and, most importantly, to measure the chlorine residuals in the treated water.[5] However, for more than 20 years, it had been the practice of PUC employees not to measure the chlorine residuals on most days and to make fictitious entries for residuals in the daily operating sheets. Stan Koebel often participated in this practice.

On May 13, Frank Koebel did not measure the chlorine residual at Well 5. It is very likely that at this time, *E. coli* O157:H7 and *Campylobacter* bacteria were overwhelming the chlorine being added at the well and were entering into the distribution system. Had Mr. Koebel measured the chlorine residual, he would

---

[4] Although there is some evidence that Well 6 was susceptible to surface contamination, there is no evidence to support a finding that contamination entered the system through Well 6 during the critical period.

[5] One of the purposes of measuring chlorine residuals is to determine whether contamination is overwhelming the disinfectant capacity of the chlorine that has been added to the water.

almost certainly have learned that there was no residual – a result that should have alerted him to the problem so that he could take the proper steps to protect the system and the community.

The next day, Sunday, May 14, Frank Koebel again checked Well 5. He followed the usual procedure and did not measure the chlorine residual. The same omission occurred on Monday, May 15, although it is not clear which PUC employee checked Well 5 on that day. Well 5 was turned off at 1:15 p.m. on May 15.

On the morning of May 15, Stan Koebel returned to work after having been away from Walkerton for more than a week. He turned on Well 7 at 6:15 a.m. Shortly after doing so, he learned that a new chlorinator for Well 7 had not been installed and that the well was therefore pumping unchlorinated water directly into the distribution system. He did not turn off the well; rather, he allowed the well to operate without chlorination until noon on Friday, May 19, when the new chlorinator was installed.[6]

On the morning of May 15, another PUC employee, Allan Buckle, took three water samples for microbiological testing. The sampling bottles were labelled "Well 7 raw," "Well 7 treated," and "125 Durham Street." I am satisfied that these samples were not taken at the locations indicated, but rather were most likely taken at the Walkerton PUC workshop, which is near to and downline from Well 5. It was not unusual for PUC employees to mislabel the bottles so that they did not reflect the actual locations at which water samples were taken.

The samples taken by Mr. Buckle, together with one other sample taken from the distribution system by Stan Koebel and three samples from a watermain construction site in town, were forwarded to A&L Canada Laboratories for testing. These samples are very significant, for reasons I explain below.

The samples were received by A&L on Tuesday, May 16. It takes a minimum of 24 hours to perform microbiological tests. On Wednesday, May 17, A&L telephoned Stan Koebel and advised him that the three samples from the construction site, which came from water pumped from the Walkerton distribution system, were positive for *E. coli* and total coliforms.

---

[6] After Well 5 was turned off at 1:15 p.m. on May 15, Well 7 was the only source of supply until Well 5 was turned on again on Saturday, May 20. Well 6 did not operate during this time.

A&L also reported to Mr. Koebel that the Walkerton water system samples "didn't look good either." One of those samples had undergone the more elaborate membrane filtration test, and the resulting plate was "covered" with total coliforms and *E. coli*. A&L faxed the results from the construction site samples to the PUC that morning and faxed those from the Walkerton water system samples in the early afternoon. The faxed report showed that three of the four samples from the Walkerton system had tested positive for total coliforms and *E. coli*, and that the samples that had undergone membrane filtration testing showed gross contamination.

A&L did not forward these results to the MOE's area office in Owen Sound. As a result, the local health unit[7] was not notified of the results until six days later, on May 23. I discuss the significance of this delay below.

The first public indications of widespread illness occurred on Thursday, May 18.[8] Two children were admitted to the Owen Sound hospital with symptoms including bloody diarrhea, a large number of children were absent from school, and members of the public contacted the Walkerton PUC office to inquire about the safety of the water. A staff member, who discussed the matter with Stan Koebel, assured them that the water was safe.

The next day, the scope of the outbreak grew quickly. More students stayed home from school. Residents in a retirement home and a long-term care facility, along with many others in the community, developed diarrhea and vomiting. A local doctor saw 12 or 13 patients with diarrhea.

Also on that day, Dr. Kristen Hallet, a pediatrician in Owen Sound, suspecting that the illnessees of the two children admitted to the hospital the previous day had been caused by *E. coli*, contacted the local health unit. The health unit began an investigation, during which its staff spoke to persons in authority at schools, the local hospitals, and the retirement home in Walkerton, as well as to the PUC's general manager, Stan Koebel.

When the health unit reached Mr. Koebel by telephone in the early afternoon of Friday, May 19, he was told that a number of children were ill with diarrhea and stomach cramps, and he was asked whether there was any problem with

---

[7] The Bruce-Grey-Owen Sound Health Unit.
[8] People had begun to experience symptoms several days before this, but there do not appear to have been public indications of an outbreak until May 18.

the water. Mr. Koebel replied that he thought the water was "okay." By then, he knew of the adverse results from the May 15 samples. He did not disclose the adverse results in the conversation with the health unit, nor did he disclose the fact that Well 7 had operated without a chlorinator from May 15 until noon that day. During another call from the health unit later that afternoon, Mr. Koebel repeated his assurances about the safety of the town's water.

The health unit did not issue a boil water advisory until two days later, on Sunday, May 21, at 1:30 p.m. I am satisfied that if Mr. Koebel had been forthcoming with the health unit on May 19 about the adverse sample results or about the fact that Well 7 had operated without chlorination, as he should have been, a boil water advisory would have been issued that day.

After speaking with staff of the health unit on May 19, Mr. Koebel began to flush and superchlorinate the system. He continued to do so throughout the following weekend. As time passed, he successfully increased the chlorine residuals both at the wellheads and in the distribution system.

I am satisfied that Mr. Koebel was concerned during the weekend about people becoming ill from the water and that he did not know that *E. coli* could be fatal. He believed that superchlorinating the water would destroy any contaminants present in the water. However, I am also satisfied that Mr. Koebel withheld information from the health unit because he did not want health officials to know that he had operated Well 7 without a chlorinator. He knew that having done so was unacceptable and was concerned that the operation of Well 7 without a chlorinator would come to light. There is no excuse for Mr. Koebel's concealing this information from the health unit. Ironically, it was not the operation of Well 7 without a chlorinator that caused the contamination of Walkerton's water. As I said above, the contamination entered the system through Well 5, from May 12 (or shortly afterward) until that well was shut off at about 1:15 p.m. on May 15.

As early as Thursday, May 18, and Friday, May 19, some people in the community believed that there was something wrong with the water and began to take steps to prevent further infection. For example, on May 19, Brucelea Haven, a long-term care facility, decided to boil the municipal water or use bottled water. Mr. and Mrs. Reich, whose seven-year-old daughter had been admitted to the hospital in Owen Sound, decided that their family, as well as their employees, should drink only bottled water.

On Saturday, May 20, a stool sample from one of the children at the Owen Sound hospital tested positive for *E. coli* 0157:H7 on a presumptive basis. By this time, the outbreak was expanding very rapidly.

On May 20, the health unit spoke to Stan Koebel on two occasions. Mr. Koebel informed the health unit of the chlorine residuals in the system, but again he did not reveal the results from the May 15 samples or the fact that Well 7 had been operated without chlorination. The health unit took some comfort about the safety of the water from Mr. Koebel's reports that he was obtaining chlorine residual measurements in the distribution system. Over the course of the day, as concern spread within the community, the health unit relied on what Mr. Koebel said and assured callers that the water was not the problem.

On Saturday afternoon, Robert McKay, an employee of the Walkerton PUC, placed an anonymous call to the MOE's Spills Action Centre (SAC), which functions as an environmental emergency call centre. Mr. McKay was aware of the adverse results from the construction site, but not of those from the other samples taken on May 15. He informed the SAC that samples from Walkerton's water system had failed lab tests.

An SAC staff member contacted Stan Koebel that day in the early afternoon. Mr. Koebel led the caller to believe that the only recent adverse results from the system were those from the construction project. He did not reveal that there had also been adverse results from the distribution system samples.

Also on Saturday afternoon, staff at the health unit contacted Dr. Murray McQuigge, the local Medical Officer of Health, at his cottage. He returned to Owen Sound to direct the investigation.

Shortly after noon on Sunday, May 21, the laboratory at the Owen Sound hospital confirmed the earlier presumptive test for *E. coli* O157:H7 and announced an additional presumptive result from another patient. This was the first occasion on which there was confirmation of the specific pathogen involved. The health unit responded by issuing a boil water advisory that afternoon at 1:30 p.m. The boil water advisory was broadcast on the local AM and FM radio stations, but not on the local CBC radio station, on television, or by way of leaflets. Some people in the community did not become aware of the advisory that day. Dr. McQuigge called Brockton's mayor directly to advise him, but did not ask him to do anything, and the mayor took no steps to further disseminate the warning to the community.

In the afternoon of Sunday, May 21, Stan Koebel received calls from the health unit and the SAC. Again, he did not disclose the adverse results from the May 15 samples. The health unit took water samples from 20 different locations in the distribution system and that evening delivered them to the Ministry of Health laboratory in London for microbiological testing.

Throughout the day of May 21, there was a rapid increase in the number of people affected by the contamination. By the end of the day, the Walkerton hospital had received more than 270 calls concerning symptoms of diarrhea and serious abdominal pain. A child, the first of many, was airlifted from Walkerton to London for emergency medical attention.

On Monday, May 22, at the urging of the health unit, the MOE began its own investigation of the Walkerton water system. When the MOE asked Stan Koebel if any unusual events had occurred in the past two weeks, he told them that Well 6 had been knocked out by an electrical storm during the weekend of May 13, but he did not mention the operation of Well 7 without a chlorinator or the adverse results from the May 15 samples.

When asked by the MOE for documents, Mr. Koebel produced, for the first time, the adverse test results faxed to him by A&L on May 17. He also produced the daily operating sheets for Wells 5 and 6 for the month of May but said he could not produce the sheet for Well 7 until the next day. Later, he instructed his brother Frank Koebel to revise the Well 7 sheet with the intention of concealing the fact that Well 7 had operated without a chlorinator.

On Tuesday, May 23, Mr. Koebel provided the MOE with the altered daily operating sheet for Well 7. That day, the health unit was advised that two of the water samples it had collected on May 21 had tested positive for *E. coli*. Both these samples were from "dead ends" in the system, which explains why the contaminants were still present after Mr. Koebel's extensive flushing and chlorination over the weekend. When informed of these results, Stan Koebel told the health unit about the adverse samples from May 15 for the first time.

By Wednesday, May 24, several patients had been transferred by helicopter and ground ambulance from Walkerton to London for medical attention. The first person died on May 22, a second on May 23, and two more on May 24. During this time, many children became seriously ill, and 27 people developed HUS. Some will probably experience lasting damage to their kidneys as well as other long-term health effects. In all, 7 people died and more than 2,300 became ill.

1.3.4   The Physical Causes

As mentioned above, I have concluded that microbiological pathogens – namely, *E. coli* O157:H7 and *Campylobacter jejuni* bacteria – entered Walkerton's water system through Well 5 starting on or shortly after Friday, May 12.

The extraordinary rainfall between May 8 and May 12, 2000, greatly assisted the transport of the contaminants to the entry point for Well 5. Well 5 was a shallow well: its casing extended just 5 m below the surface. All of its water was drawn from a very shallow area between 5 m and 8 m below the surface. More significantly, the water was drawn from an area of highly fractured bedrock. Because of the nature of the fracturing, the geology of the surrounding bedrock, and the shallowness of the soil overburden above the bedrock, it was possible for surface bacteria to quickly enter into a fractured rock channel and proceed directly to Well 5.

The primary, if not the only, source of the contaminants was manure that had been spread on a farm near Well 5 during late April 2000. DNA typing of the animals and the manure on the farm revealed that the *E. coli* O157:H7 and *Campylobacter* strains on the farm matched strains that were prevalent in the human outbreak in Walkerton. It is important to note that the owner of this farm is not to be faulted in any way. He used what were widely accepted as best management practices in spreading the manure.

Water samples taken from the system support the conclusion that Well 5 was the entry point for the contamination. The first test results indicating *E. coli* contamination in the system were from the samples collected on May 15. These samples were probably taken from a location near and immediately downline from Well 5 – the PUC workshop. In the immediate aftermath of the outbreak, beginning on May 23, the raw water at Well 5 consistently tested positive for *E. coli*. Significantly, tests of the raw water at Wells 6 and 7 during this period did not show the presence of *E. coli*. The experts who testified agreed that there was "overwhelming evidence" that the contamination entered through Well 5.

It is not possible to determine the exact time when contamination first entered the system. I conclude, however, that the residents of Walkerton were probably first exposed on or shortly after May 12. This conclusion is supported by the epidemiological evidence, the evidence of the health care institutions that treated the ill and vulnerable groups, anecdotal evidence from residents, and the timing of the heavy rainfall. It is also consistent with the findings of the Bruce-Grey-

Owen Sound Health Unit and of Health Canada, which both concluded that the predominant exposure dates were between May 13 and May 16, 2000.

Well 5 was the primary source of water during the period when contamination entered the system, while Well 6 cycled on and off, and Well 7 was not in operation.

The applicable government document, the Chlorination Bulletin,[9] required a water system like Walkerton's to treat well water with sufficient chlorine to inactivate any contaminants in the raw water, and to sustain a chlorine residual of 0.5 mg/L of water after 15 minutes of contact time.[10] One important purpose of the chlorine residual is to retain a capacity for disinfection in treated water as it moves throughout the distribution system. Another is to provide a way to determine whether contamination is overwhelming the disinfectant capacity of the chlorine that has been added to the water. If the required chlorine residual of 0.5 mg/L had been maintained at Well 5 in May 2000, when the contaminants entered the system, substantially more than 99% of bacteria such as *E. coli* and *Campylobacter* would have been killed. For practical purposes, this would have prevented the outbreak.[11]

In May 2000, the operators of the Walkerton system chlorinated the water at Well 5 but routinely used less than the required amount of chlorine at that well and at the others operated by the Walkerton PUC. The bacteria and other organic matter that entered the system on or shortly after May 12 overwhelmed the chlorine that was being added. The amount of contamination at the time was very likely so great that the demand it put on the chlorine would have overwhelmed even the amount of chlorine needed to maintain a residual of 0.5 mg/L under normal conditions.

As I point out above, the Walkerton operators did not manually monitor the chlorine residual levels at Well 5 during the critical period. Had they done so, it is very probable that the operators would have detected the fact that the chlorine residual had been overwhelmed, at which point they should have been

---

[9] MOE, "Chlorination of Potable Water Supplies," Bulletin 65-W-4 (March 1987).
[10] In this report, the terms "required residual" and "residual of 0.5 mg/L" should always be taken as including the qualifier "after 15 minutes of contact time."
[11] This statement is subject to the qualification that had a large increase in turbidity accompanied the contamination, that might have prevented the chlorine from eliminating the contaminants. In my view, it is most unlikely that this is what actually occurred.

able to take the proper steps to protect public health.[12] Although daily monitoring would not have prevented the outbreak, it is very probable that it would have significantly reduced the outbreak's scope. Instead, the contamination entered the system undetected.

Even more importantly, the outbreak would have been prevented by the use of continuous chlorine residual and turbidity monitors at Well 5.[13] Walkerton did not have continuous chlorine residual and turbidity monitors at any of its wells in May 2000.

Well 5 was supplied by a groundwater source that was under the direct influence of surface water. For such sources, the Ontario Drinking Water Objectives (ODWO)[14] require the continuous monitoring of chlorine residuals and turbidity.[15] Had properly designed continuous monitors been in place at Well 5, the monitors would have automatically sounded an alarm so that the appropriate corrective action could have been taken to prevent contamination from entering the distribution system.

1.3.5   The Role of the Walkerton Public Utilities
Commission Operators

Two serious failures on the part of the Walkerton PUC operators directly contributed to the outbreak in May 2000. The first was an operational problem: the failure to take chlorine residual measurements in the Walkerton water system daily. As I stated above, had the PUC operators manually tested the chlorine residual at Well 5 on May 13 or on the days following, as they should have done, they should have been able to take the necessary steps to protect the

---

[12] It would have been a relatively simple process for a competent water operator to interpret the implications of the lack of a chlorine residual, turn off the well, and alert the community to the problem.

[13] An important purpose of installing continous monitors is to prevent contamination from entering the distribution system. In reaching the conclusion that continuous monitors would have prevented the Walkerton outbreak, I am assuming that the MOE would have required that any such monitors be properly designed for the circumstances at Well 5. The monitors would thus have included an alarm as well as, in all probability, an automatic shut-off mechanism, because Well 5 was not staffed 24 hours a day and because the town had alternative water supplies – Wells 6 and 7.

[14] Unless otherwise indicated, the term "ODWO" refers to the 1994 version of that document.

[15] The requirement for turbidity monitoring was to take four samples a day or to install a continuous turbidity monitor. For ease of reference, I refer to this as "continuous turbidity monitoring." As a practical matter, one would install a continuous monitor rather than take four samples a day.

community. It is very likely that daily testing of chlorine residuals would have significantly reduced the scope of the outbreak.

The second failure relates to the manner in which the PUC operators responded to the outbreak in May 2000. This failure is primarily attributable to Stan Koebel. When Mr. Koebel learned from test results for the samples collected on May 15 that there was a high level of contamination in the system, he did not disclose those results to the health unit staff who were investigating the illnesses in the community. On the contrary, starting on May 19, he actively misled health unit staff by assuring them that the water was safe. Had Stan Koebel been forthcoming about the adverse results or about the fact that Well 7 had operated for more than four days that week without a chlorinator, the health unit would have issued a boil water advisory on May 19 at the latest, and a minimum of 300 to 400 illnesses would probably have been prevented.

The two persons who were responsible for the actual operation of the water system were Stan and Frank Koebel. Stan Koebel had been the general manager of the PUC since 1988. In May 2000, he held a class 3 water operator's licence, which he had received through a grandparenting process. At the Inquiry, Stan Koebel accepted responsibility for his failures and apologized to the people of Walkerton. I believe he was sincere.

The evidence showed that under the supervision of Mr. Koebel, the Walkerton PUC engaged in a host of improper operating practices, including misstating the locations at which samples for microbiological testing were taken, operating wells without chlorination, making false entries in daily operating sheets, failing to measure chlorine residuals daily, failing to adequately chlorinate the water, and submitting false annual reports to the MOE. Mr. Koebel knew that these practices were improper and contrary to MOE guidelines and directives. There is no excuse for any of these practices.

Although Stan Koebel knew that these practices were improper and contrary to the directives of the MOE, he did not intentionally set out to put his fellow residents at risk. A number of factors help to explain, though not to excuse, the extraordinary manner in which the Walkerton PUC was operated under his direction. Many of the improper practices had been going on for years before he was general manager. Further, he and the other PUC employees believed that the untreated water in Walkerton was safe: indeed, they themselves often drank it at the well sites. On occasion, Mr. Koebel was pressured by local residents to decrease the amount of chlorine injected into the water. Those residents objected to the taste of chlorinated water. Moreover, on various occasions, he received mixed messages from the MOE about the importance of several of its own requirements. Although Mr. Koebel knew how to operate the water system mechanically, he lacked a full appreciation of the health risks associated with a failure to properly operate the system and of the importance of following the MOE requirements for proper treatment and monitoring.

None of these factors, however, explain Stan Koebel's failure to report the test results from the May 15 samples to the health unit and others when asked about the water, particularly given that he knew of the illnesses in the community. It must have been clear to him that each of these questioners was unaware of those results. I am satisfied that he withheld information about the adverse results because he wanted to conceal the fact that Well 7 had been operated without chlorination for two extended periods in May 2000.[16] He knew that doing so was wrong. He went so far as to have the daily operating sheet for Well 7 altered in order to mislead the MOE. In withholding information from the health unit, Mr. Koebel put the residents of Walkerton at greater risk. When he withheld the information, Mr. Koebel probably did not appreciate the seriousness of the health risks involved and did not understand that deaths could result. He did, however, know that people were becoming sick, and there is no excuse for his not having informed the health unit of the adverse results at the earliest opportunity.

Frank Koebel had been foreman of the PUC since 1988. He was the operator who, on May 13 and May 14, went to Well 5, failed to measure chlorine residuals, and made false entries in the daily operating sheet. As was the case with his brother, Frank Koebel also deeply regretted his role in these events.

Most of the comments I have made about Stan Koebel apply equally to Frank Koebel, with one exception: Frank Koebel was not involved in failing to disclose the May 15 results to the health unit. Yet on his brother's instructions, he did alter the daily operating sheet for Well 7 on May 22 or May 23 in an effort to conceal from the MOE the fact that Well 7 had operated without a chlorinator.

---

[16] In addition to the period of May 15 to May 19 referred to above, Well 7 had also been operated without chlorination from May 3 to May 9.

As I point out above, the contamination of the system could have been pre-vented by the use of continuous monitors at Well 5. Stan and Frank Koebel lacked the training and expertise either to identify the vulnerability of Well 5 to surface contamination or to understand the resulting need for continuous chlorine residual and turbidity monitors. The MOE took no steps to inform them of the requirements for continuous monitoring or to require training that would have addressed that issue. It was the MOE, in its role as regulator and overseer of municipal water systems, that should have required the instal-lation of continuous monitors. Its failure to require continuous monitors at Well 5 was not in any way related to the improper operating practices of the Walkerton operators. I will discuss this failure of the MOE below.

1.3.6   The Role of the Walkerton Public Utilities Commissioners

The Walkerton PUC commissioners were responsible for establishing and con-trolling the policies under which the PUC operated. The general manager and staff were responsible for administering these policies in operating the water facility. The commissioners were not aware of the operators' improper chlori-nation and monitoring practices. Also, while Well 5's vulnerability had been noted when it was approved in the late 1970s, those who served as commis-sioners in the decade leading up to the tragedy were unaware of Well 5's clear and continuing vulnerability to contamination and the resulting need for con-tinuous monitors.

The evidence showed that the commissioners concerned themselves primarily with the financial side of the PUC's operations and had very little knowledge about matters relating to water safety and the operation of the system. Inap-propriately, they relied almost totally on Stan Koebel in these areas.

In May 1998, the commissioners received a copy of an MOE inspection report that indicated serious problems with the manner in which the Walkerton water system was being operated. The report stated that *E. coli*, an indicator of unsafe drinking water quality, had been present in a significant number of treated water samples. Among other things, the report emphasized the need to maintain an adequate chlorine residual. It also pointed out other problems: the PUC had only recently begun to measure chlorine residuals in the distri-bution system, was not complying with the minimum bacteriological sam-pling requirements, and was not maintaining proper training records.

In response, the commissioners did nothing. They did not ask for an explanation from Mr. Koebel: rather, they accepted his word that he would correct the deficient practices, and they never followed up to ensure that he did. As it turns out, Mr. Koebel did not maintain adequate chlorine residuals, as he had said he would, and did not monitor residuals as often as would have been necessary to ensure their adequacy. In my view, it was reasonable to expect the commissioners to have done more.

The commissioners should have had enough knowledge to ask the appropriate questions and to follow up on the answers that were given. However, if they did not feel qualified to address these issues, they could have contracted with an independent consultant to help them evaluate the manner in which Stan Koebel was operating the system and to assure themselves that the serious concerns about water safety raised in the report were addressed.

Without excusing the role played by the commissioners, it is important to note that, like Stan and Frank Koebel, they did not intend to put the residents of Walkerton at risk. They believed that the water was safe. They were distraught about the events of May 2000. Moreover, it appears from PUC records that they performed their duties in much the same way as their predecessors had. That approach seems to have been inherent in the culture at the Walkerton PUC.

Even if the commissioners had properly fulfilled their roles, it is not clear that Mr. Koebel would have changed the PUC's improper practices. However, it is possible that he would have brought the chlorination and monitoring practices into line, in which case it is very probable that the scope of the outbreak in May 2000 would have been significantly reduced. Thus, the failure of those who were commissioners in 1998 to properly respond to the MOE inspection report represented a lost opportunity to reduce the scope of the outbreak.

1.3.7   The Role of the Municipality[17] and the Mayor

The municipality's role was limited, given that at the relevant times the water system was operated by a public utilities commission. I focus on three occasions following which, it has been suggested, the municipality should have

---

[17] Before the amalgamation that resulted in the formation of the Municipality of Brockton on January 1, 1999, the relevant authority was the Town of Walkerton.

taken steps to protect drinking water or the community's health but did not do so: a November 1978 meeting at which MOE representatives suggested land use controls for the area surrounding Well 5; the receipt of the 1998 MOE inspection report; and the issuance of the boil water advisory in the early afternoon of May 21, 2000.

I conclude that the Town of Walkerton did not have the legal means to control land use in the vicinity of Well 5. Further, at the 1978 meeting, the discussion about controlling land use revolved primarily around the former Pletsch farm. In fact, however, the bacterial contamination of the Walkerton water system originated elsewhere.

Given that the control and management of the waterworks were vested in the Walkerton PUC, the Walkerton town council's response to the 1998 inspection report was not unreasonable. The council was entitled to rely on the PUC commissioners to follow up on the deficiencies identified in the report.

Brockton's mayor, David Thomson, was in an ideal position to assist the local health unit in disseminating the boil water advisory on May 21 and May 22. But Dr. Murray McQuigge did not request any assistance. Even though the mayor knew that the people of Walkerton were becoming ill, he did not offer to help inform them about the boil water advisory. Although others in his position might have done so, I conclude that the mayor should not be faulted for having failed to offer assistance.

Further, I conclude that it was not unreasonable for Mayor Thomson and other members of Brockton's municipal council to refrain from invoking the Brockton Emergency Plan. Due consideration was given to taking this extraordinary step. The primary benefit of invoking the plan would have been to assist in publicizing the boil water advisory. By the time the municipal council was considering whether the plan should be invoked, the existence of the boil water advisory was already well known within the community.

1.3.8   The Role of the Public Health Authorities

I consider the role of the Bruce-Grey-Owen Sound Health Unit in relation to the events in Walkerton in three separate contexts: its role in overseeing the quality of the drinking water in Walkerton over the years leading up to

May 2000, its reaction to the privatization of laboratory testing services in 1996, and its response to the outbreak in May 2000.

In the normal course of events, the health unit exercised its oversight role by receiving notice of reports of adverse water quality and MOE inspection reports, and responding to such reports when it considered a response to be necessary. It would have been preferable for the health unit to have taken a more active role in responding to the many adverse water quality reports it received from Walkerton between 1995 and 1998 and to the 1998 MOE inspection report. During the mid- to late 1990s, there were clear indications that the water quality in Walkerton was deteriorating.

On receiving adverse water quality reports, the local public health inspector in Walkerton would normally contact the Walkerton PUC to ensure that follow-up samples were taken and chlorine residuals maintained. Instead, when he received the 1998 MOE inspection report, he read and filed it, assuming that the MOE would ensure that the problems identified were properly addressed. Given that there was no written protocol instructing the local public health inspector on how to respond to adverse water reports or inspection reports, I am satisfied that he did all that was expected of him.[18]

Even if the health unit had responded more actively when concerns arose about the water quality in Walkerton in the mid- to late 1990s, it is unlikely that such responses would have had any impact on the events of May 2000. The actions required to address the concerns were essentially operational. The MOE was the government regulator responsible for overseeing Walkerton's water system. After the 1998 inspection report, it directed the PUC to remedy a number of operational deficiencies, but then failed to follow up to ensure that the proper steps were taken. I am satisfied that it was appropriate for the health unit to rely on the MOE to oversee operations at the Walkerton PUC and to follow up on the 1998 inspection report.

After laboratory testing services for municipalities were assumed by the private sector in 1996, the health unit sought assurance from the MOE's Owen Sound office that the health unit would continue to be notified of all adverse water

---

[18] It would have been preferable for the Ministry of Health and the health unit to have provided clear direction to health unit staff on how to respond to adverse water quality reports and MOE inspection reports. I will be making recommendations in the Part 2 report of this Inquiry to clarify the respective roles of local health units and the MOE in overseeing municipal water systems.

quality results relating to communal water systems. It received that assurance, both in correspondence and at a meeting. I am satisfied that the health unit did what was reasonable in reacting to the privatization of laboratory services.

The health unit was first notified of the outbreak in Walkerton on Friday, May 19, 2000. It issued a boil water advisory two days later. In the interval, health unit staff investigated the outbreak diligently. There were several reasons why the health unit did not immediately conclude that the water was the problem. Initially, a food-borne source was the prime suspect. However, because water was a possible source of the problem, the health unit staff contacted Stan Koebel twice on May 19 and twice again on May 20. Each time they were given information that led them to believe the water was safe. The health unit had no reason not to accept what Stan Koebel told them. His assurances pointed the health unit staff away from water as the source of the problem.

Moreover, the symptoms being reported were consistent with *E. coli* O157:H7. Infection with *E. coli* O157:H7 is most commonly associated with food, not water – indeed, it is often referred to as "the hamburger disease." The health unit was not aware of any reported *E. coli* outbreak that had been linked to a treated water system in North America. Further, illnesses were surfacing in communities outside Walkerton, a pattern that tended to indicate a source that was not water-borne.

In my view, the health unit should not be faulted for failing to issue the boil water advisory before May 21. I recognize that others in the community suspected there was something wrong with the water and took steps to avoid infection. They are to be commended for their actions. However, issuing a boil water advisory is a significant step requiring a careful balancing of a number of factors. Precaution and the protection of public health must always be paramount, but unwarranted boil water advisories have social and economic consequences and, importantly, have the potential to undermine the future credibility of the health unit issuing such an advisory. In revisiting the exercise of judgment by professionals like the health unit staff, one must be careful about the use of hindsight. In view of the assurances provided by Mr. Koebel about the safety of the water, I am satisfied that the health unit was appropriately prudent and balanced in the way in which it investigated the outbreak and decided to issue the boil water advisory.

In this respect, I do not think that the failure of the health unit to review its Walkerton water file between May 19 and May 21 made any difference to the time at which the boil water advisory was issued. The most recent relevant evidence of water quality problems in the file was more than two years old. I accept the evidence of Dr. McQuigge and others that in May 2000, more timely information was needed about Walkerton's water. The health unit sought that information and was assured by Stan Koebel that all was well.

The health unit disseminated the boil water advisory to the community by having it broadcast on local AM and FM radio stations. It also contacted several public institutions directly. Evidence showed that some local residents did not become aware of the boil water advisory on May 21. In his evidence, Dr. McQuigge acknowledged that if he faced a similar situation again, he would use local TV stations and have pamphlets distributed informing residents of the boil water advisory. That would have been a better approach, because the boil water advisory should have been more broadly publicized.

1.3.9   The Role of the Ministry of the Environment

The Ministry of the Environment (MOE) was and continues to be the provincial government ministry with primary responsibility for regulating – and for enforcing legislation, regulations, and policies that apply to – the construction and operation of municipal water systems.[19] In this regard, the MOE sets the standards according to which municipal systems are built and operated. It also approves the construction of new water facilities, certifies water plant operators, and oversees the treatment, distribution, and monitoring practices of municipal water facilities. The overall goal is to ensure that water systems are built and operated in a way that produces safe water and does not threaten public health.

As pointed out above, there were two serious problems with the manner in which the Walkerton water system was operated that contributed to the tragedy in May 2000. The first was the failure to install continuous chlorine residual and turbidity monitors at Well 5. The failure to use continuous monitors at Well 5 resulted from shortcomings of the MOE in fulfilling its regulatory and

---

[19] I refer to "municipal water systems" frequently throughout this report. For readability, I use the term interchangeably with "municipal waterworks," "municipal water facilities," "communal water systems," and similar terms.

oversight role. The PUC operators did not have the training or expertise either to identify the vulnerability of Well 5 to surface contamination or to understand the resulting need for continuous monitors. It would be unreasonable for the MOE to expect that all operators of small water systems like Walkerton's would have the expertise necessary either to identify water sources that are vulnerable to contamination or to understand the need to install continuous chlorine residual and turbidity monitors where such vulnerability exists. Continuous monitors at Well 5 could have prevented the outbreak. It is simply wrong to say, as the government argued at the Inquiry, that Stan Koebel or the Walkerton PUC were solely responsible for the outbreak or that they were the only ones who could have prevented it.

The second problem with the operation of the Walkerton's water system was the improper chlorination and monitoring practices of the PUC. I have discussed those above. Without in any way excusing the PUC operators for the manner in which they disregarded MOE requirements and directives, I am satisfied that the MOE should have detected those practices and ensured that they were corrected. Had the MOE done so, the scope of the outbreak would probably have been significantly reduced.

I have concluded that a number of MOE programs or policies[20] involved in the regulation and oversight of the Walkerton water system were deficient – some more so than others. The MOE's "deficiencies" all fall into the category of omissions or failures to take appropriate action, rather than positive acts. As a result, the effects of those deficiencies on the events in Walkerton must be measured by their failure to address one or both of the two problems at Walkerton referred to above. In that sense, the deficiencies can be measured by their failure to prevent the outbreak, to reduce its scope, or to reduce the risk that the outbreak would occur. Viewed in this light, some of the deficiencies are more closely connected to the tragedy than are others.

Responsibility for the MOE's deficiencies rests at different levels of the ministry. Walkerton fell within the jurisdiction of the MOE's Owen Sound office. Some of the deficiencies with government programs that I identify affected Walkerton through the activities of the Owen Sound office. Some also arose from the activities of the MOE's central offices in Toronto.

---

[20] According to the mandate, I am to report on "the effect, if any, of government policies, procedures and practices." This phrase is obviously intended to include government programs. Throughout this report, I use the terms "policies" and "programs," depending on the context, to refer to this part of the mandate.

I have chosen to discuss issues relating to the privatization of laboratory testing services and budget reductions in separate chapters because those issues involve decisions made by the Cabinet, not just by the MOE.

The most significant deficiencies associated with the MOE relate to the approvals program, the inspections program, the preference for voluntary rather than mandatory abatement, and the water operator certification and training program. I will briefly describe the main deficiencies I have identified.

1.3.9.1 *The Approvals Program*

Well 5 was constructed in 1978, and the Certificate of Approval for the well was issued in 1979. However, no operating conditions were attached to the Certificate of Approval. From the outset, Well 5 was identified as a potential problem: the groundwater supplying the well was recognized as being vulnerable to surface contamination. The approval of the well without imposing explicit operating conditions was consistent with the MOE's practices at that time.

Over time, MOE practices changed and it began to routinely attach operating conditions to Certificates of Approval, including conditions relating to water treatment and monitoring. By 1992, the MOE had developed a set of model operating conditions that were commonly attached to new Certificates of Approval for municipal water systems. There was, however, no effort to reach back to determine whether conditions should be attached to existing certificates, like the one for Well 5.

The ODWO was amended in 1994 to provide that water supply systems using groundwater that is under the direct influence of surface water should continuously monitor "disinfectant residuals (equivalent to free chlorine)" – a type of chlorine residual – and turbidity. Even at that point there was no program or policy to examine the water sources supplying wells referred to in existing Certificates of Approvals to determine whether a condition should be added requiring continuous monitoring. Well 5 used groundwater that was under the direct influence of surface water, and the MOE should therefore have required the installation of continuous monitors at that well following the 1994 ODWO amendment.

The MOE never did add any conditions to the Certificate of Approval for Well 5. I am satisfied that a properly structured approvals program would have addressed the need to update the Certificate of Approval for Well 5, both after the 1994 amendment to the ODWO and when the MOE practices for newly issued certificates changed in the 1990s. The installation of continuous chlorine residual and turbidity monitors at Well 5 would have prevented the Walkerton tragedy. It is very probable that the inclusion of the model operating conditions relating to the maintenance of a total chlorine residual of 0.5 mg/L after 15 minutes of contact time, coupled with effective enforcement, would have significantly reduced the scope of the outbreak.

1.3.9.2 *The Inspections Program*

The MOE inspected the Walkerton water system in 1991, 1995, and 1998. At the time of the three inspections, problems existed relating to water safety. Inspectors identified some of them, but unfortunately two of the most significant problems – the vulnerability of Well 5 to surface contamination, and the improper chlorination and monitoring practices of the PUC – went undetected. As events turned out, these problems had a direct impact on the May 2000 tragedy.

In the course of the inspections, Well 5 was not assessed, and therefore was not identified as a groundwater source that was under the direct influence of surface water. The inspectors proceeded as if Well 5 were a secure groundwater source, and their reports made no reference to the surface water influence. This occurred even though information that should have prompted a close examination of the vulnerability of Well 5 was available in MOE files. In my view, the inspections program was deficient in that the inspectors were not directed to look at relevant information about the security of water sources.

The second problem not addressed in the three inspection reports was the improper chlorination and monitoring practices of the PUC, discussed above. The evidence of these practices was there to be seen in the operating records maintained by the PUC. A proper examination of the daily operating sheets would have disclosed the problem. However, the inspections program was deficient in that the inspectors were not instructed to carry out a thorough review of operating records.

Although the MOE was not aware of the Walkerton PUC's improper chlorination and monitoring practices, I am satisfied that if the ministry had properly followed up on the operational problems identified in the 1998 inspection report, the unacceptable treatment and monitoring practices would have (or at least should have) been discovered. Specifically, *E. coli* was being detected in the treated water with increasing frequency and three successive inspections had measured chlorine residuals in treated water at less than the required 0.5 mg/L. Moreover, the Walkerton PUC had repeatedly failed to submit the required number of samples for microbiological testing. All of this should have led the MOE to conduct a follow-up inspection after 1998, preferably an unannounced inspection. However, two years and three months later, when the tragedy struck, no further inspection had even been scheduled.

I am satisfied that a properly structured and administered inspections program would have discovered, before the May 2000 outbreak, both the vulnerability of Well 5 and the PUC's unacceptable chlorination and monitoring practices. Had these problems been uncovered, steps could have been taken to address them, and thus to either prevent the outbreak or substantially reduce its scope.

1.3.9.3 *Voluntary and Mandatory Abatement*

In the years preceding May 2000, the MOE became aware on several occasions that the Walkerton PUC was not conforming with the ministry's minimum microbiological sampling program and that it was not maintaining a minimum total chlorine residual of 0.5 mg/L. Despite repeated assurances that it would conform with the MOE's requirements, the PUC failed to do so. These ongoing failures indicated a poorly operated water facility. The MOE took no action to legally enforce the treatment and monitoring requirements that were being ignored. Instead, it relied on a voluntary approach to abatement. This was consistent with the culture in the MOE at the time.

After its inspection of Walkerton's water system in 1998, the MOE should have issued a Director's Order to compel the Walkerton PUC to comply with the requirements for treatment and monitoring. It is possible that if the MOE had issued such an order in 1998, the PUC would have responded properly, taken the treatment and monitoring requirements more seriously, and brought its practices into line. If, however, the PUC had continued to ignore the newly mandated requirements, it seems likely that with proper follow-up the MOE would have discovered that the PUC was not in compliance and would have been in a position to ensure that the appropriate corrective actions were taken. As I have said, proper chlorination and monitoring would have made a difference in May 2000.

1.3.9.4 *Operator Certification and Training*

Stan and Frank Koebel had extensive experience in operating the Walkerton water system, but they lacked knowledge in two very important areas. They did not appreciate either the seriousness of the health risks arising from contaminated drinking water or the seriousness of their failure to treat and monitor the water properly. They mistakenly believed that the untreated water supplying the Walkerton wells was safe.

Managing a municipal water system involves enormous responsibility. Competent management entails knowing more than how to operate the system mechanically or what to do under normal circumstances. Competence must also include an appreciation of the nature of the risks to water safety and an understanding of how protective measures, like chlorination and chlorine residual and turbidity monitoring, work to protect water safety. Stan and Frank Koebel did not have this knowledge. In that sense, they were not qualified to hold their respective positions with the Walkerton PUC.

Stan and Frank Koebel were certified as class 3 water operators at the time of the outbreak. They had obtained their certification through a "grandparenting" scheme based solely on their experience. They were not required to take a training course or to pass any examinations in order to be certified. Nonetheless, I conclude that at the time when mandatory certification was introduced, it was not unreasonable for the government to make use of grandparenting, provided that adequate mandatory training requirements existed for grandparented operators.

After the introduction of mandatory certification in 1993, the MOE required 40 hours of training a year for each certified operator. Stan and Frank Koebel did not take the required amount of training, and the training they did take did not adequately address drinking water safety. I am satisfied that the 40-hour requirement should have been more focused on drinking water safety issues and, in the case of Walkerton, more strictly enforced.

It is difficult to say whether Stan and Frank Koebel would have altered their improper practices if they had received appropriate training. However, I can say that proper training would have reduced the likelihood that they would have continued their improper practices.

1.3.9.5 *Other Deficiencies*

The deficiencies I have described above are the most significant in terms of the effect of MOE policies on the tragedy in Walkerton. However, there were other shortcomings in MOE policies and programs that are relevant to the events in Walkerton. These inadequacies arose in the MOE's management of information, the training of its personnel, and the use of guidelines rather than legally binding regulations to set out the requirements for chlorination and monitoring. I summarize these deficiencies in this section.

The MOE did not have an information system that made critical information about the history of vulnerable water sources, like Well 5, accessible to those responsible for ensuring that proper treatment and monitoring were taking place. On several occasions in the 1990s, having had access to this information would have enabled ministry personnel to be fully informed in making decisions about current circumstances and the proper actions to be taken.

By the mid-1990s, when the water quality at Walkerton began to show signs of deterioration, certain important documents were no longer readily accessible to those who were responsible for overseeing the Walkerton water facility. Indirectly, at least, the lack of a proper information system contributed to the failures of the MOE referred to above.

With respect to training, evidence at the Inquiry showed that personnel in the MOE's Owen Sound office were unaware of certain matters that were essential to carrying out their responsibilities in overseeing the Walkerton water facility. In particular, several environmental officers were unaware that *E. coli* was potentially lethal. It would seem critical that those who are responsible for overseeing municipal water systems, and who might have to coordinate responses to adverse water results, should fully appreciate the potential consequences of threats to water safety.

The effect of this lack of training on what happened in Walkerton in May 2000 is difficult to measure, but it may have had an impact on some decisions affecting Walkerton relating to the inspections and abatement programs.

In the exercise of its regulatory and oversight responsibilities for municipal water systems, the MOE developed and regularly applied two sets of guidelines or policies: the ODWO and the Chlorination Bulletin. I am satisfied that matters as important to water safety and public health as those set out in these guidelines should instead have been covered by regulations – which, unlike guidelines, are legally binding. Two possible effects on Walkerton arose from the use of guidelines rather than regulations. Stan and Frank Koebel, despite their belief that the untreated water at Walkerton was safe, would no doubt have been less comfortable ignoring a legally binding regulation than ignoring a guideline.

Moreover, the use of guidelines may have affected the MOE's failure to invoke mandatory abatement measures and to conduct a follow-up to the 1998 inspection. Had the Walkerton PUC been found to be in non-compliance with a legally enforceable regulation, as opposed to a guideline, it is more likely that the MOE would have taken stronger measures to ensure compliance – such as the use of further inspections, the issuance of a Director's Order, or enforcement proceedings.

I note, however, that prior to the events in Walkerton there was no initiative, either from within or outside the MOE, to include these guidelines' requirements for treatment and monitoring in legally enforceable regulations.

1.3.9.6 *Summary*

I am satisfied that if the MOE had adequately fulfilled its regulatory and oversight role, the tragedy in Walkerton would have been prevented (by the installation of continuous monitors) or at least significantly reduced in scope.

It is worth observing that since the Walkerton tragedy, the government has recognized that improvements were needed in virtually all of the areas where I identify deficiencies and has taken steps to strengthen the MOE's regulatory or oversight role. In my view, though, more changes are required. I make some specific recommendations regarding the MOE's role in this report, and I will make extensive recommendations about the regulation and oversight of water systems in the Part 2 report of this Inquiry.

1.3.10   The Failure to Enact a Notification Regulation

At the time of the Walkerton outbreak, the government did not have a legally enforceable requirement[21] for the prompt and direct reporting of adverse results from drinking water tests to the MOE and to local Medical Officers of Health. This contributed to the extent of the outbreak in Walkerton in May 2000.

For years, the government had recognized that the proper reporting of adverse test results is important to public health. The ODWO directs testing laboratories to report any indicators of unsafe water quality to the local MOE office, which in turn is directed to notify[22] the local Medical Officer of Health. The Medical Officer of Health then decides whether to issue a boil water advisory.

When government laboratories conducted all of the routine drinking water tests for municipal water systems throughout the province, it was acceptable to keep the notification protocol in the form of a guideline under the ODWO rather than in a legally enforceable form – that is, a law or regulation. However, the entry of private laboratories into this sensitive public health area in 1993, and the wholesale exit of all government laboratories from routine testing of municipal water samples in 1996, made it unacceptable to let the notification protocol remain in the form of a legally unenforceable guideline.

This was particularly so since at the time, private environmental laboratories were not regulated by the government. No criteria had been established to govern the quality of testing, no requirements existed regarding the qualifications or experience of laboratory personnel, and no provisions were made for the licensing, inspection, or auditing of such laboratories by the government.

Starting in 1993, a small number of municipalities began to use private laboratories for microbiological testing. In 1996, however, as part of the government's program of budget reductions, the government stopped

---

[21] Although in this section I refer to such requirements as "regulations," I note that the government could also have passed a statute instead of a regulation.
[22] The terms "notify" and "report" are used interchangeably in the documents, the evidence, and this report.

conducting any routine drinking water tests for municipalities – that is, it fully privatized laboratory testing.[23]

At the time, the government was aware of the importance of requiring testing laboratories to directly notify the MOE and the local Medical Officer of Health about adverse test results. At the time of privatization in 1996, the MOE sent a guidance document to those municipalities that requested it. The document strongly recommended that a municipality include in any contract with a private laboratory a clause specifying that the laboratory notify the MOE and the local Medical Officer of Health directly of adverse test results. There is no evidence that the Walkerton PUC either requested or received this document.

Before 1996, the government was aware of cases in which local Medical Officers of Health had not been notified of adverse test results from municipal water systems. After privatization in 1996, the government did not implement a program to monitor the effect of privatization on the notification procedures followed whenever adverse results were found. When the MOE became aware that some private sector laboratories were not notifying the ministry about adverse results as specified in the ODWO, its response was piecemeal and unsatisfactory. Importantly, senior MOE management did not alert the local MOE offices that they should monitor and follow up on the notification issue.

In 1997, the Minister of Health took the unusual step of writing to the Minister of the Environment to request that legislation be amended, or assurances be given, to ensure that the proper authorities would be notified of adverse results. The Minister of the Environment declined to propose legislation, indicating that the ODWO dealt with this issue. He invited the Minister of Health to address the matter through the Drinking Water Coordination Committee, which included staff from both of their ministries. Nothing else happened until after the tragedy in Walkerton. Only then did the government enact a regulation requiring laboratories to directly notify the MOE and the local Medical Officer of Health about adverse test results.

---

[23] I use the term "privatization" throughout this section. This term is used extensively in the evidence, in many documents, and in the submissions of the parties. In the context of this Inquiry, the term refers to the government's 1996 discontinuation of all routine microbiological testing for municipal water systems – a move that resulted in the large majority of municipal systems turning to private sector laboratories for routine water testing. Municipalities are not required to use private laboratories: a few larger municipalities operate their own. Practically speaking, however, the large majority have no option other than to use private laboratories.

I am satisfied that the regulatory culture created by the government through the Red Tape Commission review process discouraged any proposals to make the notification protocol for adverse drinking water results legally binding on the operators of municipal water systems and private laboratories. On several occasions, concerns were expressed by officials in the Ministry of Health, as well as in the MOE, regarding failures to report adverse water results to local Medical Officers of Health in accordance with the ODWO protocol. Despite these concerns, the government did not enact a regulation to make notification mandatory until after the Walkerton tragedy. The evidence showed that the concept of a notification regulation would likely have been "a non-starter," given the government's focus on minimizing regulation.

The laboratory used by Walkerton in May 2000, A&L Canada Laboratories, was unaware of the notification protocol outlined in the ODWO. A&L notified the Walkerton PUC, but not the MOE or the local Medical Officer of Health, of the critical adverse results from the May 15 samples. Both the fact that this was an unregulated sector and the fact that the ODWO was a guideline, not a regulation, help explain why A&L was unaware of the protocol.

In my view, it was not reasonable for the government, after the privatization of water testing, to rely on the ODWO – a guideline – to ensure that laboratories would notify public health and environmental authorities directly of adverse results. The government should have enacted a regulation in 1996 to mandate direct reporting by testing laboratories of adverse test results to the MOE and to local Medical Officers of Health. Instead, it enacted such a regulation only after the Walkerton tragedy.

If, in May 2000, the notification protocol had been contained in a legally enforceable regulation applicable to private sector laboratories, I am satisfied that A&L would have informed itself of the protocol and complied with it. The failure of A&L to notify the MOE and the local Medical Officer of Health about the adverse results from the May 15 samples was the result of the government's failure to enact a notification regulation. Had the local Medical Officer of Health been notified of the adverse test results on May 17, as he should have been, he would have issued a boil water advisory before May 21 – by May 19 at the latest. An advisory issued on May 19 would very likely have prevented the illnesses of at least 300 to 400 people, although it is unlikely that any of the deaths would have been avoided.[24]

1.3.11 Budget Reductions

The budget reductions had two types of impact on Walkerton. The first stemmed from the decision to cut costs by privatizing laboratory testing of water samples in 1996 and, in particular, the way in which that decision was implemented. As discussed above, the government's failure to enact a regulation to legally require testing laboratories to promptly report test results indicating unsafe drinking water directly to the MOE and the local Medical Officer of Health contributed to the extent of the May 2000 Walkerton outbreak.

The second impact on Walkerton of the budget reductions relates to the MOE approvals and inspections programs. The budget reductions that began in 1996 made it less likely that the MOE would pursue proactive measures that would have identified the need for continuous monitors at Well 5 or would have detected the Walkerton PUC's improper chlorination and monitoring practices – steps that would, respectively, have prevented the outbreak or reduced its scope.

The MOE's budget had already been reduced between 1992 and 1995. After the new government was elected in 1995, however, the MOE's budget underwent substantial further reductions. By 1998–99, the ministry's budget had been reduced by more than $200 million – resulting, among other effects, in its staff complement being cut by more than 750 employees (a reduction of over 30%). The reductions were initiated by the central agencies of the government,[25] rather than from within the MOE, and they were not based on an assessment of what was required to carry out the MOE's statutory responsibilities.

Before the decision was made to significantly reduce the MOE's budget in 1996, senior government officials, ministers, and the Cabinet received numerous warnings that the impacts could result in increased risks to the environment

---

[24] If the boil water advisory had been issued on May 18, approximately 400 to 500 illnesses would have been avoided. It is possible that one death might have been prevented.

[25] The "central agencies" include the Management Board Secretariat, the Ministry of Finance, the Cabinet Office, and the Premier's Office.

and human health. These risks included those resulting from reducing the number of proactive inspections – risks that turned out to be relevant to the events in Walkerton. The decision to proceed with the budget reductions was taken without either an assessment of the risks or the preparation of a risk management plan. There is evidence that those at the most senior levels of government who were responsible for the decision considered the risks to be manageable. But there is no evidence that the specific risks, including the risks arising from the fact that the notification protocol was a guideline rather than a regulation, were properly assessed or addressed.

In February 1996, the Cabinet approved the budget reductions in the face of the warnings of increased risk to the environment and human health.

1.3.12   Other Government Programs

The Inquiry heard evidence about a number of other government programs or policies that I conclude did not have an effect on the events in Walkerton. However, I consider it useful to briefly set out the nature of some of this evidence and the reasons for my conclusions. I do so in Chapter 12 of this report.

1.4 The Scope of the Mandate

An Order-in-Council sets out the mandate for this Inquiry. Those parts of the mandate that relate to the events in Walkerton are as follows:

2.   The commission shall inquire into the following matters:

(a)   the circumstances which caused hundreds of people in the Walkerton area to become ill, and several of them to die in May and June 2000, at or around the same time as *Escherichia coli* bacteria were found to be present in the town's water supply;

(b)   the cause of these events including the effect, if any, of government policies, procedures and practices;

....

[i]n order to make such findings and recommendations as the commission considers advisable to ensure the safety of the water supply system in Ontario.

I am satisfied that the mandate should be interpreted broadly in order to fully
reflect the purpose for which the Inquiry was called. Like many public inquiries, this Inquiry was called in the aftermath of a tragedy. The public was shocked
by what had happened in Walkerton. People had assumed that treated drinking water was safe. There were questions from every quarter about how this
happened, how it could have been prevented, what role public officials played,
and what had happened to the government programs that were intended to
prevent such tragedies from occurring.

The public's interest and concern are fundamental to the purpose for which
the Inquiry was called. This Inquiry is intended to address all of the legitimate
questions about what happened in Walkerton and why. The mandate should
not be interpreted in a manner that leaves any of those questions unanswered.

Paragraph 2(b) of the Order-in-Council directs me to report on "the cause" of
the tragedy, including "the effect, if any, of government policies, procedures
and practices." I am satisfied that the term "cause" should not be interpreted in
the same manner that is used in determining issues related to civil or criminal
liability. This Inquiry has a different purpose from that of either civil or criminal proceedings.[26] The purpose of the Inquiry is not to make findings of liability or responsibility in a legal sense, but rather to report on all the circumstances surrounding the events in Walkerton and all the causes of those events
so as to help ensure the safety of drinking water in the future. Understanding
what went wrong in Walkerton should, in itself, prove helpful in the future to
those responsible for regulating, managing, and operating water systems.

I am satisfied that I should report not only on acts or events that directly
"caused" the outbreak in a positive sense, but also on those failures or omissions
that did not prevent the outbreak, reduce its scope, or reduce the risk that the
outbreak would occur. By way of example, I note that many government policies
or programs are intended to reduce the risk that drinking water will be unsafe.

---

[26] I note that paragraph 3 of the Order-in-Council specifically precludes me from making findings
of civil or criminal liability. It reads as follows: "The commission shall perform its duties without
expressing any conclusion or recommendation regarding the civil or criminal liability of any person
or organization. The commission, in the conduct of its inquiry, shall ensure that it does not interfere
with any ongoing criminal investigation or criminal proceedings, if any, relating to these matters."

Given the language of paragraph 2(b) of the Order-in-Council, I have no doubt that the mandate directs me to report on the failures of any of these policies or programs to achieve their intended purposes. Likewise, I should also report on the failures of others to take steps that would have reduced the risk that the Walkerton tragedy would occur.

For the purposes of calling evidence, I asked my counsel to err on the side of inclusion. If matters were possibly relevant to the mandate, the evidence was to be called. However, the fact that evidence was called about a particular matter does not in itself mean that there is a connection to the events of May 2000. In determining what matters warrant comment or assessment in this report, I have attempted to take a common sense approach and to be guided by what the public might reasonably expect, based on the evidence at the Inquiry. I am careful not to draw conclusions about matters that are so removed from the events in Walkerton that a connection between those matters and the tragedy would be based on little more than speculation.

I want to make three points about the manner in which I have expressed certain conclusions. Because this is not, strictly speaking, a legal proceeding, in certain cases I have not made "findings of fact" based either on a balance of probability (the civil test) or on proof beyond a reasonable doubt (the criminal test). Instead of making findings of fact, in some instances I have set out my conclusions by expressing them in terms of the probability or likelihood of something happening or not happening. In some cases I increase the certainty of my conclusion by using the qualifier "very." For readability, I use the words "probable" and "likely" interchangeably. One should not read a different meaning into the use of the two different words in similar contexts.

Several of my conclusions are qualified by rather remote possibilities. For the sake of the reader, I do not repeat qualifications that fall into the "possible but unlikely" category in all instances. This is particularly true in sections 1.2 and 1.3 above, but it occurs in the body of the report as well. I have, however, set out my qualifications very precisely whenever I first reach a conclusion in the body of the report.

Finally, throughout the report, I occasionally use terms such as "fault," "responsible," and "accountable," which could have a legal connotation. I do not intend, in this report, to reach any conclusions in law. Readers should attach the normal, non-legal meaning to words of this nature.

1.5 Recommendations

A purpose of the Inquiry is to inquire into and report on what happened and the causes of the tragedy, including how it might have been prevented. I do not interpret the mandate as narrowly limiting my findings and conclusions to only those that trigger recommendations. Knowing what happened in Walkerton will assist in a general sense in ensuring the future safety of drinking water in Ontario.

In the Part 2 report of this Inquiry, I will be making comprehensive recommendations relating to all aspects of the drinking water system in Ontario, including the protection of drinking water sources; the treatment, distribution, and monitoring of drinking water; the operation and management of water systems; and the full range of functions involved in the provincial regulatory role. Here in the Part 1 report, however, I do include some recommendations – those that relate to the findings I reach in this report. The recommendations included in this report are not intended to be comprehensive. They will fit into and form part of the broader framework being recommended in the Part 2 report.

1.6 The Role of the Coroner

The role of the Chief Coroner of Ontario, Dr. James Young, particularly in Part 1 of the Inquiry, deserves special mention. The Chief Coroner and I met early in the process to discuss issues arising from the potential overlap between the Inquiry and a coroner's inquest, in case he should decide to call one. We agreed that it would be helpful and appropriate for the Chief Coroner to participate in the Inquiry by applying for standing, and the Chief Coroner was granted standing in both parts of the Inquiry. His counsel attended all of the hearings in Part 1 and made an excellent contribution, both through cross-examination and in closing submissions. My own understanding benefited greatly from this contribution.

In addition, the Chief Coroner initiated an investigation in the immediate aftermath of the outbreak. Dr. Karen Acheson, regional coroner for the Walkerton area,[27] was called to testify about that investigation at the Inquiry.

---

[27] Dr. Karen Acheson is the regional coroner for South Georgian Bay, which includes Bruce County, where Walkerton is located.

Further, the Chief Coroner arranged for a panel of experts in epidemiology, microbiology, and the clinical treatment of hemolytic uremic syndrome to determine which deaths in Walkerton, if any, were associated with the outbreak. This panel was also called to testify at the Inquiry, and its findings were received as expert evidence.

In closing submissions, the Chief Coroner, through his counsel, provided an extensive analysis of the evidence called in Part 1 of the Inquiry. In addition, he included a very helpful list of suggested recommendations directed at ensuring the future safety of Ontario's drinking water. In this report, I have adopted many of the recommendations suggested by the Chief Coroner. In the Part 2 report of this Inquiry, I will be addressing and including many more.

At the outset, I agreed with the Chief Coroner that I would discuss with him the substance of the conclusions I have reached in this report. I have done so, in very general terms. In this regard, I followed a process similar to that followed by the Commission of Inquiry into the Air Ontario Crash at Dryden, Ontario. I should note that the Chief Coroner's investigation of the deaths in Walkerton continues: he has delayed his decision regarding whether to call an inquest until after the release of my report.

Finally, I wish to express my sincere appreciation to the Chief Coroner, his staff, and his counsel for the assistance and cooperation they have provided throughout the Inquiry.

Chapter 2   The Impact on Walkerton

Contents

Chapter 2   The Impact on Walkerton

2.1 Introduction

The water contamination in Walkerton in May 2000 was a terrible tragedy. Seven people died and more than 2,000 became ill. Those who became ill endured enormous suffering: their families, their friends, and the entire community felt a deep sense of shock and sorrow. Compounding this suffering was the nature of the tragedy. In Walkerton, as in most other places, people trusted the drinking water and those who operated and oversaw the water system. This trust was shattered, and in the months that followed the outbreak, the people of the town anguished over why the tragedy had happened and what it meant for the future.

It is not possible to capture here the full nature of the suffering caused by the outbreak. However, in an effort to reflect the severity, as well as the diversity, of the impacts on people's lives, this chapter recounts some of the stories of personal hardship caused by the outbreak. These stories are a vital part of the Inquiry. This chapter also provides information about the general health effects of the bacteria that contaminated the water and about the number of people who died or became ill.

2.2 Personal Suffering

The people of Walkerton have endured, and continue to endure, this ordeal with dignity and resilience. They obviously care very much for each other. Their pain has been enormous, and it will undoubtedly continue for a long time. Some of the town's residents, particularly the children, may experience serious long-term health effects; others continue to suffer from the unexpected loss of their loved ones.

Although they will no doubt always remember the tragedy, it is clear that the people of Walkerton are coming to grips with what has happened. During my brief stay in Walkerton, it seemed to me that their strength and their sense of community are serving them well. I am sure that Walkerton will continue to be, as it was before, a wonderful place to live, work, and raise a family.

In July 2000, I convened hearings in Walkerton over the course of four days and invited people to come and talk about the impact of the water contamination on their lives. This gave them an opportunity to speak about their own experiences as well as those of their families and friends, and to offer their thoughts about how the outbreak had affected their community. More than 50 presentations were made by individuals, groups, and families. Some were made in public; others, when requested, were made in private. Transcripts of the hearings are available as part of the public record of the Inquiry, and they will remain as a lasting account of the hardship endured by the community.

I cannot repeat here all of the personal stories I heard during the July 2000 hearings. Instead, I will relate some stories that I think show the different kinds of suffering experienced by so many in May 2000 and the months that followed. In recounting these stories, I rely to a significant extent on the words used by the people who told them.[1]

2.2.1 Tracey Hammell and Her Son Kody

Tracey Hammell is a Walkerton mother who told her story in a private meeting. Her two-year-old son Kody became ill and, as she said, he ended up being "the sickest little guy down there, next to the people that died." She was still at home with him two months later when she told her story in July 2000. By that time, because he was hemolytic and uremic, Kody was unable to go to daycare or to be under anyone else's care because it was feared that he would "catch everything that's going."

During the May long weekend, the Hammell family was having a garage sale. On Friday, Kody suddenly began to vomit. Mrs. Hammell took him inside to change his diaper and noticed that it was bloody. "I couldn't even tell what it was," she said. "I had never seen that before."

On Saturday morning, Mrs. Hammell woke up to find Kody violently ill. At 10:00 a.m., she phoned the hospital but was told that the hospital was "backed up" and that she should not come in just yet. "Well, when can I come?" she asked. "He's really sick." The hospital staff told her to wait until 4:00 p.m. and to get fluids into her son in order to prevent dehydration. "Do whatever you have to do to get it in him," they said: "get a syringe."

---

[1] I should note for the record that these stories do not represent testimony under oath, as was the case in the Inquiry's formal hearings in Part 1.

Mrs. Hammell followed their advice. She got a syringe and "shoved water down his throat." The water may still have been contaminated, but she did not know that. Finally, she phoned the hospital again around 12:30 p.m. and said, "You've got to see him. He's lifeless. His eyes are rolling in the back of his head … [He has] diarrhea every two minutes. He can't take it anymore."

With her mother and husband, Mrs. Hammell took Kody to the hospital, which was extremely busy. The Hammells persisted, however, and a hospital bed was found in Owen Sound. Kody was given a blood test, which confirmed that he was infected with *E. coli* O157:H7. One doctor told the family there was no treatment. "All we can do is wait for him to get better," he said, as recollected by Mrs. Hammell.

Eventually they were airlifted to London. In the helicopter, Mrs. Hammell asked the doctor whether her son might die. "Yes, he could," the doctor replied. "We hope to get him there in time." Fortunately, Kody survived the trip and arrived at the hospital in London, where he was to be put on dialysis the following morning. Again, Mrs. Hammell was told there was a chance Kody wasn't going to make it. That night, he started to have heart failure and was put on dialysis. While at the hospital, he underwent surgery twice. Finally, Mrs. Hammell said, the doctors told her: "We're sorry, but we've done all we can do … It's up to prayer and the child's body to do the rest."

Then one day, Mrs. Hammell recalled, the doctor ran down the hall toward her exclaiming, "Yippidy-do-dah. You did it. He finally made the turn." The dialysis had at last taken hold. According to the doctors, Mrs. Hammell said, it was a "pure miracle" that Kody had turned himself around and survived. Throughout the endeavour, Mrs. Hammell surprised herself at how strong she could be. But since then, she has occasionally come to the point where she has thought: "Oh my goodness, why am I so depressed and how come I can't stop crying? … It's scary just not knowing what's going to happen to him next." She said she worries constantly for her son:

> I guess for the rest of his life I'm going to be scared if he gets a cold, and I hope it doesn't affect the fluid on his lungs and I hope it doesn't affect his heart … Just every little virus I don't want him to get because, you know, it's harder on the rest of his organs.

2.2.2 Betty and Norm Borth

Betty Borth kept a diary tracing the illness of her husband, Norm. It is a graphic account of his 23 days in hospital in Walkerton and London after becoming ill with *E. coli* O157. As Mrs. Borth told the Inquiry, it is a "very personal" story, one that "may make a few feel uncomfortable."

Norm was 66 years old at the time of the outbreak. He became ill on Friday, June 2. A retired bricklayer, he had been cutting and splitting firewood in the bush when he returned home, saying he felt sick and exhausted. That evening and night, Norm experienced diarrhea consisting of "pure blood and mucus" every 15–20 minutes. Betty phoned the hospital at 6:30 a.m. the next morning and was told to bring him in at 8:00 a.m. But she had difficulty getting him there. "It took me one and a half hours to get him out of the house," she said, "because the bloody diarrhea would not slow up."

Shortly after he was admitted to the hospital, Norm was put on intravenous. The bloody diarrhea continued every 15 minutes, and he was getting weaker; he felt sick to his stomach and the cramps were beginning to get very painful. He was frightened because "he knew people had died," Betty said. "We had been to the funeral home three times in the past week."

By Saturday night, Norm was too weak to get out of bed. The nurses had to put a diaper on him. Betty was joined by their daughter, Michelle, and together they changed and washed Norm constantly, "cleaning up after his trips to the toilet." His blood pressure continued to be high, and his arms and legs began to swell. Despite his abdominal cramps, Norm could not receive painkillers because of the *E. coli*. "Even his skin hurts when you touch him," Betty wrote in her diary. His diabetes of 20 years was now "out of control."

On Monday, June 5, the decision was made to airlift Norm to the hospital in London. He was moved the next day. When Betty and Michelle arrived in London, Norm was being assessed by a kidney specialist. He underwent X-rays, which was a very painful procedure for him. Norm's abdomen was distended, he was still on intravenous, the diarrhea continued, and the swelling in his arms and legs grew even worse.

Norm's condition did not improve for over a week, and the infection continued until Sunday, June 18. Even then, the swelling in his elbows, wrists, ankles, and knees did not go away. Finally, on Sunday, June 25, he was released from the hospital. "We are both very excited," Betty wrote. "Sunday he comes home with six prescriptions to be filled." However, Norm was readmitted to hospital for a short time early in July, and by the time Betty gave her testimony, he was still very weak.

2.2.3 The Family of Betty Trushinski

Betty Trushinski, aged 56, died as a result of the outbreak. She is survived by her husband, two daughters, and a son – all of whom met with me privately in Walkerton – as well as by many other family members.

At the time they met with me, the Trushinski family members were deeply immersed in grief. Betty Trushinski's husband, Frank Trushinski, showed me photos of his wife and of their family. One photo showed Mrs. Trushinski working on her deck, one of their projects. She was able to enjoy the deck for only a month before she died. "I just had to come to show [the photos] to show to you what type of person she was," Mr. Trushinski said. "I loved her very much, and there's not one day that goes by that I don't have a good cry with her."

Mrs. Trushinski's children also expressed their feelings of deep loss for their mother. "She was young, energetic, enthusiastic, and vibrant," said one of her daughters, Janice King. "She didn't hold an office of high power or wealth," said Mrs. King, "but daily she showed acts of kindness and charity … We had over 945 people come through the wake telling us how she impacted their life, how she made differences in their life." Her daughter continued:

> She died in the hospital away from her home, hooked up to machines and tubes in a coma. She suffered terribly for ten days. She never had a chance to understand her illness. She couldn't put her affairs in order or say goodbye. There was no time. She just got sicker and sicker … and we were always ten steps behind the illness. Her dreams of her retirement with Dad and travelling were stolen, all because the water was unsafe and nobody told her.

Mrs. Trushinski's son, Terry Trushinski, also spoke. He recalled telling his mother about how his own little boy was growing up, but said that now he cannot share those experiences with her. "I was born and raised in Walkerton and have lots of memories of this town," he said, but now I can't remember anything. When I think of Walkerton I think of *E. coli* and the death of my mother. I find it difficult to be in Walkerton. I don't enjoy it like I once did ... This tragedy has affected me every day.

2.2.4 Indirect Impacts

In addition to the heartrending suffering caused by illness and loss of life, the Walkerton community suffered in many indirect ways. Children were unable to attend their own schools, businesses throughout the region suffered, and residents experienced a high degree of anxiety in the aftermath of the tragedy. Many people came forward to tell me about these indirect impacts.

Many said they came to feel unsafe in their own community and did not know when they would be able to trust that life would continue as it had before the outbreak. In the words of Lois Steffler, a local resident, "Our lives have been turned upside-down." She continued:

> It has affected our lives in the sense that you can't seem to get your feet back on the ground ... I haven't slept since the *E. coli* thing started because you could hear the helicopter go over morning, noon and night. Your skin stood up because you didn't know who was it, who's sick this time? Are they going to live? ...

> [I]n my family alone my mother has been sick and my aunt has been sick and you don't know, like, a month or two months down the road, is everything going to flare up then and you are going to find out the long-term effect on people? You don't know.

There were also some unexpected side-effects of the outbreak, such as the reaction that some people had to the chlorine that was used to disinfect Walkerton's water supply in the aftermath. Although the residents could not drink the local water for more than six months, they continued to use it for washing and household functions. I heard from B.L., a Walkerton resident who, it turned out, had a serious sensitivity to chlorine. She needed to drink a lot of water because of a pre-existing bowel condition and became sick during the outbreak. During the decontamination, she became bedridden after chlorine was put into the water pipes leading to her house. She called a poison control telephone number and was told to get out of Walkerton for 24–48 hours.

While staying with her sister, B.L. coughed for two days and had to go to hospital. She was told that if she did not leave Walkerton until after the decontamination process was finished, she risked burning her lungs.

There was also significant impact on businesses in Walkerton. The financial losses suffered by local residents are discussed in a paper prepared for the Part 2 report of this Inquiry. Here I would like to briefly tell some of the stories of the local business owners themselves. Among others, I heard from Rick Lekx, president of the Walkerton District Chamber of Commerce, and from Gary McGregor, owner of the Pizza Delight in Walkerton. They told me that their livelihoods were affected when people stopped coming through the area, and they do not know how long recovery will take.

Mr. Lekx spoke about the rolling shocks to businesses as news of the outbreak emerged. The first businesses to be significantly affected were restaurants, which were forced to close because they relied on the town's water supply and needed to protect their customers. The motels and bed & breakfasts lost bookings. Retail stores experienced significantly less business, in some cases as little as 10% of the norm. Tourism operators throughout the region were similarly affected. Some businesses found it necessary to lay off employees.

As businesses turned to alternative water sources, many reopened in the weeks after the outbreak. Mr. McGregor, however, told me that they experienced disruptions because tests on the water system would cause the businesses to close down and reopen intermittently, until a stable water delivery system was in place. As a result, he had to lay off all the staff at his Pizza Delight. Even working toward remedying the situation "required an enormous investment in time and effort" by the staff of the Walkerton District Chamber of Commerce and by volunteers in community.

2.3 General Health Effects

Most of the people who died or became ill in Walkerton were infected with one of two bacteria: *Escherichia coli* O157:H7 and *Campylobacter jejuni*. Some background information about these bacteria and the ways in which they can affect human health may shed more light on the impact of the outbreak and on the threats posed by these pathogens. The following information is intended to complement the poignant stories recounted above. It provides an indication of the potentially serious consequences of the microbiological contamination of drinking water.

2.3.1   *Escherichia coli* O157:H7

Escherichia coli is a species of bacteria that normally inhabits the large intestines of mammals, including humans. Most *E. coli* bacteria are harmless to healthy humans and do not cause disease. However, some forms of *E. coli* are enteropathogenic, meaning they cause disease through the intestines.

E. coli O157:H7, a subgroup of *E. coli*, produces verotoxins that cause hemorrhagic colitis and, in some cases, hemolytic uremic syndrome (HUS). It was one of the two primary pathogens involved in the Walkerton outbreak. The minimum infective dose in young children is generally 10–200 live bacteria, but in adults it may be higher, as many as 1,000–10,000 live bacteria.

Cattle are a common reservoir of *E. coli* O157:H7. The bacteria can be transmitted from cattle to humans through contaminated raw meat, unpasteurized milk, apple cider, and water, among other means. Secondary transmission through person-to-person contact is also possible. In Ontario, the incidence of *E. coli* O157:H7 infection in humans is highest in cattle-producing areas, such as Bruce and Grey Counties in Southwestern Ontario, and in some regions in Eastern Ontario.

On average, 17% of people exposed to *E. coli*-contaminated water become ill. Incubation periods for *E. coli* O157:H7 range from 16 hours to eight days.[2] In the overwhelming majority of cases, the incubation period is three or four days.

A person infected with *E. coli* O157:H7 will experience intestinal disease marked by diarrhea that lasts an average of (but sometimes longer than) four days. Bloody diarrhea often occurs 24 hours after the onset of illness, and the infected person may experience severe abdominal pain. The illness usually resolves itself without treatment (other than rehydration and electrolyte replacement) after about four days. Infected people may continue to shed *E. coli* O157:H7 in their stools for many months.

---

[2] The incubation period for a pathogen is the period of time between one's exposure to the pathogen and the onset of illness.

In some people, particularly children under five years of age and the elderly, *E. coli* O157:H7 infection can have more serious consequences. In particular, it may cause hemolytic uremic syndrome (HUS), in which the verotoxins produced by *E. coli* O157:H7 cause acute kidney failure, anemia, and low platelet counts. Sometimes the small blood vessels of the brain are also affected by the verotoxin produced by *E. coli* O157:H7. HUS is a life-threatening condition.

Approximately 10–15% of children infected with *E. coli* O157:H7 develop HUS. Of these children, approximately 80% will need at least one blood transfusion to maintain their hemoglobin, and about 50% require kidney dialysis to treat the HUS. Roughly 10% of those who recover from kidney failure will have permanent damage to their kidneys that may interfere with their growth. When they become adults, these children may require a kidney transplant. Approximately 5% of children who contract HUS from *E. coli* O157:H7 will die.

The overwhelming majority of the adults who develop HUS from *E. coli* O157:H7 are the very elderly. The mortality rate for very elderly people afflicted with HUS is higher than that for children because the very elderly are generally more vulnerable to the disease because of pre-existing health conditions. For example, a person with pre-existing lung and heart problems often cannot withstand the fluid shifts associated with diarrhea.

It is generally believed that once a person has been exposed to verotoxin-producing *E. coli* O157:H7, she or he will develop protective antibodies to prevent subsequent reinfection by the same strain of *E. coli*. There is some suggestion that diarrhea-induced HUS can recur; however, there is no evidence of reported cases of *E. coli* O157:H7-induced HUS recurring.[3]

2.3.2 *Campylobacter jejuni*

Campylobacter jejuni is the most common type of *Campylobacter* bacteria that causes human illness. It was also implicated in the Walkerton outbreak. *C. jejuni* is frequently found in the feces of domestic fowl, cattle, swine, sheep, goats, and wildlife, including birds and deer. Most human infections are caused

---

[3] It is possible, though very rare, for a person who has experienced *E. coli* O157:H7–induced HUS to experience another form of HUS that is not associated with diarrhea. Recurrent HUS is uncommon, but possible, among people with certain types of non–diarrhea-induced HUS. HUS that is caused by *E. coli* O157:H7 is diarrhea-induced.

by the ingestion of contaminated foods, usually undercooked poultry. *C. jejuni* can also be passed to humans through unpasteurized milk, direct contact with animals, person-to-person transmission, and, of course, water.

C. jejuni bacteria proliferate in the bowel wall. Approximately half of those people infected with *C. jejuni* experience symptoms such as diarrhea, cramping, fever, and acute abdominal pain; the other half do not develop symptoms. Approximately a third of those who experience symptoms develop bloody diarrhea and, in 0.15% of people infected (usually the elderly, young children, and infants), the bacteria spread in the bloodstream.

The infective dose for *C. jejuni* is about 100,000 live bacteria, and the average incubation period is three to four days. Approximately 20% of people exposed to *C. jejuni* bacteria become ill.

Diarrhea associated with *C. jejuni* lasts an average of two to seven days, but in 10–20% of cases it may continue for more than a week. About 5–10% of those people who suffer from diarrhea as a result of *C. jejuni* infection experience a relapse after recovering from the first episode. The vast majority of people recover fully from *C. jejuni* infection and experience no long-term adverse effects, but 0.05% of infected people develop nerve damage (Guillain Barre syndrome), and 0.6% develop reactive arthritis. The reactive arthritis rarely lasts more than several months.

C. jejuni does not usually have the severe consequences associated with *E. coli* O157:H7. The fatality rate is much lower for *C. jejuni* (0.1%) than for *E. coli* O157:H7 (0.8%), and there is no known association between *C. jejuni* and HUS.

2.4 Deaths and Illnesses

The Office of the Chief Coroner and its expert review panel identified seven deaths associated with the Walkerton outbreak. In four cases, the sole cause of death was infection as a result of the outbreak. In three cases, infection contributed to death, but other factors also played a role. In those three cases, *E. coli* was the probable organism responsible for contributing to one death, and *C. jejuni* for the other two. Further details about the results of the investigation into deaths associated with the outbreak, as they relate to the issue of the onset of illness in the community, are discussed in Chapter 4 of this report.

It is estimated that a total of 2,321 people became sick as a result of the out-break. This calculation is based on the work of the Bruce-Grey-Owen Sound Health Unit and a Health Canada team that carried out epidemiological and environmental investigations to determine the cause and scope of the out-break. I discuss the methodology used to carry out this work in Chapter 4 as it relates to the physical cause of the contamination. In this section, I briefly outline the conclusions reached about the number and types of illnesses caused by the outbreak.

To determine the scope of the outbreak, Health Canada developed a case defi-nition that included anyone who had developed certain symptoms associated with *E. coli* O157:H7 or *C. jejuni* between April 15 and June 30, after expo-sure to Walkerton water. In terms of symptoms, the case definition included anyone who had diarrhea or bloody diarrhea, produced stool specimens posi-tive for *E. coli* O157:H7 or *C. jejuni*, or who had HUS.

By August 31, 2000, Health Canada and the local Health Unit had identified 1,346 people as meeting the case definition. Of these, 65 were hospitalized, 27 developed HUS, and seven died. Of the 1,346 identified cases, 675 people submitted stool samples, of which 163 were positive for *E. coli* O157:H7, 97 were positive for *C. jejuni*, 12 were positive for both, and 20 tested positive for other pathogens.[4]

Of the 675 people who submitted stool samples, 57% submitted samples that tested negative for both *E. coli* and *Campylobacter*. A negative test result does not necessarily mean the person was not infected. It might also mean that (1) the person had stopped or was intermittently shedding the bacteria, (2) the culture was not tested before the bacteria died, (3) the culture was mishandled, or (4) another pathogen was responsible for the symptoms. Accordingly, it is possible that some or all of the people who tested negative were in fact infected, or had previously been infected.

Using the results of a descriptive study, Health Canada also identified a signifi-cant number of unreported cases of illnesses. This is to be expected in milder cases of illness, where the primary symptoms are gastrointestinal illness. In the

---

[4] Those testing positive for other pathogens included 7 for *Campylobacter coli*, 2 for *Escherichia coli* VT, and 11 for *Salmonella, Yersinia*, or *Aeromonas*. In addition, 815 stools were examined for ova and parasites. There were 4 positive *Giardia* and 2 positive *Cryptosporidium* results. Only 39 stools were examined for viruses: all tested negative.

descriptive study, 740 Walkerton residents were identified as having become sick in May, whereas the expected number of cases, based on the attack rate for the bacteria, was 1,286. Thus, Health Canada and the Health Unit estimated that reports were received from only 58% of the expected cases (740 of 1,286) and, accordingly, that 42% of the cases of illness in the community went unreported. By applying this estimate of the rate of unreported illness to the number of identified cases (1,346), Health Canada estimated that a total of 2,321 people became ill as a result of the outbreak.[5]

---

[5] This assumes that the reporting rate was the same for both residents and non-residents of Walkerton and that it remained the same throughout the outbreak.

Chapter 3   The Events in Walkerton in May 2000

Contents

Chapter 3   The Events in Walkerton in May 2000

3.1   Overview

From May 8 to May 12, 2000, heavy rainfalls in Walkerton caused flooding. Because the operators of the Walkerton water system did not check the chlorine residual levels, they were unaware that contaminated water was entering the distribution system.

Samples from the water system were collected on May 15 and sent to the laboratory for microbiological analysis. The testing laboratory reported to Stan Koebel, the general manager of the Walkerton Public Utilities Commission (PUC), on May 17 that there were high levels of total coliforms and *Escherichia coli* (*E. coli*) in the water system. By May 18, the first symptoms of the outbreak emerged. Two children who had bloody diarrhea and abdominal pain were admitted to the hospital, and about 20 were absent from school.

In the succeeding days, the scope of the outbreak expanded. On May 19, the Bruce-Grey-Owen Sound Health Unit contacted the Walkerton PUC to ask about the quality of the water. It was reassured by the general manager that the water was fine. The same reassurances were received by the health unit on the following day. The general manager did not disclose the adverse water results received on May 17, nor did he reveal that a well had been operating for several days without chlorination. On May 21, the health unit issued a boil water advisory as a precautionary measure. On May 23, it received results from water samples it had collected indicating that *E. coli* was present in the Walkerton water supply.

When the Ministry of the Environment (MOE) initiated an investigation of the Walkerton water system on May 22 and May 23, the PUC operators altered the daily operating sheets to conceal the fact that the system had operated without chlorination.

In this chapter, I will describe the events of May 2000. In subsequent chapters, I will address the roles various parties played in those events and set out my conclusions where appropriate.[1]

---

[1] For the reader's assistance, I have included a description of the participants after Chapter 15 of this report.

3.2 The Walkerton Water System

In May 2000, the Walkerton water system was supplied by three groundwater wells: Wells 5, 6, and 7.

Well 5 is located on Wallace Street, in the southwest area of Walkerton. Constructed in 1978, it is a shallow well, drilled to a depth of 15 m. Well 5 was capable of providing approximately 56% of the water needs of the town. The well water was disinfected by the use of sodium hypochlorite, a bleach solution.

Well 6 is situated approximately 3 km west of Walkerton, in the former Township of Brant, adjacent to Bruce County Road 2. Built in 1982, the well had a depth of 72.2 m and was considered a deep-drilled well. It was capable of providing 42–52% of Walkerton's water requirements. Disinfection was provided by chlorine gas.

Well 7, located a short distance west of Well 6, was constructed in 1987 and has a depth of 76.2 m. It is capable of providing 125–140% of the daily water used by the Town of Walkerton. As was the case for Well 6, disinfection was provided by chlorine gas.

The water distribution system in Walkerton included 41.5 km of watermains as well as two standpipes, which provided water storage and pressure equalization for the system. It is estimated that in the Walkerton system, between 33 and 35 locations were "dead ends." There is a greater risk of bacterial contamination in dead ends, because water does not adequately circulate in them and may become stagnant. The water system had a reserve capacity of 20 hours.

The Walkerton PUC had a computerized control system for the wells and standpipe operation known as SCADA (Supervisory Control and Data Acquisition). It controlled the water operation 24 hours a day, 7 days a week, and stored data from the system.

In the next chapter, I conclude that the vast majority, if not all, of the contamination entered the Walkerton system through Well 5 and that the residents of the town first became exposed to the contamination on May 12 or shortly after.

3.3   May 1 to May 14

On May 5, Stan Koebel, the general manager of the Walkerton PUC, left Walkerton for a conference in Windsor that was sponsored in part by the Ontario Water Works Association. He did not return to Walkerton until May 14. His brother Frank Koebel, the foreman of the Walkerton PUC, was responsible for the waterworks operation while Stan Koebel was away.

Before leaving, Stan Koebel was aware that Well 7 was pumping unchlorinated water into the distribution system. Well 7, which had not operated since March 10, had been activated on May 2. On May 3, Mr. Koebel instructed his brother to remove the existing chlorinator at Well 7. Stan Koebel expected his brother to install the new chlorinator, which had been on the PUC premises since December 1998, while he was attending the conference in Windsor.

Frank Koebel did not install the chlorinator while Stan was away, and Well 7 operated without a chlorinator from May 3 to May 9. It was the only well operating during this period. This was clearly contrary to the Ontario Drinking Water Objectives (ODWO) and Bulletin 65-W-4, "Chlorination of Potable Water Supplies," commonly known as the Chlorination Bulletin. Although both Stan and Frank Koebel were aware that chlorination was required at all times, they believed that unchlorinated water from Well 7 was safe because it was from a deep well. PUC staff would frequently drink raw unchlorinated water at the well because it was "cold, clear, and clean" and had a better taste than chlorinated water.

On May 9, Well 7 was turned off and Wells 5 and 6 were activated. Well 5 operated continuously until May 15, with the exception of the period from 10:45 p.m. on May 12 until 2:15 p.m. on May 13, and it was the primary source of water for the town. Well 6 cycled on and off during this period.

It rained heavily in Walkerton from May 8 to May 12: 134 mm of rain fell during these five days. The heaviest rainfall occurred on May 12, when 70 mm fell. On the evening of May 12, flooding was observed at Well 5, and at about 10:45 p.m. that well stopped pumping water. No explanation has been offered as to why this happened. None of the witnesses said they turned the well off, and the SCADA system was set so that the well should have continued pumping. The well began to operate again on May 13 at 2:15 p.m. Someone could have turned off the well because of a concern that there was flooding, but there is no evidence to support this suggestion; nor is there evidence as to how Well 5 was turned on again.

On May 13, Frank Koebel performed the routine daily check of the operating wells. The purpose of the daily checks was to enter data on pumping rate flows and chlorine usage, and, most importantly, to measure the chlorine residuals in the treated water. However, for more than 20 years, it had been the practice of PUC employees on most days not to measure the chlorine residual but rather to make a fictitious entry for the chlorine residual on the daily operating sheet. PUC employees routinely entered a chlorine residual of 0.5 mg/L or 0.75 mg/L, even though they were setting the chlorine dose being added to the water below these amounts.

According to the daily operating sheet for Well 5, Frank Koebel checked the well on May 13 at 4:10 p.m. and entered 0.75 mg/L as the chlorine residual. There are no entries for Well 6 on May 13. I am satisfied that Frank Koebel did not in fact check the chlorine residual at Well 5 on May 13. The PUC did not use enough chlorine to achieve a residual nearly that high, and clearly the 0.75 mg/L shown as the chlorine residual for May 13 is false. The entry that day followed the pattern of making fictitious entries over the years.

I am also satisfied that at the time Frank Koebel checked the well on May 13, contamination was most likely entering the distribution system through Well 5. Had he tested the chlorine residual on May 13, it is very likely that he would have learned that there was no residual, which should have alerted him to the problem of incoming contamination.[2] It is likely that contamination had already entered the distribution system by then, but nonetheless steps could have been taken at that time to reduce the scope of the problem.

On the next day, May 14, Frank Koebel again checked Well 5 and followed the same procedure, entering a fictitious chlorine residual of 0.75 mg/L on the daily operating sheet. Here too, I am satisfied that he did not check the residual at the well. Had he done so, he almost certainly would have detected that contamination was entering the system.

---

[2] A properly qualified operator would readily recognize that the absence of a chlorine residual indicated that the demand being exerted by contaminants in the raw water was exceeding the chlorine dosage being added to the water.

3.4   Monday, May 15

Stan Koebel arrived at the Walkerton PUC office at 6:00 a.m. He checked the SCADA system and learned that Well 7 was not operating. Mr. Koebel turned on the well, assuming that by then the new chlorinator had been installed.

At approximately 7:30 a.m., Allan Buckle, a PUC employee, informed Stan Koebel that the new chlorinator at Well 7 had not yet been installed. Nevertheless, Mr. Koebel allowed Well 7 to continue pumping unchlorinated water into the distribution system. From May 15 to May 19 at noon, at which time the installation of the new chlorinator was completed, the water that entered the distribution system from Well 7 was not chlorinated. At 1:15 p.m. on May 15, Well 5 was shut off, and from then until the following Saturday, May 20, Well 7 was the only source of supply. Well 6 did not pump water during this time.

On May 15, an entry of 0.75 mg/L chlorine residual at Well 5 was made on the daily operating sheet. Again, I am satisfied that no one measured the chlorine residual at Well 5 on that day. Had the chlorine residual been measured then, it is virtually certain that there would have been none and that PUC staff would have been alerted to the problem of incoming contamination.

It was the practice of PUC employees to collect samples for bacteriological tests every Monday from the operating wells and from the distribution system. On the morning of May 15, Mr. Buckle was instructed to collect samples at Well 7. PUC employees, including Mr. Buckle, would routinely label samples as having been taken at sites where they were not in fact collected. Mr. Buckle had four bottles labelled "Well 7 raw," "Well 7 treated," "125 Durham Street," and "902 Yonge Street." He testified that he filled the bottles labelled "Well 7 treated," "Well 7 raw," and "125 Durham Street" with raw water from Well 7. As I find in Chapter 4 of this report, I am satisfied that none of the samples from May 15 were in fact taken at the site of Well 7. Two of these samples, as well as the sample labelled "902 Yonge Street," tested positive for *E. coli*. The evidence is overwhelming that the contamination entered the system through Well 5, not Well 7.[3] Stan Koebel testified that PUC staff, including Mr. Buckle, sometimes collected samples at the PUC workshop, which was close to and

---

[3] In Chapter 4 of this report, I point out that Well 6 was susceptible to surface contamination. However, there is no evidence to suggest that contamination actually entered through Well 6 during the critical period.

down the line from Well 5, rather than at the site on the label of the sample bottle. The fourth sample was collected at 902 Yonge Street by Stan Koebel.

Samples were also collected from the Highway 9 project on May 15. At that time, the installation of the new watermain on Highway 9 was almost complete. The construction project involved the replacement of 615 m of watermain in southwest Walkerton between Wallace Street and Circle Drive. The consulting engineer was B.M. Ross and Associates Ltd., and the contractor was Lavis Construction Ltd. Before connecting the new watermain to the Walkerton water system, it was necessary to test water samples from the main. Wayne Greb from Lavis Construction and Dennis Elliott from B.M. Ross asked Stan Koebel if water samples from the Highway 9 site could be sent to the same laboratory that would test samples collected that day from the Walkerton system. Mr. Koebel agreed, and three samples were collected from two hydrants at the Highway 9 project. Mr. Greb and Mr. Elliott asked Mr. Koebel to write the words "Please rush" on the laboratory submission form (also called the "chain of custody" form) because the contractor was anxious to complete the job. The date prescribed by the Ministry of Transportation for the completion of the construction work, May 12, had already passed, and financial penalties could be imposed on contractors who failed to complete the work by the prescribed date.

On May 15, Mr. Koebel sent the three "rush" samples from the Highway 9 project, four from the Walkerton system, and eight from the subdivisions of Chepstow and Geeson to A&L Canada Laboratories. The samples were accompanied by two separate submission forms. The first form listed the three samples from Highway 9 (#1 hydrant new main, #4 hydrant new main, and #4 hydrant new main), and presence-absence testing was requested.

The second form listed 20 sampling sites but had entries for only 4 from the Walkerton system and 8 from Chepstow and Geeson.

A&L was requested to perform presence-absence and membrane filtration testing on the sample labelled "Well 7 treated" from the Walkerton system as well as on two samples from Chepstow and Geeson. Presence-absence testing was to be conducted on all of the 12 samples submitted to the lab.

Stan Koebel knew that the list of samples on the second submission form contained inaccurate information. He knew that the sample described as "Well 7 treated" could not be treated water because the well was pumping unchlorinated water and that the sample labelled "125 Durham Street" had been collected not at this site but at a different location. When Mr. Koebel was asked at the Inquiry for an explanation for this misinformation, he answered, "Simply convenience, or just couldn't be bothered." It was not unusual for PUC sampling bottles to be mislabelled in this fashion.

3.5   Tuesday, May 16

Before discussing the events of May 16, it is useful to briefly describe the history of the Walkerton PUC's relationship with A&L Canada Laboratories.

A&L was a private laboratory. Although it had performed chemical testing for the PUC, it had only begun to conduct microbiological tests for the PUC on May 1. Previously, these tests had been done by G.A.P. EnviroMicrobial Services Inc. In April, Stan Koebel received a letter from G.A.P. indicating that the laboratory would no longer conduct routine drinking water analysis such as presence-absence and membrane filtration tests. Mr. Koebel decided to retain A&L to perform the microbiological tests. When he contacted Robert Deakin, the laboratory manager at A&L, Mr. Koebel indicated that the PUC was changing laboratories because it had received a "wacky result" from the previous laboratory. As Mr. Koebel testified, this in fact was not the reason that G.A.P. was no longer analyzing water samples from the Walkerton PUC. When asked at the Inquiry to explain this statement to A&L, Mr. Koebel said, "I thought it was up to G.A.P. to make these announcements."

On May 1, when Mr. Koebel first sent samples to A&L, he did not include all the samples listed on the chain of custody form, and he sent an insufficient volume of water to perform the requested tests. A&L contacted Mr. Koebel and explained that the presence-absence test required 100 mL of water, that the coliform and *E. coli* membrane filtration test required a further 100 mL of water, and that another 100 mL of water was necessary for the heterotrophic plate count. Despite this conversation, Mr. Koebel repeated the same procedure in the samples he sent to A&L on May 15, sending only enough water samples to perform presence-absence tests and a membrane filtration test on one sample – the one labelled "Well 7 treated."

On May 16, A&L received the two chain of custody forms and the samples collected from the Walkerton water system, the Highway 9 project, and the two suburban divisions. A&L staff observed that eight samples listed on the Walkerton form had not actually been sent by the PUC. Moreover, although Mr. Koebel had requested A&L to perform presence-absence and membrane filtration tests, the requisite water volumes again had not been shipped. Mr. Deakin asked his assistant supervisor, Cathy Doyle, to contact Mr. Koebel and explain the proper sampling volumes.

Ms. Doyle spoke to Stan Koebel before 10:00 a.m. on May 16. Mr. Koebel said that the PUC would provide the appropriate water volumes in the next set of samples to be tested by A&L. He then asked whether the results for the "rush" tests were available. Ms. Doyle responded that A&L had only recently received the samples for Walkerton and that they were being processed.

Mr. Deakin called Stan Koebel later that day to explain that A&L required a minimum of 24 hours to perform the microbiological tests. He stated that if a significant finding was discerned during the 24-hour testing period, A&L would contact Mr. Koebel. In that conversation, Mr. Deakin raised the subject of Well 5. The results of the presence-absence tests performed on the May 1 samples, which were reported on May 5, had indicated that both the raw and the treated samples from Well 5 tested positive for total coliforms. Mr. Deakin wanted to know whether the "wacky results" referred to earlier by Mr. Koebel were reflected in the May 5 lab results. Mr. Koebel did not give a clear answer to the question. When Mr. Deakin asked Mr. Koebel why samples from Well 5 had not been forwarded to A&L with the May 15 shipment, he simply replied that Well 5 was "off line," which Mr. Deakin interpreted as meaning "not operational." In fact, Well 5 was operating on the morning of May 15. It was turned off at 1:15 p.m.

It is worth noting that Well 5 was not sampled on May 8, the week following the positive results received on May 5. Thus, the last bacteriological samples for Well 5 before the Walkerton outbreak were taken on May 1.

3.6 Wednesday, May 17

When Mr. Deakin arrived at A&L at approximately 8:30 a.m. on May 17, the laboratory technician had analyzed the samples from Walkerton. Mr. Deakin was informed that there were several positive results. He examined the samples and asked the technician to begin the report to the Walkerton PUC.

Mr. Deakin telephoned Stan Koebel in the early morning of May 17. He told Mr. Koebel that each of the three "rush" samples were positive for *E. coli* and total coliforms and that "the distribution samples didn't look good either." Mr. Deakin identified the samples that had adverse results. He stated that he was unable to specify the number of colony forming units (cfu) because most of the samples had only been subjected to the presence-absence test. However, Mr. Deakin did state that in the one sample from the Walkerton water system that had undergone the membrane filtration test, the plate was covered with both coliforms and *E. coli*. Although Mr. Koebel may have been focusing on the problem with the Highway 9 rush samples at this point, he certainly had information alerting him to the fact that there might be a problem in the distribution system. To be fair to him, on several previous occasions distribution samples had tested positive for *E. coli*; however, subsequent sample results had been negative.

On the morning of May 17, A&L faxed the results from the Highway 9 project to the PUC. These results indicated that the three hydrant samples were positive for total coliforms and *E. coli*. The report for the second set of samples from the Walkerton water system was faxed by A&L in the early afternoon of May 17. The sample labelled "Well 7 treated" was positive for *E. coli* and total coliforms. Membrane filtration testing was also conducted on this sample. The results showed massive contamination: coliform bacteria greater than 200 cfu/100 mL, *E. coli* greater than 200 cfu/100 mL, and a heterotrophic plate count of 600 cfu/1 mL. The presence-absence results from the samples labelled "125 Durham Street" and "902 Yonge Street" were also positive for total coliforms and *E. coli*. The sample labelled "Well 7 raw" had negative results. As I have said above, the bottles were mislabelled. I have concluded that none of the samples came from Well 7, so the anomaly of raw water being negative and treated water being positive need not be resolved.

The date on A&L's fax machine was set incorrectly: it was set 11 hours and 13 minutes ahead of the actual time and showed p.m. instead of a.m. Although the date stamped on the lab reports to the Walkerton PUC are, respectively, "May 17 8:27 p.m." and "May 18 1:50 a.m.," I am satisfied that they were in fact sent 11 hours and 13 minutes earlier – that is, on May 17 at 9:14 a.m. and 2:37 p.m., respectively.

 Neither the MOE nor the local Medical Officer of Health received notice of these adverse laboratory results. These results were sent only to Mr. Koebel at the PUC, because it was the policy of A&L to forward laboratory reports solely to its clients unless directed otherwise. Mr. Deakin was unaware of section 4.1.3 of the ODWO, a guideline stating that the lab should notify the MOE district office of indications of unsafe drinking water. The May 17 results were indicators of unsafe drinking water. I discuss the issue of the failure of the government to enact a regulation mandating notification by a testing laboratory to the MOE and the local health unit in Chapter 10 of this report.

On May 17, Mr. Koebel informed Dennis Elliott, the site supervisor for B.M. Ross, that the samples from Highway 9 had failed. Rechlorination, the flushing of the new watermain, and the collection of additional samples were necessary.

3.7 Thursday, May 18

New samples were collected from the Highway 9 project on May 18. The contractor, through its agent Philip Analytical Services, submitted three samples, this time to MDS Laboratory Services Inc. in London. Philip Analytical, an environmental laboratory that conducted chemical testing, regularly sent samples to MDS for microbiological analysis. The work order submitted to MDS requested that three samples – "BM1," "BM2," and "BM3" (identification numbers assigned by Philip Analytical) – undergo tests for total coliforms and *E. coli*. No information appeared on the work order to indicate that the samples were from a municipal drinking water system or from a hydrant. Testing on these samples was conducted by MDS on May 19.

Frank Koebel was aware on May 18 that adverse lab results from the Highway 9 construction project had been received from A&L. On that day, Frank Koebel had a discussion with Dennis Elliott of B. M. Ross and Wayne Greb of Lavis Construction regarding the connection of the new main on Highway 9 to the Saugeen Fuel and Filter building (previously the Canadian Tire building). One reason for the connection was fire protection. The owners of the building had also been pressuring the contractor to clean the area for the upcoming grand opening of Saugeen Fuel and Filter. Frank Koebel agreed to complete the connection on the condition that its water would not be consumed by people in the building and that the tap would be kept running to prevent backfeed into the system.

Meanwhile, on May 18, illnesses were emerging in the community.[4] Two children were admitted by Dr. Kristen Hallett, a pediatrician, to the Owen Sound hospital: a seven-year-old girl with bloody diarrhea, and a nine-year-old boy with abdominal pain and a fever who developed bloody diarrhea later that evening. Dr. Hallett spoke with the parents of the two patients to determine if there was a link between the children. Both children were from Walkerton and were pupils at Mother Teresa School. Dr. Hallett examined the stools of the two patients and noticed that they were similar. She suspected that the children had contracted *E. coli* O157:H7 and sent the stool samples from the two patients to the hospital laboratory for analysis.

Other members of the Walkerton community were also ill on May 18. At least 20 students at Mother Teresa School were absent, and although the evidence is not entirely clear, I am satisfied that by May 18, members of the public had begun contacting the staff at the Walkerton PUC to inquire about the safety of the water. They were told by a staff member, who had discussed the issue with Stan Koebel, that the water was fine.

It was also on May 18 that Stan Koebel instructed his brother Frank, foreman of the PUC, to install the new chlorinator at Well 7. It seems more than coincidental that the instruction to install the chlorinator was given on the same day that the public first contacted the Walkerton PUC regarding the safety of water due to illness in the community and on the day after Stan Koebel first learned that there might be contamination in the Walkerton water distribution system. I am satisfied that on May 18, Stan Koebel at least suspected there could be a problem with the water. He was very likely concerned that Well 7 had been operating without a chlorinator, a situation that he knew was contrary to government requirements.[5]

Mr. Koebel was also concerned about contamination in the new watermain on Highway 9. The valve connecting the new main to the distribution system had been opened on May 11, 12, 15, and 17 for the swabbing, flushing, and chlorination procedures on the construction project. He may have thought that

---

[4] Although some people had experienced symptoms before May 18, public indications of an outbreak emerged on that day.

[5] I use the word "requirements" to describe the provisions set out in the ODWO and the Chlorination Bulletin. As I discuss in Chapter 9 of this report, these documents were in fact guidelines, not regulations. However, the MOE had made it clear to Mr. Koebel on several occasions that the water at Walkerton was to be treated with chlorine and that a chlorine residual of 0.5 mg/L was to be maintained after 15 minutes contact time.

the new main was one of the possible sources of the contamination in the distribution system.

On the evening of May 18, the Walkerton PUC held a meeting. As was his usual practice, Stan Koebel presented the manager's report. In it, he stated that the PUC was awaiting sample results from the Highway 9 project, but he did not disclose to the PUC commissioners that adverse results from the Highway 9 project had been received, nor did he reveal the failed samples from the Walkerton water system. Moreover, Mr. Koebel indicated in his report that "we are currently rebuilding the chlorine equipment at our #7 pumphouse." He did not disclose, nor were the commissioners aware, that the new chlorinator had been stored at the pumphouse for over a year and a half and that Well 7 had been pumping unchlorinated water from May 3 to May 9 and again from May 15 to the time of the meeting. At this point, Mr. Koebel was obviously concerned about the adverse results and about a possible connection between those results and the fact that Well 7 had been operating without chlorination.

3.8   Friday, May 19

The scope of the outbreak expanded rapidly. Eight people with a three-day history of diarrhea and stomach cramps were examined at the Walkerton hospital emergency department. Bloody diarrhea had prompted these individuals to visit the hospital. More than 25 students at Mother Teresa School were ill, and 8 students at the Walkerton Public School suffering from stomach pain, diarrhea, and nausea were sent home. On the same day, three residents at a retirement home, Maple Court Villa, developed diarrhea and vomiting, and a number of residents at Brucelea Haven, a long-term care facility, contracted diarrhea; two of the residents developed bloody diarrhea. A local physician, Dr. Donald Gill, examined 12 or 13 patients, all of whom were suffering from diarrhea.

At approximately 9:00 a.m., Dr. Hallett placed a telephone call to Dr. Murray McQuigge, the local Medical Officer of Health. This was the first contact with the Bruce-Grey-Owen Sound Health Unit regarding the emerging outbreak. Early that morning, Dr. Hallett had learned that in addition to the two children she had seen on Thursday, other people in the community were ill. She had conducted a food history investigation with the parents of her two patients and suspected that *E. coli* O157:H7 was the causative agent and that contaminated water was the source of the infections. Dr. Hallett spoke to Mary Sellars,

Dr. McQuigge's executive assistant, and advised her that two young patients had been admitted to the Owen Sound hospital. The pediatrician explained that the children had diarrhea and that stool samples had been sent to the laboratory for analysis. She also indicated that the illnesses were not confined to the two pediatric patients and that several other people in the community were experiencing the same symptoms. Ms. Sellars said that she would leave a note containing this information on Dr. McQuigge's desk. Dr. Hallett called the health unit again that day to ensure that the matter was addressed.

At approximately noon, David Patterson, assistant director of health protection at the health unit, listened to the voice-mail message from Ms. Sellars that described Dr. Hallett's call. Mr. Patterson instructed Beverly Middleton, a public health inspector in Owen Sound, to contact Dr. Hallett, and in a telephone call later that afternoon, Ms. Middleton learned that two children had been admitted to the Owen Sound hospital. Dr. Hallett told Ms. Middleton that people were concerned that something was "going on" in Walkerton. Ms. Middleton informed the doctor that she had no knowledge of any unusual events in Walkerton.

At approximately 2:00 p.m., Ms. Middleton received a call from JoAnn Todd, managing director at Maple Court Villa. It was the policy of the retirement home to contact the local Medical Officer of Health if three or more residents in a 24-hour period developed the same symptoms. Ms. Todd described the outbreak protocol of the home, the symptomatology of the three residents, and the date of the onset of symptoms. Ms. Middleton issued an outbreak number and asked Ms. Todd to initiate stool collections and a patient line-listing (a list of the names of patients who had been examined).

Ms. Middleton contacted administrative staff at Mother Teresa School, the school attended by the two pediatric patients at the Owen Sound hospital. She was informed that 25 students were ill with diarrhea, some of them with bloody diarrhea, and that 4 other students had been sent home from school that day with abdominal pain and nausea. The school receptionist reported that a parent of a student had stated that something was wrong with the Walkerton water. She indicated that she was not aware of problems with the town's water supply. Ms. Middleton then spoke with the Walkerton Public School, which had also observed increased absenteeism among its student population, and learned that eight children were ill and had been sent home. These children were also suffering stomach pain, diarrhea, nausea, and vomiting.

In a conversation with the Walkerton hospital emergency department, Ms. Middleton was informed that eight patients with a three-day history of diarrhea and stomach cramps had been examined but that there had been no hospital admissions. The physician-on-call, Dr. Donald Gill, had left the hospital, and Ms. Middleton telephoned him at his office to discuss the medical histories of these individuals.

James Schmidt, the public health inspector in the Walkerton office of the health unit, also received calls on May 19 concerning illness in the community. Ruth Schnurr, an administrator at Mother Teresa School, reported to the Walkerton office that 25 students were ill – abnormally high absenteeism for that time of the academic year. Some of these students lived in the town of Walkerton, others in the countryside; and the students were in various grades and different classrooms. Ms. Schnurr believed that water was the source of the illnesses. Mr. Schmidt also received a call from a member of the public regarding the number of sick students at Mother Teresa School. He did not pass the information received on May 19 to Beverly Middleton of the health unit's Owen Sound office.

Although there were suspicions in the community that water was the source of the outbreak, Mr. Patterson, Ms. Middleton, and Mr. Schmidt did not believe at this point that water was responsible for the illnesses. Their experience was that the common source of outbreaks that have symptoms of this nature is food, not water. However, because the quality of the water had been questioned by members of the community, the health unit's public health officials decided to investigate this issue.

Mr. Schmidt contacted the Walkerton PUC in the early afternoon. By that time, the chlorinator at Well 7 had been installed and the well was pumping chlorinated water into the distribution system. Stan Koebel, who was returning from a meeting in Southampton, spoke to Mr. Schmidt on his cellphone. The telephone record shows that this call was placed at 2:21 p.m. on May 19.

Mr. Schmidt told Mr. Koebel that a number of children at Mother Teresa School were ill with diarrhea and stomach cramps. When Mr. Schmidt asked Mr. Koebel if there were any problems with the water supply, Mr. Koebel replied that he "thought the water was okay." There are differences in the testimony of Mr. Schmidt and Mr. Koebel regarding the details of the conversation that took place between them. I do not think anything turns on the differences. However, where such differences occur, I prefer the evidence of

Mr. Schmidt. It is clear that Mr. Schmidt was asking about the safety of the water and that Mr. Koebel led him to believe that everything was "okay."

I am satisfied that by this point in time, Mr. Koebel was aware of the adverse results from samples collected by the PUC on May 15 at Highway 9 and from the Walkerton water system. I do not accept the evidence of Mr. Koebel that he had not seen the adverse results from the Walkerton system when he spoke to Mr. Schmidt on May 19. There is overwhelming evidence to the contrary. Mr. Koebel had been told by Mr. Deakin about those results on May 17; the fax of the results had been on his desk since the afternoon of May 17. Later on the afternoon of May 19, he told his brother Frank Koebel that he was concerned about contamination in the distribution system, and on May 23 he told a town council meeting that he had received the lab report on May 19.

In his conversation with Mr. Schmidt, Mr. Koebel did not disclose any of the adverse results or the fact that Well 7 had been operating without a chlorinator that same week. Mr. Koebel may have expected A&L to notify the MOE's district officer, who would at some point notify the health unit of the adverse test results, as had been the case in the past. However, it was clear to Mr. Koebel that at this point, Mr. Schmidt was unaware of the results in the May 17 reports from A&L. Even though he was advised by Mr. Schmidt that children at Mother Teresa School were ill with diarrhea and stomach cramps, Mr. Koebel reassured Mr. Schmidt that the water quality was fine.

At 4:00 p.m. on May 19, Mr. Patterson contacted Stan Koebel to discuss the calls received by the health unit from members of the public concerned about the quality of the water. Mr. Koebel again stated that he thought the water was fine. Mr. Patterson asked whether anything unusual had occurred in the water system. Mr. Koebel responded that there had been watermain construction in the south part of town near Mother Teresa School and that the mains were undergoing a flushing procedure. He also stated that a new chlorinator had been installed at the well on the previous day, May 18. This statement was not accurate: the chlorinator had not been installed until May 19 at noon. Again, Mr. Koebel did not reveal the adverse results from the Highway 9 project or the Walkerton system, nor did he disclose that Well 7 had been pumping unchlorinated water from May 3 to May 9 and from May 15 to May 19.

Mr. Patterson and other members of the health unit continued to investigate the cause of the outbreak. Their training and experience led them to believe that outbreaks with these symptoms were generally caused by food. The information amassed by health officials on May 19 showed that children of elementary school age and residents of a retirement home and a nursing home had contracted bloody diarrhea. The illnesses appeared to be affecting the very young and the very old. Although this is typical for *E. coli* O157:H7, public health officials at the health unit were perplexed, because these two age groups do not generally eat the same food or attend the same functions. However, having received assurance from Mr. Koebel that the water was fine, public health officials continued to investigate possible food-borne sources. They believed that there had never been an *E. coli* O157:H7 outbreak in a treated water system like Walkerton's, and the municipal treated drinking water supply was therefore low on their index of suspicion.

Even before the health unit issued a boil water advisory, some individuals in Walkerton believed that their water might be the source of the illnesses and took measures in their homes and workplaces to prevent further infections. (It was not until Sunday, May 21, at approximately 1:30 p.m., that the health unit advised the Walkerton community not to drink the municipal water.) On May 19, Brucelea Haven decided to institute its own boil water procedures – the first time such procedures had been implemented at the nursing home. Robert McKay, an employee of the Walkerton PUC who was on sick leave, also began to boil water at his home on May 19. Similarly, Mr. and Mrs. Reich, the parents of the seven-year-old girl who had been admitted to the Owen Sound hospital on May 18, decided that their family as well as their employees should drink only bottled water. Members of their extended family made the same decision.

At 4:30 p.m., after his conversations with Mr. Schmidt and Mr. Patterson, Stan Koebel went to the PUC shop and met Frank Koebel and Allan Buckle. He asked Frank about the status of the chlorinator at Well 7 and was told that it had been installed that day. Stan Koebel told the others that the samples from Highway 9 had failed the laboratory tests. After Mr. Buckle left, Stan Koebel told Frank Koebel that he was concerned about bacteriological contamina- tion in the distribution system. He said that the PUC office had received calls from Walkerton residents, that the health unit had asked if the water was safe for consumption, and that he had indicated that the water was "okay."

After Stan Koebel's conversation with Mr. Patterson on the afternoon of May 19, he decided to flush and to increase the chlorine in the Walkerton water system. He had told Mr. Patterson he would take these "precautionary measures." Significantly, this was the first time that Mr. Koebel had flushed watermains after receiving an adverse test result. He decided to use Well 7, which a few hours earlier had had a new chlorinator installed. He testified that the fact that Well 7 had pumped unchlorinated water into the distribution system from May 15 until noon on May 19 did not influence his decision to flush the watermains. I do not accept this evidence. By this time, he knew that people in Walkerton were sick, he was aware of contamination in the system, and he had not told Mr. Schmidt or Mr. Patterson about the results of the adverse water samples or that Well 7 had been operating without a chlorinator when he was asked about the safety of the water.

I accept that on May 19, Mr. Koebel was concerned that people in Walkerton were becoming sick and that he was hoping to prevent further illness by increasing the chlorination in the water system. But he was also hoping that if he was successful in eradicating the contamination from the distribution system, the next set of microbiological samples sent to the laboratory would yield negative results from the distribution system. He was very concerned, I believe, that it should not come to light that Well 7 had operated for a significant length of time without a chlorinator. Indeed, as I point out below, on May 22, he took steps to alter the operating records for Well 7 to conceal this fact.

I do not think, however, that on May 19 or during the following weekend, Stan Koebel fully understood the seriousness of the health risk posed to the community by his failure to disclose the adverse results to the local health unit. This is exemplified by the fact that during the weekend, he continued to drink water from a fire hydrant and a garden hose, and on May 22 he filled his daughter's swimming pool with municipal water. It is also clear that Mr. Koebel was not aware of the existence of *E. coli* O157:H7, nor that this bacteria was potentially lethal.

At approximately 5:00 p.m. on May 19, Mr. Koebel began to intensively flush and increase the chlorine levels in the Walkerton water system. This activity continued until May 22. Mr. Koebel testified that he selected the hydrant at Mother Teresa School on May 19 because it was a location at which the system would draw "fresh chlorinated water" from Well 7. He tested the chlorine residual at the school at 5:45 p.m. and received a low reading of 0.01 mg/L. He continued to measure the chlorine residual at both Well 7 and Mother Teresa School throughout the evening, until 11:00 p.m. His recorded measurements appear in Table 1. It is not clear whether the residual measurements at Well 7 were taken after 15 minutes of contact time. Given the PUC sampling practices, this is highly unlikely.

Table 1 Chlorine Residual Measurements, May 19, 2000

Well 7

6:30 p.m.	0.50 mg/L
9:30 p.m.	0.63 mg/L
11:00 p.m.	0.90 mg/L

Mother Teresa School

5:45 p.m.	0.01 mg/L
7:00 p.m.	0.02 mg/L
8:00 p.m.	0.06 mg/L
9:30 p.m.	0.08 mg/L
10:30 p.m.	0.10 mg/L

3.9 Saturday, May 20

On Saturday morning, the laboratory at the Owen Sound hospital determined that the stool sample from one of the two children whom Dr. Hallett had examined on May 18 was presumptive positive for *E. coli* O157:H7. The laboratory notified the Bruce-Grey-Owen Sound Health Unit of the presumptive result and indicated that the confirmatory result would be available the next day. The other child who had been admitted to the Owen Sound hospital on May 18 had normal fecal flora.

The outbreak continued to spread on May 20. The Walkerton hospital was extremely busy throughout the day. It received more than 120 calls from concerned residents, half of whom complained of bloody diarrhea, and 20 to 30 people were examined by staff in the Walkerton hospital's emergency department.

The health unit continued to investigate the cause of the outbreak. At 9:50 a.m., David Patterson was notified of the presumptive positive *E. coli* O157:H7 result from the patient at the Owen Sound hospital. He passed this information to Ms. Middleton, who contacted the Walkerton hospital, explaining to emergency department staff that a potential complication of *E. coli* O157:H7 is hemolytic uremic syndrome (HUS), which could have serious implications for the young and the elderly. She also advised the staff not to dispense anti-diarrheal medication, because it could exacerbate the condition of patients with *E. coli*. Ms. Middleton faxed information to the Walkerton hospital on *E. coli* O157:H7, HUS, and the management of diarrheal infections. She also contacted the hospitals in Hanover and Owen Sound: she was concerned that if a parent with a child suffering from bloody diarrhea arrived at a busy emergency department at the Walkerton hospital, the parent might travel to Hanover or Owen Sound to obtain medical attention.

At 11:00 a.m., Mr. Patterson asked James Schmidt to contact Stan Koebel and advise him of the ongoing illnesses. Mr. Schmidt was also asked to obtain the current chlorine residual levels in the water system and to ensure that the system would be monitored throughout the weekend. Mr. Patterson did not instruct Mr. Schmidt to review the Walkerton water file to obtain information on sample results in past weeks. It was not until several days later, on May 24, that the health unit examined the Walkerton file.

In his discussion with Stan Koebel, Mr. Schmidt learned that the system was being flushed and that the chlorine residual levels were 0.1 to 0.4 parts per million (ppm) in the distribution system and 0.73 ppm at the wellhead. Mr. Schmidt did not ask Mr. Koebel for water test results from the previous few weeks, nor did Mr. Koebel offer information about the adverse samples from the Walkerton system and the Highway 9 construction project that he had received earlier that week.

Mr. Schmidt informed Mr. Patterson by voice mail of the chlorine residual measurements. When Mr. Patterson received this information, he was relatively confident that the water supply was secure. He believed that if chlorine residual levels existed in the distribution system, there would be no bacteria in the water supply.

At about 1:30 p.m., Mr. Patterson decided to contact Dr. Murray McQuigge, the local Medical Officer of Health, at his cottage. He informed Dr. McQuigge that two children from Walkerton with bloody diarrhea were in the Owen Sound hospital and that one of them had a stool culture that was presumptive *E. coli* O157:H7. Mr. Patterson reported that several people in the Walkerton area had also developed bloody diarrhea. Ten stool cultures had been submitted to the laboratory for analysis, but the results were not yet available. Dr. McQuigge indicated that if more cases of *E. coli* O157:H7 were reported by the hospital laboratory, the patients should be interviewed to obtain additional information about their illnesses. He returned to Owen Sound in the early evening of May 20.

At 3:00 p.m., Mr. Patterson informed Stan Koebel that an individual had reported to the hospital that he had heard on CKNX FM 102, a local radio station, that the water in Walkerton should not be consumed. Mr. Patterson asked Mr. Koebel to contact the radio station to correct the impression that there were problems with the Walkerton water and to reassure concerned members of the public. Mr. Koebel was reluctant to comply with this request.

He told Mr. Patterson that the watermains were being flushed and that the chlorine residual levels ranged from 0.1 to 0.3 ppm. Mr. Patterson again asked Mr. Koebel whether there had been any unusual events in the water system. Mr. Koebel responded that there had been watermain construction and that the chlorinator had been replaced – activities that Mr. Patterson considered standard in a water system. Again, Mr. Koebel did not disclose the adverse results from the May 15 samples or the fact that Well 7 had been operating without a chlorinator.

Mr. Patterson instructed Mr. Schmidt to travel to Walkerton and to take chlorine residual readings with a swimming pool kit at different locations. At approximately 4:00 p.m., Mr. Schmidt informed Mr. Patterson that he had visited five sites at various locations in Walkerton and was unable to detect chlorine residual levels at any of these locations. However, the minimum level detectable by the pool test kit was 0.5 ppm, and the information received by the health unit from Mr. Koebel was that the chlorine residual levels in the distribution system at that time were below 0.5 ppm.

Throughout May 20, the community continued to be concerned that the water was unsafe. The Walkerton hospital received many calls with questions regarding the quality of the water. Donald Moore, the administrator of Brucelea Haven, contacted the health unit to ask whether the water was safe for consumption. Mr. Patterson told Mr. Moore that the PUC had assured the health unit that there was nothing wrong with the water and that it was safe to drink. The health unit continued to believe that because *E. coli* O157:H7 is usually a food-borne and not a water-borne disease, it was unlikely that the illnesses had been transmitted through a municipal treated water system.

Robert McKay, an employee of the Walkerton PUC, was also concerned that a problem existed with the water supply. He was on sick leave from the PUC because of an injury. In discussions with Frank Koebel on May 18 regarding his return to work, Mr. McKay had learned that water samples from the Highway 9 construction project had failed. He had first noticed flushing in the vicinity of Mother Teresa School on May 19, the day he learned that 20 to 25 students at the school were ill. On May 20, Mr. McKay again observed flushing at a hydrant near the school. At the Inquiry, he said that it was "basically wearing on me … I presumed something was wrong" and "I just wanted someone to come and look into it."

Mr. McKay contacted the MOE's Spills Action Centre (SAC) in the early afternoon of May 20. He decided not to disclose his identity, because he was worried that he would be reprimanded by Stan Koebel if it became known that he had raised concerns about the Walkerton water system. At the time of Mr. McKay's anonymous call, Christopher Johnston and Paul Webb were on duty at the SAC. Mr. Johnston was informed by Mr. McKay that samples from the Walkerton system had failed the lab tests. In attempting to obtain further details on the adverse results to determine whether the problem was a chemical parameter, turbidity, or total coliforms, Mr. Johnston asked the anonymous caller whether the samples contained total or fecal coliforms. Mr. McKay was unable to provide this information and simply stated that the samples had failed. He then gave Mr. Johnston a contact number for the Walkerton PUC and indicated that Mr. Johnston should speak with either Stan or Frank Koebel.

Following this conversation, Mr. Johnston left a message at the number provided by the anonymous caller. He also contacted the South Grey Bruce Police Services and spoke with the dispatcher. Mr. Johnston explained that he was seeking information about the water system and asked the dispatcher for a contact number for the manager of the Walkerton PUC. The dispatcher stated that she had had a conversation with either a pharmacist or a doctor who had indicated that the water was fine.

Mr. Johnston made contact with Stan Koebel at 1:19 p.m. on May 20. He informed Mr. Koebel of the anonymous call regarding the failed water samples. The following is an excerpt of their conversation:

Christopher Johnston:	I just want to inquire and find out what's going on, that's all.
Stan Koebel:	We had a fair bit of construction and there is some concern – I'm not sure, we're not finding anything … but I am doing this [flushing and chlorinating] as a precaution …
Christopher Johnston:	So you haven't had any adverse samples then?
Stan Koebel:	We've had the odd one, you know, we're in the process of changing companies, because the other company, it closed the doors, so

> we are going through some pains right now
> to get it going.

It was Mr. Johnston's understanding that adverse sample results had been received during construction at the Walkerton PUC in past weeks. Mr. Koebel knew that the SAC wanted information on the adverse samples, yet he did not inform Mr. Johnston that A&L's Certificate of Analysis indicated that the water samples from the wells and distribution system in Walkerton had tested positive for total coliforms and for *E. coli*. Even on his own evidence, Mr. Koebel had looked at the fax results by this time.

Mr. Johnston prepared an Occurrence Reporting Information System (ORIS) report after his conversation with Mr. Koebel. The ORIS reports form a repository of information that enables MOE staff to easily access information collected on previous work shifts. The ORIS report stated that there had been "minimal adverse sampling" in the system while watermains were being replaced and that the chlorine residual levels on May 19 had been 0.1 mg/L at 5:00 p.m. and 1.0 mg/L at 11:00 p.m.

At 9:30 p.m., Robert McKay made another telephone call to the SAC. He wanted to know what actions had been taken by the SAC as a result of his call earlier that day. Mr. McKay had developed diarrhea, and his daughter had experienced the same symptoms a few days before. He was worried that the water in Walkerton was contaminated and was "wondering if we were getting sick."

Mr. McKay told the SAC that he had been unwell that day, that 25 students from Mother Teresa School were reportedly ill, and that 2 or 3 individuals had been sent to the Owen Sound hospital because there was blood in their stools. The SAC official indicated that the manager of the Walkerton PUC had been contacted. He further stated that water was the responsibility of the province's Ministry of Health. Mr. McKay thought that the MOE regulated water quality and was dissatisfied with the actions of the SAC. He told the SAC official that he was boiling water at his residence, that many people were sick, and that this was not a normal situation. He also requested the telephone number of the Ministry of Health and was informed that the ministry's Barrie office was the one closest to Walkerton.

Mr. McKay telephoned the Ministry of Health's Barrie office at 9:38 p.m. and was told to contact the emergency number of the health unit in Simcoe County.

He called that number and was advised to contact the Bruce-Grey-Owen Sound Health Unit, because Walkerton was not in Simcoe County.

At approximately 10:00 p.m., Mr. McKay made another telephone call to the SAC to inform officials that he had had no success with the Barrie telephone number. As had been the case in his two previous calls to the SAC, Mr. McKay did not reveal his identity. The SAC official who responded to this call undertook to contact the local MOE office. Mr. McKay pointed out that Walkerton used an unlicensed operator, an issue he had discussed in previous months with MOE official Larry Struthers. He said that he thought that if he alerted the SAC to the fact that the Walkerton PUC violated rules, the SAC might dispatch an official to Walkerton more quickly.

Stan Koebel worked intensively to flush and increase the chlorination in the Walkerton water system. On May 20, he spent 12 hours, from 6:00 a.m. to 6:00 p.m., at various locations in the water system, including 130 Wallace Street, Ellen Avenue, the intersection of Highway 9 and Wallace Street (the location of the new main), and the Walkerton Fire Hall. Frank Koebel assisted him for part of the day. At 10:45 a.m., Stan Koebel decided to turn on Well 5, which had been out of service since May 15. The chlorine residual levels recorded by Stan Koebel on May 20 for Well 5, Well 7, and Mother Teresa School appear in Table 2.

It is unlikely that Mr. Koebel allowed 15 minutes of contact time before he measured the chlorine residuals at Wells 5 and 7. As I discuss in Chapter 4 of this report, the raw water at Well 5 was probably still contaminated. The chlorine residuals shown for Well 5 in Table 2 are not a reliable indicator of the residuals in the water that was entering the distribution system: those residuals were proably lower.

Table 2   Chlorine Residual Measurements, May 20, 2000

Mother Teresa School

6:30 a.m.	0.12 mg/L
12:25 p.m.	0.23 mg/L
3:40 p.m.	0.19 mg/L

Well 5

11:00 a.m.	0.30 mg/L
5:30 p.m.	0.48 mg/L
6:00 p.m.	0.51 mg/L

Well 7

6:00 a.m.	0.68 mg/L
3:50 p.m.	0.70 mg/L

It is noteworthy that the chlorine residual level at Mother Teresa School decreased from 0.23 mg/L at 12:25 p.m. to 0.19 mg/L at 3:40 p.m. This change is consistent with contaminated water from Well 5, which was turned on that morning, exerting a higher chlorine demand.

Results from MDS Laboratory Services Inc. on May 20 confirmed that there were high counts of *E. coli* and total coliforms on May 18 in samples submitted from the Highway 9 construction project. Three samples had been sent to MDS by Philip Analytical Services on behalf of its client B.M. Ross. Daniel Ormerod, an environmental analyst with MDS who had 12 years' laboratory experience in microbiology, conducted the analysis and read the plates. The results of the three samples in cfu/100 mL were as follows – sample 1: *E. coli* 9, total coliforms 26; sample 2: *E. coli* 14, total coliforms 43; sample 3: *E. coli* 10, total coliforms 78.

The results were reported on May 20 to both Philip Analytical and B.M. Ross. Because of the large amount of business transacted between MDS and Philip Analytical, MDS entered the results directly into Philip Analytical's computer via modem. MDS faxed the three sample results to B.M. Ross at approximately 3:00 p.m.

It was the practice of MDS to report municipal or drinking water samples that contained *E. coli* and total coliforms not only to its client but also to the local Medical Officer of Health and to the MOE's district office. However, Mr. Ormerod was unaware that these three samples were from a municipal water system. He had not seen the document from B.M. Ross to Philip Analytical on which "hydrant" was inscribed. Consequently, neither the local health unit nor the MOE received these results on the afternoon of May 20.

3.10 Sunday, May 21

The outbreak of illness continued to expand on May 21, when more than 140 telephone calls were made to the Walkerton hospital by concerned members of the public. Many people suffering from diarrhea and abdominal pain were examined by the emergency department. Two more patients were admitted to the Owen Sound hospital.

When Gord Duggan, the news editor at local radio station CKNX, contacted Dr. Murray McQuigge on Sunday morning, he was informed that there were several cases of diarrhea in the Walkerton area and that the Bruce-Grey-Owen Sound Health Unit was investigating the illnesses. Dr. McQuigge told the news editor that he was reasonably confident about the quality of the water and advised Mr. Duggan to contact the Walkerton PUC to obtain further information on the water supply.

The information provided to Mr. Duggan by Dr. McQuigge was the subject of radio newscasts on May 21 on both CKNX AM 920 and FM 102. The 11:00 a.m. report announced that a number of Walkerton residents were ill with diarrhea. It stated that the Walkerton hospital had received 100 calls from people suffering from diarrhea, that two children had been admitted to the Owen Sound hospital, and that one stool sample had contained *E. coli*. The newscast also reported that it was Dr. McQuigge's view that because the water in Walkerton was from a deep well, the system should be secure and not prone to contamination. The local Medical Officer of Health did not think the ill-nesses were related to the heavy rain and flooding in Walkerton in the previous week. The noon newscast on CKNX AM and FM repeated similar informa-tion with respect to illness in the community. It reported that local health unit officials were continuing their investigations throughout the weekend in an attempt to identify the source of the illnesses. It further stated:

> McQuigge says the usual suspects are food or water and he says the incubation period for diarrhea puts the contamination well before last Friday's serious flooding. As for *E. coli*, McQuigge says that's also unlikely.

Shortly before noon, the laboratory at the Owen Sound hospital contacted the health unit to confirm the earlier presumptive *E. coli* O157:H7 result. This was the first confirmation of *E. coli* O157:H7 after Walkerton residents began to develop symptoms of diarrhea and abdominal pain. The lab also reported a presumptive result of *E. coli* O157:H7 for another patient. Upon receiving this notification, Mr. Patterson consulted with Dr. McQuigge and Clayton Wardell, the director of health protection, and recommended the issuance of a boil water advisory.

The boil water advisory, issued at approximately 1:30 p.m., stated:

> The Bruce-Grey-Owen Sound Health Unit is advising residents in the Town of Walkerton to boil their drinking water or use bottle [*sic*] water until further notice. The water should be boiled for five

minutes prior to consumption. This recommendation is being made due to a significant increase in cases of diarrhea in this community over the past several days.

Although the Walkerton PUC is not aware of any problems with their water system, this advisory is being issued by the Bruce-Grey-Owen Sound Health Unit as a precaution until more information is known about the illness and the status of the water supply.

Anybody with bloody diarrhea should contact his or her doctor or local hospital.

It was decided by the health unit that the local AM and FM radio stations, CKNX and CFOS, would be contacted to announce the boil water advisory. In the past, the health unit had used radio announcements to transmit information on meningitis and rabies. It did not contact CBC Radio to disseminate information on the boil water advisory, nor did it use television on that day to inform residents that water should be boiled before consumption. Neither did it distribute handbills to the approximately 5,000 residents of Walkerton to alert them to the need for preventive measures.

Many individuals in the community did not become aware of the boil water advisory on that day. A report produced several months later by the Bruce-Grey-Owen Sound Health Unit, "The Investigative Report on the Walkerton Outbreak of Waterborne Gastroenteritis May–June 2000," indicated that only 44% of the respondents surveyed were aware on May 21 that a boil water advisory had been issued by the health unit, and that 34% of the respondents had heard the announcement on the radio.

The lack of notice was also confirmed by witnesses who testified at the Walkerton Inquiry. For example, Walkerton PUC employee Allan Buckle did not know that a boil water advisory had been issued for Walkerton until he returned to work on May 23, after the long weekend. As a result, until May 23 he did not boil water prior to consuming it. Similarly, Diana Adams, a Walkerton resident, was not aware of the boil water advisory until May 23. Ms. Adams did not generally listen to the CKNX or CFOS radio stations. During the May 2000 long weekend, she entertained family from Toronto, including her 79-year-old mother, at her Walkerton home. Her three children and other relatives drank Walkerton water throughout the weekend. On May 22, Ms. Adams' husband, the coach of their son's soccer team, attended a soccer practice. He encouraged the team to drink water because it was a warm evening. His son drank two large bottles of Walkerton water. The Adamses' three children contracted *E. coli* O157:H7.

The 2:00 p.m. newscasts on the local FM and AM radio stations reported that the health unit had issued a boil water advisory for Walkerton residents and that approximately 100 people had called the hospital because they were experiencing diarrhea. The 3:00 p.m. newscasts reiterated that a boil water advisory was in effect, and advised residents either to use bottled water or to boil water for five minutes before consuming it. The newscasts reported that a large number of people were suffering from diarrhea and that the source of the illness had not yet been determined. Similar reports were made between 4:00 p.m. and 11:00 p.m.

Jack Gillespie, general manager of CKNX, explained to the Inquiry that the frequency of an announcement depends on the perception of the seriousness of the situation. He stated that if Dr. McQuigge had informed CKNX that the problem was urgent and that the announcement should be made in 15- or 30-minute intervals, the radio station would have done so.

Both Mr. Patterson and Dr. McQuigge testified that if the health unit were again confronted with a situation similar to that experienced on the May 2000 long weekend, they would not rely only on the local radio stations to transmit urgent information. In the words of Dr. McQuigge, "If we had to do it all over again, we'd have notified the TV stations too ... [W]e've learned out of this experience, we would have put it on TV stations." He also stated that in the future, handbills would also be delivered to the homes of local residents to communicate such information.

Shortly before the boil water advisory was issued, Dr. McQuigge contacted the mayor of Brockton, David Thomson. Dr. McQuigge testified that the mayor was told that people in Walkerton were ill and that a stool culture from a patient had contained *E. coli*. He explained that the disease was serious and that people could die, and he read the text of the boil water advisory to the mayor.

Dr. McQuigge asked Mayor Thomson if he was aware of any potential food-borne sources of the illnesses. The mayor responded that on May 13, a band had played in the Walkerton arena and that pizza, pop, and candy floss had been sold. Dr. McQuigge did not think that these foods were responsible for the infections. In a discussion regarding whether the water could be the source of the illnesses in the community, Dr. McQuigge indicated that he had contacted the Walkerton PUC and had been assured that the water was safe.

At the Inquiry, Mayor Thomson recalled that he had had two calls from Dr. McQuigge. He testified that after his calls with Dr. McQuigge on May 21, he did not believe that a threat to public health existed in Walkerton. In his evidence, Mayor Thomson did not recall that Dr. McQuigge had mentioned *E. coli* or the symptoms of people who were sick. It seems likely that Dr. McQuigge would have mentioned these matters, but in any event, the mayor was aware people were sick and that Dr. McQuigge had issued a boil water advisory because of his concern about the water and the health of the community. Dr. McQuigge did not, however, ask the mayor to do anything in response to the boil water advisory, and the mayor did not do anything. He did not contact anyone – the PUC chair, town council, hospitals, or police or fire departments – nor did he invoke the municipality's recently developed emergency plan, the purpose of which was to provide measures to protect the health of inhabitants.

When James Kieffer, chair of the Walkerton PUC, learned on May 21 that a boil water advisory was in effect for the Town of Walkerton, he did not believe that the consumption of municipal water constituted a serious risk to the residents of Walkerton. Mr. Kieffer contacted Stan Koebel on May 21 and was informed that Mr. Koebel was flushing the water system and that the chlorine levels had been increased. Mr. Kieffer and his family continued to drink unboiled water until May 23.

In the early afternoon of May 21, Dr. McQuigge placed a call to the SAC to inform officials that there was an *E. coli* outbreak in Walkerton. Paul Webb, an SAC official, made reference to an anonymous caller who had reported that adverse results had been received by the Walkerton PUC. He also stated that there was watermain construction in Walkerton and that the chlorine residual level in the system was 0.1 mg/L. Both the health unit and the SAC discussed the reassurances from the PUC regarding the quality of the water. Dr. McQuigge said, "We're really into something … [W]e've got over 120 cases of something and we think it's *E. coli*, bloody diarrhea."

At approximately 2:00 p.m., Mr. Patterson contacted Stan Koebel to discuss the boil water advisory. Mr. Koebel was clearly anxious: he told Mr. Patterson that he wished the health unit had given him advance notice of the boil water advisory. Mr. Koebel reported that the chlorine residual levels in the system were 0.34 mg/L and 0.43 mg/L and that there had been flushing for 16 hours at Mother Teresa School. When Mr. Koebel asked for advice, Mr. Patterson responded that although this was not his area of expertise, he thought the chlorine levels in the system should be increased.

That afternoon, the SAC received a further call from the health unit and was informed that there were 2 confirmed cases of *E. coli* O157:H7 and 50 cases of bloody diarrhea. The SAC also called Mr. Koebel to discuss the *E. coli* cases and the boil water advisory. Again, Mr. Koebel did not disclose the May 17 A&L report indicating the presence of *E. coli* in the water distribution system. At the hearings, Mr. Koebel was asked whether he deliberately avoided disclosing adverse results from samples collected on May 15. His response was, "I guess that's basically the truth." I am sure that Mr. Koebel hoped that the lab results from samples to be collected on May 23 would indicate that total coliforms and *E. coli* were no longer present in the Walkerton system.

Assisted by his brother Frank, Stan Koebel flushed the Walkerton system for approximately three and a half hours on May 21. He flushed for a shorter period of time and at fewer locations than he had the previous day, because "with the amount of chlorination we were getting into the system, [I] thought it would help to have the chlorine ... settle in and kill off the bacteria." Well 5 did not operate for most of the day: it had been shut down at 1:15 a.m. on May 21. Flushing began at the site of Mother Teresa School on May 21. The chlorine residual measurements recorded by Mr. Koebel for May 21 are shown in Table 3.

After the boil water advisory was issued, the health unit established a strategic team to address the outbreak in Walkerton. The team met twice a day. A strategic team meeting was convened at 2:30 p.m. to develop a coordinated approach to the Walkerton outbreak. It was attended by Dr. McQuigge, Clayton Wardell, David Patterson, Beverly Middleton, and Mary Sellars. A review of events to date was presented, and the information provided by Stan Koebel to the health unit was discussed. The discussion concerned watermain construction at the PUC, the installation of the new chlorinator, the flushing of the system, and the chlorine residual levels of 0.34 mg/L and 0.43 mg/L. Ms. Middleton was asked to notify Maple Court Villa and Brucelea Haven, as well as the hospitals in Walkerton, Bruce-Grey, Mount Forest, and Wingham, that a boil water advisory had been issued by the health unit, that *E. coli* O157:H7 was the suspected illness, and that a case number had been assigned for all laboratory tests connected with the outbreak. The MOE, the Bluewater

Table 3   Chlorine Residual Measurements, May 21, 2000

Mother Teresa School

12:05 p.m.	0.32 mg/L
12:30 p.m.	0.34 mg/L
3:30 p.m.	0.30 mg/L

902 Yonge Street

10:45 a.m.	0.34 mg/L
4:15 p.m.	0.39 mg/L
7:15 p.m.	0.48 mg/L
9:15 p.m.	0.69 mg/L

7 Brown's Avenue

3:40 p.m.	0.46 mg/L

Well 7

12:45 p.m.	0.78 mg/L
1:15 p.m.	0.89 mg/L
2:40 p.m.	0.92 mg/L
3:00 p.m.	1.34 mg/L

130 Wallace Street

12:20 p.m.	0.10 mg/L
3:20 p.m.	0.20 mg/L

Fire Hall

12:55 p.m.	0.47 mg/L

4 Park Street

12:00 p.m.	0.26 mg/L
4:00 p.m.	0.38 mg/L

School Board, and the Bruce-Grey District Catholic School Board were also to be notified of the boil water advisory by health unit staff.

Although the hospitals and school boards were apprised of the Walkerton outbreak and the boil water advisory on May 21, neither Maple Court Villa nor Brucelea Haven was contacted by the health unit. Ms. Middleton testified that this was an oversight on her part. As a result, not until May 23 were these institutions informed by the health unit that water should be boiled before consumption. Dr. McQuigge stated that this omission could have placed the elderly at an increased risk of contracting *E. coli* O157:H7. Fortunately, both Brucelea Haven and Maple Court Villa had, on their own initiative, taken steps to ensure that these facilities' residents did not drink water from the Walkerton system. The health unit had also not notified the Walkerton Jail, which had 30 inmates and 39 staff members, of the boil water advisory on May 21. On May 22, several staff were ill and inmates began to develop flu-like symptoms. The nurse who examined the inmates learned of the boil water advisory later that day and informed the Walkerton Jail.

The Walkerton hospital was informed of the boil water advisory at 3:30 p.m. on May 21. Before that, hospital staff had not been aware that water was under investigation by the health unit as a possible cause of the outbreak. In the 48-hour period between May 19 and May 21, although hospital staff had communicated with the health unit at least five times, the health unit had never informed the hospital that water was a possible source of transmission of the illnesses. In fact, Ms. Middleton had told hospital staff on at least two occasions that it was not necessary to boil the water. She believed that if water was responsible for the illnesses, the contamination would likely have occurred on the weekend of May 12 and that the bacteria were no longer in the water supply by May 19.

When the Walkerton hospital was notified of the boil water advisory on May 21, its building services department was instructed to shut off the water supply to the drinking fountains, post signs on the ice machines, and obtain an alternative source of water. The hospital's food services department purchased water from a local store for the evening and made arrangements with a supplier to deliver ice and water the following morning. Staff in food services were instructed to discard food that had been prepared with water, including juice, Jell-O, and vegetables that had been rinsed in tap water. The patient units of the hospital were advised to empty water jugs and not to use ice. Nurses discussed measures to be adopted with patients, such as using bottled water for drinking and brushing teeth, using waterless handwashing solution, and giving no baths, except to newborns, who were to be immersed in water that had been boiled and then cooled.

Over the next few days, the Walkerton hospital implemented a number of additional measures: bleach was used to wash dishes; there was a shift from a water-based to a chemical-based disinfection system for hospital equipment; the laundry department added a chemical to the rinse cycle; changes were made to products used by cleaning staff at the hospital; and an infection control nurse was made available for consultation.

The MOE also received notification of the boil water advisory from the health unit on May 21. When Philip Bye, the MOE's district supervisor in Owen Sound, arrived at his home on Sunday at 5:30 p.m., there was a message on his answering machine from the health unit's Clayton Wardell. The MOE official learned that there were 2 cases of confirmed *E. coli* O157:H7 and 50 cases of bloody diarrhea in Walkerton and that water was suspected to be the source of transmission in the illnesses. Mr. Bye was unaware that the presence of *E. coli* O157:H7 in the water system could result in deaths.

In a discussion with Mr. Wardell that evening, Mr. Bye reported that he was not aware of any significant events in connection with the Walkerton water system. Mr. Bye did not recall the 1998 MOE inspection report of the Walkerton system, nor was he aware of the April 2000 adverse results.[6]

Mr. Bye did not contact John Earl, the emergency response official on duty at the Owen Sound office, on May 21. At the time, he thought that the MOE did not need to become involved, because a boil water advisory had been issued, the health unit was investigating the source of the illnesses in the community, and the Walkerton PUC had increased chlorine levels and was flushing the water system.

By the early evening of May 21, the health unit had notified the Minister of Health and the Chief Medical Officer of Health of Ontario of the Walkerton outbreak and the boil water advisory. It discussed with Dr. Monica Naus of the Ministry of Health the need for assistance from hospitals in London and Toronto to treat Walkerton residents who were ill. It also investigated the availability of dialysis machines for pediatric cases of hemolytic uremic syndrome (HUS) and decided that ill children under the age of five should undergo a blood test every second day to determine whether they had renal failure. Dr. McQuigge asked the Ministry of Health to arrange to obtain the assistance of an epidemiologist from the federal government.

The number of Walkerton residents affected by the infection continued to rise throughout the day; by May 21, the Walkerton hospital had received a total of 270 calls from concerned individuals regarding symptoms of diarrhea and serious abdominal pain. A child was airlifted from Walkerton to London for medical attention. The health unit decided to assign more staff to investigate the outbreak.

David Patterson instructed James Schmidt to collect 20 water samples at various locations in Walkerton, including food premises, hospitals, and the health unit office. The health unit had made arrangements with the Ministry of Health laboratory in London to analyze these samples for bacteriological contamination. On the evening of May 21, Mr. Patterson obtained the water samples from Mr. Schmidt and left for London by car at midnight to deliver the samples. Mr. Patterson instructed Mr. Schmidt to repeat the sampling the

---

[6] The inspection report and the April adverse results are discussed in Chapters 4 and 9 of this report.

next day and to transport the second set of samples to the laboratory in London by 3:00 p.m.

3.11 Monday, May 22

The Walkerton outbreak continued to escalate. By Monday morning, 90 to 100 cases of *E. coli* had been reported to the health unit. The Walkerton hospital and other area hospitals continued to examine and receive calls from many patients who had symptoms of diarrhea, abdominal pain, and nausea. Brockton's mayor, David Thomson, was ill with diarrhea, stomach cramps, and nausea. Although he lived outside of town, he had consumed a few glasses of municipal water at an awards presentation in Walkerton on May 19. He assumed that he had contracted the flu and did not associate his symptoms with the outbreak in the community.

Neither Mayor Thomson nor the chair of the Walkerton PUC, James Kieffer, initiated any action on May 22 with respect to the boil water advisory or the suspected problems with the municipal drinking supply. The mayor thought that the health unit was investigating the situation and that Dr. McQuigge would contact him if the Walkerton water was the source of the illnesses.

When the MOE's Philip Bye was told on the morning of May 22 that Walkerton had approximately 100 cases of *E. coli* and that the health unit was reasonably certain that the water supply was the source of transmission of the illnesses, he did not immediately initiate an MOE investigation. It was only when Dr. McQuigge contacted Mr. Bye later that day to stress the urgency of the situation and the need for the MOE's involvement that Mr. Bye dispatched environmental officer John Earl to the Walkerton PUC. Mr. Earl was instructed to contact Mr. Patterson before meeting Stan Koebel and to obtain any information sought by the health unit.

Mr. Patterson provided Mr. Earl with detailed information on the outbreak: the "alarming" number of cases that had been reported to the local hospitals, the laboratory confirmation of *E. coli* O157:H7, and the imposition of the boil water advisory the previous day. He explained that the health unit had investigated group picnics, barbecues, and community events but could not explain the sudden and alarming rise in gastrointestinal disease in Walkerton. Mr. Patterson stated that the water system was highly suspect and that water samples had been sent by the health unit for testing at the Ministry of Health laboratory in London. He then asked Mr. Earl to obtain from the Walkerton PUC copies of the microbiological test results for the past two weeks, the chlorine residual levels at the wells and in the distribution system, the water flow records in this two-week period, and a map of the water distribution system. Mr. Patterson also asked for documentation on the recent construction and on disinfection procedures for the new watermains as well as for information on unusual events that had occurred in recent weeks. Finally, he asked Mr. Earl to investigate any breaches in the system.

Before leaving for the Walkerton PUC on the afternoon of May 22, Mr. Earl contacted the SAC to obtain information about the anonymous caller. He was provided with a copy of the occurrence report completed by Mr. Johnston in response to the May 20 call, which stated:

> Caller reports adverse water samples were found in the Walkerton distribution system on 2000/05/18. Caller reports new watermains going into service and PUC is flushing mains.

Because the anonymous caller seemed to have detailed information on the operation of the Walkerton water system, Mr. Earl thought that the contamination of the water system might be the result of intentional acts. He decided to ask Stan Koebel if there had been problems with discontented PUC staff.

When Mr. Earl arrived at the Walkerton PUC at 4:00 p.m. on May 22, Wells 5 and 7 were operating. Mr. Koebel explained that only in peak periods – those in which water demand was high – would Wells 5, 6, and 7 operate simultaneously. He also told Mr. Earl that a new chlorinator had recently been installed at Well 7.

Mr. Earl asked Mr. Koebel whether there had been any unusual events in the past two weeks. Mr. Koebel responded that Well 6 had been "knocked out" by an electrical storm, but that no unusual events had occurred in the past 14 days. Mr. Koebel did not mention the much more significant information that Well 7 had operated without a chlorinator from May 3 to May 9 and from May 15 to May 19 and that water samples collected on May 15 had contained *E. coli* and total coliforms.

The heavy rainfall and flooding of the previous weekend were discussed in the context of the potential contamination of the system by surface water. Mr. Koebel believed that surface water could have entered the system through the overflow pipe at Well 7. He explained that over the past few days he had flushed the watermains at various locations and had increased the chlorine residuals at the pumping wells.

Mr. Earl asked Mr. Koebel whether there were any problems with staff at the Walkerton PUC. Mr. Koebel replied that PUC employees were anxious that the Municipality of Brockton would assume control of the operation of the Walkerton water system but that he did not think that an employee had sabotaged or intentionally contaminated the system. Staff qualifications were also discussed. Mr. Earl was told that Stan and Frank Koebel were the primary operators of the water system and that they were certified; however, an unlicensed PUC employee occasionally monitored the Walkerton system.

At Mr. Earl's request, Stan Koebel provided a number of documents, including the following:

- a copy of Stan Koebel's notes describing his activities at the Walkerton PUC from May 19 to May 22 (this confirmed that the PUC manager had been chlorinating and flushing the system throughout the weekend);

- the A&L Canada Laboratories report of May 5, which indicated that total coliforms were present in samples at Well 5 "raw" and "treated";

- the A&L report of May 17, which indicated positive *E. coli* and positive total coliforms in samples labelled "Well 7 treated," "125 Durham Street," and "902 Yonge Street," with the "Well 7 treated" sample showing greater than 200 cfu/100 mL of total coliforms and of *E. coli*, as well as a heterotrophic plate count (HPC) of 600 cfu/1 mL;

- maps that identified the streets and watermains in Walkerton (on one of the maps, Mr. Koebel indicated the location and diameter of the watermains replaced in 2000);

- daily pumping data for April 2000, which indicated that Well 7 did not operate during this month; and

- daily operating sheets for Wells 5 and 6 for May 2000.

Mr. Earl asked Mr. Koebel to obtain documentation relating to the construction of the mains and the disinfection procedures from the firms involved in the watermain construction. He collected raw and treated samples from Well 7, as well as samples from the PUC office on 4 Park Street. Mr. Koebel told Mr. Earl that the daily operating sheet for Well 7 was not available and that it could be picked up the following day. I am satisfied that Mr. Koebel intended to revise that sheet so as to conceal the fact that Well 7 had operated without chlorination.

Mr. Earl arrived at the MOE office in Owen Sound at 6:00 p.m. and reviewed the Walkerton PUC documents. He learned from the May 17 A&L report that the water supply had had high *E. coli* counts. Mr. Patterson had specifically asked Mr. Earl earlier that day to obtain, from the PUC, adverse water sample results for the past two weeks. Although Mr. Earl knew that the health unit had conducted water sampling at different sites in Walkerton and was awaiting results from the Ministry of Health laboratory in London, he did not inform either the health unit or his supervisor, Mr. Bye, of these results on May 22. He testified that he did not consider the situation to be urgent, because a boil water advisory had been issued for the Town of Walkerton.

Throughout May 22, Stan Koebel continued to flush and increase the chlorination levels of the water system. At 11:00 a.m., he activated Well 5, which had been out of service the previous day. The chlorine residual was 0.64 mg/L. At Well 7, the following readings were recorded by Stan Koebel: 1.10 mg/L at 8:10 a.m. and 1.24 mg/L at 9:10 a.m.

The PUC manager also flushed at Mother Teresa School, 130 Wallace Street, the Fire Hall, and 34 William Street. The chlorine residuals at various locations, as reported by Stan Koebel, are reproduced in Table 4.

At 6:30 p.m., the health unit's outbreak team met to plot an epidemiological curve. At the health unit's request, the Walkerton, Hanover, and Owen Sound hospitals had forwarded patient line-listings – the names of patients who had been examined at these hospitals – to the health unit. Throughout May 22, public health staff contacted these patients to obtain their residential addresses as well as information about onset dates of symptoms, the patients' consumption of Walkerton water, and the dates that stool samples had been collected from the patients.

As the outbreak team began to plot the epidemiological curve, it became apparent that most individuals in Walkerton had become ill at about the same time. The peak of the onset of symptoms occurred on May 17, indicating that

Table 4   Chlorine Residual Measurements, May 22, 2000

Mother Teresa School

7:30 a.m.	0.20 mg/L
11:05 a.m.	0.38 mg/L

902 Yonge Street

7:00 a.m.	0.58 mg/L
11:45 a.m.	0.70 mg/L

Fire Hall

9:20 a.m.	0.89 mg/L

7 Brown's Avenue

11:30 a.m.	0.66 mg/L

130 Wallace Street

7:45 a.m.	0.77 mg/L

34 William Street

10:45 a.m.	0.38 mg/L
3:00 p.m.	0.26 mg/L

6 Campbell Street

9:40 a.m.	0.75 mg/L

4 Park Street

4:00 p.m.	0.68 mg/L

the illnesses appeared to be attributable to a common event. The health unit officials believed that the likely dates of transmission of *E. coli* O157:H7 were May 12, 13, and 14.

A large map of Walkerton was placed on the wall of the health unit's office, and the patients' addresses were highlighted on it. When the process was complete, the map was, in the words of Mr. Patterson, "covered with yellow highlighting." The infection was widespread – the patients lived throughout the area served by the Walkerton water distribution system.

On the evening of May 22, the health unit concluded that the municipal water supply was causing the *E. coli* O157:H7 outbreak in Walkerton. Although the health unit had not been informed of the May 17 adverse microbiological report from A&L, both the epidemiological curve and the highlighted map indicated that water was the common element linking the residents.

3.12 Tuesday, May 23

John Earl returned to the Walkerton PUC on the morning of May 23 to obtain the outstanding documents from Stan Koebel and to collect more samples from the pumphouses. He was given the annual water records from 1997 to April 2000. Mr. Earl was also provided with the daily operating sheet for Well 7, which had been altered by Frank Koebel on May 22 or 23 on Stan

Koebel's instructions. Stan Koebel had asked his brother to "clean up" the May 2000 daily operating sheet for the MOE because "it was a mess" and "the arithmetic was bad." Frank Koebel completed a new daily operating sheet for Well 7 and destroyed the original one. The intent of creating the new sheet was to conceal the fact that Well 7 had operated in May without a chlorinator.

The daily operating sheet as amended by Frank Koebel indicated that Well 7 did not operate between May 3 and May 9. Those were in fact some of the dates in May on which Well 7 pumped unchlorinated water into the distribution system. Frank Koebel also entered chlorine residual levels in the daily operating sheet for May 11, 12, and 13 – days on which there was no chlorinator at Well 7 and on which that well did not operate. For those dates, he inscribed numbers under the column "chlorine used in previous 24 hours."

Similarly, a chlorine residual level of 0.3 mg/L was entered for May 18, as well as a level of 0.5 mg/L for May 19 at 10:15 a.m. (The chlorinator at Well 7 had not been installed until noon on May 19.) At the Inquiry, Frank Koebel stated, "I'll have to take responsibility" for the fictitious numbers. He testified that he had composed these numbers on the daily operating sheet for Well 7 "so it would look better to the MOE."

After Mr. Earl was provided with these documents, he collected samples from each of the wells and from the distribution system and took photographs of Well 7.

In his review of the daily operating sheets from May 2000, Mr. Earl observed that Wells 5, 6, and 7 did not appear to operate between May 3 and May 9. He thought this was unusual. He also found "questionable" the chlorine residual measurements for Well 5, which were all 0.75 mg/L. Mr. Earl communicated his observations to his superior, Philip Bye. He also told Mr. Bye that the A&L report dated May 17 had indicated that *E. coli* and total coliforms were present in samples labelled "Well 7" and that this well had operated without disinfectant for several days in May. This information was not conveyed to the health unit by either Mr. Earl or Mr. Bye on May 23.

On the morning of May 23, the health unit received results from the Ministry of Health laboratory in London regarding the first set of samples collected at various sites in Walkerton. Two samples contained *E. coli* and total coliforms: the sample from a store on Yonge Street west of Highway 9 had a level greater than 80 total coliforms and 69 *E. coli*, and the sample from the Bruce County administrative building had 2 coliforms and 2 *E. coli*. These two locations were served by "dead ends" in the Walkerton distribution system. Although the testing process was not completed for the second set of samples submitted by the health unit, coliforms were already visible in some of the samples.

Mr. Patterson immediately contacted Mr. Bye to inform him of these results. He also conveyed the findings of the outbreak team regarding the epidemiological curve and the Walkerton map indicating that residents from all sections of the town had contracted the infection. Again, the MOE did not inform the health unit of the failed results from samples collected at the PUC on May 15.

At approximately 9:45 a.m., Mr. Patterson called Stan Koebel to notify him of the adverse results received by the health unit and asked him for the date of the last set of microbiological tests from the Walkerton PUC. When Mr. Koebel replied that samples had been collected on May 15, there was silence, and he then told Mr. Patterson for the first time that those samples had failed. He also told Mr. Patterson that the chlorinator had operated intermittently. Mr. Koebel was distraught. He testified that he realized then that his attempts at flushing and chlorinating the system from May 19 to May 22 had not been successful in eradicating the contamination. When he asked Mr. Patterson for advice, Mr. Patterson told him to be open and honest and to inform the PUC commissioners of what had transpired.

Mr. Patterson immediately informed Dr. McQuigge and the chair of the board of health, Bill Twaddle, about the adverse results from the May 15 samples. Dr. McQuigge called Brockton mayor David Thomson to request a meeting between the health unit and the Brockton municipal council. Mr. Bye was also asked to attend the meeting. Initially, the meeting was to be held at Newman's Restaurant in Walkerton, but it was rearranged to be held in the Brockton council chambers because this venue was considered to be more appropriate. Although there are discrepancies in the evidence about the arrangements for this meeting, I think nothing turns on the differences.

At approximately 11:30 a.m., Dr. McQuigge held a joint press conference at the Walkerton hospital with the hospital staff to communicate to the public the seriousness of the situation and to advise the public of precautions to be taken. He reported that since May 18, a total of 160 patients had been examined at the Walkerton, Owen Sound, and Hanover hospitals and that 400 calls had been received from concerned members of the public. Eleven people had been admitted to hospital, and three patients were in serious condition. Dr. McQuigge discussed the positive *E. coli* results from samples analyzed by the Ministry of Health laboratory and stated that exposure to the infection likely occurred on May 12, 13, or 14. He explained that the risk of renal failure was 7% and that the death rate was expected to be between 1% and 3%. Intravenous support and dialysis were the sole forms of treatment. Dr. McQuigge cautioned that antibiotics and diarrhea medications should not be administered to ill persons, because they increased the risk of hemolytic uremic syndrome (HUS).

The meeting at Brockton council chambers, which began at 2:15 p.m., was attended by officials from the health unit, the MOE, the PUC, and the Municipality of Brockton. Dr. McQuigge reviewed the chronology of events from May 19. He stated that water linked the illnesses and that an event between May 12 and May 15 was responsible for the outbreak. *E. coli* O157:H7 had been confirmed in nine patients, and a 2-year-old child was on life support. Dr. McQuigge said that the situation was serious. In fact, a 66-year-old woman had died on May 22 and the 2-year-old child he mentioned died on May 23.

Mr. Bye announced at the meeting that the MOE was initiating an investigation of the Walkerton water system. He suggested four ways in which the water could have become contaminated: watermain replacement, backwash through the floodgate at Well 7, the failure of the chlorinator, and the contamination of sumps or cisterns due to flooding. Mr. Bye recommended increasing the chlorine levels in the water system, urged the Municipality of Brockton to take immediate action, and suggested that an independent agency assume control of the water system and that the municipality contact its engineering firm. The PUC would be required to report to the MOE on measures initiated to address the problems. Mr. Bye stated that he was prepared to meet with municipal officials and the engineering firm the next morning.

Stan Koebel was then asked by Dr. McQuigge whether he wished to contribute to the meeting. The PUC manager began to discuss the new watermains, and it became evident that he had no intention of disclosing the events that had compromised the quality of Walkerton's drinking water. He did not discuss the adverse results received from A&L the previous week, nor did he reveal that Well 7 had operated without a chlorinator. Dr. McQuigge became agitated. He interrupted Mr. Koebel and said, "Stan, come clean." He asked Mr. Koebel probing questions. Mr. Koebel admitted that samples collected at the PUC on May 15 had failed the microbiological tests. He said that intensive flushing and chlorination of the water system began on May 19, but he did not disclose that Well 7 had operated without chlorination.

Dr. McQuigge told participants at the meeting that the *E. coli* outbreak in Walkerton was unprecedented in Canada. Members of the municipal council asked Dr. McQuigge a number of questions about the timing and the issuance of the boil water advisory. When he was asked whether the public could have been notified of the outbreak at an earlier date, Dr. McQuigge stated that the health unit had been aware of only two cases of bloody diarrhea on May 19. On May 20, some individuals who resided outside Walkerton were ill, which created confusion as to whether the outbreak was confined to the town. However, by May 21, the volume of calls received by the Walkerton hospital, as well as the positive stool cultures, confirmed that the problem was in Walkerton. It was also learned that an ill patient in Hanover had consumed water in Walkerton. Dr. McQuigge stated that the health unit continued to investigate the source of transmission of the infection and, despite assurances from the PUC, believed that the common link was the water. As a precautionary measure, the health unit issued a boil water advisory on May 21 at 1:30 p.m.

In response to a question regarding the dissemination of information on the boil water advisory, Dr. McQuigge said that he had contacted Mayor Thomson and the local radio stations on May 21. In his view, the holiday weekend had had no impact on the time at which the public was notified of the boil water advisory. He told officials at the meeting that it was not until May 23 that the health unit had conclusive evidence that the municipal water was responsible for the illnesses in the community.

At about 3:30 p.m., as members of the health unit began to leave the meeting, words were exchanged privately between Dr. McQuigge and Mayor Thomson. Their versions of what was said differ, and much was made of this during their evidence at the Inquiry. It was Dr. McQuigge's evidence that he said, "Dave, now's the time to tell the public what you know." The mayor, on the other hand, testified that Dr. McQuigge said, "Don't you blow the whistle on me or Brockton will … " I am satisfied that Dr. McQuigge's version is the more probable. It does not make sense to me that he would have said what the mayor recalls. I am satisfied that the mayor was simply mistaken in this regard.

After Dr. McQuigge and his staff left the meeting, Mayor Thomson, Richard Radford, and other officials from the Municipality of Brockton remained to discuss the events. It was decided that contact would be made with Steve Burns of the engineering firm B.M. Ross and Associates Ltd., and a municipal council meeting was scheduled for later that afternoon.

The council meeting held in the late afternoon of May 23 was attended by both Mr. Burns and Stan Koebel. Mr. Koebel told council members that historically there had been bacteriological problems at Wells 5 and 7. He also stated that the chlorinator at Well 7 had not functioned properly. Still he did not say that Well 7 had operated in May without a chlorinator. He explained that samples collected by the PUC on May 15 had failed but said that he had not read the laboratory report until May 18 or May 19. Mr. Koebel stated that beginning on May 19, the date on which he received a call from the health unit, he had increased the chlorine residuals and that he had flushed the system throughout the May long weekend (May 20–22).

At the meeting, Mr. Burns indicated that his firm would develop an action plan for the MOE, the components of which he had discussed with Mr. Bye. The purposes of the action plan were to determine the cause of the contamination, to remedy the problem, and to ensure the proper operation of the water system. Mr. Burns said that he would continue to chlorinate and flush the system and that he had shut down Well 5 because it was a shallow well.

Before the meeting was adjourned, those at the council meeting discussed the prospect of declaring a state of emergency under the Ontario *Emergency Plans Act*. Mayor Thomson and council members took the position that Mr. Burns had the skills necessary to rectify the problems in the water system and, after receiving legal advice, concluded that there was no point in declaring an emergency pursuant to the statute.

3.13 May 24 to May 31

In the last week of May, the Walkerton hospital continued to receive many calls from individuals who were vomiting and suffering from diarrhea. Staff hours in both the laboratory and the emergency department of the hospital doubled, and the number of patients examined remained high. According to statistics compiled by the hospital, the greatest number of emergency room registrations per day in April 2000 was 55. This number is to be contrasted with the number of patients who visited the Walkerton hospital's emergency department from May 24 to May 31, as shown in Table 5.

Table 5   **Patient Visits, Walkerton Hospital Emergency Department,**
                May 24–31, 2000

Date	Number of Patients
May 24	113
May 25	117
May 26	106
May 27	111
May 28	87
May 29	116
May 30	64
May 31	106

By May 24, some patients had developed mixed infections of *Campylobacter* and *E. coli* O157:H7. The symptoms for *Campylobacter* are similar to those for *E. coli* – diarrhea and abdominal pain. By May 24, four people, including a two-year-old child and a resident at Brucelea Haven, had died. Several patients were transported by air or ground ambulance from Walkerton to London for medical attention.

Physicians at the Walkerton hospital sought additional medical and support staff to meet the needs of the community. Elective surgery was cancelled. The maternity ward of the hospital was closed, and patients were transported to hospitals in Owen Sound, Hanover, and Kincardine. A pediatrician from Toronto's Hospital for Sick Children travelled to Walkerton and remained at the site of the Walkerton hospital until June 14. Julie Stratton, an epidemiologist from Health Canada, arrived in Walkerton on May 24 to assist the Bruce-Grey-Owen Sound Health Unit. She was later joined by Dr. Jeff Wilson of Health Canada's Laboratory Centre for Disease Control and Dr. Andrea Ellis of Health Canada's Centre for Infectious Disease Prevention and Control.

The health unit at this time was concerned that its credibility was being challenged. Some individuals in the community were criticizing it for not having issued a boil water advisory until May 21, and at a meeting of the outbreak team on May 24, David Patterson stated, "There have been complaints from the public with finger-pointing and lots of anger."

Dr. McQuigge decided that he would make public statements through the media to maintain the credibility of the health unit. At the Inquiry, he testified:

> At that time, the health unit's credibility was being called into ques-
> tion … and we very much needed the public to believe that we were
> a credible agency, because we were giving a great amount of advice
> that we really needed the public to follow and that they really needed
> to follow in order not to get any sicker.

Dr. McQuigge was concerned that Mayor Thomson had not disclosed to the public that the Walkerton PUC had received adverse results during the week of May 15 and that the chlorinator had not been functioning properly for some time. He wished to explain to the public that the health unit had waited two days to issue a boil water advisory because it had not been notified of these adverse results or that a chlorinator had not functioned properly for a period of time.

On May 25, Dr. McQuigge read a prepared statement on CTV's *Canada AM* and CBC Radio's *Metro Morning* program in Toronto. On *Canada AM*, he stated that the health unit had contacted the Walkerton PUC on May 19 and May 20 and had been told on those occasions that the water was safe and secure. The health unit had not been informed of the results of samples collected on May 15 indicating the presence of *E. coli* and total coliforms in the water distribution system. Nor had it been aware on these dates that the chlorinator at Well 7 had not been functioning properly. Despite assurances from the PUC, the health unit had decided to advise the people of Walkerton on May 21 not to drink the water. As a result of these non-disclosures, it had focused its investigation on potential food sources for the illnesses pervading the community. Not until May 23 had it become aware of this undisclosed information from the PUC.

Dr. McQuigge was interrupted by *Canada AM* host Wei Chen as he read the public statement, and in response he stated that deaths could have been prevented if the Walkerton PUC had notified the health unit when it received the laboratory results on May 17. A similar statement was made by Dr. McQuigge on *Metro Morning*, hosted by Andy Barrie:

> [T]his is a statement I would much prefer not to have made. Yester-
> day, there were questions of the Chief Medical Officer of Health of

Ontario and myself about whether we acted with all possible speed to warn the citizens of Walkerton that their water might be contaminated. I would like to discuss this and tell you what we know now …

Last night the Chief Medical Officer of Health in Ontario and myself decided that we could no longer wait for the results of the Ministry of the Environment's investigation. We felt that the people and public of Walkerton should know that what has happened and is happening is not a mystery. This could have been prevented …

People have died and people may die yet. I am saddened by that because I think this could have been prevented.

At the Inquiry, much was made of the fact that Dr. McQuigge's comments were inaccurate and reflected badly on people other than Stan Koebel, including possibly the mayor. Dr. McQuigge testified that in his opinion, the deaths in Walkerton would probably not in fact have been prevented even if the sample results from the PUC had been reported to the health unit on May 17 or May 18 and a boil water advisory had been issued at that time; he stated that the number of people infected with E. coli O157:H7 might have been reduced if the health unit had issued a boil water advisory on May 17 or May 18 rather than May 21.[7] It is unfortunate that Dr. McQuigge's comments to the media on May 25 were not entirely accurate, but I accept that he needed to make a statement for the reason he articulated and that his misstatements were entirely innocent and understandable, given the pressure he was under and the circumstances leading up to his statement.

At this time, remedial actions were initiated at the Walkerton PUC. Mr. Burns presented the action plan at a meeting on May 24 that was attended by officials from the Municipality of Brockton and the MOE. Tony Emonds, a drinking water specialist at the MOE office in Toronto, commented that the action plan was reasonable and appropriate. Mr. Burns and MOE officials toured the Walkerton water system. Mr. Emonds observed that the system's first consumer was in close proximity to Well 5. When the potentially offending overflow pipe at Well 7 was examined, Mr. Emonds noticed "sewage or similar

---

[7] I note that the epidemiological evidence discussed in Chapter 4 of this report indicates that a boil water advisory on May 18 could possibly have prevented one death. As stated in Chapter 10 of this report, I think it is too speculative to discuss the possibility of a boil water advisory on May 17.

waste water type sludge … visible in grass feet from the discharge point." The MOE officials collected water samples from various sites at the PUC.

On May 25, A&L faxed to the Walkerton PUC the results of the water samples that had been collected on May 23. A&L reported high counts of *E. coli* and total coliforms in the "raw" water sample from Well 5: 200 total coliforms (cfu/100 mL), 33 *E. coli* (cfu/100 mL), and a heterotrophic plate count of 9 (cfu/1 mL). The samples from Well 7 "raw" contained 15 heterotrophic units (cfu/1 mL), and those from 4 Park Street contained 3 heterotrophic units (cfu/ 1 mL). The samples from 130 Wallace Street, Well 7 treated, 125 Durham Street, and 902 Yonge Street were all negative by the presence-absence test.

Upon receiving these results, Stan Koebel contacted Robert Deakin at A&L and asked Mr. Deakin if he could recall their conversation of May 18. Mr. Deakin thought that this comment was "very strange," because the date of his conversation with Mr. Koebel had been May 17 – the day the two faxes with the adverse "rush" hydrant sample results and the distribution sample results were sent to the Walkerton PUC.

On May 25, the Municipality of Brockton decided to retain the Ontario Clean Water Agency to operate the Walkerton system. Ultimately, this was achieved through a resolution of the PUC, because it retained legal control over the waterworks. On that day, the MOE issued a Field Order to the Municipality of Brockton pursuant to the *Ontario Water Resources Act*. It required an action plan to be submitted to the MOE that included a statement of Brockton's response to the contamination of the water supply, the preparation of a report on the possible causes of the contamination, and the appointment of a qualified operating authority to oversee the operation to ensure the safety of the drinking water. In compliance with the Field Order, Mr. Burns filed an action plan with the MOE on May 26.

On the evening of May 26, Garry Palmateer, president of G.A.P. EnviroMicrobial Services Inc., was interviewed by Brian Stewart on CBC Television's *National Magazine*. The G.A.P. laboratory had tested the water in Walkerton from 1996 to April 2000. Mr. Palmateer stated that on five occasions between January and the end of April 2000, coliforms were detected in the distribution system or at the wells of the Walkerton PUC. The five adverse results had been reported to the MOE's district office in Owen Sound, but only one of these was an indicator of unsafe water that required notification to the health unit. Through an oversight on that occasion, the MOE did not notify the health unit.

Dr. McQuigge, who watched the television interview, was surprised to learn this information; the MOE had not informed the health unit of these adverse results. Although Dr. McQuigge had met with Mr. Bye on several occasions in the previous few days, the April samples had not been mentioned.

On May 27, a meeting took place between the health unit and the MOE, whose officials conceded that in violation of the Ontario Drinking Water Objectives, the MOE had failed to notify the health unit of the adverse results it had received from the Walkerton PUC on April 10. The MOE was required to notify the health unit if there were coliforms in consecutive samples from the same point in the distribution system or from multiple samples on a single submission. At the meeting, the MOE stated that since May 1, 2000, it had not received notification of water results from the Walkerton system. Both the MOE and the health unit had been unaware that G.A.P. no longer conducted microbiological testing for Walkerton.

In the last days of May and in succeeding months, the Walkerton hospital continued to treat many individuals in the community who had contracted *E. coli* O157:H7 and *Campylobacter*. In May 2000, a total of 1,829 individuals sought medical attention at the Walkerton hospital's emergency department – 66% above the normal rate. In addition, from May 17 to the end of May, approximately 850 calls were made to the hospital by people who were vomiting, had abdominal pain, and were suffering diarrhea. In June 2000, the number of patients registered at the Walkerton hospital emergency department was 39% above the normal rate. According to the estimates of the health unit and Health Canada, 2,321 individuals became ill as a result of the outbreak. At least 65 people were hospitalized, 27 people developed hemolytic uremic syndrome (HUS), and 7 people, ranging from 2 to 84 years of age, died as a result of the Walkerton outbreak.

In the following months, the MOE continued its investigation, and the Ontario Clean Water Agency flushed, chlorinated, and instituted other measures in an attempt to restore safe drinking water to the residents of Walkerton. The Bruce-Grey-Owen Sound Health Unit outbreak team continued to meet. The boil water advisory was lifted on December 5, 2000.

Chapter 4   The Physical Causes of the Contamination

Contents

Chapter 4   The Physical Causes of the Contamination

4.1   Overview

The physical causes of the contamination of the Walkerton water system in May 2000 were the subject of extensive evidence. In this chapter, I consider a variety of possible sources, including the three municipal wells operating in May 2000, watermain construction along a section of Highway 9, possible interference with the integrity of the distribution system, and the application of biosolids or septage near municipal wells. In determining the causes, I review several important sources of information, including the geology and hydrogeology of the surrounding area, information respecting possible sources of the *Escherichia coli* and *Campylobacter* contamination, meteorological data, bacteriological sample results, records of the location of each well and the volume of water pumped by it, and epidemiological data.

I conclude that the primary, if not the only, source of the contamination was manure that had been spread on a farm near Well 5, although I cannot exclude other possible sources. The manure was applied in late April 2000, before a period of significant rainfall occurring from May 8 to 12. The survival time of *E. coli* in soil is such that large numbers of *E. coli* on the farm could easily have survived after the manure application. DNA typing of the animals and the manure on the farm revealed *E. coli* O157:H7 and *Campylobacter* strains on the farm that matched the human outbreak strains predominating in Walkerton in May 2000. An August 2000 test demonstrated that as Well 5 pumped, *E. coli* levels increased in Well 5 as well as in two monitoring wells between the farm and Well 5. I note at the outset that Dr. David Biesenthal,[1] the farm's owner, engaged in accepted farm practices and cannot be faulted for the outbreak.

I conclude that the entry point of this contamination into the municipal drinking water supply was through Well 5. The overburden in the area of Well 5 was shallow, and there were likely direct pathways – such as fence post holes and a reversing spring by the north side of Well 5 – through which the contamination travelled from the surface to the bedrock and the aquifer.

Further, Well 5 was a shallow well, whose casing extended only 5 m below the surface. All of the water drawn from the well came from a very shallow area

---

[1] Dr. David Biesenthal is a veterinarian.

between 5.4 m and 7.7 m below the surface. More significantly, this water was drawn from an area of highly fractured bedrock. This fracturing, and the geological nature of the surrounding bedrock, made it possible for surface bacteria to quickly enter into fractured rock channels and proceed directly to Well 5. Raw water contamination by coliforms and fecal coliforms was indicated in the initial pump tests in 1978 and continued to May 2000.

In the immediate aftermath of the tragedy, samples of raw water taken at Well 5 consistently tested positive for *E. coli*. Significantly, neither Well 6 nor Well 7 samples tested positive for *E. coli* during this period. The only distribution system samples testing positive for *E. coli* were from two "dead ends" that were closer to Well 5 than to the other two active wells. A positive *E. coli* sample from June 6, 2000, taken from a spring discharging near Well 5, indicated that a large area of bedrock underlying Well 5 was contaminated.

The experts who testified at the Inquiry all agreed that there was "overwhelming evidence" that contamination entered by way of Well 5. I am satisfied that although Well 6 and, to a lesser extent Well 7, may be vulnerable to surface water contamination, the overwhelming evidence points to Well 5 as the source of the Walkerton system's contamination in May 2000.

It is not possible to determine the exact time when contamination first entered the water distribution system. However, I conclude that the residents of Walkerton were probably first exposed to the contamination on or shortly after May 12. It was at this time that Well 5 was the primary supply well, contributing the most significant amounts of water to the distribution system. This conclusion is supported by the epidemiological evidence, the evidence of the health care institutions that treated the ill and vulnerable groups, anecdotal evidence from residents, and the timing of the heavy rainfall. It is also consistent with the findings of the Bruce-Grey-Owen Sound Health Unit and of Health Canada, which both concluded that the predominant exposure dates were between May 13 and May 16, 2000.

The applicable government technical document relating to disinfection, the Chlorination Bulletin, states that a water system like Walkerton's must treat well water with a chlorine dose sufficient to satisfy the chlorine demand caused by substances in the raw water and to sustain a chlorine residual of 0.5 mg/L after 15 minutes of contact time. The evidence is clear that if such a chlorine residual had been maintained at Well 5, considerably more than 99% of bacteria such as *E. coli* and *Campylobacter* would have been killed. For practical purposes this would have prevented the outbreak.[2]

In May 2000, the operators of the Walkerton water system chlorinated the water at Well 5, but routinely used less chlorine than was required. The incoming contamination overwhelmed the chlorine being added. However, the amount of contamination was likely so great that the demand it put on the chlorine would have overwhelmed even the amount of chlorine needed to maintain a residual of 0.5 mg/L after 15 minutes of contact time under normal conditions.

Nonetheless, the outbreak could have been prevented. Walkerton did not have continuous chlorine residual or turbidity monitors at Well 5. Such monitors could have sounded an alarm and shut off the pump when the chlorine residual dropped.[3] Compounding this shortcoming, the Walkerton operators did not even manually monitor the chlorine residual levels daily during the critical period. Daily monitoring would very likely have enabled the operators to take steps to significantly reduce the scope of the outbreak.[4]

As the contaminated water spread through the system, people began to fall ill. The epidemiological data establishes that individuals started to experience symptoms around May 16 or 17, indicating an exposure date beginning on May 12 or soon afterward. This is consistent with the conclusion that significant rainfall from May 8 to 12 probably caused the contamination from the farm manure to enter the aquifer and then spread to Well 5. The first test results indicating *E. coli* contamination in the system were collected on May 15. On May 19, the Walkerton Public Utilities Commission (PUC) began to flush and superchlorinate the system, and a boil water advisory was issued by the local Medical Officer of Health on May 21.

At the end of this chapter, I review and reject a number of other possible sources of the contamination, including new construction, breaks, repairs, and cross connections in the distribution system, and the spreading of biosolids.

---

[2] This statement is subject to the qualification that a large increase in turbidity accompanying the contamination may have prevented the chlorine from disinfecting the contaminants. In my view, it is most unlikely that this is what happened in May 2000.

[3] It would have been necessary to have a continuous turbidity monitor because it is possible, although very unlikely, that an increase in turbidity would have accompanied the contamination, thus interferring with the effective operation of a continuous chlorine residual monitor.

[4] I note that it would not be difficult for any properly trained water operator to appreciate the significance of the low or non-existent chlorine residuals and to take the appropriate corrective action.

4.2   The Multi-Barrier Approach to Municipal Water Systems

Before turning to a discussion of the circumstances giving rise to the outbreak in Walkerton, it is useful to briefly describe the multi-barrier approach to ensuring the safety of drinking water in communal or municipal water systems.

Experts at the Inquiry repeatedly stated that a multi-barrier approach is necessary to ensure safe drinking water. This approach includes at least five elements: the source of the water, water treatment, the distribution system, the monitoring of water quality, and the response to adverse water test results.

4.2.1   Source

Drinking water comes mainly from two types of sources: groundwater (e.g., wells and springs), and surface water (e.g., lakes, rivers, and reservoirs). Groundwater is often the source of drinking water in smaller communities, as is the case in Walkerton. Larger communities in Canada, such as the City of Toronto, are more often supplied with surface water.

Groundwater is generally considered to be less prone to microbial contamination than is surface water, because as groundwater travels through the subsurface, a filtration of particles occurs, including the filtration of micro-organisms. The travel times for groundwater may be very long, making sudden microbial contamination even less likely. As a result, groundwater may require less treatment than surface water does. In some circumstances, however, groundwater may be "under the direct influence" of surface water: surface contamination can travel rapidly through natural cracks, fractures, or surface features such as springs or ponds to gain direct access to groundwater. When this occurs, groundwater should be treated and monitored with the same concern for sudden microbial contamination as is the case with surface water.

4.2.2   Treatment

The main purposes of water treatment are to ensure that the water is safe to drink and that it is aesthetically pleasing, with good taste and no odour.

The treatment of water attempts to eliminate three classes of contaminants: (1) microbial contaminants such as bacteria (e.g., *E. coli*), viruses, and protozoa (e.g., *Giardia* and *Cryptosporidium*); (2) chemical contaminants (e.g., metals and pesticides); and (3) radiological contaminants.

Guidelines providing baseline safety standards have been developed by the federal, provincial, and territorial governments to address microbial, chemical, and radiological parameters in drinking water. At the material times, these guidelines appeared in two publications of the Ministry of the Environment (MOE): the Ontario Drinking Water Objectives (ODWO) and the Chlorination Bulletin.

Disinfection is a treatment process designed to inactivate harmful or disease-causing organisms. In North America, chlorination is the most common method of disinfection. When chlorine is added to untreated or "raw" water, it reacts with many common substances, including ammonia, iron, and organic material (including micro-organisms such as bacteria). In sufficient amounts, chlorine can inactivate disease-causing micro-organisms.

The amount of chlorine added to disinfect water is known as the "chlorine dose." Reactions, including those that inactivate micro-organisms, will consume some or all of the chlorine dose. These chlorine-consuming reactions are called "chlorine demand." The chlorine dose minus the chlorine demand provides the "chlorine residual." The presence of a chlorine residual, after enough time has passed for the chlorine-consuming reactions to be completed, indicates that there was a sufficient amount of chlorine available to react with all of the chlorine-demanding substances, including the micro-organisms.

Section 3.1.2 of the Chlorination Bulletin (applicable in May 2000) provides that a total chlorine residual of at least 0.5 mg/L after 15 minutes (preferably 30 minutes) of contact time before the water reaches the first consumer "will" be provided at all times. It states that it is preferable that "most of the residual be a free residual." A free chlorine residual is the most effective disinfecting agent; it must be contrasted with a total chlorine residual and a combined chlorine residual. When chlorine is added to water, it dissociates into hypochlorous acid and hydrochloric acid. Hypochlorous acid is the compound that is the prime disinfecting agent in a free chlorine residual. However, it is very reactive and will quickly combine with other compounds (e.g., ammonia) to produce chloramines, which provide a "combined chlorine residual" and lower the free residual. Although a combined chlorine residual is more stable and has disinfectant ability, it will not act as quickly to destroy bacteria as will a free chlorine residual. The total chlorine residual less the free chlorine residual is the combined chlorine residual.

A failure in the treatment process can occur if equipment malfunctions or if there is a sudden change in the quality of the water and the treatment process cannot respond quickly enough to the change in source water quality. When the amount of contamination entering the system suddenly increases, the chlorine demand usually rises. If the chlorine dose is not increased to exceed the chlorine demand, the chlorine residual decreases. Where a fixed chlorine dose has been injected, a decrease in the chlorine residual level indicates increased chlorine demand in the water, a situation commonly caused by organic contamination.

Additional treatment barriers, such as coagulation, sedimentation, and filtration, are often required for surface waters when chlorine disinfection alone does not provide for the adequate safety of the water supply.

4.2.3   Distribution System

The distribution system is the network of pipes between the water source/ treatment system and the consumer's plumbing system. It also includes the storage of treated water in water towers and reservoirs. The fact that a distribution system itself exerts a chlorine demand heightens the need to maintain a chlorine residual. In addition, contamination of the distribution system can occur as a result of watermain breaks, the construction of new mains, or the infiltration of water from the surrounding ground into the distribution system pipes.

In recent years, there has been an increased emphasis on the quality of the water in the distribution system. The longer water remains in the distribution system, the greater the risk of its quality deteriorating. It is believed that for a distribution system to be secure, it should be built with as few dead ends as possible because dead ends inhibit water circulation and create an increased risk of nuisance bacterial growth and related water quality deterioration.

4.2.4 Monitoring

Monitoring involves the collection of samples and the taking of measurements to ensure that the system is working properly and that the water is safe. It focuses on health-related parameters such as the presence of bacteria as well as on aesthetic parameters.

Monitoring generally involves two components: (1) monitoring of raw water and treatment process performance (e.g., the measurement of chlorine residual or turbidity); and (2) the monitoring of the actual product – the treated water. Because it is virtually impossible to monitor all possible harmful organisms, "indicator organisms" are monitored; they indicate the possible or likely presence of a disease-causing organism. In microbiological monitoring, for example, the total coliforms test measures a broad grouping of various bacteria, including those associated with fecal contamination. If total coliforms are found in water samples, additional tests are conducted to determine if fecal contamination of the water has occurred. Because most water-borne diseases are caused by micro-organisms in fecal wastes, such a contamination of drinking water constitutes an unacceptable risk.

In addition to stipulating the primary disinfection process, the Chlorination Bulletin also provides that "a chlorine residual should be maintained in all parts of the distribution system." This has generally been interpreted to mean that a detectable residual should be present in the distribution system.

4.2.5 Response

This component of the multi-barrier approach involves appropriate responses to failing process measures or adverse water quality. For example, the failure to detect a chlorine residual indicates that the chlorine dose is insufficient to meet the chlorine demand, in which case, the disinfection may have failed. Specific notification and operational procedures exist for adverse quality measures such as microbiological results. These procedures include further sampling to confirm an adverse result, flushing watermains, and increasing the disinfectant dose. Another possible response to adverse results is issuing a boil water advisory.

In summary, the multi-barrier approach includes five elements designed to ensure safe drinking water in communal systems: a good source of water, effective treatment of the water, a secure distribution system, continuous monitoring of the system, and an appropriate response to adverse results.

4.3   Well 5

4.3.1   Warning Signs at the Time of Construction

From its inception, Well 5 was recognized as a vulnerable well that might be under the direct influence of surface water. I find, however, that no appropriately thorough analysis of the well's vulnerability was conducted from the time of its construction in 1978 until the tragedy of May 2000. I discuss below the initial hydrogeological and bacteriological results obtained at the time of Well 5's construction that indicated surface water influence.

Before bringing Well 5 online, Ian D. Wilson Associates Ltd., professional engineers, submitted a report, "Testing of the Town of Walkerton Well 4," dated July 28, 1978.[5] The length of the well casing was 18 feet (5.5 m). The Wilson report noted that the well had two water-bearing zones: one at 18–19 feet (5.5–5.8 m) and another at 23–24 feet (7.0–7.3 m). The geological materials at 18–19 feet (5.5–5.8 m) were noted to be "brown broken soft limestone" and, at 23–24 feet (7.0–7.3 m), "brown very fractured, soft limestone." The area from 0–8 feet (0–2.4 m) was brown, sandy, mixed clay with stones and mixed sand with gravel, and from 8–13 feet (2.4–4.0 m) it was brown, broken, soft limestone with shale. A 72-hour pump test revealed dewatering throughout the "shallow aquifer." The water level in a test well 11 feet (3.4 m) away lowered by 7.54 feet (2.3 m); in a test well 205 feet (62.5 m) away, it lowered by 5.77 feet (1.8 m); and in a farm well 471 feet (143.6 m) away, it lowered by 5.39 feet (1.6 m).

The Wilson report noted that a wet area in the vicinity of Well 5 was spring-fed partly through old disused concrete cribbings. During a pump test, water flowing from two nearby concrete cribs was stopped completely, showing that water normally reaching these two spring discharge points was intersected by the well.

The report concluded that the aquifer was probably recharged from gravelly spillway deposits to the west, southwest, and possibly to the south of the well.

---

[5] Initially referred to as Well 4, the well subsequently became Well 5.

It noted that these granular materials readily absorb precipitation, transporting it through the overburden, where it would reappear at the surface as springs or move downward to augment groundwater flow. The report noted: "Water moving through these friable deposits to the bedrock surface would enter the rock system in areas of fracture and weathering. Flow would then continue along these fracture or fissure zones. Well [5] intersected two of these zones at the test site."

As a result of these concerns, the Wilson report recommended that the pumping rate and pumping water level in Well 5 should be carefully monitored. The report cautioned that "if due to overpumping the water level approaches the upper water zone at 18 feet, the rate should be reduced or the well rested until the level resumes a safe depth." This was never made a condition of operation.

Bacteriological samples taken during the pump test indicated that bacterial contamination entered Well 5 between 12 and 24 hours after the start of the pump test (see Table 1).

Table 1   Walkerton Well 5, Pump Test Results, 1978

Time After Pumping Started	Total Coliforms/100 mL	Fecal Coliforms/100 mL
12 hours	0	0
24 hours	4	2
36 hours	8	0
48 hours	12	12
60 hours	8	6
72 hours	2	2
72 hours[6]	0	0

The presence of total and fecal coliforms in the water raised concerns about contamination from the surface and led to recommendations that consideration be given to controlling land uses in the immediate area. There was nothing done in this regard.

---

[6] The results of this sampling "are difficult to explain," according to the Wilson report, since it is a duplicate of the preceding sampling.

The nitrate content of the water (up to 5.0 mg/L) was within the MOE's permissible criterion of 10 mg/L for nitrate measured as nitrogen, but was still somewhat elevated. Nitrate is an oxidized form of nitrogen, whose most common source in water is chemical fertilizers; it may also result from organic (human and animal) waste. Nitrates are highly water soluble, so they cannot be filtered and do not degrade in groundwater. Unlike bacteria, nitrates do not die off. Once they enter an aquifer, they persist in the groundwater. Nitrates are often a sign of agricultural activities influencing a groundwater source.

In Chapter 9 of this report, I describe in detail the process that was followed at the time Well 5 was approved by the MOE. It is sufficient for present purposes to note that the Certificate of Approval issued on January 22, 1979 contained no operating conditions.

4.3.2   Early Bacteriological and Chemical Results

During the period 1978–80, two MOE environmental officers conducted a number of inspections of Well 5. These inspections clearly revealed concerns about surface water influence on Well 5 and the potential for the well's contamination. These concerns were based on the proximity of agricultural uses, the shallow well with a shallow overburden, fluctuating turbidity, microbiological test results showing fecal coliform contamination, and changes in spring water pumping levels. At the time, however, no steps were taken to either implement more stringent analytical or testing requirements, or to make revisions to the well's Certificate of Approval. During the 1980s, when the MOE did not conduct any inspections of this water system, these early inspectors' concerns were lost to time.

The first inspections of the new Well 5 were conducted on several occasions in 1978 and 1979. The inspector's report noted that the water level in Well 5 in March 1979 rose to between 3 feet (0.9 m) and 4 feet (1.2 m) below ground level, later dropping continuously to a depth of approximately 11.5 feet (3.5 m). The inspector concluded: "This increase in the pumping level coincided generally with the spring thaw and period of rain. This appears to confirm the relatively direct communication between this aquifer and the surface." The inspector recommended that Well 5 be monitored regularly to ensure that the parameters such as nitrates, total organic carbon, and phenols, which indicated contamination originating from the surface, did not increase beyond acceptable levels. He also noted that it had been recommended that the Town of Walkerton endeavour to exercise some control over surface activities in the area to the south and west of Well 5, and that any efforts to control land use activities in this area should be continued.

Several routine inspections of the PUC works were carried out during the period of June 1979–October 1980, approximately a year and a half after Well 5 was put in service. The inspector concluded that Well 5 was a shallow-drilled well susceptible to influence from surface activities due to the shallow overburden protecting the aquifer. His inspection report records raw water contamination by coliforms and fecal coliforms. In 1979, both coliform and fecal coliform counts were as high as 32 organisms per 100 mL. In 1980, of the 42 samples taken, four were adverse. The highest bacterial density was 260 total coliforms and 230 fecal coliforms per 100 mL. This water was seriously contaminated: these levels of fecal coliform contamination should not be found in a secure groundwater source. None of the treated water samples was of adverse quality. The inspection report concluded:

> The bacteriological quality of Well 5 reveals a variable bacteria density in the raw water throughout the year. The variation in the bacteria density reflects surface activities within the influence of the aquifer. It is recommended that Well No. 5 continue to be monitored on a regular basis in the future to confirm the suitability of the water quality at all times.

The turbidity results were also significant. The first report, in 1979, recorded that turbidity in Well 5 had been tested on nine occasions and that turbidity ranged from 0.10 to 0.54 formazin units (roughly equivalent to nephelometric turbidity units, or NTU). At no point did turbidity exceed the maximum acceptable concentration limit of 1.0 NTU as stipulated in the February 1978 version of the Ontario Drinking Water Objectives (ODWO). These turbidity results must be contrasted with the results recorded in the second report. Ten turbidity samples were taken between March 1979 and September 1980. Turbidity ranged from 0.15 NTU to 3.5 NTU; it exceeded the maximum acceptable level stipulated in the ODWO on two occasions (3.5 NTU and 1.8 NTU) and was at the maximum acceptable concentration of 1.0 NTU on one occasion. This degree of fluctuation of turbidity and such peak concentrations would not be expected in a secure groundwater source.

In the period 1978–80, the two inspectors both recognized the potential for the contamination of Well 5 based on various factors: the shallow overburden, the proximity of agricultural uses, fluctuating turbidity, microbiological test results showing fecal coliforms, and the changes in spring water pumping levels. I find that both the fecal coliform results and fluctuating turbidity, particularly in light of concerns raised by the Wilson report at the time of the well's construction, should have prompted further investigations by the MOE. Indeed, a former MOE approvals engineer testified that the fluctuations in turbidity and the level of nitrates set out in the second report, combined with raw water results from Well 5 indicating significant fecal contamination, were a cause for concern and indicated potential surface water influence. He remarked that if this kind of information had been received by him as a result of a monitoring condition in a Certificate of Approval, he would have directed either a hydrogeological or an engineering investigation to determine whether there was direct surface water influence and whether a continuous chlorine monitor should be required.

Indeed, after the May 2000 outbreak, a hydrogeological investigation undertaken by Golder Associates Ltd., discussed below, concluded there was direct surface water influence on Well 5.

4.3.3   Bacteriological Sampling Results: Wells 5, 6, and 7 and the Distribution System, 1990–2000

In this section, I review historical bacteriological sampling results from January 1990 to April 2000.[7] I conclude that the quality of water from Well 5, raw and treated, deteriorated during that decade.

The data are not entirely reliable. This is in part due to an improper practice of the Walkerton PUC operators to occasionally take samples at convenient locations other than those printed on the sample bottles and sample submission forms. A significant number of samples were taken at the tap in the Walkerton PUC shop that might have been labelled as either well samples or distribution system samples. Other samples taken at the wells were labelled as having come from some place in the distribution system. I refer to these practices elsewhere in this report as mislabelling sample bottles or locations.

The reliability of the bacteriological sampling result is also affected by the fact that water drawn from the tap at the PUC workshop is only a few minutes'

----
[7] No records are available for the period October 1980–June 1990.

travelling distance from the chlorine injection point at Well 5. Therefore, this water did not receive the 15 minutes of chlorine contact time required for complete disinfection. As a result, these samples tend to reflect the water quality at Well 5. The importance of this fact is that the number of adverse samples from Well 5 may have been higher than was recorded and, correspondingly, the number of adverse samples from the distribution system and from Wells 6 and 7 may have been lower than was recorded.

Although I am not able to rely on the stated location of any sample as properly indicating the sample's source among the three wells, I am satisfied that the bacteriological results demonstrate that Well 5 had a significant coliform detection rate in the raw and treated water. The presence of coliforms in treated water indicates inadequate disinfection because these bacteria are very vulnerable to proper chlorination.

The Bruce-Grey-Owen Sound Health Unit kept track of all sample results during the period when the Palmerston Public Health Laboratory was testing the Walkerton water (January 1990 to September 1996). The results appear in Table 2.

The Ministry of Health's Palmerston Public Health Laboratory stopped testing Walkerton's municipal water in September 1996, when the ministry's public health laboratories withdrew from municipal water testing as part of the government's policy to privatize that activity.

From September 1996 to April 2000, bacteriological testing was performed by G.A.P. EnviroMicrobial Services Inc. under the direction of Garry Palmateer. He prepared a summary of coliform and *E. coli* detections in the Walkerton distribution system water from October 1996 to April 2000 (see Table 3).

Mr. Palmateer testified that in his experience (as well as that of the Ministry of Health's Central Public Health Laboratory in Etobicoke) the expected background level of total coliforms detection in a distribution system was approximately 4% and, for *E. coli*, less than 1%. This includes the level of total coliforms one would expect to find in a distribution system due to biofilm growth, and takes into account sampling errors for *E. coli*.

Tables 2 and 3 indicate that the quality of Well 5 water, both raw and treated, appears to have been deteriorating over the decade. Coliform detection in Well 5 raw water went from approximately 2.6% in the Palmerston laboratory

**Table 2   Walkerton Water Microbiological Sample Results
Provided by Palmerston Public Health Laboratory,
January 1990–September 1996**

Sampling Location[8]	Number of Samples	Total Coliforms		E. coli	
		Positive Samples	Percentage	Positive Samples	Percentage
Well 5 raw	349	9	2.6%	1	0.3%
Well 5 treated	351	7	2.0%	1	0.3%
Well 6 raw	10	2	20.0%	0	0%
Well 6 treated	29	1	3.4%	0	0%
Well 7 raw	335	12	3.6%	2	0.6%
Well 7 treated	335	18	5.4%	5	1.5%
Distribution system	1,234	33	2.7%	6	0.5%
Total	**2,643**	**82**	**3.1%**	**15**	**0.6%**

**Table 3   Walkerton Water Microbiological Sample Results
Provided by G.A.P. EnviroMicrobial Services Inc.,
October 1996–April 2000**

Sampling Location[9]	Number of Samples	Total Coliforms		E. coli	
		Positive Samples	Percentage	Positive Samples	Percentage
Well 5 raw	116	13%	11%		<1%
Well 5 treated	115	8%	7%	1	<1%
Well 6 raw	25	3%	12%	0	0%
Well 6 treated	24	1%	4%	0	0%
Well 7 raw	98	3%	3%	0	0%
Well 7 treated	99	1%	1%	0	0%
Distribution system	471	12%	3%	4	<1%
Total	**948**	**41%**	**4%**	**6**	**<1%**

---

[8] Sampling locations may be incorrectly identified.
[9] Sampling locations may be incorrectly identified.

period to 11% in the G.A.P. laboratory period. Well 5 treated water coliform detection went from 2.0% in the Palmerston laboratory period to 7% in the G.A.P. laboratory period. Well 6 appears to have been undersampled in comparison with the other wells. Well 6 raw water had the highest coliform detection rate (20% in the Palmerston laboratory raw water tests and 12% in the G.A.P. laboratory raw water tests). Well 7 treated water positive samples declined from 5.4% in the Palmerston laboratory period to 1% in the G.A.P. laboratory period. The *E. coli* results all fall within the normal background rate of 1% or less. I will discuss the bacteriological samples taken immediately before and after the May outbreak in section 4.7.

4.3.4   Geology and Hydrogeology

Both geology and hydrogeology are crucial factors in understanding why the contamination in May 2000 was able to enter Well 5.

Geology refers to the study of rocks and the solid parts of the earth, and hydrogeology involves the study of the occurrence, movement, and quality of water beneath the earth's surface. The geology of the area around Well 5 involved a bedrock highly susceptible to fracturing. Well 5 drew its water from a shallow, highly fractured rock zone. The overburden – the area between the top of the bedrock and the surface – was very shallow. The significance of these geological factors is that a point source breach in the overburden could be connected to a fractured channel linked to the aquifer. This could lead to minimal natural filtration and a swift transport of living bacteria directly into the aquifer.

The hydrogeological features of significance here include the speed at which water will flow in such a highly fractured rock environment. They also include the presence of springs near Well 5 that stopped flowing when the well pump was operated and drew surface water into the well.[10] Tracer testing conducted after the tragedy revealed that surface tracer materials placed in those springs were transported into the well within a few hours after the well was turned on. These springs provide another route by which contaminated surface water could swiftly transport living bacteria into the well.

---

[10] It is not known whether this also occurred when the well pump was not operated.

Well 5 is located near the southwest limit of the former Town of Walkerton, near the end of Wallace Street. It was constructed in 1978 to a total depth of 15 m. The overburden (the depth from the surface to bedrock) is 2.5 m. The bedrock surrounding Well 5 is composed of limestone and dolomite carbonate rocks that are susceptible to dissolution and fracturing. The upper portion of the bedrock below the overburden is a very permeable, highly porous, fractured rock material, extending approximately 7.5 m. The casing of Well 5 extends to only 5 m below the surface. All of the water entering Well 5 comes from a shallow zones ranging from 5.5 to 7.4 m below the surface.

Well 5 was equipped to be capable of pumping approximately 20.5 L/second or 1,771 m³/day. This is just over 55% of the average daily flow required by the Town of Walkerton. Farm fields that are fertilized with manure lie to the west of Well 5. To the immediate north and east of Well 5 is a low, wet area that receives discharge from one or two springs.

All underground aquifers are replenished by surface water. In a secure groundwater source, however, surface water infiltrates through the overburden (generally a variety of soils, sand, silt, or clay) and again through bedrock. Such natural filtration will often take years. Since bacteria such as *E. coli* O157:H7 will live in water for weeks or months, and in soil for six months or longer, they are expected to be physically removed from the water flow and to die during this natural filtration process. In a secure groundwater source, there is no *direct* influence of surface water bacterial contamination on the groundwater source. However, certain factors may influence the effectiveness of the filtration process, such as a relatively direct connection between surface water and the aquifer. Where there is a direct connection between a well or aquifer and surface water, living bacteria may directly enter the groundwater source well.

4.3.5   Points of Entry

The area around Well 5 has a number of potential surface connections that were possible means by which contamination entered the well in May 2000. Among these are point source breaches in the area's overburden, which allow the rapid transport of water through the bedrock. Examples of possible point source breaches include fence post holes on the nearby farm, sand or gravel lenses, and improperly abandoned wells. Almost all of the water entering Well 5 comes from a highly fractured and weathered zone of bedrock. Well 5's casing ends within this zone, which is riddled with a finely scaled network of fractures in direct hydraulic connection with the overburden. Therefore, if contaminants breached the overburden, they would enter the fracture network and be carried to Well 5 in a short time.

Springs near Well 5 are another possible point of entry to the aquifer. There are two springs within 30 m of Well 5: one on the north and the other on the south side of the access road near Well 5. These springs have been observed to stop flowing when Well 5 is being pumped. During the flow distribution profiling conducted by Golder Associates Ltd.[11] on June 15, 2000, the spring north of the access road stopped flowing, water lying on the surface of the ground around the spring flowed back down into the ground, and within an hour, turbid water entered the well. This phenomenon is known as a "reversing spring": the spring flows normally from the ground, then reverses and flows into the ground.

On September 19, 2000, a tracer test was conducted on this spring by Golder Associates. Tracer materials were injected in the vicinity of the north spring. and Well 5 was operated. The tracer test confirmed a direct surface water connection at Well 5 through the north spring. Tracer materials were detected in the water from Well 5 within 60 minutes (electrical conductivity from sodium chloride) and within 77 minutes (sodium fluorescein, a green fluorescent dye) of their introduction in the vicinity of the north spring near Well 5. The sodium fluorescein was also observed to appear in the south ditch, near the well, where the south spring discharges, while the south spring continued to flow. Therefore, it is possible that surface water contaminated by bacteria may have entered Well 5 through the north spring in May 2000.

Dr. Stephen Worthington, a hydrogeologist called by the Concerned Walkerton Citizens, also conducted tests focusing on the connection between Well 5 and the north and south springs. He agreed with Golder Associates that the north spring may in certain conditions be a reversing spring, allowing surface water to flow into the aquifer from which Well 5 draws water. When he conducted a pump test, the springs on the north side of the road reversed in response to the pumping.

---

[11] Golder Associates Ltd. prepared a report for the Municipality of Brockton after the outbreak. The report is discussed in more detail below.

Dr. Worthington also observed the springs following a heavy (70 mm) rainfall on June 22, 2001. The daily average discharge at the springs was 10 L/second to 20 L/second. Following this rainfall the discharge increased to 30 L/second. He concluded that at times of heavy rain, particularly in spring, the flow from the springs is more than Well 5 can pump. He also found that the catchment area for the springs goes across the field where the manure – which I conclude was the source of the contamination – was applied. This provides a link between the springs near Well 5 and the source of contamination. However, in his view, the discharge of the springs near Well 5 was probably greater than the pumping rate of Well 5 around May 12, 2000. This makes it unlikely that the pumping of Well 5 drew local surface water into the springs and then into the well in May 2000.[12]

I also note that in a report dated November 23, 2000, Dr. Worthington concluded, on the basis of further fluorescein tracer tests, that surface water from Silver Creek (see Figure 1 on page 127) travels rapidly to the springs near Well 5. However, I am not able to conclude whether this is the case. The results from these tests were equivocal. Dr. Worthington did no background fluorescein analysis, and the small peaks detected were consistent with periods of rain that could have flushed background concentrations from surface pollutants into the groundwater.

In either event, I note that the geological and hydrogeological features of the area increased the risk of contamination entry to the aquifer. Water flow through fractured limestone and dolomite channels may increase dramatically, both in terms of distance and speed. Fracture zones within the bedrock may have a low porosity that permits a very high velocity of water, and water (with contaminants) may enter an aquifer many kilometres from the well itself. Where a relatively direct connection exists between the surface and a fractured channel, living bacteria may flow into an aquifer because of the speed at which surface bacteria are introduced into the aquifer by flowing through these fractures. This is in contrast to the more normal steady infiltration through overburden and bedrock, during which the bacteria are naturally filtered and die off. Direct connections through features such as springs may also lead to the entry of bacteria.

---

[12] I tend to agree with Dr. Worthington's conclusion in this regard.

4.3.6   Groundwater Under the Direct Influence of Surface Water

Because groundwater under the direct influence of surface water is vulnerable to contamination, additional treatment and monitoring steps need to be taken to ensure the safety of drinking water. I am satisfied that Well 5 was a groundwater source under the direct influence of surface water.

When Well 5 was approved in 1978, the 1973 version of the Chlorination Bulletin was in effect. Although the bulletin did not use the phrase "groundwater under the direct influence of surface water," it used a similar concept, providing that continuous and adequate chlorination be used when "groundwater sources are or may become contaminated, as in fractured limestone areas."

Because of concerns in 1978 that Well 5 was a groundwater source that might become contaminated, the MOE recommended that the water from Well 5 be treated with chlorine and that a chlorine residual of 0.5 mg/L after 15 minutes of contact time be maintained. The prevailing practice was to make recommendations for matters of this nature, not to include them as conditions in a Certificate of Approval.

In 1994, the ODWO were amended to include the concept of "groundwater under the direct influence of surface water." This amendment was modelled on the U.S. Environmental Protection Agency's Surface Water Treatment Rule. One of the purposes of the 1994 amendment was to require continuous chlorine monitors for groundwater sources that were found to be under the direct influence of surface water.

The MOE did not, however, publish any technical bulletins or guidelines listing factors that would indicate when a groundwater source was considered to be under the direct influence of surface water. For the purposes of my analysis, I have reviewed four sources of information that may indicate direct surface water influence on a groundwater source:

• **Biological Indicators** – The key biological indicators are fecal bacteria, including *E. coli*, in raw water. Given the relatively short lifespan of these organisms, the presence of fecal bacteria in a groundwater source indicates the presence of a source of fecal contamination, a short travel time from the surface, and a lack of adequate natural filtration by subsurface materials surrounding a well intake screen. Other biological indicators of surface water influence include algae, aerobic sporeformers, *Giardia*,

Cryptosporidium, and human enteric viruses. The latter three pathogens would also indicate a fecal contamination source, but they are not normally monitored.

- **Physical and Chemical Indicators** – A fluctuation of turbidity is not expected in a secure groundwater source. Generally, turbidity should be relatively low (i.e., less than 1 NTU) and should not fluctuate considerably. Fluctuations in chemical parameters such as organic nitrogen or nitrates, total organic carbon and pH, or the physical parameter of electrical conductivity, may also indicate surface water influence. None of these chemical or physical parameters is uniquely indicative of fecal contamination.

- **Hydrological and Hydrogeological Indicators** – Any interaction between surface water features (e.g., springs, ponds) and wells may indicate that surface water is directly entering the aquifer from which the well draws water. Fracturing of the bedrock, thinness of overburden, point source breaches, and improperly abandoned wells may contribute to the entry of surface water.

- **Well Construction Indicators** – Holes in the well casing, improperly maintained backflow valves, and other aspects of well construction may provide a direct route for surface water entry.

Using these four indicators, I am satisfied that Well 5 was a groundwater source under the direct influence of surface water. The 1978 Wilson report, the early MOE inspection reports, and microbiological tests taken in the 1990s revealed the presence of *E. coli* in water samples from Well 5.

Physical and chemical tests also pointed to surface water influence. The fluctuating turbidity results in the 1980 inspection report were significant. As a rule, turbidity does not fluctuate in secure groundwater sources. The 1979 inspection report noted that an increase in the water level in Well 5 generally coincided with the spring thaws and rains, which the inspector said confirmed the relatively direct communication between the aquifer and the surface. The 1978 Wilson report noted that a pump test interrupted the flow of nearby springs. Both inspectors in 1979 and 1980 raised concerns about the influence of surface water. Finally, Well 5 was a shallow well with the casing extending only 5 m below the surface. All of the water-bearing zones were also very shallow and in an area of highly fractured bedrock.

In 1994, the ODWO were amended to provide extra monitoring for wells supplied by groundwater sources under the direct influence of surface water operating without filtration. Section 4.2.1.1 of the ODWO provided for continuous chlorine residual monitoring and turbidity monitoring by taking four grab samples a day or by continuous monitoring. For simplicity, I refer to this as continuous turbidity monitoring.[13] After the amendment, the MOE did not institute a program to reclassify existing wells.

I am satisfied that had the MOE instituted a program of reclassification after 1994, the information in its files was sufficient to show that Well 5 was under the direct influence of surface water. At a minimum, there was sufficient information to trigger an investigation that would have certainly revealed that situation. After 1994, the evidence that Well 5 came within this classification increased as the years passed. *E. coli* continued to show up in bacterial samples taken from the well. Between November 1995 and February 1998, there were five separate occurrences of adverse results, including *E. coli*. Still no steps were taken to reclassify Well 5, and, as a result, the MOE did not require the Walkerton PUC to install a continuous chlorine residual and turbidity monitors.

Had Well 5 been so classified, and had the requisite monitoring equipment been installed, the contamination entering the well in May 2000 would have been identified, and appropriate alarms could have shut down the pump. Continuous monitors would have prevented the outbreak.

An important purpose of installing continuous monitors is to prevent contamination from entering the distribution system. In reaching the conclusion that continuous monitors would have prevented the Walkerton outbreak, I am assuming that the MOE would have required that any such monitors be properly designed for the circumstances at Well 5. The monitors would thus have included an alarm as well as, in all probability, an automatic shut-off mechanism, because Well 5 was not staffed 24 hours a day and because the town had alternative water supplies –Wells 6 and 7.

Some might suggest that the operators of the Walkerton system would not have operated these monitors properly. However, if the MOE – which would have been responsible for approving the installation of these monitors – had any doubt that monitors would be operated properly, the obvious step would

---

[13] As a practical matter, a continuous turbidity monitor, which costs only about $8,000, makes more sense than taking four samples a day.

have been to require an automatic shut-off device or alternative fail-safe mechanism. A shut-off mechanism would have involved only minimal additional expense.

In Chapter 5 of this report, I reject the suggestion that the PUC operators would have turned the pump at Well 5 back on if it had been automatically shut off. For the same reasons, I also reject any suggestion that the PUC operators, even if properly trained about the importance of continuous monitors, would not have responded appropriately to an alarm signalling that contamination was about to enter the distribution system.

4.4   The Source of Contamination

4.4.1   The Area Surrounding Well 5

Another important element in determining the cause of the contamination in May 2000 is identifying a source of contamination. I am satisfied that the primary, if not the only, source was the manure application in April 2000 on the Biesenthal farm near Well 5. In this section I set out a description of the farming and manure storage and application practices used on that farm. As discussed in the epidemiological evidence below, cattle from the Biesenthal farm were found by "DNA" typing to have the same strain of both *E. coli* O157:H7 and *Campylobacter* as the predominant human outbreak strain in Walkerton in May 2000. I am satisfied as to the strength of the link between this possible source, the location of the farm and Well 5, and the outbreak of illness and death in Walkerton.

In the spring of 2000, Dr. David Biesenthal was operating a cow calf operation on land near Well 5, on Lots 18 to 21 on the concession south of Durham Road. Figure 1, an aerial photo taken on September 9, 2000, shows the farm and Well 5.

The farmhouse can be seen in Figure 1. The barn is to the east of the farmhouse. A small paddock surrounds the barn on two sides. There is a fence around the paddock area where the manure storage pad was located, and another fence around the yard. The fence post holes around the paddock were dug by backhoe, to a depth of about 1.25 m. The fence post holes were approximately 2.4 m apart. The overburden was likely 2.5 m to 4 m deep, so the fence post holes penetrated a significant portion of the overburden.

Figure 1   Aerial View of Biesenthal Farm, September 9, 2000

Photo: Marc Bolduc, RCMP

Dr. Biesenthal farmed a total of 133 acres (54 ha). As can be seen in Figure 1, Lot 18 borders the west bank of Silver Creek. In 2000, it was the main area used for grazing. Lot 19 borders the east bank of Silver Creek and was used for grain crops and cut forage. These two lots drain toward Silver Creek. Lot 20 was used for grain crop production and contains the livestock barn and yard. There is also a small paddock used for calving and grazing for a brood mare; Lot 20 also provided some cut forage. Lot 21 was used for cut forage. The land and buildings on Lot 21 are the Gutscher property, formerly the Pletsch property. Dr. Biesenthal took forage from Lot 21 but did not own the land. Most of the natural drainage from Lots 20 and 21 is to the east, presumably feeding the spring and wetland close to Well 5. The soil is loam. The depth to bedrock on Lots 20 and 21 ranges from 1.5 m to 7 m.

4.4.2   Animal Husbandry and Manure

In 1999–2000, Dr. Biesenthal maintained a breeding herd of about 40 Limousin cows and heifers. The cows calve mainly in the barn from December to April. Animals from other operations are brought onto the farm in late April or early May and are sold off in the fall, together with calves from the previous winter. A maximum of 95 head of cattle may be on the farm during the spring and summer.

During the late fall and winter, the cattle are confined to the barn, the associated concrete apron, and the small paddock that surrounds the barn on two sides. In the spring, the animals are put out to the main pasture in the field to the west of Silver Creek but are allowed access to the barn to drink. Silver Creek has been fenced off and bridged to prevent animals from defecating into the stream.

On the Biesenthal farm, the manure is "solid manure." The animals are provided with straw bedding; this is typical of many beef and dairy operations. The cattle's feces and urine are mixed with the straw to form a solid manure with about 19% dry matter. In Ontario, the proportion of dry matter in solid beef-cattle manure ranges from 18% to 63%.

Manure is typically applied to the farm fields as fertilizer in the late fall before freeze-up and in the spring before planting. In November 1999, the Biesenthals applied all the manure they had in storage – approximately 105 tons[14] – to the field on Lot 20 north of the barn and paddock. The application rate was approximately 12 tons/ha. Manure was incorporated into the soil within 24 hours after application by using a disc harrow. The depth of incorporation was approximately 7 cm.

Manure accumulated from November through April was stored on an open concrete pad in the paddock area. There was no runoff system to collect feces or urine. The farmer used a tractor scraper to transfer manure from the barn and the yard onto the concrete pad. The concrete pad was able to hold approximately 200 days' manure production.

A significant rainfall occurred on April 20–21, 2000. On April 22, approximately 24 hours later, 70 tons of manure stored on the concrete pad were

---

[14] The system of measurement (Imperial, U.S., or metric) was not specifically identified.

removed and spread on the east front field of Lot 20. Again, the application rate was approximately 12 tons/ha. Within 24 hours, manure was incorporated into the top 7 cm of soil using a disc harrow. About 73 tons of manure were exported to another farm.

The application rate of 12 tons of manure per hectare represents approximately 120 g fresh weight per square metre, which is less than 25 g dry weight per square metre. Fresh manure can contain between 10^6 to 10^9 fecal coliforms per gram dry weight. Although few of the organisms would move below the cultivation depth, and in the weeks after the application many would have died, a significant source of fecal coliforms was applied and incorporated into the soil near Well 5 on April 22. At its closest point, manure was applied 81 m from Well 5.

It is important to note that Dr. Biesenthal's manure handling, storage, and spreading practices were consistent with what are considered "best management practices" by the Ontario Ministry of Agriculture, Food and Rural Affairs. Therefore, although it is virtually certain that the contamination that caused the outbreak originated on his farm, Dr. Biesenthal cannot be faulted.

4.4.3   The Lifespan of *E. coli* O157:H7 in Soil

Studies done on the survival of *E. coli* O157:H7 in various soil types indicate survival times of at least 10 to 25 weeks. Dr. Michael Goss, chair of the University of Guelph's land stewardship program, and Dr. Pierre Payment, an environmental microbiologist specializing in waterborne pathogens and a member of the Walkerton Commission's Expert Review Panel, agreed that for loam soil, studies have demonstrated the survival of *E. coli* O157:H7 at 25 weeks. Further, cooler soil temperatures tend to promote longer survival times.

Dr. Goss testified that *E. coli* will survive longer when they are infiltrated into the soil because they are not subject to drying or ultraviolet light, as they are when at or near the surface. The manure applied on April 22 was incorporated into the soil within 24 hours of spreading. As a result, by May 12, most of the bacteria in this incorporated manure were still likely to be viable, except those exposed at the soil surface. Rain prior to May 12 would be expected to infiltrate the soil, thereby encouraging the movement of bacteria close to the soil surface into the deeper layers, where their viability is enhanced. In these circumstances, *E. coli* in the front east field could survive for up to 6 months.

4.5   Wells Supplying the System in May

In seeking to determine the cause of the contamination, I have considered which wells were pumping and thereby supplying water to the distribution system during the relevant times. Through the critical period of May 10 to May 15, Well 5 was the primary well, providing most of the water to the distribution system.

Discrepancies exist between the manually prepared daily operating sheets for Well 7 and the electronic Supervisory Control and Data Acquisition (SCADA) system records. These discrepancies relate to the days on which Well 7 was operated, as well as to the volumes pumped. The SCADA system generates electronic records of pump operating times and water volume. I do not rely upon the Well 7 daily operating sheet for the month of May 2000. The daily operating sheet for Well 7 for May was rewritten on May 22 or May 23. It is not accurate. For example, the daily operating sheet shows that no wells were operating within Walkerton's water system during the period from May 3 through May 9. This is impossible, because the water system has, at most, two days' storage capacity.

I am satisfied that the electronic SCADA records more accurately depict when the wells were operating than do the daily operating sheets.[15] The SCADA information shows reasonable and consistent pumpage cycling and pumpage values. In the result, I find that:

- Well 7 did not operate from March 10 to May 2, 2000. Well 7 was the only well supplying the system from May 2 at 7:45 a.m. to May 9 at 1:45 a.m.

- Well 5 operated continuously from May 9 at 9:15 a.m. to May 12 at 10:45 p.m. It started again May 13 at 2:15 p.m. and ran continuously until May 15 at 1:15 p.m. It was off until May 20 at 10:45 a.m.

- Well 6 cycled on and off between May 9 at 6 p.m. and May 13 at 5 p.m. There is no data for some times before and after that period, but it seems unlikely that Well 6 was turned on again after May 13 at 6 p.m.

---

[15] I note that the SCADA data for Well 6 are incomplete, partly because of a power failure on the weekend of May 13–14.

- Well 7 was turned on again on May 15 at 6:15 a.m. and operated until May 19 at 10:30 a.m.

The chlorinator at Well 7 was removed before noon on May 3, and the new chlorinator was not installed until May 19. Therefore, unchlorinated water was supplied to the distribution system through Well 7 from May 3 at noon until May 9 at 1:45 a.m., and again from May 15 at 6:15 a.m. until May 19 at 10:30 a.m. The evidence is that the new chlorinator was installed by noon on May 19.

As I conclude below, the epidemiological and other evidence indicates that the water supply likely became contaminated on or shortly after May 12. Well 5 was the primary source of water from May 9 to the early morning of May 15. Well 6 was the secondary source during this period. Well 7 was not in operation during this key period; it was turned on again at 6:15 a.m. on May 15 and operated without chlorination until shortly before noon on May 19. I am satisfied that the exposure to the infection started some time before Well 7 was turned on and that there must have been another source of the contamination.

The volume of water pumped into the system is also important. As can be seen in Table 4, Well 7 provided most of Walkerton's water from May 3 to 9. However, Well 5 was providing the majority of the water to the distribution system from May 10 to 15, which I find to include the crucial contamination period.

Table 4   Summary of Well Flow, May 2000: Volume Pumped (m³)[16]

	3	4	5	6	7	8	9	10	11	12	13	14	15	16	17
	W	T	F	S	S	M	T	W	T	F	S	S	M	T	W
Well 5	12	12	12	12	14	11	12	1811	1725	1868	1181	1514	1530	418	12
Well 6[17]	7	7	7	7	7	7	NR	873	264	989	1104	NR	NR	NR	NR
Well 7	2249	2891	2809	2813	3288	3299	2914	17	3	10	12	14	548	2931	2470
Daily Total	2268	2910	2828	2832	3309	3317	2926	2701	1992	2867	2297	1528	2078	3349	2482

---

[16] NR = not recorded.

[17] From May 3 to May 8 inclusive, May 10, and May 13, SCADA pumpage for Well 6 was calculated from midnight to midnight. The SCADA system did not properly record pumpage from Well 6 on May 9 or from May 14 to May 18 inclusive.

4.6   Rainfall

Environment Canada meteorologist Heather Auld testified with respect to the estimated rainfall in Walkerton in the April–May period. On April 20–21, 35.8 mm of rain fell in the Walkerton area. The cumulative total monthly rainfall for April was 50 mm. Rainfall estimates for early May appear in Table 5.

Table 5   Estimated Rainfall, Walkerton, May 1–12, 2000

Date	Rainfall (mm)	Cumulative Monthly Total (mm)
May 1	5.5	5.5
May 8	15.0	20.5
May 9	15.0	35.5
May 10	20.0	55.5
May 11	12.5	68.0
May 12	70.0	138.0

Environment Canada took into account the surface weather, radar results, real time measurements, and climate data to estimate the rainfall amounts for May 8 to May 12, 2000. Walkerton received 70 mm of rainfall on May 12. It also had significant rainfall in the preceding days, beginning on May 8. A total of about 134 mm of rain fell in Walkerton during the five-day period of May 8 to May 12.[18]

Meteorologists measure the significance of rainfalls by "return periods." A return period estimate is the average time interval between an event level. A 10-year return period for an event or storm would mean that an average of 10 such events could be expected to occur in a 100-year period. Ms. Auld estimated that the 134 mm rainfall for the five day period from May 8 to May 12 could be expected to recur, on average, once every 60 years for the month of May. It was clearly a significantly wet period. The May 12 rainfall by itself corresponded to a return period of less than 10 years. The record one-day rainfall for Walkerton, recorded in 1964, was 125 mm.

Most of this very heavy rain on May 12 fell between 6 p.m. and midnight. Environment Canada did not have records indicating the time of day at which

---

[18] Ms. Auld testified that between 130 and 140 mm of rain fell between May 8 and 12, and her "best guess" was 134 mm.

the rain fell, but a hydrology study completed several months later[19] concluded that approximately 60 mm fell between 6 p.m. and midnight, contributing to a total of 72.4 mm for the entire day of May 12. This is consistent with the Environment Canada daily estimate.

4.7 Adverse Samples

I find that the bacteriological samples taken both immediately before and after the May 2000 outbreak support the conclusion that Well 5 was the source of the contamination in May. The turbidity data is inconclusive.

4.7.1 April 2000 Sampling Results

The April 2000 results from the Walkerton water system indicate an emerging issue concerning water quality at Well 5.[20] On three of four April sample dates, Well 5 raw water tested positive for total coliforms. On April 3, Well 5 raw and treated water and two distribution system samples tested positive for coliforms, whereas coliforms were not detected in samples from Well 6 and two other distribution system samples. On April 11, coliforms were shown to be present in Well 5's raw water. A presumptive positive finding regarding one distribution system location was not confirmed on further testing. The remaining distribution samples and Well 6 samples did not contain coliforms. On April 17, both Well 5 raw and Well 5 treated water tested positive for total coliforms. But total coliforms were not detected in distribution system samples. Finally, on April 24, both Well 5 samples and the two distribution system samples were negative. There were no samples from Well 7 in April 2000 because that well was not operating from March 10 to May 2, 2000.

4.7.2 Early May Samples

Bacteriological samples taken on May 1 indicate that samples labelled "Well 5 raw" and "Well 5 treated" both tested positive for total coliforms and negative for *E. coli*. All other samples from May 1 were negative. The next samples were taken on May 8. Those samples were labelled "Well 7 raw," "Well 7 treated,"

---

[19] By Stantec Consulting Ltd., for B.M. Ross and Associates Ltd.
[20] These comments are of course subject to the mislabelling issue I discussed above.

"125 Durham Street," and "902 Yonge Street," respectively – the latter two being two locations in the distribution system. All these samples were negative for both total coliforms and *E. coli*.

4.7.3   May 15 PUC Sampling

Two sets of samples were taken on May 15. One set of three samples came from the Highway 9 construction project, which is discussed in the next section. The regular weekly samples submitted by the Walkerton PUC on May 15 included four samples from the Walkerton distribution system.

The May 15 sample apparently containing Well 7 raw water did not contain either total coliforms or *E. coli*. However, the samples apparently consisting of treated water from Well 7 and the two locations in the distribution system all came back positive for both total coliforms and *E. coli*. The membrane filtration result for the sample labelled "Well 7 treated" had total coliforms greater than 200 cfu/100 mL and *E. coli* of 200 cfu/100 mL.

Allan Buckle, an employee of the Walkerton PUC, testified that on May 15, Frank Koebel, the PUC's foreman, asked him to take samples from Well 7. Mr. Buckle went to Well 7, and when he arrived there, the well was running without a chlorinator.

Mr. Buckle testified that he arrived at Well 7 with four prelabelled sampling bottles: one for the raw tap, one for the treated tap, one for 125 Durham Street, and one for 902 Yonge Street. He said that he filled the sample bottle labelled "raw water" from the raw water tap at Well 7 and filled two sample bottles with water from the treated tap at Well 7. He stated that on his return to the PUC shop, he gave the remaining bottle labelled "902 Yonge Street" to Stan Koebel. I have concluded that Mr. Buckle erred in saying he took the samples at Well 7 and that it is most likely that Mr. Buckle took the three samples at the PUC shop, which is near and just down the line from Well 5.

It is clear that the locations shown on the three samples that Mr. Buckle says he took were, in fact, inaccurate. All of the experts agreed that it was inexplicable that total coliforms and *E. coli* could be absent in "raw water" at the same time that a sample of the "treated water" was grossly contaminated (total coliforms greater than 200 cfu/100 mL; *E. coli* 200 cfu/100 mL; heterotrophic plate count (HPC) 600 cfu/1 mL). Further, even according to Mr. Buckle, the sample he had labelled "125 Durham Street" was incorrect; he did not go to 125 Durham Street on May 15. In addition, since Well 7 was operating on May 15 without a chlorinator, it is most improbable that one sample from Well 7 would be negative while the other two were positive.

Moreover, Mr. Buckle testified that he regularly misrepresented the sites of samples. For example, on May 15, all the samples represented as having come from two small waterworks unconnected to the Walkerton water system were actually taken at the pumphouses for the sake of convenience. However, some were labelled as distribution system samples. The PUC shop was a more convenient location than was Well 7 for taking water samples for the Walkerton system.

Most importantly, the other evidence is overwhelming that Well 5 was contaminated but Well 7 was not. The logical conclusion is that these samples were taken from a location near Well 5, most probably at the PUC shop.[21] Indeed, Stan Koebel ventured that this was the case. He, as much as anyone, was aware of Mr. Buckle's practices when taking samples.

Accepting that the May 15 samples came from the PUC shop, it still remains to be explained how one of those samples was negative. There is no clear explanation, although one possibility arises from the fact that all service connections, like the PUC shop, are essentially dead ends. One possible explanation for the May 15 results (assuming that they came from the PUC shop) was that the PUC shop's tap had not been used over the May long weekend. The first sample taken may have been clear water that had been in the pipe before the May 12 storm. The remaining samples, even if they were taken at the same location, would contain contaminated water that entered the system after the storm. No one has suggested any other explanation.

4.7.4   May 15 Highway 9 Project Samples

All of the three samples taken from the hydrants on the Highway 9 new watermain project on May 15, 2000, tested positive for both total coliforms and *E. coli* in a presence-absence test. No numerical counts were taken.

---

[21] It is also possible that Mr. Buckle took the samples at Well 5. For the purposes of my analysis, there is no difference.

Allan Buckle testified that on May 15 he received a call and was told to pick up four empty sample bottles and take them to the Highway 9 project. There he was to meet PUC general manager Stan Koebel and a representative of the contractor, Lavis Construction Ltd., at a hydrant they were flushing near the Ministry of Transportation shed at the intersection of Highway 9 and Wallace Street. Mr. Buckle testified that he took two of the bottles and filled them with water from a hose attached to the hydrant. He stated that the contractor also filled two bottles that Mr. Buckle believed were taken from another hydrant near the Energizer Canada plant, on Highway 9 east of the Ministry of Transportation shed.

Dennis Elliott of B.M. Ross and Associates Ltd., who was a site inspector for the Highway 9 construction, also testified with respect to the collection of bacteriological samples at the Highway 9 project. He stated that the collection of bacteriological samples from the flushed line containing water from the municipal water system began at 11:15 a.m. on May 15. Mr. Elliott testified that he and the contractor filled two sample bottles at the hydrant near the Ministry of Transportation shed at Wallace Street, and that a third sample bottle was filled from the easterly hydrant at the Energizer Canada plant. Mr. Elliott then took the three samples to the PUC office on Park Street, where they had earlier arranged to ship the samples out with the regular Monday samples. He had requested that the samples be marked "rush."

I note that Mr. Elliott's testimony is inconsistent with Mr. Buckle's. Mr. Buckle testified that he took four bottles over to the construction site and that he himself filled two of those bottles while the contractor filled two other bottles. Testifying with the benefit of contemporaneously made notes, Mr. Elliott gave evidence that he, together with the contractor's foreman, Wayne Greb, filled three bottles and that Mr. Elliott delivered those bottles to the PUC. On this point, I prefer Mr. Elliott's evidence. Only three bottles were in fact forwarded to the laboratory for testing.

4.7.5   May 18 Highway 9 Samples

Because of the fact that samples taken on the Highway 9 project on May 15 were positive for total coliforms and *E. coli,* further samples were taken on May 18 and submitted to MDS Laboratory Services Inc. in London. Two samples were taken from the hydrant nearest the Ministry of Transportation shed at the intersection of Highway 9 and Wallace Street. One sample showed a concentration of total coliforms of 26 cfu/100 mL and *E. coli* at 9 cfu/100 mL. The other sample showed total coliforms of 43 cfu/100 mL and *E. coli* at 14 cfu/100 mL. The sample taken from the hydrant nearest the Energizer Canada plant recorded total coliforms of 78 cfu/100 mL and *E. coli* at 10 cfu/100 mL.

4.7.6   May 21–23 Samples

Stan Koebel began flushing and superchlorinating the distribution system on May 19. A significant number of samples were taken by the Bruce-Grey-Owen Sound Health Unit, the MOE, and the PUC in the period May 21 through May 23. Very significantly, all of the Well 5 raw water samples showed contamination by both total coliforms and *E. coli*. None of the samples from either Well 6 or Well 7 showed any total coliforms or *E. coli*. Finally, the only distribution system samples that showed either total coliforms or *E. coli* contamination were from two locations in the southwest area of town near Well 5, both of which were at dead ends of the water distribution system.

James Schmidt took samples from the distribution system for the health unit on May 21, May 22, and May 23; they were analyzed at the Ministry of Health laboratory in London. Of the 21 samples taken on May 21, only two were adverse. The Yonge Street and Highway 9 store sample had total coliforms of greater than 80 cfu/100 mL and *E. coli* at 69 cfu/100 mL. The sample from the Bruce County administration building had total coliforms of 2 cfu/100 mL and *E. coli* at 2 cfu/100 mL. The location of these two adverse samples is significant. Both were located in the southwest end of town and were closer to Well 5 than to either of the other two wells. More importantly, each of the locations was at a dead end in the system. The water flow would stagnate in the dead ends and, after contamination had been introduced, bacteria there would be less likely to be killed by flushing and increased chlorination.

On May 22, all of the distribution samples taken by the health unit tested negative except for the same two locations: the fast food outlet south of the intersection at Yonge Street and Highway 9, and the Bruce County administration building on Park Street. Concentrations of total coliforms of greater than 80 cfu/100 mL and *E. coli* of greater than 50 cfu/100 mL were found in the sample taken at the fast food outlet. For the sample taken at the Bruce County administration building, total coliforms were 20 cfu/100 mL and

E. coli were 10 cfu/100 mL. The only well tested was Well 7, and both the raw water and treated water samples were negative.

On May 22, John Earl from the MOE took samples that were tested at the ministry's central laboratory. Two samples were taken at 4 Park Street, one from the raw water at Well 7, and one from Well 7 treated water. All these samples tested negative.

On May 23, the MOE, the PUC, and the health unit took more water samples. The samples taken by the MOE of the raw water at Well 5 showed total coliforms in a concentration greater than 300 cfu/100 mL and *E. coli* at 100 cfu/100 mL. A sample of treated water taken from Well 5 showed concentrations of total coliforms greater than 300 cfu/100 mL and *E. coli* at 120 cfu/100 mL. The samples taken from the treated water at Well 6 and the raw water at Well 7 were clear on that day, as were the three distribution system samples.

On May 23, the PUC also took samples, which were tested by A&L Canada Laboratories. The Well 5 raw samples showed total coliforms greater than 200 cfu/100 mL and *E. coli* at 33 cfu/100 mL. Well 7 raw and treated samples were clear, as were the distribution system samples. Finally, on May 23, all the health unit distribution system samples were negative, except for the one from the fast food outlet and the Bruce County administration building. The results for the samples taken on May 23 at the fast food outlet were total coliforms of 17 cfu/100 mL and *E. coli* at 11 cfu/100 m1, while the Bruce County administration building showed readings of total coliforms 2 cfu/100 ml and *E. coli* 2 cfu/100 ml.

4.7.7   Soil and Water Samples Taken Near Well 5 After the Outbreak

Both soil and water samples taken near Well 5 after May 2000 revealed the presence of *E. coli*. Soil bacteriological results from 23 bore holes at 12 locations near Well 5 indicated the presence of significant total coliform bacteria above the detection limit in all bore holes except one, and *E. coli* in bacteria from five of the 23 bore holes. Near-surface samples in some of the bore holes had total coliform counts of 2,800 cfu/100 g, 1,000 cfu/100 g, 1,600 cfu/100 g, and 7,400 cfu/100g.[22] Elevated *E. coli* counts were also noted for the same samples, ranging from 70 cfu/100 g to 940 cfu/100 g. Mr. Palmateer's evidence was that typical surface and subsurface soil coliform populations can exceed 100,000 cells/100 g and 200,000 cells/100 g, respectively, so these results are not excessive. I note, however, that the *E. coli* levels in these samples near Well 5 were significantly higher than the levels in soil samples taken near Wells 6 and 7.

Particularly important are pump test results obtained by Golder Associates Ltd. from two monitoring wells located west-northwest of Well 5 in late August 2000. Monitoring Well 12D is located on the Biesenthal farm, near the paddock area, approximately 225 m west of Well 5. Monitoring Well 2D is located 105 m west-northwest of Well 5, in a grassy area adjacent to the woods.

E. coli results after a 32-hour pump test are shown in Table 6. The results indicate continuing high *E. coli* counts on the Biesenthal farm in late August 2000. They also demonstrate that as Well 5 pumped, *E. coli* levels increased in both of the monitoring wells and in Well 5, implying some hydrogeological connection between the farm and Well 5.

Table 6   *E. coli* Results After Pump Test (cfu/100 mL)

Monitoring Well 12D		Monitoring Well 2D	Well 5
Before pumping	>8,000	< 10	< 1
After pumping	12,000	900	20

Another significant result was a June 6, 2000, water sample taken from the spring adjacent to Well 5, which had a count of 80 *E. coli* cfu/100 mL. This indicates that *E. coli* persisted in a significant region around Well 5 for at least three weeks after the contamination and outbreak. Further, Dr. Robert Gillham testified that this spring discharges a few gallons per minute, and it does so continuously. In his view, this sample result from the spring indicates that a large area of bedrock near Well 5 must have been contaminated.

---

[22] Bacterial counts generally decreased in deeper samples in these bore holes. It is important to note that bacterial levels in soil samples are expected to be much higher than they are in drinking water samples, particularly for total coliforms, which include natural soil bacteria, in contrast with *E. coli,* which are reliable indicators of fecal contamination.

4.7.8   DNA and Epidemiological Typing

The results of the DNA typing of animal and human samples are most persuasive. A clear link exists between the bacteria found in cattle manure on the Biesenthal farm near Well 5 and the human outbreak strains of *E. coli* O157:H7 and *Campylobacter*. I am satisfied that the primary, if not the only, source of the contamination was manure from this farm, although I cannot rule out other possible sources of contamination.

Dr. Andrew Simor is an infectious diseases specialist and head of the Department of Microbiology at the Sunnybrook and Women's College Health Sciences Centre in Toronto. An expert in molecular and epidemiological typing, he testified about the molecular and epidemiological typing methods used to classify pathogens found in human stools, animal fecal samples, and water samples during the Walkerton outbreak investigation. Polymerase chain reaction (PCR) testing of *E. coli* O157:H7 involves extracting the DNA from an organism and identifying verotoxin genes by enzyme immunoassay. PCR testing will confirm a verotoxin-positive *E. coli* O157:H7. Verotoxin-negative strains of *E. coli*, even *E. coli* O157:H7, will not cause human illness. PCR testing demonstrates whether *E. coli* O157:H7 is verotoxin-positive; it does not identify whether strains of the bacteria taken from different samples are related or derive from a common source.

Epidemiological typing is used to characterize organisms in order to determine if they represent the same strain, such as a common source in an outbreak.

Epidemiologically related isolates derived from a single precursor share common characteristics that differ from those of unrelated strains. There are hundreds, if not thousands, of *E. coli* O157:H7 strains that can cause human disease. To determine whether the same strain of *E. coli* O157:H7 is causing the disease, microbiologists resort to typing the organisms found in fecal and environmental samples. Three forms of epidemiological typing were used for that purpose in this investigation: phage-typing, serotyping, and pulsed-field gel electrophoresis (PFGE).

- Phage-typing involves characterizing isolates by their susceptibility or resistance to a variety of bacteriophages, which are viruses that can infect bacteria.

- Serotyping detects cell wall antigens; it is commonly used to type *Campylobacter*. Both phage-typing and serotyping involve looking at the properties of bacteria.

- Pulsed field gel electrophoresis (PFGE) is the gold-standard method of typing. PFGE involves looking at the molecular properties (the DNA) of the organism and is a type of "DNA fingerprinting." In PFGE, enzymes are used to extract DNA fragments that are then separated by size on electrophoresis gel. This produces a particular DNA pattern. When PFGE results have the same pattern, the bacteria are of the same strain.

The epidemiological evidence of the link between the human outbreak strains of both *E. coli* O157:H7 and *Campylobacter* and those found on the Biesenthal farm persuades me that the source of these bacteria was the Biesenthal farm. Health Canada sampled potential animal reservoirs within a 4-km radius of the three municipal well sites, as well as testing deer droppings in the vicinity of the wells. All wildlife specimens were negative for *Campylobacter* and *E. coli* O157:H7. Of the 13 livestock farms tested, *Campylocbacter* bacteria were found on 11 of the farms. *E. coli* O157:H7 and *Campylobacter jejuni* were found on only two farms. One was the Biesenthal farm near Well 5, and another was a farm within a 4-km radius of Wells 6 and 7.

The Bruce-Grey-Owen Sound Health Unit report indicates that there were 174 confirmed stool samples of human *E. coli* O157:H7 infection. Of these, 94% were PFGE type A or A4, the same strains as were found in cattle and manure at the Biesenthal farm. In contrast, the PFGE pattern of the *E. coli* found in cattle on the other farm, within the 4-km radius of Wells 6 and 7, was PFGE type A1. There were only two human cases of PFGE type A1.

Importantly, while *Campylobacter coli* and *C. jejuni* were identified on both the Biesenthal farm and the other farm, only the phage types of the *Campylobacter* on the Biesenthal farm matched the predominant human outbreak strain (phage type 33), and the majority of these isolates had a similar surface antigenic profile upon serotyping to those seen in the human cases. The phage types of the *Campbylobacter* on the other farm did not match the human outbreak strains.

Since not all of the cattle on the farms were tested and the testing did not take place until June 13, there may have been other strains present on, for example, the Biesenthal farm that simply were not identified by the Health Canada team.

These findings show a reservoir of bacteria that match the human outbreak strain in the vicinity of Well 5 during the time frame of the outbreak. Although no samples were taken from the Biesenthal farm before the outbreak, Dr. Andrea Ellis[23] testified that it is reasonable to assume that these bacteria may have been present in early May or late April, given the ecology of *E. coli* on farms.[24]

The evidence of typing is very strong. Based on available PCR, phage-type, serotype, and PFGE results, I find that the *E. coli* O157:H7 and *Campylobacter* isolates from the vast majority of human patients and from the Biesenthal farm cattle and manure were genetically related and that the farm was likely the source of the vast majority, if not all, of the contamination.

4.7.9   Other Microbiological Evidence

Raw and treated water samples taken from Well 5 on May 23 demonstrated gross microbiological contamination, with total coliform concentration greater than 300 cfu/100 mL and *E. coli* at 102 cfu/100 mL. These samples were sent to the Ontario Ministry of Health and Long-Term Care (MOH) laboratory for PCR tests to look for the DNA specific to *E. coli* O157:H7 bacteria. The laboratory identified the verotoxin gene for *E. coli* O157:H7, indicating that this bacteria had been present in the water at Well 5. No *E. coli* O157:H7 bacteria were found in samples of Well 6 or Well 7 water taken near the time of the outbreak. Indeed, no confirmed *E. coli* O157:H7 were ever found in Well 6 or Well 7 samples.

There was one anomalous result of an environmental sample taken from a pipe at a pond near Well 6. G.A.P. EnviroMicrobial Services Inc. was retained by

---

[23] Dr. Andrea Ellis is section head of the Outbreak Response and Issues Management, Division of Enteric, Food-borne and Water-borne Diseases, Population and Public Health Branch, Health Canada.

[24] In his report dated November 23, 2001, Dr. Stephen Worthington interpreted the health unit data and concluded that the evidence "strongly suggests" that the bacteriological contamination in May 2000 came from a number of different sources at a number of different farms. Dr. Ellis disagreed. She is an epidemiologist. As such, she noted that: "Had the contamination actually come from multiple wells and multiple farms then we would not expect to find almost 90% of the patients infected with the identical strain of E. coli O157." She also noted the consistency of molecular sub-typing results across several different methods – PFGE, phage typing, and serotyping – a consistency not found on any of the other livestock farms tested in the area of the wells and a factor not considered by Dr. Worthington. I prefer the evidence of Dr. Ellis in this regard.

the Ontario Clean Water Agency to conduct an environmental investigation after the outbreak. There is an excavated pond about 100 m from Well 6. A plastic pipe connects this pond near Well 6 to another pond on private property, which in turn is fed by an artesian spring. A water sample taken from the pipe by Garry Palmateer of G.A.P. on June 8, 2000, was found to contain *E. coli* O157:H7. The MOH Central Public Health Laboratory confirmed that the PFGE results from the *E. coli* O157:H7 water sample were verotoxin-positive and matched the predominant human outbreak strain.

There is no obvious explanation for the presence of this strain of *E. coli* O157:H7 at that location on June 8. There are many possibilities: bacteria may have been transported by an animal or bird to the pipe, or an infected human may have shed the pathogen; ironically, it may also have been transported on the footwear of someone involved in investigating the cause of the outbreak. Apparently the pond is part of a decorative garden fertilized with compost. Further, it is partly fed by a domestic well, and the pipe drains water from the area of a private home and septic system. Whatever the explanation, this single result from that location on June 8, when lined up with the other available evidence, falls far short of suggesting that *E. coli* O157:H7 entered the distribution system through Well 6 during the May outbreak.

4.8   Expert Evidence

The experts who testified at the Inquiry all shared the view that Well 5 was the entry point for the contamination point into the system.[25] Their opinions were, in general, based on the factors I have discussed above. The remaining issue is the pathway the contamination followed in travelling to the intake for Well 5. Broadly stated, the issue is whether the contamination entered by surface flooding in the area surrounding the well or by subsurface transport to the aquifer. Although a definitive answer is not possible, it appears more likely that the contamination entered through the fractures or conduits through the bedrock and into the aquifer that fed Well 5, rather than by way of overland flow. However, I cannot rule out the latter or a combination of both. I will briefly review the expert evidence.

---

[25] In late November (after conducting further tests), Dr. Stephen Worthington stated that Well 6 and/or Well 7 could have been a secondary source of contamination. His opinion, however, goes no further than to state that Well 6 and to a lesser extent Well 7 may be susceptible to surface contamination. There is no evidence to support a conclusion that contamination in fact entered the system through Wells 6 and 7 in May 2000.

Dr. Robert Gillham is a professor of earth sciences and industrial research chair in groundwater remediation at the University of Waterloo. He is also a member of the Walkerton Commission Expert Review Panel. He testified that the evidence that Well 5 was the source of the contamination was "overwhelming." For him, the most compelling evidence was the hydrogeological conditions at the well and the depth of the well, the *E. coli* measured in both the well water and the spring near Well 5 in June (indicating the presence of a large body of groundwater in the vicinity containing *E. coli*), and the fact that an identifiable source of contamination existed within the groundwater catchment area of Well 5.

Conversely, the pumping schedule and conditions at Wells 6 and 7 made those wells an improbable source. Dr. Gillham testified that although Well 6 was vulnerable to surface contamination, that well was an improbable contributor to the May 2000 outbreak. On June 8, 2000, *E. coli* O157:H7 was identified in a single sample – from the pipe between two ponds – not in groundwater samples or well samples. Dr. Gillham was of the view that Well 7 would not have contributed. He found that there was weak (if any) evidence that Well 7 was vulnerable, and that there was no evidence that it contributed to the outbreak.

Dr. Gillham further noted the difference between the hydrogeological settings of Wells 5, 6, and 7. The bedrock fracturing at Well 5 is much greater than it is at the other two locations. There is a highly weathered zone, with a close spacing of horizontal and vertical fractures, which provides a good vertical connection with the upper 3–4 m of weathered bedrock. Much less water would move through the vertical fracturing near Wells 6 and 7. He also noted that the major water-producing zones for Well 6, and especially for Well 7, were significantly deeper than those for Well 5.

Dr. Gillham noted a hydraulic connection to the surface of both Wells 6 and 7, but the degree of this connection is unclear. The chemistry of water from Well 7[26] is very different from that of water from Well 5 or 6, which suggests that each well has a different source of water. Dr. Gillham concluded that "there remains no doubt that Well 5 was the source of contamination. It cannot be stated that Well 6, and perhaps Well 7 to a degree, are totally absent of risk. Nevertheless, there is no evidence that they contributed to the April and May 2000 outbreak."

---

[26] Based on nitrate, sulfate, sodium, and chloride concentrations.

Dr. Gillham considered three possible pathways of the contaminated water:

- an infiltration of contaminated water at the potential source areas, followed by horizontal flow in the bedrock;

- an overland flow from the source areas, resulting in the inundation of the area around Well 5, followed by a rapid infiltration through springs and seeps; and

- an infiltration at point sources in areas where the overburden has been breached, followed by horizontal flow in the bedrock.

Dr. Gillham concluded that the first of these possible pathways – the infiltration followed by lateral transport in the bedrock – was improbable. He found that the overburden acts as a semi-confining layer; the residence time in the overburden could be up to a year, and he cited low *E. coli* in soil samples as well as generally low *E. coli* in the monitoring wells. With respect to the second possible pathway, he found this to be topographically unfavourable, given the rise of land between the Biesenthal farm and Well 5, and found the hydrologic modelling to be inconclusive. He also cited the continuing discharge of *E. coli* from the spring near Well 5. Dr. Gillham found the third posible pathway – point source infiltration caused by breaching of the protective overburden, followed by rapid transport to the bedrock – to be the most likely explanation. In preferring the third pathway, he cited the high concentrations of *E. coli* in the bedrock at monitoring Well 12 near the Biesenthal farmyard. He also cited the August pump tests in which *E. coli* increased at monitoring Well 2, monitoring Well 12, and Well 5 after pumping.

A consulting engineering firm, B.M. Ross and Associates Ltd., was retained by the Municipality of Brockton to investigate the cause of the outbreak. Golder Associates Ltd. was subcontracted to carry out a hydrogeological study. Like Dr. Gillham, the authors of the B.M. Ross report concluded that Well 5 was the most probable source of the contamination. Daniel Brown, of Golder Associates, was the senior hydrogeologist responsible for the report. He also agreed that there was an overwhelming case for Well 5 being the cause of the outbreak in May 2000. The factors leading him to this conclusion included the shallowness of the overburden; the shallowness of the aquifer itself; a known source of *E. coli* O157:H7 close to Well 5; the timing of the pumping of the various wells, taking into account the incubation periods for *E. coli* and *Campylobacter*; the laboratory results, including the heavy contamination of

Well 5 from May 23 to June 5 and the satisfactory results from Wells 6 and 7 in this period; and microbiological and epidemiological evidence.

The B.M. Ross report concluded that the mechanism for transporting contaminants to Well 5 could be either via the aquifer or by overland flow. B.M. Ross developed a hydrological model suggesting that the combination of saturated soil conditions due to rainstorms from May 8 onward, combined with the intensity and depth of precipitation on May 12, could have caused ponded water on Lot 20 of the Biesenthal farm to overcome a topographical divide so that waters from the barnyard area could have reached Well 5. The report concluded that the confluence of factors required for such ponding and flow would be a very rare occurrence and may never have happened before.

Dr. Stephen Worthington is a karst hydrogeologist and, as noted above, was called by the Concerned Walkerton Citizens. He also testified that in his opinion, Well 5 was the overwhelming source of contamination.[27] Dr. Worthington also stated that the overland flow theory was less likely than the point source infiltration theory. He discounted the potential for overland flow causing water to enter the aquifer through the reversing spring because of the volume of water flowing from this spring in May. His conclusion is consistent with Dr. Gillham's: some breach through the thin overburden in the proximity of Well 5 allowed the bacteria to enter the aquifer. The shallowness of the overburden was critical to Dr. Worthington's opinion.

A fourth expert testified about the pathway of the contamination. Dr. Michael Goss, chair of the University of Guelph's land stewardship program, was critical of the overland flow theory. He noted that:

*   by May 12, rain would have promoted the infiltration of bacteria that were close to the soil surface into deeper layers;

*   fall tining, root pores, tillage practices, and crop location and growth would also encourage infiltration into the soil and help to prevent surface runoff; and

*   the crops showed no sign of damage from the significant ponding assumed by the B.M. Ross model.

---

[27] I noted above the qualification to his opinion in his report of November 23, 2000.

All of the experts support the conclusion that Well 5 was the source of the contamination in May 2000. The preponderance of evidence indicates that the contamination most likely entered Well 5 by way of a point source breach of the overburden, and was then swiftly transported through the bedrock to the aquifer supplying the well. I agree with this conclusion. I am, however, unable to entirely rule out the overland theory.

4.9   The Timing of the Contamination

It is impossible to determine the exact time when the contamination first entered the system. I conclude, however, that the residents of Walkerton were probably first exposed on or shortly after May 12. This conclusion is supported by the epidemiological evidence, the evidence of the health care providers that treated the ill and vulnerable groups, anecdotal evidence from residents, and the timing of the heavy rainfall.

The main causes of illness and disease in the population were two bacteria: *E. coli* O157:H7 and *C. jejuni*. The incubation period for most cases of *E. coli* O157:H7 and *C. jejuni* is approximately three to four days. In Walkerton, the onset for illness of the majority of cases occurred after May 12. There was a significant clustering of illnesses between May 17 and 19 and a smaller cluster between May 22 and May 24.

Well 5 was the main source supplying the system from May 9 to May 15. Well 6 cycled on when needed, though it appears to have been out of service from the evening of May 13 onward as a result of an electrical mishap. Well 7 was not operating from May 9 until May 15 at 6:15 a.m. The conclusion that the contamination entered the system on or shortly after May 12 is consistent with a conclusion that Well 5 was the source of the contamination and inconsistent with Well 7's having been the source. It does not rule out Well 6 as a source of contamination.

4.9.1   The Onset and Clustering of Illnesses: Epidemiological Evidence

After the outbreak, the Bruce-Grey-Owen Sound Health Unit and Health Canada conducted an epidemiological study of the illnesses and deaths associated with the contamination of the Walkerton water system. They concluded that the predominant exposure dates were between May 13 and May 16.

Dr. Andrea Ellis supervised a Health Canada team assigned to conduct epidemiological and environmental investigations in order to determine the outbreak's cause and scope. The epidemiological team developed a case definition to help determine the outbreak's scope. A "case" was defined as a person who:

- had diarrhea or bloody diarrhea; or

- produced stool specimens positive for *E. coli* O157:H7 or *C. jejuni*; or

- had hemolytic uremic syndrome (HUS); and

- experienced the onset of illness between April 15 and June 30, after exposure to Walkerton water.

As discussed in Chapter 2 of this report, the health unit, using the case definition, estimated that 2,321 people became ill as a result of the outbreak. It prepared an epidemic curve based on a person's self-reporting of the date of the onset of illness (see Figure 2). The curve demonstrates that the onset of illness for the majority of cases of illness began after May 12 and continued until early June. In general, a significant clustering of cases of illness occurred between May 17 and May 19. A second, smaller cluster of cases of illness occurred between May 22 and 24.

Dr. Pierre Payment testified that the first general cluster (or peak of cases of illness), occurring from May 17 to May 19, included cases of bloody diarrhea, whereas the second general cluster of cases of illness, occurring from May 22 to May 24, did not. He concluded that the second cluster probably involved a pathogen different from that involved in the first cluster. Dr. Payment also testified, on the basis of epidemiological information, that five peaks of cases of illness occurred in the Walkerton outbreak. This observation suggests the involvement of multiple pathogens. The peaks, or clusters, of cases of illness are shown in Table 7.

The health unit's epidemic curve indicates a small number of people who reported an onset date of illness before May 14 and whose stool cultures tested positive for *E. coli* O157:H7. However, the stool cultures were not taken and confirmed until late May. Accordingly, in Dr. Ellis's view, it is not certain that these people were experiencing illness due to *E. coli* O157:H7 infection before May 14. One must therefore be careful in attaching a great deal of weight to

Figure 2   **Epidemic Curve, Walkerton, 2000**
Number of cases (n=1335) Date of onset missing for 11 reported cases

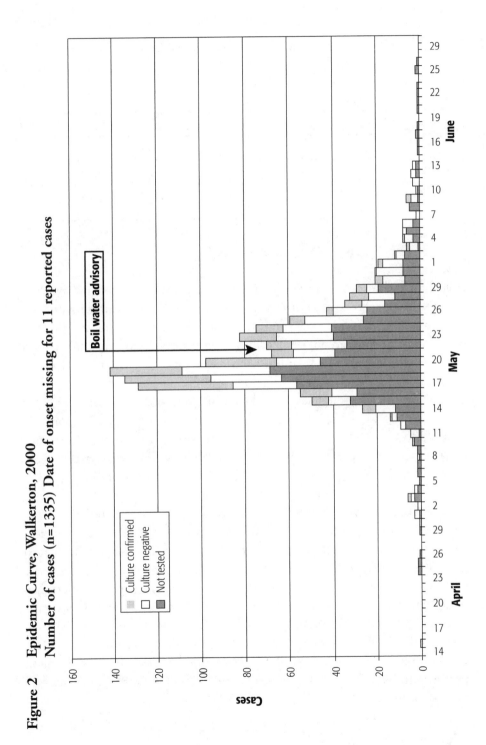

these reports. This becomes important in trying to determine the time that the contamination first entered the system.

Table 7   Clusters or Peaks of Cases of Illness, Walkerton, May 2000

Type of Pathogen or Symptom	Date of Peak
C. jejuni cases	May 19–21
Cases involving bloody diarrhea	May 17–20
E. coli cases	May 19–22
Cases involving other symptoms	May 17–20 May 21–25

4.9.2   Other Evidence Regarding Onset Dates

In addition to the health unit's report recording the self-reported information, the other major source of information about the outbreak was the institutions responsible for treating those who became ill. This evidence indicates that the onset of diarrhea began on May 16. Based on a three- to four-day incubation period, the earliest exposure appears to be between May 12 and May 14.

The Walkerton hospital emergency department's records of patient visits and telephone inquiries are an important source of information. Before the May 2000 outbreak, the number of patients who visited the emergency department of the Walkerton hospital each month was approximately 1,100. In May 2000, there were 1,829 visits – 66% above the normal rate.

In April 2000, the maximum number of emergency room registrations for any day in the month was 55. On May 16, May 17, and May 18, the number of patients who visited the emergency department of the Walkerton hospital ranged from 36 to 50, which the hospital administrator, Dianne Waram, testified was within the normal range. On May 19, there were 48 visits to the emergency room, which also was within the range of normal use. The people visiting the hospital on May 19 included eight patients who had experienced three days of diarrhea that had turned bloody, which prompted them to come to the hospital. Assuming an onset date of diarrhea symptoms of May 16 for these eight patients and allowing for a three- to four-day incubation period indicates a likely exposure date of May 12 or May 13.

On May 20, and for two weeks after that , the number of visits to the Walkerton hospital significantly exceeded the range of normal use. Table 8 shows the number of patients examined in the emergency department from May 20 to June 3.

Table 8   **Walkerton Hospital Emergency Department, Patients Examined, May 20–June 3, 2000**

Date	Number of Patients
May 20	67
May 21	58
May 22	84
May 23	84
May 24	113
May 25	117
May 26	106
May 27	111
May 28	87
May 29	116
May 30	64
May 31	106
June 1	95
June 2	81
June 3	62

A chart prepared by the Walkerton hospital documents the number of telephone calls to the emergency department between May 14 and May 31 that were related to the symptoms associated with *E. coli*. On May 14, May 15, and May 16, the hospital did not receive any calls pertaining to *E. coli*–type symptoms. Table 9 shows the incidence of these calls from May 17 to May 28.

An additional 90 calls related to *E. coli* were made to the emergency department by members of the public from May 29 to May 31, totalling 848 calls from May 17 to May 31. Individuals reported diarrhea and vomiting and sought information on measures they should take. Given that the first phone calls were received on May 17 and May 18, a three- to four-day incubation period indicates a likely exposure date between May 13 and May 15.

Table 9   **Telephone Calls to Walkerton Hospital Emergency Department Concerning** *E. coli*–**type Symptoms, May 17–28, 2000**

Date	Number of Calls
May 17	1
May 18	4
May 19	6
May 20	121
May 21	141
May 22	51
May 23	80
May 24	137
May 25	78
May 26	29
May 27	47
May 28	63
Total	758

Donald Moore, the administrator of the Brucelea Haven nursing home, testified that the first cases of illness occurred there on May 17. Using a three- to four-day incubation period suggests a likely exposure date from May 13 to May 14.

Catherine Reich testified that she called Mother Teresa School on May 18 to tell the secretary that her daughters were ill and would not be attending school. She was told by the secretary that 20 other children were ill and out of school. Ms. Reich's daughters had been sick since May 16. At about 8:30 p.m. that day, one of her daughters was admitted to the Owen Sound hospital under the care of Dr. Kristen Hallett. Also on May 18, in the afternoon, a young boy was admitted to the Owen Sound hospital under the care of Dr. Hallett. This boy had bloody diarrhea as of the evening of May 18.

On May 19, JoAnn Todd, administrator of the Maple Court Villa retirement home, reported an enteric outbreak among the resident population when three residents became ill with vomiting and diarrhea.

Further, on May 20, a third child (age two and a half) was admitted to the Owen Sound hospital with gastroenteritis. On May 21, this child experienced abdominal cramping, fever, vomiting, and bloody diarrhea. After developing symptoms of HUS, she was transferred to London, and on May 23 she died as a result of *E. coli* O157:H7 infection.

The health unit received the first laboratory results from the Owen Sound hospital indicating the presence of *E. coli* O157:H7 in a patient's stool sample on May 20. Later results indicated that *C. jejuni* was also present in many of the patients.

4.9.3   The Onset of Illnesses Leading to Death

The Office of the Chief Coroner and its Expert Review Panel identified seven deaths associated with the Walkerton outbreak. Information about the deaths is summarized in Table 10, in order of the onset date of illness. This evidence is consistent with the conclusion that the contamination probably entered the system on or shortly after May 12.

Table 10   Deaths Associated with the Walkerton Outbreak, 2000

Date of Onset	Date of Death	Did the Outbreak Cause Death or Contribute to Death?	Probable Outbreak Organism
May 18	May 22	Contribute	*E. coli* O157:H7
May 18	May 23	Cause	*E. coli* O157:H7
May 19	July 25	Contribute	*C. jejuni*
May 19	May 24	Cause	*E. coli* O157:H7
May 20	May 29	Contribute	*C. jejuni*
May 20	May 30	Cause	*E. coli* O157:H7
May 21	May 24	Cause	*E. coli* O157:H7

As mentioned, the average incubation period from infection to onset of symptoms for both *E. coli* O157:H7 and *Campylobacter* is three to four days. This is consistent with the evidence regarding the incubation period for the person who died on May 23, who was the only non-resident of Walkerton to die as a result of the outbreak. The period between her last exposure to Walkerton water and the onset of her symptoms provides a general indication of the length of the incubation period for *E. coli* O157:H7 in the Walkerton outbreak. Her last exposure to Walkerton water was on May 14, and the date of the onset of her symptoms was May 18. Therefore, her likely incubation period was four days, which is in keeping with the experts' evidence.

Since the maximum incubation period for *E. coli* O157:H7 is eight days and the shortest period is approximately one day, the outside exposure dates for the five people whose deaths were caused or contributed to by *E. coli* O157:H7 – who all began experiencing symptoms between May 18 and May 21 – are May 10 and May 20. However, given that the evidence indicates that the average incubation period for *E. coli* O157:H7 is three to four days, it is likely that these five people were exposed to the *E. coli* O157:H7 bacteria between May 14 and May 18.

Similarly, given that the maximum incubation period for *C. jejuni* established in the evidence is 10 days, the earliest possible exposure dates for the two people whose deaths were contributed to by *C. jejuni* – who began to experience symptoms on May 19 and May 20, respectively – are May 9 and May 10, respectively. Since the evidence indicates that the average incubation period for *C. jejuni* is three to four days, these two people were probably exposed to the *C. jejuni* bacteria between May 15 and May 17.

4.10 The Chlorine Dosage at Well 5 and Residuals in the System

Given my conclusion that the contamination entered the system through Well 5, why did the chlorine added at Well 5 not disinfect the water by killing the bacteria?

To reiterate, essentially the chlorine dose minus the chlorine demand equals the chlorine residual. It is the chlorine residual that assures disinfection. If the chlorine demand exceeds the chlorine dose, there will be no chlorine residual remaining to achieve disinfection. When heavily contaminated water enters a source such as Walkerton's Well 5, where the chlorine dose administered at the wellhead was regularly below 0.5 mg/L, the chlorine demand exerted by the contamination could completely eliminate the chlorine residual, permitting viable bacteria to enter the distribution system. It is important to specify a treatment requirement in terms of chlorine residual because chlorine demand can change as a result of fluctuating raw water quality. If chlorine demand rises, then the chlorine dose must be increased to ensure that the chlorine residual is maintained.

Water from Well 5 was disinfected by a sodium hypochlorite injection system. The sodium hypochlorite contained 12% chlorine. The solution was diluted with water in a mixing tank before being injected into the water that was pumped from the well to the distribution system. There is some uncertainty about how much the Walkerton PUC diluted the sodium hypochlorite before injection. PUC records reported a "dilution factor" of 10/30, which I take to mean 1 part sodium hypochlorite solution to 3 parts water (a dilution factor of 1 in 4). Based on information obtained from Stan Koebel through his counsel, the dilution factor actually used by the PUC was closer to 1 in 6 – that is, 1 part sodium hypochlorite to 5 parts water, based on mixing 5 gallons of sodium hypochlorite with water to make 30 gallons of solution in the mixing tank.

Dr. Peter Huck, a professor and NSERC chairholder in water treatment at the University of Waterloo and a member of the Walkerton Commission Expert Review Panel, calculated the maximum chlorine dose possible at Well 5, based on his assessment of the capacity of the feed pump used at the well in May 2000, the flow recorded by SCADA data, and assuming no dilution of the 12% sodium hypochlorite solution. He concluded that in these circumstances, the maximum chlorine dose that could be placed in the water leaving Well 5 was 2.3 mg/L. Assuming the information provided by Stan Koebel about a 1-in-6 dilution factor, Dr. Huck calculated that the maximum chlorine dosage at Well 5 would be reduced to approximately 0.4 mg/L. This is significant, because it means that given its chlorination practices, the Walkerton PUC could not possibly have met the Chlorination Bulletin's requirement of maintaining a chlorine residual of 0.5 mg/L after 15 minutes of contact time.

Stephen Burns, of B.M. Ross and Associates Ltd., calculated the chlorine dosage at Well 5 in a different manner than did Dr. Huck. Mr. Burns calculated the average for January through April 2000 based on chlorine consumption records and recorded pumpages. Using this information, Mr. Burns calculated the average dosage at Well 5 to be 0.44 mg/L.

The evidence of both Dr. Huck and Mr. Burns is that it was highly unlikely, given the practices of the Walkerton PUC, that a chlorine dose of 0.5 mg/L was ever introduced into the water at Well 5.

There is no reliable evidence of the chlorine demand of the raw water entering any of the wells before the outbreak. It is, however, clear that in order to cause the degree of illness evident in May 2000, a significant glut of contamination entered the system and was not disinfected at the well site.

There is also no reliable information about the normal chlorine demand of the Walkerton water distribution system before May 2000. Mr. Burns noted that in early June, prior to the extensive swabbing and superchlorination program implemented by the Ontario Clean Water Agency, the difference between residuals at the pumphouses and those in the distribution system was generally greater than 0.6 mg/L. This would seem to indicate a high chlorine demand in the distribution system. That high level of demand would be a function of the chemistry of the water, the large amount of iron piping, the extensive biofilm[28] in the distribution system, and other conditions of that nature. Mr. Burns was of the view that on the basis of his calculations of average dosages, and the demand exerted by the distribution system of 0.6 mg/L, on average, there would under normal circumstances have been no chlorine residual in the distribution system.

I am reluctant to place too much weight on the 0.6 mg/L difference between chlorine residuals at the wells and in the distribution system as measured in early June 2000. Chlorine demand may in some circumstances be a function of chlorine dosage. For example, as more chlorine is applied, interactions may occur that would not otherwise have occurred, such as more biofilm dissolution or interactions with iron piping. By early June, the system had been subjected to significantly higher than previous chlorination levels, including the superchlorination initiated on May 19, as well as significant flushing. The chlorine demand in the system measured in early June may well have appeared higher as a result of higher chlorine dosage. The chlorine demand at the lower chlorine dosage typically applied by the PUC would likely have been substantial but possibly lower than the 0.6 mg/L dosage that was estimated in June 2000, when high chlorine doses were applied to the system.

However, I conclude that it is likely that the chlorine residual level in the distribution system under normal operating conditions was very low. I say this on the basis of the dilution practices at Well 5, the practice of the PUC staff to keep chlorine doses at low levels, the degree of interactions with iron piping, and the amount of biofilm in Walkerton's water distribution system. If the incoming contaminated water in May 2000 had an unsatisfied chlorine demand – as it surely did – then the residual in the system, if there was any, would likely have been be consumed quite rapidly.

---

[28] Biofilm is an accumulation of bacterial growth on the inside of water distribution system pipes. The biofilm in the Walkerton water distribution system consisted primarily of *Leptothrix*, a harmless soil bacterium.

4.11   Chlorine and Turbidity Monitoring at Well 5

Continuous chlorine residual and turbidity monitors would have prevented the outbreak. It is very probable that daily chlorine residual monitoring would have significantly reduced the amount of contamination that entered the system.

During the relevant time, the MOE had two requirements for monitoring chlorine residual for groundwater sources. The first applied to the more vulnerable groundwater sources: those that were under the direct influence of surface water. Section 4.2.1.1 of the ODWO provides that groundwater that is under the direct influence of surface water and not undergoing filtration should be monitored for disinfectant residual (equivalent to free chlorine) by continuous monitoring.

It also required that groundwater sources under the direct influence of surface water should monitor turbidity levels, using a grab sample, every four hours or by continuous monitoring. For the sake of simplicity, I will refer to this requirement relating to turbidity as a requirement for a continuous turbidity monitor. It is important to combine continuous chlorine residual monitoring with effective turbidity monitoring. In some instances, turbidity can reduce the disinfection effectiveness of chlorine. In section 4.2.1.1, the ODWO states that "[v]iable coliform bacteria have been detected in waters with turbidities higher than 3.8 NTU even in the presence of free chlorine residuals of up to 0.5 mg/L and after a contact time in excess of thirty minutes."

Increases in turbidity may indicate excessive contamination, even when chlorine residual monitoring may not disclose the problem. Turbidity rises can interfere with disinfection because they are often accompanied by substances that result in increased chlorine demand. Turbidity may also result from aggregated bacteria and particulates in which bacteria can be embedded and thereby protected from disinfection.

For the reasons set out previously, I have found that Well 5 was a groundwater source under the direct influence of surface water; it therefore should have had continuous chlorine residual and turbidity monitors.

There is a strong probability that when the contamination entered Well 5 in May 2000, the increased chlorine demand overwhelmed the chlorine dose being applied at the well; resulting in inadequate disinfection of the water.

The Chlorination Bulletin sets out chlorine residual monitoring requirements of treated water before it enters the distribution system. Section 3.1.2 of the Chlorination Bulletin provides:

> The chlorine residual test must be performed as frequently as needed to ensure that an adequate chlorine residual is maintained at all times. Such considerations as raw water quality and the resultant variation in chlorine demand, and changing flow rates must be taken into account.

Under this requirement, chlorine residuals are taken manually by waterworks operators. This is the method ostensibly employed by the Walkerton PUC. For years, dating as far back as 1979, the operators of the Walkerton PUC purported to monitor chlorine residuals on a daily basis. Daily entries of chlorine residuals were made in the daily operating sheets. At the time Well 5 was approved in 1979, it was agreed between the Walkerton PUC and the MOE that chlorine residuals would be monitored daily. Through its inspection program, the MOE was aware that the PUC purported to take residuals daily, and it accepted this procedure.

Until the spring of 1998, the Walkerton PUC operators used a colorimetric chlorine residual analyzer that was able to measure chlorine residuals up to a level of 0.5 mg/L in units of one tenth (e.g., 0.1, 0.2, 0.3, 0.4, 0.5, and so on). After 0.5 mg/L, the next possible measurement was 0.75 mg/L. In early 1998, they began using a more sophisticated HACH digital chlorine residual analyzer, which measured residuals in units of 0.01 mg/L.

The evidence at the Inquiry disclosed that for many years, the Walkerton PUC operators did not regularly take chlorine residuals on a daily basis. Rather, the PUC employees who attended the well house would usually write a number, nearly always either 0.5 or 0.75, in the appropriate column of the daily operating sheet, falsely indicating that a residual had been taken and an acceptable reading obtained. On some occasions – it is not clear how often – chlorine residuals were in fact taken. It was never the practice of the Walkerton PUC operators to take turbidity readings during their daily attendances at the well sites.

I will set out my conclusions about the conduct of these operators in greater detail in Chapter 5 of this report, when I discuss their roles in these events. It is sufficient for the purposes of discussing the physical cause of the events of

May 2000 to note that their practice was, on most occasions, not to take chlorine residuals and to make misleading entries in the daily operating sheets.

This practice continued in May 2000. The daily operating sheet for Well 5 shows chlorine residuals for each of the nine days that Well 5 operated during the period from May 1 to May 15 as being 0.75. Given that the quality of raw water varies and that the instrument used in May to measure chlorine residuals measurer in use in May was calibrated to measure differences as small as 0.01 mg/L, there is no possibility that these were accurate numbers. No one suggested that they were. Of particular relevance to the issue of the physical cause are the entries for May 10 to May 15 inclusive. Each entry, as I have said, was 0.75. If the contamination entered the system during this period, as I have found that it did, and if chlorine residual readings had been taken, they would have disclosed either no chlorine residual or a residual significantly less than 0.75. I have no doubt that during this critical period, no chlorine residual readings were in fact taken at Well 5. That is most unfortunate, because if daily chlorine residual readings had been taken during this period there is a strong likelihood that the chlorine demand of the incoming contamination was such that no residual would have been present and that the appropriate measures – either increasing the chlorine dosage or shutting off the well – could have been taken.

One possible exception to the point that taking chlorine residual readings would have disclosed the incoming contamination arises from the fact the readings might have been taken precisely when there was no contamination in the incoming well water. That seems most unlikely, given the enormous amount of contamination that was disclosed by test results from samples taken on May 15 and the fact that the raw water at the well days later continued to be massively contaminated.

Another possible exception to the effectiveness of daily chlorine residual monitoring as an alarm mechanism would be the presence of high turbidity, which in some circumstances could possibly preclude a drop in the chlorine residual. However, given the massive amount of contamination that entered the system, it is most unlikely that high turbidity operated in this manner at the time the Walkerton water system became contaminated in May 2000.

Until the outbreak, there was a dearth of data concerning turbidity at Well 5.[29] In the aftermath of the outbreak, turbidity was closely monitored and some very high turbidity levels were detected in samples taken from fire hydrants. I am satisfied, however, that these readings do not support a finding that there was a major influx of turbidity in conjunction with the contamination.

On May 24, the Central Ontario Analytical Laboratory tested turbidity at 33 locations. Of the 33 samples, 19 exceeded the maximum acceptable concentration for turbidity. I am reluctant to place any weight on the May 24 results as indicating that excessive turbidity entered the water system after May 12. What appear to be very high distribution system results were, in fact, taken from hydrants that were not flushed immediately before they were sampled. Therefore, a sample containing 85 NTU was taken from a hydrant near Walkerton Daycare, but it is not known when the hydrant was last flushed. The same is true of an 18 NTU reading derived from a sample purportedly taken at "Sacred Heart High School." These high readings do not reflect water quality throughout the distribution system. Similarly, they do not assist me in determining whether turbidity entered the system on May 12 or afterward and do not indicate turbidity levels at Well 5 at the time of contamination.

Importantly, there is no evidence of cloudy water or excess turbidity being observed by residents of Walkerton at any time after May 12. Cloudiness in water starts to become visible above 5 NTU, and the ODWO established an aesthetic objective of 5 NTU for turbidity at the point of consumption. Had there been a turbidity problem in the distribution system during the outbreak that resulted in counts of anywhere near those found on May 24, it is most probable, given the outbreak, that residents would have recalled it.

Assuming, however, that there was turbidity, turbidity samples should have been taken daily. They were not. Section 4.2.1.3 of the ODWO provides that daily turbidity monitoring was voluntary unless routine microbiological sampling indicated no adverse water quality. Clearly, Well 5 did not come within this exception.

---

[29] Turbidity in the Well 5 water was measured on ten occasions in 1979–80. On two of these occasions, the turbidity levels of 1.8 NTU and 3.5 NTU exceeded the maximum acceptable concentration, and on another it was at the maximum level of 1 NTU. Over the next 20 years, turbidity was recorded on only six occasions. In each instance, it was below the maximum acceptable concentration of 1 NTU.

The failure of the Walkerton PUC to take daily turbidity samples is another example of a government guideline that was not followed by the PUC. However, it should be noted that MOE inspectors, although aware that turbidity monitoring was not being conducted, did not object. Nevertheless, the point is that if there was turbidity, proper monitoring should have disclosed that problem.[30]

That brings me back to the failure of the PUC to take chlorine residual readings daily, as it was expected to do. Had it done so, it is very likely that the PUC would have discovered the incoming contamination within 24 hours or possibly 48 hours. The result of this monitoring – the monitoring that the PUC ostensibly did and that the MOE expected it to do – would not likely have prevented the outbreak, but it could have led to steps that would have greatly reduced the outbreak's scope of the illnesses and probably reduced the number of deaths in the community.

Before leaving this issue, there is a further matter that needs comment: the requirement for chlorine residuals is that a level of 0.5 mg/L after 15 minutes of contact time be maintained. The 15 minutes of contact time give the contamination an opportunity to exert its full demand on the chlorine. Chlorine residual readings taken before 15 minutes of contact time may therefore be higher than would be the case after the full 15 minutes. It is not clear that when the PUC operators actually did take residuals, they waited 15 minutes before obtaining a reading. However, in the end, that does not matter – because, as I have found, PUC operators did not take residuals during the critical period.

4.12 The Operation of Well 7 Without a Chlorinator

Well 7 was operated without a chlorinator during two periods in May: from May 3 to May 9 and from May 15 to May 19. In these periods, Well 7 was Walkerton's only source of water. This raises the question of whether operating Well 7 without a chlorinator caused, or contributed to the extent of, the contamination of the water distribution system.

---

[30] Because I consider it unlikely that there was turbidity in sufficient amounts to have rendered chlorine residual monitoring ineffective, I do not, in this report, analyze the failure of the MOE to require daily turbidity monitoring.

The total volume of the system, excluding the standpipes, is approximately 1,100 m³. The average length of time that the water resides within the system is less than one day. This means that on an average day, all the water will be used up and replaced by new water within 24 hours. The total volume of the standpipes is approximately 4,900 m³, only a portion of which is active volume. Normally the standpipes are kept reasonably full to provide both the required pressure and water for fire protection.

When Well 5 began pumping on May 9, Well 7 had been providing water without chlorination since May 3. Given the average residence time of water in the system and the practice of maintaining low chlorine residuals, there was essentially no chlorine residual in the distribution system when Well 5 began pumping on May 9. Dr. Huck was of the opinion that if most of the *E. coli* entering Well 5 did so on the May 12 weekend, it is unlikely that Well 7's operation without chlorination from May 3 to May 9 had a significant impact. The reason for this opinion is that between May 9 and May 12, the unchlorinated Well 7 water would have been largely displaced. Since the distribution system is not homogeneous, there may have been specific areas where the earlier presence of unchlorinated Well 7 water might have made a difference, but Dr. Huck stated that with existing information it was impossible to quantify any such effect. I accept Dr. Huck's opinion, and agree that the operation of Well 7 without a chlorinator from May 3 to May 9 did not cause or contribute to the extent of the contamination in May 2000.

Well 7 was also operated without a chlorinator from May 15 to 19. Well 5 was turned off on May 15 at 1:15 p.m. and was not turned on again until May 20. Starting on the late afternoon of May 19, Stan Koebel superchlorinated the system. The contamination had entered the system by the time Well 7 was turned on without a chlorinator on May 15 at 6:15 a.m. The operation of Well 7 without a chlorinator did not add to the contamination. The contaminated water from Well 5 would have remained in the system for at least 24 hours after Well 5 was turned off on May 15 at 1:15 p.m. It remained in dead ends for much longer.

The effect of operating Well 7 without a chlorinator in this later period was to exclude any disinfecting assistance that might have been provided by that well's water mixing with the contaminated water in the distribution system. Both the ODWO and the Chlorination Bulletin merely require the level of chlorine residual in the distribution system to be "detectable." In this system, even if the chlorination in Well 7 had been maintained at the proper level, it is unlikely that achieving only a "detectable" disinfectant residual in the distribution system would have been an amount great enough to significantly eliminate bacteria that had entered through another source.

The general purpose of a distribution system disinfectant residual is to depress biofilm growth and potentially to address point source disturbances in the distribution system; it is not intended to eliminate massive contamination that was not eradicated at source. It is impossible to measure the extent to which operating Well 7 without a chlorinator from May 15 to May 19 may have contributed to the extent of the distribution system's contamination, but it is fair to say that it would likely not have been great.

4.13 Wells 6 and 7

Much of the information regarding Wells 6 and 7 has been dealt with above in the discussion of my reasons for finding that the evidence supports contamination entering through Well 5. The microbiological water samples indicated gross contamination at Well 5 immediately after the outbreak and no contamination at Wells 6 and 7. There is a clear epidemiological link between the farm beside Well 5 and the predominant human outbreak strains of both *E. coli* O157:H7 and *Campylobacter*. The pumping schedule of the wells indicates that Well 5 provided most of the water in the crucial period of May 10 to May 15. Having discussed that evidence thoroughly above, in this section I focus on the hydrogeological setting of Wells 6 and 7 and their physical construction. I find it most unlikely that either Well 6 or Well 7 caused or contributed to the outbreak of May 2000.

Well 6 is located approximately 3 km west of Walkerton in the former Brant Township, adjacent to Bruce County Road 2. It is slightly more than 3 km northwest of Well 5. Well 6 was constructed in 1982 to a depth of 72.2 m. Depth to bedrock was 6.1 m, with a casing to 12.5 m. Well 6 is equipped to be capable of pumping approximately 16.9 L/second to 21.3 L/second, or 1,460 m³/day to 1,832 m³/day. This represents approximately 42–52% of the water requirements of the system.

Flow profiling carried out by Golder Associates Ltd. found that 50% of the flow was found at a depth of 19.2 m; 5% from 27.7 m to 29.3 m; 25% from 34.4 m to 35.3 m; 15% from 47.2 m, 50.4 m, and 54.0 m; and 5% from 61.6 m or greater. The Golder investigation concluded that much of the water comes from intermediate producing zones that are hydraulically connected to shallow water in the nearby wetland and to a nearby private pond. Dr. Robert Gillham was of the view that there was probably less than 1 m of overburden between the bottom of the pond and the top of the bedrock, and very little protection for the aquifer.

Dr. Gillham also noted a connection between Well 6 and springs in the area. However, given that the first water-bearing zone is approximately 17 m below the surface, this connection between surface water and Well 6 is not as direct or extensive as that at Well 5.

Four holes in the upper section of Well 6's casing were observed during Golder Associates Ltd.'s investigation. It is not known whether these holes played any part in the occasional adverse bacteriological sample results that have been observed in the raw water from Well 6, but it is unlikely that they contributed to the contamination in May 2000. Two test wells (TW1-82 and TW2-82) are located near Well 6. Their potential to contaminate Well 6 was also assessed; the results were inconclusive.

Well 7 is located approximately 357 m northwest of Well 6. It was constructed in 1987 to a total depth of 76.2 m. Depth to bedrock was 6.1 m, the well with casing extending to 13.7 m. Well 7 is capable of pumping approximately 50.8 L/second to 56.8 L/second or 4,390 m^3/day to 4,908 m^3/day. This is about 125–140% of the average daily water use. Disinfection is provided by a gas chlorination system similar to that at Well 6. Since Well 7 is capable of supplying the entire demand for the system, it is also equipped with a standby diesel generator.

Water-producing zones based on flow profiling by Golder Associates Ltd. indicated that 50% of the flow came from below 72.4 m; 10% from between 72.4 m and 68 m; 30% from between 68 m and 51.5 m; and 10% from between 51.4 m and 45.7 m.[31] Well 7's water-producing zones are significantly deeper than those at Well 5. At Well 5, 100% of the water came from a depth of 5.5 m to 7.4 m. Well 6 drew 50% of its water at 19.2 m, a level deeper than Well 5. At Well 7, at least 88% of the water came from a depth of 45.7 m.

---

[31] Dr. Worthington offered a different interpretation of this data. According to this interpretation, 29% of the flow comes from below 67 m in the well, compared with the 60% attributed to this zone by Golder Associates Ltd.

Both Wells 6 and 7 are artesian. However, because the top of the wellhead for Well 6 is elevated above the static water level in the well, that well does not discharge when it is not being operated. Well 7 discharges to surface when not being pumped. In May 2000, a 100-mm-diameter overflow pipe at Well 7 discharged water to the adjacent wetland when the well was not in use. This overflow pipe was equipped with a flap gate to prevent surface water from entering the well if the overflow pipe were submerged. If the pump was not on, water would flow from the pipe and there would be no problem. Some concern existed that if the pump was operating, surface water could enter through the flap gate into the well.

One small area of significant casing corrosion was found in Well 7 at a depth of 11.7 m. A test well (TW1-86) is located 2.1 m north of the Well 7 pumphouse. There is no indication of a seal around the casing at surface. It was determined that there is a poor cement bond throughout the 14.2 m of casing associated with this test well. These features could allow surface water or shallow groundwater to infiltrate this test well and ultimately affect Well 7. Golder Associates Ltd. noted a hydraulic connection between TW1-86 and Well 7 between depths of 44.8 m and 67.8 m.

There is a possible hydraulic connection between Wells 6 and 7. When Well 6 was pumped, the water levels decreased in both Well 7 and the pond adjacent to Well 6. However, because of the depth of the water-producing zones in Well 7 (45 m to 75 m), and in the light of certain water chemistry results, it is unlikely that Well 7 was under the direct influence of surface water, and hence it is unlikely that it was the source of the contamination.

Differences in water chemistry (high sulfate/low chloride in Well 7, high chloride/low sulfate in Well 6) suggest different sources of water for Wells 6 and 7. Furthermore, the relatively high nitrate concentration in Well 6 (2.52 mg/L to 9.34 mg/L) and the low nitrate concentration in Well 7 suggest a surface connection for Well 6 but no surface connection for Well 7.

4.13.1 Soil Samples

In August 2000, Golder Associates Ltd. drilled 15 bore holes at nine locations in the vicinity of Wells 6 and 7. Sixteen soil samples from six of the bore holes were analyzed for total coliforms and *E. coli*. The results indicated the presence of total coliform bacteria above the detection limit in at least one sample from each bore hole and the presence of *E. coli* in only one sample from one bore hole. Most of the counts were very low – less than 10 cfu/100 g to 40 cfu/100 g. The highest number of total coliforms was found in a near-surface sample that had a count of 1,600 cfu/100 g. The only *E. coli* count was from a bore hole sample at the detection limit of 10 cfu/100 g. The occurrence of bacteria in the bore hole samples for the areas of Wells 6 and 7 was notably lower than in bore hole samples from the area of Well 5, discussed above.

4.13.2   Pump Test Results

Golder Associates Ltd. also conducted pump tests of Wells 6 and 7 in late August and early September 2000. Those pump tests included the monitoring of water levels in nearby surface waters, private wells, and special monitoring wells. When Well 6 was pumped, water levels decreased in both Well 7 and the pond closest to Well 6.

Well 6 is susceptible to direct inputs of shallow groundwater because it has a shallower producing zone at 19.2 m. Groundwater quality tests for Well 6 indicated variable water quality; nitrate levels, turbidity, and iron concentrations fluctuated widely among zones. Well 6 exceeded the ODWO for hardness, iron, turbidity, and aluminum levels. Nitrate ranged from 2.52 mg/L to 9.34 mg/L in the individual sample zones. The majority of bacteriological results were negative from each zone. Although individual samples from two zones yielded initial positive bacteriological accounts, replicate samples from each zone yielded no organisms.

Water samples from Well 7 were of good chemical quality, and only one sample had any bacteria (2 cfu/100 mL).

Following the pump test, the results of bacteriological analyses for Well 6 groundwater samples showed low levels (1 cfu/100 mL to 26 cfu/100 mL) of total coliform organisms in 12 of the 20 samples collected during the 48-hour test, and no detectable *E. coli* bacteria. In addition, 11 of the 16 samples showed low but detectable levels of aerobic sporeformers, an indicator of surface water influence. Two of the 11 samples from Well 7 showed detectable aerobic sporeformers, and no detectable total coliform or *E. coli* bacteria were found.

4.13.3 Other Hydrogeological Evidence

Dr. Worthington also considered Wells 6 and 7. There are two springs relatively close to Wells 6 and 7. At what Dr. Worthington designated "Spring B" and described as "very close to Well 7," the flow in February 2001 was about 13 L/second, increasing to 25 L/second in April and May. By the beginning of July, Spring B was backflowing into the aquifer and potentially contaminating it. By late July, Spring B had dried up. Dr. Worthington was of the view that when Well 7 was pumped, electrical conductivity changes at Spring B occurred in response, with a lag time of one to three hours. He also noted that during a 72-hour pumping test at a test well near Well 7, the discharge of Spring B dropped by 5.2 L/second. In his view, these factors show a probability that when the spring discharge is low, surface water can be drawn into the aquifer and can travel directly through karst conduits into the pumping wells.

In July 2001, Dr. Worthington found that when Well 7 had been pumping continuously, Spring B ceased flowing, reversed its flow, and then began flowing into the aquifer. On that day, Well 7 tested positive for total coliforms.

When asked directly whether the discharge from springs A and B would have backed-up and been a source of possible contamination, Dr. Worthington replied: "I think that it would be impossible that there was backflow into the aquifer." In his view, contamination by surface water at springs A and B would generally occur at times of low spring discharge (i.e., low water flow). I find nothing in Dr. Worthington's November 23 report to change this assessment.

4.14 Other Possible Sources of Contamination

The Inquiry also heard evidence about seven other possible contamination entry points to the Walkerton water system (see Table 11). I examine each of these possible contamination entry points below. In my view, it is most unlikely that the contamination was caused by any of these possible entry points.

Table 11   Additional Potential Sources of Contamination of the Walkerton Water System

Location Type	Specific Locations	Possible Entry Mechanism
New construction	• Highway 9 (Kincardine Highway) • Old Durham Road • Ellen Avenue	• Contamination could enter when a new main is opened to an existing main if the new main is contaminated.
Fire events	• Orange Street near Willow Street	• System depressurization during fire could allow contamination to enter.
Breaks and repairs	• Four locations in March 2000	• The system is locally depressurized to carry out repairs; this could allow contamination to enter.
Storage structures (standpipes)	• Standpipe No. 1 • Standpipe No. 2	• Contamination could enter through overflow or a vent.
Cross-connections	• Private wells (8 locations) • Cisterns (many locations) • Sanitary sewage facilities	• If the well or cistern is a source and if it is pressurized to a level greater than system pressures, contamination could be discharged to the system. • If there is a connection between the sewage collection and water distribution systems, contamination could enter.
Flooding of the distribution system	• Flooding occurred May 12, 2000	• If the distribution system was depressurized and open at a flooded location, contamination could enter.
Biosolids and septage	• Fields adjacent to Wells 5, 6, and 7	• Entry could occur through a well. • The aquifer could be contaminated by surface spreading.

4.14.1   New Construction

Extensions of the water distribution system were occurring at two separate locations in the middle of May 2000: Highway 9 (the Kincardine Highway) from Circle Drive west to Wallace Street, and Old Durham Road east of Elm Street. A third location, Ellen Avenue, in the southern part of the municipality, had a new watermain constructed in March 2000. The new main remained connected but was isolated from the existing mains by means of a closed gate valve until May 16.

For the existing water distribution system to become contaminated as a result of new construction, it would be necessary for contamination to enter the new watermains and then pass into the existing main when the two are opened to one another. It would also require the new main to have a higher pressure, which could occur either by pressurizing the new main (such as would occur during testing) or, alternatively, by depressurizing the existing main while there is some pressure in the new main.

4.14.1.1 *Highway 9 (Kincardine Highway)*

Construction on the Highway 9 watermain project began on April 6, 2000. The project involved the replacement of 615 m of watermain in the south-western part of Walkerton, along Highway 9, between Wallace Street and Circle Drive. It was at the system's southwestern extremity, on a dead end. The consulting engineer on the project was B.M. Ross and Associates Ltd., and the contractor was Lavis Construction Ltd.

On April 17, Lavis Construction began to install the new watermain. The installation was completed on May 11. Swabbing was carried out to remove debris from the watermain. The valve near the intersection of Circle Drive and Highway 9, referred to as "15+999," was opened on May 11 to enable water from the distribution system to fill the main for swabbing. The valve was again opened on May 12 because water from the distribution system was required to move a chlorine solution through the new watermain. The chlorine solution remained in the watermain during the weekend of May 13–14.

The chlorine solution was flushed from the new watermain on May 15. The valve at Circle Drive was again opened to allow water from the distribution system to enter the new main. Flushing continued until the chlorine residual had decreased to 0.8 mg/L. Three samples were taken: two from the hydrant near the Ministry of Transportation shed at the intersection of Highway 9 and Wallace Street, and one from the hydrant at the Energizer Canada plant, east of that intersection.

All three hydrant samples tested positive for total coliforms and *E. coli*. Dennis Elliott of B.M. Ross testified that although total coliforms were commonly detected in the first sampling after the standard construction industry disinfection process, this was the first occasion in his experience when *E. coli* had been detected in samples from a new watermain that had undergone that process.

Further disinfection flushing and sampling were undertaken. The new watermain was rechlorinated on May 17, and water was drawn from the distribution system through a hydrant. The chlorine solution remained in the new watermain from the afternoon of May 17 to the morning of May 18. Flushing began on the morning of May 18. Again a valve was opened, allowing water from the distribution system to enter the new main. When the chlorine residual had decreased to less than 1.0 mg/L, a second sampling was taken at the same three sites. All these samples also tested positive for both *E. coli* and total coliforms.

On May 18, Mr. Elliott had a discussion with Frank Koebel regarding the connection of the new main to the old Canadian Tire building (now known as the Saugeen Fuel and Filter building). It was explained that the owners of Saugeen Fuel and Filter were anxious for the construction area to be cleaned up before the firm's grand opening. The connection was also necessary to address fire protection concerns. As a result, on May 19, before the results from the second sampling had been received from MDS Laboratory Services Inc., the new watermain was connected to Saugeen Fuel and Filter. The owners of the building were told not to drink the water and were asked to leave a tap running to prevent backflow from the new watermain.

Until May 19, the new main at the Highway 9 project was connected to the existing system only when it was necessary to fill the new main with water. The direction of the flow on these occasions was away from the existing system. However, on May 19, the new valve connecting the watermain to Saugeen Fuel and Filter remained open.

Steve Burns of B.M. Ross concluded that the Highway 9 watermain construction did not cause or contribute to the contamination. His reasons included the following:

- The watermain was situated on a dead end. There was little risk of water moving from the dead end to the distribution system.

- The circumstances of the connection made it unlikely that there was backflow.

- The connection of Saugeen Fuel and Filter to the distribution system occurred on May 19, after the water in the system had become contaminated.

- The likely source of contamination in the samples collected from the Highway 9 project on May 18 was from Well 5.

Another consulting engineering firm, Dillon Consulting Ltd., also investigated the potential for this new watermain to have contributed to the contamination of the Walkerton water system. Dillon Consulting reported as follows:

Although we identified some potential areas where local contamination could occur, there appears to be very little possibility that these events could have contributed to the general contamination of the water system. The location of the connection on a dead end main, and the only conduit between the new and existing mains being through a closed valve, further suggests that any contamination would have difficulty migrating to the remainder of the distribution system.

On the basis of our review, there appears to be a very low likelihood that the activities surrounding the construction of the main contributed to the general contamination of the water system.

For the reasons given by Mr. Burns and Dillon Consulting, I am of the view that the Highway 9 construction did not cause or contribute to the contamination.

4.14.1.2 *Old Durham Road*

This new watermain is located on Old Durham Road, in the northeast part of the community. The main, an extension of an existing dead end main on Old Durham Road, was constructed to provide service to a new municipal industrial park. Its connection to the existing distribution system occurred on May 19, 2000. The project consultant noted that the connection was made in relatively dry conditions and that no specific problems were identified. The new watermain is located approximately 600 m from Standpipe No. 2. There were no reports or indications of any depressurizations of the system occurring at or about the time of the connection.

I conclude that the Old Durham Road construction did not contribute to the contamination of the Walkerton water system. This conclusion is based on the following reasons:

- No connection of the new watermain to the existing watermain occurred until May 19, 2000, which is after the onset-of-illness date.

- The watermain was a dead end connected to a dead end with a closed valve between the existing and new watermains. It is not possible for water to transfer from a (new) non-pressurized system to an (existing)

pressurized system. If the valve leaked, water would flow from the existing watermain to the new watermain.

- No depressurization of the existing system is reported to have occurred;
  depressurization would be a prerequisite for contamination to enter the
  existing system.

- The watermain is in the outer part of the water distribution system; this
  location reduces the probability that any contamination would spread
  quickly through the system, as did occur.

4.14.1.3 *Ellen Avenue*

Approximately 150 m of watermain was constructed on Ellen Avenue between
February 14 and March 2, 2000. The watermain was flushed, pressure tested,
and chlorinated in March. On March 7, a bacteriological sample was taken
and submitted to the Ministry of Health laboratories for analysis. The results
were reported on March 8 as 0 total coliforms and 0 *E. coli*.

On May 16, construction personnel working at a house on Ellen Avenue
attempted to use water from a building service connection, but no water was
available. This indicated that the new watermain was still isolated from the
distribution system as a result of closed valves. The PUC was contacted, and it
opened the valves on the same day.

Garry Palmateer of G.A.P. EnviroMicrobial Services Inc. provided an opinion
concerning whether or not stagnant water that had tested satisfactorily in early
March could have caused the observed *E. coli* contamination. He concluded
that in his opinion, "it was essentially impossible for the contamination of the
water main to have occurred to the extent to cause the outbreak of *E. coli*
O157:H7 in Walkerton, Ontario."

4.14.2   Fire Events

During urban fire events, firefighters typically connect pumping equipment to
fire hydrants. There is the possibility that the pumping equipment could reduce
local system pressures to the point where contamination could be pulled into
the water distribution system, through leaking pipes or cross-connections. For

the contamination observed in Walkerton to have been the result of a fire event, at least one of the following occurrences would have been necessary:

- a fire event in April or early May 2000, near a connection to the water system;

- local depressurization of the distribution system;

- a source of *E. coli* O157:H7 contamination near the fire;

- a means of entry to the system (i.e., a cross-connection); and/or

- hydraulic conditions in the water system capable of causing the contamination to be distributed throughout the system.

The only fire event between April 5 and May 30, 2000, in which a connection to the water distribution system occurred was on May 1. The fire occurred at 11 Orange Street, in the northeastern part of the system. Connections were made to the distribution system at two locations near the fire. At no time was the water distribution system depressurized. The recollection of on-site firefighters as set out in the B.M. Ross report was that system pressures were approximately 550 kPa (80 psi). The fire occurred at a level lower than that of most of the water system. The system supply points (including Standpipe No. 2) are between Orange Street and the balance of the distribution system. Further, no apparent source of *E. coli* O157:H7 was identified in the area of Orange and Elm Streets. I am satisfied that the fire events did not cause the system contamination in May 2000.

4.14.3   Breaks and Repairs

Watermain breaks and repairs are another possible means of contamination. Repairs usually involve isolating the break location by closing adjacent system valves, excavating down to the watermain, installing a clamp over the break, and then opening the valves to repressurize the watermain. Break locations are typically wet, and disinfection is not normally practical. Theoretically, contamination could occur at the point of the repair and then be distributed throughout the system when the main is repressurized. For the contamination in Walkerton to have resulted from a watermain break and repair, the following conditions would have been necessary:

- a source of *E. coli* O157:H7 contamination near the break location; and

- water system hydraulic conditions capable of causing the contamination to be distributed throughout the system.

The Walkerton PUC "Water Leaks Record Book" lists four leaks for the period January 1 to June 1, 2000; they all occurred in March (see Table 12). The break locations are dispersed throughout the water distribution system. Each location was observed in June 2000; all are urban locations within easy reach of travelled roads or parking areas. None is located in obvious drainage pathways for agricultural runoff.

Garry Palmateer of G.A.P. EnviroMicrobial Services Inc. provided an opinion regarding the probability of a watermain break or repair in March 2000 causing the observed contamination. He noted two hypothetical possibilities:

- a simultaneous sanitary sewer break, at the watermain break location, that would cause raw sewage to enter the watermain; or

- cow manure being flushed into the main during the repair.

No sanitary sewer breaks occurred on the dates of the watermain breaks in Walkerton. Further, there are no obvious sources of cow manure near any of the break locations. Although the locations could be affected by surface runoff, they are all in road or parking areas and it is unlikely that the runoff contained manure. Finally, bacteriological analysis results for samples taken from the distribution system in March and April 2000 were reviewed. Although total coliforms were identified in April, none of the samples showed *E. coli* contamination. I conclude that breaks in or repairs of the water distribution system did not cause the contamination in the system.

Table 12   Watermain Break and Repair Locations, Walkerton, March 2000

Date of Break/Repair	Location	Type
March 22	130 Wallace Street	Watermain break
March 23	McGivern Street at Ridout Street	Watermain break
March 27	Colborne Street at Lutheran Church	Watermain break
March 28	6 Amelia Street	Watermain break

4.14.4 Storage Structures (Standpipes)

The Walkerton water system has two standpipes for storage. They are located in the southwestern (No. 1) and northeastern (No. 2) part of the distribution system. It is possible for storage facilities to become contaminated through openings such as overflows and vents. Birds and animals have occasionally been known to enter at these locations. During the initial stages of the water distribution system investigation by B.M. Ross & Associates Ltd., both standpipes were completely drained and examined. They were then gradually filled and placed back in service. Each standpipe was filled until water passed through the overflow. In late May 2000, staff of Collingwood Utilities Services inspected Standpipe No. 2. They reported that no sources of contamination were observed. Staff of the Ontario Clean Water Agency (OCWA) reported similar results with respect to Standpipe No. 1. Further, the mode of operation of the standpipes is to fill and empty from a single pipe on the basis of system pressures and demands. If a standpipe became contaminated, it would be highly unlikely that contamination would spread quickly throughout the distribution system, as it is reported to have done. The contamination would tend to stay in, or near, the storage structure.

No source of contamination was observed in either standpipe. In addition, *E. coli* O157:H7 is typically associated with cattle or sewage. The standpipe overflows and vents are on the top of the structure and are therefore not susceptible to agricultural contamination. I conclude that there is no probability that the water storage structures were the source of the contamination.

4.14.5 Cross-Connections

A cross-connection is a physical connection, direct or indirect, that provides an opportunity for non-potable water to enter a conduit, pipe, or receptacle containing potable water. In the Walkerton water system in May 2000, there were cross-connections to the distribution system from several private wells and several hundred cisterns, each of which was a possible source of contamination. Cisterns are storage tanks, typically located in the basements of homes, designed to store rainwater from a roof's runoff systems. Cistern water is generally "softer" in terms of calcium carbonate hardness and is frequently used for laundry systems.

Activities undertaken by OCWA during the disinfection of the water distribution system established that there were approximately 30 private water systems (wells) and approximately 470 cisterns, many of which were cross-connected to the municipal distribution system.

Private non-potable systems, including cisterns and wells, can be a source of contamination if they discharge contaminated water into the distribution system. For this to occur, they must be contaminated, they must operate at pressures greater than those in the distribution system, and there must be no functioning backflow prevention device (i.e., check valve, closed gate valve, or backflow preventer) between the private system and the communal distribution system.

Professional staff from B.M. Ross visited eight private wells on May 24, 2000, to establish whether or not the connected well was a likely source of contamination. Water samples were also taken. With the exception of the one well at RR 4, Walkerton, which had a sample result of 33 units for total coliforms and 0 for *E. coli*, all other locations had negative results for both parameters.

During the disinfection of the distribution system, contractors working under the direction of OCWA identified additional cross-connected wells. All these wells were located on residential properties in the developed urban areas. With the exception of the water system at the Energizer Canada plant, all of the systems are small. Even if they were contaminated, it would be extremely unlikely for the contamination to be distributed throughout the water system from a single small source. Inspections at the Energizer Canada plant confirmed that check valves or closed gate valves were in place.

In conclusion, although the multiple cross-connections to private systems and cisterns represented a potentially serious problem (that has since been addressed), I find it unlikely that any of these systems was the cause of the outbreak in Walkerton.

4.14.6   The Flooding of the Distribution System

On the evening of May 12, 2000, heavy rains fell in Walkerton and the surrounding area. Surface flooding occurred in several locations in Walkerton. For surface flooding to interact with the water supply and cause contamination, it would be necessary for the surface water to be contaminated and for one of the following additional situations to occur:

*   inflow to a wellhead or similar water supply source; or

*   inflow to a reservoir opening (i.e., a vent); or

*   inflow to a watermain that is depressurized and open to the atmosphere.

The water wells and storage structures were visually examined for openings during the last week of May 2000, and it was determined they were not subject to flooding.

With respect to the water distribution system, it has been established that no depressurizations of the system occurred on May 12 or May 13. The Walkerton PUC did not report any. There were no fire events and no breaks in the system. Further, a review of the SCADA pumpage records confirms that one or more well pumps were operating continuously at normal discharge rates, which indicates that there was normal system pressurization.

Although significant surface flooding did occur on the evening of May 12 and morning of May 13, there was no apparent interaction between the flooding and either the storage structures or the water distribution system.

4.14.7   Biosolids and Septage

The Inquiry also heard evidence as to whether the land application of biosolids or septage in the Walkerton area could have caused or contributed to the contamination. Biosolids and septage are regulated under the *Environmental Protection Act*,[32] the Waste Management Regulation,[33] and the 1996 Guidelines for the Utilization of Biosolids and Other Wastes on Agricultural Land. Under the Waste Management Regulation, biosolids, or "processed organic waste," means waste that is predominantly organic in composition and that has been treated by aerobic or anaerobic digestion or other means of stabilization. It includes sewage residue from sewage works that are subject to the provisions of the *Ontario Water Resources Act*.[34] Hauled sewage, also known as

---

[32] *Environmental Protection Act*, R.S.O. 1990, c. E-19.
[33] Waste Management Regulation, R.R.O. 1990, Reg. 347.
[34] *Ontario Water Resources Act*, R.S.O. 1990, c. O-40.

septage, includes waste removed from a cesspool, a septage tank system, a privy vault or privy pit, a chemical toilet, a portable toilet, or a sewage holding tank.

Biosolids may be applied to land only in places where an MOE district office has approved such an application by way of an Organic Soil Conditioning Site Certificate of Approval. Septage also requires a Certificate of Approval for a hauled sewage disposal site. These sites are subject to inspection by the MOE.

In the fall of 1999, biosolids were spread on three sites in the vicinity of Walkerton. The last dates of spreading on those three sites were September 16, September 20, and October 19, 1999. Each of the sites is north and east of Wells 5, 6, and 7. Indeed, the three sites are all east of the Saugeen River watershed, so they are on the other side of the watershed divide from the wells. The closest site for a land application of biosolids to Well 5 was approximately 3 km north and east of Well 5. Although Certificates of Approval for biosolids application had been issued for sites closer to Well 5, there was no land application of biosolids on any of these sites in 1999 or 2000.

Regarding septage, there are no approved septage sites in the immediate Walkerton area. The closest sites are in Chepstow, northwest and downstream of Walkerton. Before May 2000, there were no sites upon which septage was applied near the town of Walkerton.

In the fall of 1999, it was determined that biosolids from the Walkerton sewage treatment plant were not acceptable for disposal on land because of their heavy mineral content. As a result, the last land application of these biosolids was the October 1999 application mentioned above. After October 1999, no biosolids from the Walkerton sewage treatment plant were land-applied on the sites for which Certificates of Approval had been issued.

I am satisfied that there was no septage application in the area. Further, I am satisfied that with regard to the application of biosolids, both the dates (in September and October 1999) and the location (on the other side of the Saugeen River divide, 3 km from Well 5) rule out the fall 1999 land application of biosolids as the source of the contamination in May 2000.

4.15 Summary

The conclusions I have reached in this chapter are as follows:

- The primary, if not the only, source of the contamination of the Walkerton water system was manure that had been spread on a farm near Well 5, although I cannot exclude other possible sources.

- The entry point of the contamination was through Well 5. Well 6 and, to a lesser extent, Well 7 may be vulnerable to surface contamination. However, there is no evidence to support a conclusion that the contamination entered through either Well 6 or Well 7 in May 2000.

- The residents of Walkerton were probably first exposed to the contamination on or shortly after May 12.

Chapter 5   The Role of the Public Utilities Commission Operators

Contents

Chapter 5 The Role of the Public Utilities Commission Operators

5.1   Overview

Two serious failures on the part of the Walkerton Public Utilities Commission (PUC) operators directly contributed to the outbreak in May 2000. The first was the failure to take daily chlorine residual measurements in the Walkerton water system. If the Walkerton PUC operators had measured the chlorine residual manually at Well 5 on May 13 or on the days following, as they should have done, they would almost certainly have discovered that incoming contamination was overwhelming the chlorine that was being added to the water. They should then have been able to take the necessary steps to protect the community. Although daily monitoring of the chlorine residual probably would not have prevented the outbreak, it is very likely that it would have significantly reduced its scope.

The second failure relates to the manner in which the PUC operators responded to the outbreak in May 2000. This failure is primarily attributable to Stan Koebel. When Mr. Koebel learned from test results for the samples collected on May 15 that there was a high level of contamination in the system, he did not disclose the results to the health officials in the Bruce-Grey-Owen Sound Health Unit (the local health unit) who were investigating the outbreak of illnesses in the community. Instead, he misled them by assuring them that the water was safe. Had Mr. Koebel been forthcoming about these results, the local health unit would have issued a boil water advisory by May 19 at the latest, and 300 to 400 illnesses would probably have been prevented.

In this chapter, I will review the roles of the operators of the Walkerton PUC in relation to the events in May 2000. The two people who exercised managerial or supervisory control over the water system were Stan Koebel and his brother Frank Koebel.

Stan Koebel had been the general manager of the Walkerton PUC since 1988. In May 2000, he held a class 3 water distribution operator licence, which he had received through a grandparenting process. At the Inquiry, Mr. Koebel accepted responsibility for his failures and apologized to the people of Walkerton. I believe he was sincere.

The evidence showed that under his supervision, the PUC engaged in a host of improper operating practices. These practices included mislabelling sample bottles[1] for microbiological testing, failing to adequately chlorinate the water, failing to measure chlorine residuals daily, making false entries on daily operating sheets, submitting false annual reports to the Ministry of the Environment (MOE), and operating wells without chlorination. There is no excuse for these improper practices.

Although Stan Koebel knew that these practices were improper and contrary to the directives of the MOE, he did not intentionally set out to put his fellow residents at risk. A number of factors help to explain, though not to excuse, the extraordinary manner in which the Walkerton PUC was operated under Mr. Koebel's direction. For example, many of the improper practices had been going on for years before he became general manager. Further, he and the other PUC employees believed that the untreated water in Walkerton was safe: indeed, they themselves often drank it at the well sites. On occasion, Mr. Koebel was pressured by local residents to decrease the amount of chlorine injected into the water. Those residents objected to the taste of chlorinated water. Moreover, on various occasions, he received mixed messages from the MOE itself about the importance of several of the MOE requirements. Although Mr. Koebel knew how to operate the water system mechanically, he did not have a full appreciation of the health risks associated with failing to properly operate the system and of the importance of following the MOE requirements for proper treatment and monitoring.

None of these factors, however, explain Stan Koebel's failure to report the test results from the May 15, 2000, samples to the local health unit and others when asked, particularly given that he knew of the illnesses in the community. It must have been clear to him that those to whom he spoke were unaware of these results. I am satisfied that he withheld information about the adverse results because he wanted to conceal the fact that Well 7 had been operated without chlorination for two extended periods in May 2000. He deceived both the local health unit and the MOE, and in doing so, he put the residents of Walkerton at greater risk. When he withheld the information, he probably did not appreciate the seriousness of the health risks involved and did not understand that deaths could result. He did, however, know that people were becoming sick, and he should have informed the health unit of the adverse results at the earliest opportunity.

---

[1] The sites at which the samples were collected were misrepresented.

Frank Koebel had been the foreman of the Walkerton PUC since 1988. He was the operator who, on May 13 and May 14, went to Well 5, failed to measure the chlorine residuals, and made false entries in the daily operating sheet. Like his brother, Frank Koebel was also sincerely sorry for the role he played in these events.

Most of the comments I have made about Stan Koebel apply equally to Frank Koebel, with one exception: Frank Koebel was not involved in failing to disclose the May 15 results to the local health unit. He did, however, on his brother's instructions, alter the daily operating sheet for Well 7 on May 22 or May 23 in an effort to conceal from the MOE the fact that Well 7 had operated without a chlorinator.

Stan and Frank Koebel lacked the training and expertise either to identify the vulnerability of Well 5 to surface contamination or to understand the resulting need for continuous chlorine residual and turbidity monitors. The MOE took no steps to inform them of the requirements for continuous monitoring or to require training that would have addressed the issue.

5.2   The Qualifications of the Supervisors

5.2.1 Stan Koebel

Stan Koebel was the general manager of the Walkerton PUC in May 2000. Although he was certified as a class 3 operator of a water distribution system, there were significant gaps in his knowledge about the possible threats to the safety of water and the importance of treatment and monitoring practices.

Mr. Koebel began his employment at the Walkerton PUC in 1972, at the age of 19. He had a Grade 11 education. His father was the foreman of the Walkerton Works Department at the time.

Mr. Koebel initially worked on the water system under the supervision of the general manager of the PUC, Ian McLeod, but beginning in 1976 he focused more on electricity after completing the lineman apprentice program. In 1981, Mr. Koebel was promoted to the position of foreman and became responsible for PUC employees who worked on both water and electricity. When Mr. McLeod retired in 1988, Mr. Koebel became the general manager of the PUC.

As general manager, Mr. Koebel had the important responsibility of ensuring that safe drinking water was supplied to the residents of Walkerton. Yet he was not required to complete any courses or undergo an examination to qualify as the senior operator of the water system. When Mr. Koebel became the general manager in 1988, the only course he took was a leadership seminar on the supervision of employees. The course had no content relating to the operation of a water system.

In 1987, the MOE had introduced a voluntary grandparenting program for water operators. Mr. McLeod had submitted Stan Koebel's name to the MOE in 1988, and Mr. Koebel had been certified as a class 2 operator. He had not been required to pass a test. In the years that followed, his certification was renewed as a matter of course. He had been recertified in 1996 after the Walkerton water system was reclassified as a class 3 water distribution system, again without the MOE assessing his knowledge and skills. In May 2000, he held a class 3 water distribution licence with an expiry date of February 2002.

There was a good deal that Mr. Koebel did not know about matters relating to the provision of safe water. Mr. Koebel testified that he had never read section 4.1.2 of the Ontario Drinking Water Objectives (ODWO) – the section on the indicators of unsafe water. He did not know what *Escherichia coli* was, nor was he aware of the implications to human health of *E. coli* in drinking water. He was unaware that the presence of *E. coli* or fecal coliforms in a sample from the distribution system indicated that the water was unsafe. Moreover, he had never read the section of the Chlorination Bulletin on the importance of maintaining a total chlorine residual of at least 0.5 mg/L after 15 minutes of contact time and before the first consumer is supplied with water. He did not understand the distinction between total chlorine and free chlorine, two important concepts in the Chlorination Bulletin. Nor had Mr. Koebel read the section of the Chlorination Bulletin regarding notifying the MOE of adverse bacteriological results. Mr. Koebel stated that he did not fully understand such terms as "turbidity" and "organic nitrogen": consequently, he did not always fully comprehend portions of the MOE inspection reports on the Walkerton system and correspondence from the MOE's Owen Sound district office.

Section 17 of Ontario Regulation 435/93, passed in 1993 pursuant to the *Ontario Water Resources Act*, provides that every operator employed at a waterworks facility must receive at least 40 hours of training each year. The provision further states:

(2)   The training may include, for example, training in new or revised operating procedures, reviews of existing operating procedures, safety training and studies of information and technical skills related to environmental subjects.

(3)   The owner shall ensure that records are maintained of the training given under this section including the names and positions of operators who attend training sessions, the dates of training sessions, the duration of each training session and the subjects considered at each training session.

Stan Koebel interpreted the meaning of "training" in this regulation unreasonably broadly. In his view, marketing and leadership courses, a cardiopulmonary resuscitation course, or simply accompanying an MOE environmental officer on an inspection of the water plant constituted "training" for the purposes of the regulation. In the training logs for 1998 and 1999, Stan Koebel showed 16 hours' credit for attending a marketing course and 6 hours for the MOE inspection of the Walkerton water system by Michelle Zillinger in 1998, despite the fact that the inspection took only 2 hours.

Stan Koebel went to some conferences on waterworks during his employment at the PUC. He attended annual conferences sponsored by the Ontario Municipal Waterworks Association, he went to meetings put on by the Georgian Bay Waterworks Association, and he participated in workshops put on by the Ontario Water Works Association. Although chlorine disinfection and turbidity in wells and surface water were discussed at some of these conferences and workshops, Mr. Koebel testified that he did not adequately understand the importance of chlorinating the Walkerton water supply. He believed that the water was safe without chlorination, and he himself frequently drank the untreated water.

It is clear that Stan Koebel did not receive training even close to the required amount – 40 hours a year – and that much of what he recorded as training was not focused on water safety issues. It is important to note that his failure to receive the required training was not related to a shortage of funds at the Walkerton PUC, which allotted between $1,500 and $3,000 a year for training. The PUC had large reserves, and there is no evidence to suggest that requests for training funds were ever denied by the commissioners.

5.2.2 Frank Koebel

Frank Koebel was the foreman of the Walkerton PUC in May 2000. Like his brother Stan Koebel, he was poorly informed about matters relating to water safety. He had been hired by the PUC in 1975 at the age of 17. He had a Grade 12 education. In 1983, he became a journeyman lineman after completing courses at the Ontario Hydro Training Centre in Orangeville. Before 1988, about 75% of his time was devoted to waterworks and 25% to hydroelectric power. He became the foreman of the PUC in 1988, the year his brother Stan became the general manager.

Frank Koebel had also received his certification through the voluntary grandparenting process. Ian McLeod had submitted Mr. Koebel's name to the MOE in 1988, and Frank had been certified as a waterworks operator that year. He had received his class 2 and later his class 3 water distribution system operation certification without being required to complete any courses or undergo any examinations to test his skills and knowledge. A letter sent to him by the Ontario Environmental Training Consortium in 1996 stated that the Walkerton facility had been reclassified on the basis of new criteria and that his licence had:

> been upgraded to a Water Distribution Class 3 ... The upgrade was assessed under the Voluntary Grandparenting provision Regulation 435/93. Therefore, you will not be required to write an examination. Your hours of additional education/training were not assessed at this time.

Frank Koebel had never read the ODWO sections concerning microbiological and chemical testing or its provisions on measures to be taken in case of adverse sample results. He was unaware that the presence of *E. coli* was an indicator of unsafe drinking water. He was not familiar with the Chlorination Bulletin, which provided important information on the monitoring of water systems, minimum chlorine residuals, and chlorination equipment. Frank Koebel believed that Walkerton had good-quality water at source and that chlorinating it was unnecessary. As was the case with Stan Koebel, the terms "organic nitrogen," "turbidity," and "total and free chlorine" had little meaning for him. Despite the fact that he was the PUC foreman, Frank Koebel was not familiar with Ontario Regulation 435/93, which addressed the licensing of operators, the classification of waterworks facilities, and mandatory training requirements.

Frank Koebel testified that he had had the opportunity to attend courses on the operation of a waterworks. He had never been told that he could not participate in a training course because there was not enough money. Although Mr. Koebel had attended some conferences on the operation of a waterworks, he had not taken full advantage of the training opportunities because he had been "busy either with the hydro or the water" and could not "be away any length of time." He had never taken a course on chlorination in the 25 years that he had worked at the Walkerton PUC. Mr. Koebel acknowledged at the hearings that he did not have the requisite knowledge to perform his job as foreman of the PUC.

5.3   Improper Operating Practices

The evidence disclosed that for over 20 years, the Walkerton PUC had engaged in a number of improper operating practices that significantly increased the risk of producing unsafe drinking water. One of these, the failure to monitor chlorine residuals daily, contributed directly to the outbreak in May 2000. However, to properly understand the seriousness of the operating deficiencies in Walkerton, it is useful to review each of these practices. They show a serious disregard for MOE requirements and repeated failures by Stan Koebel to do what he said he would.

5.3.1 Microbiological Sampling

5.3.1.1   *The Importance of Sampling*

The Ontario Drinking Water Objectives (ODWO) require that samples from a municipal water system undergo microbiological testing. The importance of such testing is explained in sections 3.1 and 4.1 of the ODWO:

> *Microbiological quality of drinking water is the most important aspect of drinking water quality because of its association with water-borne diseases.* Typhoid fever, cholera, enteroviral disease, bacillary and amoebic dysenteries, and many varieties of gastro-intestinal diseases can be transmitted through water ...

> *Contamination by sewage or excrement presents the greatest danger to public health associated with drinking water,* and microbiological

testing provides the most sensitive means for the detection of such pollution ... Occasional outbreaks of water-borne diseases emphasize the continuing importance of strict supervision and control over the microbiological quality of drinking water supplies. [Emphasis added]

The ODWO prescribes both the frequency and the locations at which water samples are to be collected. For a population the size of Walkerton's, samples are to be taken weekly from the raw water source, the point at which the treated water enters the distribution system. Concerning the number of samples to be collected from the distribution system, the ODWO states that if the population does not exceed 100,000, a minimum of eight samples and a further one sample per 1,000 population are to undergo microbiological testing each month. Since Walkerton had a population of approximately 5,000, a minimum of 13 samples should have been collected monthly from the distribution system.

It was the practice of employees at the Walkerton PUC to collect water samples on the first working day of each week and to send them to a laboratory for microbiological testing. Prior to 1996, the samples from the Walkerton water system were analyzed at the Ministry of Health's laboratory in Palmerston. After the provincial privatization of laboratory testing in 1996, G.A.P. EnviroMicrobial Services Inc. tested the samples from Walkerton. This arrangement continued until the end of April 2000, when A&L Canada Laboratories began to conduct the bacteriological analyses for the Walkerton PUC.

Over the years, there were two significant and recurring problems in the microbiological sampling practices of the Walkerton PUC: sample bottles were routinely mislabelled by PUC staff, and an insufficient number of samples were collected. A discussion of these two problems follows.

5.3.1.2   *Mislabelling*

Each Monday (or Tuesday, if Monday was a holiday), Stan and Frank Koebel (and sometimes Allan Buckle, a PUC employee who was not a licensed operator) collected the water samples. Normally, the practice was to take four samples for each well in operation: one from the raw water, one from the treated water before it entered the distribution system, and two from the distribution system. Thus, if two wells were in operation on a testing day, eight samples would be collected and sent for testing. It was the expectation of the laboratory and the MOE that PUC staff would place a label on each bottle to identify the site at which the sample had been collected. For years, the PUC staff collected water samples at locations other than those indicated on the sample bottles sent to the laboratory.

Stan and Frank Koebel, as well as Allan Buckle, testified that they frequently collected water samples at the wells and labelled the bottles as having come from sites in the distribution system. They would go to one of the wells and fill one bottle with raw water and another with treated water. A third bottle would be filled from the treated tap at the well but would be labelled as having come from the distribution system. Stan Koebel generally filled a fourth bottle with water from the PUC office or his home. Mr. Buckle stated that 99.9% of the samples he labelled as having come from 125 Durham Street, a site in the distribution system, were actually collected from the treated tap at Well 7. The practice of mislabelling samples also occurred at Geeson and Chepstow, two subdivisions where PUC employees also collected samples.

Stan and Frank Koebel understood that if a sample was taken at the pumphouse and not from the distribution system, it would not provide information on the quality of the water in the system. PUC operators and the MOE might therefore not be alerted to any problems in the distribution system. When asked why they had routinely mislabelled sample bottles, Stan Koebel's response was "complacency," and Frank Koebel's was that he "didn't need the aggravation." This practice saved them time – although, I would note, not much time.

Another practice of PUC employees was to fill sample bottles labelled "Well 5 treated" and "Well 5 raw" with water from the PUC shop at 130 Wallace Street. The explanation given for this practice was that Well 5 "was very close to the [PUC] shop and it was time saving."

5.3.1.3 *Insufficient Sampling*

MOE inspection reports, as well as correspondence from the MOE throughout the 1990s, specified the number of samples to be submitted by the PUC for microbiological analysis. For many years, however, the Walkerton PUC did not collect the number of samples required by the ODWO.

In the report of the 1991 MOE inspection of the Walkerton system, bacteriological quality monitoring was listed as a deficiency. The inspection report recommended that monitoring be upgraded from 9 to 13 samples, which were to be collected monthly at various locations in the distribution system. On June 23, 1995, Stan Koebel received a letter from Willard Page, district manager of the MOE office in Owen Sound, which set out the minimum recommended number of microbiological samples to be collected for the town. The letter said that raw and treated water sampling was to be conducted weekly and that a total of 13 samples was to be collected from the distribution system each month.

In the report of the 1995 MOE inspection of the Walkerton system, the inspector noted that the PUC was still failing to meet the minimum requirements of the bacteriological sampling program.[2] In the summer of 1997, Walkerton was placed on a list of municipalities that were not conforming to the minimum sampling programs. The list was compiled by the MOE for the purpose of issuing a Director's Order for these water systems. After Stan Koebel undertook to comply with the minimum sampling program, Walkerton was removed from the MOE list in the fall of 1997.

Despite Mr. Koebel's previous assurance, by the time of the MOE inspection in February 1998, the Walkerton PUC still had not satisfied the requirements of the minimum sampling program. Only 8 or 9, rather than the required 13, bacteriological samples were being collected from the distribution system each month. Mr. Koebel told the inspector in February that the PUC would comply immediately, but again it failed to do so. In a letter dated May 6, 1998, which forwarded the inspection report, Philip Bye, supervisor of the MOE's Owen Sound office, threatened to issue a Director's Order if the PUC did not comply. In his letter of response dated July 14, 1998, Stan Koebel said that the PUC would comply by the end of July. It appears that in the following months, the PUC more or less complied by taking the required number of samples. But Mr. Koebel's conduct to that point showed a serious disregard for proper operating practices.

---

[2] The "minimum requirements of the bacteriological sampling program" were set out under the ODWO as a guideline. In 1995, the MOE initiated the Minimum Recommended Sampling Program, based on the ODWO. Both of these programs are referred to as the "minimum sampling program" or "minimum bacteriological sampling program" throughout this report.

5.3.2 Inadequate Chlorination

The operators of the Walkerton PUC routinely failed to add the required amount of chlorine at the well sites. The Chlorination Bulletin states that "disinfection, to kill pathogenic organisms, is the most important step in any water treatment process." The standard mandated by the bulletin for groundwater sources, unless the supply has been "proven free of hazardous bacteriological contamination," is a total chlorine residual of at least 0.5 mg/L after 15 minutes (preferably 30 minutes) of contact time before the water reaches the first consumer.

It was clear to the Walkerton PUC as early as 1979 that a 0.5 mg/L chlorine residual was to be maintained at Well 5. In its application for a Certificate of Approval for Well 5, the PUC submitted a hydrogeological report prepared by Ian D. Wilson Associates that described Well 5's vulnerability to contamination. Fecal coliforms had been found in water samples from the well at various times in a 72-hour period. The report recommended that because the bacteriological testing indicated "pollution from human or animal sources," the supply "should definitely be chlorinated and the bacteria content of the raw and treated water should be monitored."

During their review of the PUC's application for a Certificate of Approval for Well 5, MOE staff had raised concerns about the security of the water source that supplied Well 5 in a memo dated October 24, 1978. To discuss these concerns, a meeting was held on November 23, 1978, between representatives of the PUC, the Town of Walkerton, the MOE's Owen Sound office, and the MOE's Approvals Branch. The participants at the meeting reached an understanding that the PUC would maintain a minimum chlorine residual of 0.5 mg/L at Well 5, after 15 minutes of contact time, before the water reached the first consumer.

The importance of maintaining a 0.5 mg/L chlorine residual after 15 minutes of contact time at all three wells was pointed out in the reports of both the 1995 and 1998 MOE inspections.[3] John Apfelbeck, the inspector who

---

[3] In the report of the 1991 inspection, Brian Jaffray of the MOE had recommended maintaining a chlorine residual level of between 0.3 mg/L and 0.5 mg/L. The residuals he had obtained during that inspection were 0.3 mg/L and 0.35 mg/L and therefore conformed with what he understood a proper residual to be. However, his reference to 0.3 mg/L as the lowest acceptable residual was in error, at least for Well 5, because from the time of that well's approval the expectation was that the Walkerton PUC would maintain a minimum total chlorine residual of 0.5 mg/L after 15 minutes of contact time.

conducted the 1995 inspection, wrote that it was important to ensure that "an adequate chlorine residual is maintained in water in the distribution system at all times" and that a "minimum total chlorine residual of 0.5 mg/L after 15 minutes [of] contact time must be maintained in the water discharged to the distribution system from all wells at all times."[4] The MOE inspector in 1998, Michelle Zillinger, also observed that the minimum total chlorine residual level of 0.5 mg/L was not being maintained by the PUC; under the heading "Action Required" in her inspection report, she included the maintenance of a total chlorine residual of 0.5 mg/L after 15 minutes of contact time.

Stan Koebel testified that the reports of the 1995 and 1998 MOE inspections made it abundantly clear that a "minimum total chlorine residual of 0.5 mg/L after 15 minutes' contact time must be maintained in the water discharged to the distribution system for all active wells, at all times." Evidence of Mr. Koebel's belief is found in the chlorine residual entries in column 11 of the daily operating sheets. On the daily operating sheets for the wells in the 1980s, the 1990s, and the year 2000, the operators nearly always entered 0.5 mg/L or higher as the chlorine residual at the three wells. As will be discussed below, most of the chlorine residual entries in the daily operating sheets are fictitious.

Neither Stan nor Frank Koebel thought it necessary to adhere to the MOE guideline by maintaining a minimum total chlorine residual of 0.5 mg/L. Most of the PUC staff believed that Walkerton had good-quality water at source and that it was unnecessary to disinfect the water. Their lack of education and training undoubtedly contributed to this view. PUC employees themselves would readily drink raw water at the well because it was clean and clear and "always tasted better than the treated [water]." Stan Koebel testified that he generally set the chlorinator to slightly less than 0.5 mg/L and that Frank Koebel would lower it to approximately 0.3 mg/L several times a month. Stan Koebel testified that one of the reasons they added less than the required amount of chlorine was that they had received complaints from town residents from time to time that the water had too much chlorine, which affected its taste. Stan Koebel testified that he considered "any" amount of chlorination in the distribution system to be sufficient, even 0.01 mg/L, the lowest measurement on a HACH digital chlorine residual analyzer.

---

[4] The 1995 inspection led to a report released in January 1996.

The only objective evidence of the amount of chlorine actually added by the PUC employees is found in the chlorine residual measurements taken by the three MOE inspectors in 1991, 1995, and 1998. In all, the inspectors took nine residual readings of the treated water at the well sites. All measured less than 0.5 mg/L: they ranged from 0.12 mg/L to 0.40 mg/L, and the average was 0.27 mg/L. It is clear that as a matter of practice, the operators of the Walkerton system added significantly less chlorine than was required.

5.3.3 The Failure to Monitor Chlorine Residuals Daily

The Chlorination Bulletin says that the chlorine residual test "must be performed as frequently as needed to ensure that an adequate chlorine residual is maintained at all times." Considerations such as raw water quality, variation in chlorine demand, and changing flow rates "must be taken into account."

To ensure that the minimum total chlorine residual levels of 0.5 mg/L were maintained, it was necessary to measure the chlorine residuals on a daily basis. The daily operating sheets were designed to record the chlorine residual levels for the operating wells on each day of the month.

At the November 1978 meeting concerning the vulnerability of Well 5, the MOE representatives, the PUC, and the Town of Walkerton reached an understanding that the PUC would monitor the chlorine residuals daily and record the results on the daily operating sheets. According to the minutes of the meeting, "the importance of maintaining a chlorine residual at all times was emphasized in light of the presence of bacteria in the well water."

The importance of measuring the chlorine residuals on a daily basis was also stressed in MOE policy documents. In addition, the reports of the 1995 and 1998 inspections emphasized the importance of maintaining a minimum chlorine residual of 0.5 mg/L after 15 minutes of contact time. One could *maintain* a residual only if regular (daily) monitoring was taking place. Despite clear directions from the MOE, PUC staff did not measure the chlorine residuals each day. The PUC operators testified that the chlorine residuals were measured only about once a week.

This problem was exacerbated, moreover, by the fact that the method frequently used by PUC staff to test the chlorine residuals was inaccurate. Although the Walkerton PUC had used a HACH digital chlorine residual analyzer since

1998 and a chlorometric tester before that to measure the chlorine residuals, Stan and Frank Koebel, as well as Allan Buckle, often used the "bubble method" to obtain a "guesstimate" of chlorine residuals. The bubble method involved looking at a glass-encased bubble on the gas chlorinators at Wells 6 and 7: numbers inscribed on the bubble indicated whether chlorine was entering the system. PUC employees testified that if the bubble showed numbers between 2 and 3 or between 4 and 5, chlorine residuals of 0.5 mg/L and 0.75 mg/L, respectively, would be entered on the daily operating sheets for the well.

Even when the PUC operators actually measured chlorine residuals, they did not generally wait for the required 15 minutes of contact time. As a result, the residual readings they noted may have been higher than if they had waited 15 minutes. Further, until 1998, the PUC operators did not measure chlorine residuals in the distribution system, as specified in the ODWO. After the 1998 MOE inspection, Stan Koebel began measuring chlorine residuals in the distribution system, but he did so only sporadically.

The failure to monitor chlorine residuals daily flowed directly from the practice of underchlorinating the water: there was little sense in measuring a residual unless the goal was to achieve the required level. It can also be attributed to Stan and Frank Koebel's ignorance of the importance of maintaining a chlorine residual.

5.3.4 Inaccurate Operating Sheets

Because the PUC operators added inadequate levels of chlorine and did not monitor chlorine residuals daily, they made false chlorine residual entries in the daily operating sheets to conceal their improper practices.

In November 1978, at the meeting of the MOE and the Walkerton PUC about the vulnerability of Well 5, it was understood that the PUC would maintain daily operating sheets for that well. The information in the daily logs was to include the date and time of record taking, the name of the operator on duty, the meter reading, the pumping rate, the chlorine solution, and the chlorine residual reading. Although it was not included as a condition on the well's Certificate of Approval, there was an expectation at the November 1978 meeting that the PUC would monitor the chlorine residuals daily at Well 5, maintain a minimum chlorine residual of 0.5 mg/L after 15 minutes of contact time, and record the results on the daily operating sheets.

The practice of making false entries for chlorine residuals in the daily operating sheets began almost immediately. At the time of the 1979 MOE inspection, the residuals recorded in the daily operating sheets differed from the residuals measured by the inspector. It was evident in that year's inspection of Well 5 that inaccurate numbers had been inserted by PUC operators in the "chlorine residual" column of the daily operating sheet. The 1979 inspection report noted that in contrast to the 0.3 mg/L chlorine residual measured by the inspector, the operating authority had recorded a chlorine residual of 0.5 mg/L. A comparison of the daily operating sheets and the chlorine residuals measured by the MOE inspectors in 1995 and 1998 shows similar discrepancies, although it is not clear whether the residual readings were entered into the daily operating sheets at the same time as the inspections occurred.

For more than two decades before May 2000, chlorine residual readings were entered on the daily operating sheets for all the operating wells for days on which the residuals were not actually measured by PUC staff. Occasionally, false entries were made in the column that designated the operator. Stan Koebel acknowledged at the Inquiry that other people's initials would sometimes be inserted in the "operator" column of the daily operating sheets. Mr. Buckle testified that since he was not licensed to operate the waterworks, he was reluctant to inscribe his initials as the operator on the daily operating sheet. Moreover, entries in the columns "chlorine solution level" and "chlorine used in previous 24 hours" sometimes contained fictitious numbers.

The daily operating sheets for the wells in the 1980s and the 1990s reveal that either 0.5 mg/L or 0.75 mg/L was generally entered as the chlorine residual. Most of the chlorine residuals recorded in 1998, for example, are 0.75 mg/L, and as Stan Koebel acknowledged, virtually all of the entries on the 1999 daily operating sheets are false.[5] Fictitious entries in the daily operating sheets continued until the outbreak in May 2000.

5.3.5 Inaccurate Annual Reports

Stan Koebel began to submit annual reports to the MOE in 1998. The annual reports were based on information in the daily operating sheets and consequently contain inaccurate and misleading information. For example, in the

---

[5] It is, of course, virtually impossible to detect the same residual day after day for a month, let alone for an entire year.

"Annual Summary of Treated Water and Waste Water Flows, Turbidity and Disinfectant Residual" for 1998, the numbers for "Treated Disinfectant" are based on false chlorine residual measurements in the daily operating sheets for the three wells. In fact, Mr. Koebel calculated an average of the falsified numbers, a 0.60 mg/L chlorine residual, for the MOE. Similarly, the "Annual Summary of the Distribution System Bacteriological Data" for that same year contained inaccurate information. Entries in that report for "Number of Samples with Detectable Residual" and "Treated Disinfectant Average Residual" are also based on fictitious numbers. At the Inquiry, both Stan and Frank Koebel agreed that MOE officials would be misled by such records and therefore would not be alerted to potential drinking water risks to the health of Walkerton's residents.

5.3.6 The Operation of the Wells Without Chlorination

The ODWO says that waterworks operators must take measures to ensure that the disinfection process is functioning at all times. According to the Chlorination Bulletin, chlorination is the primary method for water disinfection and is "the one step in water treatment specifically designed to destroy pathogenic organisms and thereby prevent water-borne diseases." Moreover, the Chlorination Bulletin requires continuous and adequate disinfection for water supplies obtained from a surface water source or from a groundwater source that is or "may be" contaminated. The 1995 and 1998 MOE inspection reports also stated that a 0.5 mg/L total chlorine residual after 15 minutes of contact time was to be continuously maintained at all three wells.

Despite the requirement for continuous disinfection in MOE policy documents and in the inspection reports, the Walkerton PUC operators at times allowed a well to operate without chlorination. Again, they believed that the water in Walkerton was of good quality at its sources and were not convinced of the need for chlorination. It was therefore not a concern to either Stan or Frank Koebel that a well would sometimes operate without a chlorinator for a few days.

For two lengthy periods in May 2000, Stan and Frank Koebel allowed Well 7 to pump unchlorinated water into the system. From May 3 to May 9 and from May 15 to May 19, the well operated without a chlorinator.

On May 3, the chlorinator at Well 7 was removed by PUC staff on Stan Koebel's instructions. When Stan Koebel left Walkerton on May 5 for a conference in Windsor, he was aware that Well 7 was pumping unchlorinated water and that this situation would reduce the chlorine residual in the distribution system. During Stan Koebel's absence from Walkerton between May 5 and May 14, Frank Koebel did not install the new chlorinator. The well pumped unchlorinated water into the distribution system until May 9, when it was turned off.

When Stan Koebel returned to the Walkerton PUC on May 15, he reactivated Well 7. Well 7 again operated without chlorination from May 15 until May 19, the day on which the new chlorinator was installed by PUC staff.

Both Stan and Frank Koebel knew that it was wrong to allow a well to pump unchlorinated water. This explains the "revisions" made by Frank Koebel, on his brother's instructions, to the May 2000 daily operating sheets on May 22 or May 23. The brothers were attempting to conceal the fact that Well 7 had operated without a chlorinator. I discuss this issue in more detail below.

5.4   The Relationship Between the Walkerton Public Utilities Commission and the Ministry of the Environment

The MOE's Owen Sound office was the provincial regulator responsible for overseeing the Walkerton facility. I will review the manner in which the MOE exercised this oversight role in a later chapter. In this section, I discuss the relationship from the perspective of the Walkerton PUC. The message received by Stan Koebel from the MOE, no doubt unintended by the ministry, was that although the requirements for treating, monitoring, and testing the water were important, they were not important enough to cause the MOE to take any steps to ensure that they were followed.

As the PUC's general manager, Stan Koebel was involved in MOE inspections of the Walkerton system in 1991, 1995, and 1998. As will be discussed, Mr. Koebel did not address many of the deficiencies identified in the three MOE inspection reports. Several of the deficiencies specified by MOE inspectors in the early and mid-1990s had still not been addressed by the time of the 1998 MOE inspection – the last before the outbreak. Sometimes Mr. Koebel did not understand the terms used or was not conversant with MOE guidelines, policies, and legislation. On other occasions, he simply did not do what he said he would. The MOE threatened to take, but never actually took, decisive steps to ensure compliance with its requirements.

Although staff at the PUC, with the exception of Stan Koebel, did not accompany MOE officials on inspections of the Walkerton water system or read MOE inspection reports, they were aware of any impending inspections. The MOE would contact the PUC to inform Mr. Koebel that the facility would be inspected in about a week. In turn, Mr. Koebel would instruct the PUC staff to clean the pumphouses, to ensure that the equipment operated properly, and to ensure that records were "presentable." Frank Koebel testified that he had never experienced an unannounced "spot check" by MOE inspectors in his 25 years of employment at the PUC.

When Stan Koebel was notified of the upcoming November 1991 inspection, he took measures to ensure that the chlorinators were working properly, that the chlorine was set at a sufficiently high level,[6] and that the pumphouses were clean. Mr. Koebel accompanied the MOE inspector, Brian Jaffray, on his inspection of the premises. During the approximately two-hour inspection, Mr. Jaffray visited the wells, collected water samples, and took notes on the system.

The inspection report was sent to the PUC several months later, in March 1992. Three issues were identified as deficient: the lack of weekly bacteriological quality monitoring, flow calibration problems, and the absence of a contingency plan. It was recommended that the bacteriological quality monitoring be upgraded to 13 samples a month from the distribution system and that these samples be collected at various locations throughout the system. As previously mentioned, only nine distribution system samples were being collected each month by PUC staff.

It is clear from the evidence that Mr. Koebel was aware at least as early as 1990 that the PUC was not satisfying the MOE sampling requirements. In that year, Stan Koebel signed a grant application prepared by B.M. Ross and Associates Ltd. That document, which sought funds for a needs study of the Walkerton water distribution system, stated that the MOE bacteriological objectives were not being met.

It was also recommended in the report of the 1991 inspection that a chemical/physical quality monitoring program be established. The PUC was instructed to submit to the MOE an annual report containing a bacteriological summary of the raw and treated sample results, the chemical and physical results, a

---

[6] Even at that, the chlorine levels measured by the inspector were only 0.3 mg/L and 0.35 mg/L.

description of any plant upsets and corrective action, and a list of waterworks extensions or modifications.

Prior to the MOE inspection in October 1995, Stan Koebel received two important letters from the district manager of the MOE's Owen Sound office. The letters, dated June 6, 1995, and June 23, 1995, respectively, specified the minimum number of samples to be collected at the Walkerton waterworks and stipulated that the PUC was to notify the MOE as soon as possible of any treated water or distribution system bacteriological analysis indicating unsafe drinking water quality. Mr. Koebel was also provided with a copy of the ODWO.

Mr. Koebel stated that before the May 2000 tragedy, it had been his understanding that the laboratory, not the waterworks operator, would notify the MOE of adverse results. He testified that he had likely read only portions of the June 1995 correspondence from the MOE and had therefore assumed that he had no obligation to contact the MOE's Owen Sound office regarding unsafe drinking water results in either treated or distribution system water samples.

In October 1995, Stan Koebel was advised of another upcoming MOE inspection. Preparatory steps were taken to ensure that the chlorination equipment was operating properly and that the premises were clean. In John Apfelbeck's two-hour inspection of the Walkerton water system, he collected samples from the three wells and tested the chlorine residuals. The measurements obtained by Mr. Apfelbeck on October 31, 1995, ranged from 0.12 mg/L to 0.4 mg/L.

The MOE inspection report that was sent to the Walkerton PUC on January 29, 1996, stated that *E. coli* had been present in one or more samples on three sampling occasions. It emphasized "the importance of ensuring that an adequate chlorine residual is maintained in the distribution system at all times" and "that a minimum total chlorine residual of 0.5 mg/L after 15 minutes [of] contact time must be maintained in the water discharged to the distribution system from all wells at all times."

The report also noted the absence of a physical/chemical quality monitoring program as a deficiency: in the report of the 1991 inspection, the PUC had been asked to establish such a program. The report further noted that the PUC continued to fail to meet the requirements of the minimum bacteriological sampling program. I note that this failure persisted despite the recommendation in the previous inspection report and the MOE's two June 1995 letters to Mr. Koebel setting out the required sampling program. A further deficiency specified in the report of the 1995 inspection was that the Walkerton PUC was not complying with the requirements in Ontario Regulation 435/93 for keeping records of training received by waterworks operators. Finally, the report stated that the safety guidelines in the Chlorination Bulletin were not being met: wells that used chlorine gas were not equipped with chlorine leak detection equipment and alarms, and the doors to Wells 3 and 6 were not equipped with panic bars.

About four months after Mr. Koebel received the report of the 1995 inspection, he wrote a letter to the MOE's Owen Sound office in response to the deficiencies identified by Mr. Apfelbeck. It is clear from his letter that he had not addressed many of the deficiencies.

Much of the letter was cast in the future tense. Mr. Koebel stated that physical and chemical sampling "will" be done by A&L Canada Laboratories and that all wells "will" have a minimum total chlorine residual of 0.5 mg/L after 15 minutes of contact time. He also discussed the provisions of the Chlorination Bulletin and said that Wells 3 and 6 "will" have panic bars by the end of 1996; Wells 6 and 7 "will" have leak detection equipment, including an alarm; and an automatic chlorine residual monitor "is" proposed for the 1997 budget.

In the letter, Mr. Koebel failed to discuss one of the deficiencies identified in the inspection report: non-compliance with Ontario Regulation 435/93. Mr. Koebel testified that he had "missed it" and that Larry Struthers, the MOE environmental officer responsible for Walkerton, did not raise the issue with him later.

The last MOE inspection before the May 2000 tragedy occurred on February 25, 1998. Like her predecessors, Michelle Zillinger gave advance notice of the inspection to Stan Koebel. A few days before the inspection, changes were made to the daily operating sheets. In particular, Stan Koebel changed a dash in the "chlorine residual" column for Wells 6 and 7 on February 20, 1998, to reflect a chlorine residual of 0.4 mg/L. His explanation was that Allan Buckle had likely taken the readings on February 20 but failed to record the chlorine residuals.[7]

---

[7] The February 1998 daily operating sheet was unusual in that it included entries that, like 0.4 mg/L, broke from the established pattern of 0.5 mg/L and 0.75 mg/L, thus creating a more realistic picture of what the residuals would have looked like if they had actually been measured.

The MOE inspection report received by Mr. Koebel on May 6, 1998, indicated that many of the deficiencies identified in the 1995 inspection had still not been addressed. The number of adverse bacteriological results had increased. *E. coli*, an indicator of unsafe drinking water quality, had been present in a number of treated water samples from Wells 5 and 7 and at several locations in the distribution system. Moreover, the minimum total chlorine residual level of 0.5 mg/L was not being maintained. On the day of the inspection, the chlorine residual at Well 7 was 0.4 mg/L and the reading at Well 6 was 0.35 mg/L.

Ms. Zillinger's inspection report said that "given the frequency of adverse bacteriological results, it is imperative that the required chlorine residuals be maintained in the distribution system." It also said that according to the daily operating sheets, the chlorine residual levels had occasionally fallen below the required 0.5 mg/L. Ms. Zillinger also discussed the MOE's June 23, 1995, letter to the PUC stipulating that a disinfectant residual must be detected in 95% or more of the distribution samples collected each month. Despite this letter, Stan Koebel had not been monitoring the chlorine residuals in the distribution system.

Again, it was noted that the Walkerton PUC was not satisfying the requirements of the minimum recommended sampling program. Only 8 or 9 bacteriological samples were being collected each month from the distribution system, rather than the required 13 samples. In the covering letter that accompanied the inspection report, the MOE threatened to issue a Director's Order pursuant to section 52(2) of the *Ontario Water Resources Act* if the PUC did not conform with the minimum sampling program. However, the MOE did not invoke any mandatory abatement measures, like issuing a Director's Order, to ensure that compliance would ensue.

Two other deficiencies from the 1995 inspection remained outstanding: the failure to maintain training records as required by Ontario Regulation 435/93 and the failure to develop a contingency plan for the waterworks.

After the 1998 inspection, Stan Koebel failed, as he had in the past, to address several of the deficiencies identified in the report. His explanation was that he had had other priorities. When he wrote to Philip Bye on July 14, 1998, most of the problems in the system had not been remedied. The letter to the MOE's Owen Sound office was again cast in the future. Mr. Koebel wrote that the PUC "will" be maintaining a minimum total chlorine residual of 0.5 mg/L and that "hopefully" it "will" be purchasing equipment "in the future" to ensure the continuous maintenance of a 0.5 mg/L chlorine residual. In fact, he had no intention of increasing the chlorine residual to 0.5 mg/L. His explanation at the Inquiry was that he was "trying to get a balance between customer complaints and meeting the Ministry of the Environment's guidelines." Nor did Mr. Koebel purchase continuous chlorine residual monitors.

Mr. Koebel also wrote in the letter to Mr. Bye that the PUC "will" be working on a contingency plan by the end of 1998; no plan was completed by that time. He stated that the PUC "will" be upgrading employee Robert McKay to class 3 certification for water treatment and water distribution. But by May 2000, the month of the tragedy, Mr. McKay still had only a class 1 licence. At the hearings, Mr. Koebel stated that if a Director's Order had been imposed by the MOE, the PUC would have responded to the deficiencies identified in the 1998 inspection report.

Michelle Zillinger testified that she did not think any actions had been taken by environmental officers at the MOE's Owen Sound office to follow up on the February 1998 inspection of the Walkerton waterworks. Although the MOE did not determine whether the deficiencies had been remedied, Mr. Bye sent a letter to Mr. Koebel on August 10, 1998, thanking him for the PUC's "cooperation and attention to the concerns raised in the status report." Moreover, Donald Hamilton, an environmental officer at the MOE's Owen Sound office, wrote to Stan Koebel on January 15, 1999:

> The Ministry conducted an inspection of your facility on February 5 [sic, 25], 1998. There has been a noticeable improvement in the operation of your water works since that time. I thank you for your effort and cooperation in this regard.

In his testimoney, Mr. Koebel acknowledged that two years before the May 2000 tragedy, he was given a clear "road map" by Ms. Zillinger of exactly what he had to do to ensure that the drinking water in Walkerton was safe. Yet he did not take the necessary actions to address several of the deficiencies identified in the 1998 inspection report, and he reverted to the improper chlorination and monitoring practices. When asked at the Inquiry to provide an explanation for his inaction, his response was "complacency."

The MOE was aware in the years leading up to May 2000 that the Walkerton PUC was not conforming with several ministry requirements.[8] Despite repeated assurances, the PUC failed to fulfill its undertakings to the MOE. It was clear to the MOE environmental officers during the three inspections in the 1990s that the PUC was not complying with the minimum bacteriological sampling program and that it was not maintaining minimum total chlorine residuals of 0.5 mg/L. Nevertheless, the MOE took no action to make legally enforceable the requirements that were consistently being ignored by the PUC. Neither a Director's Order nor a Field Order under the *Ontario Water Resources Act* was issued. Instead, the MOE chose a voluntary approach to abatement. While in no way excusing Stan Koebel's disregard for MOE requirements, the ministry's failure to take stronger measures in the face of his repeated failures likely sent the unintended message that these requirements – all in the form of guidelines and recommendations, rather than legally enforceable regulations – were not important enough for the MOE to ensure that they were followed.

5.5 The Relationship Between Stan Koebel and the Public Utilities Commissioners

Stan Koebel was responsible for reporting to the public utilities commissioners on the operation of the water system. The commissioners were unaware of the improper operating practices of PUC staff, because Mr. Koebel was not forthcoming about the manner in which he operated the system. They spent next to no time addressing matters related to the quality of Walkerton's water, relying almost completely on Stan Koebel to provide safe water to the town's residents.

James Kieffer, chair of the PUC, testified that during the ten years in which he served as a commissioner, water quality was not generally discussed at the monthly PUC meetings. In the time devoted to water issues, discussions focused on financial matters and impending projects at the waterworks, rather than on the quality of Walkerton's drinking water. Particularly since the end of 1998, after Ontario's *Energy Competition Act* came into effect, most of the discussions at the PUC centred on the restructuring of the electrical utilities.

---

[8] Stan Koebel never disclosed to MOE officials that he was not taking samples from the distribution system at the specified locations, that he was not measuring chlorine residuals daily, that the annual records contained fictitious entries, that he operated wells without chlorinators from time to time, and that he had not read the ODWO or the Chlorination Bulletin. MOE officials, for their part, never questioned his qualifications to operate a municipal water system.

Commissioner Richard Field testified at the hearings that 75% of the meetings were devoted to hydro issues.

As will be discussed in Chapter 6 of this report, the PUC commissioners had little training in or understanding of the water system. The terms "*E. coli*" and "chlorine residual" were unfamiliar to them, as were the indicators of unsafe drinking water outlined in the ODWO. They did not know about the requirements in the Chlorination Bulletin. Nor were the commissioners aware of the requirement in Ontario Regulation 435/93 that waterworks employees should receive a minimum of 40 hours' training annually.

Although the commissioners reviewed the reports of the 1995 and 1998 MOE inspections of the Walkerton water system, they did not understand many of the deficiencies that were identified in the reports. When the 1998 report was presented at the PUC meeting on May 20, 1998, Stan Koebel discussed the inadequate number of samples collected from the water system, not the occasions when *E. coli* had been found in the system or the failure to maintain the required chlorine residuals. Mr. Koebel was not questioned at the meeting about the large number of samples that contained *E. coli*, largely because the commissioners were unfamiliar with this bacteria and did not know that it could be fatal.

During the approximately 12 years in which he was general manager of the PUC, Mr. Koebel failed to adequately inform the commissioners, either through the monthly manager's report or in discussions at the monthly PUC meetings, about problems in the system that could compromise the water quality in Walkerton. He did not alert the commissioners to adverse sample results received from the laboratory, and he was not candid about the amount of chlorination entering the system. In fact, Mr. Koebel misled the commissioners on a number of occasions.

For example, at the meeting on October 12, 1999, subsequent to the enactment of the *Energy Competition Act*, the issue of whether the Municipality of Brockton should assume control of the Walkerton waterworks was discussed. Prior to the meeting, Mr. Koebel prepared a presentation taking the position that the Walkerton PUC should retain its employees and equipment and continue to operate the water system. It stated that the PUC and its staff were "still providing the best service and promoting the best interest of the utilities customers," as they had been doing since 1953. The presentation also said that staff "carries out daily sampling for chlorine residual." Stan Koebel knew that this statement was false: chlorine residual testing generally took place only once a week, and fictitious chlorine residual measurements were regularly inscribed on the daily operating sheets. In addition, the presentation implied that sedimentation and filtration processes were used by the PUC to treat the water supply, when in fact they were not.

Another example of Stan Koebel's misstatements to the commissioners occurred on May 18, 2000, at the time of the Walkerton outbreak. The manager's report presented at the PUC meeting that day stated that "we are currently rebuilding the chlorine equipment at our #7 pumphouse." Mr. Koebel did not disclose that Well 7 had operated without a chlorinator from May 3 to May 9 and from May 15 to the date of the meeting. In fact, the commissioners were unaware that the new chlorinator for Well 7 had been at the PUC since December 1998 and had not yet been installed. They were also unaware that adverse results had been received from A&L Canada Laboratories on May 17 or that members of the public had contacted the PUC to inquire about the quality of the water because people in Walkerton were becoming ill.

5.6   Well 5: Continuous Monitors

One of the causes of the tragedy in May 2000 was the failure to install continuous chlorine residual and turbidity monitors at Well 5. Neither Stan nor Frank Koebel was aware of the seriousness of the vulnerability of Well 5 to surface contamination. Nor were they familiar with the 1994 amendments to the ODWO requiring continuous monitoring of chlorine residual and turbidity levels to protect public health.

Stan and Frank Koebel both believed that the reason for the development of Well 5 in 1978 was that the PUC wished to provide Walkerton residents with softer water. Well 5 was referred to as a "band-aid" or "stop-gap" solution in attempts by the PUC to supply softer water. Frank Koebel believed that Well 5's water would be softer because Well 5 was a shallow well. He did not think that Well 5 was more vulnerable to contamination than was a well drilled to a deeper depth. In his view, any drilled well was a safe well.

Stan and Frank Koebel were also not familiar with the findings of the 1978 Ian D. Wilson Associates report, a copy of which was in the PUC office. This report stated that the bacteriological testing of samples at Well 5 indicated pollution from human or animal sources and that shallow aquifers were susceptible to pollution. It recommended that the Town of Walkerton purchase property in the vicinity of Well 5 to protect the water supply. The report also recommended that the bacterial content of the treated and raw water should be monitored and that the supply "should definitely be chlorinated." Stan Koebel testified that he was unaware of the recommendation that the town should acquire land surrounding Well 5 because of the well's vulnerability to surface contamination. He did not turn his mind to the possibility that farming activities could result in contamination of the water at the well.

In the years following the release of the report, Stan Koebel acknowledged that he did become somewhat concerned about the impact of surface activities on Well 5's water quality. For example, correspondence from the MOE in 1990 discussed Mr. Koebel's concern about the installation of fuel tanks near the well. At the hearings, Mr. Koebel stated, "I was concerned about a possible fuel leak down the road and getting into the aquifers, thereby [into] our main water supply." He also became aware from the laboratory reports in the 1990s that on several occasions, Well 5 samples contained total coliforms and *E. coli*. The vulnerability of Well 5 to contamination was also adverted to in the 1992 "Water Distribution System Rehabilitation Needs Study." Nevertheless, he did not understand eiher the degree to which the well was susceptible to contamination from surface activities or the serious consequences of such contamination.

In the 1994 amendments to the ODWO, section 4.2.1.1 was changed to require water supply systems that serve populations of 3,300 or more, and that use groundwater that is under the direct influence of surface water without filtration, to continuously monitor chlorine residuals.[9] The 1994 amendments also required such systems to monitor turbidity levels either continuously or by taking grab samples every four hours. As discussed in Chapter 4 of this report, installing continuous monitors at Well 5 would have prevented the tragedy in May 2000.

In the 1997 capital budget of the PUC, $6,000 was allocated to acquire an automatic chlorine residual monitor for Well 7. However, it was never purchased. A chlorine residual monitor was, however, mentioned by Stan Koebel in his July 14, 1998, letter to the MOE, in which he responded to the deficiencies it had noted in its 1998 inspection. Mr. Koebel wrote:

---

[9] More specifically, the requirement is to continuously monitor "disinfectant residuals (equivalent to free chlorine)" – a type of chlorine residual.

> We will be maintaining a total chlorine residual of 0.5 mg/L for all
> our active wells. Hopefully we will be purchasing equipment in the
> future to ensure [that a] residual of 0.5 mg/L is kept up at all times.

Mr. Koebel did not purchase a continuous chlorine residual monitor after the 1998 inspection to assist in fulfilling his undertaking to continuously maintain a 0.5 mg/L chlorine residual at all active wells. However, the MOE never required, or even requested, the PUC to do so.

There is no evidence to suggest that either Stan or Frank Koebel was aware of the 1994 ODWO amendments. The MOE took no steps to bring these amendments to their attention. Moreover, the MOE did not require waterworks operators to take training specifically focused on issues relating to identifying vulnerable water sources or understanding the need for continuous monitoring where such vulnerability exists. It is interesting to note that when Stan Koebel did consider purchasing a chlorine residual monitor, it was for Well 7, the most secure of the three water sources, and not for Well 5, the most vulnerable. He obviously did not know about Well 5's vulnerability to surface contamination and did not have the training or expertise either to identify that vulnerability or to understand the connection between vulnerable water sources and the need for continuous monitoring.

5.7   The Working Environment at the Walkerton
Public Utilities Commission

Evidence was introduced at the Inquiry regarding the working environment at the Walkerton PUC. It falls into two categories: (1) alcohol consumption at the workplace by PUC employees, and (2) the pressure arising from the passage of the *Energy Competition Act* in 1998 and from municipal amalgamation in 1999. Although the working environment, particularly in the months leading up to the outbreak, was far from satisfactory, I am not satisfied that it contributed to the outbreak.

Alcohol had been consumed by the Walkerton PUC staff for many years before the tragedy occurred. Beer was stored in the refrigerator at the PUC shop. Frank Koebel had a drinking problem. PUC employees Allan Buckle and Robert McKay testified that they sometimes smelled alcohol on Frank Koebel's breath and noticed that his speech was slurred. On at least one occasion, Stan Koebel drove his brother home during the working day because of Frank Koebel's excessive drinking.

In 1997 and 1998, Frank Koebel suffered two heart attacks. In 1998, he spent five weeks at the Homewood Institute in Guelph to deal with his alcohol problems and recover from the second heart attack. Stan Koebel decided at that time to prohibit the storage of alcoholic beverages in the refrigerator at the PUC shop.

Drinking beer at the workplace was symptomatic of a cavalier, undisciplined attitude among PUC staff. However, the improper operating practices do not appear to have been the result of drinking beer on the job. Apparently that practice had ended after Frank Koebel's heart attack, whereas the improper operating practices continued. While clearly unacceptable, I do not believe that drinking alcohol on the job was responsible for the May 2000 tragedy.

The working environment at the PUC was also affected by the passage of the *Energy Competition Act* and by municipal amalgamation.

In January 1999, the Town of Walkerton, the Township of Brant, and the Township of Greenock amalgamated to establish the Municipality of Brockton. The Townships of Brant and Greenock had two communal wells: one in the Chepstow subdivision and the other on Geeson Avenue. After the amalgamation, the Walkerton PUC became responsible for operating these wells. Thus, the amalgamation somewhat increased the work of PUC employees.

The enactment of Ontario's *Energy Competition Act* (Bill 35) also had an impact on the operation of the water system in Walkerton. This legislation required municipalities to decide by November 2000 whether to retain, sell, or lease their electrical utilities. Stan Koebel said that he had spent an inordinate amount of time on the issue of electrical restructuring and that only 5% of his time had been devoted to the water operation at the PUC. He testified that by April 2000, he was uncomfortable with the manner in which the PUC was operating:

> There [were] too many ongoing projects that I wasn't getting a handle on, and being away too often for the amalgamation talks with the electricity side, not spending enough time in our own utility. I felt like I was losing it.

At this time, the Municipality of Brockton was also contemplating whether the Walkerton PUC's water operation ought to become a department of the municipality. On May 1, 2000, John Strader, superintendent of the Works Department, presented a report to the Brockton municipal council that described the duties of a prospective waterworks supervisor employed by the municipality.

Staff at the PUC were concerned that if Brockton assumed responsibility for the waterworks, there would be a surplus of workers and PUC employees would be laid off. As Frank Koebel said, "There was a lot of uncertainty amongst us. Nobody knew whether we were going to have the same position as [we] were holding at that time." Stan Koebel was anxious that the municipal council was making decisions on waterworks projects and was imposing charges to customers for water services without consulting him. He testified, "I was getting a feeling I was left out there."

Robert McKay was also concerned about his continued employment at the Walkerton PUC. In March or April 2000, he contacted the MOE's Owen Sound office to obtain information on the rules and regulations applicable to persons who do not hold a licence as a waterworks operator. He was informed by Larry Struthers, an environmental officer at the Owen Sound office, that unlicensed operators were not permitted to collect water samples or take readings at a water treatment plant. After hearing this, Mr. McKay decided that if necessary he would "bump" Allan Buckle, who was not certified as a waterworks operator. Mr. McKay believed that pursuant to the collective agreement, he had seniority over Mr. Buckle. Mr. Struthers did not ask Mr. McKay, during their conversation, whether the Walkerton PUC employed unlicensed operators.

Although additional stress resulted from the possible restructuring of the waterworks and from the municipal amalgamation, I am satisfied that this stress did not contribute to the outbreak in May 2000. The improper operating practices – the failure to chlorinate and to monitor chlorine residuals daily – had been going on for years and would have continued regardless of the *Energy Competition Act* or municipal amalgamation.

5.8   The Operators' Response to the May 2000 Outbreak

I have already described the actions of Stan and Frank Koebel in May 2000 in some detail in Chapter 3 of this report. In this section, I will highlight the relevant events and my conclusions.

Stan Koebel failed to inform the Bruce-Grey-Owen Sound Health Unit in a timely way about the adverse test results derived from samples taken on Monday, May 15, from the Walkerton water system and from a watermain construction project along a section of Highway 9. If the local health unit representative had been informed of these matters when he first contacted Mr. Koebel about the illnesses reported in Walkerton on Friday, May 19, 300 to 400 people would probably have been spared infection.

On May 15, at 6:15 a.m., Stan Koebel turned on Well 7. It had no chlorinator. The well operated from then until shortly before noon on Friday, May 19, without a chlorinator.

On May 15, the Walkerton PUC sent a number of water samples to A&L Canada Laboratories for microbiological testing. These included three samples from the Highway 9 construction site and four samples from the Walkerton system.

On May 17, Robert Deakin of A&L telephoned Mr. Koebel and indicated that the three construction site samples and three of the Walkerton system samples had tested positive for both total coliforms and *E. coli*. Later that day, Mr. Deakin faxed the test results for both sets of samples to the Walkerton PUC. One of the Walkerton system samples, which had undergone the more extensive membrane filtration test, showed massive contamination.

Starting on May 18, residents of Walkerton began to telephone the PUC and ask questions about the safety of the water. They were assured by a staff member, who had consulted with Stan Koebel, that the water was fine. Stan Koebel then instructed Frank Koebel to install the new chlorinator at Well 7.

That evening, Stan Koebel attended the Walkerton PUC's monthly meeting. As was his practice, he submitted a manager's report in writing. He did not disclose to the commissioners that he had received adverse samples from the construction project and the Walkerton distribution system or that Well 7 had been operating without chlorination.

When the health unit's local public health inspector, James Schmidt, contacted Stan Koebel on the next day, May 19, and inquired whether there were any problems with the water system, Mr. Koebel responded by saying that he "thought the water was okay." The same day, David Patterson of the health unit contacted Mr. Koebel to discuss inquiries from the public about the quality of Walkerton's water. Mr. Koebel assured Mr. Patterson too that the water was fine.

It was no coincidence that within half an hour of speaking to Mr. Patterson, Stan Koebel went to the PUC shop at 130 Wallace Street. He wanted to make sure that the chlorinator at Well 7 had been installed: he was told that it had been, on that day. He told both Frank Koebel and Allan Buckle that the samples from the Highway 9 construction project had contained bacterial contamination. After Mr. Buckle left, Stan Koebel also told Frank Koebel that he was concerned that there was bacteriological contamination in the distribution system. He also told his brother that the PUC office had received telephone calls from town residents and from the health unit, asking if the water was safe to drink.

Starting on the evening of May 19 and throughout the following long weekend (May 20 through May 22), Stan Koebel increased the chlorination and intensively flushed watermains in Walkerton's water distribution system. He said that he did this as a "precautionary measure" in response to the adverse water test results and because of his having learned that people in Walkerton were becoming sick. Despite his concern that the water was contaminated, Mr. Koebel certainly hoped and probably believed that the increased chlorination would make the water safe. Although by May 19 he must have been seriously concerned that the water was making people ill, I am satisfied that he did not know that *E. coli* was potentially lethal.

When the local health unit's James Schmidt contacted Stan Koebel on May 20, Mr. Koebel informed him that the system was being flushed and that the chlorine residual levels were 0.1 to 0.4 parts per million (ppm) in the distribution system and 0.73 ppm at the wellhead.

Later on May 20, Christopher Johnston of the MOE's Spills Action Centre (SAC) contacted Stan Koebel as a result of Robert McKay's anonymous call regarding failed water samples. Inexcusably, when asked directly whether there had been adverse samples, Mr. Koebel failed to inform Mr. Johnston that analyses of samples taken from a municipal well and from the distribution system had shown the presence of total coliforms and *E. coli*.

At about 3:00 p.m. on May 20, David Patterson of the local health unit tele-phoned Stan Koebel and advised him that someone had reported having been warned by a radio station against drinking Walkerton water. But Mr. Koebel was not comfortable about going public with a claim that the water was safe. During this conversation, Mr. Koebel informed Mr. Patterson that he was con-tinuing to flush the watermains and that the chlorine residual levels ranged from 0.1 to 0.3 ppm. In response to Mr. Patterson's question as to whether there had been any unusual events in the water system, Mr. Koebel again re-ferred to the watermain construction and the replacement of the chlorinator. He did not mention the adverse test results or the fact that Well 7 had operated without a chlorinator from May 3 to May 9 and from May 15 to May 19.

Mr. Koebel testified that he was contacted by the mayor of Brockton, David Thomson, on the next day, May 21, and that during their conversation, he assured the mayor that he thought the water was "okay." According to his testimony, he contacted the mayor later that day, after learning of the boil water advisory. He testified that he did not tell the mayor about the adverse test results in either of these calls.

When James Kieffer, the PUC's chair, contacted Stan Koebel after learning of the boil water advisory on the afternoon of May 21, Mr. Koebel was again presented with an opportunity to tell the truth about the adverse sample results and the fact that Well 7 had operated without chlorination. Mr. Koebel told Mr. Kieffer only that he was flushing the system and that the chlorine levels had been increased.

Similarly, when on May 21 the SAC again contacted Mr. Koebel, this time to discuss the boil water advisory, Mr. Koebel maintained his approach of delib-erately avoiding the disclosure of adverse results from samples collected on May 15.

Stan Koebel's attempt to avoid any detection of the PUC's operation of Well 7 without chlorination continued through his meeting with MOE environmental officer John Earl on May 22. Instead of telling the truth, he referred to Well 6 having been "knocked out" by an electrical storm, clearly implying that nothing else out of the ordinary had occurred. When asked, however, he pro-vided a number of Certificates of Analysis to Mr. Earl, including the certificate pertaining to the water samples collected on May 15 from the municipal water system, reflecting *E. coli* and total coliforms contamination. This was the first disclosure of these results. He still did not indicate that Well 7 had operated without a chlorinator. When asked for Well 7's daily operating sheet, Mr. Koebel said that he would provide it the following day.

When Mr. Earl returned to the Walkerton PUC the next day, May 23, Mr. Koebel gave Mr. Earl what purported to be the May 2000 daily operating sheet for Well 7. This document had actually been created by Frank Koebel on May 22 or May 23 to conceal the fact that Well 7 had operated without a chlorinator. It falsely indicated that Well 7 had not operated between May 3 and May 9. It also reflected chlorine residual levels for five days when no chlorinator had been installed at the well.

It was only on May 23 that Stan Koebel began to tell the truth to the local health unit. Even then, he was telling only parts of the truth. In a telephone call with David Patterson, Mr. Koebel was informed that samples collected by the health unit had revealed the presence of bacteria in the water system. Mr. Patterson then asked for the date of the last set of microbiological tests from the Walkerton PUC. Mr. Koebel told Mr. Patterson that samples had been taken on May 15, and then, on being asked for the results, after a pause, told him that the samples had all "failed." However, Mr. Koebel still did not disclose the fact that Well 7 had operated without a chlorinator.

At the meeting in the Brockton municipal council chamber that afternoon, Dr. Murray McQuigge asked Mr. Koebel whether he had anything to say. Mr. Koebel began to discuss new watermains, again implying that they could have caused the contamination. Only after being asked direct questions by Dr. McQuigge did Mr. Koebel admit that the May 15 PUC samples had failed the microbiological tests. He still did not disclose the fact that Well 7 had operated without a chlorinator.

At the council meeting that followed the meeting convened by Dr. McQuigge, Mr. Koebel said that the chlorinator at Well 7 had not functioned properly. In fact, there had been nothing wrong with the unit removed on May 3. He continued to withhold the important fact that Well 7 had been operated without chlorination. Although he admitted that the PUC's May 15 samples had failed, he claimed not to have read the laboratory report until May 18 or May 19. He did not tell the municipal councilors that on May 17, Robert Deakin had told him that the May 15 samples were positive for *E. coli* and total coliforms, and that the plate containing the single sample that had undergone membrane filtration was covered with both types of bacteria.

By May 18, Stan Koebel knew of the adverse results from the May 15 samples and knew that there might be contamination in the water system. He also knew on that day that people were becoming sick. He was alarmed because he had been operating Well 7 without a chlorinator since May 15. He knew that doing so was wrong and did not want this improper practice to come to light.

Mr. Koebel not only did not disclose the truth about Well 7 when it would have been appropriate to do so, he also did not disclose the adverse test results from the May 15 samples. On May 19, after the chlorinator at Well 7 was installed, he began to flush and chlorinate the system. He must have recognized that the adverse results would eventually become known but hoped that by then, resampling and testing would show that the system was free of contamination. He did all this, I am satisfied, to conceal the fact that Well 7 had been operated without chlorination. Indeed, he went so far as to have his brother Frank Koebel alter the daily operating sheet for Well 7 to conceal the truth about Well 7.

Ironically, Well 7 was not the source of the contamination.

5.9   Allan Buckle

Allan Buckle, who had a Grade 10 education, did not hold a licence as a waterworks operator. He was hired by the Walkerton PUC in 1992 as a general labourer. His responsibilities included repairing water leaks, digging post holes, cutting grass, and weeding. Mr. Buckle did not understand the importance of maintaining a 0.5 mg/L chlorine residual after 15 minutes of contact time, nor did he know that it is dangerous to operate a well without chlorination. He did not know what *E. coli* is, and he did not understand that the presence of *E. coli* is an indicator of unsafe water. Nevertheless, Mr. Buckle collected water samples, measured chlorine residuals in the system, and completed the daily operating sheets for the wells. Both Stan and Frank Koebel instructed him to perform these tasks, despite his lack of certification.

Given Mr. Buckle's lack of training and certification, he should not have been involved in operating the PUC water system. Both Stan Koebel as general manager and Frank Koebel as foreman had the responsibility to ensure that only certified employees collected samples, measured the chlorine residuals, and completed the daily operating sheets. Both Stan and Frank Koebel taught Mr. Buckle improper operating practices, including the mislabelling of water samples and the use of inaccurate methods for measuring the chlorine residual levels. Stan and Frank Koebel must bear responsibility for instructing Mr. Buckle to operate the water system and for teaching him improper operating practices.

5.10 Robert McKay

There was no evidence to suggest that Robert McKay engaged in improper practices in the operation of the water system. Mr. McKay began his employment at the PUC in May 1998, after working for approximately nine years at the Norwich and Brighton Public Utilities. He spent most of his time at the Walkerton PUC working on hydro. In early May 2000, Mr. McKay underwent knee surgery; as a result, he was on sick leave from May 9 to June 5, 2000 – a period that encompassed the time of the outbreak.

5.11 Conclusions

Stan and Frank Koebel engaged in a host of improper and unsafe operating practices during the years leading up to the May 2000 tragedy, some of which had a direct impact on the outbreak. The failure to measure daily chlorine residuals at Well 5 on May 13, or on the following days, was a lost opportunity to detect the contamination and to take the necessary steps to protect the community. As I have found in Chapter 4 of this report, although daily chlorine residual monitoring would not have prevented the outbreak, it is very probable that it would have significantly reduced the outbreak's scope.

Stan and Frank Koebel lacked the training and expertise either to identify the vulnerability of Well 5 to surface contamination or to understand the resulting need for continuous monitors. The MOE took no steps to inform them of the requirements for continuous monitoring or to require training that would have addressed the issue.

Finally, Stan Koebel's repeated failure to disclose the adverse results from the May 15 samples to the local health unit and others led to a delay in the issuance of the boil water advisory. If Mr. Koebel had been forthcoming, as he should have been, it is likely that between 300 and 400 illnesses would have been avoided.

Chapter 6 The Role of the Walkerton Public Utilities Commissioners

Contents

Chapter 6   The Role of the Walkerton Public Utilities Commissioners

6.1   Overview

The commissioners of the Walkerton Public Utilities Commission (PUC) were responsible for establishing and controlling the policies under which the PUC operated. The general manager, Stan Koebel, and the staff were responsible for administering these policies in operating the water facility. The commissioners were not aware of the operators' improper chlorination and monitoring practices; nor were they warned about the vulnerability of Well 5 to surface contamination and the resulting need for continuous monitors.

The evidence showed that the commissioners primarily concerned themselves with the financial side of the PUC's operations and had very little knowledge of matters relating to water safety and the operation of the system. They relied almost totally on Stan Koebel in these areas. The commissioners did not set any policies addressing operational issues and did not raise questions with Mr. Koebel, even when it should have been apparent to them that there were serious concerns about water safety and the manner in which Mr. Koebel was operating the waterworks.

In May 1998, the commissioners received the 1998 Ministry of the Environment (MOE) inspection report, which indicated serious problems in the operation of the Walkerton water system. The report stated that *Escherichia coli*, an indicator of "unsafe" drinking water quality, had been present in a significant number of treated water samples. Consequently, the report emphasized the need to maintain an adequate chlorine residual. It also pointed out other significant problems: the operator was not complying with the minimum sampling program, had only recently started to measure chlorine residuals in the distribution system, and was not maintaining proper training records.

The commissioners' response was to do nothing. They did not even ask for any explanation from Mr. Koebel: rather, they accepted his word that he would correct the deficient practices and then left the matter, without ever following up. As it turns out, Mr. Koebel did not maintain adequate chlorine residuals, as he said he would, and did not monitor residuals to ensure that they were adequate. In my view, it was reasonable to expect the commissioners to have done more.

Without excusing the commissioners, it is important to note that, like Stan and Frank Koebel, they did not intend to put the residents of Walkerton at risk. They believed that the water was safe. They were genuinely distraught about the events of May 2000. Moreover, it appears from the PUC records that they performed their duties in much the same way as their predecessors had. That approach seems to have been inherent in the culture at the Walkerton PUC.

Even if the commissioners had done more, it is not clear that Mr. Koebel would have changed the PUC's improper practices. However, if they had done more, it is possible that he would have brought the chlorination and monitoring practices into line, in which case it is very probable the outbreak in May 2000 would have been significantly reduced. Thus, the failure of those who were commissioners in 1998 to properly respond to the MOE inspection report represented a lost opportunity to reduce the scope of the outbreak.

6.2 The History of the Walkerton Public Utilities Commission

The Town of Walkerton and, more recently, the Municipality of Brockton have owned Walkerton's water system since it was constructed. The town operated the waterworks until 1951, when it passed a bylaw, under what is now section 38(1) of the *Public Utilities Act*,[1] to create a public utilities commission. Thereafter, the Walkerton PUC operated the town's water facilities and electricity system.

From the outset, the Walkerton PUC had three commissioners: two were directly elected, and the third, the mayor of the town, served in an *ex officio* capacity. Commissioners were elected for terms of three years, and one of the elected commissioners served as chair. Consistent with the practice throughout Ontario, commissioners were paid a small annual honorarium, which most recently was $2,188 for the chair and $2,000 for each of the other two commissioners. For years, the elected commissioners were acclaimed.

---

[1] Section 38(1) of the *Act* provides: "Subject to subsections (2) to (6), the council of a municipal corporation that owns or operates works for the production, manufacture or supply of any public utility or is about to establish such works, may, by by-law passed with the assent of the municipal electors, provide for entrusting the construction of the works and the control and management of the works to a commission to be called The Public Utilities Commission ..." Subsection (6) provides that upon repeal of the bylaw establishing the commission, the control and management of the works are vested in the municipal council and the commission ceases to exist.

On January 1, 1999, by order of the Minister of Municipal Affairs and Housing, the Town of Walkerton was amalgamated with the adjoining Townships of Brant and Greenock to form the new Municipality of Brockton. As part of the amalgamation, the Walkerton PUC was dissolved and a new public utilities commission (still called the Walkerton Public Utilities Commission) was established. The new PUC continued to treat and distribute water, and to deliver electricity, to the former Town of Walkerton.[2] In addition, it assumed operational responsibility for two smaller water systems in the former Townships of Brant and Greenock: those serving the Geeson and Chepstow subdivisions.

After the November 1998 passage of the *Energy Competition Act* (Bill 35) and the amalgamation, the Municipality of Brockton considered the question of whether the water operations should be transferred to the municipality or an affiliated corporation, or whether they should be left in the PUC. By the time the water supply became contaminated in May 2000, the municipal council had not yet reached a decision. Immediately after the outbreak on May 25, 2000, the Walkerton PUC convened a special meeting and passed a resolution retaining the services of the Ontario Clean Water Agency to operate the water system.

In November 2000, the ownership and control of the PUC's electricity distribution system was transferred to two related companies, Westario Power Inc. and Westario Power Services Inc. On January 8, 2001, the Brockton municipal council passed bylaws effectively dissolving the Walkerton PUC.

6.3 The Legal Status of Public Utilities Commissions

Although municipalities are creatures of the province, public utilities commissions (PUCs) are creatures of municipalities, albeit under provincial legislation. A PUC has all the powers, rights, and privileges conferred on a municipality by the *Public Utilities Act*. It functions as a local or special-purpose board of the municipality. The municipality has the power to dissolve[3] or make prescribed changes to the PUC[4] (e.g., change the composition of the board, remove powers from the PUC, and transfer powers from the PUC to the municipality).

---

[2] The sewage collection and treatment system has been operated by the municipality's public works department throughout; it was never transferred to the PUC.
[3] *Public Utilities Act*, R.S.O. 1990, c. P.52, s. 45.
[4] *Municipal Act*, R.S.O. 1990, c. M. 45, s. 210.4.

A PUC operates under the *Public Utilities Act* as a separate corporation that can enter into agreements, sue, and be sued. It has the power to make decisions concerning its day-to-day management, including obtaining, treating, and distributing water, hiring and firing employees, maintaining equipment, setting rates for the utility, and collecting those rates. Water consumers contract directly with the PUC concerning the provision of water and the rates for its use. The municipality, however, remains responsible for the capital borrowing required for public utility purposes. The municipality also generally has ownership of the assets, including real property, used by the PUC for its operations.

6.4 The Responsibilities of Public Utilities Commissioners

The *Public Utilities Act* provides no express guidance regarding the duties of public utilities commissioners beyond indicating that the constituting bylaw entrusts "the control and management of the works" to the commission.[5] Although there are undoubtedly differences from one community to another, it appears that generally, public utilities commissioners function in a manner similar to that of the directors of a corporation. Typically, they are involved in setting policy and in determining the overall direction of the commission, but they are not directly active in its management. They are responsible for hiring and evaluating senior management, who in turn are responsible for supervising the PUC employees' work performance and ensuring that those employees are properly qualified and trained. Commissioners receive periodic reports from senior management, review and approve budgets, and are advised of significant issues relating to operational matters.

When the commissioners are elected,[6] there is no assurance they will have any knowledge of or experience in water treatment and distribution. The Province does not provide them with training or orientation. There is no requirement that PUC commissioners in Ontario receive training. However, in practice, after taking office, many communities' commissioners receive some orientation from those who are involved in the ongoing management and operation of the system.

Since there is no express direction in the *Public Utilities Act* or elsewhere concerning the roles and responsibilities of public utilities commissioners, I must

---

[5] *Public Utilities Act*, ss. 38(1) and 41(1).
[6] I discuss the role of the mayor, who served as an *ex officio* commissioner, below.

be cautious in making assessments about the roles played by individual commissioners. With this in mind, I approach this analysis by looking only to the
minimum that I consider could reasonably be expected of them by the public
who elected these officials to oversee the operation of the water system.

Commissioners often come to the task with little or no background in operating
a water system and are paid only a small honorarium. They cannot be expected
to spend large amounts of time educating themselves. It is not surprising if
many do not develop a sophisticated understanding of how a system operates;
that is the role of senior management. Nonetheless, commissioners do seek
election to an office that has the ultimate supervisory responsibility for the
safety of water. They should be expected to acquire some knowledge to properly carry out their duties.

The Inquiry heard testimony from an experienced PUC manager, Kent
Edwards, of the Windsor Public Utilities Commission, that the extent to which
commissioners acquaint themselves with the laws, regulations, and guidelines
applicable to the operation and management of waterworks is a matter of individual choice for reasonable, prudent persons. In his view, public utilities commissioners in Ontario are generally concerned with the water being safe, but
they do not have an obligation to be acquainted with the Ontario Drinking
Water Objectives, to know the importance of maintaining an adequate chlorine residual, or to inform themselves of the dangers of unsafe drinking water.
A specific knowledge of particular pathogens such as *E. coli* would not normally be within their area of expertise. The same would hold true for municipal councillors when a municipality operates a water system.

In contrast, a more rigorous role for public utilities commissioners was proposed in a paper presented at an Ontario Municipal Waterworks Association
conference in October 1997. The paper's authors suggest that commissioners
should acquaint themselves with relevant legislation, regulations, guidelines,
and standards, and that they should review and monitor the operations to
ensure compliance with requirements and guidelines. I recognize, however,
that this was only a suggestion by experienced commissioners and that there is
no legislative framework requiring commissioners to do any of these things.

What is expected of public utilities commissioners may vary, depending on the
size and complexity of the water system for which they are responsible. Under
no circumstances, however, can they choose to relinquish their supervisory
role and leave all responsibility to senior management. In my view it is reasonable

to expect, as a minimum, that commissioners absorb enough knowledge, over time, to ask intelligent questions of senior management, to evaluate the performance of senior management, and, if issues of serious concern arise, to inform themselves of what is necessary to address those issues. It is also reasonable to expect more in this regard from a commissioner who has served for a longer period of time or from a commissioner who has been a PUC chair.

In terms of the functions performed by public utilities commissioners, the first is generally to hire competent senior management. Normally, commissioners can rely on certification by the province as a satisfactory indicator of competence. As a minimum, it is reasonable to expect commissioners to receive periodic reports from the senior management, evaluate the performance of senior management, set the overall policy direction for the commission, raise questions about serious water safety issues that come to their attention through management reports or external reports, and satisfy themselves that appropriate steps are being taken to address these issues.

I do not think any of this is particularly onerous. To expect less would render the position of commissioner virtually meaningless, at least as far as water safety is concerned. In the event that commissioners consider they lack the expertise to fulfill this role, it is reasonable to expect they would engage the services of consultants to assist them in the performance of their duties.

The comments I have made have focused on commissioners who are directly elected. Some aspects of the evidence of James Bolden, the former mayor of Walkerton, and David Thomson, Brockton's current mayor, implied that *ex officio* PUC members had different and lesser responsibilities than did those who were directly elected. I note that this position was not maintained in submissions made on their behalf. In my view, a mayor who serves as an *ex officio* commissioner has the same responsibilities as do those directly elected to the office of public utilities commissioner. There is nothing to indicate otherwise in the legislation, the relevant bylaws, or in any other legal authority. I think the public would expect, reasonably, that a mayor serving as an *ex officio* commissioner would perform his or her duties as I have described.

In fact, it would be unworkable if the *ex officio* commissioner were to have any lesser responsibilities than do directly elected commissioners. It would be up to the *ex officio* commissioner to cast the deciding vote in the event the other two commissioners differed on an issue. It would make no sense to have a different standard of responsibility for one of three commissioners.

In the Part 2 report of this Inquiry, I will make extensive recommendations about the governance and operation of municipal water systems. I will include recommendations about the responsibilities of those who perform a role similar to that of public utilities commissioners.

6.5 The Expertise of the Walkerton Public Utilities Commissioners

I heard evidence from the four individuals who at the time of the outbreak had most recently been commissioners of the Walkerton PUC: James Kieffer, whose ten years as a commissioner included eight years as chair of the PUC; James Bolden, who served as Walkerton's mayor and an *ex officio* commissioner for approximately 14 years; Richard Field, who was a PUC commissioner from December 1997 to November 2000; and David Thomson, who became Brockton's mayor and an *ex officio* commissioner in January 1999. Their evidence raises two serious concerns. First, they had a poor understanding of matters that affected the PUC's ability to provide safe drinking water. Second, they relied almost completely on Stan Koebel in matters of water safety and waterworks operation.

6.5.1   The Lack of Knowledge

The public utilities commissioners had little, if any, knowledge about matters relating to water safety and the operation of a waterworks facility. They did not receive any orientation when they were first elected. James Kieffer, a long-time chair of the Walkerton PUC, testified that he received no guidance from anyone when he became a commissioner. "It was an education process from the Chair … and the Mayor … as I worked up through the process." Mr. Kieffer did not read any material or take any courses when he became chair. Similarly, when James Bolden, a former mayor and *ex officio* commissioner, assumed his role as commissioner in 1981, he received no orientation about his duties and responsibilities. He received no books or pamphlets about the PUC and did not view the wells. He just listened, and in this way he said he brought himself up to speed.

The dearth of information to assist PUC commissioners in understanding their responsibilities to oversee the waterworks may have contributed to their failure to take a more active role. But it is also clear that they did not make full use of the resources at their disposal. For example, the Municipal Electric Association's Commissioner and Senior Manager Handbook describes the role of a municipal utility commissioner. It encourages commissioners to acquaint themselves with the legislation under which utilities operate and to learn about the utility's operations from the general manager. The handbook includes a chart reflecting the relationship between commissioners and managers and provides a sample job description for the general manager of a utility. This information is clearly relevant to both electrical and water utilities. Of the two commissioners who received a copy of the handbook, one (Mr. Kieffer) read some of it and the other (Mr. Field) read none at all.

Further, of the four public utilities commissioners who testified at the Inquiry, only Walkerton's former mayor, James Bolden, had read the *Public Utilities Act* and the Ontario Drinking Water Objectives (ODWO). Paradoxically, Mr. Bolden said that he had once read the ODWO but could not recall the contents subsequently. He also did not know what a chlorine residual was, or that *E. coli* could be fatal. Neither Mr. Kieffer, the chair, nor Mr. Field had read the ODWO. They did not know what a chlorine residual was, and did not know what *E. coli* was. Neither of them was aware that Ontario Regulation 435/93 requires waterworks employees to take a minimum of 40 hours' training annually, even though this requirement had been raised in both the 1996 and 1998 inspection reports. Mr. Kieffer was the only witness who was asked about his knowledge of the Chlorination Bulletin and turbidity. He had not read the bulletin and did not know what turbidity was. Mayor Thomson had not read the ODWO and did not know that *E. coli* could be harmful in water.

In Chapter 9, I deal with the approval of Well 5, a vulnerable source that at the time of its approval was seen as a temporary solution to Walkerton's water supply problems. There, I make the point that both the PUC and the MOE lost sight of the fact that Well 5 was intended to be a temporary solution. In addition, I find that by the 1990s, the PUC commissioners were unaware of Well 5's vulnerability to surface contamination.

When he began his initial term as mayor and public utilities commissioner, Mr. Bolden understood that Well 5 would be used only for a short time. He was surprised to learn that it was still in use in 1989, when he began his second term as mayor. Mr. Bolden came to understand that it would not be used in the late fall, winter, and early spring. He testified that the potential for Well 5 to be contaminated was never discussed at a PUC meeting. Only after the events of May 2000 did he become aware that the water drawn from that well was susceptible to surface contamination due to the shallow overburden. Similarly, when asked what knowledge he had of Well 5 being susceptible to contamination, Mr. Kieffer replied he had "absolutely none."

This evidence is inconsistent with the fact that Mr. Kieffer and Mr. Bolden reviewed the 1992 needs study conducted by B.M. Ross and Associates Ltd., which refers to Well 5 as "the second primary supply well" and as "a shallow drilled well [that] may be susceptible to contamination from surface activities due to shallow overburden protecting the aquifer." At the time of its completion, the needs study was presented to the commissioners, including Mr. Bolden and Mr. Kieffer. However, it appears that if they had read the study, they did not absorb the information about Well 5.

Mr. Thomson, who possessed very little knowledge of the Walkerton water system before becoming Brockton's mayor, came to know that Well 5 was drilled into bedrock, but he did not know that it was a shallow well until after the outbreak.

6.5.2 The Reliance on Stan Koebel

The Walkerton public utilities commissioners took a very narrow view of their role, which they saw as almost exclusively limited to budgeting and financial aspects of the operation. The minutes of the commissioners' meetings for the decade leading up to the tragedy reflect that limited focus. Richard Field told the Inquiry that he understood his role to consist of attending meetings, reviewing the minutes of previous meetings, and looking after the PUC's finances.

Mr. Kieffer testified that although the public utilities commissioners relied on Stan Koebel to inform them of any major concerns, Mr. Koebel never identified a problem that had to be addressed. During his decade-long tenure as a commissioner, Mr. Kieffer could only recall two occasions – after the PUC's receipt of the reports of the MOE inspections carried out in 1995 and 1998 – when water quality was discussed. Even then, Mr. Kieffer did not ask Mr. Koebel any questions about the quality of the water being provided to the people of Walkerton. Mr. Thomson testified that he did not ask to see adverse sample results but expected Stan Koebel to advise him of them. There was no policy requiring Mr. Koebel to report on any particular matters, including adverse quality reports. As it turns out, he did not report adverse results to the commissioners. In short, with two exceptions, the commissioners did not discuss water quality issues with Mr. Koebel.

The commissioners also failed to formally review or evaluate Mr. Koebel's performance as the PUC's general manager. There was no job description, no process for a periodic evaluation, and no performance criteria. The PUC did retain outside engineering consultants from time to time to assist with the construction and replacement of watermains. However, those consultants were never asked to do an evaluation of either the operating systems or the operators, and then report directly to the commissioners. Stan Koebel was the sole contact between the PUC and its consultants.

The needs study that was completed in 1992 focused on the water distribution system and, especially, on developing a long-term watermain rehabilitation program. Given that purpose, it is not surprising that the study did not involve an evaluation of the PUC's operating procedures. In fact, the study's only reference to system operation was a summary description of the town's supply wells and standpipes.

The commissioners' failure to ask questions and exercise some oversight of the operation of the system is significant in the case of their reaction to one document in particular: the 1998 MOE inspection report.

6.6 The 1998 Ministry of the Environment Inspection Report

The MOE's 1998 inspection report, together with Philip Bye's covering letter of May 6, 1998, was circulated to public utilities commissioners and tabled at a PUC meeting on May 20, 1998. The commissioners at the time were James Kieffer, Richard Field, and Mayor James Bolden.

The inspection report raised significant issues about water quality that were serious enough to alert even an uninformed reader about problems with the operation of the system. The report disclosed repeated indicators of unsafe water quality, a need to ensure that a minimum chlorine residual was maintained, inadequate records of operator training, and the fact that the operators continued to take an insufficient number of water samples. The last two problems had been identified in the previous MOE report, two years earlier, which had been provided to Mr. Kieffer, at least. (Mr. Bolden denied receiving it, and

Mr. Field was not a commissioner in 1996.) Mr. Bye's covering letter for the 1998 report emphasized the seriousness of the situation.

The minutes of the May 20, 1998, commissioners' meeting reflect Stan Koebel's assurance that three items raised in the report had been addressed. They contain no discussion, however, of the repeated indications of unsafe drinking water. When asked about the 1998 report's references to the presence of *E. coli* and unsafe drinking water quality, Mr. Kieffer said Mr. Koebel had not suggested that there was a major problem and that the commissioners relied on Mr. Koebel to alert them to major concerns. Mr. Bolden testified that *E. coli* gave him cause for concern, but the commissioners were told that the "chlorine concentration ... would look after the situation." Mr. Bolden did not recall asking Mr. Koebel any questions about *E. coli* when the report was discussed at the meeting, nor does he recall any discussion on the subject between Mr. Koebel and any of the other commissioners. This is consistent with Stan Koebel's testimony that there was no discussion about the presence of *E. coli* in the water. Mr. Bolden testified he could not recall the subject ever coming up at another commissioners' meeting.

The commissioners did not inquire about the circumstances that gave rise to the concerns in the report. It appears that Mr. Koebel assured the commissioners that he would comply with each of the items identified for action in the inspection report. The commissioners accepted Mr. Koebel's response and never followed up to determine whether he was in fact doing what he said he would. Included in Mr. Koebel's response was the assurance that the PUC would maintain a minimum total chlorine residual of 0.5 mg/L. The operators did not maintain a residual at that level of course; nor did they monitor chlorine residuals on a daily basis – a practice that is necessary to maintain the adequate residual.

I am satisfied that the concerns raised in the 1998 MOE inspection report about the water system's operation were such that the commissioners should have taken steps to ensure that those concerns were addressed. It was not sufficient to simply rely on Mr. Koebel, whose management of the operation was shown to be lacking. If the commissioners felt ill-equipped to address these matters themselves, they should have sought the assistance of someone independent of Mr. Koebel who had the necessary expertise.

I recognize that eight months later, Mr. Koebel presented the commissioners (who by then no longer included Mr. Bolden) with a letter from the MOE indicating that there had been noticeable improvement in the operation of the

PUC. That letter, however, does not excuse the commissioners' failure to respond in a proactive manner when the inspection report was received, and in the months following.

6.7 Portraits of the Commissioners

6.7.1 James Kieffer

Mr. Kieffer was a public utilities commissioner for ten years and the chair of the Walkerton PUC for eight years. He was acclaimed in each election. He has lived in Walkerton all his life and operates a number of businesses, including an agency for the Ministry of Transportation that deals with driver and vehicle licences. He is involved in several voluntary organizations and has a history of public service.

During the time that Mr. Kieffer was a commissioner, he learned very little about water treatment and water safety issues. He attended one conference jointly presented by the Ontario Municipal Waterworks Association and the American Water Works Association's Ontario Section, but does not appear to have benefited, at least in terms of informing himself about water safety issues. Like the other commissioners, he relied entirely on Stan Koebel in this critical area.

In my view, the people of Walkerton were entitled to expect more. The consequences of Mr. Kieffer's lack of knowledge and his total reliance on Stan Koebel were most apparent when the 1998 inspection report was received. Mr. Kieffer said he read that report either before or after the May 20, 1998, meeting. At the time, he was unfamiliar with the ODWO, the Chlorination Bulletin, the significance of *E. coli*, and the nature of a chlorine residual. He did not ask any questions about the report. Rather, he relied on Stan Koebel to tell the commissioners about any concerns, and Mr. Koebel did not express any concerns about the safety of water.

6.7.2 Richard Field

Richard Field was first elected by acclamation as a commissioner in 1997, and he was acclaimed to serve in that office again after the amalgamation in January 1999. He has lived in Walkerton since 1975. He owned and operated an appliance store in town from 1975 to 1990 and was active in a number of community organizations. He served as a volunteer firefighter for ten years.

Like Mr. Kieffer, Mr. Field had virtually no knowledge of matters relating to water treatment and water safety. He too relied almost totally on Mr. Koebel in this area. He did not read the ODWO or the utility commissioners' and senior managers' handbook published by the Municipal Electrical Association. He did not know what chlorine residuals or *E. coli* were. He also did not know that training requirements existed for waterworks operators.

Although the fact that Mr. Field was a commissioner for a relatively short time might provide some explanation for his lack of knowledge, it does not explain why he did not read the 1998 MOE inspection report or Mr. Bye's covering letter. He did not ask any questions when that report was presented at the meeting of May 20, 1998, and he, like the other commissioners, did not take any steps to ensure that Mr. Koebel followed up on the concerns raised in the report.

I am satisfied that Mr. Field should have done more to fulfill his role in overseeing the safety of the water, particularly in responding to the MOE's 1998 inspection report.

6.7.3   James Bolden

James Bolden is a former mayor of Walkerton. He was born and raised in Walkerton and worked for Canada Post for 33 years, until 1994. He served on town council from 1972 to 1976 and as reeve from 1977 to 1980. From 1980 to 1984, and again from 1988 until the amalgamation in 1998, he was the mayor of Walkerton. As mayor, he was an *ex officio* commissioner of the PUC.

Mr. Bolden's level of knowledge and his approach to his responsibilities as a commissioner in relation to the operation and safety of waterworks were essentially the same as those of Mr. Kieffer and Mr. Field. After serving for approximately 14 years as a commissioner, he had almost no knowledge of water safety issues and relied entirely on Stan Koebel in this critical area.

Mr. Bolden was a commissioner in May 1998, when the MOE's 1998 inspection report was tabled. He said he found the report's warnings about water quality disturbing but believed that chlorine solved problems relating to the presence of *E. coli*. However, Mr. Bolden did not inquire into why the chlorine had not worked on the occasions when *E. coli* was detected in the treated water, why the operators had not been monitoring chlorine residuals in the distribution system until recently, and why the other deficiencies noted in the inspection report were occurring. Like the other commissioners, he did nothing to follow up and ensure that Mr. Koebel took the required corrective action.

I am satisfied that the people of Walkerton had a right to expect more of Mr. Bolden, particularly in relation to the 1998 inspection report. He, like Mr. Kieffer and Mr. Field, did not respond adequately to that report.

6.7.4   David Thomson

David Thomson became Brockton's first mayor when the municipal amalgamation took effect on January 1, 1999. He became an *ex officio* commissioner of the Walkerton PUC and held that office at the time of the outbreak in May 2000. Mayor Thomson has had a long career in elected office, dating back to 1966. He grew up on a farm in the former Township of Brant, near Walkerton, and took over the family farm in 1953. He now operates a beef cattle farm with three of his sons. Mayor Thomson understood that, as an *ex officio* commissioner, his role extended beyond financial issues to include responsibilities for protecting the health of local residents. Like the other commissioners, he had little knowledge of the way in which the water treatment facility was operated or of matters relating to water safety. He too relied very heavily on Stan Koebel.

Mayor Thomson was not a commissioner when the MOE's 1998 inspection report was presented to commissioners. After becoming a commissioner, he did not ask to see it. Mayor Thomson was a commissioner for only a short period of time, which gives some explanation for his lack of knowledge and his reliance on Mr. Koebel.

Mayor Thomson should, however, have taken more steps to inform himself about the nature of the operation, especially water safety issues, for which he had responsibility. That said, nothing happened during his tenure that should have alerted him to the operating problems of the waterworks. Moreover, I note that shortly after he became a commissioner, Stan Koebel tabled the letter of January 15, 1999, from Donald Hamilton of the MOE, which said that there had been a noticeable improvement in the performance of the Walkerton PUC.

6.8 Conclusion

The commissioners of the Walkerton PUC had little knowledge of drinking water safety and the operation of a waterworks facility. They relied almost entirely on Stan Koebel. Their shortcomings were most prominent at the time they received the 1998 MOE inspection report. The three commissioners at the time should have done more to inquire into the problems identified and to satisfy themselves that those problems were addressed. If they had succeeded in having Stan Koebel correct the improper chlorination and monitoring practices, while it is by no means a certainty, it is very likely that the scope of the outbreak would have been significantly reduced.

Chapter 7   The Roles of the Municipalities and Mayors

Contents

Chapter 7   The Roles of the Municipalities and Mayors

7.1 Overview

In this section, I consider the role of the Town of Walkerton, the Municipality of Brockton (Walkerton's successor), and two of the mayors of those municipalities in the events of May 2000. The municipalities' roles were limited, given that at the relevant times the water system was operated by a public utilities commission. I focus on three occasions following which, it has been suggested, the municipality should have taken steps in relation to the drinking water system but did not do so: the November 1978 meeting at which Ministry of the Environment (MOE) representatives suggested land use controls for the area surrounding Well 5; the receipt of the 1998 MOE inspection report; and the issuance of the boil water advisory in the early afternoon of May 21, 2000.

I conclude that at the relevant times the Town of Walkerton did not have the legal means to control land use in the vicinity of Well 5. Further, the discussion in 1978 about controlling land use revolved primarily around the former Pletsch farm. In fact, however, the bacterial contamination of the Walkerton water system originated elsewhere.

Given that the control and management of the waterworks were vested in the Walkerton Public Utilities Commission (PUC), the Walkerton town council's response to the 1998 inspection report was not unreasonable. The council was entitled to rely on the public utilities commissioners to follow up on the deficiencies identified in the report.

Brockton's mayor, David Thomson, was in an ideal position to assist the Bruce-Grey-Owen Sound Health Unit in disseminating the boil water advisory on May 21 and May 22. Even though the mayor knew that the people of Walkerton were becoming ill, he did not offer to help inform them about the boil water advisory. But Dr. McQuigge did not request any assistance. Although others in Mayor Thomson's position might have done so, I am not satisfied that the he should be faulted for having failed to offer assistance.

Further, I conclude that it was not unreasonable for Mayor Thomson and other members of Brockton's municipal council to refrain from invoking the Brockton Emergency Plan. Due consideration was given to taking this extraordinary step. The primary benefit of invoking the plan would have been to assist in publicizing the boil water advisory. By the time the municipal council was considering whether the plan should be invoked, the existence of the boil water advisory was already well known within the community.

7.2 The Town of Walkerton's Failure to Control Land Use in the Vicinity of Well 5

Control of land use in the vicinity of Well 5 is also addressed in Section 9.2 of this report. In order to minimize the repetition of facts relating to this issue, I will refer here only to those facts that are essential in understanding the Town of Walkerton's role in this respect.

Walkerton's mayor at the time (an *ex officio* commissioner of the Walkerton PUC) attended the November 23, 1978, meeting at which the MOE's representatives recommended that "consideration should be given to controlling activities in areas adjacent to the new well which may contribute to aquifer contamination." The meeting's minutes show that the then mayor, Neil MacDonald, stated that "Mr. [Percy] Pletsch would probably be very hesitant to sell the farm to the PUC." Nonetheless, the PUC commissioners agreed that Mr. Pletsch "should be approached in order that the potential effects on the new well supply of land use activities on the Pletsch farm could be fully discussed."

Elsewhere I conclude that the commissioners' agreement cannot be characterized as an implied condition attaching to the Certificate of Approval issued to the Walkerton PUC in relation to Well 5. I now consider whether the Town of Walkerton can be faulted for not acting on the MOE representatives' recommendation.

Basic to this consideration is the fact that the Town of Walkerton lacked the legal power to control land use on the Pletsch property. Although Well 5 was in Walkerton, the Pletsch farm, only a few metres away, was in Brant Township. The Town of Walkerton lacked the power to control activities in another municipality.

Municipalities generally have the power to expropriate property for purposes related to making, maintaining, and protecting utility works. This power is apparently not limited to property within the geographical boundaries of the expropriating municipality. However, as long as the control and management of the waterworks were entrusted to the Walkerton PUC, the PUC – not the municipality – was empowered to expropriate property in order to preserve the purity of the water supply.

Finally, it must be noted that the Pletsch farm was the only specific property on which land use might have been controlled that was referred to by the participants at the meeting of November 1978. There does not appear to have been any discussion about controlling land use on the farm of Dr. David Biesenthal or about other possible sources where the *Escherichia coli* and *Campylobacter jejuni* bacteria that contaminated Walkerton's water system might have originated.

Given all of this, I conclude that the failure of the Town of Walkerton and its officials to act on the MOE representatives' recommendation to control land use activities on the Pletsch farm is not reasonably connected to the outbreak in May 2000.

7.3 The Town of Walkerton's Response to the 1998 Ministry of the Environment Inspection Report

As is discussed in Section 9.3 of this report, the 1998 MOE inspection report raised troubling issues concerning the operation of Walkerton's waterworks. Chief among them was the presence of *E. coli* – an indicator of unsafe drinking water quality – in treated water samples. As a consequence, the report's author, Michelle Zillinger, emphasized the need to maintain an adequate chlorine residual. The report alluded to other problems, including the failure to comply with the minimum sampling program under the Ontario Drinking Water Objectives.

A copy of the report was sent to Walkerton's clerk-treasurer, Richard Radford, and the report was placed on the agenda for the town council meeting of June 8, 1998, as an information item. At that meeting, Mary Robinson-Ramsay, a municipal councillor, expressed her concern about the PUC's non-compliance and the detection of *E. coli* bacteria. From her standpoint, the solution to these problems was to provide what she termed "regular and on-going technical expertise." She identified the options of either retaining a consulting engineer to take supervisory responsibility or hiring a municipal director of public works (either for the new municipality that was to come into existence on January 1, 1999, or to be shared with another municipality). But there was very little reaction to the points she raised, except for the idea of passing a resolution concerning the role of the MOE. Ms. Robinson-Ramsay concluded that the options she had identified were not pursued because the council only had six months left in its mandate.

The council meeting minutes reflect the following under the heading, "Information":

> Min. of Environment — *Status Report* — *Walkerton Waterworks* — Council debated this report and supported a motion being brought forward to request MOEE controls on water quality be left in place on a province wide basis. Councillor Ramsay and the CAO[1] will work on this motion for presentation at a future meeting.

When the motion was brought before the council on June 15, 1998, it was for a resolution that council "urge the Government of Ontario to maintain the Ministry of the Energy and the Environment [*sic*], as the guardian of water quality, ensuring basic, healthy water standards for all Ontarians." As a result, a letter was written by the town's chief administrative officer to the Premier of Ontario. The Premier responded and thanked Mr. Radford for informing him of the council's resolution. As reflected by the minutes, although the report was debated, the action taken by the town council did not directly address the serious deficiencies identified in the report.

Under section 41(1) of the *Public Utilities Act*, where a PUC has been created, the commission – and not the municipality – possesses all the powers, rights, authorities, and privileges that the statute would otherwise confer on the municipality.[2] This provision restricted the ability of the municipal council to address the problems identified in the 1998 inspection report.

In view of that fact, the question arises whether the Walkerton town council had a duty to act upon its receipt of the report. Normally, it would be sufficient for the council to satisfy itself that the PUC commissioners were aware of the situation and were taking what the commissioners considered to be appropriate steps to respond. The town council was entitled to rely upon the mayor, an *ex officio* PUC commissioner, to bring any problems to their attention. As he put it in his testimony, Mayor James Bolden was a PUC commissioner who

---

[1] In addition to being the clerk-treasurer, Mr. Radford was the chief administrative officer.
[2] *Public Utilities Act*, R.S.O. 1990, c. P 52, s. 41(1).

was "to represent town council on the commission." Unfortunately, Mayor Bolden failed to follow up in order to ensure that the report's most troubling findings were being properly addressed, and he did not bring any concerns about the PUC's response to the inspection report to the attention of the town council.

In reaching the conclusion that subsection 41(1) of the *Public Utilities Act* limited the municipal council's ability to respond to the report, I have considered whether the ability to dissolve the PUC created a duty on the council to act in the circumstances. It is true that although day-to-day PUC operations are not the concern of municipal councils, the decision to retain a PUC is. In that sense, Ms. Robinson-Ramsay was undoubtedly right when she recorded in notes she made in preparation for the June 8, 1998, town council meeting that in relation to the oversight of the PUC, "ultimately the municipality is responsible." It is also true that as of 1998, municipal councils had been empowered to dissolve public utilities commissions without the necessity of holding a plebiscite. But that did not alter the PUC's legal status, as discussed in Chapter 6 of this report. Had the legislature intended to alter the principle that a PUC exercises all the powers, rights, and privileges conferred on a municipality under the *Public Utilities Act*, it would have amended section 41(1) of the statute. It did not, and the fact remains that the town council's authority in relation to the PUC was limited to the rather stark extremes of either dissolving the PUC or permitting it to remain in existence and assuming virtually no role in its daily operations.

I want to commend Ms. Robinson-Ramsay for the diligence with which she strove to bring the report's troubling findings to the attention of other members of Walkerton's town council.

7.4 Mayor Thomson's Initial Response to the Boil Water Advisory

Brockton's mayor, and by extension, the municipality, did not take an active role when the outbreak first came to light. At approximately noon on May 21, 2000, Dr. Murray McQuigge, the local Medical Officer of Health, telephoned Mayor David Thomson at his home. Mayor Thomson disputed Dr. McQuigge's testimony that he told the mayor that the situation was serious and that people could die. However, Mayor Thomson agreed that in their brief conversation, Dr. McQuigge informed him that people in Walkerton were becoming ill. It was Mayor Thomson's evidence that Dr. McQuigge did not mention *E. coli*, nor did Dr. McQuigge describe the symptoms to him.

The evidence of the mayor and Dr. McQuigge conflicted as to whether they spoke again on May 21. Testifying with the benefit of notes made at the time, Dr. McQuigge maintained that there was a single telephone call, placed by him to the mayor, at approximately noon. Mayor Thomson testified that Dr. McQuigge again telephoned him at approximately 1:30 p.m., about 90 minutes after the first call. Mayor Thomson recalled that in this conversation, Dr. McQuigge advised the mayor that he was issuing a boil water advisory as a precautionary measure and that it would be announced by radio. Mayor Thomson recalled Dr. McQuigge saying that he did not want to "set off any alarm bells."

Dr. McQuigge did not seek Mayor Thomson's assistance in publicizing the boil water advisory, nor did the mayor offer any. As Mayor Thomson put it in his testimony: "[T]hat wasn't a consideration because I felt Dr. McQuigge was looking after it and he was the person who had the authority to do that."

It is difficult to determine what actually passed between the mayor and Dr. McQuigge. It is clear, however, that by 1:30 p.m. on May 21, the mayor was aware that people were becoming ill, that a boil water advisory had been issued, and that information about it was being disseminated only on radio.

Moreover, there were indications that Dr. McQuigge considered the situation to be serious. The mayor was unaware of any other instance in which the Medical Officer of Health had telephoned him on a holiday weekend. He knew that Dr. McQuigge had returned to Owen Sound from his cottage because Walkerton residents were becoming ill. Mayor Thomson agreed that the issuance of the boil water advisory was an unusual event – one that would be unsettling for Walkerton residents.

After his telephone call from Dr. McQuigge, Mayor Thomson did nothing about the crisis for two days. He did not call emergency meetings of the municipal council or the PUC. He did not ask if he could help Dr. McQuigge. In fact, the council meeting of May 23 was convened at Dr. McQuigge's instance. For the balance of May 21 and on May 22, Mayor Thomson did not even telephone Stan Koebel, although it should be noted that Mr. Koebel's evidence was that the mayor called him the morning of May 21 and that he called the mayor later that same afternoon. Nor did Mayor Thomson contact the police or the fire department, both of which might have been helpful in disseminating word of the boil water advisory. He did not contact anyone about Walkerton's drinking water following the issuance of the boil water advisory. Mayor Thomson explained his inaction by saying, "I felt that if there was a water problem, I likely would have heard from somebody on the Commission or somebody that was in charge or Dr. McQuigge." Unfortunately, many people in Walkerton did not become aware of the boil water advisory on May 21.

The question arises whether the mayor should have done more to help publicize the boil water advisory. He was certainly in a better position than Dr. McQuigge to assess the best means for publicizing the advisory and to implement any needed steps. However, Dr. McQuigge was in charge and he did not ask Mayor Thomson to do anything. Dr. McQuigge possesses a commanding personality; as his own counsel put it, he is "no shrinking violet." As a consequence, I hesitate to criticize the mayor for his inaction in a situation in which Dr. McQuigge had authority and did not request assistance. Dr. McQuigge issued the advisory and had the primary responsibility to publish it so as to protect the health of the community. Although others in the mayor's position may at least have offered assistance, I am not able to conclude that Mayor Thomson should be faulted for his inaction.

7.5   The Failure to Invoke the Brockton Emergency Plan

During the crisis of May 2000, the Municipality of Brockton did not invoke the Brockton Emergency Plan, which had been approved in a bylaw passed less than seven months earlier on December 13, 1999. Municipal emergency plans are contemplated by the *Emergency Plans Act*, which enables municipalities to pass bylaws empowering the "head of council" (in Brockton's case, Mayor Thomson or his designee) to declare a state of emergency and to act as necessary to protect the health, safety, and welfare of their residents. One of the express aims of the comprehensive Brockton Emergency Plan was to ensure that prompt factual information was provided to all relevant officials, the news media, and concerned individuals.

The plan imposed specific duties on Mayor Thomson, including determining whether an emergency existed, calling a special council meeting so that a resolution could be passed, and, if an emergency were found to exist, notifying the Solicitor General of Ontario through Emergency Measures Ontario. If an emergency were declared, the mayor was also under a duty to approve news releases and public announcements.

Dr. McQuigge thought that the emergency plan should have been invoked. It was his evidence that he expected this to occur after his telephone call to Mr. Thomson on May 21, 2000, in which he informed the mayor that the situation was serious. A staff member of the Bruce-Grey-Owen Sound Health Unit even contacted Emergency Measures Ontario on May 25 to inquire as to why it had not been invoked. In Dr. McQuigge's view, invoking the emergency plan would have helped communicate information about the outbreak. Although Dr. McQuigge could have requested that the emergency plan be invoked, he made no such request of Mayor Thomson and, as I said above, did not ask for help in publishing the boil water advisory.

At its meetings on May 23 and 24, 2000, Brockton municipal council discussed but decided against invoking the municipality's emergency plan. It is safe to conclude that by then nearly everyone in the community would have known of the boil water advisory. When asked to explain the rationale for not invoking the plan, Mayor Thomson said, "[W]e felt that we brought an engineer [Steve Burns] in, we were bringing all the experts in, we felt we had it under control ..." Furthermore, the municipality's discussions with Emergency Measures Ontario did not disclose any benefit to invoking the plan. Subsequently, Mayor Thomson was advised that this view was shared both by counsel in the Ministry of the Solicitor General's legal services branch and by Dr. James Young, who, in addition to being Chief Coroner of Ontario, is the assistant deputy solicitor general in charge of public safety.

Mayor Thomson and other members of Brockton's municipal council were under no duty to invoke the plan. Instead, their duty was to consider whether to do so. On the evidence, I am satisfied that they met this duty. Further, it has not been shown that invoking the plan would have achieved any benefit in managing the crisis. In practical terms, the potential benefit of invoking the emergency plan, insofar as limiting the outbreak, would have been to assist in publicizing the boil water advisory. However, as I have noted above, by the time the municipal council was convened and had considered the issue, the existence of the boil water advisory was well known. Finally, given that no request was made to Mayor Thomson by Dr. McQuigge on May 21 for assistance in publicizing the boil water advisory, I conclude that the mayor and municipal council should not be faulted for not considering the issue until May 23.

Chapter 8   The Role of the Public Health Authorities

Contents

Chapter 8   The Role of the Public Health Authorities

8.1 Introduction

In this section I consider the role of the Bruce-Grey-Owen Sound Health Unit in relation to the events in Walkerton in three separate contexts: its role in overseeing the quality of drinking water at Walkerton over the years leading up to May 2000, its reaction to the privatization of laboratory testing services in 1996, and its response to the outbreak in May 2000.

In the normal course of events, the health unit exercised its oversight role by receiving notice of reports of adverse water quality and Ministry of the Environment (MOE) inspection reports and responding when necessary. It would have been preferable for the health unit to have taken a more active role in responding to the many adverse water quality reports it received from Walkerton between 1995 and 1998, and also to the 1998 MOE inspection report. During the mid- to late 1990s, there were indications that the water quality in Walkerton was deteriorating.

On receiving adverse water quality reports, the local public health inspector in Walkerton would normally contact the Walkerton Public Utilities Commission (PUC) to ensure that follow-up samples were taken and that chlorine residuals were maintained. Instead, when he received the 1998 MOE inspection report, he read and filed it, assuming that the MOE would ensure that the problems identified were properly addressed. Given that there was no written protocol instructing the local public health inspector on how to respond to adverse water reports or inspection reports, I am satisfied that he did all that was expected of him.[1]

Even if the health unit had responded more actively when concerns arose about the water quality in Walkerton in the mid- to late 1990s, it is unlikely that such responses would have had any impact on the events of May 2000. The actions required to address the concerns were essentially operational in nature. The MOE was the government regulator responsible for overseeing Walkerton's waterworks. After the 1998 inspection report, the MOE directed the PUC to

---

[1] It would have been preferable for the Ministry of Health and the Bruce-Grey-Owen Sound Health Unit to provided clear direction to health unit staff on how to respond to adverse water quality reports and MOE inspection reports. I will be making recommendations in the Part 2 report of this Inquiry to clarify the respective roles of the local health unit and the MOE in overseeing municipal water systems.

remedy a number of operational deficiencies, but then failed to follow up to ensure that the proper steps were taken. I am satisfied that it was appropriate for the health unit to rely on the MOE to oversee operations at the Walkerton PUC and to follow up on the 1998 inspection report.

After laboratory testing services were assumed by the private sector in 1996, the health unit sought assurance from the MOE's Owen Sound office that the health unit would continue to be notified of all adverse water quality results relating to communal water systems. It received that assurance, both in correspondence and at a meeting. I am satisfied that the health unit did what was reasonable in reacting to the privatization of lab services.

The health unit was first notified of the outbreak in Walkerton on Friday, May 19, 2000. It issued a boil water advisory two days later. In the interval, its staff investigated the outbreak diligently. There were several reasons why the health unit did not immediately conclude that the water was the source of problem. Initially, a food-borne source was the prime suspect. However, because water was a possibility, the health unit staff contacted the PUC's general manager, Stan Koebel, twice on May 19 and twice again on May 20. Health unit staff were given information that led them to believe the water was safe. They had no reason not to accept what Stan Koebel told them. His assurances led the health unit's investigation away from concluding that water was the source of the problem.

Moreover, the symptoms being reported were consistent with *Escherichia coli* O157:H7 – sometimes called "the hamburger disease" – which is most often communicated through food, not water. The health unit was not aware of any reported *E. coli* outbreak that had ever been linked to a treated water system in North America.

In my view, the health unit should not be faulted for failing to issue the boil water advisory before May 21.

I recognize that others in the community suspected that the water was the source of the contamination and took steps to avoid infection. They are to be commended for their actions. However, issuing a boil water advisory is a significant step, requiring a careful balancing of a number of factors. Precaution and the protection of public health must always be paramount; however, unwarranted boil water advisories have social and economic consequences and, most importantly, have a potential to undermine the future credibility of the health unit issuing such an advisory. I am satisfied that the health unit was appropriately prudent and balanced in the manner in which it investigated the outbreak and decided to issue the boil water advisory.

In this respect, I do not think that the health unit's failure to review its Walkerton water file between May 19 and May 21 made any difference. The most recent relevant evidence of water quality problems in that file was more than two years old. I accept the evidence of Dr. Murray McQuigge and others that at that point, more timely information about water quality was needed. The health unit sought that information and was assured by Stan Koebel that all was well.

The health unit disseminated the boil water advisory to the community by having it broadcast on local AM and FM radio stations. It also contacted several public institutions directly. Evidence showed that some people did not become aware of the boil water advisory on May 21. In his evidence, Dr. McQuigge acknowledged that if he faced a similar situation again, he would use local television stations and have pamphlets distributed informing residents of the boil water advisory. That would have been a better approach, because the boil water advisory should have been more broadly publicized.[2]

8.2 The Public Health Branch

The Public Health Branch is part of the Ministry of Health and Long-Term Care. The Director of the Public Health Branch is also the Chief Medical Officer of Health of Ontario.[3]

The role of the Public Health Branch is:

- to manage funding for public health programs;

- to provide the Minister of Health with advice pertaining to public health; and

- to provide advice and assistance to local health units.

---

[2] There were no written protocols or guidelines from the Public Health Branch of the Ministry of Health about ways of disseminating boil water advisories. I am making specific recommendations for a protocol for issuing boil water advisories in the Part 2 report of this Inquiry.
[3] This has been a combined position since 1987.

Dr. Richard Schabas, the former Chief Medical Officer of Health of Ontario, regarded the third element above as being the most important because it entails the Public Health Branch acting as a central resource for the public health system and as a principal adviser and director for local health units.

In this age of new and emerging pathogens, the Public Health Branch has a great deal to offer to health units, particularly smaller ones, which may not have the special expertise and resources to deal with these issues. In the case of Walkerton, the local Medical Officer of Health contacted and received assistance from the Public Health Branch from the onset of the outbreak.

8.3 Boards of Health and Health Units

Boards of health are established as corporations without share capital under the *Health Protection and Promotion Act*. Under the Act, a board of health must be established for every "health unit" in the province.[4] A health unit is an official health agency established by a group of municipalities to provide community health programs. Health units are funded by the province and the local municipalities on a cost-sharing basis. They are administered by the local Medical Officer of Health, who reports to the board of health.

Boards of health are composed of elected local representatives and provincial appointees. Every board of health is required to ensure that certain mandatory public health programs and services are provided in accordance with minimum provincial standards.[5] Boards of health are expected to deliver additional programs and services in response to local needs.

8.4 The Medical Officer of Health

The office of the local Medical Officer of Health is established by the *Health Protection and Promotion Act*. The appointment of the Medical Officer of Health

---

[4] A health unit is defined under the legislation as the area of jurisdiction of a board of health. The term "health unit" is commonly used to describe the agency and is used interchangeably with the term "board of health." Nothing turns on this. In most instances, I use the term used in the evidence – "health unit" – to describe the agency.

[5] These programs and services are described in the "Mandatory Health Programs and Services Guidelines," issued by the Ministry of Health's Public Health Branch in December 1997. These guidelines present minimum standards for programs and services.

must be approved by the Minister of Health. The appointment is made by Order-in-Council.

The Medical Officer of Health reports directly to the board of health on issues relating to public health concerns and to the delivery and management of public health programs and services under the Act. The employees of the health unit are subject to the direction of, and are responsible to, the Medical Officer of Health in respect of their duties that relate to the delivery of public health programs or services under the legislation. The Medical Officer of Health is given powers of entry to premises, as well as powers to make orders directing persons to perform certain actions or restraining them from doing so.

The independence of the Medical Officer of Health from local political pressures is an essential component of the public health system. Although the Medical Officer of Health must be accountable to the board of health, which is composed of local politicians, he or she must be equipped to make difficult decisions that may not be popular with these politicians. To preserve his or her independence, a Medical Officer of Health can be dismissed only with the written consent of two-thirds of the members of the board of health, as well as that of the Minister of Health.

The existing legislative scheme that requires every board of health to appoint a full-time Medical Officer of Health is a provision that enhances the security and independence of the office.

8.5 Mandatory Programs and Services

The Province sets minimum standards for programs delivered by health units.[6] Standards for individual programs outline the minimum requirements to be met in order for each program to contribute to provincial goals for public health. The standards are divided into three general areas: chronic diseases and injuries, family health, and infectious diseases.

For the purposes of drinking water, two individual programs in the area of infectious diseases are important. The first is the Control of Infectious Disease Program, the purpose of which is "to reduce the incidence of infectious diseases

---

[6] The standards are set out under the "Mandatory Health Programs and Services Guidelines," ibid.

of public health importance." Both *E. coli* O157:H7 and *Campylobacter* are reportable diseases under this program.

The second important program is the Safe Water Program, the purpose of which is to reduce the incidence of water-borne illness. One of its objectives is to ensure that community water systems meet the health-related goals of the Ontario Drinking Water Objectives (ODWO) and the Canadian Drinking Water Quality Guidelines. In terms of the relevant standard, the Safe Water Program requires health units to: maintain an ongoing list of all drinking water systems, receive reports of adverse drinking water test results from those systems, have a written protocol for dealing with adverse results, and "act immediately" in accordance with the ODWO "to protect the health of the public whenever an adverse drinking water result is received."[7]

8.6 The Bruce-Grey-Owen Sound Health Unit

8.6.1 Background

The Owen Sound Health Unit was established in 1911, the Bruce County Health Unit in 1946, and the Grey County Health Unit in 1963. Owen Sound and Grey County amalgamated their health units in 1967. In 1989, these health units were amalgamated to form the Bruce-Grey-Owen Sound Health Unit,[8] which serves a population of more than 150,000 people.

Dr. Murray McQuigge was appointed as the Medical Officer of Health for the Bruce-Grey-Owen Sound Health Unit in 1990. In May 2000, the director of health protection was Clayton Wardell. The health unit had three assistant

---

[7] This standard was issued in 1997. Under the 1989 standard, the health unit was required to "*monitor* the quality of drinking water" rather than to "receive all reports of adverse drinking water test results" (emphasis added). The significance of the change from "monitoring" to "receive all reports" was canvassed in the evidence. Some witnesses testified that the change in language did not substantively change the role of the health unit; others said it did.

It is important that the role and responsibilities of the health unit be clarified, and I will be making recommendations to that effect. However, in my view, the change in the 1997 guidelines did not play a part in the manner in which the Bruce-Grey-Owen Sound Health Unit exercised its oversight role of Walkerton.

[8] The Bruce-Grey-Owen Sound Health Unit board of health has twelve members: four municipally elected members from the County of Bruce, four municipally elected members from Grey County, two elected members from the City of Owen Sound, and two provincial government appointees.

directors: David Patterson, Jim Paton, and Sue Askin.[9] It employed 108 active staff in four offices: Owen Sound (the head office), Walkerton, Southampton (a branch office), and Durham (a branch office). Walkerton, the second-largest office, employs between 15 and 20 staff. In 1999, the health unit's annual budget was $5,632,000.[10]

8.6.2   The Medical Officer of Health

Dr. McQuigge was responsible for the overall administration of the health unit, including its budget. He had a reporting responsibility to the board of health that included providing sufficient information to ensure that the board was able to carry out its tasks and make informed decisions. He attended all meetings of the board and its committees and submitted regular and special reports as required.

Dr. McQuigge had reporting responsibilities to the Ministry of Health's Public Health Branch. He was required to keep the ministry informed of the health unit's delivery of programs.

Dr. McQuigge was also required to promote the coordination of community health services. This involved regular contact with, and education of, relevant groups and individuals in the community.

Dr. McQuigge acted as a medical adviser to staff on program service delivery and advised health workers about mandatory reportable diseases. He was also required to ensure that adequate emergency plans were in place in both the health unit and the community to deal with outbreaks of disease and other public health emergencies.

---

[9] In May 2000, Mr. Patterson was responsible for the Control of Infectious Disease Program. Previously, he had been responsible for the Safe Water Program. In July 1999, responsibility for the Safe Water Program was transferred to Mr. Paton. When the events in Walkerton occurred in May 2000, Mr. Patterson was filling in for Mr. Paton, who was on vacation.

[10] Of this amount, the Province and the municipalities each provided 37.1% of the funding. An additional 13.5% came from the Province for 100% funded provincial programs. 12.3% of the funding came from other sources.

8.7 Overseeing the Safety of Drinking Water

8.7.1 Procedures and Policies

The health unit exercised its oversight role for communal water systems as it applied to the quality of the water provided to the public "when the water comes out of the tap." It was the responsibility of the MOE to monitor communal systems to ensure that the infrastructure and operational procedures of a water facility were sufficient to deliver safe water. Drawing the line between the jurisdiction of the MOE and that of the health unit is not always easy.

The health unit's role with respect to municipal water systems was limited. The MOE exercised the lead oversight role for the construction and operation of municipal water systems, as well as for the certification and training of water operators. As a result, the amount of time spent on municipal water systems by the health unit was minimal. For example, in 1999, only 0.17% of all of the time spent by the infectious disease group on the Safe Water Program was directed to municipal water systems.[11]

In May 2000, the health unit had a public health inspection policy and procedure manual. One of the goals was to ensure that water provided for human consumption was "potable." The manual lists certain activities to be carried out in fulfilling this goal, including "monitoring"[12] the quality of drinking water from public and designated private water supplies; providing advice and information on the treatment of water supplies and the health effects associated with those supplies; and interpreting water analysis reports for the public. With respect to the monitoring role, the manual provides that for public water supplies, it may be sufficient to review the operator's or MOE's records if adequate samples are being taken.

On the whole, the health unit did not have extensive procedures and policies for overseeing municipal water systems. Virtually no guidance was provided to public health inspectors about how to respond to adverse water quality reports or to MOE inspection reports. However, the evidence is also clear that the

---

[11] In total, 1.2 out of 10.5 full-time equivalent employees in the infectious disease group (11.19%) were committed to the Safe Water Program. Of this time devoted to the Safe Water Program by the infectious disease group, only 1.54% was related to municipal water systems.

[12] "Monitoring" for the purpose of this policy means reviewing bacterial and/or chemical sample results and other relevant information pertaining to a water supply. Sampling by health unit personnel should not be assumed.

Public Health Branch provided little, if any, guidance to local health units on the development of protocols relating to a health unit's role in overseeing municipal water systems.

8.7.2 The Receipt of Adverse Results

Upon receiving adverse water quality reports, the practice of the health unit office in Walkerton was to contact the PUC and ensure that a follow-up sample was taken and that the proper corrective action was pursued if warranted. The health unit dealt with adverse results on an individual basis and did not review the trends indicated by results over time. Before the privatization of laboratory testing services in 1996, the health unit received all test reports – positive and negative – and would have been in a position to assess overall trends if it chose to do so. After privatization, however, the health unit received only reports of unsafe water quality; monitoring trends would have been more difficult for them.

In any event, the health unit did not, either before or after 1996, view the monitoring of water quality trends as one of its functions; if anything, it relied on the MOE to do that. I am satisfied that a properly structured program overseeing the potability of drinking water should have regard for more than just the most recent test results. Putting specific results in a broader context would be the preferred approach.

However, I note that there is no guideline from the Public Health Branch of the Ministry of Health directing a health unit to do this. The 1989 guidelines directed health units to "monitor" the quality of the water, but provided no further guidance as to the nature of monitoring. The word "monitoring" was dropped from the 1997 guidelines.

Moreover, the resources available to the Bruce-Grey-Owen Sound Health Unit were under pressure in recent years, and it was unlikely that a public health inspector would have enough time to review trends. In the circumstances, I do not think that the way in which the health unit responded to adverse quality reports in Walkerton was unreasonable.

In any event, even if the public health inspector had reviewed Walkerton's water test results to look for trends, it is unlikely that there would have been an impact on the events of May 2000. At most, concerns about deteriorating water quality would have led to a discussion involving the PUC and the MOE about the operational procedures necessary to safeguard the water. The health unit could be expected to emphasize to the PUC and the MOE the increasingly frequent adverse results, the need for adequate treatment, the need to take the appropriate corrective action, and the importance of informing the health unit of ongoing problems. The MOE was largely aware of these matters. The responses that were necessary were essentially operational. It was up to the MOE – not the health unit – to determine what steps needed to be taken regarding treatment and monitoring, and to ensure that they were implemented. I address the MOE's role in the next chapter.

I am satisfied that clear, province-wide guidelines should be issued by the Public Health Branch, directing local health units how to address adverse quality reports. This guideline should specify the nature and extent of any response and should contain clear directions about the respective roles of the MOE and health units. I set out my recommendations at the end of this chapter.

8.7.3   The Receipt of Ministry of the Environment Inspection Reports

In a meeting held on May 2, 1997, between the health unit and the MOE's Owen Sound office, Philip Bye, the area supervisor for the MOE, encouraged the health inspectors to read inspection reports. He said that all municipal supplies would be inspected by March 31, 1998, and that detailed reports would be forwarded to the health unit.

Dr. McQuigge received a copy of the 1998 inspection report relating to Walkerton from the MOE.[13] As was his normal practice, he did not read the report and had his secretary forward it to the Health Protection Department. David Patterson testified that he scanned the covering letter but did not read the contents of the report. The clerical staff forwarded the inspection report to James Schmidt, the public health inspector responsible for Walkerton, who testified that he read it but took no further action.

That report indicated that there were a number of occasions on which E. coli had been detected in the treated water and distribution system, and it identified several operating deficiencies at the Walkerton PUC. Some parties suggested

---

[13] I will address only the 1998 report, since it was the most proximate to the May 2000 events and since it dealt with the most serious issues of water quality.

to the Inquiry that Mr. Schmidt should have been more concerned with the safety of the water at Walkerton – that he should have looked into the matters raised in the report and taken steps to ensure that the actions required by the report were in fact implemented by the PUC. I think that would be expecting too much of Mr. Schmidt, for two reasons.

First, there were no guidelines from the Public Health Branch to the health units that set out the steps to be followed on the receipt of an MOE inspection report. As a result, there were no guidelines from the health unit to the public health inspectors regarding what should be done with a report of this nature. Second, the MOE was responsible for following up on the report. The MOE was the lead ministry, the inspection was an MOE inspection, and the concerns raised in the report – while clearly relating to water quality – required corrective actions that were operational in nature.

The actions required of the PUC by the MOE in the 1998 inspection report were a reasonable response to the problems identified. If they had not been a reasonable response, then perhaps the health unit should have become more involved. Following the inspection, difficulties at Walkerton arose because the Walkerton PUC did not do what it was reasonably directed to do by the MOE in the inspection report. It would not have made sense for the health unit to have duplicated the MOE's efforts in ensuring that an operator complies with the actions required by the MOE. If the MOE is satisfied, then it seems reasonable that a health unit should also be satisfied that the appropriate actions have been followed.

The inspection report directed the operators to maintain a chlorine residual of 0.5 mg/L after 15 minutes of contact time. That was the proper way to address concerns about water quality. The MOE should have ensured from an operational standpoint that this was done. Similarly, it should have ensured the proper monitoring of chlorine residuals: either manually, or by way of installing the appropriate monitoring equipment.

In my view, the local public health inspector should have discussed with the MOE and the PUC operator the significance of the adverse water quality results disclosed in the 1998 inspection report.[14] However, I do not think

---

[14] Also, the public health inspector probably should have noted that he had not received all of the adverse water quality reports shown in the inspection report; he then should have taken steps to ensure that he received the reports in the future. However, even if he had done so and had raised that with the MOE, I do not think there would have been any effect on the events of May 2000.

that in this case it would have mattered. The inspection report identified the seriousness of the situation. The required responses were operational in nature. The MOE had already correctly identified those responses and, as I conclude in Section 9.3, should have conducted a follow-up inspection to ensure the PUC did what it was directed to do. The health unit was entitled to rely on the MOE to do that. The failure to act was the MOE's, not the health unit's.

The manner in which a health unit should respond to an MOE inspection report was another area of uncertainty in the public health system. As I have said before, there was no centralized guideline or protocol. Dr. Colin D'Cunha, the current Chief Medical Officer of Health, testified that if he had read the 1998 inspection report relating to Walkerton, he would have followed up with some action.

Dr. Alexander Hukowich, the Medical Officer of Health for the Haliburton, Kawartha and Pine Ridge District Health Unit, testified that in the year 2000, he developed a template to be used by public health inspectors upon the receipt of an MOE inspection report. The inspectors were asked to complete the template after reviewing the report and meeting with the operator. The Medical Officer of Health was to be advised of anything that he or she should be made aware of. I believe that this is a useful initiative by Dr. Hukowich.

However, Dr. McQuigge and others did not follow the practice described by Dr. Hukowich. That speaks to the uncertainty and the lack of uniform or helpful guidance from the Public Health Branch.

At the end of this chapter, I have included my recommendation for a province-wide direction relating to the receipt of inspection reports.

8.7.4   The Discontinuation of Public Laboratory Testing

In 1996, the Government of Ontario discontinued the provision of laboratory testing services for municipal treated water systems. Municipalities like Walkerton were thereafter required to use private sector laboratories.

The government did not enact a regulation mandating private laboratories to notify the MOE and the local Medical Officer of Health about any adverse water quality results. Concerns were raised by a number of public health authorities about the reliability of the process then in place. The Bruce-Grey-Owen Sound Health Unit raised the issue with the MOE district office and received assurances that the notification process would be followed and that the health unit would be notified of adverse results.

I am satisfied that the health unit acted appropriately. The failure here rests with the government for not enacting a legally binding regulation mandating that the proper authorities be notified of adverse results as part of the implementation of its decision to discontinue routine testing by provincial laboratories.

There was a good working relationship between the MOE's Owen Sound office and the Bruce-Grey-Owen Sound Health Unit. Although there were no formalized meetings or communications between them, there were a number of ad hoc meetings to deal with particular issues as they arose.

The health unit's Water Quality Committee met on September 12, 1996. The minutes of that meeting indicate a concern about the transfer of water testing from the Ministry of Health to the private sector. They also indicate that the health unit had earlier notified Willard Page, the district supervisor in the MOE's Owen Sound office, in a letter dated August 30, 1996, of its concerns about the discontinuation of testing by the government laboratories. The minutes state: "It is an MOEE responsibility to set up a suitable protocol. They are aware of our concerns through correspondence from Dave Patterson and the Public Health Lab. The Municipality is ultimately responsible to ensure delivery of potable water."

In a responding letter to Mr. Patterson dated October 24, 1996, Mr. Page stated that MOE staff would report all adverse results received to the health unit. In a memo to all public health inspectors dated November 22, 1996, Mr. Patterson expressed concerns about the transition of the laboratory work: "This transition has been poorly handled. Much confusion has been caused by stakeholders taking contradictory positions. The Public Health Laboratory has continued service to save jobs." Mr. Patterson testified that the transition occurred rapidly and that it did not appear to have been coordinated.

A significant meeting was held on May 2, 1997, at the request of the health unit, concerning the discontinuation of routine analytical testing by government laboratories. The notice of the meeting set out the agenda, which included the ODWO, private laboratory analysis procedures, and notification of adverse results.

At this meeting, Philip Bye, at that time the new supervisor of the MOE's office in Owen Sound, expressed three concerns with the existing arrangements in light of the discontinuation of government testing. First, he felt that the notification requirement should have the force of a regulation. Second, he felt that the ODWO should be changed to provide that the private laboratory be required to immediately notify the health unit of an adverse result, and to provide for an opportunity for discussion between the health unit and the MOE regarding the operational aspects of the system. Third, he was concerned about the absence of a dedicated inspection program in respect of private communal water systems. Mr. Bye also indicated that the ODWO was being revised in the near future to require the operating authority to contact the health unit directly. This differed from what the ODWO then required – that the laboratory notify the MOE District Officer, who in turn would notify the Medical Officer of Health and the operating authority. The ODWO was never revised as Mr. Bye suggested.

At the meeting, Mr. Bye also stated that the MOE staff would contact all major municipal waterworks operators to confirm that they were carrying out the required bacteriological sampling program, to confirm that they were aware of the current notification requirements, and to determine which laboratory they were using for water sampling. With the information obtained, the MOE prepared and circulated a list of municipalities not conforming to the minimum sampling program.[15]

In my view, the health unit acted appropriately in responding to the privatization of laboratory services. It sought and received assurances from the MOE that notification of adverse results would take place. It was entitled to rely on those assurances. As I conclude in Chapter 10, when laboratory testing services were privatized, the provincial government should have enacted a regulation requiring mandatory notification.

---

[15] It is not clear whether and to what extent the MOE confirmed that municipal waterworks operators were aware of the current notification requirements, or whether the MOE determined which laboratories were being used by various municipalities.

8.8 The Boil Water Advisory

8.8.1 Boil Water Advisories Generally

Section 4.1.3 of the ODWO provides that the Medical Officer of Health can issue advice in the form of a boil water advisory where the circumstances warrant. Furthermore, section 13 of the *Health Protection and Promotion Act* provides the Medical Officer of Health or a public health inspector with the legislative authority to issue boil water orders.[16]

There is a distinction between a boil water order and a boil water advisory. A boil water advisory – a term used in the ODWO – is issued by health units to advise consumers not to drink water. A boil water order is more appropriate for directing operators of food premises, and water producers or distributors, to boil water before providing it to consumers.

The Bruce-Grey-Owen Sound Health Unit's public health inspection policy and procedure manual contains a procedure for dealing with boil water advisories. Procedure IV-50 provides that the presence of total coliform organisms in a treated water supply may indicate inadequate treatment, or contamination, in the distribution system. The procedure requires the investigation of the water supply for chlorine residuals and the collection of additional samples. The MOE must be informed of any boil water advisory issued in respect of any system under its jurisdiction. The procedure also provides that with regard to a treated supply, the advisory can be lifted if a satisfactory residual is present and one satisfactory sample has been received. The unapproved revision of this procedure of April 2000 did not change the procedure.

The Public Health Branch of the Ministry of Health did not provide local health units with a boil water advisory protocol. Dr. Colin D'Cunha testified that such a protocol was not developed because it was felt that the ODWO and the exercise of professional judgment by the Medical Officer of Health or a public health inspector addressed the issue. However, such a protocol is now being developed; clearly it is necessary.

---

[16] *Health Protection and Promotion Act*, R.S.O. 1990, c. H-7, s. 13.

8.8.2 The Timeliness of the Boil Water Advisory

The Bruce-Grey-Owen Sound Health Unit was first notified of the outbreak in Walkerton on May 19, 2000. It issued a boil water advisory two days later, at approximately 1:30 p.m. on May 21. In the interval, it actively pursued an investigation to determine the source of the illnesses that were being reported. Some parties to the Inquiry argued that the health unit should have issued the boil water advisory sooner. I am satisfied that the health unit acted responsibly and should not be faulted for the timing of the issuance of the advisory.

Issuing a boil water advisory involves exercising a good deal of judgment. Important information received by the health unit during its investigation pointed away from water as being the source of the illnesses in Walkerton. Shortly after it began the investigation, on the afternoon of May 19, the health unit twice contacted the PUC's general manager, Stan Koebel, and was assured there was no problem with the water. It spoke to Mr. Koebel twice again on May 20 and received further information indicating that the water was safe. The health unit had no reason not to accept what Mr. Koebel told it.

Moreover, the symptoms being reported by those who had become ill were consistent with *E. coli* O157:H7 (sometimes called the "hamburger disease"), which is typically associated with food sources, not water. Importantly, the local Medical Officer of Health, Dr. Murray McQuigge, was not aware at that time of any reported *E. coli* outbreak that had ever been linked to a treated water system in North America. For those who were considering the possibility of *E. coli* contamination, water was low on the list of suspects. Moreover, there were reports of illnesses outside of Walkerton. This also tended to point away from water as the source of the problem.

In addition, Stan Koebel told the health unit that starting on the evening of May 19, he would flush and chlorinate the water system as a precaution. On May 20, the health unit was advised that there were chlorine residuals in the distribution system. This provided some comfort that the water, at least by then, was not contaminated.

From the outset, the health unit actively pursued various potential sources for the outbreak. It followed all leads. There is no question that the health unit staff worked diligently throughout the weekend and in the days that followed. There was no lack of effort on their part to investigate the outbreak and to safeguard the health of the community.

With one exception, which I mention below, the health unit took the proper steps in communicating with hospitals, health care officials, the PUC, and others in the community.

Those who argue that a boil water advisory should have been issued earlier point to a number of factors. They say that some people in the community suspected the water. Dr. Kristen Hallett did, as did the Brucelea Haven long-term care facility. Brucelea Haven took protective action. The pattern of ill-nesses among the young and old pointed away from a common food source and supported the conclusion that water was the problem. There were rumours in Walkerton that water was the source, and some of these rumours were passed on to the health unit.

All of this is, of course, correct. These factors supported the notion that water may have been the problem. However, in response, the health unit took the logical step of investigating the water. Health unit staff contacted the operator of the water system to determine whether there had been any recent events related to water safety. Had the health unit's questions to the PUC been answered in a straightforward manner, a boil water advisory would have been issued on May 19. It is not reasonable to expect the health unit to immediately have gone behind the answers it received from the Walkerton PUC. Unfortu-nately, for a time, those answers tended to steer the health unit away from concluding that water was the source of the outbreak.

There was some suggestion that the failure of the health unit staff to review the Walkerton water file on May 19 contributed to a delay in issuing the boil water advisory. In particular, it has been suggested that if the file had been reviewed on that date, a boil water advisory would have been issued earlier than May 21. As a result, the argument goes, the impact of the outbreak would have been lessened.

Several witnesses agreed that if the cause of the outbreak was water-related, information from the previous week or two would be most relevant. The infor-mation in the water file was dated: the May 1998 inspection report was the most recent relevant information. That information was of limited assistance in view of the information received from the PUC that there were no recent problems with the drinking water. Even if the health unit had referred to the file, I am satisfied that it would not have done anything differently, in view of the assurances it received from Stan Koebel.

One further aspect of the health unit's response requires comment. Before the boil water advisory was issued, representatives of the health unit advised members of the public that it was safe to drink the water because of the assurances given by the PUC. Mr. Patterson also encouraged Stan Koebel on May 20 to contact a local radio station and inform its listeners that the water was safe; Mr. Koebel did not do so. In giving the advice to the public about the safety of the water, the health unit representatives relied upon the PUC assurances and the belief that if the source of the contamination was water, the bacteria would no longer be in the distribution system, given the incubation period for bacteria. They also relied on the fact that the system was being flushed and chlorinated. As well, the health unit staff continued to believe that because E. coli O157:H7 is essentially a food-borne disease, the likelihood that the illness was transmitted through a treated water system was low.

In my view, the health unit staff should have advised the public of the precise situation as it existed at that time: the source of the outbreak was still unknown, water had not been ruled out as a factor, and the investigation was continuing. Even though the PUC was obtaining positive chlorine residuals from the distribution system, it was nonetheless possible that contamination could have been found in the system's dead ends. Some people, armed with this knowledge, may have elected to continue drinking the water; others would have decided not to.

In summary, I am satisfied that the health unit should not be faulted for failing to issue the boil water advisory before May 21 at 1:30 p.m.

8.8.3 The Dissemination of the Boil Water Advisory

It would have been preferable if the boil water advisory had been disseminated more broadly on May 21. The advisory was broadcast on the local AM and FM radio stations, CKNX and CFOS. In the past, the health unit had used radio effectively to convey information about infectious diseases. The health unit did not contact either CBC Radio or the television stations because it did not think they would be as effective in disseminating this type of information in a rural community such as Walkerton. Also, the health unit had not used these media in the past to disseminate such information. Although faxes containing notices of the boil water advisory were sent to the newspapers on May 21, because this was a long weekend, local newspapers could not publish this information until May 23. Further, the health unit did not distribute pamphlets or handbills to the residents of Walkerton to alert the citizens to the measures they should take.

The health unit staff notified area institutions of the boil water advisory on May 21. Hospitals in Bruce and Grey Counties and area physicians were informed of the advisory on the same day, as was the MOE. However, because of the oversight of a staff member, Maple Court Villa and Brucelea Haven were not notified until May 23. Fortunately, both Brucelea Haven and Maple Court Villa had taken steps to ensure that these facilities' residents did not drink water from the Walkerton system. The Walkerton Jail was not directly notified and only came to learn of the boil water advisory on May 22. That was unfortunate. On May 21, Dr. McQuigge informed the mayor of Brockton and the directors of education for both area school boards of the advisory. The Minister of Health and the Chief Medical Officer of Health of Ontario were also notified on May 21. The local health unit also communicated with area physicians and hospitals concerning treatment.

After May 21, a number of steps were taken by the health unit to disseminate the boil water advisory. Background information and notices were sent to area hospitals, physicians, laboratories, and food establishments. Meetings were held with local hospitals and physicians. Media releases, interviews, and press conferences were provided regularly. Information was posted on the health unit's Web site to inform the public of the latest developments. As well, informal communications with the appropriate authorities continued through the crisis.

At the Inquiry, Mr. Patterson and Dr. McQuigge testified that if they faced a similar situation again, they would use the local television stations to inform the residents about the boil water advisory. Dr. McQuigge also confirmed that it would have been a good idea to have had pamphlets delivered door-to-door. That would have been a better approach, because the boil water advisory should have been more broadly publicized. I note that at the time, there was no protocol from the Public Health Branch addressing the manner for disseminating boil water advisories; I am recommending that there should be such a protocol.

After the outbreak, Dr. Andrea Ellis, the Health Canada epidemiologist who assisted the health unit, investigated the effectiveness of the boil water advisory. Questions were asked about when and how people heard about it. Of the residents using Walkerton water, 56% had heard about the boil water advisory on May 21, 18% had heard about it on May 22, and 8% had been informed of it on May 23. Interestingly, 17% claimed to have heard about it before

May 21. In addition to the survey evidence, the Inquiry heard direct evidence from Walkerton residents that they had not heard about the advisory on the day it was issued, May 21.

From Dr. Ellis's investigation, it is apparent that the boil water advisory was very effective in influencing people's behaviour. The respondents to the Health Canada survey stated that, after learning of the advisory, they used an alternative source of water 94% of the time for drinking water, 91% of the time for mixing other drinks, 82% of the time for brushing their teeth, and 86% of the time for washing fruit and vegetables; and that they followed the recommendations for the use of chlorinated water for hand washing 82% of the time. Dr. Ellis commented that the level of compliance observed in Walkerton appeared to be much higher than in previously reported studies.

In summary, it would have been better if the health unit had disseminated its boil water advisory more broadly on May 21. I recommend that a protocol for boil water advisories be developed.

8.9 Recommendations

The following recommendations relate to the roles of the local Medical Officers of Health as they apply to communal water systems. I will deal with this topic more extensively in the Part 2 report of this Inquiry.

I recommend the following:

Recommendation 1: The *Health Protection and Promotion Act* should be amended to require boards of health and the Minister of Health, acting in concert, to expeditiously fill any vacant Medical Officer of Health position with a full-time Medical Officer of Health.

Recommendation 2: Random assessment should be conducted on a regular basis by the Minister of Health, or his or her delegate, pursuant to the *Health Protection and Promotion Act*, of public health boards in Ontario to ensure their compliance with the Mandatory Health Programs and Services Guidelines of the Public Health Branch. Further, the Public Health Branch or the Minister of Health's delegate should continue to track, on an annual basis, trends in non-compliance by public health boards in Ontario, in order to assess whether altered programs and services guidelines are required and whether resourcing allocations by the Province of Ontario require adjustment to ensure full compliance.

Recommendation 3: The role of the local Medical Officers of Health and health units in relation to public health issues concerning treated and untreated municipal water systems should be clarified and strengthened. In particular, clarification is required as to whether local Medical Officers of Health are required to implement a proactive approach to responding to adverse drinking water sample test results upon receiving notification of these results.

Recommendation 4: Written guidance – developed in cooperation with local Medical Officers of Health and the MOE – should be provided to local Medical Officers of Health by the Public Health Branch. It should include steps to be taken by Medical Officers of Health upon receipt of MOE inspection reports and adverse drinking water sample test results.

Recommendation 5: Regular meetings should be scheduled between the local MOE office and local health unit personnel to discuss public health issues, including issues related to waterworks facilities as documented in MOE inspection reports. Any affected operator or laboratory should be invited to attend the meeting.

Recommendation 6: Upon the implementation by the MOE of the Integrated Divisional System (management information system), access to it should be made available to local health units and, where appropriate, to the public. This should include access to profiles of municipal water systems and to data concerning adverse drinking water quality sample test results, as included in that database.

Recommendation 7: The Public Health Branch should develop a Boil Water Protocol – a written protocol outlining the circumstances in which a boil water advisory or a boil water order could and should be issued. I will be commenting on the government's current draft proposal in the Part 2 report.

Recommendation 8: The Boil Water Protocol should be developed by the Public Health Branch in consultation with Medical Officers of Health, municipalities, and the MOE. The Boil Water Protocol should provide guidance concerning an effective communications strategy for the dissemination of a boil water advisory or order.

Chapter 9   The Role of the Ministry of the Environment

Contents

Chapter 9   The Role of the Ministry of the Environment

9.1   Introduction

9.1.1   Overview

In this section I will address the role of the Ministry of the Environment (MOE) in relation to the events of May 2000.[1] The MOE was and continues to be the provincial government ministry with the primary responsibility for regulating – and for enforcing legislation, regulations, and policies that apply to – the construction and operation of communal water systems.

Before addressing the MOE's role in detail, I want to repeat a point I made in Chapter 5 of this report. Stan Koebel and the others at the Walkerton Public Utilities Commission (PUC) are responsible for their own actions and for the consequences of those actions. Failures by the MOE in overseeing the operation of the Walkerton water system do not excuse those actions, nor do they lessen the responsibilities of the individuals involved. But given that the MOE was responsible for overseeing the construction and operation of the Walkerton water facility, its activities must also be considered in order to determine if it adequately fulfilled its role and, if not, whether a proper exercise of its responsibility would have prevented the outbreak, reduced its scope, or reduced the risk that the outbreak would occur.

At the Inquiry, the government argued that I should find that Stan Koebel was the sole cause of the tragedy in Walkerton and that I should also find that government failures, if any, played no role – the suggestion being that if it were not for Stan Koebel's failures, the tragedy would not have happened. I reject that argument completely. It totally misconceives the role of the MOE as overseer of communal water systems, a role that is intended to include ensuring that water operators and facilities perform satisfactorily. When there is a failure in the operation of a water facility, as there was in Walkerton, the question arises whether the MOE in its role as overseer should have prevented the failure or minimized the risk that it would occur. If the answer is yes, I am satisfied that the Inquiry's mandate directs me to report on any deficiencies in the manner in which the MOE exercised its oversight role.

---

[1] In this chapter, I do not address the issues of the privatization of water testing and the notification procedures to be followed when adverse test results are found. I discuss those issues in Chapter 10 of this report.

The government's argument also ignores the fact that the only thing that could have completely prevented the outbreak in Walkerton was the use of continuous chlorine residual and turbidity monitors at Well 5. The failure to use continuous monitors at Well 5 resulted from shortcomings of the MOE in fulfilling its regulatory and oversight role, not from failures of the Walkerton PUC operators. The MOE knew (or should have known) that the PUC operators lacked the training and expertise necessary to identify the vulnerability of Well 5 to surface contamination and to understand the resulting need for continuous monitors.

In Chapter 5 of this report I identified two serious problems in the operation of the Walkerton water system that contributed to the tragedy in May 2000.

The first problem was the failure to install continuous chlorine residual and turbidity monitors at Well 5. As a result of an amendment to the Ontario Drinking Water Objectives (ODWO) in 1994, continuous monitors were required for water systems that operated without filtration and were supplied by groundwater sources under the direct influence of surface water.[2] Well 5 was such a system, but continuous monitors were not installed. Continuous monitors would have prevented the outbreak.

The second serious problem with the operation of Walkerton's water system was the improper chlorination and monitoring practices of the Walkerton PUC. The PUC's personnel routinely failed to maintain the required minimum total chlorine residual of 0.5 mg/L after 15 minutes of contact time, failed to monitor chlorine residuals daily, and made false entries in the PUC's daily operating sheets. It is very likely that proper chlorine residual monitoring on a daily basis would have significantly reduced the outbreak's scope, although it would not have prevented the outbreak.

I have concluded that the MOE failed in several respects to fulfill its oversight role in relation to Walkerton's water system. Some MOE programs or policies were deficient because they should have identified and addressed one or both of the two operational problems at Walkerton referred to above, but did not do so. Other programs or policies were deficient because they reduced the likelihood that the two problems would be identified and addressed. In summary, the deficiencies are as follows:

---

[2] The phrase "under the direct influence of surface water" appears in the ODWO. Throughout this report, in my discussion of Well 5 I use the phrase interchangeably with "vulnerable to surface (water) contamination."

- After the 1994 amendment to the ODWO, the approvals program should have identified Well 5 as a water system supplied by a groundwater source that was under the direct influence of surface water and therefore should have required the installation of continuous monitors. The approvals program should also have attached a condition to Well 5's Certificate of Approval mandating the PUC to maintain a minimum total chlorine residual of 0.5 mg/L after 15 minutes of contact time.

- The inspections program should have detected the vulnerability of Well 5 to surface contamination and noted the need for continuous monitoring. It should also have detected the improper chlorination and monitoring practices of the Walkerton PUC and ensured that the PUC took the necessary steps to correct the practices.

- After the 1998 inspection, the MOE should have issued a Director's Order to compel the Walkerton PUC to comply with MOE water treatment and monitoring requirements.

- The MOE did not have an information system that made critical information about the history of vulnerable water sources, like Well 5, accessible to those responsible for ensuring that the proper treatment and monitoring were taking place.

- The MOE's training requirements for water operators (e.g., Stan Koebel and Frank Koebel) should have been more focused on drinking water safety issues and more strictly enforced.

- In recent years, a serious decline occurred in the training made available to MOE employees. Some of those with responsibility for overseeing Walkerton's water system did not fully understand the requirements of the ODWO or that Escherichia coli (E. coli) could be lethal.

- The MOE used guidelines rather than legally enforceable regulations in setting out the standards and procedures to be followed in ensuring the safety of drinking water.

I have used the word "deficiencies" to describe the problems I identify in the MOE because they all fall into the category of omissions or failures to take appropriate action, rather than positive acts. As a result, the effects of those deficiencies on the events in Walkerton must be measured by their failure to prevent the outbreak, to reduce its scope, or to reduce the risk that the outbreak would occur. Viewed in this light, some of the deficiencies are more closely connected to the tragedy than are others. In the sections where I discuss each of the deficiencies separately, I will set out my conclusions on the effect, if any, of each deficiency on the events of May 2000.

In measuring the effects of the MOE deficiencies on the events of May 2000, it is necessary in some instances to assess whether the Walkerton PUC or Stan Koebel would have acted differently if the treatment and monitoring requirements[3] had been legal obligations – for instance, a regulation, a condition in a Certificate of Approval, or a Director's Order – rather than a legally unenforceable guideline. There is no certainty, of course, about how the PUC would have reacted in such circumstances. However, on balance, I conclude that with proper oversight and enforcement, it is likely that the PUC would have treated and monitored the water as required. It is possible that the fact of a legal requirement would in itself have been sufficient to compel compliance. Assuming, however, that this was not the case, then a proper inspections program would probably have detected the improper practices (at this point, breaches of legal requirements) and ensured that proper treatment and monitoring took place.

It is worth noting that since the Walkerton tragedy, the government has recognized that improvements were needed in virtually all of the areas where I identify deficiencies and has taken steps to strengthen the MOE's regulatory or oversight role.

9.1.2   The Oversight Role of the Ministry

The MOE sets the standards according to which communal water systems are built and operated. It also approves the construction of new water facilities, certifies water plant operators, and oversees the treatment, distribution, and monitoring practices of communal water facilities. The overall objective is to

---

[3] Although the requirements were established by guideline and thus were not, strictly speaking, legally required, I refer to the maintenance of a minimum total chlorine residual of 0.5 mg/L after 15 minutes of contact time and the monitoring of chlorine residuals as "treatment and monitoring requirements" throughout this report, in view of their necessity for the safe operation of a water system relying on disinfection through chlorination.

ensure that water systems are built and operated in a manner that produces safe water and does not threaten public health.[4]

Many of the deficiencies I identify are, in part, a reflection of the general level of comfort among MOE personnel regarding the safety of treated water in systems operated by municipal authorities. Before the year 2000, Ontario had experienced relatively few instances in which contamination of municipally operated treated drinking water systems had led to a publicly reported outbreak, although in recent years there had apparently been an increase.[5] During the years immediately preceding the Walkerton outbreak, an attitude developed within the MOE that municipalities, as the owners of Ontario's water systems, should bear more of the responsibility for the safety of the water and that the MOE, as overseer, should assume a lesser role.

For years there had been a culture within the MOE of working cooperatively with municipalities and trusting the municipalities to do what was expected of them. Budget and resource reductions in the 1990s significantly increased the pressures to limit MOE activities and to prioritize workloads differently. Overseeing communal water systems became less of a priority.

By way of example, in 1995, in anticipation of budget cutbacks, MOE managers across the province were asked to identify non-core programs. They viewed communal water as one of the few non-core MOE programs. As well, the MOE's priorities policies, developed after 1995, viewed the ministry's role in relation to communal water systems as being an advisory role: the municipality was considered responsible for delivering safe water, and the local Medical Officer of Health was considered responsible for determining when water was unsafe.

It clearly makes sense for the MOE to cooperate with municipalities and to rely on them to do those things that are expected of them, but in my view the MOE went too far in this direction. This was particularly so for small municipalities, like Walkerton, where the operators were less likely to be sophisticated

---

[4] As an example, an MOE document titled "Approval Process and Drinking Water Sampling and Monitoring" (June 1996) provided that "[t]he public also expects the MOE/government to take the lead role in protecting the public health through the production of uniformly safe drinking water. This has been achieved with numerous MOE programs that include approval of treatment plant design and operation, development of guidelines, procedures and collection of data."

[5] Here I refer to the *Cryptosporidium* outbreaks in Waterloo in 1993 and in Collingwood in 1996, and the *Giardia* outbreak in Thunder Bay in 1998.

and knowledgeable about threats of contamination and about requirements for ensuring the safety of drinking water. It was also the case for municipalities, again like Walkerton, that had shown a pattern of failing to follow MOE requirements or to do what they said they would do. In such situations, careful oversight was essential.

The process of supplying drinking water raises serious public health concerns. A properly structured system for ensuring the safety of drinking water should have multiple barriers: if one protective measure fails, there must be another to back it up. The experts who testified at the Inquiry repeatedly emphasized the need for multiple barriers – that is, for a robust system with built-in safeguards.

Having the MOE serve as overseer provides an important safeguard to ensure that the practices of water operators are sufficient to deliver safe drinking water to the public. Proper provincial oversight reduces the risks arising from the failure of an operating system. In my view, the MOE failed in several respects to fulfill its oversight role in the case of Walkerton.

9.1.3 The Organization of the Ministry

The MOE is organized into divisions, branches, and district and area offices to carry out its functions. Those functions include setting standards, planning and monitoring activities that have an impact on the environment, and delivering programs. Since its creation in 1971,[6] the MOE has undergone a number of reorganizations.

Currently, the Operations Division of the MOE is its most "front-line" division. "Environmental officers" in the Operations Division deal with the public daily. Most of the front-line services of the Operations Division are regionalized and divided among the Northern, Central, Eastern, West Central, and Southwestern Regions. The regions are further subdivided into districts and area offices, which together may be referred to as "local" offices. Walkerton is the responsibility of the MOE's area office in Owen Sound ("the Owen Sound office"), which is part of the Barrie District and the Southwestern Region. For the purposes of this Inquiry, the other important branch of the MOE is the Environmental Assessment and Approvals Branch ("the Approvals

---

[6] At the time of its creation in 1971, the MOE was known as a department; it was designated a ministry in 1972.

Branch") of the Operations Division. The Approvals Branch, located in Toronto, is staffed by specialists in scientific and technical issues relating to the issuance of approvals for activities that are regulated by the MOE.

Although the MOE has a number of other divisions, none had a direct responsibility for the water system in Walkerton, so I need not discuss them here. For the purposes of this chapter, the most significant MOE components are the Owen Sound office and the Approvals Branch. An organizational chart of the MOE is set out at the end of this chapter.

From 1974 until the present, the MOE's Owen Sound office has been responsible for overseeing the Walkerton water system. The Owen Sound office has always been part of the MOE's Southwestern Region. In 1997, it was downgraded from a district office to an area office and was placed within the Barrie District. After the reorganization in 1997, the Owen Sound office was responsible for the geographic areas of Bruce and Grey Counties. Huron County, for which it had previously been responsible, was transferred to the Sarnia District office.

Environmental officers are the MOE's front-line employees: they are responsible for carrying out the ministry's programs. The responsibilities of the environmental officers in the Owen Sound office were broad and varied. Their responsibilities included responding to pollution incidents as well as overseeing municipal water and sewage treatment facilities, private communal water systems, wastewater disposal sites, and industrial activity. The Owen Sound office was also the government overseer for the Bruce nuclear power plant.

Environmental officers who were not assigned full-time to inspections were assigned to address a wide range of responsibilities in their geographic area. As a result, they were generalists who required knowledge of a broad spectrum of activities that fell within the office's mandate. The MOE's local offices administer a number of programs. Since the mid-1980s, this number has increased significantly. By the year 2000, environmental officers were responsible for 15 programs, one of which was the communal water program.

The Owen Sound office normally had a staff of six environmental officers. From August 1999 onward, however, the number fluctuated between four and five. The amount of time each environmental officer devoted to the communal water program was relatively small in relation to his or her overall workload. During 1999–2000, for example, the environmental officers in the Owen Sound office spent about 5% of their time on the communal water program. In all, the office had 54 municipal water systems within its jurisdiction. Therefore, the amount of time environmental officers spent on the Walkerton water system was a very small fraction of their overall workload.

I discuss the role of staff at the Owen Sound office throughout this chapter. However, I first discuss the role of the MOE's Approvals Branch as it relates to the approval of Well 5 in Walkerton.

9.2 Approvals

9.2.1 Overview

In this section, I address the process by which Well 5 was approved in 1978–79. I also address the MOE's failure to attach operating conditions to the Certificate of Approval issued for Well 5 on January 24, 1979.

Well 5 was approved without any operating conditions. Of significance to the May 2000 oubreak, there were no conditions relating to treatment, monitoring, and notification, and there was also no condition requiring continuous chlorine residual and turbidity monitoring. This approval was given despite the concerns of MOE personnel at the time about the well's location and about the vulnerability of the well to surface contamination. However, I am satisfied that the MOE's approval was consistent with the standards and practices prevailing at the time.

Over time, MOE practices and procedures relating to waterworks approvals changed: it began to routinely attach operating conditions to Certificates of Approval, including conditions relating to water treatment and monitoring. By 1992, the MOE had developed a set of model operating conditions that were commonly attached to new Certificates of Approval for municipal water systems, as appropriate. There was, however, no effort to reach back to determine whether conditions should be attached to existing certificates, like the one for Well 5.

The Ontario Drinking Water Objectives (ODWO) were amended in 1994 to provide that water supply systems using "groundwater under the direct influence of surface water" without also using filtration should continuously monitor chlorine residuals and turbidity.[7] The MOE did not, however, put in place a program to examine the water sources supplying existing wells to determine whether a condition requiring continuous monitoring should be added to their Certificates of Approval. Well 5 used groundwater that was under the direct influence of surface water, and the MOE should therefore have required the installation of continuous monitors at that well following the 1994 ODWO amendment.

The MOE's failure to "reach back" and systematically review existing Certificates of Approval, once it became standard practice in the 1990s to attach operating conditions to new Certificates of Approval, was very significant for Walkerton. The MOE never did add any conditions to the Certificate of Approval for Well 5. I am satisfied that a properly structured approvals program would have addressed the need to update the Certificate of Approval for Well 5 – both after the 1994 amendment to the ODWO and when the MOE practices for newly issued certificates changed in the 1990s.

I conclude that had the Walkerton PUC been required to install continuous chlorine residual and turbidity monitors at Well 5, the Walkerton tragedy would have been prevented. I also conclude that the inclusion of the model operating conditions relating to the maintenance of a total chlorine residual of 0.5 mg/L after 15 minutes of contact time, coupled with effective enforcement, would very likely have significantly reduced the scope of the outbreak.

Before addressing the approval of Well 5 in detail, I will briefly describe the nature of two instruments: the Certificate of Approval and the Permit to Take Water.

---

[7] ODWO (1994 revision), section 4.2.1.1. More specifically, the amendment provided for the continuous monitoring of "disinfectant residual (equivalent to free chlorine)" – a type of chlorine residual. The amendment also provided an option for turbidity level monitoring: grab samples could be taken every four hours, or turbidity levels could be monitored continuously. (The ODWO defines "turbidity" in water as a measurement that reflects "the presence of suspended matter such as clay, ... plankton and other microscopic organisms," noting that turbidity's most important health effect ... is its interference with disinfection and with the maintenance of a chlorine residual.") For convenience, I will refer to these options as "continuous turbidity monitoring." Also, I note that in many documents the terms "continuous monitor" and "continuous analyzer" are used interchangeably.

9.2.2   Approvals Instruments

The instrument now known as a Certificate of Approval existed before the passage of the *Ontario Water Resources Act* in 1957. Originally, instruments of this type were issued under provincial public health legislation. In Ontario, they date from 1884, if not earlier.

As the name suggests, the purpose of a Certificate of Approval is to grant approval for an undertaking: in this case, the construction of a municipal water system. Under the *Ontario Water Resources Act*, an approval of this sort may be granted by the MOE with certain conditions, or conditions may be imposed or altered over time.[8] It is an offence under this legislation to operate a municipal water system as large and complex as Walkerton's without MOE approval.[9]

The Permit to Take Water is of more recent origin. This instrument was introduced when the *Ontario Water Resources Act* was amended in 1961 to authorize the regulation of water taking after disputes arose in connection with the taking of water to irrigate tobacco crops. Permits to Take Water are concerned with water quantity rather than water quality. Section 34 of the *Ontario Water Resources Act* generally requires that a Permit to Take Water be obtained where a total of more than 50,000 L of water is to be taken in a single day. Permits are issued by the MOE's regional offices.

Although I heard evidence concerning the evolution and use of the Permit to Take Water, I conclude that there are no provincial government policies, procedures, or practices in relation to permits of this type that are relevant to the Walkerton outbreak. I therefore focus my discussion on the MOE's approval of Well 5.

Before May 2000, the MOE addressed most operational requirements for municipal water systems by way of a guideline or policy directive, neither of which is legally binding. Certificates of Approval authorize the construction of water systems and are not, by definition, operating licences. Nonetheless, a practice has evolved of attaching operating conditions to Certificates of Approval for water systems. When this occurs, Certificates of Approval are at least akin to operating licences. The importance of this development is that operating

---

[8] *Ontario Water Resources Act*, R.S.O. 1990, c. O-40, ss. 5, 52(4).
[9] Ibid., s. 52(7).

conditions that would otherwise have been addressed by way of legally unenforceable guidelines or policy directives become legally enforceable obligations.

When operating conditions like those relating to water treatment and monitoring are included in a Certificate of Approval, the likelihood of compliance increases. Water system operators can be reasonably assumed to be more likely to comply with legal obligations – and if they do not, enforcement by the MOE is more readily achieved.

Over time, Certificates of Approval evolved to the point where those that included operating conditions became a means of ensuring greater vigilance by the MOE over the safety of drinking water supplies.

9.2.3   The Approval of Walkerton Well 5

9.2.3.1   *The Construction of Well 5*

In 1978, when the Walkerton PUC applied for a Certificate of Approval for what became Well 5,[10] three wells existed in Walkerton: Wells 1, 2, and 3. All three produced very hard water – a condition widely considered undesirable. The water from Wells 1 and 2 was described as extremely hard and very high in sulphates. The water from Well 3, although chemically superior to that from Wells 1 and 2, was nevertheless very hard. Following its construction in 1963, Well 3 had not lived up to the hopes of Walkerton residents that it would solve the town's water problems.[11] Moreover, the Walkerton water system lacked any reserve capacity to accommodate new development in the town. It was essential that Walkerton find a new water supply.

The Walkerton PUC applied for a Certificate of Approval for Well 5 on September 27, 1978. The application indicated that construction was to begin in October of that year and would take two months. In fact, Well 5 had already been built. Its construction had been completed three months earlier, in June 1978, but the new well had not yet been connected to the distribution system.

---

[10] Initially, Well 5 was referred to as Well 4.

[11] Conventional water softeners of the time operated on an ion exchange principle, in which sodium ions replace calcium and magnesium ions. The result was that softened water had sodium concentrations as high as 575 mg/L, almost 29 times the concentration at which sodium intake was considered a risk factor for people suffering from hypertension (high blood pressure).

It was highly unusual for a municipality or PUC to construct waterworks without first obtaining a Certificate of Approval.

Despite these circumstances surrounding the construction of Well 5, I am satisfied that the fact that Well 5 was constructed before the PUC applied for approval did not influence the MOE's decision to approve it. Although the circumstances were unusual, I accept that once the MOE was satisfied that there would be sufficient disinfection at the well, it would have approved the well even if it had not already been built.

9.2.3.2 *The Wilson Report and the Ministry Review*

As part of its application to the MOE for approval of Well 5, the Walkerton PUC submitted a hydrogeological report prepared for the MOE by Ian D. Wilson Associates, dated July 28, 1978 ("the Wilson report"). The Wilson report raised concerns about the vulnerability of Well 5 to contamination. It described the thin overburden in the area supplying the well, the shallow aquifer from which water was drawn, and the effect of pumping on two nearby springs. The report also noted that when the well was operated, water flowing from the springs "stopped completely, showing that water normally reaching these two discharge points was intersected by the well," and suggested that when the well was in production, the springs would flow only intermittently.

Importantly, during a pumping test, fecal coliforms were found in water samples taken 24, 48, 60, and 72 hours after the well pump was started. Chemical analysis showed that nitrates were elevated but still within acceptable limits. Among the five conclusions reached in the Wilson report, two are set out below:

> The results of the bacteriological examination indicate pollution from human or animal sources; however, this was not confirmed by chemical analyses. The supply should definitely be chlorinated and the bacteria content of the raw and treated water supply should or would [*sic*] be monitored. The nitrate content should also be observed on a regular basis …

> The Town of Walkerton should consider establishing a water-protection area by acquiring additional property to the west and south in the vicinity of Well [5]. Shallow aquifers are prone to pollution, and farming and human activities should be kept away from

the site of the new well as far as possible. If this area is large enough, additional, relatively soft-water supplies could perhaps be proved sometime in the future ...

These conclusions are significant because they reveal concerns, from the beginning, regarding Well 5's vulnerability to surface contamination.

MOE staff at the Owen Sound office reviewed the Wilson report as part of the ministry's consideration of the PUC's application. The results of this review are set out in an October 24, 1978, memorandum from Willard Page, then the district officer of the Owen Sound office, to the Approvals Branch.

This memorandum raised several concerns, including some of those identified in the Wilson report, about the security of the water source supplying the proposed well. Mr. Page's memorandum discussed the shallowness of the aquifer, the shallowness of the overburden, the possibility that a "nearby agricultural operation ... could be contributing to elevated levels of nitrates in the groundwater," the resultant need to monitor chemical and bacterial parameters that might reflect surface contamination, and the advisability of considering controlling any activities adjacent to the well that might contribute to aquifer contamination.

In addition, Mr. Page inquired whether the MOE's policy relating to surface water sources, which required continuous chlorine residual analysis and recording, also applied to groundwater sources with a known bacterial history. As William Hutchison, an engineer in the Owen Sound office at the time, said in his testimony, "This obviously was a sensitive source of supply and we did not know whether or not Approvals staff would consider this, for all intents and purposes, to be a surface water [source] or whether or not they would consider it to be a groundwater source."

9.2.3.3   The Meeting of November 23, 1978

As a result of concerns arising from the construction of Well 5 without approval, a meeting took place among representatives of the MOE, the Town of Walkerton, the Walkerton PUC, and the PUC's engineering consultants on November 23, 1978. Willard Page's memorandum was used as an agenda for the meeting.

The understandings reached at that meeting are critically important to what happened in May 2000. An understanding was reached that the PUC would maintain at Well 5 a minimum total chlorine residual of 0.5 mg/L after 15 minutes of contact time before the water reached the first consumer. It was also agreed that the PUC would monitor these residuals daily, and that it would record the results in daily operating sheets. Over the ensuing years, the PUC routinely failed to follow these practices. As I conclude above, this failure by the PUC had a direct impact on the events of May 2000. The importance of the meeting leads me to discuss it in some detail.

The minutes of the meeting indicate that the MOE representatives expressed concern that the Town of Walkerton had proceeded with the construction of Well 5 without first having obtained approval from the MOE. The discussion then turned to the vulnerability of the aquifer to contamination and the corresponding need to consider controlling land use in the area, the need for 15 minutes of chlorine contact time due to the presence of bacteria found in the aquifer during the pumping test, and the sampling program to be followed.

The meeting minutes reflect that in referring to the shallowness of the overburden and the aquifer and to the water's resulting vulnerability to contamination, MOE staff members from the Owen Sound office stressed that consideration should be given to controlling any activities in areas adjacent to the new well that might contribute to aquifer contamination. Specific reference was made to the nitrate concentration found in the well's water during the pumping test and to the possibility that this result may have been due to farming activity on the nearby farm owned by Percy Pletsch. Walkerton's mayor, Neil MacDonald, indicated that Mr. Pletsch would probably be very hesitant to sell the farm to the PUC. Nonetheless, the PUC representatives agreed that Mr. Pletsch should be approached so that the potential effects of his farm on the new well could be fully discussed.

In Chapter 7 of this report, I address the failure of the Town of Walkerton[12] to control land use in the vicinity of Well 5 in the years after the well was constructed and approved. I conclude that the town lacked the jurisdiction to expropriate the Pletsch farm for the purpose of safeguarding the water supply. Under the *Public Utilities Act*, it was, however, open to a PUC to expropriate property to preserve the purity of the water supply.[13] There is no evidence as to

---

[12] The Town of Walkerton was amalgamated into the Municipality of Brockton in 1999.
[13] *Public Utilities Act*, R.S.O. 1990, c. P- 52, ss. 4(4), 41(1).

whether the Walkerton PUC considered exercising this power. But in any case, acquiring the Pletsch farm would not have prevented the outbreak. As I conclude in Chapter 4 of this report, the contaminants that entered Walkerton's water system through Well 5 originated from the farm of Dr. David Biesenthal and possibly from other locations. There is no evidence to suggest that the contaminants originated from the former Pletsch property.

Those present at the meeting reached three important understandings about the treatment and monitoring of the water at Well 5. First, it was understood and agreed that the PUC was to maintain a chlorine residual of at least 0.5 mg/L after 15 minutes of contact time before the water reached the first consumer. That was the standard mandated by the Chlorination Bulletin[14] unless, in the case of a groundwater source, the supply had been proven free of bacterial contamination.

Everyone at the meeting knew that Well 5 was supplied by a vulnerable source, susceptible to contamination from surface activities. Willard Page's October 24, 1978, memorandum referred to the well's "known bacterial history." Mr. Hutchison, whose testimony described the source as "sensitive," assumed that Well 5's chlorination met the standard established by the Chlorination Bulletin. Indeed, immediately after Well 5 was put into operation, the PUC operators began to enter chlorine residuals of at least 0.5 mg/L on the well's daily operating sheets.

Second, although Mr. Page had raised the issue in his October 24, 1978, memorandum, the minutes do not reflect any discussion of the issue at the meeting. However, I am satisfied that it was understood that Well 5 would not require a continuous chlorine residual monitor, and the evidence is unequivocal that no such monitor was ever installed.

At the meeting, Ian McLeod, the general manager of the Walkerton PUC, stated that "the well supply system is manned on a 24-hour basis, 7 days per week." It is difficult to know what Mr. McLeod meant in making this statement: he died in 1993. However, it is apparent that given the size of Walkerton's water system, Mr. McLeod did not mean that someone would be present at Well 5 at all times. He probably meant that someone would be on call if an emergency arose.

---

[14] MOE, "Chlorination of Potable Water Supplies," Bulletin 65-W-4 (March 1987).

I am satisfied that the MOE representatives at the meeting did not interpret Mr. McLeod's statement to mean that a PUC staff member would in effect take the place of a continuous chlorine residual monitor: they would have known that such a plan was completely impractical. There was no suggestion in the evidence or in the submissions that anyone from the MOE understood Mr. McLeod's comment to amount to an undertaking that there would be a 24-hour-per-day surveillance of chlorine residuals.

The MOE personnel testified that in 1978, continuous chlorine residual monitors were not required for groundwater sources with known bacterial histories. I accept that this appears to be the way the Chlorination Bulletin was interpreted at the time.[15] The general disinclination to require the installation of continuous chlorine residual monitors may have stemmed from the fact that at that time, continuous monitors were costly, complicated to operate, and prone to be unreliable.

I am satisfied that on the basis of the information available to the review engineer when the PUC applied for the approval of Well 5, approval without attaching an operating condition requiring continuous chlorine residual monitoring was consistent with the standards of the day. The evidence established that the mere fact of a known bacterial history was not at that time sufficient to prompt the MOE to require continuous chlorine residual monitoring.

The third important understanding reached at the November 23, 1978, meeting was that the PUC would measure chlorine residuals on a daily basis. Only by doing that could they ensure that the proper residual was being maintained. According to the minutes, "[t]he importance of maintaining a chlorine residual at all times was emphasized in light of the presence of bacteria in the well water."

The use of daily operating sheets for the Walkerton wells had its origins in the October 24, 1978, memorandum and the November 23, 1978, meeting. The minutes of that meeting indicate that the MOE gave the town's consulting engineers a sample sheet outlining the records that the ministry recommended that the municipality keep. Most importantly, the records to be kept on a daily basis included those relating to the chlorine solution level and strength (that is,

---

[15] At the time, the Chlorination Bulletin provided that a continuous monitor was required when "poor raw water quality and/or minimum supervision indicated a hazard," regardless of whether the source was surface water or groundwater.

the amount and strength of the chlorine added to the raw water), and the chlorine residual in the treated water at the well.

Mr. Hutchison pointed out in his testimony that daily operating sheets are critical for the proper operation of a water system. Recording this information helps the MOE inspectors assess the water system and helps the water operator monitor chlorine demand[16] at the well. This information is essential because it alerts the operator to the presence of contaminants that require a higher chlorine dose. A significant variation in chlorine demand also provides a good reason to install a continuous chlorine residual monitor.

The understandings reached at the November 23, 1978, meeting about how the PUC would treat and monitor the water at Well 5 were not included as conditions in the well's Certificate of Approval. There is no question, however, that these were the understandings regarding how Well 5 would be operated. In the years that followed, the PUC nevertheless routinely underchlorinated the water, failed to monitor residuals daily, and made false entries in the daily operating sheets.

9.2.4 The Terms of the Approval

9.2.4.1 The Failure to Impose Conditions

Consistent with the practice that prevailed at the time, no operating conditions were attached to the Certificate of Approval issued for Well 5 in January 1979. Instead, the MOE relied on assurances given by the PUC at the meeting on November 23, 1978, that it would treat and monitor the water as agreed. At the time, it was not considered practical to impose conditions relating to land use in the vicinity of groundwater sources. Donald Carr, an engineer in the Approvals Branch at the time, testified that he had understood that enforcing such a condition would have been very difficult or even impossible.

---

[16] As discussed in Chapter 4 of this report, the amount of chlorine added to disinfect water is known as the "chlorine dose." Reactions, including those that inactivate micro-organisms, consume some or all of the chlorine dose: these chlorine-consuming reactions are called "chlorine demand." The chlorine dose minus the chlorine demand provides the "chlorine residual." The presence of a chlorine residual after enough time has passed for a chlorine-consuming reaction to be completed indicates that there was enough chlorine available in the chlorine dose to react with all the chlorine-demanding substances, including micro-organisms – and thus indicates that the water has been successfully disinfected (i.e., harmful or disease-causing micro-organisms have been inactivated).

I am satisfied that the practice in 1979 was to issue Certificates of Approval without attaching express (i.e., explicit) operating conditions relating to treatment, operating, monitoring, and notification, and also without conditions relating to land use in the vicinity of groundwater sources. I accept the evidence that the approval of Well 5 without conditions was consistent with the standard practice at the time.

In the evidence, MOE staff suggested that the understandings reached at the meeting of November 23, 1978, such as those relating to treatment, monitoring, and possible land-use protection measures, were implied conditions in the Certificate of Approval for Well 5. Along these lines, James Jackson, a senior MOE lawyer and principal adviser to the Approvals Branch, testified that all the foundation material underlying an application for a Certificate of Approval dictated the scope of the resulting certificate. In that sense, the material could be said to impose implied conditions on the certificate. However, implied conditions of the kind he was referring to are not enforceable by way of prosecution or legal proceeding. They would become legally enforceable only if the Certificate of Approval were amended to impose an express condition or if a Director's Order were issued.

I am satisfied that in practical terms, the concept of implied conditions, in the sense referred to by Mr. Jackson, was no substitute for express conditions on a Certificate of Approval.

A direct consequence of the MOE's failure to impose operating conditions on Certificates of Approval was that this approach denied the MOE a mechanism for the immediate enforcement of treatment and monitoring requirements. To rectify this situation, the MOE eventually began attaching conditions to newly issued Certificates of Approval. However, as I discuss below, the ministry never reached back in a systematic way to attach conditions to existing Certificates of Approval like the one for Well 5.

9.2.4.2 *Sending the Wrong Signals*

An important consequence of issuing an unconditional Certificate of Approval was that it might communicate the wrong signals. Water operators might be inclined to treat their assurances to the MOE more casually than they would treat legally binding conditions in a Certificate of Approval. Moreover, a more casual approach was reinforced by the MOE's reliance on legally unenforceable guidelines, rather than on enforceable standards, as a means of setting out operating requirements such as those involving chlorination and monitoring.

The events immediately following the issuance of Well 5's Certificate of Approval also sent an unfortunate message to the Walkerton PUC that the requirements for treating the water for Well 5 that had been discussed at the November 23, 1978, meeting were not actually as important as the MOE had indicated at the time.

Shortly after the November 23 meeting, the PUC's consulting engineers wrote to the Approvals Branch to propose a means of providing the necessary 15 minutes of chlorine contact time at Well 5 before the treated water reached the first consumer. The purpose of requiring 15 minutes of contact time is to give the chlorine the opportunity to disinfect the water effectively – that is, to destroy any bacterial contaminants in the water. According to the consultants' proposal, the most effective method for achieving the required contact time was to install a 55-m section of oversized pipe, or "force main," running parallel to the existing watermain from Well 5. The force main would allow water from Well 5 to circulate long enough to allow adequate contact time for disinfection.

The MOE accepted this solution and included a requirement to construct the force main in the Certificate of Approval for Well 5 that the ministry issued on January 24, 1979. However, the Approvals Branch did not require the PUC to certify that Well 5 had been constructed in compliance with the Certificate of Approval before the well was put into operation. As it turned out, the force main was never built. The PUC put Well 5 into service in January 1979, pumping water to the first consumer without the required contact time.

The MOE inspectors who prepared an inspection report on June 4, 1979, noted that Well 5 was being operated without the force main, which they recognized was necessary for achieving the required contact time. They noted that the PUC had said that the force main would be installed by the spring of 1979, but that by the time of the report's preparation in June, the PUC was giving consideration to an alternative proposal. A June 4, 1979, letter from Willard Page to the Walkerton PUC enclosing the inspection report clearly recognized that the force main had not been installed and noted the potential public health implications of failing to ensure adequate chlorine contact time.

In August 1979, seven months after Well 5 was put into operation, the Town of Walkerton applied for a Certificate of Approval to cover a proposed alternative method of ensuring that houses near Well 5 would be provided with water only after at least 15 minutes of chlorine contact time. This solution, which involved connecting those houses directly to the existing distribution system rather than to the pipe that connected Well 5 to the system, was approved on October 19, 1979, and a second Certificate of Approval was issued.

However, there is no evidence that during the nine months in which Well 5 operated without providing 15 minutes of contact time, the MOE directed the PUC not to use Well 5 until a solution was found. The implicit message from the MOE to the PUC was that the 15-minute requirement was not important enough to insist on. Clearly this was the wrong signal to send about the importance of adequate chlorination at Well 5.

9.2.5 The Follow-up to the Approval

9.2.5.1   *The 1979 Inspection*

After Well 5 began operating, the MOE carried out a number of on-site inspections. The first inspection report – which was issued, as discussed above, on June 4, 1979 – presented further information about the surface connection to the aquifer supplying Well 5. It referred to the coincidence of an increase in Well 5's pumping level with either spring thaw or a period of rain. When presented with this information at the Inquiry, William Gregson, formerly of the MOE's Approvals Branch,[17] agreed that it was consistent with the view that Well 5 was under the influence of surface water, and he agreed that this was known by the MOE in 1979.[18] The 1979 report went on to note that any efforts to control land use near the well should be continued.

Despite the information referred to in this inspection report about the influence of surface water on Well 5, there was no communication from the Owen Sound office to the Approvals Branch, and no steps were taken to require a continuous chlorine residual monitor for the well.

---

[17] Mr. Gregson was formerly the assistant director and the acting director of the Approvals Branch. At the time of his testimony, he had recently retired as manager of the branch's Certificate of Approval Review Section.

[18] This information became very important in 1994, when the ODWO was amended to require continuous chlorine residual and turbidity monitors for water supply systems using groundwater sources that are under the direct influence of surface water. Because Well 5 was such a system, the MOE should at that point have required the installation of continous monitors at the well.

In addition, the inspection report noted what was probably the origin of the improper chlorine residual monitoring practices followed by the Walkerton PUC over the ensuing years. The report said that "on February 27, 1979, a chlorine residual measurement taken at Well #5 indicated a residual of approximately 0.30 mg/L. This was less than the residual of 0.5 mg/L which was measured by the operating authority." The MOE did nothing to ascertain a reason for the discrepancy.

9.2.5.2   Well 5: A Temporary Solution?

Anecdotal evidence existed that Well 5 was initially considered to be a temporary solution to Walkerton's water problems and that it was not intended to be operated indefinitely. Some called it a "band-aid solution." However, the Certificate of Approval was not time limited, and there is no document recording an intention that the well was not to be used by the Walkerton PUC over the longer term.

Over time, both the Walkerton PUC and the MOE's Owen Sound office seem to have lost sight of the initial thought that Well 5 was a temporary solution to Walkerton's water problems. This is perhaps understandable, because in the years after the 1980 inspections, the well had performed reasonably satisfactorily.

There were no formal, structured inspections of the Walkerton water facility between 1980 and 1991. In the years after the 1980 inspections until the 1991 inspection, few, if any, adverse microbiological results were reported. It was Mr. Hutchison's evidence that the inspection carried out in November 1991 disclosed virtually no problems with Well 5. Although Well 5 remained a source that was vulnerable to contamination from surface activities, that concern was alleviated by what he termed "14 years' history of half-decent operation."

9.2.6   The Failure to Update the Certificate of Approval

9.2.6.1   Evolving Practice: 1980s–1990s

The Approvals Branch began to impose express conditions on Certificates of Approval in the mid-1980s. This practice evolved very slowly and sporadically, on a site-specific basis, and in time moved to the inclusion of model conditions in new or amended Certificates of Approval.

Initially, the ODWO formed the basis for express conditions attaching to newly issued Certificates of Approval for waterworks. As an example, adherence to the ODWO was mandated through the inclusion of a condition requiring the applicant to "comply with the requirements of the Ontario Drinking Water Objectives, as amended from time to time."

As early as 1986 or 1987, an MOE committee studied the development of model conditions for inclusion in waterworks Certificates of Approval, but given the atmosphere of cooperation with municipalities that the MOE had enjoyed, the committee did not consider this initiative to be a priority.

Over time, however, Approvals Branch staff developed generic conditions that were included in the guide used by engineers who were reviewing applications for approval. In September 1992, the MOE's Approvals Branch issued its "Review Procedures Manual for Approval of Municipal and Private Water and Sewage Works," which contained model conditions for waterworks Certificates of Approval. In June 1996, the MOE published a document titled "Approval Process and Drinking Water Sampling and Monitoring," which further refined the model conditions to be attached to waterworks Certificates of Approval. These model conditions included requirements for maintaining a total chlorine residual of 0.5 mg/L[19] after 15 minutes of contact time and for the water system owner to notify the district manager and the local Medical Officer of Health when results failed to meet the ODWO standards or when unchlorinated water was introduced into the distribution system. MOE staff testified that the former condition could be appropriate when (as was the case with Well 5) the water source had a known bacterial history or in cases where there was relatively direct communication between the aquifer and the surface. The latter condition would likely have been included in all new Certificates of Approval for facilities with chlorinated groundwater.

However, despite increasing recognition within the Approvals Branch of the value of imposing operating conditions on Certificates of Approval relating to the operation of the water system, there was no centralized system of tracking Certificates of Approval issued before 1989. This situation significantly impeded any concerted effort to review existing Certificates of Approval to determine whether they should be updated by including operating conditions.

---

[19] The conditions actually refer to a residual of "0.2 (0.5) mg/L." The higher requirement, 0.5 mg/L, would have applied to Walkerton Well 5 because it was a water supply that had not been shown to be free of hazardous bacterial contamination. See s. 3.1 of the Chlorination Bulletin.

The Approvals Branch was not alone in recognizing the merit in imposing express conditions on Certificates of Approval. Citing the lack of "enforceable criteria or Certificate of Approval limits with which to regulate and ensure compliance for most ... water facilities," the 1992 report of the provincial government's Sewage and Water Inspection Program (SWIP) proposed either the enactment of a legally binding regulation regarding the operation of sewage and water treatment facilities or the issuance of a new Certificate of Approval to every facility, providing uniform operating conditions that established standards for such items as monitoring and water quality criteria. This proposal was not acted upon by the MOE until after the Walkerton outbreak. Only then was the absence of operating conditions in existing Certificates of Approval comprehensively addressed.

Prior to the Walkerton outbreak, Approvals Branch staff waited until applications to amend unconditional Certificates of Approval were made before adding conditions to them. They reasoned that approved equipment had a limited lifespan and that Certificates of Approval could be updated to include conditions when an application was made to alter, extend, or replace existing water supply systems.

In addition to waiting for applications for amendments, the Approvals Branch also relied on local MOE offices to identify municipal water systems requiring the imposition of operating conditions. But it was uncommon for the local offices to suggest the amendment of existing Certificates of Approval in order to provide for the inclusion of express conditions. Moreover, although there existed a process by which the MOE's Investigation and Enforcement Branch could sponsor amendments of existing Certificates of Approval, Julian Wieder, currently a program manager with that branch, testified that this process was used to amend Certificates of Approval involving solid and hazardous wastes but did not point to any instances involving water supply systems.

The hit-and-miss process followed by the Approvals Branch of waiting for an application from an operator to amend a Certificate of Approval before adding operating conditions resulted in the uneven inclusion of such conditions in Certificates of Approval across the province. The Walkerton PUC did not apply for an amendment for the Certificate of Approval for Well 5, and thus the need for including operating conditions did not come to the attention of the Approvals Branch.

9.2.6.2 *The Failure to Add Model Conditions for Well 5*

I am satisfied that when the MOE in the 1990s, and by 1996 at the latest, began to routinely attach model conditions to newly issued Certificates of Approval, it would have been reasonable to have developed a program or practice of reviewing all existing certificates to see if such conditions were appropriate. The practice of waiting for applications for an amendment or of relying on MOE local offices before doing so was random and inexact.

In his testimony, William Gregson agreed that had a review of the Certificate of Approval for Well 5 been conducted in 1996, when the MOE published the refined model conditions, it would have been appropriate to amend the certificate by including the following model conditions:

1. construction and operation of disinfection facilities in such a manner that the total chlorine residual in the treated water reaching the first consumer connection and the effective contact time are maintained at all times to a minimum of 0.5 mg total chlorine per litre of water after 15 minutes of contact time;[20]

2. installation of continuous water quality monitors and indicators with alarm systems in order to monitor free or total chlorine residual in treated water at the point(s) of entrance to the distribution system;[21]

3. maintenance of bacteriological and chemical monitoring programs, as required by the 1994 ODWO revision;

4. the taking of all necessary steps within the owner's authority "to ensure protection of the source of water supply (the groundwater aquifer) from contamination";

5. notification of the MOE district manager and the local Medical Officer of Health by the water system's "owner" – a term that is defined in the Certificate of Approval and that could therefore include the operator – if

---

[20] Although Mr. Gregson's evidence was that a condition requiring the maintenance of a chlorine residual of only 0.2 mg/L after 15 minutes of contact time would have been appropriate, this higher standard would actually have been required, given that the source had not been "proven free of hazardous bacterial contamination" and therefore did not fall under the Chlorination Bulletin's exception permitting the maintenance of a chlorine residual of 0.2 mg/L.

[21] By this time, the 1994 amendment to the ODWO, referred to in note 7, was in effect.

any analytical result exceeds the maximum acceptable concentration of a health-related parameter or shows deteriorating bacteriological water quality as defined in the ODWO; and

6.   notification of the MOE district manager and the local Medical Officer of Health by the "owner" when unchlorinated water is introduced into the distribution system.

I have already noted that despite having had the legislative and policy tools to conduct a review of existing Certificates of Approval, the MOE did not carry out a systematic review to identify certificates in need of updating. I am satisfied that if the MOE had conducted such a review, it would have added the model conditions to the Certificate of Approval for Well 5.[22]

The MOE's failure in this regard did not escape the attention of the Provincial Auditor. In a report finalized in March 2000 but not issued until October of that year, the Provincial Auditor found that the MOE did not have an adequate system for reviewing the conditions of existing Certificates of Approval in order to ensure that they met current environmental standards. The Provincial Auditor pointed out that the approximately 130,000 approvals issued before 1986 were recorded on a manual card index system, which made it impractical to determine whether they required updating.

The Provincial Auditor recommended that the MOE improve its information systems so that all Certificates of Approval could be assessed regarding the extent to which they needed to be updated with new conditions, develop systems that would allow for updating certificates in a timely and efficient manner, and establish action plans and timetables for updating certificates. The MOE agreed with these recommendations: its response stated that reviews of priority sectors, including water, had already been undertaken or were in progress to improve the currency of certificates. It also stated that the Integrated Divisional System (IDS) – the information management system that the ministry is developing – would, once fully implemented, enable the MOE to assess over time the extent to which Certificates of Approval needed to be updated.

---

[22] Model condition 2, set out above, includes the "installation of continuous water quality monitors." I discuss the MOE's failure to require continuous monitors after 1994 in section 9.3.

9.2.6.3 *The Failure to Update After the 1994 ODWO Amendments*

In 1994, the ODWO was amended to provide that water systems using ground-water that is under the direct influence of surface water and without filtration should continuously monitor chlorine residuals.[23] In Chapter 4 of this report, I conclude that the water drawn from Well 5 was groundwater that was under the direct influence of surface water. After the 1994 ODWO amendment, the Certificate of Approval for Well 5 should have been updated to include a condition requiring the installation of continuous chlorine residual and turbidity monitors to allow an adequate response when the chlorine residual fell below the prescribed minimum or the turbidity exceeded a pre-determined level.

The 1994 revision to the ODWO also provided that water supply systems using groundwater that is under the direct influence of surface water and without filtration should monitor turbidity levels, either continuously or by taking grab samples every four hours. By then, continuous chlorine residual monitors had improved and no longer required chemical buffers and pH adjustment. They were also less expensive and more reliable than they had been in 1979, when Well 5 was approved. One witness estimated that a continuous chlorine residual monitor equipped with an alarm and a recorder would cost approximately $8,000 and that a continuous turbidimeter would cost approximately the same amount. An automatic shut-off device would add only minimal additional cost for each of the monitors.

Before the 1994 ODWO amendment, the Chlorination Bulletin required continuous chlorine residual monitors for "sources where poor water quality and/or minimum supervision indicates a possible health hazard." That requirement was less precise than the one in the 1994 ODWO amendment, and apparently the MOE did not interpret it as requiring continuous monitoring in situations like the one that existed at Well 5. In any event, I am satisfied that after the 1994 amendment to the ODWO, there ceased to be any reason for failing to properly assess Well 5.

The importance of continuous monitoring is clear. The 1994 amendment to the ODWO was directed at providing increased protection for safeguarding public water supplies. The inclusion of the more specific test for "groundwater under the direct influence of surface water" should have triggered steps by the

---

[23] ODWO (1994 revision), s. 4.2.1.1. See note 7 regarding the specific requirement for continuous monitoring.

MOE to ensure that municipal water supply systems received the protection of continuous monitoring where warranted.

After the 1994 amendment, the MOE did not initiate any program or practice for assessing existing municipal water sources to determine if they were ground-water sources under the direct influence of surface water and thus required continuous monitoring. The new requirement was applied to newly issued Certificates of Approval or in some instances to situations in which Certificates of Approval required updating. The result of not reaching back to review existing certificates was that some municipal water systems – either newly approved systems or those seeking amendments to existing Certificates of Approval – had the increased protection offered by continuous monitoring, while others did not. In a matter so important to public health, this inconsis-tent approach was not acceptable.

This situation was exacerbated by the MOE's failures to instruct inspectors of municipal water systems to assess whether existing wells posed problems when reviewed in the light of the new provision, to notify water system operators of the amendment, and to direct them to assess whether continuous monitors should be installed.

Moreover, the evidence showed that as late as the spring of 2001, the MOE had yet to formulate criteria for determining what constituted "groundwater under the direct influence of surface water." Instead, this determination was left to the discretion of review engineers.

Because there was no systematic review of existing Certificates of Approval, the MOE did not require continuous monitoring for Well 5. Had a proper review and assessment taken place, along with proper follow-up, I am satisfied that Well 5 would have been identified as a groundwater source under the direct influence of surface water and that continuous monitors would have been installed. I have found above that continuous monitors would have pre-vented the outbreak in May 2000.

I am satisfied that the Walkerton PUC operators did not have the training and expertise either to identify the vulnerability of Well 5 to surface contami-nation or to understand the resulting need for continuous monitors. The MOE knew or should have known that this was the case. It is no answer to the failure of the MOE to carry out a systematic review of existing Certificates of Approval to say that it relied on water operators like Stan Koebel to do so: the

MOE did not even bring the 1994 ODWO amendment to the attention of water operators.

Further, I reject the submission of counsel for the Province of Ontario that if continuous chlorine residual and turbidity monitors with alarms had been installed at Well 5, and if in May 2000 the alarms had shut Well 5 down, Stan Koebel would have reacted by turning the well back on and allowing it to continue to pump contaminated water into the distribution system. First, I note that Stan Koebel was not in Walkerton at the critical time when the monitors would have shut the pump off: Frank Koebel was in charge of the system during the relevant period.

In any event, Stan and Frank Koebel's deficient chlorination and recording practices were born not out of malice or lack of industry, but out of the misguided conviction the water was safe without proper chlorination. Had Well 5 been shut down because the chlorine demand had used up all of the chlorine injected or because the turbidity had exceeded acceptable levels, the shutdown would have made it clear to them that the water was contaminated and unsafe. I do not accept that either Stan or Frank Koebel would have pumped what they knew to be contaminated water into the system.

9.2.6.4 *Resources in the Approvals Branch*

In Chapter 11 of this report, I discuss the budget and resource cuts experienced by the MOE between 1992 and 1998. As the need for a systematic review of existing Certificates of Approval became apparent, staff reductions in the Approvals Branch compromised the branch's ability to conduct that review. In his evidence, however, Mr. Gregson seemed to suggest that the failure to conduct such a review was not connected to staff reductions.

He testified that a "relatively small number of additional resources" would have been required in order to undertake a systematic review of existing waterworks' Certificates of Approval to determine whether to attach conditions relating to the following issues: continuous chlorine residual and turbidity monitoring, maintenance of minimum chlorine residuals, adherence to the minimum bacteriological sampling program,[24] and notification of the local Medical Officer of Health regarding adverse samples. If that was in fact the case, one wonders why it was not done.

The Provincial Auditor's report of the year 2000 set out a different view from that held by Mr. Gregson. It said that MOE management had advised that updating existing approvals would require "significant workload and expense" for the MOE. Whatever the size of the additional resources needed, I am satisfied that a systematic review would have required additional work at a time when staff reductions were taking place and that the shortage of resources made it most unlikely that such a review would be carried out.

As previously mentioned, it was only after the Walkerton tragedy that the MOE took steps to review and update existing Certificates of Approval. All Certificates of Approval for municipal water treatment plants must now be renewed every three years. Municipalities are now required to submit a professional engineer's report to the MOE in relation to each waterworks. The intent is to consolidate all Certificates of Approval so that there will be a single certificate for each of the 700 municipal water supplies and to include in each certificate the appropriate conditions.

9.2.6.5   *The Impact on the Events of May 2000*

Had the MOE included a condition in its Certificate of Approval for Well 5 requiring the maintenance of a chlorine residual of 0.5 mg/L, it is likely that with proper oversight and enforcement, the PUC would have complied with the requirement. I refer to proper oversight and enforcement because if the PUC had not complied with such a condition, a proper inspections program would probably have detected the improper practices – by then, breaches of legal requirements – and ensured that proper treatment and monitoring took place.

As I pointed out above, it is very likely that daily chlorine residual monitoring would have significantly reduced the scope of the outbreak in May 2000. Had the MOE required continuous monitors for Well 5, the protection would have

---

[24] The "minimum bacteriological sampling program" was set out under the ODWO as a guideline. In 1995, the MOE initiated the Minimum Recommended Sampling Program, based on the ODWO. Both of these programs are referred to as the "minimum sampling program" or "minimum bacteriological sampling program" throughout this report.

been even greater. I am satisfied that continuous monitors would have prevented the outbreak.

9.2.7   The Approval of Wells 6 and 7

Walkerton had two other operating wells in addition to Well 5. Well 6 was approved in 1983, and Well 7 in 1987. I have found that although Well 6 may be susceptible to surface contamination, there is no evidence to support a conclusion that the contamination entered the system through Well 6 in May 2000. In view of this fact, I do not propose to review the approvals process for Well 6.

I have also found that the contamination did not enter the system through Well 7. However, the process involving the approval for Well 7 provides another example of the implicit messages sent by the MOE to the Walkerton PUC and to Stan Koebel that it was not essential that they follow MOE requirements, even when these requirements were a legal obligation, as they were in this case.

The Certificate of Approval for Well 7 was issued on October 22, 1987. An October 15, 1987, memorandum from Mr. Hutchison of the MOE's Owen Sound office to the Approvals Branch suggested including conditions that required (1) a monitoring program addressing the impact of operating Well 7 alone, and Wells 6 and 7 together, on shallow and deeper aquifers in the area, and (2) the submission of a report concerning that program within 15 months. Monitoring the performance of conditions attached to Certificates of Approval was the responsibility of the MOE's regional and local offices.

The Walkerton PUC failed to satisfy the condition in the Well 7 Certificate of Approval for seven years. The MOE treated the issue in a most offhand manner. When the 15-month period passed, there was no follow-up. When Brian Jaffray, who conducted the November 19, 1991, inspection of the Walkerton water system, noted that the condition required the submission of a report by June 1, 1989, he gave the PUC until June 1, 1992, to provide it. The report was not submitted to the MOE until September 26, 1994 – seven years after the condition was attached to the Certificate of Approval and more than five years after the report was due.

Although this situation was unsatisfactory, apparently it was not uncommon. A 1996 MOE internal audit of the approvals process referred to the fact that between 6,000 and 7,000 Certificates of Approval were issued annually and found that:

> given the volume, the district staff are unable to plan site visits effectively, except for the most critical Certificates of Approval. Our review of procedures at district offices disclosed that few site visits are being done. In fact, as documented in the workplan of the regional offices, monitoring of approvals conditions is assigned the lowest priority.

As for ensuring the operators' compliance with reporting conditions of the kind imposed on the Walkerton PUC in relation to Well 7, the internal auditors concluded:

> Our review of procedures at district offices disclosed that due to the large volumes of certificates of approvals and due to lack of resources district staff were unable to monitor reporting requirements imposed on the proponents effectively.

9.2.8   Recommendations

The following recommendations will form part of the broader set of recommendations that will be set out in the Part 2 report of this Inquiry.

Recommendation 9: The MOE should develop criteria for identifying "groundwater under the direct influence of surface water."

Recommendation 10: The MOE should maintain an information data system that includes all relevant information arising from an approval application process – in particular, information relating to the quality of source water and relevant details from expert reports and tests.

Recommendation 11: The MOE should require continuous chlorine and turbidity monitors for all groundwater sources that are under the direct influence of surface water or that serve municipal populations greater than a size prescribed by the MOE.

Recommendation 12: All Certificates of Approval should be limited to a specific period of time, probably five years, and be subject to a renewal process that considers the current circumstances, including recent indicators of water quality. Conditions should be added as required.

In the Part 2 report, I will be making recommendations about the nature and form of operating conditions for municipal water systems.

9.3 Inspections

9.3.1 Overview

An essential element of the MOE's oversight role of municipal water systems is its inspections program. The frequency and nature of inspections have varied over time. In the years immediately preceding the outbreak in May 2000, the MOE inspected the Walkerton water system on three occasions, the last being in February 1998, more than two years before the outbreak.

At the time of the three inspections, problems existed relating to water safety. Inspectors identified some of these problems, but unfortunately two of the most significant – the vulnerability of Well 5 to surface contamination, and the improper chlorination and monitoring practices of the PUC – went undetected. As events turned out, these problems had a direct impact on the May 2000 tragedy.

During the three inspections, Well 5 was not assessed, and therefore was not identified as a groundwater source that was under the direct influence of surface water. The inspectors proceeded as if Well 5 were a secure groundwater source, and their reports made no reference to the surface water influence. This occurred even though information existed in MOE files that should have prompted a close examination of the vulnerability of Well 5 – that is, the 1978–79 material relating to the MOE's approval of Well 5, along with the reports from the 1979 and 1980 inspections, the first inspections completed after the well was put into operation.

Even after problems with the water quality at Well 5 began to emerge in the 1990s, the inspectors who saw these results did not refer to the critical information on file describing the vulnerability of the well. There were no instructions from the MOE directing inspectors to refer to this type of information, even in the face of indicators of deteriorating water quality.

The second problem not addressed in the three inspection reports from the 1990s was the improper chlorination and monitoring practices of the Walkerton PUC. Evidence of these improper practices was readily apparent in the operating records maintained by the PUC. A proper examination of the PUC's daily operating sheets for any extended period would have shown a pattern of entries for chlorine residuals – repeatedly either 0.5 or 0.75, with almost no other entries (whether higher, lower, or in between those two measurements) for more than 20 years – that should have raised suspicion about the integrity of the numbers and led to questions about the chlorination and monitoring practices. Unfortunately, inspectors were never instructed to carry out this type of thorough examination. Michelle Zillinger, the 1998 inspector, looked only at the current month's daily operating sheets for two of the three wells and did not notice anything unusual. Because those sheets did not contain only 0.5 or 0.75 entries, they showed a more believable range of residuals.

Although the MOE was not aware of the Walkerton PUC's improper chlorination and monitoring practices, I am satisfied that if the ministry had properly followed up on the deficiencies noted in the 1998 inspection report, the unacceptable treatment and monitoring practices would have (or at least should have) been discovered.

However, two years and three months later, when the tragedy struck, no further inspection had even been scheduled. That was a serious failure on the part of the MOE, because a follow-up inspection could have made a significant difference to the outcome in May 2000.

The failure to detect these two significant problems in the Walkerton water system is the result of four flaws in the inspections program:

1.   the failure to give inspectors adequate instructions to review relevant material in MOE files, especially following the 1994 ODWO amendments that required continuous chlorine residual and turbidity monitors for groundwater sources under the direct influence of surface water;

2.   the failure to give inspectors clear instructions concerning the review of operating records for the purpose of assessing the operator's treatment and monitoring practices;

3.   the failure to conduct a follow-up to the 1998 inspection; and

4.   the failure to make unannounced inspections.

The MOE inspections program was thus seriously flawed as it applied to Walkerton. A properly structured and administered inspections program would have discovered, before the May 2000 outbreak, both the vulnerability of Well 5 and the PUC's improper chlorination and monitoring practices. Had these problems been uncovered, corrective action could have been taken to address them. With proper follow-up, such steps would either have prevented the outbreak or substantially reduced its scope.

9.3.2 The Ministry Inspections in Walkerton

By way of background, it is useful to review briefly the history of inspections of the Walkerton water system. Since the MOE took over the functions of the Ontario Water Resources Commission in 1972, it has conducted on-site inspections of municipal water systems for the purposes of ensuring that the facilities are properly maintained and operated to enable them to meet treated water quality standards. In 1974, when the MOE was decentralized, creating six regions and 22 districts, the responsibility for conducting inspections was transferred to the district offices. The policy-making role, including providing instructions about the nature, process, and frequency of inspections, remained with the provincial level of the MOE.

During the late 1970s, the MOE conducted regular inspections. For example, inspection reports were prepared for Walkerton in 1979 and 1980, and both were preceded by several site visits by the inspectors. Starting around 1980, however, the frequency of formalized inspections declined dramatically. Inspections became essentially reactive, and after the 1980 inspection, the MOE did not conduct a formal inspection again until 1991. During the intervening period, environmental officers made periodic visits to Walkerton, but there was no formalized inspection and no records were maintained setting out the results of these informal visits.

In 1988, the Provincial Auditor conducted an audit of the MOE's inspections program and found that most treatment plants had not been inspected in at least two years. He noted that the purpose of regular inspections was primarily preventive and proactive, and recommended annual inspections of all water treatment plants. In response, the MOE established the Sewage and Water Inspection Program (SWIP), under which, after an initial inspection, water facilities were to be inspected every two years. Initially SWIP was administered by the regions, but in 1994 the responsibility for conducting inspections under SWIP was returned to the district offices. After this transfer, the frequency of inspections varied but the program emphasized the need to more frequently inspect facilities that had historical problems or significant deficiencies.

In the 1990s, the Walkerton water facility was inspected on three occasions: November 1991, October 1995, and February 1998. The inspections disclosed several serious problems. In each instance, the Walkerton PUC was not complying with the minimum sampling program and the total chlorine residuals measured by the inspectors of the treated water at the wells then in operation were all less than the required 0.5 mg/L. The review of the bacteriological results in 1995 and 1998 showed that adverse results were noted in the Walkerton system on three and eight occasions respectively, including the presence of *E. coli* on a significant number of occasions. In their reports, the inspectors pointed out the seriousness of these findings and emphasized the need to maintain a minimum chlorine residual of 0.5 mg/L after 15 minutes of contact time.

The inspections also had notable failures. Most significantly, they did not address the vulnerability of Well 5, nor did they uncover the improper chlorination and chlorine residual monitoring practices of the Walkerton PUC. These failures resulted from the flaws in the program that I discuss below. Although the conclusions regarding the failures of the inspections program apply, to some extent, to all three inspections, I will focus on the last inspection, in February 1998. The failure of that inspection to detect the problems at Walkerton is most closely related to the outbreak. In addition, by that time the problems were both well established and readily apparent.

The 1998 inspection was conducted by Michelle Zillinger, who was an experienced environmental officer. She had joined the MOE in 1986 as an environmental officer level 3 and served in various positions until October 1997, when she was transferred to the Owen Sound office. By then, she had been promoted to environmental officer level 4. In Owen Sound, her duties were mainly confined to proactive routine compliance inspections of municipal water and sewage treatment facilities. She had considerable experience in conducting inspections. In the early 1990s, she completed a two-year secondment to SWIP, and she continued as a SWIP inspector after 1994, when the program was delivered by local MOE offices. Over the years, Ms. Zillinger had attended regular meetings for SWIP inspectors, at both the regional and provincial level.

I am satisfied that Ms. Zillinger carried out her inspections, including her 1998 inspection of the Walkerton water system, in accordance with what she understood her instructions from the MOE to be. Although it was not necessary to hear evidence from Brian Jaffray and John Apfelbeck, the inspectors who conducted the 1991 and 1995 inspections, I have no reason to doubt that they were also competent and carried out their inspections as directed by the MOE. The inspection flaws I have identified are not those of the individual inspectors; they are the responsibility of the MOE. The flaws relate to the directions the MOE gave its inspectors and the manner in which the inspection program was applied to Walkerton. Let me turn, then, to each of these flaws.

9.3.3 The Lack of Instructions to Inspectors Regarding Ministry Files

The quality of a well's source water is critical to determining the types of treatment and monitoring that may be required. I am satisfied that when positive *E. coli* results appear repeatedly in the raw and treated water from a particular well – as in the case of Well 5 in the years leading up to the 1998 inspection – a properly structured inspections program should direct an inspector to look for information in MOE files, and elsewhere if necessary, that addresses potential problems with the source water for that well.

Operators of small water systems like Walkerton's are unlikely to have the same level of expertise or sophistication as the environmental officers who conduct MOE inspections. Interpreting the implications of deteriorating water quality results may entail more experience and knowledge than some operators have. One of the purposes of an inspection should be to identify situations that require analysis, assessment, and possibly action – especially where those situations may go beyond the expertise of the local operator.

For this type of assessment to be thorough and effective, it is essential that an inspector be armed with the relevant available information. None of this is particularly surprising or demanding. Nonetheless, the inspections program in which Ms. Zillinger operated did not point her in this direction. Like the two previous inspections in the 1990s, the inspection conducted by Ms. Zillinger in 1998 did not address the significant concerns about Well 5's vulnerability to surface water contamination.[25]

The primary source of instructions to inspectors of water treatment facilities during the 1990s was the standardized inspection forms prepared by the MOE. Although the content of inspection forms varied from time to time, the matters to be reviewed in MOE files as part of an inspection did not change significantly.

The inspection forms used by the three Walkerton inspectors required them to examine the Certificates of Approval and Permits to Take Water for wells in use at the time. However, neither the inspection forms nor any other instructions provided to inspectors directed them to review historical data or MOE files that might contain information about the quality of the water sources, even in the face of water test results showing deteriorating water quality from a particular source.[26] Moreover, no time was allocated to inspectors for the extensive effort that may have been involved in locating and assessing information of this nature.

9.3.3.1   *The 1998 Inspection*

In preparation for the inspection, Ms. Zillinger reviewed the most recent inspection report, the Certificates of Approval for the three wells then in use, and the Permits to Take Water from those wells. All of these items were in the Walkerton water file in the Owen Sound office. Significantly, she did not review several very important pieces of information that were kept in other MOE files or storage facilities. She did not consider important material that was assembled when Well 5 was approved in 1978 and 1979. This included the Wilson Report of 1978, Willard Page's memo of October 24, 1978, and the minutes of the meeting of November 23, 1978 – all of which addressed the vulnerability of Well 5. Ms. Zillinger was unaware that the MOE had recommended land-use protection measures because of what had been found in the chemical and

---

[25] Information that was critical to making a proper assessment about the quality of the water entering the system through Well 5 was available in MOE files or storage areas. However, it was contained in files or storage areas that the inspectors were not directed to review; some of these files or storage areas were not even accessible to an inspector. I discuss these issues in section 9.6.

[26] Other sources of instructions were found in "how-to" tools such as the Compliance Guideline and Delivery Strategies documents, management correspondence, and presentations to staff.

microbiological testing of the well's water. She was also unaware that these measures had never been implemented. She did not review the 1979 and 1980 inspection reports, or a letter of October 21, 1982, from Mr. Page of the MOE's Owen Sound office to the Walkerton PUC – all of which expressed concern about the vulnerability of Well 5 to surface contamination.

In her report, Ms. Zillinger expressed serious concerns about the eight occasions on which adverse bacteriological results had occurred since the last inspection, several of which included the presence of *E. coli* in the Walkerton system. Five of those results were labelled as coming from Well 5. If Ms. Zillinger had considered all the material in MOE files relating to Well 5, she would have learned that the siting and hydrogeological features of the well rendered it vulnerable to surface contamination.

The need for having available the relevant information of the type I am referring to was at least indirectly recognized in 1999, in an internal review and evaluation of the MOE's inspections program. That review recommended developing an information management system and standard business practice for the planned inspections program, to be used, in part, "as a tool for identifying and targeting high risk facilities." As it stood, the information systems available to MOE inspectors did not include such critical information as that indicating the vulnerability of Well 5 to surface contamination. I will be addressing the deficiency of the MOE's information systems in section 9.6.

Significantly, Ms. Zillinger's supervisor, Philip Bye, was not aware of either a written protocol or a direction regarding how an inspector should prepare for an inspection of a water treatment plant, other than the instructions implicit in the inspection form itself. He testified that it was his expectation that the inspector would review the file to prepare for the inspection, at least to the extent of reviewing the previous inspection report. However, the absence of a written protocol opened the door for inconsistencies in the material an inspector would review before carrying out an inspection.

A related flaw in the MOE's inspections program arose in 1994, when the ODWO was amended. As discussed above, the 1994 amendments introduced a requirement for continuous chlorine residual and turbidity monitoring for groundwater sources under the direct influence of surface water.

By the time Mr. Apfelbeck and Ms. Zillinger conducted their inspections in 1995 and 1998, respectively, the 1994 ODWO amendment – intended to provide greater protection for more vulnerable groundwater sources – was in effect. After making this amendment, the MOE should have drawn this new requirement to the attention of inspectors. This would have allowed inspectors to ensure, as part of an inspection, that they reviewed all material and information in MOE files that might be helpful in assessing whether the new requirement applied to wells they were inspecting – especially if there were recent adverse *E. coli* test results in the water from those wells.

The MOE did not, however, give inspectors any instructions relating to the amendment.[27] The inspection forms were not amended to reflect this new category of water source – groundwater under the direct influence of surface water – and its increased monitoring requirements.

In the same vein, the inspectors were not invited to bring the 1994 amendment to the attention of water systems operators, nor were they invited to inquire into the operators' competency either to assess the vulnerability of water sources to surface contamination or to understand the resulting need for continuous monitors. As a result, Ms. Zillinger had no discussion with Stan Koebel about the need to consider the installation of a continuous monitor at Well 5.

9.3.3.2   *The Impact on the Events of May 2000*

It is not possible to say with certainty whether Ms. Zillinger, armed with this additional information about the vulnerability of Well 5, and especially with knowledge of the 1994 ODWO amendments, would have done anything differently in conducting the 1998 inspection. In her testimony, she said that if she had known of the concerns about Well 5, it would have heightened her level of concern. She said she might "have pursued different directives or different courses of action" had she possessed that knowledge. Two other MOE witnesses, John Earl of the Owen Sound office and Donald Carr of the MOE's Water Policy Branch, said that if they had possessed all of the available information about Well 5 before the outbreak, they would have taken steps to

---

[27] Nor, as I point out in section 9.2, did the MOE institute a systematic review of existing Certificates of Approval to assess whether water sources supplying wells came within the amendment so as to require continuous monitoring. To make matters worse, the MOE did not have any program or practice of drawing the amendment to the attention of water facility operators so that they could assess whether their source(s) came within the amendment.

look into the possibility of a problem, and possibly would have ordered a hydro-geological study of the well. William Gregson, formerly a senior member of the Approvals Branch, was of the view that the 1979 inspection report alone showed Well 5 to be "hydraulically under the influence of surface water."

I am satisfied that a proper review of the available material would have led to the conclusion that Well 5 was under the direct influence of surface water – or, at a minimum, that a hydrogeological study of Well 5 was required. The conclusion, however reached, would have led to the installation of continuous chlorine residual and turbidity monitors at the well.

Moreover, had inspectors been directed to inquire, after the 1994 ODWO amendments, into the issue of whether groundwater sources then in use were under the direct influence of surface water, a review of the historical data and hydrogeological information in MOE files would have been essential. I am satisfied that if Mr. Apfelbeck in 1995 or Ms. Zillinger in 1998 had looked at this information, they would have set in motion a process to conclude that Well 5 was under the direct influence of surface water. That process would have resulted in the installation of continuous monitors at Well 5.

9.3.4 The Lack of Clarity in the Instructions to Review Operator Records

The instructions given to inspectors about what operator records should be reviewed as part of an inspection have varied from time to time, and there has been a lack of consistency and clarity in those instructions. When Ms. Zillinger inspected the Walkerton water facility in February 1998, neither the inspection form she used nor any other instruction she received from the MOE directed her to examine the daily operating sheets for any specific period before the month of the inspection. She examined only the sheet for the current month, February 1998, and as a result she did not see the suspicious pattern of daily chlorine residual entries for the months and years preceding her inspection. She did not, therefore, detect the unacceptable treatment and chlorine residual monitoring practices of the Walkerton PUC. I am satisfied that the inspections program was deficient in that inspectors were not directed to review the records of an operator for a period of at least one year before the time of an inspection.

A protocol in the *Report on Municipal Sewage and Water Treatment Plant Inspections*[28] directs inspectors as to how they should plan for the inspection of a water system. It indicates that before the inspection, the inspector should request certain information from the operator, such as a summary of the bacteriological sampling results for the previous year. It also offers guidelines on how to conduct the inspection itself. The inspector is required to review the previous three years of bacteriological and chemical data to determine whether the treated water quality meets the ODWO. Further, the inspector is required to document the method and frequency of the chlorine residual monitoring performed on the water.

James Mahoney, an MOE employee[29] who had had considerable experience in the MOE's inspections program, testified that there was no written protocol to supersede the 1989 protocol. He said that this was because inspections had not changed significantly since 1989. However, the 1989 protocol was not circulated widely, nor was it available on the MOE Web site. Tim Little, who also had had broad experience in the MOE,[30] testified that he never saw the 1989 protocol and that at least since 1995, when he worked there, it was not available in the Southwestern Region, which included Walkerton. Even if an inspector was aware of the 1989 protocol, it did not provide clear direction regarding the review of chlorine residuals.[31]

A sample inspection form in the 1989 SWIP report did make express reference to an "annual review of records" under the disinfection heading. It seems to direct the inspector to review chlorine residuals for a one-year period. Mr. Mahoney testified it was his experience that an inspector would review one year of chlorine residuals in the course of an inspection. However, he also said that the extent of the review is a matter of professional judgment by the inspector.

The three inspection reports of the Walkerton system in the 1990s are also of interest in terms of the instructions they give to an inspector. The 1991 and

---

[28] This report created the Sewage and Water Inspection Program (SWIP) in 1989. The protocol referred to is found in Appendix 4 of the report.

[29] MOE, Regional Program Coordinator, Kingston, seconded to the Drinking Water Regulation Implementation Team.

[30] MOE, Supervisor in the Assistant Director's Office, Southwest Region, seconded to the Drinking Water Regulation Implementation Team.

[31] On this topic, the protocol required the inspector to document only the method and frequency of the measurement of chlorine residuals.

1995 reports each have a section entitled "Record Keeping/Data Submission," which asks the question "Is a daily operational sheet maintained?" However, there is no specific direction as to the documents or period that should be addressed with respect to daily operating sheets. Sometime after 1995, the inspection form was redesigned by the MOE and the "record keeping" section was removed. Thus, Ms. Zillinger did not have the benefit of this section during her inspection in 1998.

The 1991 and 1995 inspection forms also required the inspector to record the annual average chlorine residual. This might imply that the inspector should review more than one month of chlorine residual entries on the daily operating sheets. However, this requirement was also unclear. In the absence of a specific direction to review the operator's records, an inspector might choose to rely on information provided by the operator to compile the annual average residual.

It appears unlikely that the two inspectors in Walkerton in 1991 and 1995 reviewed the operating sheets for any extended period, since they made no mention of suspicious repetitive entries. These suspicious entries went back as far as 1979. In any event, as previously mentioned, the inspection form used by Ms. Zillinger in 1998 did not require the annual chlorine residual to be set out.

The important point here is that the inspection form used by Ms. Zillinger in 1998 did not instruct her to review daily operating sheets of the water system, let alone to review the operating sheets for any specific period. The significance of this lack of instructions should not be understated. An inspector like Ms. Zillinger has a great many things to prepare and review in the course of an inspection. She also has a limited time to do them. In these circumstances, it would be unreasonable to count on an inspector to divert time and effort away from the parts of an inspection that he or she has been instructed to complete, in order to pursue other areas. Given the importance of chlorine residual monitoring to the safe operation of a water system, it was very important for inspectors to be given clear written instructions concerning how to evaluate an operator's residual monitoring practices.

9.3.4.1 *The 1998 Inspection*

During her inspection of February 25, 1998, Ms. Zillinger examined the operating sheets for Wells 6 and 7, but only for the month of February. She did not examine the February operating sheet for Well 5. In the sheets she did examine, the entries for chlorine residuals departed somewhat from the usual pattern, which was to record only residuals of either 0.5 mg/L or 0.75 mg/L. Instead, the February sheets showed a few residuals under 0.5 mg/L. Operating sheets for the months preceding February 1998 were not available at the well sites, and Ms. Zillinger did not ask to see them.

When Ms. Zillinger was shown the earlier operating sheets at the Inquiry, with the repeated entries of 0.5 mg/L or 0.75 mg/L, she observed that there was no variability from day to day or from week to week. This, she suggested, might have led her to be "somewhat suspicious" of the results. She said it would "bring into question the reliability of the data to see the same result every day." I agree with that observation.

Ms. Zillinger's suspicions would likely have been further aroused if she had noticed the unusual coincidence that the only month in which lower-than-required levels were recorded was February 1998, the month of the inspection. She also might have thought it unusual that the chlorine residuals obtained by the previous inspector in 1995 for the five wells then in use were also below the required level, ranging from 0.12 mg/L to 0.4 mg/L. The "coincidence" that the only unacceptable chlorine residuals were those noted at the times of inspections would probably have raised questions about the other entries and, from there, would have led to questions about the PUC's actual chlorine monitoring practices. If the entries of residuals were not in fact accurate, obvious questions would arise about the amount of chlorine being used and the way in which the residuals were being measured. The fact of inaccurate entries, one would hope, would enable a competent inspector to uncover what was actually taking place.[32]

When Ms. Zillinger was asked about her responsibility as an inspector with regard to the daily operating sheets, she replied that it was to conduct a "cursory" or "brief" review of these sheets in order to determine whether the operator was regularly recording information about flow and chlorine use. She would

---

[32] I note that all but one of the entries in the daily operating sheets for the days of the 1995 and 1998 inspections were 0.5 mg/L. These are inconsistent with the measurements taken by the inspectors. However, I do not attach any significance to the difference because there was no evidence that the entries had been made at the time the inspectors were on site. It is worth noting that when environmental officer John Earl examined the daily operating sheets for Well 5 on May 22, 2000, he found it "questionable" that the chlorine residuals were all 0.75 mg/L, and he advised his superior, Philip Bye, about this. Not surprisingly, Mr. Earl was suspicious.

ensure that the operator was in fact performing a chlorine residual test each day for the operating well. She would confirm that the residuals did not fall below a certain prescribed minimum level that would ensure adequate disinfection. Although these are the types of things that she would look for in the daily operating sheets, it was not her practice to go behind the current month's sheet, especially if, as she recalled was the case in Walkerton, those sheets were not at the well site. She testified that she understood her practice was in accordance with what was expected of her by the MOE.

The credibility of Ms. Zillinger's evidence in this respect is strongly supported by a memorandum she wrote to her superior, Mr. Bye, on June 4, 1998, within a month of completing her report on the Walkerton water system. The memo dealt with a new inspection form introduced by the MOE in 1998 that differed from the previous form in not including a number of sections that had existed in the previous form.

In her memo, Ms. Zillinger raised concerns about the new form's lack of clear directions from the MOE regarding what inspectors should do when conducting inspections of water systems. The "plant treatment requirements" section of the new inspection form, she wrote, was the only section that related directly to chlorination. That section required inspectors to simply indicate whether chlorination was being provided. Ms. Zillinger asked Mr. Bye whether this meant inspectors were no longer required to consider other issues, such as whether the operator maintained adequate chlorine residuals and contact time, among other issues. Further, she asked her supervisor whether inspectors were still expected to check chlorine residuals at the time of the inspection and compare the results to those of the operator.

Ominously, Ms. Zillinger also asked in her memo whether inspectors were expected "to review any plant records for completeness/accuracy," such as "daily operating logs" and "water quality analysis records." Further, she called for a written protocol to clarify what management expected of its inspectors and to promote consistency across the ministry.

Several months later, Mr. Bye included Ms. Zillinger's comments in a memo to the chair of a committee responsible for the review of the planned inspection reports. In the memo, Mr. Bye suggested there was a need to formulate protocol documents for each type of planned inspection. He said the protocols should clearly define the specific factors to be assessed under each heading of the inspection report. He suggested that, with the protocol documents, inspectors would have a more clear understanding of their inspection responsibilities.

Apparently there was no response.

9.3.4.2   *The Impact on the Events of May 2000*

Chlorination and chlorine residual monitoring practices are critical to the safe operation of drinking water systems that rely on chlorination for disinfection. It is difficult to think of anything more important. If nothing else, a properly structured inspections program should determine the adequacy of operators' practices relating to chlorination and the monitoring of chlorine residuals. Such a program should do so by clearly instructing inspectors to review an operator's daily operating sheets, where the relevant information is recorded. Further, inspectors should be instructed to review a historical sampling of operating sheets beyond the month in which the inspection occurs. An operator's typical practices are unlikely to be revealed simply by examining the operating sheets for a single month. A proper assessment of the adequacy of chlorination and monitoring practices therefore requires a more extensive examination of the operating sheets.

Some MOE inspectors examined daily operating sheets for the previous year. Others, like Ms. Zillinger, did not; but in either case there was no clear direction from the MOE as to what should be done. Ms. Zillinger's memo of June 4, 1998, speaks directly to the issue.

The 1989 sample inspection form referred to an "annual review of records," apparently referring to chlorine residuals. By the time Ms. Zillinger came to inspect the Walkerton system in February 1998, the reference to an annual review was no longer in the inspection form, at least not in the one used by the MOE's Owen Sound office. No evidence was presented about why this was the case. I am satisfied that the MOE's inspections program was lacking in that it failed to clearly set out which operator records should be examined by an inspector.

In the case of Walkerton, if Ms. Zillinger had reviewed the previous year's daily operating sheets, she would likely have uncovered the unacceptable treatment and monitoring practices of the PUC. In this event, she or others in the MOE would certainly have taken steps to ensure that in the years that followed, the

PUC properly monitored chlorine residuals daily, as it was expected to do. It has been suggested that even if she had unearthed the problems, it would not have mattered, because despite any steps the MOE might have taken, the PUC operators would have continued as they always had. I simply do not accept that. Surely if the MOE had known what had been going on in Walkerton, with proper follow-up it could have ensured conformance with the treatment and monitoring requirements. To suggest otherwise is to accept an abdication of responsibility by the MOE.

Although it may be true that in some cases a dishonest operator could avoid the detection of his or her improper practices, even by a competent and thorough inspection, that is not the case here. The PUC operators, perhaps because of their incompetence, made entries that would have rendered their improper practices easily detectable by a properly structured inspections program.

As I point out above, if the PUC had been monitoring chlorine residuals daily, the influx of contamination through Well 5 would very likely have been detected within 24 hours of its entry into the system. A proper response would have been to take corrective action, which could have significantly reduced the scope of the outbreak.

9.3.5   Follow-up Inspections

Walkerton was inspected three times in the 1990s. After the last inspection, in 1998, two years and three months elapsed before the tragedy. No further inspection had been scheduled. By the time of the 1998 inspection, at the very latest, it was clear to the MOE that Walkerton's water system had significant operating deficiencies. As a result, there should have been a follow-up inspection in 1999 and, if necessary, another in 2000. Unfortunately, this was not done. I find this failure to be a serious flaw in the way in which the MOE's inspections program was applied to Walkerton.

9.3.5.1 *Inspection Frequency*

The MOE's policy regarding both the frequency and the use of follow-up inspections has varied greatly over the years. There were frequent inspections of the Walkerton PUC in the 1970s, one overall inspection in 1980, and three inspections in the 1990s.

When the Sewage and Water Inspection Program was implemented in 1990, the goal of the MOE was to inspect all water treatment plants annually for compliance. However, due to staffing limitations and other program requirements, it was recognized that some time would pass before this goal would be reached. It was also recognized that larger, more complex plants or "problem plants" might require more frequent inspections.

In fiscal year 1991–92, most plants, including Walkerton's, were inspected. In 1992, it was decided that inspections were to be undertaken once every two years, again with "problem plants" receiving greater attention.

In 1994, the Provincial Auditor recommended that the MOE give priority to follow-up inspections for those plants identified as having significant compliance problems, instead of relying on a two-year inspection cycle of all water treatment plants. In response, the MOE stated that "inspection frequency will be based on risk assessment factors rather than routine cycles so that plants with historic problems will be inspected more frequently."

One senior MOE witness, Robert Shaw,[33] testified that after 1994, inspections were to be completed once every four years unless a significant deficiency was found, in which case a plant was to be inspected in the following year. After 1998, the MOE considered inspections of water treatment plants to be optional. However, when inspections were undertaken, priority was to be given to those with significant deficiencies.

9.3.5.2   *Red Flags Regarding the Walkerton Water System*

Over the years, many "red flags" had indicated that Walkerton required careful supervision by the MOE. On many occasions, the PUC had disregarded MOE requirements and directions. This started as early as 1978, when the PUC constructed Well 5 without the MOE's prior approval and then put it into operation without complying with the specifications in the Certificate of Approval. It continued in 1982, when the PUC, again without obtaining a Certificate of Approval, began installing a 2.5-km-long trunk main connecting Well 3 with the then-proposed Well 6. The MOE ordered the PUC to cease construction on that project until a Certificate of Approval was granted. In

---

[33] Regional Director, Central Region, Operations Division.

1987, when Well 7 was approved, a condition was included in the Certificate of Approval that was to be met within 15 months. It took the PUC almost seven years to comply.

In the 1990s, two even more serious problems became apparent to the MOE. The first was that the PUC continued to disregard the requirements for microbiological water testing that are set out in the ODWO. The 1991 inspection revealed that Walkerton was not complying with the ODWO and led to a recommendation that its microbiological monitoring program be upgraded. In a June 6, 1995, letter to the PUC, Mr. Page stated that it was essential for the monitoring program required by the ODWO to be implemented and maintained and that he trusted the PUC to take the necessary steps in order to comply. Shortly afterward, the PUC received a province-wide MOE letter, dated June 23, 1995, directing the PUC to implement and maintain a minimum sampling program. The program, which was set out in an appendix to the letter, included provisions for bacteriological, physical, and chemical sampling based on ODWO requirements.

In the 1995 inspection, it was found that the minimum sampling program had not been implemented. In response, Stan Koebel stated that he would comply. He did not. In July and August 1997, Walkerton was placed on a list of municipalities that were not conforming to their minimum sampling programs. This list had been compiled for the purpose of issuing Director's Orders. However, that fall, Walkerton was taken off the list after Mr. Koebel again undertook to comply. Because of Mr. Koebel's undertaking, the MOE did not issue an order. At the same time, it took no steps to confirm compliance.

During her inspection in 1998, Michelle Zillinger discovered that the PUC was still not meeting the requirements of the minimum sampling program. At the time of the inspection, Mr. Koebel told her that he would comply immediately. By the time the report was issued on May 6, he still had not complied. In a letter responding to the 1998 inspection report, dated nearly five months after the inspection, Mr. Koebel advised: "We *will be* up to the minimum sampling program by the end of July 1998" (emphasis added). In other words, he was still not complying. Although Philip Bye testified that through Michelle Zillinger, he had instructed Donald Hamilton, the environmental officer responsible for Walkerton at the time, to monitor the situation and to follow up, the 1998 visit by the MOE to the Walkerton water system was the last before the events of May 2000.

The second problem that should have become apparent to the MOE was that the Walkerton PUC was not adequately chlorinating the water. During each of the three inspections in the 1990s, the inspectors measured the chlorine residual of the treated water at the wells in Walkerton. All nine samples measured the chlorine residual at below the recommended level of 0.5 mg/L after 15 minutes of contact time.[34]

In 1995 and 1998, the inspectors recommended and emphasized the importance of maintaining adequate chlorine residuals after 15-minute contact time. Evidence at the Inquiry disclosed that the PUC may have changed its practice of underchlorinating for a brief time after the 1998 inspection. However, it soon reverted to the practice of inadequately chlorinating the water and entering false chlorine residuals in the daily operating sheets. The MOE, of course, was unaware that Walkerton continued to underchlorinate its water after the 1998 inspection because there were no further inspections before the outbreak.

The PUC's failures to follow the minimum sampling program and to adequately chlorinate the water went to the core of what is necessary to provide safe water. By 1998, the seriousness of these failures was compounded by increasing signs that the quality of the water in the Walkerton system was deteriorating. The 1995 inspection report refers to three adverse results in which *E. coli* was found in the distribution system. The 1998 report refers to an additional eight occasions on which there were adverse bacteriological results, several of which included *E. coli*. Five of these results were labelled as having come from the treated water at Well 5, and several others from within the distribution system.

Both reports emphasized that the presence of *E. coli* in treated water is an indicator of unsafe drinking water quality. Other witnesses agreed. Dr. Richard Schabas and Dr. Colin D'Cunha, the former and present Chief Medical Officers of Health for Ontario, respectively, testified that the adverse results disclosed in the 1998 inspection report were of sufficient concern to warrant follow-up action. Goff Jenkins, a long-time MOE employee with expertise in drinking water, agreed.

---

[34] In the 1991 report, Brian Jaffray recommended maintaining a level of between 0.3 mg/L and 0.5 mg/L. The residuals he obtained during that inspection were 0.3 mg/L and 0.35 mgL, and therefore conformed with what he understood a proper residual requirement to be. But his reference to 0.3 mg/L was in error for Well 5, because from the time of its approval the expectation had been that the Walkerton PUC would maintain a minimum total chlorine residual of 0.5 mg/L after 15 minutes of contact time at that well. In any event, at the time of the 1995 inspection report, four of the five samples taken by the inspector were under even 0.3 mg/L, reaching as low as 0.12 mg/L. The remaining sample was 0.4 mg/L.

I recognize that Garry Palmateer of G.A.P. EnviroMicrobial Services Inc. testi-fied that the frequency of adverse results at Walkerton between 1996 and 2000 was not unusual and that he did not perceive a potential public health hazard there. However, I am satisfied that these results indicated a potential problem, particularly in view of the operating deficiencies of the Walkerton PUC that were known to the MOE.

Willard Page said that after the 1995 inspection, it was evident that the Walkerton water system was a problem that should have been observed or monitored carefully. Even more serious problems were found during the in-spection in 1998. In her report, Ms. Zillinger set out three items under the heading "Action Required":

1. A minimum total chlorine residual of 0.5 mg/L, after 15 min. contact time, must be maintained in the water discharged to the distribution system for all active wells, at all times. A disinfectant residual must be detected in 95% or more of the monthly samples collected from the dis-tribution system.

2. The municipality must ensure that records are maintained documenting that a minimum of 40 hours of waterworks-related training has been provided to each operator each year. These records must contain all of the information outlined in s. 17(3) of Ontario Regulation 435/93.

3. The operating authority must immediately modify its water quality moni-toring program to meet the requirements of the Ministry's minimum recommended sampling program. Failure to meet all of the requirements of the program will result in the issuance of a s. 52(2) *Ontario Water Resources Act* Direction.

Ms. Zillinger recommended to her supervisor, Mr. Bye, that he issue a Director's Order with respect to the third item. He decided against issuing such an order, and I will review that decision in section 9.4. Instead, Mr. Bye sent a strongly worded letter *threatening* to issue an order if the PUC failed to comply. On July 14, 1998, Stan Koebel responded that he would comply with each of the items set out in Ms. Zillinger's report. There was no follow-up inspection to ensure that he did.

9.3.5.3   *The Failure to Conduct a Follow-up Inspection*

Apart from the issue of whether the MOE should have issued a mandatory order after the 1998 inspection, I am satisfied that it should have followed up that inspection with another inspection in 1999 and, if necessary, yet another after that.

One of the primary purposes of an inspections program should be to address problems like those found at Walkerton during the period leading up to and including the 1998 inspection. Time and again, the PUC general manager's assurances that the faulty practices would be corrected had proved unreliable.

The time had come when it was no longer acceptable for the MOE to rely on Mr. Koebel's assurances. It needed to follow up the 1998 inspection with a further on-site inspection within the following year in order to satisfy itself that the PUC was employing proper operational procedures that were critical to the safety of the water. It is reasonable to expect that a proper inspections program would have done so.

Robert Shaw, currently the director of the MOE's Central Region, seemed to suggest in his testimony that the ministry's policy at the time did not require a follow-up inspection in these circumstances. The problems at Walkerton were very serious. If in these circumstances the MOE policy did not mandate a follow-up inspection in the following year, it should have.

9.3.5.4   *The Resources of the Inspections Program*

Starting in 1995, the number of inspections began to decrease significantly. This coincided with and was likely related to significant budget and staff reductions in the MOE.[35] It is also likely that the overall reduction in inspections resulted in fewer follow-up inspections. James Merritt, a former assistant deputy minister of the MOE Operations Division, testified that there was a reluctance in some areas to conduct inspections because "the day was eaten up with reactive work" and that the staff would feel this to an even greater extent about follow-ups after inspections.

---

[35] These reductions are discussed in detail in Chapter 11 of this report.

Before his departure in 1997, testified Willard Page, then the district manager in Owen Sound, budget and staffing reductions had resulted in reductions in the frequency of inspections, site visits, and contacts between the MOE and the waterworks. This is consistent with other evidence concerning the activities at the MOE's Owen Sound office. From 1994–95 to 1999–2000, the number of annual planned inspections fell from 25 to 10, the number of actual inspections per year went from 16 to 10, and the amount of employee resources expended on communal water decreased from 10.17% to 5.12%. Starting in 1995–96, the number of inspections fell by about 50% ministry-wide.

There is no direct evidence that the failure to conduct a follow-up to the 1998 inspection in Walkerton was related to these reductions. I note, however, that the number of inspections conducted by the Owen Sound office and the amount of time spent on the communal water program in Owen Sound decreased significantly from 1994–95 to 1999–2000. This was due, at least in part, to the program planning process and delivery strategies implemented throughout the MOE to manage increased workloads after the budget and staff reductions.

I am not certain that a follow-up to the 1998 inspection would have been conducted had the budget reductions not taken place. It is fair to say, however, that after the budget reductions, the resulting refocusing of program priorities made it less likely that a follow-up inspection would occur.

9.3.5.5   *The Impact on the Events of May 2000*

The question then becomes whether a follow-up inspection would have made a difference to the outcome in May 2000. The three earlier inspections did not uncover the improper chlorination or chlorine monitoring practices. However, I am satisfied that a follow-up inspection, particularly if unannounced, should have discovered the unacceptable treatment and monitoring practices.

The 1998 inspection report directed the Walkerton PUC to maintain a chlorine residual of 0.5 mg/L after 15 minutes of contact time. Despite the assurance given by the Walkerton PUC in its letter dated July 14, 1998, it continued to treat the water inadequately at its wells and failed to maintain the required chlorine residual.

During a follow-up inspection, the inspector would have taken chlorine residual measurements and would have seen that, as in the preceding three inspections, the measured chlorine residuals of the treated water at the Walkerton wells were below the required 0.5 mg/L. By that point, it is reasonable to expect that the inspector would have been put on notice that proper treatment was not occurring on a regular basis. On looking into the matter, he or she would have discovered the pattern of failing to chlorinate adequately, failing to measure chlorine residuals daily, and recording false entries in the daily operating sheets. Once all this was discovered, the MOE had the necessary tools to ensure that adequate treatment and chlorine monitoring would take place in future. Had that occurred, it is very likely that the scope of the outbreak in May 2000 would have been substantially reduced.

It is worth noting that since the Walkerton tragedy, the government has recognized the importance of more frequent inspections and has initiated a program of annual inspections for all municipal water systems.

9.3.6 Unannounced Inspections

9.3.6.1 *Ministry Policy Regarding Unannounced Inspections*

It is self-evident that the enforcement of legislation and government guidelines is enhanced by visits that are made without advance notice. Unannounced inspections enable an assessment to be done under normal working conditions rather than in a situation possibly structured to accommodate the inspection.[36]

Unannounced inspections were contemplated by the MOE's policy. When the Sewage and Water Inspection Program (SWIP) was created in 1990, the MOE provided for unannounced visits to water treatment plants. The report of the meeting that created SWIP provided that, starting in April 1991, unannounced visits would be the normal way to conduct inspections. However, the 1989 protocol, which gave instructions to inspectors, directed them to contact the operating authority in advance to obtain certain information. For example, the operator was to be asked to provide summaries of the bacteriological sampling program and results for the previous year.

---

[36] Three MOE witnesses with experience in enforcement, Julian Wieder, Gordon Robertson, and Nancy Johnson, testified that they agreed that unannounced inspections were valuable for these reasons.

James Mahoney of the MOE testified that at the beginning of SWIP, the intent was to conduct unannounced inspections but that this was not carried out for a practical reason: smaller systems have facilities that are not continuously staffed. If an inspector was traveling some distance to do an inspection, it was prudent to have a person available at the facility to provide the inspector with the records to review. The practice was to provide notice of less than a week. This did not provide a great deal of time for the operator to "falsify things in a way that's going to really escape detection."

During the 1990s, unannounced inspections were within the discretion of an inspector, but there was no policy or practice within the MOE to give an inspector guidance or criteria on which to rely in exercising that discretion. Very few unannounced inspections were conducted in the Owen Sound office.

9.3.6.2 *The Impact on the Events of May 2000*

The three inspections of the Walkerton water system in the 1990s were announced in advance. In each case, the inspector made arrangements with Stan Koebel to attend on an arranged day.

It is not surprising that some operators might take advantage of announced inspections by creating an appearance of compliance. Stan Koebel testified that once inspections were arranged, he took steps to ensure that the pumphouses looked appropriate and that the chlorinators were working properly.

Mr. Koebel may also have taken the following steps to prepare for Ms. Zillinger's inspection in February 1998. The daily operating sheets for the month of February were the only operating sheets available at the well sites. They recorded varying chlorine residuals, some of which were less than the required 0.5 mg/L. These entries broke from the pattern of the previous months and years, during which either 0.5 mg/L or 0.75 mg/L was almost always recorded. The timing of this variation seems to be more than merely coincidental. Stan Koebel knew that the practice of not monitoring chlorine residuals and making false entries was wrong. He may also have known that chlorine demand can vary and that by making what I have called "suspicious repetitive entries," he ran the risk of being caught. He may well have changed the usual practice in anticipation of the inspection. As it turned out, Ms. Zillinger looked only at the February operating sheets for Wells 6 and 7 and therefore did not become suspicious about the integrity of the numbers recorded.

That said, it is difficult to say with any certainty whether, had the MOE used unannounced inspections in the 1990s, the inspectors would have discovered the unacceptable practices. At most, I can say that unannounced inspections would have increased the likelihood that those practices would have been discovered.

I am satisfied that the MOE should have carried out unannounced inspections, particularly for a problem water system like Walkerton's. If it had done an unannounced inspection to follow up on the 1998 inspection, the improper practices of the PUC would likely have been discovered and corrective action could have been taken.

9.3.7 Recommendations

Here I will set out recommendations for improving the inspections program that arise from the evidence I heard in Part 1. The Part 2 report of this Inquiry, which will address broader issues for the regulation and oversight of municipal water systems, will incorporate these recommendations.

Recommendation 13: The MOE's inspections program for municipal water systems should consist of a combination of announced and unannounced inspections. The inspector may conduct unannounced inspections when he or she deems it appropriate, and at least once every three years, taking into account such factors as work priority and planning, time constraints, and the record of the operating authority.

Recommendation 14: The MOE should develop and make available to all MOE inspectors a written direction or protocol, for both announced and unannounced inspections:

- outlining the specific matters to be reviewed by an inspector in preparing for the inspection of a water system;

- providing a checklist of matters that an inspector is required to review, as well as matters that it may be desirable to review, during an inspection of a water system; and

- providing guidance concerning those matters to be discussed with the operator of a water system during an inspection.

Recommendation 15: As a matter of policy, inspections of municipal water systems, whether announced or unannounced, should be conducted at least annually. The government's current program for annual inspections should be continued.

Recommendation 16: There should be a legal requirement that systems with significant deficiencies be inspected at least once per year. Ontario Regulation 459/00, also known as the Drinking Water Protection Regulation, should be amended to require that an inspection be conducted within one year of any inspection that discloses a deficiency as defined in the regulation. In this regard, deficiencies include any failure to comply with the treatment, monitoring, or testing requirements, or with specified performance criteria, set out in the regulation or in the accompanying drinking water standards.

Recommendation 17: The government should ensure that adequate resources are provided to ensure that these inspections are thorough and effective.

Recommendation 18: Copies of MOE inspection reports should be provided to the manager of the water system, the members of the operating authority, the owner of the water system, the local Medical Officer of Health, the MOE's local office, and the MOE's Approvals Branch.

Recommendation 19: The MOE should establish and require adherence to time lines for the preparation and delivery of inspection reports and operator responses, and for the delivery of interim status reports regarding remedial action.

9.4 Voluntary and Mandatory Abatement

9.4.1 Overview

Closely connected with the MOE's failure to conduct a follow-up to the 1998 inspection was the ministry's failure to make use of mandatory abatement measures after the 1998 inspection in order to address the operational problems at the Walkerton PUC. Instead, the MOE relied on a voluntary approach to abatement.

After the 1998 inspection report, the MOE should have invoked mandatory measures to require the PUC, among other things, to maintain a minimum chlorine residual of 0.5 mg/L. Had the MOE done so, and had there been proper follow-up, it is possible that the PUC would have complied. If the PUC had not complied, it is quite likely that the MOE would have detected a failure to comply and would have been in a position to ensure that appropriate corrective actions were taken. In either event, it is likely that the scope of the outbreak would have been significantly reduced.

One of the serious consequences of continually using a voluntary approach to correcting the operating deficiencies at Walkerton was to reinforce Stan Koebel's belief that the MOE requirements – found in guidelines, not in legally binding regulations – were not essential to the safety of the drinking water. The MOE's failure to insist that Mr. Koebel conform to MOE requirements, as well as its continued use of a voluntary approach, tended to support Mr. Koebel's misplaced confidence in the safety of the water even when the PUC's treatment and monitoring did not comply with MOE requirements.

9.4.2   Ministry Policies and Practices

9.4.2.1   *Voluntary and Mandatory Abatement*

Abatement is a term that describes measures taken by the MOE to bring about compliance or conformity with its requirements. In the case of water treatment plants, those requirements, in broad terms, focus on ensuring that treated water is free of contamination and that public health is protected.

When the MOE encounters a situation of non-conformance or non-compliance requiring corrective action,[37] it has the choice of proceeding by way of either voluntary or mandatory abatement. Voluntary abatement, as the term suggests, describes the process under which the MOE asks or directs an operator to take certain measures, without resorting to legal compulsion.

---

[37] "Non-compliance" is a term used to describe the failure to adhere to a legal obligation. "Non-conformance" describes a situation in which there is a failure to follow a non-legal requirement contained in a guideline or a policy statement.

Voluntary abatement may take a variety of forms: a letter, a violation notice, a recommendation in an inspection report, a phone call, or even an oral instruction during a field visit. Depending on the nature of the problem, voluntary abatement may involve establishing a program to be undertaken by a water utility within prescribed time limits.

Mandatory abatement is a more prescriptive response to a problem. It too may take several forms. The MOE may issue a control document – either a Director's Order or a Field Order[38] – requiring the operator to carry out the desired measures. Alternatively, the MOE may choose to amend an authorizing document, such as a Certificate of Approval, in order to direct the operator to do what is required. The hallmark of mandatory abatement, whatever form it takes, is that the required measures are compelled by a legal obligation and are subject to enforcement proceedings. Thus, mandatory abatement can convert a non-binding requirement under a government guideline or policy into a legally enforceable prescription, similar to a provision in legislation or a regulation.

Breaches of legally enforceable requirements – whether they are set out in legislation, regulations, ministry orders, or authorizing documents – are subject to enforcement proceedings. In the case of the MOE, those proceedings are generally handled by the Investigation and Enforcement Branch, although an MOE abatement officer may also lay charges. However, when the breach is only of a guideline or policy, and not of a legally binding obligation, enforcement proceedings are not an option.

9.4.2.2 *The Ministry's Compliance Guideline*

Environmental officers are frequently called upon to use either voluntary or mandatory abatement measures. After 1995, the key document that assisted them in choosing one or the other was the MOE Compliance Guideline. In 1995, the ministry conducted a program to train environmental officers from across the province in applying this guideline.

The Compliance Guideline has several criteria for pursuing mandatory abatement, including an unsatisfactory compliance record, deliberate non-

---

[38] Director's Orders and Field Orders are provided for under the *Ontario Water Resources Act*, R.S.O. 1990, c. O-40, and the *Environmental Protection Act*, R.S.O. 1990, c. E-9.

compliance, repeated violations, and unsatisfactory progress in a voluntary program. In these situations, the guideline suggests that mandatory abatement should be pursued unless it is decided that a voluntary program would be appropriate. The reasons for this decision are documented in an occurrence report. The guideline also provides that the MOE will issue no more than two written warnings before mandatory abatement is initiated. In no case will the MOE tolerate unsatisfactory progress on a voluntary abatement program beyond 180 calendar days.[39]

Despite the direction in the guideline, evidence at the Inquiry showed that MOE officials believed that a great deal of discretionary latitude existed even when the criteria for mandatory abatement were present. This came from a deeply rooted culture across the MOE that favoured a voluntary abatement approach whenever possible.

9.4.2.3 *The Culture of Voluntary Abatement*

MOE staff appear to have been reluctant to use mandatory abatement instruments, such as orders; rather, they sought voluntary compliance. The former district manager of the Owen Sound office, Willard Page, testified that in the late 1970s the MOE took a voluntary compliance approach in dealing with municipal water systems. He said that he was a proponent of voluntary abatement, as opposed to legal action, and that this philosophy had guided his career. In his view, it was more productive to avoid mandatory enforcement unless there was no alternative. Mr. Page saw municipalities as cooperative institutions that, for the most part, voluntarily followed recommendations relating to drinking water. He stated that his emphasis on voluntary compliance, prevailed in the MOE, and that he had followed it until his retirement in 1997.

According to Kevin Lamport, an MOE investigator from the Owen Sound office, some abatement officers were more likely than others to prefer voluntary abatement, as opposed to mandatory abatement or to passing matters on quickly to the Investigations and Enforcement Branch (IEB) for investigation. He said that in the Owen Sound office, the MOE staff who had started in the 1970s or earlier tended to prefer a voluntary approach. However, he did not

---

[39] This 180-day limit relates to any one period of unsatisfactory progress and not to the length of the program.

think that the Owen Sound office was any less willing than other MOE offices to refer matters to the IEB.

9.4.2.4 *The Shift Toward Mandatory Abatement*

In 1997, the culture of favouring voluntary abatement gradually began to change. In the fall of that year, the MOE compiled a list of municipalities that were not conforming with the ministry's minimum sampling program. This list ultimately led to a number of Director's Orders being issued.[40] In 1999, an internal MOE audit noted studies that had concluded that enforcement measures provide a better assurance of compliance than do voluntary approaches.[41]

In March 2000, the MOE issued a directive to its staff to follow a mandatory abatement approach. The directive stated that the MOE needed "a stronger/ tougher enforcement program." To implement this, it instructed staff to move the "pendulum ... more towards mandatory abatement and further away from voluntary abatement." Unfortunately, this directive had no effect on the MOE's supervision of the Walkerton waterworks before the events in May 2000. Since the Walkerton tragedy, the MOE has introduced policies strongly favouring mandatory abatement and the strict enforcement of government requirements.

9.4.3 Voluntary Abatement for the Walkerton Water System

In section 9.3, I described the checkered history of the Walkerton PUC with respect to MOE requirements for treatment and monitoring. I will not repeat the details here, but will recap briefly. During the 1990s, the PUC continually failed to follow the MOE's minimum sampling program. Further, on each of the three occasions on which the MOE had inspected the Walkerton PUC, the PUC had failed to maintain the required chlorine residual of 0.5 mg/L.

---

[40] As I have mentioned, Walkerton, which was initially on the list, was taken off in the fall of 1997 because Mr. Koebel assured the MOE that he would follow the program.

[41] In 2000, the culture of pursuing voluntary rather than mandatory abatement also generated external criticism. In the 2000 Provincial Auditor's report, the MOE was called upon to strengthen its enforcement activities by taking appropriate actions in response to violations, and by following up on a more timely basis. The Provincial Auditor also recommended that the MOE ensure that its policies and procedures manuals encourage the use of more stringent compliance measures where appropriate.

When Stan Koebel responded by letter, in July 1998, to the 1998 inspection report, the Walkerton PUC was still not conforming with the minimum sampling program. By then, the MOE had issued at least seven directives, in one form or another, telling the PUC to conform with the sampling program. Some of these directives were accompanied by threats that the failure to conform would result in a Director's Order. None of this made any difference to Mr. Koebel. In most instances, he responded by saying that he would conform and then not doing so. The pattern repeated itself time and again. By July 1998, he was still not complying; once again, he said that he would.

In his letter, dated July 14, 1998, Mr. Koebel stated that the PUC "will be maintaining a minimum total chlorine residual of 0.5 mg/L for all of our active wells." He also referred to continuous monitoring: "Hopefully, we will be purchasing equipment in the future to ensure a residual of 0.5 mg/L is kept at all times." The MOE accepted these assurances. Mr. Koebel, of course, did not maintain a chlorine residual of 0.5 mg/L: there was no legal requirement to do so. Once again, the MOE accepted his representations.

9.4.3.1   *The Failure to Issue a Director's Order in 1998*

In section 9.3, I concluded that the MOE should have conducted a follow-up inspection after Ms. Zillinger's 1998 report to ensure that the PUC had addressed the deficiencies she noted. I am also satisfied that, for essentially the same reasons, the MOE should have used mandatory abatement to ensure that the PUC complied with Ms. Zillinger's directions in the inspection report.

In her report, Ms. Zillinger identified three deficiencies and directed specific corrective action for each. Briefly, the actions required were to maintain a minimum chlorine residual of 0.5 mg/L, to keep proper training records, and to comply with the minimum sampling program.

Ms. Zillinger recommended to her supervisor, Philip Bye, that he issue a Director's Order with regard to the third matter – the need to comply with the minimum sampling program. He declined to do so. Instead, he instructed Ms. Zillinger to write a strongly worded letter, for his signature, *threatening* to issue a Director's Order if the PUC continued to fail to comply.

In his evidence, Mr. Bye gave a number of reasons for his decision not to invoke mandatory measures. He mentioned that the PUC was taking bacteriological samples and that the water was being chlorinated, although he acknowledged that the number of samples being collected was five fewer than required per month and that the chlorine residual occasionally fell below the required minimum. Mr. Bye also pointed out several other facts: that an MOE environmental officer was instructed to follow up in order to ensure compliance; that Mr. Koebel's July 1998 letter gave assurances that he would comply; and that throughout the fall of 1998, Mr. Bye did not receive any calls from the laboratory, the operating authority, or the Bruce-Grey-Owen Sound Health Unit about problems with Walkerton.

In my view, the wrong decision was made. I am satisfied that the MOE should have resorted to mandatory abatement in response to Ms. Zillinger's report and that the mandatory measures should have included each of the three corrective actions noted in her report. Mandatory abatement could have taken the form of a Director's Order. Alternatively, it could have been accomplished by amending the Certificates of Approval for the operating wells. The legal effect of either response would have been the same. The key point is that by this time, the MOE should have converted the corrective actions noted in Ms. Zillinger's report into legal obligations.

There was some suggestion at the Inquiry that the situation at Walkerton did not fit squarely within the Compliance Guideline's criteria for mandatory abatement. This was supposedly because the most serious issues with the PUC involved *non-conformance* with MOE guidelines, rather than *non-compliance* with legal obligations.[42] Several of the criteria in the Compliance Guideline refer to situations involving non-compliance, as opposed to non-conformance. The guideline also speaks of moving to mandatory abatement only after issuing two warnings and only in situations where there has been a failure to follow a voluntary program.

I do not propose to analyze whether the criteria in the Compliance Guideline, if interpreted narrowly, captured the Walkerton situation as it existed in 1998. If they did not, they should have. It is inconceivable to me that the MOE would issue guidelines for the use of mandatory abatement that would not have applied to the situation in Walkerton as described. Surely the repeated failures to conform, the broken promises, and the ignored warnings were enough to require mandatory measures.

---

[42] For an explanation of the difference between these terms, see note 37.

Before issuing a Director's Order, the MOE must first send a notice of its intention, which provides the operator with an opportunity to respond. The director of the Central Region, Robert Shaw, testified that even if Mr. Bye had issued a notice of a Director's Order in May 1998, that order would likely not have been issued, because Mr. Koebel, in his letter of July 14, 1998, agreed to comply with everything required by the inspection report.

I disagree with that approach. By July 1998, Mr. Koebel's assurances had no value. Mr. Shaw's view may have been influenced by the MOE culture favouring voluntary rather than mandatory measures. Mr. Bye's decision not to issue a Director's Order was consistent with that culture. I accept that many others in the MOE at that time would likely have made the same decision as Mr. Bye.

When Mr. Bye decided not to issue a Director's Order, he was unaware of Well 5's history of vulnerability. Like Ms. Zillinger, he had not seen the earlier files on Well 5 and did not know about the well's susceptibility to surface contamination. Had he known about these concerns, he would probably have attached more importance to the recent adverse results that showed *E. coli* in the treated water at Well 5 and in the distribution system. This underlines the significance of the MOE's failure to ensure that such information was readily accessible to those in the MOE who were making decisions about the safety of drinking water. I discuss the lack of an adequate information system in section 9.6.

I also observe that at the time he decided not to issue a Director's Order, Mr. Bye was not aware that *E. coli* could be lethal.[43] Although it is not possible to say that knowing the potential consequences of *E. coli* would have made any difference to his decision, it was certainly something that he should have known, and it might have tipped the scales in favour of mandatory measures.

I said above that a Director's Order should have been issued for each of the three action items in Ms. Zillinger's report. One of those items was to maintain a minimum chlorine residual of 0.5 mg/L. I appreciate that Ms. Zillinger's recommendation to Mr. Bye related only to the minimum sampling program. But in view of the deteriorating water quality at Walkerton, maintaining an adequate chlorine residual was so important that it should have been made a legal requirement.

---

[43] For that matter, neither Ms. Zillinger nor any of the other environmental officers who had oversight responsibilities for Walkerton were aware of this fact.

By 1998, the MOE had for several years been routinely attaching conditions regarding minimum chlorine residuals to Certificates of Approval for newly approved water systems. This approach made the minimum residuals a legal requirement. I see no reason why the same effect could not have been achieved by imposing a Director's Order as part of the abatement process on Walkerton's water system, where the PUC had shown disregard for the chlorination requirements. To comply with the requirements that would have been included in such a Director's Order, the PUC would have had to provide adequate chlorine and to monitor residuals regularly.

It is possible that if the MOE had taken the mandatory measures I suggest, either the PUC operators would have complied or the PUC commissioners, having been made aware of those measures, would have ensured compliance.[44] If, despite the legal requirement, the PUC had continued to fail to comply, then the MOE, with proper follow-up, should have discovered the non-compliance and ensured that the necessary corrective steps would be taken. Such actions would very likely have significantly reduced the scope of the outbreak in May 2000.

9.4.3.2 *The Impact on Stan Koebel*

I have found that Stan Koebel was primarily responsible for the inadequate chlorination and monitoring practices at Walkerton, which contributed to the outbreak in May 2000. Mr. Koebel was clearly wrong in failing to follow the MOE's requirements, and for that there is no excuse. But Stan Koebel believed the water was safe and, despite what he was told by the MOE about the need to chlorinate, he apparently thought he knew better. He did not fully understand the seriousness of the health risks involved or the importance of proper operating practices. This was due to a lack of training and qualifications; but it was also fuelled, I believe, by the MOE's failure to take appropriate action in the face of Mr. Koebel's repeated disregard of MOE requirements.

The requirements to treat and monitor residuals and to test for bacterial contamination were set out in guidelines, not regulations. They had no legal effect – and that in itself was not conducive to encouraging someone like Stan

---

[44] Walkerton's mayor at the time, James Bolden, who was also an *ex officio* PUC commissioner, testified that if the report had been accompanied by a Director's Order, the commissioners would have taken the report more seriously and ensured compliance.

Koebel to adhere to them. No doubt he was aware that disregarding a guideline is very different from breaching a legal requirement.

Added to this was Mr. Koebel's relationship with the MOE. This relationship was characterized, on Mr. Koebel's part, by breaches of MOE directives and broken promises. On the MOE's part, it was characterized by idle threats and failures to follow up. Although Mr. Koebel eventually complied with the minimum sampling program, the MOE's latitude on this issue for an extended period sent the message that, although the program might be a good idea, it was by no means essential to the safety of the drinking water. This message was reinforced by the very title of the program: the Minimum *Recommended* Sampling Program.

So too with the requirement to maintain a minimum chlorine residual of 0.5 mg/L. At the time of the three inspections, and likely on some other occasions when *E. coli* was found in the Walkerton system, Mr. Koebel was told about the importance of maintaining the minimum residuals. Unlike the situation with the minimum sampling program, though, he never met this requirement, at least on a regular basis. To do so, he would have had to increase the chlorine dosage normally added at the wells and then measure the residuals daily to ensure that the required residual was maintained.

The MOE clearly told Mr. Koebel on many occasions that it considered his deficient operating practices to be matters of concern and emphasized the importance of conforming to its guidelines. However, its failure to use mandatory measures to ensure compliance likely undermined the seriousness of this message.

9.4.4   The Ministry's Responses to the Adverse Results in Walkerton in 2000

Between the end of January and mid-April 2000, the MOE received five confirmed reports of total coliforms in samples taken at Walkerton – all relating to the treated water at Well 5 and the distribution system.[45] Counsel for the

---

[45] The first adverse result was from the treated water at Well 5 on January 31. The next three results were from the water at Well 5 (one sample) and from the distribution system (two samples) on April 3. The fifth result was from, once again, the treated water at Well 5 on April 17.

Municipality of Brockton argued that, in light of the multiple occurrences of total coliforms, the MOE should have pursued a more active response and, indeed, that this was required under the MOE's Delivery Strategies policy.[46] The policy states that repeat or multiple occurrences may indicate a systemic problem with a water system warranting further evaluation or action.[47]

The MOE staff responded to these reports of adverse results in various ways. First, they did nothing with respect to the adverse sample taken on January 31, 2000, because it was not from the distribution system.

Second, with respect to the adverse samples taken on April 3, Larry Struthers, of the MOE's Owen Sound office, testified that he considered them to be indicators of "deteriorating" water quality under the ODWO and that he there-fore called the Walkerton PUC on April 10. However, because there were two adverse results from different points in the distribution system, these samples were actually indicators of "unsafe" water quality, and the local health unit should have been notified. Through an oversight, Mr. Struthers did not notify the Bruce-Grey-Owen Sound Health Unit.

Third, John Earl, of the Owen Sound office, telephoned the Walkerton PUC on May 2 after he became aware of the "questionable" samples collected on April 3 and April 17. The PUC advised him that resamples had proved satis-factory and faxed him these results to confirm.

These adverse results – three from the treated water in Well 5, and two from the distribution system – over a period of roughly three months, raised con-cerns about the security of the water source for that well. It would have been preferable for the MOE to have responded by doing more than telephoning the PUC. However, in the result, I do not think that a stronger response would have affected the outcome in May 2000.

The January 31 and April 17 samples showed total coliforms in a single sample from Well 5 treated water. At worst, these samples were indicators of

---

[46] The Delivery Strategies policy was developed by the MOE to prioritize tasks undertaken by ministry personnel.

[47] The policy further states that, if any program priority is known or can reasonably be expected to be present, there is a need for staff to be involved in order to assess the issue and determine whether there are any adverse effects, environmental impairments, or other violations.

"deteriorating" drinking water quality under section 4.1.4 of the ODWO,[48] and the specified response is to notify the MOE district officer "so that an inspection of the sampling sites can be undertaken to determine the cause." Further, section 4.1.4 states that "[s]pecial samples should be taken" as provided by section 4.1.3.1,[49] and, if these samples are positive, "then corrective action ... will be initiated" as provided by section 4.1.3.[50]

In response to the April 17 result, MOE staff telephoned the PUC and determined that the follow-up samples were negative. It appears that this response did not conform to the most obvious interpretation of section 4.1.3.1, in that special samples were not taken. However, the evidence showed that MOE officials routinely interpreted this section as requiring only telephone calls to ensure that follow-up samples tested negative for total coliforms and *E. coli*.

With regard to the April 3 samples, Mr. Struthers simply made a mistake in failing to note that the two samples from the distribution system were taken on the same day and that this was an indicator of "unsafe" water quality that

---

[48] Section 4.1.4 of the ODWO reads as follows:

> Any of the following conditions indicate a deterioration in drinking water quality:
> a)   total coliforms detected as a single occurrence (but not *Escherichia coli* or other fecal coliforms);
> b)   samples contain more than 500 colonies per mL on a heterotrophic plate count analysis;
> c)   samples contain more than 200 background colonies on a total coliform membrane filter analysis;
> d)   *Aeromonas* spp., *Pseudomonas aeruginosa, Staphylococcus aureus; Clostridium* spp. or members of the Fecal Streptococcus (*Enterococcus*) group are detected.
>
> If any of these conditions occur, the MOEE district officer should be notified so that an inspection of the sampling sites can be undertaken to determine the cause. Special samples should be taken as indicated in 4.1.3.1, if these are positive then corrective action as outlined in 4.1.3 will be initiated.

[49] Section 4.1.3.1 reads, in part, as follows (emphasis in original):

> **Special sampling** shall consist of a minimum of 3 samples to be collected for each positive sampling site. ... The measurement of the chlorine residual in the vicinity of the positive sampling site may assist in determining the extent of the contamination within the distribution system, and may be used to determine the appropriate corrective action.

[50] Section 4.1.3 provides for specific corrective action to be taken, based on the presence of indicators of unsafe water quality, including notification "of the MOEE District Officer who will immediately notify the Medical Officer or Health and the operating authority to initiate collection of **special samples** and/or take corrective action" (emphasis in original). Corrective action includes "immediately increasing the disinfection dose and flushing the mains to ensure a total chlorine residual of at least 1.0 mg/L or a free chlorine residual of 0.2 mg/L to all points in the affected part(s) of the distribution system." If satisfactory chlorine or disinfectant residuals are not detected, then a boil water advisory may be issued by the Medical Officer of Health.

should have been reported to the local health unit. Even if he had reported those results, however, it is unlikely that this would have made any difference to the actions taken by the Bruce-Grey-Owen Sound Health Unit in response to the outbreak in May 2000. The evidence indicated that the health unit would not have issued its boil water advisory earlier than Sunday, May 21, even if it had been informed by Mr. Struthers of the April 3 results.

I do not think that the adverse samples received in January and April 2000, disclosing total coliforms but not *E. coli* in the water system, should have by themselves led to mandatory abatement. However, I have concluded that by this point, the MOE should have taken mandatory measures. The significance of the samples is that they gave a further opportunity to review the situation at Walkerton in order to determine whether mandatory measures were necessary. However, given that it was the district supervisor at the Owen Sound office who decided, in 1998, not to issue a Director's Order, it seems unlikely that an environmental officer, such as Mr. Struthers or Mr. Earl, would have reached a different conclusion in 2000 after addressing the adverse samples. The problem is not so much with the way in which the environmental officers responded to the samples, but rather with the MOE's general failure to take mandatory measures.

9.5 Operator Certification and Training

9.5.1 Overview

Stan and Frank Koebel had extensive experience in operating the Walkerton water system but lacked knowledge in two very important areas. First, they did not appreciate the seriousness of the health risks arising from contaminated drinking water. Second, they did not understand the seriousness of their failure to treat and monitor the water properly. They believed that the untreated water supplying the Walkerton wells was safe: indeed, they themselves frequently drank unchlorinated water.

Managing a communal water system entails enormous responsibility. Competent management includes knowing more than how to operate the system mechanically or what to do under "normal circumstances." Competence, for those managing a water system, must also include appreciating the nature of the risks to the safety of the water as well as understanding how protective measures, such as chlorination and chlorine residual and turbidity monitoring, protect water safety and why they are essential. Stan and Frank Koebel lacked this knowledge. In that sense, they were not qualified to hold their respective positions with the Walkerton PUC.

In this section, I will review two MOE programs that are relevant to the issue of the qualifications of the Koebel brothers: the operator certification program and the operator training program. Under the operator certification program, Stan and Frank Koebel were certified as water distribution class 3 operators[51] at the time of the outbreak. They had obtained their certification through a "grandparenting" scheme based solely on their experience. They were not required to take any training courses or to pass any examinations in order to be certified. Nonetheless, I conclude that given the standards of the day and the practical considerations that arise when introducing a certification program, it was not unreasonable for the MOE to use grandparenting when introducing mandatory certification in 1993, provided that adequate mandatory training requirements existed for grandparented operators.

After 1993, under the operator training program, the MOE required 40 hours of training per year for each certified operator. Stan and Frank Koebel did not take the required amount of training, and the training they did take did not adequately address drinking water safety. I am satisfied that the 40-hour requirement should have been more clearly focused on drinking water safety issues and, in the case of Walkerton, more strictly enforced.

It is difficult to say whether Stan and Frank Koebel would have altered their improper operating practices if they had received appropriate training. However, I can say that proper training would have reduced the likelihood that they would have continued those improper practices.

9.5.2 The Walkerton PUC Employees

I have described the qualifications of Stan and Frank Koebel in Chapter 5 of this report, which deals with the role of the operators. I will briefly review their backgrounds here.

---

[51] Throughout this report, I refer to this licence as a "water operator's licence" or "operator's licence."

9.5.2.1 *Stan Koebel*

Stan Koebel began his employment with the Walkerton PUC when he was 19 years old, having completed Grade 11. He started as a labourer in 1972 and, after completing an apprenticeship and an examination, was a hydro lineman from 1976 to 1980. In 1981, he was appointed to the position of foreman, and in 1988, upon the retirement of his predecessor, Ian McLeod, he became general manager.

Stan Koebel described his initial training in how to operate a water system as "basically seeing and hands on." He never completed a course in which he had to pass an examination in order to qualify as an operator of a water system. He first obtained certification in 1988, through a voluntary grandparenting scheme.

In the mid-1990s, the MOE increased the classification of the Walkerton water distribution system from a level 2 to a level 3 classification. The 1995 inspection report indicated that, although the system had been upgraded to level 3, operating staff had not yet been upgraded to that level. Mr. Koebel subsequently applied for upgrading, and the MOE upgraded his designation in 1996 to a class 3 operator.[52] Throughout all of this, the MOE did not require him to take any courses or examinations.

As of May 2000, Mr. Koebel held a class 3 operator's licence with an expiry date of February 2002. No one had ever interviewed Mr. Koebel about his level of knowledge or competence. He believed that the Walkerton water sources were "okay," and he regularly drank unchlorinated water. He did not believe that the water needed to be treated to the extent required by the MOE, that is, having a minimum total chlorine residual 0.5 mg/L after 15 minutes of contact time. Although he had received some information on chlorination, his comfort about the safety of the Walkerton water resulted, in part, from his superficial knowledge of both the threat posed by potential contaminants and the importance of disinfection by chlorine.

I recognize that Mr. Koebel stood to benefit at the Inquiry by taking the position he was not qualified to operate the Walkerton water system and by attempting to minimize his level of knowledge about the risks that his practices posed to his community. One cannot excuse his repeated failures to do what he was told. However, I am satisfied that his improper practices were not

---

[52] This designation was as a class 3 distribution operator, as opposed to treatment operator.

the result of any malice or ill will. He did not properly appreciate the risks that his practices posed, nor did he understand the necessity of chlorination and monitoring.

9.5.2.2   *Frank Koebel*

Frank Koebel was hired by the Walkerton PUC in 1975, when he was 17 years old. His older brother, Stan, was already working there. Frank Koebel had completed Grade 12 and had attended trade school to learn to be an auto mechanic. He never took any courses related to the operation of a water system. He was given the opportunity to do so, but felt that he was too busy and could not take the time off. Over the years, he did attend between 13 and 20 water systems conferences sponsored by the Georgian Bay Waterworks Association.

When Stan Koebel became the PUC's general manager in 1988, he recommended that Frank Koebel replace him as foreman, which he did. Like his brother, Frank Koebel first obtained a waterworks operator licence in 1988 through a grandparenting process, without taking a course or passing an examination. After the Walkerton water system was upgraded, his certification was upgraded to a class 3 operator's licence[53] without any training or examination. As of May 2000, Frank Koebel held a class 3 licence that was due to expire in February 2002.

Since becoming the PUC's foreman in 1988, Frank Koebel had spent about 25% of his time dealing with water and the other 75% dealing with electricity. He testified that he did not think he had sufficient technical training to do his job and that he should have been more aware of the regulations and requirements. The PUC did possess manuals relating to water systems, but Frank never read them, nor did he ever see any other PUC employees reading them. He thought that Walkerton had good-quality water, and if the chlorinator broke down for a short period of time, "it wasn't a major issue."

---

[53] As with Stan Koebel, this was a licence for a class 3 distribution operator, as opposed to treatment operator.

9.5.2.3 *Other PUC Employees*

Robert McKay was first employed in Walkerton in May 1998. While employed at the PUC, he held a journeyman lineman certificate and a water operator's class 1 licence.[54] He had obtained the latter designation in 1991 through the grandparenting process while employed by another community's PUC.

Mr. McKay was employed almost exclusively on the electrical side of the Walkerton PUC. He rarely collected water samples from any of the wells in Walkerton, nor did he see water test results while he was employed by the PUC. He was unaware of the PUC's improper treatment and monitoring practices. None of his actions as a PUC employee are connected to the outbreak of May 2000.

Allan Buckle was hired by the PUC in 1992 as a maintenance worker. He did not have a waterworks operator's licence. With the approval of Stan and Frank Koebel, he read the chlorine residuals at the wells in Walkerton, made entries on the daily operating sheets, and took samples for laboratory tests. Frank Koebel had shown Mr. Buckle how to take water samples, check the meters, and complete the daily operating sheets. When Frank was busy with other tasks, he permitted Mr. Buckle to check the wells. Because he did not have an operator's licence, Mr. Buckle should not have been taking water samples and measuring chlorine residuals. However, Stan and Frank Koebel bear responsibility for involving an uncertified operator in these tasks.

9.5.3 The Grandparenting of Water Operators

The certification of water operators began in Ontario in 1987 with a voluntary certification program. The purpose of certifying water operators was to protect Ontario's drinking water by ensuring that operators had the required knowledge and experience to perform their duties, by promoting professionalism, and by establishing and maintaining operator standards.

There was a "grandparenting" provision for operators, meaning that those who had experience and education could be certified without meeting the examination requirements. The educational requirement for class 1 and 2 operators was 12 years of elementary and secondary school education; there was no

---

[54] Mr. McKay's licence was for both distribution and treatment.

requirement for training. Relevant work experience could be substituted for education.

The deadline for applying for a grandparented voluntary licence was October 1990. Stan Koebel applied for his certification[55] in February 1988. His application indicates that he had completed 12 years of school education and 15 years of related employment experience. Although Mr. Koebel signed the application, it does not appear that he was the person who actually filled out the form. He testified that it was Ian McLeod's idea that he apply for grandparenting. In 1988, he was granted certification as a class 2 operator for a three-year period.

Stan Koebel testified that he had had only 11 years of education, rather than the required 12, when he applied for certification. The general practice in such cases would be to refer the application to an advisory board to decide whether his experience could be substituted for the minimum educational requirement. My belief is that Stan Koebel would have been grandparented even if he had accurately stated in his application that he had 11 years of education.

Frank Koebel also applied for voluntary certification in February 1988. He had 12 years of elementary and secondary school, 4 years of trade school, and 10 years of related employment experience. Like his brother, he was granted certification as a class 2 operator in 1988.

Operators who were certified through the voluntary grandparenting process did not have to meet any additional requirements to renew their licences.

Certification was made mandatory for water operators in June 1993 under Ontario Regulation 435/93. When this requirement was introduced, operators were given a second opportunity to apply for grandparenting. The deadline for doing so was February 1, 1994. Stan and Frank Koebel both applied for and received grandparented certification.[56]

Under Ontario Regulation 435/93, grandparented licences expire after three years, within which time the operator must pass an examination. In practice, however, the regulation has been applied in such a way that people who were

---

[55] "Certification" refers to the Ontario Water and Waste Water Utility Operator's Certification.
[56] When an operator applied for grandparenting, employers were required to sign the applications to confirm the operator's length of employment. However, they were not asked to comment on the ability or knowledge of the employee, and the MOE did not check references.

grandparented under the voluntary program, such as Stan and Frank Koebel, are not subject to the requirement to upgrade, prior to renewal, by taking an examination.[57]

Although I will be making recommendations in the Part 2 report of this Inquiry to strengthen Ontario's certification program, it should be noted that Ontario was, and still is, ahead of many other provinces in this area. In 1993, Ontario was one of two provinces, along with Alberta, that required the mandatory certification of operators.[58]

Jurisdictions that have made certification mandatory have used grandparenting as a transitional measure. Alberta used grandparenting when it introduced mandatory certification in 1993. Further, all of the other provinces except Quebec have used grandparenting to some degree in their voluntary certification programs. In the United States, most states use grandparenting as part of their certification programs. Indeed, the Inquiry heard evidence that many U.S. states have legislated the requirement for grandparenting in order to prevent current employees from being negatively affected by certification.

One of the main purposes of the 1987 and 1993 grandparenting provisions was to ensure that experienced operators would maintain their employment.[59] Another purpose was to ensure that there would be enough experienced licenced operators to meet Ontario's needs. Introducing mandatory certification without grandparenting might have created a serious shortage of water operators. Quite reasonably, transition to a program of full testing was required. As of 2001, approximately 75% of operators had obtained their certification by passing examinations.

It appears that municipalities are becoming more discriminating in their hiring practices. Max Christie, the president of the Ontario Municipal Waterworks Association and an experienced water system manager, testified that he could not think of a municipality that would now hire an operator who did

---

[57] Those who were not grandparented under the voluntary program could be grandparented under the regulation for a period of three years; after that, however, they were required to pass an examination for renewal. If they failed, their licence would be downgraded by one class.

[58] All other provinces except Quebec had a voluntary certification program in place. Since that time, Nova Scotia has introduced mandatory certification programs. Saskatchewan has passed legislation that will require certification over a transition period of five years, and Quebec is also moving in that direction.

[59] The Canadian Union of Public Employees and the Ontario Public Service Employees' Union were both in favour of grandparenting to protect the seniority rights of employees.

not have at least two years of postsecondary education. Further, both he and Brian Gildner, a former MOE policy adviser, testified that certification by examination is only one way to ensure that operators are competent. It provides the owner of the water system with a measure of the operator's competence in terms of his or her knowledge of the theory behind the operation of a water system.

In the result, I am satisfied that the MOE's use of grandparenting as a means of obtaining certification was consistent with and, indeed, ahead of the practices of many other jurisdictions. Ontario has moved more quickly than most provinces toward mandatory certification and toward requiring training and examination for all operators who are being certified. That evolutionary process should continue.

Although one of the consequences of granting Stan and Frank Koebel certification without a training and examination requirement may have been that they had less knowledge than they should have had, I do not think that it is reasonable to expect the Province of Ontario to have moved toward mandatory training and testing prior to certification any more quickly than it did. However, it was important that the grandparenting process for certification be accompanied by sufficient training for water operators after they obtained certification.

9.5.4   The Training of Water Operators

For years, the MOE offered training courses to water operators. By 1999, it no longer offered such courses. The important issue, however, is not whether the MOE provided the training but whether it took adequate steps to ensure that operators had proper training from some source. For completeness, I will begin by briefly describing the history of the MOE's involvement in the delivery of training programs.

The predecessor to the MOE, the Ontario Water Resources Commission, first offered training to water operators in 1959. In 1970, the MOE created a training centre in Brampton. Partly as a result of voluntary certification measures in 1987, the MOE funded the establishment of the Ontario Environmental Training Consortium (OETC). The aim of the OETC was to provide training for operators across the province, through community colleges. At the same time, the MOE maintained a training program through its Brampton training centre.

Until 1990, OETC courses were heavily subsidized by the MOE. Participants were charged about $60 for a course that actually cost $400–$500 per week. In 1990, to ensure that the community colleges could offer these courses in a competitive manner, the MOE subsidy for the training of operators was removed and the full price was charged. This had two effect: it encouraged larger municipalities to train in-house and encouraged private sector trainers to enter the market.

Ontario Regulation 435/93, enacted in 1993, made certification mandatory and required 40 hours of continuing education each year for water operators. Between 1990 and 1995, the OETC offered courses using MOE materials through 16 community colleges. In 1995, however, it ceased coordinating operator training, and training was transferred to the Ontario Clean Water Agency (OCWA). Then, in 1999, OCWA restricted training to its own staff.

The role of the MOE is now limited to advertising available courses. It evaluates courses very generally, to see whether they have the correct type of content and duration to assist with certification examinations, but the MOE does not specifically approve or accredit courses.

Between 1974 and 1995, more than 17,600 people participated in the MOE's training courses through its training centre in Brampton. Also, from 1990 to 1995, an additional 1,450 people participated in OETC courses offered through community colleges.

The elimination of MOE training courses was no doubt a part of the budget and staff reductions that took place within the MOE in the 1990s. I discuss these in detail in Chapter 11 of this report.

When the price of courses increased, it became difficult for smaller communities to pay for training. When certification became mandatory in 1993, these communities focused on certification courses for their operators rather than on process-related training. Access to training was still a problem for operators in remote communities because of the cost of the courses, the expenses of travel, and the fact that there might not have been any replacement staff to operate the water system while they attended courses.

According to the MOE files, no operators from the Walkerton PUC attended any of the ministry's courses. This was highly unusual, because it was common for most PUC employees and municipal employees to attend MOE training.

Although Stan Koebel obtained certification under the voluntary certification program, he was unaware that the OETC offered courses to assist with certification or that until 1990 the MOE offered courses at a subsidized rate to operators. There were, however, other training opportunities available, and the important issue is not whether the MOE provided the training itself but whether, as regulator, it took steps to ensure that water operators like Stan and Frank Koebel received adequate training.

9.5.5 Training Requirements Under Ontario Regulation 435/93

In 1993, when the MOE provided for mandatory certification but allowed for a grandparenting regime, the need for operator training became readily apparent, particularly for grandparented operators. It was especially important that the training focus on issues relating to water safety. For grandparented operators, mandatory training could ameliorate some of the concerns that might arise from the lack of a testing requirement.

Ontario Regulation 435/93 requires water operators to have 40 hours of continuing education per year and requires that records be kept detailing such training. I do not think that the amount of training required – 40 hours – is necessarily deficient. However, I find that two problems exist with the training requirements in relation to the operators in Walkerton. The first problem is the failure to require training that is sufficiently focused on water safety issues. The second is the MOE's unwillingness to enforce compliance with the training requirements under the regulation.

Although there may be some benefit in requiring training for other matters, the main focus of the mandatory training program should have been on the protection of public health. However, the regulation does not clearly set out what constitutes training for the purposes of the required 40 hours per year. As examples, the regulation states that the training may include training in new or revised operating procedures, reviews of existing operating procedures, safety training, and studies of information and technical skills related to environmental subjects.[60]

---

[60] O. Reg. 435/93, s.17(2).

There is no requirement for the training to focus on technical issues involving water treatment or distribution, or on human health issues such as the significance of pathogens in drinking water. The Inquiry heard testimony from Brian Gildner that if the entire 40 hours of training had been spent entirely on workplace safety issues, that would not have been a contravention of the regulation. Further, Max Christie testified that there should be more definitive guidance in the legislation concerning what is expected.

Importantly, in relation to the events in Walkerton, after the 1994 ODWO amendment requiring continuous monitors for groundwater that is under the direct influence of surface water, there was no requirement for training with respect to assessing the vulnerability of water sources or understanding the need for continuous chlorine residual and turbidity monitoring.

9.5.6 The Training of Walkerton PUC Employees

Stan Koebel testified that he was not aware of specific criteria regarding what constituted training for purposes of Ontario Regulation 435/93. But his interpretation of training seemed to stretch common sense. For example, after the 1998 inspection, he included in his training log the time that he spent during the inspection with Ms. Zillinger (recording six hours, although he spent only two hours with her). He referred to this as "MOE updates." Mr. Koebel also included time he spent explaining the water system to a new employee as training, both for himself and the new employee. Had the criteria for training been more specific and more focused on water safety issues, it would have been more difficult for Stan Koebel to adopt such a liberal interpretation of training.

The second problem with the training requirements is that the MOE did not strictly enforce compliance with O. Reg. 435/93. Compliance was especially important in the case of certified operators like Stan and Frank Koebel, who had never been tested. Further, in both of the MOE inspections that took place after the regulation came into force, the Walkerton PUC was found to be violating the regulation. In fact, the PUC's "training log" was created after the 1998 inspection.

Section 17 of O. Reg. 435/93 requires the maintenance of records documenting compliance with the requirement of 40 hours of annual operator training.

At the time of the 1998 inspection, Ms. Zillinger found that the Walkerton PUC did not have a record demonstrating that such training had been provided. There was no follow-up; nor was there an inquiry into whether the PUC employees had completed the required 40 hours of training.

Because the Walkerton PUC did not maintain accurate training logs as required by O. Reg. 435/93, it is impossible now to determine how much training Stan and Frank Koebel underwent between 1993 and 2000 or to determine the exact nature of that training. The regulation stipulates that they should each have taken at least 240 hours of training by the year 2000. I am satisfied from the evidence that neither of them took this amount of training, and I am also satisfied that a great deal of what they considered to be training was not focused on water safety issues. Stan and Frank Koebel are primarily responsible for their failure to take the required amount of training. However, the MOE's failure to require training that was specifically focused on water safety, as well as its failure to enforce the training requirements in O. Reg. 435/93, reinforced the Koebels' lax approach to training.

Although more training focused on water safety would certainly have been preferable, it is difficult to determine whether Stan and Frank Koebel would have altered their practices if they had received that training. What I can say is that if they had received more training directed to important issues concerning water safety, the likelihood that they would have continued their improper practices would have been reduced.

9.5.7   Recommendations

In the Part 2 report of this Inquiry, I will be making extensive recommendations with respect to the operation of municipal water systems. I will include in those recommendations the following, which emerge from the findings I have made above.

Recommendation 20: The government should require all water system operators, including those who now hold certificates voluntarily obtained through the grandparenting process, to become certified through examination within two years, and to be periodically recertified.

Recommendation 21: The materials for water operator course examinations and continuing education courses should emphasize, in addition to the technical requirements necessary for performing the functions of each class of operator, the gravity of the public health risks associated with a failure to treat and/or monitor drinking water properly, the need to seek appropriate assistance when such risks are identified, and the rationale for and importance of regulatory measures designed to prevent or identify those public health risks.

Recommendation 22: The government should amend Ontario Regulation 435/93 to define "training" clearly, for the purposes of the 40 hours of annual mandatory training, with an emphasis on the subject matter described in Recommendation 21.

Recommendation 23: The government should proceed with the proposed requirement that operators undertake 36 hours of MOE-approved training every three years as a condition of certification or renewal. Such courses should include training in emerging issues in water treatment and pathogen risks, emergency and contingency planning, the gravity of the public health risks associated with a failure to treat and/or monitor drinking water properly, the need to seek appropriate assistance when such risks are identified, and the rationale for and importance of regulatory measures designed to prevent or identify those public health risks.

Recommendation 24: The MOE should inspect municipal water systems regularly for compliance with Ontario Regulation 435/93, enforce the regulation strictly, and follow up when non-compliance is found in order to ensure that operators meet certification and training standards.

9.6 The Accessibility of Information

9.6.1 Ministry of the Environment Information Systems

I have discussed above the MOE's failure on several occasions in the 1990s to take note of the vulnerability of Well 5 to surface contamination and to use that information in making decisions about what to do at Walkerton. Well 5's vulnerability was well documented in MOE files, dating from 1978 to 1982. On several occasions in the 1990s, it was important to have access to this information in order to make fully informed decisions about current circumstances and the proper actions to be taken. I refer here to the three inspections of the Walkerton water system, the several occasions when environmental officers received adverse water quality reports showing *E. coli* in the treated water at Well 5 and in the distribution system, and the situation in 1994, after the ODWO was amended, at which point a systematic review of water sources should have been undertaken. On occasions like these, it was important for the MOE to be able to properly assess contamination threats in order to determine whether further steps needed to be taken to ensure the safety of the water.

None of the MOE personnel with responsibility for Walkerton in the 1990s reviewed the information in the ministry's files about the vulnerability of Well 5 to surface contamination. There were several sources of this information. Located in the Approvals Branch file for Well 5 were the PUC's application to construct well 5, the hydrogeologist's report supporting the application, MOE correspondence and memoranda, and minutes of meetings between the MOE and the PUC. Relevant information also existed in the 1979 and 1980 inspection reports and in a letter, dated May 21, 1982, from Willard Page of the MOE's Owen Sound office to the Walkerton PUC.

However, by the mid-1990s, when the water quality at Walkerton began to show signs of deterioration, these documents (or copies of them) were no longer being filed or stored in a manner that was readily accessible to those who were responsible for overseeing the Walkerton water facility.

In 1994, the MOE's Owen Sound office received a directive from the MOE's Records Branch in Toronto concerning the destruction of documents in the office. As a result, many pre-1986 documents were either shredded or archived at a location away from the office. Thus, from the mid-1990s onward, the Owen Sound office's file on Walkerton – the "Walkerton water file" – included the Certificates of Approval and the Permits to Take Water for the three operating wells, copies of the most recent inspection reports, and all adverse test results after 1995.

Four consultants' reports relating to the Walkerton water system were kept in the MOE's Owen Sound office in various places, separate from the Walkerton water file. One report – the 1992 needs study by B.M. Ross and Associates Ltd. – was kept on a shelf in the filing room with other consultants' reports. The other three – including the very important 1978 Ian D. Wilson Associates report on Well 5 ("the Wilson report") – were in the storage area in another part of the building. The evidence showed that none of the people who were responsible for overseeing the Walkerton system during the mid- and late 1990s had easy access to anything other than the Walkerton water file and the 1992 needs study.

The MOE did not maintain a computerized information management system designed to include information about the quality of source water for municipal water systems. The computerized information system to which MOE personnel, like those responsible for overseeing Walkerton, would routinely have access was the Occurrence Reporting Information System (ORIS). The ORIS was designed to keep track of occurrence reports that were ordinarily prepared to record occasions when water facility operators were not complying with regulations or other legally binding obligations, or to record instances when matters were referred to the MOE's Investigation and Enforcement Branch. Although a report of this nature might refer to the quality of source water, by no means would this always be the case. In the case of Walkerton, the ORIS materials no reference to the vulnerability of Well 5 as described in the 1978 hydrogeology report.

9.6.2   The Impact on the Events of May 2000

The upshot of all of this is that MOE personnel such as Philip Bye, the district supervisor; Michelle Zillinger, the 1998 inspector; and the other environmental officers who dealt with Walkerton did not have ready access to, and did not refer to, the historical information about the vulnerability of Well 5. Knowledge about the source and quality of the water supplying a municipal water system and about the types of contamination threats to which it may be susceptible is critical to determining the proper treatment, monitoring, and microbiological testing requirements for a facility. MOE personnel who are confronted with test results that reveal deteriorating water quality at a particular well may be called upon to determine whether the treatment and monitoring programs used by the well's operator are adequate. To do so, they require as much information as possible about the quality of the water source.

The information about the vulnerability of Well 5 should not have been permitted to disappear from institutional memory. All the MOE witnesses who were asked considered this information to have been important in making effective decisions about Well 5 when the quality of water began to deteriorate in the mid- to late 1990s. The information should therefore have been readily accessible to the MOE personnel who dealt with Walkerton.

The MOE's failure to have a proper information storage and retrieval system contributed to several of the failures in the oversight programs that I have described above. Had there been a proper information system, the Approvals Branch could have more easily identified Well 5 as a candidate for continuous chlorine residual and turbidity monitoring. Furthermore, the MOE's inspections and abatement programs would have been more likely to identify the seriousness of the problems at Walkerton and to initiate the appropriate corrective action.

9.6.3   Recommendation

As a result of the above, I would make the following recommendation:

Recommendation 25: The MOE should proceed expeditiously to complete the design and implementation of the management information system now under development (that is, the Integrated Development System, or IDS). That system should include the capacity for the creation and maintenance over time, in electronic form, of water system operator profiles consisting of any hydrogeological or other consultant's report relating to the water system; relevant operator chlorine residual measurements; past inspection reports; drinking water test results for a reasonable period; all operator responses to inspection reports; and all applicable Certificates of Approval, Permits to Take Water (PTTW), Field and Director's Orders, occurrence reports, and information concerning the safety and security of public water sources and supplies.

9.7 The Training of Ministry Personnel

9.7.1   The Lack of Adequate Training

Evidence at the Inquiry showed that the MOE personnel in the Owen Sound office who dealt with Walkerton were unaware of certain matters that were essential to carrying out their responsibilities in overseeing the Walkerton water facility. For example, Philip Bye, the Owen Sound district supervisor; Michelle Zillinger, the 1998 inspector; and John Earl and Larry Struthers, the two other environmental officers who dealt with Walkerton, were all unaware that *E. coli* was potentially lethal. It would seem essential that those who have the responsibility to oversee communal water systems and who might be required to direct or coordinate responses to adverse water quality reports should fully appreciate the nature and potential consequences of important threats to water safety and human health.

In addition, some of the environmental officers were unaware of, or at least unclear about, certain provisions of the ODWO – the government guideline they were responsible for enforcing. In July 1999, for instance, Mr. Earl did not know he was required by the ODWO to notify the Bruce-Grey-Owen Sound Health Unit of the presence of *E. coli* in the Walkerton water system.

Moreover, there were differing views about the interpretation of some aspects of section 4.1.2 of the ODWO, which defined indicators of unsafe water quality. Further, none of those who had responsibility for the Walkerton water system followed the procedures specified in section 4.1.4, which directs the inspection of sampling sites after a notification of indications of "deteriorating" water quality. They also did not follow the procedures specified in section 4.1.3.1, which deals with taking special samples after a notification of indications of "unsafe" water quality. There was evidence that it was not the general practice of MOE personnel to take either of these steps. What this reveals, it seems to me, is the lack of a coordinated ministry-wide training program to address the interpretation and application of the drinking water guidelines.

The failures of MOE personnel to have a uniform understanding of certain provisions specified in the ODWO, or to follow other provisions, are problems that should have been addressed through appropriate training.

I am careful here to point to a lack of training, rather than to the failings of certain individuals. I am confident that if the individuals involved had received the proper training about the health risks associated with *E. coli* or about the content and interpretation of the ODWO, they would have used that information appropriately in carrying out their duties.

9.7.2 The Impact on the Events of May 2000

The effect, if any, of this lack of training on what happened in Walkerton in May 2000 is difficult to measure. I am satisfied that it did not have any direct effect. At most, it may have had an impact on some of the decisions affecting Walkerton that were made in the MOE's inspections and abatement programs.

I have discussed those decisions in detail elsewhere in this report, so in this section I will set out only my conclusions about the lack of training. First, if Philip Bye had known that *E. coli* is potentially lethal, it is more likely that he either would have issued a Director's Order in response to the 1998 inspection report or would have ensured that the 1998 inspection was properly followed up. However, it is by no means certain that knowing this one additional fact would have led him to take either of these steps.

Second, John Earl's failure to notify the Bruce-Grey-Owen Sound Health Unit of the adverse results showing the presence of *E. coli* in the Walkerton water system in July 1999 had no effect on the actions of the health unit in responding to the crisis in May 2000. I accept the evidence that even if the health unit had been informed of that result, Dr. Murray McQuigge and his staff would not have issued the boil water advisory any earlier than they did.

Third, even if the environmental officers who received results indicating deteriorating water quality had then inspected the sampling sites as specified in the ODWO, it is unlikely that they would have become aware of the two operational problems that contributed to the outbreak: the lack of continuous monitors at Well 5 and the improper treatment and monitoring practices of the PUC. Moreover, because the MOE did not in practice perform such inspections, additional training might have reinforced that approach instead of leading to additional inspections.

Fourth, the MOE's failure to insist that PUC operators follow the special sampling procedures specified for use when *unsafe* water quality is indicated falls into the same category as the immediately preceding conclusion, which relates to the less serious situation of *deteriorating* water quality. Although it is surprising, given the clear language of section 4.1.3.1 of the ODWO, that MOE personnel did not require water operators to take special samples, it is nevertheless most unlikely that even if MOE personnel had required the Walkerton PUC to follow the special sampling procedures, there would have been any effect on the outbreak in May 2000. Further, given the ministry-wide practice of not requiring operators to follow the special sampling procedures, additional training might have led the MOE to question the utility of the provision and to decide to delete the requirements so that the guideline would comply with MOE practices.

Finally, although the environmental officers' differing interpretations of some ODWO provisions is a matter of serious concern, I do not conclude that this confusion led to any of the failures of oversight functions that affected the events of May 2000.

All of that said, it is necessary not to lose sight of the importance of training MOE personnel. The overall approach has been for MOE staff in local offices to act as generalists who can work on the ministry's wide range of program areas. As a result, environmental officers do not normally have specialized expertise in issues relating to drinking water when they begin to work on the MOE's communal water program. For this reason, regular training for MOE staff in technical and regulatory issues that relate to drinking water is very important.

I will be addressing the issue of training in depth in the Part 2 report of this Inquiry. However, because of its importance, I think it is useful to briefly summarize my findings about the deficiencies in the present MOE training program and to set out recommendations that flow from those findings.

9.7.3 The Trends in the Ministry's Training Program

During the 1990s, two trends emerged in the training program for MOE personnel that need to be addressed. First, there was a substantial reduction in the MOE's training budget. Second, there was a reduction of training in technical areas.

The first trend shows that the MOE's training expenditures have substantially eroded over the past decade. MOE training expenditures were reduced by approximately 30% in the five-year period from 1995–96 to 1999–2000 alone.[61] It can also be seen in the reductions to the MOE's "learning ratio."[62] The learning ratio declined from 0.92% in 1989–90 to 0.36% in 1993–94. It climbed back up to 0.95% in 1997–98 and to 1.17% in 1999–2000; however, this resulted from the significant staff reductions in 1996 and 1997, rather than from any increase in training programs.

The second trend, the shift away from technical training, was accompanied by a move toward management and administrative training.[63] On several occasions, MOE documents expressed concern about the lack of technical training. Most recently, an MOE human resources plan in 2000-2001[64] reported that the MOE has difficulties attracting and retaining skilled personnel in a number of areas. Science professionals were identified as a priority for the next few years. As such, special efforts should be made to recruit, develop, and retain individuals in designated science positions.[65] Technical training within the MOE is clearly an essential part of ensuring that an adequate base of technical knowledge exists in the ministry.

The MOE's human resources plan recognized that the MOE competes with other government and private sector organizations to retain technical staff. Skilled personnel often leave the MOE after they have developed their knowledge and expertise. Also, the demographics of MOE staffing indicate that many technical specialists will retire within the next few years.

---

[61] Specifically, the combined total of Actual Salaries (includes all salaries paid to OPS training staff) and Actual Other Direct Operating Expenditures (includes all OPS training costs other than salaries) fell from $1,021,200 to $698,700. (The time periods indicated reflect fiscal years.) Three factors contributed to the significant reductions: (1) there were fewer employees after 1997–98; (2) one position was transferred to the Shared Services Bureau in 1999; and (3) the basic training of water system operators was transferred to OCWA in 1995.

[62] The "learning ratio" is the amount spent by the MOE on staff development as a proportion of total salaries and wages.

[63] The aim was to help career development with courses on career counselling and résumé-writing.

[64] MOE, "Human Resources Business Plan and Learning Plan for Fiscal Year 2000–2001."

[65] According to the MOE human resources plan, positions with a strong emphasis on science demand skills that, combined with advanced scientific education, require extensive on-the-job experience and knowledge that is gained only through time and investment in learning.

9.7.4 Recommendations

Recommendation 26: A full needs assessment for training should be undertaken for MOE technical staff, and a component of that assessment should focus on communal drinking water.

Recommendation 27: The MOE, on the basis of the needs assessment, should develop and maintain both introductory and advanced mandatory courses for environmental officers pertaining to communal drinking water systems. These courses should emphasize science and technology, including all matters that could present a risk to public health and safety; emerging pathogen risks; existing, new, and emerging treatment technologies; the limits of particular technologies; and the proper interpretation and application of government regulations, guidelines, and policies.

Recommendation 28: The MOE should devote sufficient resources to technical training to allow the ministry to meet the challenges outlined in its "Human Resources Business Plan and Learning Plan for Fiscal Year 2000–2001."

9.8 The Ontario Drinking Water Objectives and the Chlorination Bulletin

In exercising its regulatory and oversight responsibilities for municipal water systems, the MOE developed and regularly applied two sets of guidelines or policies: the Ontario Drinking Water Objectives (ODWO) and the Chlorination Bulletin.

The ODWO sets out matters critical to the production and delivery of safe drinking water, including the maximum acceptable concentrations in drinking water of substances that could threaten human health, the method and frequency of microbiological testing, the corrective steps to be taken when samples exceed certain limits, and the monitoring requirements for various types of water sources.[66]

---

[66] The ODWO also includes a notification protocol to be followed when indicators of unsafe water quality are found. I address this issue in detail in Chapter 10 of this report.

The Chlorination Bulletin contains guidelines for the disinfection of potable water and distribution systems, including detailed information about when disinfection is required, minimum chlorine residuals, chlorination equipment, and monitoring.[67] The Chlorination Bulletin makes clear that disinfection to kill pathogenic organisms is the most important step in any water treatment process.

The MOE's use of guidelines rather than legally binding regulations to set out the requirements for producing safe drinking water had two possible effects on the events in Walkerton. First was the effect on the PUC operators, particularly Stan Koebel. As I point out above, Stan Koebel routinely failed to follow many of the operational requirements set out in the ODWO and the Chlorination Bulletin. The very nature of a "guideline" implies that it includes practices and standards that are recommended and encouraged but that are not mandatory in all situations.

Stan and Frank Koebel, who genuinely believed that the untreated water in Walkerton was safe, would no doubt be more comfortable about not following a guideline than about not following a legally binding regulation. That said, it must be recognized that the MOE repeatedly informed Stan Koebel of the importance of complying with the guidelines, and still he failed to do so. While it is far from certain that the presence of a regulation would have made a difference to the way in which Stan Koebel operated the water system, it is fair to say that he would have been more likely to follow a legally binding requirement than a guideline.

The second possible effect of the use of guidelines is that it may have affected the MOE's decisions with respect to invoking mandatory abatement measures and conducting a follow-up to the 1998 inspection. Had the Walkerton PUC been found to be in non-compliance with a legally enforceable regulation, as opposed to non-conformance with a guideline, it is more likely that the MOE would have taken stronger measures to ensure compliance, including the use of enforcement proceedings and further inspections. If the MOE had followed either of these courses of action, it would likely have detected the improper practices of the Walkerton PUC and taken steps to ensure that they were corrected.

---

[67] The provisions of the ODWO and the Chlorination Bulletin are more fully discussed in Chapter 4 of this report.

It is important to note, however, that before May 2000 there was no initiative, or even suggestion, either from within the MOE or externally, to make a regulation mandating the treatment, monitoring, and testing practices and standards found in the ODWO and Chlorination Bulletin. Although the use of a regulation to address some or all of the matters in the ODWO and Chlorination Bulletin seems like a sensible approach, the culture that prevailed in the MOE, and among those who managed and operated the broader drinking water supply system, apparently did not recognize the advantages of such an approach.[68] For years, these matters were dealt with by way of guidelines. When it was thought that stronger measures were required, the MOE attached conditions to Certificates of Approval or issued a Director's Order. Both of these responses created legal obligations.

I am satisfied that the use of a regulation, as a general approach, is the most logical way to set out requirements for treating, monitoring, and testing drinking water. Because of the importance to public health, there is a significant benefit in making these requirements legally enforceable, where practical. Relying on conditions in Certificates of Approval and Director's Orders can be a haphazard way of addressing these matters. In August 2000, the government recognized the sense of changing its approach and passed Ontario Regulation 459/00, also known as the Drinking Water Protection Regulation, mandating requirements for treating, monitoring, and testing communal drinking water. I will be commenting on the adequacy of this new regulation extensively in the Part 2 report of this Inquiry.

The evidence disclosed a number of poorly drafted and confusing provisions in the ODWO and the Chlorination Bulletin. Here I refer to the lack of clarity in section 4.1.2 of the ODWO about whether the samples referred to include treated water samples, the uncertainty about the inspection required under section 4.1.4 of the ODWO when conditions of deteriorating water were detected, the difference between the corrective actions required by section 4.1.3 of the ODWO and section 5 of the Chlorination Bulletin, and the difference in the language used in the two guidelines to set out the requirements for continuous chlorine residual monitoring.

---

[68] In contrast, there was a strong push to include the notification protocol for adverse water quality results in a legally binding regulation after the privatization of water testing services in 1996. For reasons I develop in Chapter 10 of this report, it never took place.

Although these problems relating to the guidelines are unsettling, I do not find that any of them are linked, even indirectly, to the events in Walkerton.

9.9 The Ministry's Response to the Boil Water Advisory in May 2000

The MOE did not immediately initiate an investigation of the Walkerton water system on May 21 when it was informed that contaminated water was a suspected source of the illnesses and that the Bruce-Grey-Owen Sound Health Unit had issued a boil water advisory for Walkerton. Moreover, when the MOE learned of relevant information about the Walkerton system on May 22, after it had begun its investigation, it did not immediately pass on that information to the health unit. Although it would have been preferable for there to have been more immediate communication by the MOE to the health unit, I am satisfied that nothing turns on this failure. The boil water advisory had been issued on May 21, and it is unlikely that the health unit would have done anything differently if the MOE had provided the information sooner.[69] Despite reaching this conclusion, I think it useful to describe what, in fact, occurred.

In the early evening of May 21, Philip Bye, the area supervisor at the MOE's Owen Sound office, learned that a boil water advisory had been issued for Walkerton. He was informed by Clayton Wardell, director of health protection at the health unit, and the MOE's Spills Action Centre that two cases of *E. coli* infection and 50 cases of bloody diarrhea had occurred in the Walkerton community. Mr. Wardell reported that the health unit had issued a boil water advisory because contaminated water was suspected as the source of the illnesses. As previously mentioned, Mr. Bye was not aware that *E. coli* O157:H7 in the water system could result in deaths.

Mr. Bye told Mr. Wardell that his staff had not reported any unusual occurrences in relation to the Walkerton system. At the time, Mr. Bye did not recall the 1998 inspection report or the April 2000 sample results. Mr. Wardell indicated that the Walkerton PUC had reassured the health unit that the water was fine and that Stan Koebel had increased the chlorination and was flushing the water system.

---

[69] It is possible that, if the health unit had the adverse results of the May 15 samples on May 22, it would have disseminated the boil water advisory more broadly or make the language of the advisory stronger. However, I am not convinced on the evidence that either of these steps would have been taken.

Mr. Bye was aware on May 21 that John Earl was on duty as the emergency response officer for the MOE's Owen Sound office on the May long weekend. However, he decided that it was unnecessary to initiate an investigation of the Walkerton water system at that time because the health unit had issued a boil water advisory, the source of the illnesses was being investigated by the health unit, and the Walkerton PUC had increased the chlorine levels and was flushing the system.

The next morning, on May 22, at 10:00 a.m., Mr. Bye received another call from Mr. Wardell. He was informed that the number of *E. coli* cases had increased to 90 or 100 and that the health unit was reasonably certain the water supply was the source of the illnesses in Walkerton. Mr. Bye indicated that if the health unit required the assistance of the MOE, it should contact the Owen Sound office. Again, he did not initiate an investigation of the Walkerton system despite the increase in the number of individuals with *E. coli* and the health unit's reasonable certainty that contaminated water was responsible for the illnesses. It was only at noon on May 22 – after Dr. Murray McQuigge, the local Medical Officer of Health, stressed the urgency of an MOE investigation – that Mr. Bye requested the Spills Action Centre to dispatch Mr. Earl to the Walkerton PUC.

At 1:00 p.m., the Spills Action Centre instructed Mr. Earl to carry out "a field response to an incident of adverse water quality and disease outbreak in the town of Walkerton." Mr. Earl was told that the health unit was concerned that the contamination of the water supply was responsible for gastrointestinal illness in Walkerton. He contacted his supervisor, Mr. Bye, who instructed him to speak to David Patterson of the health unit before his departure to the Walkerton PUC and to carry out the health unit's requests.

Mr. Earl was told by Mr. Patterson that an alarming number of cases had been reported to local hospitals and that the health unit had received confirmation of *E. coli* O157:H7 in stool samples. He was told that the health unit had investigated various food sources – community events, group picnics, and barbeques – but was unable to explain the sudden increase in gastrointestinal illness in Walkerton. Mr. Patterson explained that the water system was highly suspect and that the health unit had issued a boil water advisory the previous day. He also told Mr. Earl that the health unit had sent water samples to the Ministry of Health's laboratory in London for testing.

Mr. Patterson asked Mr. Earl to obtain a number of documents from the PUC for the previous two weeks, including bacteriological test results, chlorine residual levels at the wells and the distribution system, and water flow records. The health unit also sought documentation on the recent construction of the watermains, the disinfection of the mains, and any unusual events that had occurred in past weeks. Mr. Earl was asked to investigate breaches in the water system.

Stan Koebel met Mr. Earl at 4:00 p.m. on May 22 at the PUC office. At the request of Mr. Earl, Mr. Koebel provided several documents, including: a copy of Stan Koebel's notes that described his activities at the Walkerton PUC from May 19 to 22 and that confirmed he had been chlorinating and flushing the system throughout the weekend; the A&L Canada Laboratories report of May 5 indicating that positive coliforms were present in samples at Well 5 "raw" and "treated"; the A&L report of May 17, which indicated positive *E. coli* and positive total coliforms in samples labelled "Well 7 treated," "125 Durham Street," and "902 Yonge Street.";[70] and daily operating sheets for Wells 5 and 6 for May 2000. Mr. Koebel told Mr. Earl that the daily operating sheet for Well 7 was not available and that it would be provided the following day.[71]

At the time of Mr. Earl's visit, Wells 5 and 7 were operating. Mr. Koebel explained that a new chlorinator had recently been installed at Well 7. Mr. Earl asked whether there had been any unusual events in the past two weeks, and Mr. Koebel responded that the only significant event was an electrical storm that had "knocked out" Well 6. The heavy rains and flooding on the previous weekend were discussed in the context of the potential contamination of well water by surface water. Mr. Koebel said he had flushed the watermains at various locations during the May long weekend and had increased the chlorine residual levels at the wells.

Mr. Earl also discussed staff qualifications at the PUC with Stan Koebel. Mr. Koebel said that he and Frank Koebel were the primary operators of the water system and that they were certified. Occasionally, however, a PUC employee who was not licensed would monitor the system. Mr. Earl collected

---

[70] At Well 7 treated, there were more than 200 counts of total coliforms and *E. coli* per 100 mL, and a heterotrophic plate count of 600 per 1 mL.

[71] Stan Koebel had not produced that sheet because he intended to "revise" it in order to conceal the fact that Well 7 had operated without chlorination.

raw and treated samples from Well 7 and a treated sample from the PUC office on 4 Park Street. He arranged to meet Mr. Koebel the following day.

Mr. Earl did not contact Mr. Patterson to advise him of the information he had obtained at the PUC. He knew the health unit had collected water samples in Walkerton and that it was awaiting results from the Ministry of Health's laboratory. Mr. Patterson had specifically asked Mr. Earl to obtain bacteriological test results from the previous two weeks. Mr. Earl learned from his review of the A&L Canada Laboratories report that there were high *E. coli* counts and total coliforms in water samples collected at the PUC on May 15. Yet Mr. Earl did not convey this information to the health unit. Nor, on May 22, did he inform his superior, Mr. Bye, of the results from A&L. Mr. Earl testified that he did not consider the situation to be urgent because a boil water advisory had been issued for the Walkerton community.

On the morning of May 23, Mr. Earl returned to the Walkerton PUC to collect additional information on the water system. He was provided with the daily operating sheets for Well 7 for May 2000, which, as discussed in Chapter 3, had been "revised" by Frank Koebel on his brother's instructions. Mr. Earl also received the annual water records from 1997. After receiving the documents, he collected samples from each of the wells and from the distribution system.

In reviewing the documents, Mr. Earl observed that none of the wells appeared to have operated between May 3 and May 9. He thought this was highly unusual. He also thought that the chlorine residual levels at Well 5, which were all entered as 0.75 mg/L on the daily operating sheets, were "questionable." Mr. Earl discussed the records, as well as his observations of the Walkerton system, with Mr. Bye. He indicated that there were *E. coli* and total coliforms in treated samples collected on May 15 and that Well 7 had been operating without disinfectant for several days. Mr. Earl also informed Mr. Bye that Stan Koebel had not disclosed this information to the health unit. Nevertheless, the records and information gathered by Mr. Earl on May 22 and May 23 were not provided by the MOE to the health unit.

On May 23, Mr. Bye was informed by Mr. Patterson of the results of the water samples analyzed by the Ministry of Health's laboratory; high counts of *E. coli* and total coliforms were found at a restaurant in Walkerton and at the Bruce County administration building. Mr. Bye was also told that it was clear from the epidemiological curve and patient mapping by health unit staff that all areas of Walkerton had been affected by the gastrointestinal illness. Nevertheless, Mr. Bye did not disclose to Mr. Patterson the information that Mr. Earl had collected on the Walkerton water system. When asked at the Inquiry why he failed to do so, Mr. Bye replied: "I can only assume that over the weekend, in conversations that Mr. Earl had had with Mr. Patterson, that information had been relayed."

At a meeting in the afternoon of May 23, attended by representatives of the Bruce-Grey-Owen Sound Health Unit, the MOE's Owen Sound office, the Town of Walkerton, and the Municipality of Brockton, Mr. Bye announced that the MOE would conduct an investigation of the Walkerton system. He suggested that the chlorine levels in the water system be increased and that an independent authority assume control of the water system.

On May 25, the MOE issued a Field Order to the Municipality of Brockton pursuant to the *Ontario Water Resources Act*. It required the municipality to submit an action plan on the response to the contamination of the system, to prepare a report on the causes of the contamination, and to retain a qualified operating authority to oversee the operation and to ensure the safety of the drinking water. It was on this day that the Ontario Clean Water Agency assumed control of the Walkerton water system.

9.10 Ministry Organizational Chart

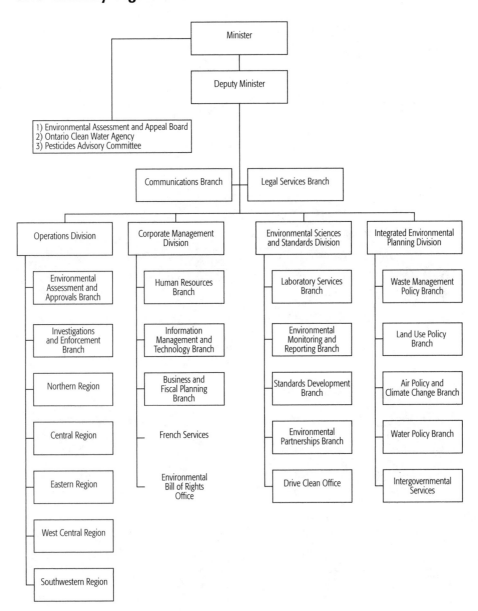

Chapter 10   The Failure to Enact a Notification Regulation

Contents

Chapter 10   The Failure to Enact a Notification Regulation

10.1   Overview

The Province of Ontario failed to enact a legally enforceable regulation[1] requiring the prompt and direct reporting[2] of test results indicating unsafe drinking water to the Ministry of the Environment (MOE) and to the local Medical Officer of Health. This failure contributed to the extent of the outbreak that occurred in Walkerton in May 2000.

For years before the outbreak in Walkerton, the provincial government had recognized that the proper reporting of test results indicating unsafe drinking water is important to the protection of public health. During those years, the Ontario Drinking Water Objectives (ODWO) directed the testing laboratory[3] to notify the local MOE office of indicators of unsafe water quality. In turn, the MOE was to notify the local Medical Officer of Health, who could then issue a boil water advisory if warranted.

When provincial government laboratories were conducting all of the routine drinking water tests for municipal water systems throughout the province, it was acceptable to set out this notification protocol as a guideline under the ODWO, rather than as a legally enforceable regulation. However, the entry of private laboratories into this sensitive public health area in 1993, and the wholesale exit of all government laboratories from routine microbiological testing for municipalities in 1996, made it unacceptable to let the notification protocol remain in the form of a legally unenforceable guideline.

This was particularly the case because private sector laboratories were not regulated by the government. There were no established criteria governing quality of testing, no requirements regarding the qualifications or experience of laboratory personnel, and no provisions for the licensing, inspection, or auditing of such laboratories by the government.

---

[1] I refer to "regulation" throughout this chapter, although I note that the government could also have passed a law instead of a regulation.

[2] The terms "notification" and "reporting" are used interchangeably in the documents, the evidence, and this report.

[3] Throughout this chapter, unless otherwise indicated, I use the terms "laboratory" and "testing laboratory" interchangeably to refer to environmental testing laboratories, as opposed to clinical testing laboratories.

For years before May 2000, the government was aware of the importance of requiring testing laboratories to directly notify the MOE and the local Medical Officer of Health about test results indicating unsafe water quality.[4] Shortly after privatization[5] in 1996, the MOE sent a guidance document to municipalities who requested it. That document strongly recommended that a municipality include in any contract with a private laboratory a clause specifying that the laboratory notify the local MOE office and the local Medical Officer of Health directly of adverse test results. Although the guidance document is referred to in correspondence sent by the MOE to the Walkerton PUC, there is no evidence that the PUC requested it or that the MOE sent it to the PUC.

The government clearly recognized that direct notification by testing laboratories to public authorities was an important measure in the protection of public health. It did not, however, enact a regulation making this type of reporting obligatory. One of the reasons for the failure to do so at the time of privatization in 1996 was the government's "distaste for regulation."

Before 1996, the government was aware of cases in which local Medical Officers of Health had not been notified of adverse test results from municipal water systems. At the time of privatization in 1996, the government did not implement a program to monitor the effect of privatization on the notification protocol followed whenever adverse results were found. Although the government encouraged municipalities to address the issue through their contracts with testing laboratories, the MOE did not review those contracts, had no assurance that municipalities were directing the laboratories to report as suggested, and had no way of knowing whether private laboratories were reporting adverse results.

When the MOE's Laboratory Services Branch and Operations Division became aware that some private laboratories were not notifying the ministry of adverse test results, as specified by the ODWO, the MOE's response was piecemeal

---

[4] The terms "adverse tests" and "adverse test results" are used interchangeably throughout this chapter to refer to test results indicating unsafe drinking water.

[5] I use the term "privatization" throughout this chapter. This term is used extensively in the evidence, in many documents, and in the submissions of the parties. In the context of this Inquiry, the term refers to the government's 1996 discontinuation of all routine microbiological testing for municipal water systems – a move that resulted in the large majority of municipal systems turning to private sector laboratories for routine water testing. Municipalities are not required to use private laboratories: a few larger municipalities operate their own. Practically speaking, however, the large majority have no option other than to use private laboratories.

and unsatisfactory. When an instance of failure to notify came to the attention of a local MOE office, it appears that the issue was dealt with locally. The local MOE offices generally did not report these failures to regional offices or to the lead region on water. More importantly, the MOE's Laboratory Services Branch, Water Policy Branch, and Operations Division failed to alert the regional or district offices that they should monitor and follow up on the notification issue.

In 1997, the Minister of Health took the unusual step of writing to the Minister of the Environment requesting that legislation be amended or that assurances be given to ensure that local Medical Officers of Health would be immediately notified of adverse results. The Minister of the Environment declined to propose legislation, indicating that the ODWO protocol dealt with this issue. He invited the Minister of Health to address the matter through the Drinking Water Coordination Committee (DWCC), which included staff from both their ministries.

Nothing else happened until after the tragedy in Walkerton. Only then did the government enact a regulation requiring testing laboratories to directly notify the MOE and the local Medical Officer of Health about adverse test results.

There was evidence that A&L Canada Laboratories, which was conducting microbiological testing for Walkerton in May 2000, was unaware of the ODWO notification protocol. As a result, A&L notified only the Walkerton PUC of the critical adverse results from the water samples taken from the Walkerton water system on May 15.

Both the fact that private laboratories doing microbiological testing of municipal water samples were unregulated and the fact that the ODWO was only a guideline, not a regulation, help explain why A&L was not aware of the notification protocol. Significantly, some other private laboratories that *were* aware of the ODWO notification protocol consciously decided not to follow it. Instead, they sent test results to their clients only, on the grounds that only a legally enforceable requirement – and not a government guideline like the ODWO – could override concerns about client confidentiality.

Even if A&L had known of the ODWO notification protocol, it would likely have followed the same procedure and notified only the Walkerton PUC of the critical adverse results from the May 15 samples.

In my view, it was not reasonable for the government, after the privatization of water testing, to rely on the ODWO – a guideline – to ensure that public health and environmental authorities were notified of adverse results. The government should have enacted a regulation in 1996 to mandate direct reporting by testing laboratories of adverse test results to the MOE and to local Medical Officers of Health. Instead, it enacted such a regulation only in August 2000, after the Walkerton tragedy.

If, in May 2000, the notification protocol had been contained in a legally enforceable regulation applicable to private laboratories, I am satisfied that A&L would have informed itself of the regulation and complied with it. The failure of A&L to notify the MOE and the local Medical Officer of Health about the adverse results from the May 15 samples was the result of the government's failure to enact a notification regulation. If the local Medical Officer of Health had been notified of the adverse results on May 17, as he should have been, he would have issued a boil water advisory before May 21 – by May 19 at the latest. An advisory issued on May 19 would very likely have reduced the scope of the outbreak.

10.2   The Role of Provincial Government Laboratories Before 1996

In the early 1990s, provincial government laboratories at both the MOE and the Ministry of Health were providing a number of testing services to municipalities, including microbiological analyses of drinking water.[6]

At the time, the MOE's Laboratory Services Branch operated one central laboratory, in Toronto, and three regional laboratories, in Kingston, London, and Thunder Bay. The regional laboratories were part of the MOE's Operations Division. Until 1996, all four MOE laboratories engaged in routine testing of drinking water for municipalities. These tests had historically been provided to municipalities free of charge. Fees were introduced in 1993. As discussed below, the three regional laboratories were closed in July 1996. At the same time, the central laboratory stopped performing routine drinking water testing.

---

[6] Microbiological analyses were also provided to the Ontario Clean Water Agency (OCWA) in its role as owner or operator of some municipal water treatment plants.

Before September 1996, there were 13 public health laboratories operated by the Ministry of Health that also provided microbiological testing of drinking water for municipalities. These municipalities were advised that all of these laboratories would stop providing this testing in September 1996. Before then, drinking water tests had been provided to the Walkerton PUC by the Ministry of Health laboratory in Palmerston.

After the MOE and Ministry of Health laboratories stopped performing routine water tests, municipalities either performed the tests internally, if they were large enough to have the resources to do so, or contracted with private laboratories to perform the tests. As discussed below, the Walkerton PUC contracted with two private laboratories after September 1996. The first, which the PUC retained from October 1996 until April 2000, was G.A.P. EnviroMicrobial Services. The second, retained from the end of April through May 2000, was A&L Canada Laboratories.

10.3 The Introduction of Fees in 1993

10.3.1 The Impact of the Decision to Introduce Fees

In January 1993, the MOE started charging fees for routine testing of drinking water for municipalities. This fee-for-service approach allowed private laboratories to enter the field of routine drinking water testing.[7]

The introduction of the fee-for-service program did not result in a significant reduction in the number of routine microbiological tests performed by the MOE laboratories. As of May 1, 1994, approximately 16 months after the introduction of fees, the MOE's Laboratory Services Branch noted that only one municipality – the Municipality of Sudbury – had switched from the MOE to a private sector laboratory. In the first 18 months after the MOE began to charge for drinking water tests, the total testing performed by MOE laboratories fell by only 6%. According to Dr. Bern Schnyder, director of the MOE's Laboratory Services Branch, this reduction could have resulted from either the introduction of private laboratory testing or a decline in the number of samples taken by municipalities.[8]

---

[7] For municipalities, routine drinking water testing includes the testing, for ODWO purposes, of microbiological, physical, and chemical parameters.

[8] When testing was free, some municipalities tested more samples than the ODWO required.

Curiously, the Ministry of Health laboratories did not implement charges for microbiological testing after the MOE decision to do so in 1993, even though the Ministry of Health was subject to the same budget reduction strategy.[9] The Walkerton PUC, which was using the Ministry of Health public health laboratory in Palmerston, continued to have microbiological tests done without charge.

10.3.2   The Failure to Regulate Private Laboratories

Throughout the 1990s, an increasing number of private laboratories in Ontario provided environmental testing – including chemical, physical, and microbiological testing – for a variety of MOE programs, including the Municipal Industrial Strategy for Abatement Program and the Air Quality Program. Starting in 1993, with the introduction of fees by the MOE, private laboratories began to move into the area of drinking water testing. Although the ministry recognized this trend, it took no steps to monitor or regulate the impact of this change on public health.

During this time, there was no regulation, whether for quality or for other purposes, relating to the private laboratories that were doing environmental testing. In the area of microbiological testing of drinking water for municipalities, there was no government requirement for the certification or accreditation of private laboratories until August 2000, when the government introduced Ontario Regulation 459/00.[10] Some private laboratories voluntarily joined the International Association for Environmental Testing Laboratories (IAETL)[11] and some voluntarily became accredited or certified by the Canadian Association of Environmental Analytical Laboratories (CAEAL),[12] but there was no requirement to do so. There was not even a requirement that private laboratories have scientists on staff.

After the MOE started charging fees for routine testing of drinking water in 1993, the Ministry of Health expressed concerns about this approach and about

---

[9] The strategy was described at the time as an "expenditure control and reduction strategy."

[10] Also known as the Drinking Water Protection Regulation.

[11] A voluntary association of private laboratories; it changed its name in January 2000 to the Canadian Council of Independent Laboratories.

[12] CAEAL's membership includes representatives from the private sector, government, and private individuals. It works with the Standards Council of Canada (SCC) to support certification, accreditation, and auditing of environmental laboratories.

the role it created for private laboratories. Ministry of Health staff[13] noted that a laboratory's overall capability of providing analytical testing is best determined through a recognized accreditation program. Unfortunately, though, accreditation was not required for environmental laboratories in Ontario. According to Ministry of Health staff, after the introduction of fees and the entry of private laboratories into this area, only the MOE and Ministry of Health laboratories "provide[d] an acceptable bacteriological testing service" for the province. However, nothing was done by either the MOE or the Ministry of Health to address this concern.[14] It should be noted that there were relatively few private laboratories actually conducting drinking water testing for municipalities at the time.

In 1994, the MOE's Laboratory Services Branch did require all laboratories performing contract analyses for the MOE itself to become accredited. The MOE was concerned that "[t]he quality of analytical data from private sector laboratories [was] not uniformly acceptable for Ministry use." By way of a memorandum dated April 25, 1994, the MOE notified private laboratories of this new accreditation requirement for those laboratories that wished to provide contract services to the MOE. The memo states:

> The reason for this change is twofold: to ensure the Ministry receives and acts on environmental analytical information which conforms to a minimum quality standard; and to recognize, and encourage improvements in, the performance of environmental laboratories in Ontario.

However, the MOE did not correspondingly direct municipalities in 1994 that they too should retain only accredited laboratories, nor did it impose any standards on private laboratories generally.

10.3.3 The Contrast to Regulation of Clinical Laboratories

The failure to regulate environmental laboratories in the 1990s can be contrasted with the stringent provincial standards that had been applied since the

---

[13] In particular, Michael Brodsky, chief of environmental bacteriology and microbiological support services at the Ministry of Health's Laboratory Services Branch, and Nicholas Paul, manager of regional services.

[14] As mentioned below, the MOE had the lead legislative role under the OWRA.

[15] The *Laboratory and Specimen Collection Centre Licensing Act*, R.S.O. 1990, c.L.1.

early 1970s to clinical laboratories – that is, laboratories that test specimens taken from humans (such as blood or stool specimens). Clinical laboratories were and continue to be regulated under the *Laboratory and Specimen Collection Centre Licensing Act*.[15] Under section 9(1) of the Act, all laboratories that test human specimens are licensed by the provincial government with renewable 12-month licences. The government can refuse to issue or renew a licence on a number of grounds, including failing to meet the standards set out in the provincial Laboratory Proficiency Testing Program.[16]

Significantly, clinical laboratories are required by Regulation 682[17] to report all positive laboratory findings with respect to reportable and communicable diseases as defined by the *Health Protection and Promotion Act* to the Medical Officer of Health. They are required to do so within 24 hours after the test is conducted. In contrast, the government did not enact a regulation requiring this same type of reporting for environmental laboratories that were testing drinking water samples until after the tragedy in May 2000.

10.4   The Move to Privatization in 1995–96

10.4.1   The Proposal for Privatization

Once the MOE laboratories began in 1993 to charge for routine microbiological testing, private sector laboratories raised a concern that public sector laboratories should not be competing directly with the private sector for routine analytical work.

By 1994, the MOE was engaged in a review of services provided by its laboratories to assess the role and scope of laboratory operations generally and to consider how private and public laboratories could provide services more effectively. Dr. Bern Schnyder, director of the MOE's Laboratory Services Branch, addressed the issue in a report dated June 6, 1994, to Dr. Peter Victor, assistant

---

[16] The provincial government, together with the Ontario Medical Association, sets the standards to be met by such clinical laboratories in this program. It is a condition of the licence that laboratories submit to proficiency testing. Laboratory inspections are performed by the Ministry of Health's Laboratory Services Branch staff.

[17] Regulation 682, R.R.O. 1990, under the *Laboratory and Specimen Collection Centre Licensing Act*. This Regulation also establishes the educational and experience qualifications required for laboratory personnel, such as the laboratory director, the technical director, laboratory technologists, and laboratory technicians. It also requires laboratories to establish a quality control program and to maintain records and submit reports to the Province.

deputy minister of the MOE's Environmental Sciences and Standards Division. In the report, Dr. Schnyder suggested reducing or eliminating routine drinking water testing for municipal water sytems and for Ontario Clean Water Agency (OCWA) water systems because this work could be effectively performed by private laboratories at no cost to the MOE.

Significantly, Dr. Schnyder noted at the time that it would require a greater involvement of MOE staff to "support, regulate, monitor and accredit environmental laboratory operations in Ontario" if the withdrawal of public sector laboratories from routine drinking water testing was pursued. In fact, however, when testing was privatized in 1996, the MOE laboratories did not "support, regulate, monitor and accredit" private laboratories, and no additional staff were dedicated to these ends.

By January 26, 1995, senior MOE officials had agreed to recommend that the MOE discontinue fee-for-service work for municipal and OCWA water and wastewater plants. Three reasons were cited for this recommendation: (1) the need to eliminate policy differences between the MOE and the Ministry of Health regarding the provision of microbiological testing of water samples (the Ministry of Health was providing these services at no cost); (2) the need to remove the perception that MOE laboratories were competing with private laboratories for work that was open to competitive bidding; and (3) the fact that competent private laboratories were available to take over the analytical work.

The Ministry of Health was not involved in the process that led to the MOE's decision to privatize water testing. It was advised of this decision in late 1995 or early 1996. According to Dr. Helen Demshar, the former director of the Ministry of Health's Laboratory Services Branch, once the MOE had decided to discontinue routine testing, the Ministry of Health had no choice but to follow suit, both because the MOE had the legislative authority to make a universal policy and because the decision was made at a very senior level of the MOE. The Ministry of Health's Laboratory Services Branch was not given an opportunity to provide input into the decision or to raise concerns.

In June 1995, Dr. Victor, in a memorandum to Richard Dicerni, an MOE deputy minister, recommended that routine drinking water tests be privatized and discussed an implementation schedule. He stated that if the reduction in staff and testing capacity associated with such a privatization was managed over three years, there would be sufficient time for the private sector to make the necessary adjustments to ensure that high-quality testing continued to be available in Ontario. He went on to say that he believed the downsizing could be accomplished within a two-year time frame. Allowing much less time than that, he said, could cause serious disruptions in the quality and availability of testing services. Thus, the original time line contemplated for the privatization of microbiological testing was two to three years.

10.4.2   The Decision to Privatize

A new government was elected in Ontario in June 1995. The MOE initiative to privatize drinking water testing that had begun shortly before the election was consistent with the policies of the new government. The decision to privatize became part of the budget reductions implemented through the MOE business plan dated January 22, 1996, and approved by Cabinet on February 28, 1996.

As mentioned, the original MOE proposal for privatization, in June 1995, was based on a time line of two to three years. After the newly elected government assumed office, this period was reduced to six months, then to four months, then to two months.[18] Municipalities were informed, in a letter dated May 15, 1996, that the MOE's laboratories would stop providing routine drinking water tests on July 13, 1996.[19] On July 17, 1996, the Ministry of Health informed municipalities that its laboratories would also stop routine testing, as of September 1996. This was the letter that affected Walkerton, because the Walkerton PUC had historically sent its water samples to the Ministry of Health laboratory in Palmerston for testing.

10.4.3   The Failure to Identify and Manage Risks

The Cabinet decision to privatize drinking water testing was based on the 1996 MOE business plan. This plan warned of increased risks to the environment and public health, but did not specifically identify risks relating to the notification procedures that private laboratories would follow when adverse results were found. The Premier of Ontario and the then Minister and Deputy

---

[18] To accommodate this compressed time frame, Dr. Schnyder met with OCWA in December 1995, before the official announcement, and told them to start arranging contracts with private laboratories.

[19] Private laboratories were informed of the decision in a letter dated May 24, 1996.

Minister of the Environment testified that they understood the risks to be "manageable." There was, however, no assessment of the risks associated with the privatization of municipal water testing, nor was there a consideration of the need for a regulation requiring testing laboratories to notify the local MOE office or local Medical Officer of Health about adverse results. The budget and resource reductions, and the associated decision-making process, are addressed in Chapter 11 of this report.

A key document written jointly by the MOE and the Ministry of Health relating to the privatization of routine drinking water tests was a briefing note dated March 22, 1996.[20] The briefing note did not raise any health concerns in relation to the privatization of such testing. It did note that the municipal sector would have concerns about the increase in testing costs and about the extra administrative work involved in contracting analytical services.

The briefing note also pointed out that in 1996, only six private laboratories in Ontario were accredited for microbiological testing. It stated that with three to four months' notice, these six laboratories were capable of supplying the required volume of drinking water tests. Dr. Bern Schnyder said that this conclusion was based on the MOE's experience with its ability to increase its own workload. Further, he stated that the MOE's Laboratory Services Branch had met with some private sector laboratories and that those laboratories had confirmed that they could "quadruple" their capability in a very short time.

No other research or analysis was done to ascertain whether private sector laboratories had the capacity and the capability to assume the work of the 17 government laboratories that would withdraw from the field, nor was there an analysis of the need to make the notification protocol specified by the ODWO a legally enforceable requirement.

As I pointed out above, the regulation that applied to clinical laboratories made it mandatory that private laboratories notify the Medical Officer of Health about communicable and reportable disease results within 24 hours. Although the Ministry of Health's Laboratory Services Branch had experience with the clinical laboratory licensing model, it did not raise this issue with the MOE's Laboratory Services Branch as a model for the regulation of environmental laboratories after privatization.

---

[20] The briefing note was addressed to three assistant deputy ministers: two in the MOE and one in Ministry of Health.

Part of the recommendation to transfer routine testing to private laboratories, as set out in the briefing note, was that the MOE and the Ministry of Health should ensure the quality of bacteriological testing by private and municipal laboratories in Ontario. They were to do so through partnership arrangements with the Standards Council of Canada (SCC) and the Canadian Association of Environmental Analytical Laboratories (CAEAL) aimed at strengthening and harmonizing provincial and national requirements for certification, accreditation, and performance evaluations of such laboratories. Once the decision to privatize was made, however, nothing was done in this regard.

The Public Health Branch of the Ministry of Health never raised a public health concern about the decision to implement laboratory privatization without also requiring laboratory accreditation. Dr. Demshar, formerly of the ministry's Laboratory Services Branch, testified that the branch had not pushed for accreditation because the MOE had the lead legislative role under the *Ontario Water Resources Act*.

Dr. Richard Schabas, the Chief Medical Officer of Health for Ontario at the time of the privatization,[21] testified that he was not consulted about the discontinuation of routine testing by government laboratories. Neither was he asked to provide input as to whether the testing should be privatized.

Dr. Schabas was consulted about how to implement the privatization. He commented that there was nothing wrong with privatization *per se*, so long as it was implemented properly and with the appropriate safeguards, including quality assurance and reporting requirements. However, Dr. Schabas expressed concern that municipalities were given only two months' notice of the privatization. He felt that this was insufficient notice to ensure proper implementation. Dr. Schabas was also surprised to learn that it was not mandatory to use an accredited laboratory.

10.4.4   The Decision Not to Require Accreditation

Before the decision was made to privatize testing in 1996, concerns about public health had been raised. These concerns dealt mainly with the issue of

---

[21] I note that the Chief Medical Officer of Health is also traditionally the director of the Public Health Branch of the Ministry of Health.

whether laboratories doing such testing should be required to be accredited by a nationally recognized body such as the SCC or CAEAL.

As it turns out, the decision not to require accreditation did not have an impact on the events in Walkerton. However, the manner in which the government approached the accreditation issue is relevant because it shows both the importance that the government put on proceeding quickly with privatization and the reservations that it had about enacting new regulations.

Since at least 1992, the International Association for Environmental Testing Laboratories (IAETL) had been lobbying for mandatory accreditation. A February 1992 briefing note recorded that IAETL had requested the MOE to recommend the use of accredited laboratories for all analytical testing done in support of regulatory programs. In fact, IAETL had expressed concern that laboratories that are not accredited might "be reducing quality conformance in an effort to cut costs in a very competitive market." It noted that mandatory accreditation would help ensure that all laboratories met the same quality guidelines.

The MOE had been informed that at the time the cost of laboratory accreditation and certification of tests was as high as $15,000 for the first year. Dr. Schnyder testified that he was concerned that mandatory accreditation could put smaller laboratories out of business. CAEAL responded quickly to meet the MOE's concern, and by September 1995 it had implemented an accreditation program for smaller laboratories that would have cost less than $5,000 per year.

Public health concerns were also raised by IAETL in a meeting with the MOE on January 13, 1994. IAETL noted that because the MOE was not bringing in mandatory accreditation, private laboratories were "not maintaining adequate quality assurance procedures because of cost cutting pressures to remain profitable."

Dr. Schnyder testified that he believed that Dr. Victor had planned to make mandatory accreditation part of the privatization package if there had been a two- to three-year transition period, as originally envisioned in Dr. Victor's 1995 recommendation regarding privatization. However, when routine testing for municipalities was privatized in 1996, the MOE did not pursue mandatory accreditation.

Dr. Schnyder recalled that Dr. Victor told him that in order to introduce mandatory accreditation, the case would have to be made to the MOE's deputy minister and to its minister. That process, along with the Regulatory Review Process,[22] would take at least one or two years. When the time frame for privatization was reduced to two months, there was no time to implement mandatory accreditation.

In addition, Dr. Victor told Dr. Schnyder that the government was attempting to consolidate or reduce the number of regulations and that the Red Tape Commission was not in favour of increased regulations. Dr. Schnyder believed that Dr. Victor felt that the newly elected government's "distaste for regulation" played a role in the decision not to make accreditation mandatory. In the same vein, George Crawford, of the MOE's Laboratory Services Branch, advised the office of the Environmental Commissioner of Ontario on October 23, 1996, that a new regulation requiring accreditation was not a direction the MOE wanted to go, in view of the general regulatory climate.

10.5 Concerns About the Lack of Notification Before and During Privatization

It seems clear that before the decision to privatize was made in 1996, the government was aware of concerns about the notification procedures being followed by private laboratories when adverse results were found. As a practical matter, the discontinuation of provincial government laboratory testing made the use of private laboratories essential unless a municipality was large enough to operate its own laboratory. Given that there were already problems with notification before privatization, the wholesale privatization of testing in 1996 enormously increased the risk that Medical Officers of Health would not be notified of adverse results. This risk should have been managed before government testing was stopped. However, after the decision to privatize was made, the need to address the risk increased dramatically.

---

[22] This process, implemented by the government elected in June 1995, set standards for the enactment of new regulations. The process is described in greater detail in Chapter 13 of this report.

10.5.1   The Survey of Medical Officers of Health in 1995

Before privatization, the government was aware that local Medical Officers of Health were not always being notified of adverse results from tests conducted by private laboratories. As a result of this concern, Dr. Chuck Le Ber of the Ministry of Health's Public Health Branch[23] sent a letter dated November 2, 1995, to all Medical Officers of Health. The letter stated that some Ministry of Health laboratories had learned that adverse test results from municipal water systems might not be being conveyed to the local Medical Officer of Health by the local MOE office, as specified by section 4.1.3 of the ODWO.

Of the 42 health units that received this letter, 21 responded to Dr. Le Ber. Only six indicated that they were being advised directly by the MOE as specified by the ODWO.[24] Dr. Le Ber reported these numbers to the Ministry of Health's Technical Advisory Committee on Environmental Microbiology. In December 1995, he presented the survey results at the annual meeting of the Association of Supervisors of Public Health Inspectors of Ontario. No similar survey was conducted after the 1996 laboratory privatization.

10.5.2   Communications with Municipalities in 1996

Communications from the MOE to municipalities at the time of privatization reflected the ministry's recognition of how important it is that testing laboratories promptly and directly notify public health authorities about adverse test results. However, some of these communications were not sent to all water systems operators or to the private laboratories that would be conducting the tests. Moreover, the government did not follow up to ensure that notification was taking place.

The letters sent to municipalities by the MOE on May 15, 1996, and by the Ministry of Health on July 17, 1996, advising them of the discontinuation of public laboratory testing said that the MOE's Laboratory Services Branch would, on request, provide municipalities with a "Guidance Document" titled "Selecting an Environmental Analytical Laboratory." This document strongly

---

[23] Dr. Le Ber is the senior veterinary consultant with the Ministry of Health, and head of the Food Safety/Safe Water Unit of the Public Health Branch.

[24] Seven indicated that they received results from the regional public health laboratory or from municipalities conducting their own testing. One reported that it received no results from anyone, and one specifically reported that it received no results from the MOE.

recommended that all environmental testing be done by laboratories that were properly accredited or certified by a national agency such as the SCC or CAEAL.

Subsequently, the MOE sent a separate addendum to the guidance document relating to the notification procedures for adverse results. This addendum was sent only to those municipalities who had originally requested the guidance document. There is no evidence that the Walkerton PUC ever requested or received a copy of the guidance document or that it received a copy of the addendum regarding notification. In the addendum, the MOE strongly recommended that any contract for the analytical testing of municipal water samples include the following requirement regarding notifying the proper authoritites of adverse results:

> In the case where a sample result for a parameter designated as health-related in the Ontario Drinking Water Objectives is above a certificate of approval limit or an Ontario Drinking Water Objective, the contracted laboratory must immediately inform the local Medical Officer of Health, the MOE District Office and the contracting agency of the exceedance.

This addendum is significant. It shows that the government recognized the importance of requiring private laboratories to immediately report adverse test results directly to the local MOE office and the local Medical Officer of Health. It also shows that the government was aware that the ODWO-recommended notification protocol was not binding and that further steps needed to be taken to ensure that adverse results were properly reported.

The Ministry of Health letter of July 17, 1996, strongly recommended that municipalities contract with laboratories that had demonstrated their competency through certification and/or accreditation. The letter enclosed a list of accredited/certified laboratories. It went on to say that Ministry of Health laboratory staff would:

> work with SCC/CAEAL to ensure that private sector and municipal laboratories have the required testing capabilities. The Ministry will continue its efforts to improve analytical testing capabilities in Ontario by making staff available to audit analytical performance and transfer new analytical methods and improvements to laboratories serving municipalities.

In fact, Ministry of Health staff did not establish any program to ensure that private and municipal laboratories had the required testing capabilities. Besides supplying auditors to CAEAL, they did nothing to audit the performance of those laboratories, and no program was established for transferring new analytical methods and other improvements to private laboratories.

10.5.3 Communications with Municipalities in 1997

In January 1997, the MOE's Laboratory Services Branch sent another guidance document to all municipalities, including Walkerton, regarding the collection of samples and the use of presence-absence tests for the bacteriological analysis of drinking water. The document states that the laboratory should, *with the permission of the treatment plant or distribution system owner*, report results indicating the persistence of coliforms or the presence of *E. coli* to both the MOE's district abatement officer and the local Medical Officer of Health, the ODWO notwithstanding.

However, the MOE did not send this guidance document to private laboratories. Similarly, private laboratories were not invited to workshops hosted by the MOE dealing with the implementation of the privatization initiative. Some may have attended because water operators informed them of the workshop.

The statement in the 1997 MOE guidance document was another recognition by the government that there was no requirement for private laboratories to report adverse results: otherwise, the document would not have had to specify that private laboratories should obtain "permission" from municipal clients to report to the MOE and the local Medical Officer of Health. And like the addendum to the earlier guidance document, this document also reflected the MOE's recognition of the importance of having testing laboratories directly notify the proper authorities about adverse test results.

10.5.4 Inadequate Communication with Private Laboratories

The only communication by either the MOE or the Ministry of Health to private laboratories about the decision to privatize testing was a letter dated May 24, 1996. The letter informed private laboratories of the government's withdrawal from routine testing and strongly recommended accreditation – noting that accredited laboratories are "preferred and…highly recommended to Ministry customers." It did not refer to the notification procedures for adverse results or to the ODWO reporting protocol.

The letter was sent by the MOE's Laboratory Services Branch to laboratories that were then members of one or more of three voluntary laboratory associations: IAETL, CAEAL, and the Central Ontario Municipal Environmental Laboratories Group (COMELG). If a laboratory was not a member of at least one of these three voluntary associations, it did not receive the letter. The MOE did not even maintain an up-to-date list of association members and did not mail similar letters to new testing laboratories after privatization was implemented.

10.5.5   The Failure to Follow Up

At the time of privatization in 1996, and in spite of knowing that there was a problem with the notification procedures being followed by private laboratories when adverse results were found, the government made no effort to ensure that testing was being done properly or that notification to the local MOE office and the local Medical Officer of Health was taking place.

The MOE's Laboratory Services Branch did not ask the MOE's Operations Division to find out the names of laboratories retained by municipal water operators. There was no follow-up or ongoing communication with private laboratories. Neither the Laboratory Services Branch nor the Operations Division established a program for systematically monitoring the performance of the private laboratories, with respect either to quality or to whether proper notification procedures were being followed.

After privatization, the MOE's Laboratory Services Branch had little communication with private laboratories or with municipalities. Although MOE Operations Division personnel had regular contact with municipal water operators, they did not inspect private laboratories. The MOE provided no instructions to its staff to inquire into whether laboratories had been told to report adverse results to the MOE or to the local Medical Officer of Health.

The failure of a private laboratory to notify the proper authorities about adverse results might be discovered during an MOE inspection of a municipal water system. However, from 1994 to 2000 inspections were scheduled only every four years unless issues of non-compliance had arisen. Moreover, a municipality might switch from a reporting laboratory to a non-reporting laboratory, and the MOE would have no way of knowing until the next inspection was conducted.

Following privatization, the MOE's Operations Division did not have any program for advising laboratories of their notification obligations or for monitoring the effects of privatization on either the notification procedures followed for adverse results or the quality of testing. Local MOE staff were never asked to provide information to their region, or to the lead MOE region on water, regarding the notification practices of private laboratories. The lead region responsible for water in the immediate post-privatization period, the Eastern Region, did not initiate any special program to monitor the impact of privatization on notification or quality issues.

Since the MOE was responsible for the ODWO, the Ministry of Health's Laboratory Services Branch did not implement any programs to monitor the effect of privatization.

10.6   Concerns About the Lack of Notification After Privatization

In the period following privatization, the government was informed on a significant number of occasions about concerns regarding the notification procedures being followed by private laboratories when adverse results were found. On each occasion, the government failed to adequately respond to the problems raised. I review five examples below.

10.6.1   The 1996 Letter to Medical Officers of Health

In November 1996, David N. Brown, a public health inspector in the Windsor-Essex County Health Unit, wrote to Dr. Le Ber, of the Ministry of Health's Public Health Branch. Mr. Brown informed Dr. Le Ber that in July 1996, three adverse tests results from a private laboratory had not been reported to the local MOE office, as specified by the ODWO. As a result, the MOE could not report the adverse results to the local Medical Officer of Health. Mr. Brown's suggested solution was for health units to "register" with private laboratories in their area so that the health units could be notified directly by the laboratories.

Dr. Le Ber proposed the "registration" solution within the Ministry of Health. The idea was vetoed by others in the ministry's Laboratory Services Branch on the grounds that it would be better not to circumvent the notification procedure identified in the ODWO. Still, Dr. Le Ber had lingering concerns.

On December 4, 1996, Dr. Le Ber wrote to all Medical Officers of Health to remind them of the ODWO notification procedure. He suggested that health units work with local MOE offices to ensure that private laboratories, as well as municipal water operators, were aware of the notification procedure. Copies of this memorandum were sent both to the MOE's Laboratory Services Branch and to the ministry's Operations Division. Despite having received the memorandum, the MOE did not take any steps to inform private laboratories of their responsibilities.

10.6.2   The 1997 E-mail Message from the MOE's Belleville Office

The issue of whether a regulation requiring private laboratories to notify the proper authorities about adverse results should be put in place was directly raised in January 1997 and considered by the MOE's Legal Services Branch. An area supervisor with the MOE's Belleville office, John Tooley, was to attend a meeting with the local health unit in February 1997. One of the agenda items was the notification procedures being followed when adverse results were found. In preparing for the meeting, Mr. Tooley wrote an e-mail message, dated January 16, 1997, to Stella Couban, a lawyer with the MOE's Legal Services Branch. He indicated to Ms. Couban that there was no guarantee that a private laboratory would notify the local MOE office of adverse results, and said:

> In fact, I can almost guarantee that the laboratory does not notify the [MOE] District Manager in the vast majority of cases. The number of deteriorating, poor and unsafe results [that the MOE learns about] have dropped dramatically since our labs do not do the analyses.

Ms. Couban responded to Mr. Tooley by e-mail on January 28, 1997, after consulting with her superiors at the Legal Services Branch. She presented three options, the third of which was for the government to enact a notification regulation.[25] Regarding this option, Ms. Couban wrote:

> I am not sure whether the concept of a regulation imposing a new
> requirement is even a starter with the current regime and its interest
> in lessening or reducing the amount of regulatory control.

In her testimony at the Inquiry, Ms. Couban said that there were three problems associated with the option of a notification regulation. First, it would involve suggesting a new regulation in the current government climate. Second, the regulation being suggested would have resource implications for front-line MOE staff at a time when their resources had been cut "fairly significantly." Finally, the suggested regulation would impose a new requirement on the private sector – a move that in her view would probably not have been "a starter" with the government at that time.

There was no MOE initiative to proceed with a notification regulation, despite the issue's having been raised on this occasion in 1997.

10.6.3   The 1997 Survey by the MOE's Owen Sound Office

On March 11, 1997, Philip Bye, of the MOE's Owen Sound office, asked environmental officer Larry Struthers to check into whether various private laboratories were reporting adverse results to local MOE offices. Mr. Struthers determined that two of the four private laboratories he checked were not reporting adverse results to the MOE. Although he informed Mr. Bye of this situation, nothing was done by the Owen Sound office and the information was not conveyed to the Southwestern Region – to which the Owen Sound office reported – or to the MOE's lead region on water.

10.6.4   The 1996–97 Reports of the Environmental Commissioner

In her October 1996 special report, Eva Ligeti, the Environmental Commissioner of Ontario, criticized the MOE for failing to assess the effects of shutting down its three regional drinking water laboratories and laying off scientists.

---

[25] Ms. Couban provided legal advice as to each option: such advice was not disclosed at the Inquiry. However, only the non-legal advice given by Ms. Couban was disclosed at the Inquiry, and that advice is discussed here.

In her 1996 annual report, which was released in April 1997, the Environmental Commissioner criticized the government regarding the decision to privatize routine water testing. Specifically, she criticized the government for not posting the decision on the Environmental Registry for public comment, and for not consulting with municipalities or the public. She commented that municipalities had had barely eight weeks to arrange for private laboratories to perform tests.

The Environmental Commissioner was also critical that the law did not require private laboratories to be certified or accredited. She concluded that the MOE had not made this a legal requirement because of costs and because such a requirement ran counter to the government's move to cut regulations.

When the 1996 annual report was released, several questions were raised in the legislative assembly concerning the decision to privatize laboratory testing. On April 22, 1997, some members asked Premier Michael Harris about the Environmental Commissioner's criticism, and the lack of a legal requirement that private laboratories be certified or accredited. In response, he said that his government took responsibility and was accountable for the decision to privatize laboratory testing.

10.6.5   The 1997 Letter from the Simcoe County District Health Unit

In July 1997, the non-reporting issue was brought to the attention of the MOE's Barrie office.[26] Ian Gray, the district manager of the office, was informed by the manager of the health unit in Simcoe County[27] that some of the private laboratories in the county were not reporting adverse results to the MOE. As a result, the health unit was not being notified. Mr. Gray testified that before receiving this information, he had been unaware of a possible problem regarding the notification procedures being followed by private laboratories.

In response, Mr. Gray wrote a letter dated July 16, 1997, to the seven private laboratories that were doing microbiological testing of drinking water in Simcoe

---

[26] The MOE's Barrie office was responsible for the Regional Municipality of Muskoka, Simcoe County, Grey County, and Bruce County, which included Walkerton. It supervised the MOE's Owen Sound office.

[27] Ted Devine, the manager of the Simcoe County District Health Unit, first telephoned Mr. Gray and then wrote him a letter dated July 4, 1997.

County. He reminded them of section 4.1.3 of the ODWO and requested that they fax unsatisfactory test results directly to the Simcoe County Health Unit.

Mr. Gray did not receive any resistance to this idea from the seven laboratories: in fact, he received no responses at all. He did not contact the local health units for the other counties in his district, including the Bruce-Grey-Owen Sound Health Unit, to inquire whether they had concerns similar to the ones raised by the Simcoe County District Health Unit. Nor did he recall contacting Philip Bye of the MOE's Owen Sound office. Finally, he did not raise this concern about the reporting of adverse results by private laboratories with the MOE's Southwestern Region, with the lead region on drinking water, or with the Water Policy Branch.

Prior to receiving Mr. Gray's letter, Lakefield Research Ltd., a laboratory performing tests for municipalities in Simcoe County, had not been notifying the MOE of adverse water sample results because of concerns about client confidentiality. Lakefield was an accredited laboratory and took the view, as did others, that reporting adverse results to anyone other than the client would breach International Standards Organization (ISO) Guide 25. After receiving Mr. Gray's letter, Lakefield changed its practice and began notifying the MOE district office of adverse results.

10.7 The Health Minister's Request of the Environment Minister

I mentioned earlier the ongoing concerns that Dr. Chuck Le Ber of the Ministry of Health had had about the fact that Medical Officers of Health were not always being notified about adverse drinking water test results. His concerns lingered after privatization was implemented in 1996. He expressed those concerns in a memorandum, dated December 4, 1996, to all Medical Officers of Health, in which he reminded them of the notification procedure under the ODWO.

Dr. Richard Schabas, Chief Medical Officer of Health for Ontario, testified that Dr. Le Ber had raised concerns on several occasions about the lack of legally enforceable reporting requirements for drinking water test results. Dr. Schabas agreed with Dr. Le Ber that a problem existed. They decided to take the highly unusual step of asking the Minister of Health to write to the Minister of the Environment to request that notification requirements be included in MOE legislation.

Dr. Le Ber drafted a memorandum for Dr. Schabas's signature, dated July 22, 1997, expressing the concern that there was no legally binding requirement for the reporting of adverse results to Medical Officers of Health. The memorandum described this situation as "a serious oversight." It concluded that the Ministry of Health needed assurances that adverse results would be reported directly to the local health unit for follow-up.

As a result of this memorandum, Minister of Health Jim Wilson sent a letter, dated August 20, 1997, to Minister of the Environment Norman Sterling. The letter requested an amendment to the *Ontario Water Resources Act*, or assurances from the MOE, that adverse drinking water test results from municipal water systems would be immediately brought to the attention of the local Medical Officer of Health. The letter said that it was important that policies or legislative procedures be in place to ensure the effective and timely reporting of adverse test results.

I note that this was one of many occasions on which Dr. Le Ber acted on his concerns about the notification issue. I am satisfied that he did all he could to raise the issue with those senior to him in the public service. He should be commended for his efforts.

It was Dr. Schabas's opinion that, for Medical Officers of Health to do their jobs properly, there was a need for mandatory reporting requirements, rather than voluntary guidelines. This was the basis of the concerns expressed in the memorandum and letter mentioned above. It was Dr. Schabas's experience that where a legal requirement exists, the level of reporting is more reliable. In this regard, he relied on his experience with clinical laboratories. Dr. Schabas testified that although his memorandum and Minister Wilson's letter recommended that legislation require municipal water operators to report adverse results, he now thought in hindsight that private laboratories should also have the same duty.

Minister Sterling responded to the letter from the Minister of Health in a letter dated November 10, 1997. On the advice of his senior advisers, he indicated that the transfer of laboratory testing to the private sector would have no effect on the notification procedure under the ODWO. He said that the ODWO clearly delineated the responsibility of municipalities and testing laboratories to ensure the immediate reporting of microbiological and other exceedances of maximum acceptable concentrations in drinking water. He invited the Minister of Health to refer the matter to the Drinking Water Coordination Committee (DWCC), which was responsible for amending the

ODWO. He did not initiate any amendment to the *Ontario Water Resources Act* or take any steps to make the notification procedure set out in the ODWO legally binding.

Minister Sterling testified that he did not recall receiving the letter from Minister of Health Wilson. He said that the first time the letter was brought to his attention was at the end of a briefing session related to another matter. He testified that his staff were of the opinion that the ODWO satisfied the Ministry of Health's concern, but he could not recall which staff member gave this opinion. Minister Sterling said that the whole issue was not high on the list of the MOE's priorities and that he had not read the ODWO by that point in time. He testified that he did not follow up to determine what had happened with the DWCC concerning this matter. He expected to receive something back as a proposal from the DWCC but never saw anything.

In his testimony, Minister Sterling acknowleged that if the failure to make the notification protocol a binding law after privatization in order to ensure timely reporting of adverse results contributed to the events in Walkerton, then he as Minister of the Environment was accountable in a political sense.

There is no question that there were serious concerns about the notification issue in the Ministry of Health and that those concerns were shared by a number of its officials. The letter from the Minister of Health was a significant warning to the Minister of the Environment that a potential problem existed regarding the notification procedure specified by the ODWO as a result of the privatization of water testing. Indeed, the letter described the situation as a "serious oversight." This letter from the Health Minister was highly unusual and underlined the public health importance of the issue. Unfortunately, the MOE did not respond in an adequate way, and the notification protocol remained in the form of a guideline.

Thus, more than two years before the tragedy in Walkerton, the government had at a very high level recognized a problem with its own guidelines, but had done nothing. As discussed in section 10.10, although an appropriate notification regulation would not have prevented the contamination of drinking water in Walkerton, it would have reduced the scope of the outbreak.

10.8   Reasons for the Failure to Enact a Notification Regulation

I do not intend to comment on the merits of the government's decision to privatize laboratory testing. That was a policy decision that was open to the government to make as part of its budget reduction program. The following comments are limited to the manner in which that decision was implemented: specifically, the failure to enact a notification regulation.

I am satisfied that at the time laboratory testing of municipal water samples was privatized in 1996, the government should have enacted a regulation requiring laboratories to notify public authorities promptly and directly of adverse results. As mentioned earlier, such a requirement was in place for private clinical laboratories.[28]

In my view, direct notification by a testing laboratory to public authorities when adverse test results are found is an important element in protecting public health. It avoids the delay inherent in having an intermediate step – that is, having the laboratories relay adverse results through the water operators. Just as importantly, it avoids the possibility of missed communications. In something as important as ensuring the prompt communication of unsatisfactory drinking water test results to public officials, there is no reason not to require direct reporting. The government was aware of the advantages of direct notification both before and after the decision to privatize.

Because it was the private sector that would be asked to directly notify public authorities, it was essential that the requirement be embodied in a legally enforceable regulation, rather than a guideline. After the Walkerton tragedy, the government moved quickly to enact a notification regulation. It should have done so in 1996, or at least on the numerous occasions afterward when serious concerns about the lack of notification came to its attention.

I am satisfied that the failure to enact a notification regulation resulted, at least in part, from the regulatory culture of the government elected in June 1995. The regulatory culture of the MOE, and of the government generally, discouraged the enactment of a new regulation to make the notification protocol for

---

[28] In Chapter 5 of this report, I concluded that Stan Koebel should have disclosed the adverse results received on May 17 to the health unit. Had he done so, the scope of the outbreak would have been reduced. However, in my view, that does not affect the conclusion that the government should have enacted a regulation mandating notification or the conclusion that if it had done so, the scope of the outbreak would have been reduced, as I describe below.

adverse drinking water results legally binding on municipal water operators and on private laboratories.

At the relevant time, the MOE was conducting a review of existing regulations to ensure that they were all justified in view of the directions being taken by the government. Any new regulation would have had to overcome the cost-benefit analysis imposed by the Red Tape Commission,[29] which discouraged regulations that imposed reporting requirements because such requirements are "complicated and create unnecessary paperwork." To impose such a legal requirement upon private laboratories might have been considered a barrier to jobs and economic growth. Moreover, because a new regulation would have to be administered and enforced, it would also increase the cost of government – another effect that would have been unpopular in the prevailing political climate.

It was also clear that the Red Tape Commission was focusing on the nature and extent of regulations under the purview of the MOE. The MOE was subject to twice as many recommendations from the commission as any other ministry.[30] In a consultation paper, the MOE stated that environmental protection agencies in many countries were reducing their emphasis on traditional "command and control" regulatory approaches. In its view, there was a trend toward using environmental management approaches that were broader than simply mandatory requirements. This paper was published in July 1996, the same month in which the routine laboratory testing was privatized. In reviewing the MOE's regulatory reform package in September 1997, the Red Tape Commission recommended that certain regulations be replaced with voluntary guidelines. In making this recommendation, the commission relied on its position that "as a matter of principle, when we ask businesses to be good corporate citizens and in effect to police themselves, those matters should be agreed upon through voluntary agreements, MOUs [Memorandums of Understanding] and other instruments outside of Regulations."

In view of this regulatory climate, it is not surprising that the MOE did not move to turn a voluntary guideline into a binding legal requirement. This is unfortunate given the information that the MOE had – both at that time and

---

[29] I discuss the Red Tape Commission and the related process of regulatory review in Chapter 13 of this report.
[30] The MOE was subject to 36 recommendations; the ministry with the next highest number of recommendations was subject to 18. The recommendations pertained to a range of regulatory issues including, but not limited to, removing regulations.

afterward – that private laboratories were not notifying the local MOE offices and Medical Officers of Health about adverse test results for municipal drinking water.

I discussed above the evidence of Stella Couban, counsel with the MOE's Legal Services Branch. Ms. Couban struck me as a conscientious public servant who gave evidence in a forthright manner. She had reviewed the terms of reference of the Red Tape Commission shortly after its report was published in January 29, 1996. She followed the evolution of the government's positions on both red tape and environmental protection through documents such as throne speeches, the 1996 consultation paper titled "Responsive Environmental Protection," and the "Less Paper/More Jobs" test.[31]

Although former Minister of the Environment Norman Sterling testified that he did not believe that civil servants should have been deterred from recommending regulations for public health purposes, I am satisfied that Ms. Couban's doubts about the prospects for enacting a notification regulation were reasonable as well as fairly based on the government's enunciated policies.

I am satisfied that her view that the concept of a notification regulation was not likely "a starter" with the government, given its interest in minimizing regulation, was a reasonable assessment of the situation. I am sure that those within the MOE who might have initiated the steps necessary to develop such a regulation would have been disinclined to do so in view of the prevailing culture.

My conclusion that there was a reluctance to enact a new regulation in conjunction with the privatization of laboratory testing is also consistent with the way in which the government addressed the issue of the accreditation and certification of private laboratories. The government was disinclined to enact a regulation to require mandatory accreditation of private laboratories that were entering the area of routine drinking water testing as a result of the government's decision to discontinue conducting such tests.

There were generally two reasons for this disinclination to require mandatory accreditation. First, if such a regulation had been introduced, there would have been significant delays in the implementation of privatization. A case would

---

[31] These and other documents, as they relate to the process of regulatory review, are discussed in greater detail in Chapter 13 of this report.

have had to be made to both the deputy minister and the minister, and regulatory review would also have had to occur, taking at least one or two years. Given the short time lines associated with the decision to privatize in 1996, there was not enough time to go through the review process for a regulation.

The second reason for the disinclination to require mandatory accreditation was the government's distaste for regulation. As mentioned, senior officials in the MOE were of the view that mandatory accreditation had not been implemented because of the prevailing culture against new regulations.

10.9   The Drinking Water Coordination Committee

The Drinking Water Coordination Committee (DWCC) was established around 1993.[32] Its mandate was to guide and coordinate the MOE's drinking water program. The DWCC's terms of reference[33] described the MOE's drinking water program as a comprehensive approach for ensuring that the drinking water produced by Ontario municipal water treatment plants is safe.[34]

The DWCC met infrequently. It held three meetings in 1995, two in 1996, one in 1997, and two each in 1998, 1999, and 2000 (March 1 and May 1, 2000). Subcommittees of the DWCC dealt with specific issues and met more frequently.

Beginning in 1997, the DWCC and its various subcommittees began to consider revisions to the ODWO. There is no evidence that the effect of privatization on notification was referred to the DWCC for consideration before the 1996 decision, or that the DWCC was requested to monitor the impact of privatization. The 1997 impetus to revising the ODWO came from a presentation made in November 1997 by James Mahoney, then the representative of the MOE's Operations Division on the DWCC.

---

[32] In addition to the Public Health Branch of the Ministry of Health, the following areas of the MOE were usually represented on the DWCC: Program Development Branch, Standards Development Branch, Science and Technology Branch, Environmental Monitoring and Reporting Branch, Laboratory Services Branch, Approvals Branch, and Operations Division regions.

[33] Although the DWCC's draft terms of reference were never finalized, they were generally accepted as accurate by DWCC panel members.

[34] The basic components of water production to which the DWCC would turn its attention included source protection, water treatment, program assessment, upgrading, public perception, and partnerships with industry and other groups such as the Ontario Water Works Association and the Association of Municipalities of Ontario.

Mr. Mahoney addressed two main issues: the ODWO minimum recommended sampling program and related compliance problems, and the notification protocol. He noted that it no longer made sense for the MOE to notify local Medical Officers of Health about adverse results, given the privatization of laboratory testing of drinking water.

Mr. Mahoney's presentation noted that when the ODWO had last been revised in 1994, public sector laboratories had been performing most of the drinking water tests for municipalities. Since public sector laboratories were therefore typically the first to know whether a maximum acceptable concentration had been exceeded, it had made sense for the MOE to notify the local Medical Officer of Health and the operating authority about such adverse results. After the 1996 privatization of drinking water testing, however, the notification procedure contained in the ODWO no longer made sense. The presentation concluded with a statement that the accountability for drinking water quality, sampling, record keeping, and reporting should rest "where it belongs: with the waterworks' owner."

Following the November 1997 presentation, an ad hoc subcommittee of the DWCC was struck to deal with ODWO issues, including the minimum sampling program in relation to smaller municipal systems and the requirements for notifying the proper authorities about adverse test results. In June 1998, the subcommittee's proposed draft revisions to the ODWO included a provision that the testing laboratory notify only the owner of the waterworks, who would then notify the local Medical Officer of Health. No proposal was made to include the MOE in the reporting loop.

Goff Jenkins, a member of the DWCC, testified that he had expressed a concern about the failure of private laboratories to report adverse results on the basis of his previous discussions with the Ministry of Health's Public Health Branch. However, the other three members of the DWCC panel who testified at the Inquiry did not recall any discussion at either the DWCC or the subcommittee about the failure of private laboratories to report adverse tests to the MOE as specified by the ODWO, and the minutes do not reflect such a concern. The members of the DWCC who testified agreed that neither the ad hoc subcommittee nor the DWCC had considered the issue that private laboratories might be less compliant with a notification protocol that was in the form of a guideline rather than a regulation.

Mr. Jenkins testified that he felt that it would have been more appropriate to have a laboratory directly notify either the health unit or the Medical Officer of Health, but that he was told that adverse results were likely proprietary information, so it would probably be inappropriate to have the laboratory report directly to the Medical Officer of Health.[35]

10.9.1 The Delay of the 1998 ODWO Revisions

In the summer of 1998, the DWCC was set to proceed with revisions to the ODWO, including revisions to the notification protocol and to the sampling requirements. The revisions were delayed at the request of the MOE's Operations Division, which was poised to issue orders enforcing the minimum sampling program and wanted a reasonable period of time for the orders to take effect before changes to the sampling requirements were implemented. The only explanation given for not proceeding separately with the changes to the notification protocol was that all of the ODWO revisions were being presented as a package and therefore were of equal importance at the time.[36]

10.9.2 The ODWO Revisions Back on the Agenda

It appears that the ODWO revisions were back on the policy agenda of the DWCC at a subcommittee meeting scheduled for February 1999. This subcommittee work was superseded by a subsequent Water Policy Branch proposal for completely revising the ODWO, rather than just the two issues on which the subcommittee had been focusing. In January 2000, the new working group proposed the following:

---

[35] Mr. Jenkins testified that he believes he was aware that some private laboratories were citing the confidentiality of data as a reason to report adverse results only to their clients (the municipalities) and not to the MOE, but he believes he had become aware of this information through his role on the Technical Liaison Committee on Water Microbiology (a joint committee of the MOE and the Ministry of Health), rather than from discussions at the DWCC. He agreed that the concern that private laboratories might not comply with the ODWO reporting protocol was not brought to the attention of the DWCC.

[36] James Janse, the director of MOE's Southwestern Region, who made the request that the revisions be delayed, testified that after the decision was made to delay the ODWO revision process, no other MOE unit, branch, or division contacted him to question the decision or to request reasons or clarification.

> Due to provincial government downsizing and restructuring from
> mid 1996 onwards, Ministry labs no longer undertake drinking water
> analyses for municipalities. The result of this change is that the
> [MOE] District Manager would not be the first to know of any
> adverse results as now there is not a reporting link through the
> Ministry's laboratories. As such, the responsibility for notifying the
> Medical Officer of Health reverts to the owner of the Works.

While agreeing that the privatization of laboratories had prompted the proposed change to the notification protocol, Donald Carr, a long-time MOE
employee, testified that it had also stemmed from the municipalities' 1998
assumption of the ownership of waterworks. The group felt that the MOE
should no longer be the "middleman" and that "since the owner was now fully
responsible for the water quality," the owner should report adverse results directly
to the local Medical Officer of Health. No changes to the notification protocol
were implemented until August 2000.

10.10 The Effect on Walkerton in May 2000

10.10.1 The Role of A&L Canada Laboratories

From October 1996 until April 2000, the Walkerton PUC retained G.A.P.
EnviroMicrobial Services Inc. to carry out routine microbiological testing of
drinking water samples from the Walkerton water system. G.A.P. was a private
laboratory that chose to follow the ODWO reporting protocol. Garry Palmateer,
the president of G.A.P., had served as the regional microbiologist for the MOE's
Southwestern Region laboratory from 1974 to 1996. Mr. Palmateer established G.A.P. after the MOE's regional laboratory closed in 1996. G.A.P. was
accredited by CAEAL and the SCC for the testing of *E. coli* and total coliforms
in water by way of both the presence-absence test and the more elaborate membrane filtration test. It withdrew from routine microbiological testing in April
2000 because of competitive pressures to cut costs.

When G.A.P. withdrew from routine testing, the Walkerton PUC retained
A&L Canada Laboratories to perform microbiological tests on the town's drinking water. A&L had performed metal and chemical tests on water for the
Walkerton PUC since 1996. A&L was a general-service, primarily agricultural, laboratory. It had not done any microbiological testing of drinking water
until January 2000, when it began to perform presence-absence tests and

membrane filtration tests for total coliforms and *E. coli*. Although A&L employed a number of scientists (primarily agronomists), it did not have a microbiologist on staff. Walkerton's was the first and only public utilities commission for which A&L performed microbiological tests on drinking water.

As of May 2000, A&L was accredited by the SCC and certified by CAEAL for tests relating to metals in soil and in water. It was also accredited for and participated in proficiency tests for various agricultural parameters. However, it was not certified or accredited for either presence-absence or membrane filtration tests for *E. coli* and total coliforms in water.

A&L tested water samples taken from the Walkerton system on four occasions: May 1, May 8, May 15, and May 23. Robert Deakin, A&L's laboratory manager, testified that he relied on the 1996 Canadian Drinking Water Guidelines for his understanding of "acceptable" levels of *E. coli* and total coliforms (0 cfu/100 mL for each). He stated that he understood that the ODWO criteria for these organisms were the same: 0 cfu/100 mL for each. However, he was not familiar with ODWO criteria for microbiology and did not review the notification protocol under the ODWO before the events of May 2000.

It would have been preferable for A&L to have been familiar with the ODWO when it undertook the microbiological testing of Walkerton's drinking water. However, both the fact that this was an unregulated sector and the fact that the ODWO was only a guideline, not a regulation, help explain why A&L was unaware of the reporting protocol. Clearly the situation would have been different if the reporting protocol had been a legal obligation.

A&L had a procedures manual that states, "It is the intent of A&L Laboratories to ensure the confidential delivery of final results to the customer." Importantly, at the time, ISO Guide 25, a document used by the SCC and CAEAL as part of the accreditation process, provided that "[t]he laboratory shall … have policies and procedures to ensure the protection of its clients' confidential information and proprietary rights, including procedures for protecting the electronic storage and transmission of results." A&L's procedures and policies had been audited by the SCC/CAEAL and had been found to conform with ISO Guide 25. Evidence was given at the Inquiry indicating that other private laboratories had similar client confidentiality concerns and would report adverse results only to the client and not to another body, such as the MOE, in the absence of legally enforceable requirements.

An argument could be made that section 8 of CAEAL's Code of Ethics permits laboratories to disclose a client's confidential information under certain circumstances. Section 8 provides that "a member shall protect the interest of his/her... client so far as it is consistent with the public welfare." In my view, this public welfare exception is ambiguous as to its effect in the face of clear provisions elsewhere in CAEAL's Code of Ethics and in ISO Guide 25 prohibiting the disclosure of a client's confidential information. Russ Calow of Lakefield Research Ltd., another private testing laboratory, testified that his laboratory had, after much discussion, decided to protect the client's confidentiality given the wording of ISO Guide 25, and because there was no clear legal document directing otherwise.

The critical samples for Walkerton were those taken by the PUC on May 15, 2000, and received by A&L on May 16. As previously discussed, the samples labelled "Well 7 treated" were positive for both total coliforms and *E. coli*, and membrane filtration tests showed both total coliforms and *E. coli* greater than 200 cfu/100 mL. Samples from two locations in the Walkerton distribution system also tested positive for both total coliforms and *E. coli* by the presence-absence test, as did three hydrant samples from a new construction site. A&L performed these tests properly and obtained accurate results.

Upon receiving the adverse results on the morning of Wednesday, May 17, A&L's Robert Deakin telephoned Stan Koebel to alert him of the results. The results from the well and the distribution system were faxed to Mr. Koebel in the early afternoon of May 17.

However, A&L did not notify the local MOE office – the Owen Sound office – of the adverse results. Mr. Deakin testified that he did not know that the ODWO specified that testing laboratories should notify the MOE of adverse results. He also testified that even if he had known, the results would have been reported only to A&L's client, the Walkerton PUC, given the laboratory's policy on customer confidentiality.

There was no legally enforceable requirement for A&L to report adverse results to the MOE. Other laboratories cited confidentiality concerns as their reason for reporting adverse results to anyone other than the contracting client. I accept Mr. Deakin's evidence that even if he had known the ODWO notification protocol, he would have done as other laboratories did: that is, in the absence of a legal requirement to do otherwise, he would have reported only to his client. However, I am also satisfied that if there had been a regulation requiring notification to the local MOE office and the local Medical Officer of Health, Mr. Deakin would have complied with the legal requirement.

10.10.2 The Reduction of the Scope of the Outbreak

If A&L had notified either the MOE's Owen Sound office or the Bruce-Grey-Owen Sound Health Unit of the results from the May 15 samples on Wednesday, May 17, I am satisfied that the health unit would have issued a boil water advisory earlier than Sunday, May 21 – by Friday, May 19, at the latest. By then the health unit was aware of complaints of illness in Walkerton. The combination of the adverse results and the complaints would have led to the issuance of a boil water advisory.

If a boil water advisory had been issued on May 19, approximately 300 to 400 illnesses would probably have been prevented, but it is very unlikely that any of the deaths would have been avoided.

It is possible that if the health unit had been notified of the adverse results on the afternoon of Wednesday, May 17, it would have issued a boil water advisory before May 19. The results showed gross contamination and no doubt would have triggered an immediate response: possibly a boil water advisory, but more likely a direction to resample, flush, and maintain adequate chlorine residuals. The results of any resampling would not have been available until the following day, May 18, at the earliest. By Thursday, May 18, complaints of illness had surfaced. If the health unit had been informed of those complaints and of the May 17 results, it might well have issued a boil water advisory at that point.

If a boil water advisory had been issued on May 18, between 400 and 500 illnesses would probably have been avoided. It is possible that one death might have been prevented.[37]

---

[37] One of the persons who died had first experienced symptoms on May 21. Assuming a three- to four-day period of incubation, it is possible that if that person had heard of a boil water advisory on May 18 and had avoided drinking municipal water without boiling it first, he or she would have avoided infection. All the others who died had experienced symptoms before May 21, making it most unlikely that a boil water advisory on May 18 would have prevented them from becoming infected.

Chapter 11 The Ministry of the Environment Budget Reductions

Contents

Chapter 11 The Ministry of the Environment Budget Reductions[1]

11.1 A Background to the Reductions

Beginning in 1992–93 and continuing until 1997–98,[2] the budget of the Ministry of the Environment (MOE) underwent very substantial reductions. The first series of reductions occurred in the early to mid-1990s. Between 1991–92 to 1995–96, the MOE's annual budget estimates fell by approximately 30% and total annual expenditures decreased by about $210 million.

After the election of the new government in 1995, there were further reductions. Shortly after the election, there was a reduction to the MOE's budget of $30.8 million. In August 1995, the central agencies of the government[3] directed the MOE to develop a plan for reducing its budget by a further 40% for 1996–97, and then by another 20% for 1997–98. These reductions added up to $200.8 million over the two-year period. In January 1998, an internal MOE document reported that the ministry had been "particularly hard hit" in comparison with other ministries. It stated that since 1995–96, the MOE budget had been reduced by 48.4%.[4]

The budget reduction targets for the MOE were not set by that ministry. They also did not involve a review of the question of whether the reductions could be achieved without sacrificing the MOE's capacity to fulfill its statutory mandate. Rather, the reduction targets were initiated by the central agencies, and the MOE's responsibility was to develop strategies for reaching those targets.

With one exception, there was no negotiation between the central agencies and the MOE about the amount of the targeted budget reductions in view of the ministry's statutory responsibilities. The sole exception occurred in 1998, when the central agencies were proposing further reductions. The Minister of the Environment at the time, Norman Sterling, was advised by his staff that the MOE had reached the point where further budget reductions would affect

---

[1] I did not address this topic in Chapter 9 of this report, when dealing with the role of the MOE, because the budget reductions involved decisions made by the Cabinet and not only the MOE.

[2] In this chapter, ranges of years indicate respective fiscal years.

[3] The Ministry of Finance, the Management Board Secretariat, the Cabinet Office, and the Premier's Office.

[4] This calculation was adjusted to remove the skewing effect resulting from the removal of capital and water grants. At the end of the chapter, I have included three tables summarizing the budget constraints, financial resources, and staffing complement of the MOE in the 1990s.

the delivery of core programs. In response, Minister Sterling negotiated with the Management Board Secretariat and with the Cabinet to reduce the impact by using non-tax revenue, generated by the MOE, to meet the budget reduction target.

The provincial government developed a new process for implementing budget reductions across all ministries beginning in 1996–97. Each ministry had to complete a form from the Management Board of Cabinet to show how that ministry would implement its budget reduction strategy. This became part of the ministry's business planning process, whereby it would complete a business plan for the ultimate approval of the Cabinet, on the recommendation of the Management Board of Cabinet and the Policy and Priorities Board of Cabinet.[5] For the MOE, one of the requirements of the business plan form was to outline the impacts of the budget reductions on the environment and on public health.

The first business plan prepared by the MOE was signed by the Minister of the Environment at the time, Brenda Elliott, on January 22, 1996. It was approved at a joint meeting of the Management Board of Cabinet and the Policy and Priorities Board of Cabinet on February 8, 1996, and ultimately by the Cabinet on February 28, 1996. The approval by the Cabinet gave the authority by which the MOE's budget was cut by $200.8 million and by which, in time, its total staff was reduced by more than 750 employees. As I discuss below, the business plan outlined risks to the environment and human health associated with the budget reductions.

11.2 The Impacts of Budget Reductions on the Events in Walkerton

In this section, I comment on the effect of the significant budget reductions on what happened in Walkerton. Before doing so, I will outline some general issues about budget reductions and discuss how I propose to address the topic.

Over the course of the Inquiry, it became evident that the impact of budget reductions was a prominent concern for many people. The reductions in the

---

[5] The Policy and Priorities Board of Cabinet is chaired by the Premier and is generally composed of the chairs of the Cabinet's policy committees. The Board supervises the strategic policy of the government.

MOE's budget were substantial, and the impacts were wide-ranging. It should be kept in mind, however, that the purpose of the Inquiry is not to review the broad impact of budget reductions on the MOE or on the provincial government as a whole. The purpose of this report is to address the budget reductions only to the extent to which they may have had an effect on the tragedy in May 2000.

I conclude that the budget reductions had two types of effects on the tragedy in Walkerton. First, with respect to the decision to privatize the laboratory testing of drinking water samples, and especially the way in which that decision was implemented, the budget reductions are connected directly to the events of May 2000. Second, in the case of the MOE's approvals and inspections programs, the budget reductions are indirectly linked to the events in May 2000 in that they made it less likely that the MOE would pursue proactive measures that would have prevented or limited the tragedy.

In Chapter 10 of this report, I discussed the decision in 1996 to discontinue all routine testing of water for municipalities at provincial laboratories – after which the large majority of municipalities, including Walkerton, had to use private sector laboratories for these tests. This decision resulted directly from the decision to reduce the MOE's budget.

As I mentioned in Chapter 10, I do not comment on the merits of the government's decision to privatize laboratory testing in this report. However, it is my opinion that the way in which the decision was implemented was deficient in that the associated risks to public health were not properly analyzed or managed, repeated warnings about the risks were not acted upon, and the standards that applied to private laboratories were not properly updated. In part, this may have occurred due to the speed with which the decision to discontinue laboratory testing was implemented, which in turn stemmed from the speed with which the Cabinet required the budget reductions from the MOE. As I have discussed, the failure to enact a notification regulation very likely resulted in an additional 300 to 400 illnesses in Walkerton, although such a regulation would probably not have prevented any deaths.

The second type of effect of the budget reductions was to reduce the likelihood that the operating problems at the Walkerton PUC would be detected, so that corrective action could be taken. To have detected those problems and initiated the necessary corrective action would not have required a superhuman effort on the part of the MOE or its personnel. However, it would have required the MOE to be proactive, especially in its approvals and inspections programs as they applied to Walkerton. The budget reductions reduced the MOE's ability to be proactive in this regard. I note that in its Statement of Environmental Values, the MOE commits to taking a proactive approach in fulfilling its statutory mandate of environmental protection.

As I discussed in Chapter 9 of this report, the MOE approvals program did not systematically review existing Certificates of Approval, like the one issued for Well 5, to determine if operating conditions for treatment and monitoring should be added, especially after the 1994 amendments to the Ontario Drinking Water Objectives.

After the budget reductions, the staff in the Approvals Branch was reduced, albeit not as substantially as staff in other areas of the MOE. Nonetheless, the introduction of a systematic program to reach back and review all Certificates of Approval to determine if conditions should be attached would have taken time and resources. I have concluded that the MOE should have implemented a program of this nature. The budget reductions made it less likely that the MOE would do so.

I have also found that the MOE should have conducted a follow-up to its 1998 inspection to ensure that the Walkerton PUC complied with MOE requirements for chlorination and monitoring. With the proper follow-up, these proactive measures would likely have resulted in the PUC's adoption of chlorination and monitoring practices that would in turn very likely have substantially reduced the scope of the outbreak in May 2000.

If a follow-up inspection of the PUC had been carried out after the 1998 inspection, it would have been conducted by the MOE's Owen Sound office. There is no direct evidence that the reason that such a follow-up inspection was not done was related to budget reductions. Indeed, the number of staff in the Owen Sound office had not been significantly reduced as a result of the budget reductions. However, it is clear that workloads had increased and that the amount of time available for overseeing municipal water systems had decreased after the reductions began in 1996. For example, at that office, from 1994–95 to 1999–2000, the number of planned annual inspections of municipal water systems fell from 25 to 10. The number of actual inspections fell from 16 to 10. The amount of time that staff in the office spent on communal water – including inspections, abatement, and enforcement – fell by about one half during the five years of budget reductions leading up to the tragedy.[6] In fiscal year 1999–2000, the entire cohort of environmental officers in Owen Sound would have been able to allot, on average, 7.7 hours to supervising each of the 54 municipal water systems in their district.[7] I am satisfied that this decreased staff time flowed from the budget reductions and the resulting work prioritization programs.

I am not certain that there would have been a follow-up to the 1998 inspection had the budget reductions not occurred. However, it is fair to say that the budget reductions made a follow-up inspection less likely.

After the substantial reductions to its budget in the 1990s, and especially after 1996, it was unlikely that the MOE would take these proactive measures in the approvals and inspections programs. To do so would have required it to propose and implement new initiatives – an unlikely step at a time when its budget was being reduced by nearly 50%. The overall approach during these years was to try to maintain existing programs to the extent possible, not to expand those programs to address new issues, however important such issues might be. Put another way, the goal was not to fill in any gaps that existed, but rather to stop those gaps from getting any wider. The orientation of the MOE's offices to problems associated with municipal water systems became more reactive than proactive.

Thus, one effect of the budget reductions was that MOE put less priority on its role in overseeing municipal water systems. The Inquiry heard evidence that starting in 1995, the number of inspections conducted by the MOE decreased dramatically, as did the number of site visits and other contacts between the MOE and municipal water systems.

At the Inquiry, it was argued by some parties that the budget reductions contributed to other problems in the MOE that had an effect on the events of May 2000. Unquestionably, the reductions increased workload pressures, caused MOE personnel to change the way they prioritized and targeted their time, and created significant morale problems among MOE staff. However, on the

---

[6] Specifically, the amount of time dedicated to the communal water program by staff at the MOE's Owen Sound office fell from 10.17% in 1994–95 to 5.12% in 1999–2000.

[7] This calculation assumes a 36-hour workweek, 48 weeks per year, with 4.8 environmental officers dedicating 5% of their time to the 54 water systems as part of the communal water program. I note that the number of environmental officers at the Owen Sound office fluctuated between four and six during 1999–2000.

evidence, I am not satisfied that there is a sufficient connection between the budget reductions and any other problems in the MOE that warrant comment by me. I will be addressing the budget reductions in the course of the Part 2 report of this Inquiry, and I will be making recommendations concerning the need to ensure that the MOE has adequate resources to allow it to carry out its role as a regulator of drinking water systems.

I now turn to a review of the budget reductions and the process by which they were carried out.

11.3 Warnings About the Impacts

On many occasions during the MOE's first business plan process in 1995 and 1996, ministry staff warned senior management, the Minister of the Environment, and the Cabinet that the impact of the budget reductions being imposed on the ministry presented risks to the environment and public health.

Several points about the possible impacts of the proposed reductions that are found in the warning documents are significant in relation to Walkerton. Warnings that the reductions would result in increased risks to the environment and human health included suggestions that the MOE would become more reactive than proactive; that the MOE's ability to monitor long-term threats to the environment would be reduced; and, importantly, that increased environmental risks would result from an inability to conduct proactive inspections[8] or to detect or control improper or illegal actions because of decreased compliance and enforcement activities.

The evidence at the Inquiry disclosed that the budget reductions did in fact result in fewer proactive inspections, as had been predicted in the warnings made by the public officials. James Merritt, a former MOE assistant deputy minister of the Operations Division, testified that staff increasingly found much of their day taken up with "reactive work," leaving little time for proactive work such as planned inspections and inspection follow-ups. Robert Shaw, the regional director of the MOE's Central Region, confirmed that the cutbacks reduced the MOE's ability to conduct proactive work. He testified that the reduction in staffing made it difficult to do more than just reactive work.

---

[8] I note that the documents did not refer specifically to water treatment plant inspections.

The business plan approved by the Cabinet identified several key impacts resulting from the reductions, including the following:

• The MOE's ability to ensure compliance with environmental standards and regulations would be reduced as a result of several factors, including a reduction in the proactive inspection of industries, a reduction in the MOE's scientific and technical expertise, and delays in developing standards and in providing expert advice on the risks of water contamination.

• The risks to the environment and human health might increase as a result of improper or illegal actions that were neither detected nor controlled through orders and prosecutions because of a decrease in compliance and enforcement activities.

• The level of front-line service would be reduced as a result of slower response times to complaints, a focus on compliance activities rather than on providing assistance with abatement actions, having less information available to provide when responding to inquiries, and reduced technical assistance being given to municipalities that were seeking to optimize their water and sewage treatment facilities.

A Management Board document dated February 5, 1996, provided advice on the MOE's business plan. In accordance with government policy, this document was prepared by Management Board analysts after reviewing the business plan proposed by the MOE. It was presented to a joint meeting of the Management Board of Cabinet and the Policy and Priorities Board of Cabinet. One impact referred to in the document was the increased risks to human health and the environment that might occur as a result of the business plan. After summarizing the impacts, the document stated that the plan provided a "[r]ealistic assessment of impacts." The document also referred to the proposal to close the MOE laboratories in order to reduce the budget, and stated that issues such as the accreditation of private laboratories still needed to be resolved.

11.4 The Cabinet Decision and the Lack of a Risk Assessment

The MOE's business plan, with its discussion of associated risks, was approved by the Cabinet on February 28, 1996. As I have mentioned, those risks were significant. The business plan warned of a reduced capacity in the MOE to detect or control violations of environmental standards because of slower response times, less information available for responding to inquiries, and reduced technical expertise.

Despite having knowledge that there could be risks, no member of Cabinet or other public servant directed that a risk assessment and management plan be conducted to determine the extent of those risks, whether the risks should be assumed, and if assumed, whether they could be managed. Although evidence was given at the Inquiry by senior civil servants, the Minister of the Environment, and the Premier that the risks were considered and that conclusions were reached that the risks were considered manageable, no analysis appears to have been made of the specific nature, scope, or extent of the risks or of how they could be managed.

Before the budget reductions, the MOE had done a functional analysis of the various work areas in the ministry. After the reductions, the MOE developed policies such as the Delivery Strategies, which prioritized the work to be done. But such analyses and policies cannot be considered to be risk assessment plans. The functional analysis was a planning tool aimed at providing an accurate picture of how and where resources were being used. The Delivery Strategies was a work-plan tool: it prioritized work for the MOE's employees. It was developed after the reductions were already in place, and it did not examine the risks arising from the reductions, whether the risks should be assumed, or how the specific risks could be managed. These analyses, policies, and strategies were an attempt by the MOE to rationally cope with budget constraints. However, none of these tools assessed the risks that resulted from the significant budget and staff reductions.

In its closing submissions at the Inquiry, the government referred to an undated memorandum from Deputy Minister of the Environment Linda Stevens to Norman Sterling, who became Minister of the Environment in August 1996. The memorandum is an undated draft; nothing in it indicates that Ms. Stevens sent, authorized, or otherwise agreed with the contents of the document, nor is there anything to indicate that it was actually forwarded to Minister Sterling. The memorandum included this statement:

> As dramatic as these constraints are, the Ministry's capacity to fulfill statutory obligations and implement new priorities was maintained.

Government counsel used this memorandum to support the suggestion that Minister Sterling relied upon assurances from his senior bureaucrats that the risks were manageable. This memorandum does not, however, demonstrate that a proper risk assessment study had been done, nor does it show a plan as to how the specific risks would be managed.

Premier Michael Harris, who chaired the Cabinet meeting at which the MOE's business plan was approved on February 28, 1996, testified that he would have asked if the impacts were a concern, but he does not recall making such an inquiry. He does not recall seeking advice regarding whether the risks could be managed. Premier Harris could not identify any documents that persuaded him that the increased risks to the environment and public health could be managed. He accepted that as chair of the Policy and Priorities Board and chair of the Cabinet, which approved the 1996 business plan, he is accountable if any of these reductions are found to have contributed to the tragedy in Walkerton.

The MOE's 1996 business plan was not released to the public after it was approved by the Cabinet. However, on May 1, 1996, the MOE published a modified business plan that did not include assessments of the adverse impacts or concerns about increased risks to the environment and human health resulting from the budget reductions. In fact, the business plan that was released to the public promised reforms "without lowering the current high level of environmental protection in Ontario."

One cannot help but question the basis for this statement, given the nature of the risks identified in the original business plan and the failure to conduct a risk assessment or develop a risk management plan.

11.5 Conclusions

The failure to properly assess and manage the risks arising from the budget reductions had one direct effect and two indirect effects on the events in Walkerton.

I am satisfied that the failure to enact a regulation mandating testing laboratories to follow a notification protocol at the time of privatization of laboratory testing services did increase the risk to public health. Although this risk was not specifically identified in the business plan or in other documents warning of risks, it is very likely that if a proper risk assessment had been done regarding the decision to discontinue provincial government laboratory testing, the need for a notification regulation would have been identified and should have been addressed. As I concluded above, the failure to enact a regulation requiring testing laboratories to notify the proper authorities promptly and directly about adverse results had a direct impact on the events in Walkerton.

In the warnings about the risks associated with the budget reductions, references were made to the loss of technical expertise and the reduction in the number of proactive inspections. Again, there was no risk assessment regarding the effects of these changes, particularly as they related to the safety of drinking water. A proper risk assessment might have identified the potential for the problems in the approvals and inspections programs that I have discussed as contributing to the events in Walkerton. Of course, it is impossible to be certain that steps would have been taken to address potential problems even if the specific risks had been identified. I can conclude only that the budget reductions made it less likely that the approvals and inspections programs would have detected and addressed the two problems at Walkerton that contributed to the outbreak: the need for continuous monitors at Well 5, and the improper operating practices of the Walkerton PUC.

11.6 Detailed Summary of the Reductions

The following tables and commentary summarize evidence heard at the Inquiry with respect to the budget and staff reductions at the MOE.

Table 1 summarizes the annual budget reductions and the constraint programs for the period 1992–2000.

Table 2 presents a survey of budgets for the period 1990–2000. As stated elsewhere, the government used various figures to measure its financial resources in any particular fiscal year. The first column in Table 2 represents the annual estimates for the MOE. An annual estimate is the allocated amount of money approved by the legislature that is given to each ministry in any particular year. The huge reduction in 1994–95 results from the creation of the Ontario Clean Water Agency (OCWA) as a separate entity, so that it was no longer part of the MOE estimates. The second column represents the MOE's actual expenditures, which include both capital and operating expenditures. These figures exclude any expenditures attributable to the Ministry of Energy,

Table 1   Summary of Budget Constraints at MOE (1992–2000)

Year	Reduction	Program
1992–1993	$82.9 million	Managed Savings Strategy, Capital and Investment Savings
1993–1994	$79.9 million	Managed Savings Strategy, Expenditure Control Program, Multi-Year Expenditure Reduction Program
1994–1995	$47.9 million	Social Control, Expenditure Control Plan Capital
1995–1996	$30.8 million + $24.6 million from OCWA* + $19.1 million from IWA** and ETF***	Operating Reduction Target
1996–1997	$200.8 million (over two years)	Business Plan Allocation Target
1997–1998	$13.5 million	Base Review Target
1998–1999	$5.0 million	Efficiency Operating Constraint
1999–2000	$4.8 million	Efficiency Operating Constraint
2000–2001		

* Ontario Clean Water Agency
** Interim Waste Authority
*** Environmental Technologies Fund

Table 2   Summary of Financial Resources of MOE (1990–91 to 2000–01)

Year	Annual Estimates	Actual Expenditures	Operating Expenditures
1990–91	$648.7 million	$645 million	$363 million
1991–92	$774.0 million	$711 million	$461 million
1992–93	$722.3 million	$671 million	$453 million
1993–94	$837.7 million	$539 million	$379 million
1994–95	$376.0 million	$328 million	$271 million
1995–96	$411.3 million	$400 million	$282 million
1996–97	$373.3 million	$367 million	$166 million
1997–98	$349.8 million	$255 million	$165 million
1998–99	$270.6 million	$213 million	$169 million
1999–00	$406.7 million	$341 million	$174 million
2000–01	$229.1 million	—	—

which was part of the MOE for a period in the 1990s. Unfortunately, information relating to fiscal year 2000–01 was not available to the Inquiry. The third column shows the MOE's operating expenditures. It too neutralizes the effect of the Ministry of Energy by excluding its expenditures for the years in which it was part of the MOE. This information was also unavailable for 2000–01.

In the five-year period after 1995–96, the MOE's annual estimates were reduced by over 44%. In the four-year period after 1995–96, the actual expenditures were reduced by approximately 15% and its operating expenditures by approximately 38%.

Table 3 surveys the MOE's staff complement during the last decade. There are three separate measures. The first column shows funded positions – that is, all positions that are actually funded by the Ministry's allocation. Where there are two figures in a box, the lower figure is the one that excludes the Ministry of Energy employees during those years when the two ministries were combined. The huge reduction in 1994–95 results from the creation of OCWA and the

Table 3   **Summary of Position and Staff Complement of MOE (1990–91 to 2000–01)**

Year	Funded Positions	FTEs	Headcount (as of March 31, excl. OCWA)
1990–91	3,317	3,024	2,306
1991–92	3,517	3,218	2,378
1992–93	3,575	3,193	2,358
1993–94	3,510 3,344	3,220	2,371
1994–95	2,554 2,408	3,310	2,208
1995–96	2,430 2,283	2,298 2,151	2,065
1996–97	1,905 1,787	2,188	1,663
1997–98	1,648 1,531	1,714	1,494
1998–99	1,509	1,582	1,418
1999–00	1,529	1,439	1,374
2000–01	1,501	1,394	—

transfer of MOE employees to the Crown agency. The second column represents FTEs (full-time equivalents) as of the end of each fiscal year. The lower of the two numbers for 1995–96 represents the MOE total excluding the Ministry of Energy. The third column is the MOE's "headcount," which excludes OCWA employees before and after its creation. The headcount includes all "classified" employees (civil servants), all "unclassified" employees employees (for example, contract employees), and all management staff. It does not, however, include staff who are on leave or are receiving Long Term Income Protection.

Whatever measure is chosen, Table 3 shows a significant reduction of staff beginning in 1995–96. Excluding the Ministry of Energy, a 34% reduction in funded positions and a 35% reduction in FTEs take place over the next five years. Headcount shows there is a 33% reduction between 1995–96 and 1999–00.

Chapter 12 Other Government Policies, Practices, and Procedures

Contents

Chapter 12 Other Government Policies, Practices, and Procedures

12.1   Introduction

The Inquiry heard evidence about several government policies, practices, and procedures that I have concluded were not causes of the outbreak in May 2000 and had only a remote, if any, connection to the events in Walkerton. However, I will briefly discuss the more significant ones here to explain my conclusions and in one instance to provide support for recommendations I will be making in the Part 2 report of this Inquiry.

The following provincial initiatives are summarized in this chapter: the *Energy Competition Act* (Bill 35); municipal restructuring; the "Who Does What" policy; provincial grants and loans to municipalities; the municipal financing of waterworks; Ontario Ministry of Agriculture, Food and Rural Affairs programs; the groundwater management strategy; employee morale in the Ministry of the Environment; and land use planning.

12.2   The *Energy Competition Act*

Until the late 1990s, public utilities commissions commonly provided both water and electricity in Ontario. This situation changed with the passage of the *Energy Competition Act*, still known as "Bill 35," which received royal assent on November 7, 1998. The Inquiry heard evidence from several witnesses that between 1998 and May 2000, municipal officials and the Walkerton Public Utilities Commission (PUC) were preoccupied with Bill 35's repercussions and were not focused on drinking water. Although this may have been the case, I do not find a connection between the passage of Bill 35 and the events in Walkerton in May 2000.

The *Energy Competition Act*, passed in response to the recommendations of the Macdonald Report,[1] paved the way for increased competition in the energy sector. It restructured the electricity distribution system in order to dismantle Ontario Hydro's monopoly and required municipalities to decide whether to

---

[1] *A Framework for Competition: The Report of the Advisory Committee on Competition in Ontario's Electricity System to the Ontario Minister of Environment and Energy* (Toronto: Queen's Printer, 1997).

keep, sell, or lease their electrical utilities by November 2000. Section 142 of the Act required a municipality that retained its electricity distribution assets to incorporate the utility under the *Ontario Business Corporations Act*. This left municipalities to decide whether to keep the remaining public utilities commissions that were responsible for water as separate entities (alone or affiliated with another corporation), or whether to turn them into municipal departments. They could do this more easily after the passage of Bill 26, the *Savings and Restructuring Act* (the "Omnibus Bill" amending the *Municipal Act*), which gave municipalities the power to disband public utilities commissions without a plebiscite.

Municipal officials and the Walkerton PUC were aware of the *Energy Competition Act* and its repercussions. In 1996, Stan Koebel and the PUC's chair, James Kieffer, wrote to the Minister of Finance urging the government to act on the recommendations of the Macdonald Report and end Ontario Hydro's monopoly. In 1998, Walkerton's town council debated the content of Bill 35 and its potential impact on the Walkerton PUC. In 1999, the Ministry of Energy, Science and Technology sponsored workshops throughout the province to inform municipal electricity distributors and corporations about the new rules and responsibilities under Bill 35. Brockton mayor David Thomson, municipal clerk Richard Radford, and Stan Koebel attended the workshop in Owen Sound. The Municipality of Brockton passed a bylaw in August 1999 to create the Brockton and District Utilities Corporation, in compliance with section 142 of the *Energy Competition Act*. All municipal hydro assets were transferred to the corporation in order to be held by it. Brockton considered sharing services with neighbouring utilities. On October 25, 1999, its municipal council passed a resolution leaving the water services under the jurisdiction of the Walkerton PUC.

The issue of whether the PUC should continue to operate what was referred to in evidence as the "water side" was still being discussed in 2000. The municipality's lawyer told the Brockton council that it had three options: leave the water side to stand alone; form an affiliate corporation; or transfer the water services to the municipality and operate it as a municipal department. Mr. Radford and Mark Gaynor, the municipal treasurer/tax collector, prepared a report for the council concluding that the third option – making water services a municipal department – was economically viable. The council decided on March 16, 2000, that the PUC would continue to exist and would provide contract services to the Brockton and District Utilities Corporation. Nonetheless, John Strader, the works superintendent, prepared a report for the council dated April 28, 2000, summarizing a meeting he had had with Stan Koebel. The report described the possibility of creating the position of waterworks superintendent within the municipal Works Department. The council decided on May 1, 2000, to have the proposed position evaluated by a compensation expert. It had not made a decision regarding Mr. Strader's report by the time the tragedy struck later that month.

James Kieffer, Richard Field, and David Thomson all testified that Bill 35 affected their roles as public utilities commissioners in that they spent a great deal of time discussing alternatives relating to the PUC's hydro responsibilities rather than those relating to water. Mr. Kieffer said that Stan Koebel would have had a job no matter what happened to the PUC. According to Mr. Kieffer, Mr. Koebel could have worked on the hydro side, even if it were operated by another company. Mr. Keiffer testified that Mr. Koebel also could have stayed with the PUC if it kept the waterworks, or could have worked for the municipality if it had taken over the waterworks.

Stan Koebel testified that before the passage of Bill 35, he spent about 20% of his time on water and the remainder on electricity; after November 1998, about 5% of his time was spent on water. He did not understand that he was to be interviewed for the position of municipal waterworks supervisor. He thought that if the waterworks responsibility were given to the municipality, he would apply for a position with the new electricity company. He felt that because of the time taken up by the discussions concerning the PUC's electricity business in relation to the waterworks, he was "losing it" – meaning, losing control.

Frank Koebel testified that Bill 35 created uncertainty among the PUC employees about whether they would be able to keep their jobs. This resulted in tension and unhappiness in the workplace. He thought that Stan Koebel would have been concerned about his own position and about the time spent in meetings trying to come up with a solution to Bill 35's requirements.

Even if the atmosphere was stressful, however, I find that the implementation of Bill 35 did not make it substantially more difficult for the PUC employees and commissioners to do their jobs properly. The problems at the PUC lay in the lax attitude toward disinfection, sampling, and monitoring, and the failure to do these things properly. No one testified that with more time to work on the water side, they would have started conforming and complying with MOE guidelines and directions. Indeed, these improper practices had gone on for years before the passage of Bill 35. Moreover, the primary problem I have found with the Walkerton PUC commissioners was their failure to properly respond to the 1998 MOE inspection report. That also preceded the passage of Bill 35.

12.3   Municipal Restructuring

I heard evidence about the impact of municipal restructuring on Walkerton. As with the Bill 35 evidence, there were suggestions in testimony that the preoccupation created by this change might have affected the ability of local officials to turn their minds to drinking water safety. I do not accept that there was a connection between municipal restructuring and the events of May 2000: I will briefly review the evidence here in order to show why.

The County of Bruce had undertaken county restructuring studies in 1975 and again in 1990. Both studies were defeated by county council and never implemented. In the fall of 1996, county council formed a restructuring committee to revisit the issue of restructuring. This process began with review of the 1990 study. Bruce County decided to initiate restructuring again after the passage of Bill 26 in order to avoid having restructuring carried out by the province on the province's terms.

Bill 26, the *Savings and Restructuring Act*, was the most significant recent change to provincial legislation affecting municipalities. Passed in 1996, the "Omnibus Bill" provided municipalities outside of regional municipalities with the necessary legislative tools to develop and implement local restructuring proposals. Amalgamation is one form of municipal restructuring. As a consequence of amalgamation, the number of municipalities in Ontario decreased from 815 to 447 between 1996 and 2001.

Part of the restructuring of Bruce County that became effective on January 1, 1999 was amalgamation of the Townships of Brant and Greenock with the Town of Walkerton to create the Municipality of Brockton. The restructuring order under the *Municipal Act* dissolved the former Walkerton PUC, but reestablished it under the same name to distribute and supply electrical power and to produce, treat, distribute, and supply water to the geographic area of the former Town of Walkerton. In March 1999, the Brockton municipal council passed a resolution to transfer responsibility for operation and maintenance of a small waterworks in Chepstow (formerly in Greenock) and another on Geeson Avenue (formerly in Brant) to the Walkerton PUC. The addition of these two water systems created additional work for the PUC staff. Staff had to drive to each of the well locations to conduct sampling, and were required to perform maintenance on the wells. The Chepstow well house was found to be substandard. Stan Koebel took primary responsibility for upgrading the Chepstow and Geeson Avenue waterworks.

Richard Radford agreed with the statement that "this was kind of a unique time with a lot of pressure and everybody was working pretty hard." However, although the PUC was given some additional responsibility, there was no indication that this responsibility rendered it incapable of attending to the safety of the drinking water supply as a whole. During the time that amalgamation was being implemented, Stan Koebel did not make a request for additional staff – nor did he tell the commissioners that the post-amalgamation structure made it impossible for him to perform his duties properly. He failed to execute his duties properly for reasons canvassed in other areas of this report.

I have considered whether municipal amalgamation resulted in the loss of an opportunity to correct the Walkerton PUC's deficient disinfection and monitoring practices after its receipt of the 1998 Ministry of the Environment (MOE) inspection report. Indeed, there was evidence that Walkerton's town council considered the option of hiring a director of public works when it discussed the report at its June 8, 1998, meeting but that this did not occur because the council was going to be replaced in January 1999. However, I am not persuaded that even if the council had held office for a full three-year term, it would have taken that significant step in the face of Stan Koebel's assurances to the PUC (on May 20, 1998) and to the MOE (in his letter of July 14, 1998) that the Walkerton waterworks system would conform to MOE directives.

12.4   The "Who Does What" Policy

The "Who Does What" provincial policy initiative reorganized and clarified provincial and municipal roles in the late 1990s, including the responsibility for waterworks. The Inquiry heard evidence on this policy, but in the end I find no clear connection between that policy and the events of May 2000. The Local Services Realignment Program implemented many of the Who Does What recommendations, including the transfer of provincially owned waterworks to municipalities. Walkerton, however, had always owned its own waterworks and was not affected by this change.

The need to redistribute responsibilities and rationalize program administration between the provincial and municipal governments had been recognized since at least as early as the 1980s. There were various attempts to discuss and negotiate what should be done, but there was no overhaul of the system until 1996. Bill 26 set up the legislative framework for reform in provincial-municipal relations. The Who Does What panel was appointed to recommend ways to make the allocation of responsibilities between local and provincial governments more efficient, and to make both levels of government more accountable. It focused on ways to eliminate a duplication of regulation in areas where there were blurred responsibilities between the two levels of government. The Transportation and Utilities Subpanel addressed water and sewage issues and reported by letter to the Minister of Municipal Affairs and Housing, Allan Leach, on November 4, 1996.

The reporting letter confirmed municipal responsibility for water and sewer infrastructure and services. It expressed the view that municipalities should own, operate, and finance water and sewer systems, and that the province should focus primarily on enforcing standards and promoting conservation. The reporting letter recommended the following: that municipalities be encouraged to move to full-cost pricing for drinking water; that once they were brought into compliance with provincial standards, provincially owned facilities should be transferred to municipalities; and that provincial grants and loans should be eliminated and municipalities should finance their own future needs on the basis of their access to the private market – except when one-time funding was needed to address health or environmental risks. The sub-panel's recommendations were accepted and adopted by the provincial government, and the question of how to bring provincial facilities into compliance was left open.

Many municipalities were affected by the Who Does What panel's report because of the resulting transfer of ownership of hundreds of waterworks systems from the province to the municipalities. The Local Services Realignment affected the transfer of water and sewage works worth $400–$500 million (in addition to the province forgiving loans worth approximately $130 million in 1985–86). Walkerton, however, had always owned its own waterworks. Richard Radford, the town's senior administrator, did not believe that the Local Services Realignment resulted in the diminution of the municipality's ability to provide safe drinking water. I agree with him.

I am satisfied that Walkerton's drinking water safety was not affected by the changes brought about by the Who Does What initiatives.

12.5   Provincial Grants and Loans to Municipalities

The Province of Ontario provided grants and loans to municipalities for waterworks and related infrastructure and programs. Provincial funding levels changed over time, and I will briefly review the amount of provincial funding received by Walkerton. It appears that Walkerton did not take advantage of all of the funding that was available to it. It is unfortunate that several of the provincial programs were primarily directed at distribution systems (infrastructure) rather than water quality (treatment and monitoring), on the assumption that groundwater was safe. In the end, however, the tragic events in Walkerton were not due to a lack of provincial grants and loans to that municipality or its successor.

Through various funding programs, the Province of Ontario has contributed approximately $4 billion to waterworks and sewage infrastructure throughout the province since 1956.

In the late 1970s and 1980s, the decision makers of the Walkerton PUC generally preferred "to solve the problems on their own" rather than apply for provincial funding for waterworks projects.

Between 1990 and 1999, Walkerton received funding under the Direct Grant Program to assist three of its projects: two sewer projects and a communal drinking water project. The latter was the replacement of a watermain on McGivern Street, for which Walkerton received $50,065.42, or 50.28% of the project cost of $99,565.25.

Walkerton received funding for four projects between 1987 and 1992 under the Lifelines Program. One of the projects related to the sanitary collection system, and three related to the water distribution system. Of the three projects, two of the grants covered 33.3% of the cost of replacing water mains ($42,447.02 of $127,353.79, and $52,897.21 of $158,707.49, respectively). The Lifelines Program also paid $9,432 toward a project cost of $16,995 (55.5%) for the water distribution system rehabilitation needs study prepared by B.M. Ross and Associates Ltd. The total amount of drinking water-related funding received under the Lifelines Program was $104,776.23.

As a result of the Canada/Ontario Infrastructure Works programs I and II, Walkerton received a total of $540,425. The Canada/Ontario Infrastructure Works program I, designed as a three-year, $2.1 billion federal cost-shared program, was introduced in 1994. Cost-sharing was one-third federal, one-third provincial, and one-third municipal. Ontario's contribution was approximately $720 million, and the projects with the province had a total value of $2.2 billion. The Canada/Ontario Infrastructure Works program II was introduced in 1997 as part of a one-year, $1.275 billion top-up to Canada/Ontario Infrastructure Works program I. This money was invested under the same cost-sharing arrangements, and Ontario's contribution was approximately $172 million. Drinking water-related infrastructure projects funded under program I included the warning and backup system for the water distribution system (actual project cost, $98,963; federal/provincial grant, $61,698), the Yonge Street watermain replacement project (actual project cost, $224,713; federal/provincial grant, $121,290), and the Hinks Street watermain replacement project (actual project cost, $93,418; federal/provincial grant, $62,278). Three sewage projects having an aggregate actual project cost of $98,463 were funded under program I. None of the $40,742 of program II funding was applied to waterworks projects.

The Provincial Water Protection Fund was a $200 million fund created in 1997 as part of the Municipal Capital and Operating Restructuring Fund. The new program was part of the Who Does What policy and was intended to fulfill the provincial government's commitment to assist municipalities in their transition to full responsibility for financing and operating water and sewage services. The fund consisted of two parts. One part provided funding for the construction of water and sewer infrastructure projects to address immediate health and environmental problems. The second part provided funding for studies of environmental issues, water and sewage system optimization, and groundwater management and regional servicing studies. These studies were intended to encourage conservation, the protection of water resources, and the reduction, elimination, or deferral of the need for capital works.

Richard Radford testified that Walkerton had evaluated the Provincial Water Protection Fund guidelines and had considered repairs to its sewage collection system and sewage treatment plant under this program. However, Mr. Radford, in consultation with the MOE, concluded that Walkerton's discretionary reserve funds were too large for the town to meet the financial eligibility criteria of the Provincial Water Protection Fund program. Consequently, the municipality did not apply for funding under this program. It should be noted that the financial eligibility criteria did not apply to the groundwater management study portion of the Provincial Water Protection Fund.

The Municipality of Brockton was notified of the groundwater management study funding. Stan Koebel requested, and the MOE sent, the groundwater management study guide and application. The groundwater management study funding could cover such initiatives as the formulation of a groundwater management plan, which identified the planning steps, including establishing well-head protection zones and groundwater protection policies. Groundwater management studies were funded within Huron and Oxford Counties – areas that faced issues similar to those faced by Walkerton.

The provincial government left it to the municipalities to apply for funding to conduct a groundwater management study. It did not target communities with problematic water sources, and no particular municipalities were encouraged to apply. It would have been preferable for Walkerton to have been encouraged to apply, because the MOE had information on file showing that the town clearly had source problems with Well 5.

Mr. Radford testified that Walkerton did not consider seeking funding under the Provincial Water Protection Fund to locate a new water source, although in 1999 it considered developing an additional groundwater source on land that it already owned.

I find that the funding structures were not a problem in themselves; rather, the Walkerton PUC did not know how to make the best use of available funding. It is, however, simply too speculative to conclude that there would have been any different outcome in May 2000 if Walkerton had applied for funding from the Provincial Water Protection Fund.

12.6   The Municipal Financing of Waterworks

The Inquiry heard evidence on the workings of municipal finance in general, and on the finances of the Municipality of Brockton and the Walkerton PUC in particular. It appears that Brockton was a fiscally conservative municipality with substantial reserve funds and the capacity to borrow more money than it did. The various provincial laws and policies on municipal finance had no connection to the events of May 2000. Nor did a shortage of municipal funds affect drinking water safety.

Municipalities can raise revenue from several sources: taxation on property assessment, payment in lieu of taxes, development charges, user fees, licence fees, fines, and transfers from the provincial and federal governments. Property taxes comprise approximately 47% of the municipal "own source" revenue of most municipalities, depending on how many residential properties are in the municipality.

Richard Radford characterized the Municipality of Brockton as fiscally conservative. The municipal finance panel members agreed that this is the case for most Ontario municipalities – for example, many do not borrow the maximum possible amount of money.

There are controls on municipal finances. Each municipality has an annual repayment limit, equivalent to 25% of municipal own-source revenue. This is the limit beyond which a municipality cannot borrow in a year without the approval of the Ontario Municipal Board.

Mr. Radford confirmed that Brockton's annual repayment limit in 2000 was $1,209,981. However, he said that in reality, the limit would never be reached because Brockton would not be able to raise enough taxes or other revenues to service the debt.

If the Walkerton PUC wanted to borrow money, it required permission from the Municipality of Brockton. The PUC was required to submit a list of its reserves at the end of each year, to be approved by the municipal council, so that these funds could be reserved for future years. The municipality had control over the PUC reserve funds, so it could actually take PUC reserves and put them into the municipality's reserve funds.

The total reserves and reserve funds for the Town of Walkerton at the end of December 1998 were $946,458. As a result of the municipal amalgamation on January 1, 1999, the municipality's debt capacity increased. The reserve funds for the Walkerton PUC were $449,401 at the end of December 1998. At the end of 1999, the balance in the PUC reserve fund was approximately $347,000. The PUC's capital reserve fund of $100,000 was deposited into the water reserve account on December 4, 1999. These funds were specifically allocated to pay for three particular watermain improvement projects.

Mr. Radford was not aware of any PUC capital project that Walkerton or Brockton had been unable to fund. He said that in-year changes did not detract from the municipality's ability to provide safe drinking water.

Walkerton and, later, Brockton had ample funds on hand – and the capacity to borrow more – to ensure that the PUC's infrastructure, equipment, and staff were sufficient to deliver safe drinking water. Neither provincial policies on municipal finance nor the financial status of Walkerton contributed to the events of May 2000.

12.7   The Privatization of Municipal Waterworks

It was argued at the Inquiry that the failure of the Walkerton PUC and the Municipality of Brockton to engage a private operator to run the Walkerton water system contributed to the events of May 2000. It was also argued that the Province did not do enough to promote municipalities' use of private waterworks operators. I find the issue too remote to reach such conclusions.

Until the PUC's dissolution in January 2001, it would have been the PUC's decision as to whether to seek an alternative operator of the Walkerton system. There is no evidence that the PUC considered the possibility of turning to an alternative operator, whether public or private, in response to the problems identified in the 1998 inspection report. I have concluded that the PUC commissioners should have required the PUC operators to respond properly to the issues raised in the 1998 MOE inspection report. One possible response was to engage an alternative operator, such as the Ontario Clean Water Agency (OCWA). However, there were several ways of addressing the issues, and it is too remote to conclude that the commissiners should be faulted for not engaging an alternative operator, or that any provincial government program prevented them from doing so.

The issue of the private sector's involvement in drinking water has been extensively canvassed in Part 2 of the Inquiry, and I will address this issue in the Part 2 report.

12.8   Ontario Ministry of Agriculture, Food and
Rural Affairs Programs

Manure is a source of nutrients for crops. The amount of nutrients available from a manure application can be analyzed to ensure that crops receive neither too many nor too few nutrients. Fertilizer applications can be adjusted to complement the application of manure. For this reason, manure application is part of the "nutrient management planning" process.

The Resource Management Branch of the Ontario Ministry of Agriculture, Food and Rural Affairs (OMAFRA) works in three areas: environmental planning, which includes the development of best management practices; engineering, which includes third-party reviews of nutrient management plans; and land use planning, which deals with provincial policy statements on agriculture. In recent years, OMAFRA's overall objectives have remained constant, but the way in which they are achieved has changed. Since 1995, the ministry's focus has been on core businesses and on working in partnerships with other ministries. OMAFRA's staff strength decreased from 2,400 full-time equivalents in 1990 to 613 full-time equivalents in 2000 – a substantial decrease, even when new partnerships and alternative service delivery are taken into account. In 1990, OMAFRA had 50 county offices and five colleges. By May 2000, it did not have any field offices but did have 13 resource centres across Ontario. In Walkerton, OMAFRA's staff decreased from ten people in the years 1990–95 to one person by fiscal year 2000–01. The move from field offices to resource centres reflects the change from a focus on individual farmers to a focus on providing more specialized expertise in specific priority areas.

12.8.1   The Ministry's Role in Groundwater Protection

Two OMAFRA representatives sit on the Ontario Farm Environmental Coalition's water quality working group.[2] At the time of the Walkerton hearings, the working group had not developed an integrated provincial groundwater strategy.

Through the 1990s, OMAFRA was aware of the bacterial threat posed by manure spreading practices to surface water and groundwater. In 1992, for example, it knew that 34% of Ontario's private wells exceeded standards for coliform bacteria, that there was a higher incidence around livestock operations, and that well maintenance and poor septic systems were issues of concern. OMAFRA's response was to disseminate information so that the risks were well understood. The Ministry focussed on environmental farm plans, nutrient management plans, and other Best Management Practices approaches.

---

[2] The Ontario Farm Environmental Coalition is a multi-stakeholder group with members from various disciplines. OMAFRA provides support and technical assistance to its working groups.

Throughout the 1990s, OMAFRA's approach to environmental protection was to develop technical guidance documents by building consensus with stake-holders. The Ministry did not develop legislation, regulations, or even official policies aimed at environmental protection during that period.

12.8.2   Environmental Farm Plans

Voluntary environmental farm plans provide a process for farmers to carry out a risk assessment on their own farms. Each farmer voluntarily attends a work-shop where the farmer answers questions related to soils, water, and activities that may introduce contamination into the environment. Such activities include pesticide use; petroleum storage; and manure storage, use and management. Participants develop action plans that establish ratings based on factors such as the distance between pesticide storage or manure application, and the farm's domestic well or a nearby stream. A poor rating on an environmental farm plan requires some immediate action. A fair rating means that the farm opera-tion has met the minimum provincial standard but an action plan is still re-quired to improve the rating to a good or best rating. The environmental farm plans do not consider factors such as subsurface geology and aquifer sensitiv-ity. Approximately 50% of the agricultural land base in Ontario is covered by environmental farm plans. As of April 30, 2000, 20–21% of the Bruce County farms had been represented at environmental farm plan workshops.

12.8.3   Nutrient Management Plans

Voluntary nutrient management planning has three components: minimum distance separation for new or expanding livestock facilities from existing or approved development (MDS II), manure storage capacity, and nutrient man-agement plans. A nutrient management plan analyzes the source of nutrients, the quantity of nutrients being put on the land, and the rate of uptake of nutrients by crops. Randy Jackiw, the Director of the Resources Management Branch of OMAFRA, conceded that nutrient management planning currently places primary emphasis on the uptake capacity of crops; the role of pathogens in the environment is only a secondary consideration.

In 1997, OMAFRA initiated the development of a provincial strategy and draft municipal bylaws for nutrient management. The work was done through the Ontario Farm Environmental Coalition's nutrient management working group. OMAFRA encourages municipalities to adopt minimum distance separation and nutrient management plan bylaws. In addition, it reviews nutrient management plans for new and expanding livestock operations that either exceed 150 "livestock units,"[3] or are greater than 50 livestock units and have a density of more than two livestock units per acre (0.4 ha). However, in its role as reviewer, the ministry does not usually perform site inspections.

In November 1998, OMAFRA's non-binding position statement for nutrient management plans recommended that farms exceeding 150 livestock units, or with greater than 50 livestock units and more than five livestock units per tillable acre (0.4 ha), have nutrient management plans.

12.8.4   Best Management Practices

The Best Management Practices booklets provide practical and affordable voluntary approaches to conserving soil and water resources. OMAFRA was one of a number of public and private sector organizations that prepared the Best Management Practices technical documents. Although the Best Management Practices approach is supported by OMAFRA as technical policy, it is not official policy (i.e., signed off by the minister, approved by Cabinet, or posted on the *Environmental Bill of Rights* registry).

Neither OMAFRA nor the MOE enforced the Best Management Practices. However, Dr. David Biesenthal – who owned the farm near Well 5 from which contaminants entered the Walkerton water system – was essentially in compliance with the Best Management Practices documents. In fact, the Best Management Practices do not address the distance between manure application and municipal wells. They only provide that the distance between manure application and watercourses or domestic wells should be at least 15 metres. At its closest, the manure at the Biesenthal farm was applied at least 85 metres' distance from Well 5. In that sense, Dr. Biesenthal's practices surpassed the Best Management Practices.

---

[3] A "livestock unit" is generally equal to one cow or two calves.

12.8.5   The Legislative and Policy Framework

As reviewed in Chapter 13 of this report, animal waste disposed of in accordance with normal farm practices is exempt from certain provisions of the *Environmental Protection Act*. The 1998 *Farming and Food Production Protection Act* defines normal farm practice to be "a practice that … is conducted in a manner consistent with proper and acceptable customs and standards as established and followed by similar agricultural operations under similar circumstances." That Act also prohibits municipal bylaws from restricting a normal farm practice carried on as part of an agricultural operation. The risk created by this legislation is that a municipal bylaw passed to establish a wellhead protection zone can be ineffective against the practice of spreading manure if the practice is deemed a normal practice by the Normal Farm Practices Protection Board.

By July 2000, it became clear that a shift from voluntary to mandatory practices was necessary and that nutrients had to be addressed in a comprehensive manner. An August 2000 assessment of several ministries' (including OMAFRA's) water management responsibilities and initiatives identified the need for greater knowledge about water- and environment-related issues, for better-coordinated monitoring, and for relevant provincial legislation and regulations. At the time of writing this report, Bill 81, the *Nutrient Management Act 2001*, had received first reading. The Bill would provide for regulations governing items such as minimum distance separation.

12.8.6   Conclusion

In my view, the government's policies or lack of policies or programs relating to agricultural activities cannot reasonably be said to have been a cause of the events of May 2000. It is speculative to draw a connection between what regulations the government may or should have enacted, and the ways in which such regulations would have applied to Dr. Biesenthal's farm or other farms from which bacteria may have originated. Moreover, I note that the manure spreading practices on Dr. Biesenthal's farm conformed to the non-binding Best Management Practices guidelines. It is far from clear that newly enacted regulations would have affected the manure spreading practices of that farm. I will be making recommendations in the Part 2 report of the Inquiry that address this sensitive and important area of agricultural operations as they relate to the safety of drinking water.

12.9   The Groundwater Management Strategy

Evidence at the Inquiry showed that the Province of Ontario lacks a ground-water management strategy – despite repeated calls for such a strategy from independent parties such as the Environmental Commissioner and the Provincial Auditor. A groundwater management strategy should provide a full understanding of the water being removed from and added to the ground-water system. It should also provide an understanding of the effects of contaminants.

A comprehensive, coherent strategy to protect and manage groundwater seems fundamental in a province that relies extensively on groundwater as a source of drinking water. However, despite this shortcoming, the evidence falls short of establishing that the lack of a strategy had an effect on what occurred in Walkerton in May 2000. It is not clear what would have been included in a groundwater strategy, how it would have applied to the areas around Walkerton, how it would have affected existing uses such as the Biesenthal farm, and how it would have interacted with other government programs like the Best Management Practices described above. In addition, had the province estab-lished a groundwater management strategy, it would have taken some time to assess specific situations such as the catchment area for the aquifer that sup-plied Well 5. Whether such a program, if implemented, would have led the MOE to address the vulnerability of Well 5 before May 2000 is speculative. In any event, I conclude above that even without a groundwater management strategy, the MOE should have been alerted to the vulnerability of Well 5 through its approvals and inspection programs. Further, it should have taken the appropriate steps to require the installation of continuous chlorine residual and turbidity monitors.

My conclusion that the lack of a groundwater management strategy was not shown to have had an effect on the events in Walkerton, however, should not be interpreted as indicating that such a strategy is not important. On the con-trary, it is essential.

I heard a great deal of evidence about the lack of a groundwater strategy. Because of the importance of this issue to the safety of drinking water, it is useful to summarize that evidence here to lend support to the recommendations I will be making with regard to source protection in the Part 2 report of this Inquiry.

Dr. Ken Howard testified:

> Most parts of the world which use groundwater extensively manage
> the water; in Ontario unfortunately we don't manage water, the
> degree of management extends simply to issuing permits to take
> water and to me issuing permits to take water is a little bit like me
> writing cheques on my bank account when I don't know how much
> money is coming in every month and how much is going out to pay
> ... the other bills ... [T]here's a big difference between issuing per-
> mits to take water and managing a resource and to manage a resource
> you really need to know how the system is working. There's abso-
> lutely no reason at all why we can't get to that stage, but I think we
> are a little bit behind the game certainly in Ontario.

Dr. Howard explained that Permits to Take Water are issued without any prior
adequate measurement of either the depletion of the resource that would result from permit use or the amount of water in the aquifer.

Other evidence established that Ontario does not have a province-wide groundwater management strategy as described by Dr. Howard. It was suggested by
another witness that budget cutbacks prevented the development of a groundwater strategy.

The Environmental Commissioner of Ontario has brought this and other
groundwater protection concerns to the attention of the Ontario government
in five consecutive annual reports released since 1996. The commissioner was
prompted to investigate provincial management of groundwater after it received
13 applications requesting a more comprehensive, preventive approach to
groundwater protection. The commissioner's first annual report, dated
1994–95 and released in June 1996, criticized the Ontario government for
reducing the budgets of the Ministry of Environment and the Ministry of
Natural Resources – the two ministries likely to take on primary responsibility
for groundwater management. The government was also criticized for reducing provincial funding to conservation authorities across Ontario by 70% and
restricting their mandate to flood control. The commissioner recommended
that Ontario's groundwater management framework be upgraded through the
participation and cooperation of the MOE, Ministry of Natural Resources,

Ministry of Consumer and Commercial Relations,[4] OMAFRA, and the Ministry of Transportation.

The MOE committed itself to develop a plan to protect Ontario's groundwater as part of its 1996 business plan. Later that year it announced that it would lead a review of groundwater management.

In the Environmental Commissioner's 1996 annual report, the commissioner again urged the government to prioritize the development of a sustainable strategy for restoring, protecting, and conserving Ontario's groundwater. The report recommended 11 elements for a comprehensive groundwater strategy.

In the 1997 annual report, the Environmental Commissioner recommended that the government make public its progress on developing a groundwater strategy and specify a completion date. The commissioner criticized the MOE for its incomplete understanding of hydrogeology as well as for its incomplete understanding of potential impacts, including the cumulative impacts, of water-taking. This criticism was echoed in the concerns raised by Dr. Ken Howard at the Inquiry.

In the 1998 annual report, the Environmental Commissioner observed that the MOE had failed to make public its progress toward a groundwater management strategy. The MOE response was to enumerate a list of water-related initiatives. The commissioner observed that the initiatives did not constitute a comprehensive groundwater management strategy.

In the 1999–2000 annual report, the Environmental Commissioner concluded that the current legal and policy framework for groundwater management was fragmented and uncoordinated. The commissioner predicted growing risks if the ministries failed to develop a groundwater management strategy. These risks included conflicts over groundwater in rural Ontario and in urban areas that rely on groundwater for municipal and industrial purposes. The commissioner again recommended that ministries develop and implement a groundwater management strategy in a timely manner in consultation with key stakeholders and the public.

---

[4] The Ministry of Consumer and Commercial Relations is now known as the Ministry of Consumer and Business Services.

The Provincial Auditor also urged the MOE to develop a groundwater strategy. The Provincial Auditor's 1996 annual report recommended the systematic monitoring of groundwater quality to safeguard the environment and human health.

In response to the findings outlined in the 1996 report, the MOE stated that such efforts were underway. In the 1998 follow-up report, the Provincial Auditor repeated both his recommendation of 1996 and the MOE response to that recommendation. He concluded: "As of June 1998, a groundwater strategy had yet to be finalized."

I will be making extensive recommendations about the protection of drinking water sources in the Part 2 report of this Inquiry.

12.10 Employee Morale in the Ministry of the Environment

Many witnesses testified that MOE employees are dedicated, conscientious, and loyal. Their concern for the environment and public health was unquestioned. Compared to other members of the Ontario Public Service, they tend to be less likely to move to another ministry. However, the significant reductions in resources and staff had an inevitable impact upon the remaining staff in the MOE. James Merritt and Robert Shaw testified that in 1997, the morale in the MOE was low because of the cutbacks.

Before the 1996–97 budget cuts, a number of cost-cutting measures were implemented by the provincial government. One such measure was the Factor 80 program, under which staff were eligible to take early retirement. Programs like this one were designed to encourage employees to leave the MOE. Andre Castel and Robert Shaw testified that such programs resulted in removing a number of individuals with significant experience at an earlier time than was normal. A significant loss of experience and "collective memory" resulted. Philip Bye testified that the MOE's Owen Sound office suffered from this loss of experience.

The layoffs in 1996 and 1997 caused employees to be concerned for their colleagues and for their own job security because there were no guarantees against further layoffs. The remaining staff were preoccupied with reacting to daily crises and complaints rather than with taking a preventive approach to environmental protection. Work planning tools, such as the Delivery Strategies, were developed to assist employees in prioritizing their work in times of reduced resources. However, as occurs in any workplace experiencing significant change and cutbacks, morale was low. Low morale emerged as an issue in the 1997 province-wide Operations Division exercise called "Planning Our Future Together." Local workshops were conducted across the province to obtain feedback in order to assist the MOE in planning for the future in a period of significant change.

The workshops indicated that the cutbacks had, predictably, led to feelings of frustration and anxiety. Employees were given the opportunity to suggest directions in which the MOE should go in this period of restraint. One concern expressed was the loss of technical expertise and assistance for the field staff, which led to a breakdown in the networks that employees had relied on in the past. The result was that employees found it difficult to access information. Another opinion expressed was that environmental officers should not be involved in the inspections of municipal operations because of the MOE's limited resources. In the MOE employees' view, the onus should be on the municipalities. In general, the workshops demonstrated a concern with heavy workloads, tight deadlines, reduced staff, and feelings of uncertainty.

I accept that morale was lowered as a result of budget and staff reductions, but I am not satisfied that low morale of MOE staff played a part in any of the MOE failures I have identified above. There was no evidence indicating that any of the MOE staff involved with Walkerton did or did not do anything because of low morale.

12.11 Land Use Planning

12.11.1 General

The Inquiry heard evidence about provincial land use policies and their relationship to municipal bylaws. The evidence raised concerns about a lack of connection between the planning process and issues relating to water-taking and the protection of drinking water. However, I do not think that the policies can reasonably be said to have had an impact on the events in Walkerton.

The primary source of the contamination was the Biesenthal farm which, prior to the amalgamation of Brockton in 1999, was outside the municipal boundary of Walkerton. Moreover, the Biesenthal farm had been in operation for years. There was no suggestion that either Walkerton or Brockton considered land use measures for any of the farms in the area of Well 5. I do not see a connection between provincial land use policies and the events in May 2000.

I heard considerable evidence about the land use planning process, and I will be making extensive recommendations in the Part 2 report of this Inquiry about land use and the protection of water sources. I will briefly summarize the evidence I heard here but will leave all of my recommendations to the Part 2 report.

12.11.2 The Provincial Role

The provincial government's role in land use planning is to develop and maintain a legislative framework through, for example, the *Planning Act* and the *Municipal Act*. The Ministry of Municipal Affairs and Housing, the lead ministry administering this legislation, issues provincial policy statements, promotes provincial interests, and advises municipalities. The Province administers and approves local planning controls. The Ministry of Municipal Affairs and Housing does receive input from six partner ministries, including OMAFRA, the MOE, and the Ministry of Natural Resources.

12.11.3 The *Planning Act*

The *Planning Act* generally requires municipalities to have official plans, which "shall have regard to" the 1996 Provincial Policy Statements. It requires Bruce County to have a plan. Municipalities not designated by the *Planning Act* have the discretion to decide whether or not to make a plan. The approval authority oversees the official plans' degree of regard to the Provincial Policy Statements. Once an official plan is in effect, all public works and bylaws must conform to it.

Recent amendments to the *Planning Act* limit the MOE's role in planning policy issues such as groundwater and surface water protection. Since provincial approval is no longer required for certain types of planning decisions, MOE expertise is not often called upon during the planning process.

12.11.4 Relevant Provincial Policy Statements

The Provincial Policy Statements make no reference to drinking water, and they protect normal farm practices in prime agricultural areas (of which Walkerton is not one). I reproduce here the Provincial Policy Statements related to land use and groundwater protection:

> PPS 1.1.1(e): A coordinated approach should be achieved when dealing with issues which cross municipal boundaries, including: 1. infrastructure and … 2. ecosystem and watershed related issues; …

> PPS 1.1.1(f): Development and land use patterns which may cause environmental or public health and safety concerns will be avoided …

> PPS 2.4.1: The *quality and quantity* of groundwater and surface water and the function of sensitive groundwater recharge/discharge areas, aquifers and headwaters will be protected or enhanced.

12.11.5 The Approval of Official Plans

The approval authority works with municipalities while they are developing their official plans and considers whether the plans "have regard to" the above Provincial Policy Statements. The Ministry of Municipal Affairs and Housing is the approval authority for official plans, unless the municipality is exempted under the *Planning Act*. Since 1996, many of the approval functions of the minister under the *Planning Act* have devolved to the municipalities by delegation or exemption. The approval authority for a local municipality may now be an upper-tier municipality such as a regional municipality council, a county council, or the Ministry of Municipal Affairs and Housing.

Once a municipality has adopted its official plan, the plan comes before the approval authority for review and approval. The approval authority can raise an issue, issue a notice of decision to modify and approve a plan, or issue a notice of its decision to refuse the plan. A plan can be refused on the basis that it does not have sufficient regard to the Provincial Policy Statements. If the plan is refused, the municipality can appeal to the Ontario Municipal Board. The Ministry of Municipal Affairs and Housing is the only provincial ministry that can initiate an appeal of a municipal planning decision to the Ontario

Municipal Board. The focus of an appeal is usually on official plans and amendments, rather than on site-specific matters.

If the MOE is concerned that a particular official plan or bylaw may have an impact on surface water or groundwater, it cannot act on its own; it must persuade the Ministry of Municipal Affairs and Housing to bring the matter before the Ontario Municipal Board. At the time of the Inquiry, the Ministry of Municipal Affairs and Housing had received only one authorized request from the MOE to launch an appeal – and that request was granted.

12.11.6 The Role of Municipalities

Municipalities can take some action if they wish to restrict activities near wells or to protect groundwater from contamination. They can purchase land in the area, expropriate the land, or pass zoning bylaws within municipal boundaries. They can also arrange a land swap, a conservation easement, or a land trust. The Ministry of Municipal Affairs and Housing does not provide municipalities with any information explaining these options.

12.11.7 Bruce County's Official Plan

The Bruce County official plan is the plan applicable to the Municipality of Brockton. The former Town of Walkerton has its own official plan for the local municipality, but it must comply with the county's plan for the upper-tier municipality. The Ministry of Municipal Affairs and Housing is the approval authority for the county's plan and any amendments to it.

Several sections in the Bruce County official plan were identified by the Ministry of Municipal Affairs and Housing as "having regard to" the Provincial Policy Statements protecting water quality and quantity. I will summarize them here.

The county's plan states that it has a general environmental policy goal to protect and enhance air, land, and water quality. Further environmental objectives include promoting environmentally sound watercourse management, encouraging the preparation of watershed plans, protecting groundwater and surface water quality, protecting headwater areas of rivers and streams, and discouraging land uses and activities that are noxious and that may contribute to air, water, or land pollution. The plan specifically states Bruce County's intention to protect headwater areas, groundwater recharge areas, and aquifers as a means of protecting groundwater and surface water from degradation.

The Bruce County plan notes, however, that the Province of Ontario did not provide for the mapping of these important geographical features. The plan encourages the preparation of watershed studies when a major development is proposed and encourages the incorporation of the results into county and/or municipal official plans. It also states Bruce County's intention to protect water quality and natural habitats that depend on water bodies for their existence. It goes as far as saying that not only should local plans implement surface water management policies, but surface water management plans "shall be required" for some forms of new development.

12.11.8 Conclusion

The Provincial Policy Statements regarding water quality are not binding, and the MOE has little input into municipal land use planning. A provincial groundwater strategy, including information such as mapped aquifers, mapped water tables, and a well water database, would significantly enhance municipalities' ability to develop official plans that reflect provincial interests in water quality and quantity. The Ministry of Municipal Affairs and Housing does not have any policies or guidelines specifically relating to the siting of wells, aquifer protection, or the protection of recharge areas, and the MOE's role in this area has been greatly reduced. I will address all of these issues in depth in the Part 2 report of this Inquiry.

Chapter 13   The Legislative, Regulatory, and Policy Framework

Contents

Chapter 13   The Legislative, Regulatory, and Policy Framework

13.1 Introduction

This chapter outlines the main legislative, regulatory, and policy framework applicable to drinking water systems in Ontario. It also includes a summary of the regulatory review process that was instituted in Ontario in 1995.

13.2 Constitutional Jurisdiction

Although constitutional jurisdiction over the environment is shared between the federal government and the provinces, water has become primarily an area of provincial jurisdiction. The *Constitution Act, 1867* grants the provinces a number of sources of regulatory authority over water. Section 109 gives them jurisdiction over natural resources. This section is reinforced by section 92A, which provides the provinces with exclusive jurisdiction over the development, conservation, and management of non-renewable resources. Additionally, section 92 provides provinces with jurisdiction over local works and under-takings, property and civil rights, all matters of a local and private nature, and municipal institutions. These powers give the provinces ample authority to regulate the management of water resources and to protect these resources from pollution.

The provincial jurisdiction over water is not, however, exclusive. The *Constitution Act, 1867* grants the federal government powers to regulate various aspects of water resource management. Section 91 provides for federal jurisdiction over seacoasts and inland fisheries – the most important source of federal authority over matters related to water. This section is the basis of the federal *Fisheries Act*, R.S.C. 1985, c. F-14, section 35(1) which prohibits the carrying on of works or undertakings that result in the harmful alteration, disruption, or destruction of fish habitat. Section 36(3) of the *Fisheries Act* prohibits persons from depositing or permitting the deposit of a deleterious substance into water frequented by fish. Regulations under the *Fisheries Act* limit effluent discharges into the aquatic environment from pulp and paper mills, petroleum refineries, chlor-alkalai plants, meat and poultry plants, metal mining operations, and potato processing plants.

The federal government has also regulated water pollution for the "peace, order and good government" of Canada, and to protect the health and safety of Canadians. It has used its criminal law power to support regulations concerning the release of toxic substances into the water. In addition, section 36 of the *Constitution Act, 1982* specifically provides that both the federal and provincial governments are committed to "providing essential public services of reasonable quality to all Canadians."

13.3 The Ontario Legislative and Policy Framework in May 2000

Although the jurisdiction over water is shared among the levels of government, the legal framework for the protection and management of water supplies that is applicable to the events of Walkerton in May 2000 consists primarily of the following provincial statutes: the *Ministry of the Environment Act,* the *Ontario Water Resources Act* and the Water and Sewage Works Regulation, the *Environmental Protection Act,* the *Environmental Bill of Rights,* the *Health Promotion and Protection Act,* and the *Public Utilities Act.*

13.3.1 The Ministry of the Environment Act

The *Ministry of the Environment Act,* R.S.O. 1990, c. M-24, as amended, gives the Minister of the Environment charge over the ministry and empowers the minister to appoint the employees considered necessary for the proper conduct of the ministry's business. The minister is responsible for administering the legislation assigned to him or her by statute, regulation, or Order-in-Council (s. 4).

13.3.2 The *Ontario Water Resources Act* and Regulation 435/93

The *Ontario Water Resources Act,* R.S.O. 1990, c. O-40, as amended (OWRA), is a primary statute for the management and protection of surface and groundwater in the province. The OWRA and its regulations

- prohibit the discharge into water of polluting materials that "may impair the quality of water";

- enable the MOE to take remedial and enforcement action to protect water quality;

- provide a regime for approvals of water taking, water wells, water supply and treatment facilities and sewage works; and

- enable the Ontario Clean Water Agency to operate municipal water and sewage works.

13.3.2.1 *The Management of Ontario's Water Supply*

The OWRA sets out a process by which Permits to Take Water are granted to large-scale water users (s. 34). Permits to Take Water were introduced under the OWRA in 1961 in response to a growing number of disputes between parties taking water from creeks or streams to irrigate tobacco crops. Under the OWRA, a person must have a permit issued by a director in order to take 50,000 L of water per day from a well or wells constructed or deepened after March 29, 1961. During fiscal year 2000–01, a total of 1,540 new and renewal Permits to Take Water were issued. There are now about 5,400 valid Permits to Take Water in the province.

Issues related to the quality of the water sought to be withdrawn are dealt with in the OWRA Certificate of Approval. The establishment, alteration, extension, or replacement of waterworks is prohibited, except in accordance with an approval issued by a director. A director may require an applicant to submit plans, specifications, and an engineer's report or to carry out tests or experiments relating to the water supply before issuing an approval (s. 52). People who establish a waterworks without first obtaining approval may be ordered by a director to provide, at their own expense, the facilities that the director considers necessary (s. 52(3)). The approval is either refused or granted under the terms and conditions that a director deems to be in the public interest (s. 52(4)). The director is also empowered to alter the terms and conditions of approval or to revoke or suspend the approval. A person is prohibited from operating waterworks unless the required approval has been granted and complied with (s. 52(7)). A similar framework is in place for approving sewage works (s. 53).

Provincial officers may inspect a waterworks to determine the causes of any impairment or to ascertain the quality of water, take samples, run tests, require equipment to be operated, and examine and remove documents (s. 15). They may also use "provincial officer's orders" or "field orders" to require a person who has contravened the OWRA, a regulation, or a term of a licence to take steps to achieve compliance and to provide an alternative water supply (s. 16).

A municipality may apply to have the Ontario Clean Water Agency (OCWA) operate waterworks or sewage works for the municipality (s. 63(1)). The municipality and OCWA then enter into an agreement by which the municipality pays OCWA to operate the facility. Before May 2000, OCWA had never operated the Walkerton Public Utilities Commission.

13.3.2.2 *The Protection of Ontario's Water Supply*

The Minister of the Environment has supervisory authority over all surface and ground water in Ontario (s. 29). The OWRA prohibits the discharge of any material into water that causes or may cause injury to any person, and requires any person who discharges polluting material into water to notify the minister (ss. 28, 30). It empowers the minister to designate its employees as provincial officers and to appoint Directors (s. 5(1)–(3)). Both provincial officers and directors may require certain actions to protect the public water supply, though directors may require more onerous actions.

A director may prohibit or regulate the discharge of sewage into any waters by any person (s. 31). He or she may also order measures to prevent the impairment of water quality, make equipment changes, or study and report on measures to control the discharge (s. 32). A director may, for the purposes of protection, define an area that includes a source of public water supply and prohibit the discharging of material that may impair water quality or the taking of water if it may diminish the amount of water available as a public water supply (s. 33).

The minister may apply to the Superior Court of Justice for an injunction prohibiting the discharge of any material that may impair water quality (s. 29(3)). If the recipient of a Director's Order or Minister's Order does not comply, the director can cause the work to be done and recover the costs from the recipient (ss. 80–84).

13.3.2.3 *The Waterworks and Sewage Works Regulation*

Ontario Regulation 435/93 (the Waterworks and Sewage Works Regulation) provides for the classification and licensing of waterworks, sewage works, and facility operators. The regulation divides facilities into four categories: wastewater collection facilities, wastewater treatment facilities, water distribution facilities, and water treatment facilities (s. 3(1)). Each type of water treatment facility is classified as a class I, class II, class III, or class IV facility, according to the facility's characteristics. These characteristics include the number of people served, flow, water supply source, raw water quality, processes, sludge/backwash water disposal, and laboratory control.

The effect of the regulation was to reclassify these facilities in 1993. In cases in which the reclassification upgraded the facility, the regulation gave operators until February 1, 1994, to apply to the director for the issuance of an operator's licence for that type of facility (s. 8). The director issued the licence if the operator met the experience qualifications set out for that class of operator, and the operator paid a fee. Under this procedure, known as "grandparenting," an operator must write and pass an examination before the licence can be renewed. If an operator fails an examination to obtain a licence, the director issues a licence one class lower than the interim licence. All licences are for three-year terms and can be renewed only after the operator passes the examination and pays the required fee.

The regulation sets out operating standards for both the owner of the facility and the operator-in-charge. The owner of the facility, or the public utilities commission, where one has been established, must ensure that

- the operator-in-charge holds a licence applicable to that facility (s. 13);

- every operator employed in the facility holds a licence applicable to that type of facility or a licence as an operator-in-training, or is a professional engineer who has been employed in the facility for less than 6 months (s. 14);

- operators and maintenance personnel in the facility have ready access to operations and maintenance manuals sufficient for the safe and efficient operation of the facility (s. 16);

- every operator has at least 40 hours of training per year (s. 17);

- records are kept regarding information about the facility, training, and the length of time each operator works as an operator-in-charge (ss. 17(3), 18, 20); and

- ensure that records and logs are accessible in the facility for at least 2 years (s. 20(6)).

The operator-in-charge, who is responsible for the overall operation of the facility, must ensure that

- all steps reasonably necessary to operate the processes within his or her responsibility are taken in a safe and efficient manner in accordance with the relevant operations manuals;

- the processes within his or her responsibility are measured, monitored, sampled, and tested in a manner that permits them to be adjusted when necessary;

- records are maintained of all adjustments made to the processes within his or her responsibility; and

- all equipment used in the processes within his or her responsibility is properly maintained, inspected, and evaluated, and that records of equipment operating status are prepared and available at the end of every operating shift (s. 19).

13.3.3   The *Environmental Protection Act*

The *Environmental Protection Act*, R.S.O. 1990, c. E-19, as amended (EPA), is Ontario's principal environmental statute. The EPA prohibits the discharge of contaminants into the natural environment (s. 14), the definition of which includes water. It sets out remedial actions that provide the proper legal basis, in combination with the OWRA provisions, for actions to protect sources of water from pollution. EPA control orders (s. 7), stop orders (s. 8), and preventive orders (s.18) are similar to the OWRA orders discussed above. Remedial orders under the EPA (s. 17), which do not have a counterpart in the OWRA, can require damage to be cleaned up.

In certain circumstances, animal wastes disposed of in accordance with normal farm practices are exempt from section 14 of the EPA, which makes it illegal to discharge contaminants into the natural environment. If the only adverse effect is "impairment of the quality of the natural environment for any use that can be made of it" (s. 1(1)(a)) then the exemption applies (s. 14(2)). If there is some other effect, such as damage to health or property, then there is no exemption (ss. 1(b)–(h), 14(2)). "Normal farm practices" are not, however, defined in the EPA. What constitutes a normal farm practice is determined by the Normal Farm Practices and Procedures Board under the *Farming and Food Production and Protection Act*, S.O. 1998, c. 1.

By extension, control orders directed at farm operations are limited to cases in which there is some adverse effect beyond impairment of the quality of the natural environment. Further, farm operations are exempt from requirements relating to Certificates of Approval (s. 9(3)). Farmers are also exempt from notifying the Ministry of the Environment of contaminant discharges resulting from the disposal of animal wastes in accordance with normal farm practices where such discharges may have adverse effects (s.15(2)).

13.3.4   The *Environmental Bill of Rights*

The *Environmental Bill of Rights*, S.O. 1993, c. 28, as amended (EBR), sets out the ways in which citizens are to be consulted before the government makes environmental decisions and provides the means for the public to scrutinize environmental compliance. The EBR defines the environment to include water. Its purposes are:

- to protect, conserve, and, where reasonable, restore the integrity of the environment;

- to provide for the sustainability of the environment; and

- to protect the right to a healthful environment.

The EBR requires certain ministries to develop, with public participation, statements of environmental values that set out how each ministry intends to be accountable for ensuring a consideration of the environment in their decisions. It requires ministries to take reasonable steps to ensure that their statements of environmental values are considered when they make decisions that might significantly affect the environment (s. 11).

The Ministry of the Environment statement of environmental values commits the ministry to place priority on preventing and then minimizing the creation and release of pollutants. It commits the ministry to exercise a precautionary approach: where uncertainty exists about the risk presented by particular pollutants or classes of pollutants, the ministry will exercise caution in favour of the environment. These guiding principles are to be incorporated in the ministry's internal management practices, Certificates of Approval, permits, licences, orders, Acts, regulations, and policies.

Additionally, before an action in respect of actual or imminent harm to a public resource resulting from noise, odour or dust from an agricultural operation can be taken, the plaintiff must have applied to, and had their application disposed of, by the Normal Farm Practices and Procedures Board (s. 84(4)).

13.3.5 The *Health Protection and Promotion Act*

The *Health Protection and Promotion Act*, R.S.O. 1990, c. H-7, as amended (HPPA), is the statutory foundation of the public health system in Ontario. The HPPA provides for the creation of public boards of health and establishes the offices of the Chief Medical Officer of Health and local Medical Officers of Health. It delineates the powers, responsibilities, and duties of each these offices and of the Ministry of Health in relation to them.

The HPPA requires that for each health unit there must be a board of health comprised of members appointed by the province and by the area municipalities (ss. 48, 49). The board of health is required to superintend, provide, or ensure the provision of mandatory public health programs and services (s. 5). This is a statutory minimum guideline for program and services, and the board normally delivers additional programs and services in response to local needs.

The HPPA empowers the Minister of Health to oversee the administration of public health in Ontario and to publish guidelines for the provision of mandatory programs and services that every board of health is required to provide (s. 7). The minister is also empowered to oversee the operation of health units and boards of health and can appoint an inspector to inspect a health unit to ascertain the extent of compliance with the Act and regulations (s. 80). He or she may appoint an assessor to ascertain whether a board of health is providing the mandatory program and services (s. 82) and is authorized to direct a board of health to do anything if it is not complying with the legislative scheme.

Every board of health must appoint a full-time local Medical Officer of Health and may appoint one or more associate medical officers of health (s. 62). The appointment of the Medical Officer of Health or the associate medical officer of health must be approved by the Minister of Health (s. 64). The dismissal of these officers must also be approved by the Minister of Health and two thirds of the members of the board (s. 66). Finally, the Medical Officer of Health is responsible to the board for the management of public health programs and services, and the employees of the board of health are subject to the direction of and are responsible to the Medical Officer of Health in respect of their duties relating to public health (s. 67).

The HPPA contains provisions concerning the contamination of drinking water that poses a health threat. It provides that every Medical Officer of Health is required to "inspect or cause the inspection of the health unit served by him or her for the purposes of preventing, eliminating and decreasing the effects of health hazards in the health unit" (s. 10). When a complaint is made to a Medical Officer of Health that a health hazard related to occupational or environmental health exists, the officer must notify the provincial ministry with primary responsibility for the matter (s.11). The officer, in consultation with the relevant ministry, is obliged to investigate the complaint to determine whether or not the health hazard exists.

When a Medical Officer of Health or a public health inspector has reasonable or probable grounds to believe that a health hazard exists and that certain actions are needed to decrease the effect of or eliminate the health hazard, he or she may issue a written order to require any person to take or refrain from taking any action specified in the order with respect to the health hazard (s. 13). The Medical Officer of Health is required to set out the reasons for the order in that order. Where the time required to put the order in writing will or is likely to substantially increase the hazard, the officer may make the order orally and without reasons.

13.3.6 The *Public Utilities Act*

The *Public Utilities Act*, R.S.O. 1990, c. P-52, as amended (PUA), provides for the powers of municipalities in respect of waterworks and other utilities and their governance. A municipality may establish, maintain, and operate waterworks and may acquire, purchase, and/or expropriate land, waters and water privileges for waterworks purposes (s. 2(1)). The PUA regulates the operation of the waterworks in respect of the power to enter on lands, to expropriate, and to lay pipe (ss. 4–5). The municipality is empowered to regulate the distribution and use of the water and to fix the prices for the use of this water (s. 8). It may supply water to land outside its borders (s. 11) and pass bylaws regulating the supply of water, the price to be paid for it, and any other matter necessary to secure for the inhabitants "a continued and abundant supply of pure and wholesome water" (s. 12).

The PUA empowers the council of a municipality, with the assent of the municipal electors, to pass a bylaw establishing a public utilities commission that is entrusted to control and manage its waterworks (s. 38(1)). In January 1996, the PUA was amended so that a public utilities commission could be dissolved by repealing the bylaw without the necessity of holding a plebiscite. Upon this repeal, the control and management of the waterworks are vested in the council and the commission ceases to exist (s. 38(6)). Such a bylaw must be passed with the assent of the municipal electors (s. 45(1)). Although the PUA permits the establishment of one commission for several public utilities (s. 40(1)), separate books and accounts must be kept of the revenues for each public utility (s. 46(1)). Any excess of revenue arising from the supply of a public utility over expenditures and authorized reserves must be paid to the municipal treasurer to pay down any debt. Upon the retirement of any debt, these moneys form part of the municipality's general revenues (s. 35).

A public utilities commission is authorized to exercise all of the powers, rights, authorities, and privileges conferred upon a municipality by the PUA while the bylaw entrusting it with control remains in force. During the life of the bylaw, the municipality may not exercise those powers, rights, authorities, and privileges. This power is, however, limited when the cost of any alterations to the works or utility services is intended to be paid out of those moneys that are required to go to the municipal treasurer (s. 41(5)). The council or the municipality must agree to these alterations.

13.4 The Ontario Policy Framework in May 2000

Ontario applied two main policy guidelines to decisions about drinking water protection and management: the Ontario Drinking Water Objectives (revised 1994), and the Chlorination Bulletin (Bulletin 65-W-4, "Chlorination of Potable Water Supplies," updated March 1987).

13.4.1   The *Ontario Drinking Water Objectives*, 1994

The *Ontario Drinking Water Objectives* (ODWO), a publication of the Ministry of the Environment's Water Policy Branch, were first introduced in 1964. Before May 2000, the ODWO was revised several times. The 1994 revision of the ODWO was the applicable version at the time of the Walkerton tragedy. The ODWO was superseded by Ontario Regulation 459/00, the Drinking Water Protection Regulation, which came into effect in August 2000.

The ODWO sets out the maximum acceptable concentrations in drinking water of substances that can cause harm to human health or that may interfere with the taste, odour, or appearance of drinking water. It also sets out how and how often samples should be tested and specifies the steps to be taken when samples are above certain limits.

The ODWO contains minimum sampling requirements. In groundwater systems, weekly samples are required of raw water and of treated water at the point at which the water entered the distribution system (s. 4.1.1). For a town the size of Walkerton, 13 samples per month would be required from the distribution system for microbiological testing, including at least one sample weekly.

The ODWO sets out three circumstances that require notification of the MOE district office:

- when drinking water is judged unsafe;

- when drinking water quality is deteriorating; and

- when the microbiological maximum allowable concentrations are exceeded.

13.4.1.1 *Unsafe Drinking Water*

The ODWO provides that drinking water is considered to be unsafe if any of the following conditions exist:

- *Escherichia coli* (*E. coli*) and/or fecal coliforms are detected in any distribution sample by any analytical method;

- total coliforms are detected in consecutive samples from the same site or in multiple samples taken from a single submission from a distribution system; or

- in communal drinking water supplies, more than 10% of the samples (based on a minimum of ten samples per month) show the presence of coliform organisms (s. 4.1.2).

If the water contains any indicators of unsafe drinking water quality, the laboratory is required to immediately notify the Ministry of the Environment's district officer, who then immediately notifies the Medical Officer of Health and the operating authority[1] to initiate the collection of special samples and/or take corrective action, including disinfection and flushing (s. 4.1.3). These measures are to be taken until the objectives are no longer exceeded in consecutive samples. The ODWO provides that if satisfactory chlorine or disinfectant residuals are not detected in the affected parts of the distribution system (or if circumstances warranted it), a boil water advisory can be issued by the local Medical Officer of Health.

13.4.1.2 *Deteriorating Drinking Water Quality*

The ODWO provides that the following conditions are indications of deteriorating water quality:

- total coliforms detected as a single occurrence (but not *E. coli* or other fecal coliforms);

---

[1] The Drinking Water Protection Regulation (Ontario Regulation 459/00) contains a new notification procedure.

- samples containing more than 500 colonies per milllilitre on a heterotrophic plate count (HPC) analysis;

- samples containing more than 200 background colonies on a total coliform membrane filter analysis;

- *Aeromonas spp.*, *Pseudomonas aeruginosa*, *Staphylococcus aureus*, *Clostridium spp.* or members of the Fecal Streptococcus (*Enterococcus*) group detected (s. 4.1.4).

When indicators of deteriorating water quality occur, the ODWO provides that the MOE district officer should be notified so that an inspection can be carried out and special samples taken. The ODWO does not indicate who is responsible for the notification or for conducting the inspection.

13.4.1.3 *Exceedance of Maximum Allowable Concentrations*

The ODWO requires that all public water supply systems using groundwater be sampled as set out in the Certificate of Approval (or according to a suggested minimum sampling program) for the following chemical and physical parameters:

- turbidity

- disinfectant residuals

- volatile organics

- inorganics

- nitrates/nitrites

- pesticides and PCBs

If the results show that the level for any of the above parameters exceeded its maximum acceptable concentration, immediate resampling is required. If the results from the resampling also indicate an exceedance, the Ministry of the Environment and the Ministry of Health should be notified. The ODWO does not state who is responsible for this notification.

13.4.1.4 *Monitoring*

The ODWO requires continuous disinfectant residual monitoring for systems serving more than 3,300 people from surface water, or groundwater under the direct influence of surface water, and where no filtration is present (s. 4.2.1.1). As well, systems using surface water, or groundwater under the direct influence of surface water, and not performing filtration, should monitor turbidity levels, using a grab sample, every four hours by continuous monitoring.

13.4.1.5 *Legal Status*

Although the ODWO were guidelines and were not legally binding in May 2000, they provided guidance to ensure that water was safe to drink. There were, however, two ways to make them legally enforceable in May 2000. First, the MOE could have made compliance with the ODWO a condition of the Certificate of Approval. Second, the ODWO or portions of them could have been made the subject of a Field Order (provincial officer's order) or a Director's Order under the OWRA and the EPA.

13.4.2   The Chlorination Bulletin

Bulletin 65-W-4, updated in March, 1987 and entitled "Chlorination of Potable Water Supplies," was first introduced in the 1970s. Known as the Chlorination Bulletin, this document is a guideline for the disinfection of potable water and distribution systems. It provides detailed information about various issues, including when disinfection is required, minimum chlorine residuals, chlorination equipment, and monitoring. The Ministry of the Environment's Standards Development Branch was responsible for developing and revising the Chlorination Bulletin, which was primarily used by the ministry's Approvals Branch to determine the minimum level of treatment of a waterworks for which a Certificate of Approval was being sought. It was also used in inspections conducted by the Operations Division to assess whether the treatment process of a particular water facility was appropriate and to make recommendations if it was not.

Continuous and adequate disinfection is required in various circumstances: when the water supply is obtained from a surface source; when groundwater sources were or might become contaminated, as in fractured limestone areas;

when the supply is exposed to contamination during treatment; or when emergency conditions, such as flooding or epidemic, indicate the need (s. 1.2).

The Chlorination Bulletin sets out that at waterworks where disinfection is required, chlorine feed equipment (both gas and hypochlorite chlorinators), should be installed in duplicate to provide uninterrupted chlorination if a breakdown occurs.

Chlorine can be present in water as either a free or a combined residual. The bactericidal effectiveness of both residual forms is markedly reduced by high pH or turbidity, but it is enhanced by a higher temperature or a longer contact time. A free chlorine residual, although it is a much more effective disinfectant, readily reacts with ferrous iron, manganese, sulphides and organic material to produce compounds of no value for disinfection (s. 3.1.1).

Chlorination is required for all surface waters and many groundwaters. A total chlorine residual of at least 0.5 mg/L after 15 minutes (preferably 30 minutes) of contact time after the filter and before the first consumer is to be provided at all times. These are minimum acceptable residuals, not targets or objective residuals. The chlorine residual is to be differentiated into its free and combined portions for recording purposes, at least to get historical information and for the purposes of problem solving (s. 3.1.2). Most of the residual is to be a free residual.

The chlorine residual test must be performed as frequently as needed to ensure that an adequate chlorine residual is maintained at all times (s. 3.1.2). In groundwater sources where poor water quality and/or minimum supervision indicated a possible health hazard, there is to be an automatic chlorine residual monitor (i.e., continuous monitoring) with an alarm system (s. 2.6). As stated above, in groundwater systems under the direct influence of surface water, a town the size of Walkerton is required by the ODWO to perform continuous chlorine residual monitoring (s. 4.2.1.1). The frequency and location of chlorine residual testing is determined by the ODWO and the Chlorination Bulletin. In groundwater systems, the ODWO requires chlorine residual testing in the distribution system to be done with the same frequency as the one required for microbiological sampling (s. 4.2.1.3). (For Walkerton, the required frequency is 13 times per month, including at least one test per week). The Chlorination Bulletin requires that a chlorine residual be maintained in all parts of the distribution system (s. 3.1.2).

The Chlorination Bulletin sets out that the amount and type of chlorine residual present when routine bacteriological samples are taken should be recorded, because this allows a more complete evaluation of the condition of the distribution system. Recording this information on the laboratory submission form might facilitate the comparison (s. 3.1.2).

As was the case with the ODWO, the Chlorination Bulletin was not legally binding in May 2000 but could have been made legally enforceable through a Certificate of Approval, a Director's Order, or a Field Order.

13.4.3   The Drinking Water Protection Regulation

In August 2000, following the Walkerton outbreak, the legal approach described above was altered with the passage of the Ontario Regulation 459/00, the Drinking Water Protection Regulation. As a result, the revised ODWO and Chlorination Bulletin are now contained in a document entitled "Ontario Drinking Water Standards" (ODWS) and referenced in the regulation. In considering an application for an approval, the director must now have regard to the ODWS (s. 4(2)). Although segments of the ODWS relating to sampling and analysis, standards, and indicators of adverse water quality are schedules to the new regulation, the ODWS as a whole is not part of the regulation. However, the regulation requires owners of water treatment systems to report quarterly on measures taken to comply with the regulation and the ODWS.

Sampling and analysis requirements, chemical and physical standards, indicators of adverse water quality, and corrective actions are now legally binding. The indicators of adverse water quality under the ODWS include the ODWO indicators of unsafe and deteriorating water quality. Chlorination is now mandatory for all waterworks, unless a variance is granted (ss. 5(3), 6). Waterworks must now use a laboratory that is accredited for the required analysis (s. 7). Rather than relying on a recommended minimum sampling program, the new regulation makes sampling mandatory (s. 7).

The new regulation clarifies some of the confusion regarding the notification of adverse results. It is now mandatory for a waterworks owner to ensure that notice is given both to the local Medical Officer of Health and the Ministry of the Environment's Spills Action Centre when analysis shows that a parameter has been exceeded or indicates adverse water quality (s. 8). It is also mandatory for private laboratories to give notice to the local Medical Officer of Health and the ministry and advise the owner of adverse water quality (s. 8). Instead of simply recommending corrective action, the new regulation makes corrective action (including resampling) mandatory and outlines the appropriate corrective action to take when an indicator of adverse quality is identified (s. 9).

The regulation also introduces four new requirements. The owner of a waterworks is now required to:

• post a warning when it does not comply with the sampling and analysis requirements for microbiological parameters or when corrective actions as outlined in the regulations have not been taken (s. 10);

• make all information regarding the waterworks and the analytical results of all required samples available for the public to inspect (s. 11);

• prepare a quarterly written report to the Ministry of the Environment and to consumers of drinking water summarizing analytical results and describing the measures taken to comply with the regulation and the ODWS (s. 12); and

• submit an independent engineer's report according to the schedule contained in the regulation and to submit triennial reports thereafter (s. 13).

13.5 The Regulatory Review Process

13.5.1 Overview

In Chapter 10 of this report, I conclude that the government's failure to enact a regulation providing for a notification protocol at the time of the privatization of routine drinking water testing was in part related to a culture of deregulation in government in 1996; following that there was a reluctance to enact new regulations. In this section, I describe in additional detail the government initiatives that created that culture. This section is intended only to provide a background for the conclusion reached in Chapter 10. I reach no new conclusions in this section.

In the "Common Sense Revolution," the Government of Ontario made commitments to cut government barriers to job creation, investment, and economic growth. It also made a commitment to reduce the size of government and to provide the people of Ontario with better for less. In carrying out these commitments, the new government, elected in 1995, promised to eliminate red tape and to reduce the regulatory burden for businesses and institutions. The vehicle to carry out these commitments was the Red Tape Review Commission, which subsequently became known as the Red Tape Commission. In its throne speech, on September 27, 1995, the government promised to initiate a "red tape review" of regulations affecting business and to eliminate any restrictions that could not be justified within 12 months of the review.

13.5.2   The Ministry of the Environment's Regulatory Review

In anticipation of the red tape review process, the Ministry of the Environment commenced a regulatory review on its own. In its review, the MOE assessed approximately 80 regulations for which it had statutory responsibility. The objective of the review was to bring about reforms to the MOE's regulations that would:

- improve the efficiency and effectiveness of environmental management;

- reduce barriers to economic renewal and competitiveness;

- reduce costs to government and regulated parties; and

- improve services to MOE clients, in part by making reductions in red tape.

After consulting stakeholders, the MOE released a consultation paper in July 1996 entitled "Responsive Environmental Protection," which concluded that Ontario needed a more responsive approach to environmental protection. That approach included the following emphases:

- focusing on environmental priorities to become more results-oriented, cost-effective, and customer-driven;

- providing the flexibility and certainty that industry needs to ensure jobs and economic growth; and

- simplifying rules and eliminating the red tape encountered by individuals, municipalities, and businesses.

Within this context, the MOE set five major directions for change:

- Focus on environment and energy priorities.

- Emphasize accountability and results.

- Simplify regulation and approvals and processes.

- Encourage continuous improvement and voluntary action.

- Ensure that regulation is clear, consistent, and current.

The fourth direction noted above related to the MOE's view that regulation was only one tool available to government to improve and protect the environment. The ministry stated that going beyond regulation meant providing incentives to achieve more than minimum regulatory requirements. It would recognize and encourage voluntarism, resource conservation, and pollution prevention by adopting new tools, including economic instruments. This direction demonstrated a strong and consistent commitment to self-regulation and industry stewardship.

13.5.3   The Red Tape Commission Regulatory Review

The Red Tape Commission was established in November 1995 as a Cabinet-level committee. It is composed of members of the legislature who are not members of the Cabinet. The commission was appointed by the Premier to review the appropriateness of existing regulatory measures, especially as they affected businesses and institutions, and to make recommendations to the Cabinet concerning the elimination or amendment of any inappropriate regulatory measures. The commission was also to design an ongoing evaluation/impact test and review process for the approval of any new regulatory measures.

A regulatory measure includes all statutes and subordinate legislation and all associated administrative policy and operational processes, directives, and actions. These may include regulations, licensing, inspection, standards, compliance, enforcement, registration, permits, approvals, certifications, and other similar procedures and processes.

The objectives of the Red Tape Commission include the following:

- Ensure that all regulatory measures reflect current government goals and needs.

- Reduce government costs in administering regulatory measures.

- Reduce the compliance costs and administrative burden to businesses and institutions, thereby improving the competitiveness and business climate for existing and new businesses.

- Move toward alternative methods of regulation, such as the establishment of performance standards and allowing business self-regulation; move away from micro-managing the compliance process.

- Establish an ongoing regulatory review process that would critically evaluate all aspects of new regulations, including the cost to government, the cost to the private sector to comply, and the overall benefit.

- Change the regulatory culture of the government and the public.

- Ensure that the health and safety of Ontarians are not adversely affected by the regulatory reform process.

In 1995, the MOE Policy Development Branch had a group of 15 employees working on regulatory review. A very large majority of their time was devoted to responding to the Red Tape Commission. By the end of 1997, three or four people were working in this group; they were involved in reviewing existing regulations and did not come forward with any new regulations at the material time.

13.5.4   Impact Tests for Regulatory Review

In furtherance of the objectives of the Red Tape Commission, the government established a succession of tests to weigh the costs and benefits of regulations under review. In July 1996, the government implemented the first of its business impact tests – the Less Paper/More Jobs test – which applied a number of criteria in the review of a regulation, including the following:

- The implementation of regulatory actions was restricted to instances in which a problem required intervention.

- The Ontario government would only legislate or regulate in areas consistent with its role and priorities.

- The benefits of the policy must outweigh the risks and consequences of lack of intervention.

- The costs to government and to the affected parties should not outweigh the benefits.

- The Ontario government should explore all realistic alternatives to legislation and regulation by government.

- The need for regulations would be assessed in early and continued consultations with affected businesses, individuals, and groups.

- The paper burden and process requirements of any legislation or regulation would be streamlined, minimized, or eliminated as much as possible.

- Enforcement and compliance would be consistent with the objectives of the policy and the risks and remedies assessed for non-compliance.

This test was elaborated upon in the Red Tape Commission's final report of January 1997, *Cutting the Red Tape Barriers to Jobs and Better Government*. In the report, specific kinds of "customer" service problems were identified. A problem identified by 68% of the respondents was: "Reporting requirements are complicated, and create unnecessary paperwork." The Red Tape Commission directed 36 of its 131 recommendations to the MOE. By way of comparison, the Ministry of Labour and the Ministry of Health received 18 and 12 recommendations, respectively. The MOE received by far the greatest attention of any ministry, and the Premier testified that it was high on the priority list of the Red Tape Commission.

In respect of the process prior to proposing a new regulation, a ministry would have to consider input from stakeholders in the regulated community and justify the regulation under the business impact test. Before approving a regulation, the Cabinet would refer it to the Red Tape Commission for its review and advice. If the MOE and the Red Tape Commission disagreed about a new regulation, each would provide its view to Cabinet for Cabinet to make the ultimate decision. The Red Tape Commission favoured regulation as a last resort.

In September 1997, the Red Tape Commission replaced the Less Paper/ More Jobs test with the Regulatory Impact and Competitiveness Test (RICT), which included the following requirements:

- Explain why intervention is required.

- List the alternatives considered, including self-management, voluntary codes, and other alternatives to government regulation, and identify groups that will be affected by the proposal. In this regard, the RICT states that small business should always be considered.

- Summarize the costs and benefits to government, business, small business, institutions, and other affected parties.

- Identify whether the administrative burden of regulation will be reduced, unchanged, or increased. Factors included in administrative burden include paper burden, recognition for new technologies, time/effort/costs to comply or receive a response, degree of overlap or duplication with other ministries, other levels of government, and clarity of communication.

- Identify the impact of Ontario's competitiveness as improved, unchanged, or decreased.

- Describe the means of the ongoing review of the legislation, regulation, or policy.

Chapter 14   The Process of Part 1 of the Inquiry

Contents

Chapter 14   The Process of Part 1 of the Inquiry

14.1 Introduction

This section of the report offers an outline of the process of Part 1 of the Walkerton Inquiry and the principles that guided the development of the process.[1] The process of Part 2 of the Inquiry[2] will be described in the Part 2 report, which will follow at a later date.

In designing the process, my counsel and I considered several recent decisions of the Supreme Court of Canada, which provided guidance on a number of issues that arise in the conduct of public inquiries.[3] We also benefited from the experiences of past inquiries, from law reform commission reports, and from academic articles.[4] To some extent, the process for Part 1 evolved as the Inquiry proceeded. As circumstances changed and new issues arose, we adapted the process in an effort to ensure that the Inquiry was thorough, timely, and fair to

---

[1] A commissioner of an inquiry has the authority to determine the procedure of the inquiry under the *Public Inquiries Act*, R.S.O. 1990, c. P-41, s. 3. According to Cory J.: "[T]he nature and the purpose of public inquiries requires courts to give a generous interpretation to a commissioner's powers to control their own proceedings under the Nova Scotia Act"; see *Phillips* v. *Nova Scotia (Commission of Inquiry into the Westray Mine Tragedy)*, [1995] 2 S.C.R. 97 at para. 175, which dealt with the application of the Nova Scotia *Public Inquiries Act*, R.S.N.S. 1989, c. 372, s. 5.

[2] The terms "the Inquiry" and "the Commission" are used interchangeably throughout this report.

[3] See *Canada (Attorney General)* v. *Canada (Commission of Inquiry on the Blood System in Canada – Krever Commission)*, [1997] 3 S.C.R. 440; *Phillips* v. *Nova Scotia (Commission of Inquiry into the Westray Mine Disaster)*, *supra*, note 1; and *Starr* v. *Houlden*, [1990] 1 S.C.R. 1366.

[4] We were assisted, in particular, by the reports of the Commission of Inquiry on the Blood System in Canada (1997), the Commission of Inquiry into Certain Events at the Prison for Women in Kingston (1996), the Commission on Proceedings Involving Guy Paul Morin (1998), the Westray Mine Public Inquiry (1997), the Commission of Inquiry into Certain Deaths at the Hospital for Sick Children and Related Matters (1984), the Niagara Regional Police Force Inquiry (1993), and the Commission of Inquiry into the Air Ontario Crash at Dryden, Ontario (1989).

We were also assisted by three reports on public inquiries: Law Reform Commission of Canada, Working Paper 17, *Administrative Law: Commissions of Inquiry* (1977); Ontario Law Reform Commission, *Report on Public Inquiries* (1992); and Alberta Law Reform Institute, Report 62, *Proposals for the Reform of the Public Inquiries Act* (1992).

We also found useful several academic works on public inquiries, including A. Paul Pross, Innis Christie, and John A. Yogis, eds., *Commissions of Inquiry, Dalhousie Law Journal*, vol. 12 (1990), 151; R.J. Anthony and A.R. Lucas, *A Handbook on the Conduct of Public Inquiries in Canada* (Toronto: Butterworths, 1985); Nicholas d'Ombrain, "Public inquiries in Canada," *Canadian Public Administration*, vol. 40, no. 1 (1997), p. 86; Marlys Edwardh and Jill Copeland, "A delicate balance: The rights of the criminal accused in the context of public inquiries," paper prepared for the Conference at Osgoode Hall Law School in Honour of Justice Peter de Carteret Cory, October 27, 1999; and Julian N. Falconer and Richard Macklin, "Current issues on standing," paper prepared for the Law Society of Upper Canada – Department of Continuing Education.

the interests of the many individuals, groups, and institutions that might be affected by the proceedings.

14.1.1   Purpose

In the *Westray* case in the Supreme Court of Canada, Mr. Justice Cory wrote that public inquiries "are often convened, in the wake of public shock, horror, disillusionment, or scepticism, in order to uncover 'the truth.'"[5] The search for the truth is a difficult undertaking in circumstances of human tragedy and suffering. The role of an inquiry in such circumstances is to find out what happened, what went wrong, and what can be done to avoid a similar tragedy in the future.

Given the tragic consequences of the water contamination in Walkerton, the importance of the "fact-finding" role was paramount. The public was shocked by what had happened, and it was widely reported that many people had lost confidence in the safety of Ontario's drinking water. They questioned the role of public officials and the government in failing to prevent such a tragedy. In a very real sense, the Walkerton Inquiry was born out of a public sense of anger and doubt. This was especially true for the residents of Walkerton, who were the people most directly affected by the outbreak.

14.1.2   A Broad Mandate

Because of the circumstances in which the Inquiry was called, its mandate was broad. The overarching purpose of the Inquiry was to make recommendations to ensure the safety of Ontario's drinking water in the future. To do this, I was directed to carry out three tasks, two of which were directly connected to the events in Walkerton. The third was, in effect, a catch-all that allowed me to consider any other matters I considered necessary to carry out the mandate. The relevant portion of the mandate reads:

The commission shall inquire into the following matters:

---

[5] *Phillips v. Nova Scotia (Commission of Inquiry into the Westray Mine Tragedy)*, [1995] 2 S.C.R. 97 at para. 62.

(a)   the circumstances which caused hundreds of people in the
       Walkerton area to become ill, and several of them to die in
       May and June 2000, at or around the same time as *Escherichia
       coli* bacteria were found to be present in the town's water
       supply;

(b)   the cause of these events including the effect, if any, of govern-
       ment policies, procedures and practices; and

(c)   any other relevant matters that the commission considers nec-
       essary to ensure the safety of Ontario's drinking water,

in order to make such findings and recommendations as the commission considers advisable to ensure the safety of the water
supply system in Ontario.[6]

14.1.3   The Division of the Mandate

Although each of the three prongs of the mandate was directed at making
recommendations, the first two were Walkerton-related. They directed me to
investigate and determine what had happened in Walkerton and why, and to
make recommendations based on those findings. The third prong was much
broader: what happened in Walkerton has provided some but by no means all
of the answers to the question of what needs to be done to ensure the safety of
our water.

Moreover, because the Walkerton part of the mandate involved a great deal
of fact-finding, it was appropriate to adopt an adjudicative, evidentiary
type of process. The broader, non-Walkerton part required a policy-based
examination of issues, practices, and experiences in other jurisdictions. The
different nature of the two exercises required two different procedural models.

Given the dual roles of the Inquiry, one of my first decisions was to divide the
Inquiry into two parts: Part 1 and Part 2. I proceeded with both parts simultaneously, providing each with a different process. Part 1 was conducted by way
of evidentiary hearings in Walkerton and was further divided into two sub-
parts, reflecting the first two heads in the mandate. Part 1A addressed the

---

[6] Order in Council 1170/2000, s. 2; see Appendix A.

circumstances of the cause of the contamination, and Part 1B addressed the effect, if any, of government policies, procedures, and practices.[7]

Part 2 of the Inquiry deals with policy issues related to safe drinking water, as reflected in the third head of the mandate. It involves a broad review of relevant issues, including public health, source water protection, and technological and management issues associated with the delivery of safe drinking water. I will deliver a separate report for Part 2 at a later date.

The primary purpose of Part 1 is to make findings regarding the historical cause of the tragedy in Walkerton and to make recommendations based on those findings. The primary purpose of Part 2 is to make recommendations regarding the broader issue of Ontario's drinking water system.

14.2 Principles

Four principles should guide the conduct of a public inquiry: thoroughness, expedition, openness to the public, and fairness. The process of the Walkerton Inquiry was designed with these principles in mind.

14.2.1 Thoroughness

Given the purpose of an inquiry, "[i]t is crucial," as Mr. Justice Cory has said, "that an inquiry both be and appear to be independent and impartial in order to satisfy the public desire to learn the truth."[8] An inquiry must be thorough to realize this duty of independence and impartiality. It must examine all of the relevant issues with care and exactitude so as to leave no doubt that all questions raised by its mandate were answered and explored.

---

[7] Part 1A preceded Part 1B. Part 1A began on October 16, 2000, and was completed on March 1, 2001. Part 1B began on March 6, 2001, and was completed on July 30. Closing submissions for both were heard from August 15 to 27, 2001.

[8] *Phillips* v. *Nova Scotia (Commission of Inquiry into the Westray Mine Tragedy), supra,* note 1, at para. 175.

14.2.2   Expedition

To remain relevant, an inquiry should be expeditious. Some inquiries have been criticized for becoming bogged down in procedural wrangling and for taking so much time that they drift into irrelevance. Expedition in the conduct of an inquiry makes it more likely that members of the public will be engaged by the process and feel confident that their questions and concerns are being addressed. Moreover, an expeditious inquiry usually costs less. In the Walkerton Inquiry, we set timelines at the beginning, and, with few exceptions, they were met. This is a testament to the commitment and hard work of all those involved, including the parties, most of whom made a substantial contribution.

14.2.3   Openness to the Public

An inquiry should be public in the fullest sense. This means that the public must have access to the inquiry so that the story that is told can be heard. Further, to maintain public confidence, the process of an inquiry must be open to public scrutiny. On this issue, I echo the reflections of Justice S.G.M. Grange, commissioner of the Inquiry into Certain Deaths at the Hospital for Sick Children, who said:

> I remember once thinking egotistically that all the evidence, all the antics, had only one aim: to convince the commissioner who, after all, eventually wrote the report. But I soon discovered my error. They are not just inquiries; they are *public* inquiries ... I realized that there was another purpose to the inquiry just as important as one man's solution to the mystery and that was to inform the public. Merely presenting the evidence in public, evidence which had hitherto been given only in private, served that purpose. The public has a special interest, a right to know and a right to form its opinion as it goes along.[9]

An inquiry must also respond to the concerns of the public, especially to those individuals most affected by its *raison d'être* – in this case, the people of Walkerton. Mr. Justice Cory expressed this role as follows:

---

[9] S.G.M. Grange, "How should lawyers and the legal profession adapt?" in A. Paul Pross, Innis Christie, and John A. Yogis, eds., *Commissions of Inquiry, Dalhousie Law Journal*, vol. 12 (1990), 151 at pp. 154–55 (emphasis in original).

Open hearings function as a means of restoring the public confidence in the affected industry and in the regulations pertaining to it and their enforcement. As well, it can serve as a type of healing therapy for a community shocked and angered by a tragedy. It can channel the natural desire to assign blame and exact retribution into a constructive exercise providing recommendations for reform and improvement.[10]

14.2.4 Fairness

The principles reviewed above all stem from the public's interest in an inquiry. It is important to remember, however, that inquiries can have a serious impact on those implicated in the process. Thus, an inquiry must balance the interests of the public in finding out what happened with the rights of those involved to be treated fairly. As the Ontario Law Reform Commission has commented, the public benefits of an inquiry must be weighed against the costs of "interfering with the privacy, reputation, and legal interests of individuals."[11]

14.3 A Description of the Process

14.3.1 Relations with the Community

Many inquiries originate in human tragedy and suffering. The residents of Walkerton – some of whom lost loved ones, others who suffered lasting physical harm, and all of whom experienced the shock and tragedy that overcame their community – clearly had a profound interest in the conduct of the proceedings. It was very important to communicate, to the greatest extent possible, with those most affected. Within a month of my appointment, Inquiry staff met with the representatives of local groups in Walkerton to discuss local views and concerns. Within two months, we held community meetings over the course of four days in Walkerton to hear directly from those

---

[10] *Phillips* v. *Nova Scotia (Commission of Inquiry into the Westray Mine Tragedy)*, *supra*, note 1, at para. 117.

[11] Ontario Law Reform Commission, *supra*, note 4, at p. 19. In particular, I derived guidance from the Supreme Court of Canada's decision in *Phillips v. Nova Scotia (Commission of Inquiry into the Westray Mine Tragedy)*, *supra*, note 1.

who wished to tell their story about the ongoing impact of the tragedy on their lives.[12] This was the Inquiry's first public event.[13]

Thereafter, all of the hearings in Part 1 were held in Walkerton. I think this was important. Walkerton was the place where the tragedy occurred, and the people living there were the most directly affected. My sense was that it was their wish, overwhelmingly, that the Part 1 hearings be held in their community.

14.3.2   The Rules of Procedure and Practice

With the above principles in mind, the Inquiry developed a set of draft rules, which were published in July 2000. These rules were, to a considerable extent, modelled on the rules of other inquiries and tailored to the circumstances and requirements of this Inquiry. Once parties were granted standing, they were given an opportunity to comment on the rules.[14]

The rules indicated that the Inquiry would be divided into two parts, as described above. Given the evidentiary nature of Part 1, the rules dealt at length with the role of those parties with standing in Part 1. They outlined the basis on which parties would be granted standing, their rights during the hearings, and the rights of witnesses. The rules also outlined the role of Walkerton Commission counsel, the manner in which evidence would be called, and the order of examinations of witnesses.

---

[12] The boil water advisory remained in effect during the first two months of the Part 1 hearings. A letter from me to the residents of Walkerton and a list of presenters at the hearings is included in Appendices C(i) and C(ii).

[13] Those who wished to tell their story *in camera*, due to its personal nature, were permitted to do so. Transcripts of those meetings, without name references, were publicly available. (Under the *Public Inquiries Act*, R.S.O. 1990, c. P-41, s. 4(b), a commissioner of an inquiry is empowered to hold hearings in the absence of the public when "intimate financial or personal matters or other matters may be disclosed … that are of such a nature, having regard to the circumstances, that the desirability of avoiding disclosure thereof in the interest of any person affected or in the public interest outweighs the desirability of adhering to the principle that hearings be open to the public.")

[14] The rules, in their final form, are included in Appendices D(i) and D(ii). Also, supplementary procedural guidelines provided to the parties are included in Appendices D(iv) and D(v).

14.3.3   Standing

In a public inquiry, those who have a direct stake in the process may be granted standing so that they can participate in the proceedings. In the case of this Inquiry, applicants for standing made written submissions and oral argument at a hearing in Walkerton, and I granted standing to a wide range of individuals and groups.[15] I wanted to ensure that a broad range of interests and perspectives would be represented so that the Inquiry was inclusive and thorough.

There were two bases on which I granted standing in Part 1. The first was the basis required under section 5(1) of the *Public Inquiries Act*:

> A commission shall accord to any person who satisfies it that the person has a substantial and direct interest in the subject-matter of its inquiry an opportunity during the inquiry to give evidence and to call and examine or to cross-examine witnesses personally or by counsel on evidence relevant to the person's interest.[16]

The definition of "substantial and direct interest" under this section is a matter of law, and I do not need to undertake a detailed review of the issues here. Suffice it to say that the definition generally includes anyone whose reputation might be damaged by the findings of the commissioner and who has a greater interest in the proceedings than that of an interested member of the public.[17]

I also granted standing to a number of groups who represented clearly ascertainable interests and perspectives that were essential to my mandate and who I thought should be separately represented before the Inquiry.[18] These groups included a municipal association, agricultural associations, environmental groups, trade unions, and an association of public health inspectors. By involving these groups in the hearings, the Inquiry benefited from a diverse array of views that would not otherwise have been brought forward. In cases in which several applicants for standing appeared to have similar perspectives, they were given a single grant of standing on the understanding they would

---

[15] My ruling on standing and funding, a supplementary ruling, and the notice of the hearing on standing are included in Appendices E(i), E(ii), and E(iii).

[16] *Public Inquiries Act*, R.S.O. 1990, c. P-41, s. 5(1).

[17] See *Gosselin v. Ontario (Royal Commission of Inquiry into Certain Deaths at the Hospital for Sick Children – Grange Commission)* (1984), Admin. L.R. 250 (Ont. Div. Ct.); and *Re The Ontario Crime Commission, Ex parte Feeley and McDermott* (1962), 34 D.L.R. (2d) 451 (Ont. C.A.).

[18] Rules of Procedure and Practice, Rule 5(b).

form a coalition. I granted standing to a total of 21 groups and individuals in Part 1.[19]

14.3.3.1 *Categories of Standing*

In granting standing to a relatively large number of parties, I knew there was a risk that the hearings could bog down, so I limited the concept of standing as much as possible to the specific interest or perspective of a party. Parties with a legal interest under the *Public Inquiries Act* were able to participate in the hearings and cross-examine witnesses on days when the hearings addressed their specific interest. Parties with a useful perspective were limited to those hearing days on which their perspective would be helpful.

This approach led to three categories of standing. Parties with the widest interests or perspectives were granted *full standing* and were entitled to participate in all of the Part 1 hearings. Those with more narrow interests or perspectives had *limited standing* and were notified in advance of the days on which they were expected to participate, subject always to an opportunity on their part to seek broader participation. Finally, a few parties with focused perspectives were granted *special standing*, which entitled them to receive documents produced by Commission counsel but not to participate in the hearings. This system made necessary a rather complex procedure to track and notify the parties regarding their attendance and funding. In the end, though, I am satisfied that the procedure allowed for greater participation in the process with efficient use of time, while at the same time avoiding unnecessary expense.

14.3.4 Funding

The Order-in-Council laying out the mandate for the Inquiry also provided as follows regarding funding for the parties:

> The commission may make recommendations to the Attorney General regarding funding to parties who have been granted standing, to the extent of the party's interest, where in the commission's

---

[19] A list of parties is included in Appendix B(i).

view, the party would not otherwise be able to participate in the
inquiry without such funding.[20]

To qualify for a funding recommendation, parties had to demonstrate that
they would not be able to participate in the Inquiry without funding. They
also had to have a satisfactory proposal that stated how they would use and
account for the funds. In recommending funding, I considered these criteria:

- the nature of the party's interest and proposed involvement in the
  Inquiry

- whether the party had an established record of concern for and a demonstrated commitment to the interest it sought to represent

- whether the party had special experience or expertise with respect to the
  Commission's mandate

- whether the party could reasonably be included in a group of others of
  similar interest

Many parties did not apply for funding. For those that did, I recommended
full funding in some cases and partial funding in others. Funding was normally recommended for a single counsel, with disbursements, for each qualify-
ing party, for those hearing days that engaged its interest or perspective. I was
pleased that the Attorney General accepted all my funding recommendations.
A total of 11 parties in Part 1 received either full or partial funding on my
recommendation.

Counsel fees and disbursements for those with funding were based on the
funding guidelines issued by the Attorney General for outside counsel who
provide legal services to the government.[21] Parties awarded funding submitted
their accounts for legal fees and expenses to an independent assessor, Mark
Orkin, Q.C., who was jointly appointed by the Attorney General and me.
Mr. Orkin reviewed and approved accounts for payment by the Attorney
General.

---

[20] Order in Council 1170/2000, s. 5; see Appendix A.
[21] Funding criteria and guidelines are included in Appendices F(i) and F(ii).

A number of parties requested funding for experts to assist them in their preparation in Part 1. I declined to recommend such funding because the Attorney General's funding guidelines did not include funding for experts for this purpose. In a few cases, the Commission did directly fund experts who were called by its counsel on the suggestion or application of a party, and in one case I recommended funding for an expert who was called as a witness by one of the parties with standing.

14.3.5 The Role of Commission Counsel

Commission counsel play a special role in a public inquiry. Their primary responsibility is to represent the public interest at the inquiry. They have the duty to ensure that all issues bearing on the public interest are brought to the Commissioner's attention. Commission counsel do not represent any particular interest or point of view, and their role is neither adversarial nor partisan.

In the case of Part 1 of the Inquiry, Commission counsel played a vital role by locating, organizing, and calling the evidence; by dealing with counsel for the parties; and by assisting in the administration of the Inquiry.[22] I was very well served by Commission counsel in this Inquiry. They performed their role with great skill and professionalism, and I am very appreciative of their assistance.

14.3.6 The Role of Investigators

Early in the process, Commission counsel contacted the Royal Canadian Mounted Police (RCMP) to ask whether an investigator could be made available to assist the Inquiry. In response, the RCMP made available an inspector from the Commercial Crime Unit and a constable to assist him. They made an important contribution by obtaining search warrants, conducting searches, and providing technical advice about our document management system. In addition, they advised the Commission regarding security issues on days when high-profile witnesses testified. The Inquiry benefited enormously from the assistance of the RCMP.

---

[22] Commission counsel sometimes called witnesses who were suggested by the parties; in two instances, the party itself called the witness.

14.3.7   Procedural Rights

14.3.7.1   *The Parties*

Individuals and institutions that were granted standing in Part 1 were afforded a range of procedural rights under both the *Public Inquiries Act* and the Rules of Procedure and Practice.[23] All had the right to counsel. Additionally, for those hearings that engaged their interest, the parties were granted:

- access to documents collected by the Commission subject to the Rules of Procedure and Practice

- advance notice of documents that were proposed to be introduced into evidence

- advance provision of witness statements of anticipated evidence that were prepared by the Commission

- a place at counsel table

- the opportunity to suggest witnesses to be called by Commission counsel, or, alternatively, an opportunity to apply to the Commissioner to lead the evidence of a particular witness

- the opportunity to cross-examine witnesses on matters relevant to the basis upon which standing was granted

- the opportunity to make closing submissions

Finally, as previously noted, parties with insufficient funds could apply for funding to support their participation.

14.3.7.2   *Witnesses*

Witnesses called at the Inquiry were also afforded procedural rights under the rules, though on a more limited basis than were parties with standing. For

---

[23] See Appendices D(i) and D(ii).

example, all had the right to be represented by counsel at the time of their testimony. Similarly, anyone interviewed by Commission counsel was entitled to have counsel present during the interview. I did not receive any applications for funding from witnesses, other than those associated with the Part 1 parties, and therefore I made no recommendations in this regard.

14.3.7.3   *Recipients of a Section 5(2) Notice*

The *Public Inquiries Act* affords special legal protection to any person who might be found by an inquiry to have engaged in misconduct. Section 5(2) of the Act provides:

> No finding of misconduct on the part of any person shall be made against the person in any report of a commission after an inquiry unless that person had reasonable notice of the substance of the alleged misconduct and was allowed full opportunity during the inquiry to be heard in person or by counsel.[24]

In accordance with this section, the Commission provided a number of persons with a "Notice of Alleged Misconduct," also known as a "section 5(2) notice."[25] If these individuals had standing before the Inquiry, they would have the opportunity to follow the evidence and respond to any allegations of misconduct made against them. Occasionally witnesses at the Inquiry who did not have standing received a section 5(2) notice after they had testified. These recipients of a section 5(2) notice were given additional procedural rights to ensure that they would be made aware of, and could respond to, any allegations of misconduct.[26] They had the right to be represented by counsel and the right to apply for funding. Furthermore, they were provided with references to those portions of the evidence that were relevant to the issues in their notice, and they were entitled to receive all exhibits or documents that Commission counsel intended to put into evidence that related to these issues.

In addition, recipients of a section 5(2) notice could participate in the hearings to the extent necessary to respond to any allegations of misconduct, and they

---

[24] R.S.O. 1990, c. P-41, s. 5(2).

[25] A sample s. 5(2) notice is included in Appendix I(i). Further, my rulings on three applications regarding s. 5(2) notices issued by the Commission are included in Appendix J.

[26] Two sample letters to a recipient of a s. 5(2) notice, outlining relevant procedural rights, are included in Appendices I(ii) and I(iii).

were entitled to call evidence and cross-examine witnesses on relevant issues. Commission counsel endeavoured to notify them of any evidence considered relevant to their interests. Recipients could also monitor the proceedings to decide for themselves whether their interests had been affected, and they could apply to recall witnesses if necessary. Finally, they could make closing submissions.

14.3.7.4 *Criminal Investigation*

One of the occasions in a public inquiry in which the public interest may conflict with a person's right to procedural fairness occurs when an individual whose testimony is relevant to the inquiry is also the subject of a criminal investigation. My mandate specifically provided that the Commission "shall ensure that it does not interfere with any ongoing criminal investigation."[27]

In the case of this Inquiry, it was widely reported before and during the hearings that there was an ongoing criminal investigation into the conduct of Stan Koebel. When he was called to give evidence, the question arose whether requiring his testimony at the Inquiry might adversely affect his right to receive a fair trial, if he were charged. Mr. Koebel's testimony was expected to be widely reported in the media, thus raising the possibility of tainting pools of jurors across the province.

Because of this concern, Commission counsel notified counsel for both the Province of Ontario and Mr. Koebel that they could apply to me for a publication ban on Mr. Koebel's testimony as one possible approach to this issue. As it turned out, no application was made, and I was not required to decide whether a publication ban was appropriate.

14.3.8 The Collection and Production of Documents

The commissioner of an inquiry is granted a number of tools to aid in the search for the truth: above all, the wide-ranging powers of investigation. A commission has the power to compel the production of documents or other information by way of a summons or search warrant from the court.[28] A

---

[27] Order in Council 1170/2000, s. 3; see Appendix A.
[28] A sample summons to a witness is included in Appendix G. A sample search warrant appears in Appendix H(ii).

commissioner can also compel persons to appear publicly as witnesses and to testify under oath. Anyone who refuses to produce relevant material or to respond to a call to testify could face punishment for contempt of court.[29]

During the Inquiry, we collected thousands of documents from various sources, including several individuals, the Walkerton Public Utilities Commission, the Municipality of Brockton, A&L Canada Laboratories, and G.A.P. EnviroMicrobial Services. By far the greatest number of documents collected, perhaps as many as one million, came from the provincial government.[30] Government documents were obtained from six provincial ministries,[31] the Ontario Clean Water Agency, the Management Board Secretariat, the Cabinet Office, and the Premier's Office. About 200,000 government documents were scanned into the Commission's database.

The process for reviewing documents, interviewing witnesses, and organizing the evidence was directed by the three lead Commission counsel. The sheer quantity of material led us to assemble a team to support the investigation by assisting in the collection and review of documents and the interviewing of witnesses. In Part 1A, two RCMP investigators played an instrumental role. In Part 1B, we relied primarily on an energetic team of junior lawyers to support Commission counsel.

Once the documents had been collected, many were scanned into the Commission database so that they could be reviewed more quickly. After they were scanned and reviewed, the documents were produced on CD-ROMs and provided to the parties,[32] who had provided a signed undertaking regarding confidentiality.[33] The parties also received regular statements of anticipated evidence for upcoming witnesses. These statements were prepared by Commission counsel on the basis of witness interviews. The Commission attempted to provide the statements one week in advance, although occasionally it was not possible to meet this target.

---

[29] These powers are granted under the Public Inquiries Act, R.S.O. 1990, c. P-41, ss. 7, 8, and 17.

[30] The provincial government reports that it produced one million documents to the Inquiry.

[31] Ministries that provided documents included: Environment; Health and Long-Term Care; Agriculture, Food and Rural Affairs; Municipal Affairs and Housing; Energy, Science and Technology; and Finance.

[32] As they became ready for production to the parties, groups of documents were scanned onto CD-ROMs, whose delivery to the parties was accompanied by a bound index of documents that were included in the CD-ROM. A total of 41 CD-ROMs were produced to the parties in 14 productions.

[33] Undertakings regarding confidentiality are included in Appendix H(iv).

A total of 447 exhibits, containing more than 3,000 documents, were entered into evidence at the hearings in Part 1. There were 95 hearing days over nine months, generating 21,686 pages of transcripts. In all, we heard from 114 witnesses.[34] Statistics aside, it was an enormous task to review and classify the documents, to identify and interview witnesses, and to digest and organize the relevant information so as to put it into evidence in a coherent way. Commission counsel, staff, the parties, and their counsel and staff spent countless hours ensuring that this process worked. As a result, with a few minor exceptions, the hearings proceeded on schedule.

14.3.9   The Role of the Government

The Inquiry's mandate in Part 1B was to examine the effect, if any, of government policies, procedures, and practices on the cause of the water contamination in Walkerton.[35] As a result, the government played an important role in the Part 1B process. Most of the documents collected for Part 1B came from the government, and most of the witnesses called are current or former government employees.

Many provincial public servants worked long and hard to search for relevant government documents in response to requests from the Inquiry. For the most part, and especially in the case of the Ministry of the Environment, large numbers of documents were produced in remarkably short periods of time.

Since the mandate focused on examining government policies, practices, and procedures, it was essential to obtain all relevant government documents. This proved to be an enormously complicated exercise. That process is described in some detail below.

---

[34] A list of witnesses is included in Appendix B(ii).

[35] The range of policies, procedures, and practices under consideration is indicated by the "Outline of Potential Issues in Part 1B," which was made available to the parties for comment and is included, in its final form, in Appendix K(i).

14.3.9.1   *Document Requests*

The Commission made 17 detailed document requests to the government be-tween June 30, 2000 and January 24, 2001.[36] The first request was made to the Ministry of the Environment (MOE). Other requests went to the Ministries of Health and Long-Term Care; Agriculture, Food and Rural Affairs; Municipal Affairs and Housing; and Energy, Science and Technology, as well as to the "central agencies," including the Ministry of Finance, the Management Board Secretariat, the Cabinet Office, and the Premier's Office. Finally, the Commission sent follow-up requests to a number of ministries and agencies, especially the MOE.

14.3.9.2   *Search Warrants*

At the request of the government, the Commission obtained search warrants from the Ontario Superior Court for each of its document requests.[37] The mechanism of a "friendly" search warrant was agreed on as a means of accom-modating the government's concerns regarding protection of privacy interests and third-party notification requirements under the *Freedom of Information and Protection of Privacy Act*,[38] while also ensuring that the Commission would receive relevant documents on a timely basis. The use of these warrants, with the exception of a warrant executed in August 2001, did not reflect any lack of cooperation on the part of the government. The warrants were executed by Inquiry staff, or RCMP investigators seconded to the Inquiry, at the time and place of document productions and searches.

The government responded to the Inquiry's requests with many waves of document productions, starting in August 2000 and generally ending in February 2001. I use the word "generally" here because some document pro-ductions from the government did not in fact end until November 2001, fol-lowing the conclusion of the scheduled Part 1 hearings.[39] I would have liked to have seen certain document productions completed more quickly, but, in

---

[36] The Commission's document request of June 30, 2000, to the MOE is included as a sample in Appendix H(i).

[37] A sample search warrant is included in Appendix H(ii).

[38] *Freedom of Information and Protection of Privacy Act*, R.S.O. 1990, c. F-31.

[39] Further, the Commission obtained and executed additional search warrants in August 2001, in an effort to enhance the comprehensiveness of document searches and productions by the Cabinet Office and Premier's Office.

fairness, they required substantial effort on the part of government staff and counsel. Further, the follow-up searches were complementary, but not essential, to the continuing hearings in Part 1B. Thus, it was rarely necessary to delay the scheduled hearings. The Commission did, however, make it clear to the government that if the late production of any documents made it necessary to call or recall a particular witness, further hearings would be scheduled for that purpose.

14.3.9.3   *Document Review*

The large volume of documents produced by the government required the Commission to put in place a special process for searching and reviewing the documents. Inquiry staff reviewed the hard copies of documents produced by the government in order to identify groups of documents that should be electronically scanned into the Commission database for a more detailed review.[40] The purpose of the initial stage of this review was to expedite the review of large numbers of documents by eliminating those that appeared to be irrelevant before they were scanned.

14.4 Cabinet Privilege

Early in the process, the government indicated that it would assert a claim of Cabinet privilege over certain government documents. In response, the Commission took the position that the breadth of its mandate to examine "the effect, if any, of government policies, procedures and practices" constituted a waiver of Cabinet privilege by the Province. The Commission further indicated that it would attempt to resolve this "threshold issue" of law by stating a case to the Divisional Court, a proceeding that would be public. The government, using the analogy of procedures under the *Criminal Code of Canada* for determining a claim of solicitor-client privilege, took the position that any issue associated with a claim of privilege should be resolved at a private hearing before the judge who issued the Inquiry's search warrants.

In the interests of avoiding lengthy court proceedings, an agreement was reached: Commission counsel would inspect documents produced by the government

---

[40] Documents not identified for scanning were stored by the government as hard copies and remained available for further review by Inquiry staff.

before any assertion of privilege. Once the Commission had identified documents that it intended to put into evidence, the government could, if it saw fit,
claim privilege. Both parties would then have an opportunity to resolve the
issue on a document-by-document basis. If the parties failed to agree, a
hearing would be held before the judge who issued the search warrants to
determine the issue of privilege – including the threshold issue of whether
privilege had been waived by the wording of the mandate – with a right of
appeal to the Court of Appeal for Ontario. The Commission also stipulated
that it would notify all parties with standing in Part 1 of the date and place of
any such hearing and would argue before the judge that the hearing should be
held in public.[41]

Government counsel claimed privilege over a number of documents, most of
which Commission counsel did not wish to put into evidence. Occasionally
a conflict occurred, but an agreement was reached that satisfied the
Commission counsel that all of the relevant portions of the document had
been put into evidence. As a result, it was unnecessary to resort to the legal
procedure described above.

14.4.1   Follow-up Searches: Electronic Searches

The Commission's document requests to the government included requests
for electronically stored, as well as hard-copy, documents. Searches for electronically stored documents are generally done through the use of keywords.
On March 20, 2001, the Commission asked the government to provide lists of
the keywords used by each of its ministries and agencies to search for and
identify documents in response to the Commission's requests. The purpose of
the request was to verify the process used by the government to locate relevant
electronically stored documents.

On April 23, government counsel provided a list of the keywords used to search
for e-mails in the MOE and another list used to search for e-mails in the
Cabinet Office and Premier's Office. They indicated that, for the remaining
ministries and agencies, a common list of keywords was not used.[42] On
April 25, Commission counsel wrote that, in its opinion, the breadth of the

---

[41] Letters outlining this agreement are included in Appendix H(iii).

[42] Rather, as indicated by government counsel, individuals generally tailored their searches of electronic documents to a particular document request. Some individuals assembled their own list of
search terms, whereas others searched all their electronic documents.

keywords used was unduly narrow[43] and requested that the government carry out additional searches based on an expanded list of keywords provided by the Commission. To expedite the process, these searches were narrowed to the office of the Secretary of Cabinet, the Premier's Office, and the office of the Minister of the Environment. On July 3, 2001, the government completed the searches and produced an additional 97 boxes of documents. The great majority of these documents were created after May 2000, and none of the documents was considered significant enough to be put into evidence.

14.4.2   Follow-up Searches: The Premier's Office

The Commission considered document productions by the central agencies important because of the key role they reportedly played in some policy decisions made under the current administration.[44] A review of documents produced by the Premier's Office made it apparent that relatively few documents had been produced, compared with the number produced by other ministries and agencies.[45] Furthermore, although the documents produced were generally identified as originating from the files of specific Premier's Office staff, it was apparent that no documents had been produced from files of the Premier's chief of staff. As a result, the Commission made a number of further requests for documents from the Premier's Office.

Government counsel responded to the follow-up requests by stating that documents relevant to the Inquiry might have been deleted by the Premier's chief of staff in the normal course. On the advice of RCMP personnel, the Commission requested that the government arrange to take a "mirror image" of the appropriate computers to obtain any relevant deleted files that were stored on

---

[43] For example, in response to the Commission's request for documents relating to reductions in the budget of the MOE, the government searched for electronic documents that included the keywords "budget cuts." However, this approach would not capture documents that used terms such as "budget reductions," "resource reductions," "cuts to budgets," or "staff cuts." Likewise, the list of keywords used to search at the Cabinet Office and Premier's Office included the term "reduc" but not "budget," "resource," "staff," or "cut."

[44] For example, see the issue paper prepared for the Inquiry by Nicolas d'Ombrain, "Machinery of government for safe drinking water in Ontario" (2001), at pp. 77–78.

[45] A total of 365 documents were produced by the Premier's Office, compared with thousands or tens of thousands produced by many ministries and hundreds of thousands by the Ministry of the Environment. Most of the five boxes produced by the Premier's Office contained only a few files of documents, and the bulk of those documents related to the post–May 2000 response of the government to the tragedy.

the hard drive.[46] The mirror image was taken on June 13, 2001, with the assistance of the RCMP. After reviewing the deleted files, Commission counsel determined that none of these files – all of which originated after May 2000 – was significant enough to be put into evidence. Following the search, however, it was considered necessary to search the deleted files on the computer servers used by the Premier's Office and Cabinet Office, and an additional search warrant was obtained for this purpose. The search of mirror images of those servers, taken in late August 2001, has been completed. However, the analysis of the deleted files, due to the size and nature of the respective hard drives, is an extensive and time-consuming process, and it is not yet complete. In the event that anything that I consider warrants comment by me is disclosed, I will issue a supplementary report.[47]

14.4.3 Certificates of Production

Clearly, Commission counsel and investigators were thorough and persistent in trying to ensure that all relevant documents were obtained. Ultimately, however, the Inquiry must rely on the word of the government that all relevant documents were produced. In this regard, we obtained certificates of productions from senior government personnel for each government ministry or agency that produced documents.[48] The certificates state, among other things, that all documents relevant to the subject matter of the Inquiry were produced.

After having heard the evidence, I conclude that the Commission obtained the documents necessary to fully and fairly review the important government policies, procedures, and practices referred to in its mandate.

14.5 The Conduct of the Hearings

In setting the schedule for gathering and hearing the evidence in Part 1, and for hearing closing arguments, our intent was to balance the principles of thor-

---

[46] Deleted files are stored on a computer hard drive until they are overwritten by the computer. A file may, however, be overwritten only in part. Making a mirror image of the hard drive makes it possible for technicians to capture any remaining deleted files before they are overwritten.

[47] Further, the review of approximately 2,700 additional documents produced by the government in November 2001 is not yet complete; I will issue a supplementary report if anything that I consider warrants comment by me is disclosed in those documents.

[48] An example of a certificate of production is included in Appendix H(v).

oughness, fairness, and expedition. With a few minor exceptions, we were able to meet the schedule.

The Inquiry benefited greatly from the division of the mandate. By separating Part 2 from the more formal evidentiary process in Part 1, the Commission was able to avoid having to review the broad, non–Walkerton-related issues in Part 2 by way of examining and cross-examining witnesses in the hearing room. Using the more formal evidentiary process in Part 2 would have been costly and cumbersome. Instead, the Commission was able to have more wide-ranging and efficient discussions in Part 2 by holding round-table meetings and informal, non-evidentiary public hearings.

Once the Part 1 hearings were underway, the Inquiry benefited greatly from the professionalism and cooperation of virtually all counsel to the parties. To keep the hearings on track, counsel frequently had to work quickly to review the documents, sometimes with very little lead time. Both Commission counsel and other counsel often worked late into the night to prepare for upcoming witnesses. The hearing days lasted longer than a normal court day, sometimes continuing for eight or nine hours. During our busiest weeks, we regularly sat into the early evening.

I considered, but did not impose, time limits on cross-examinations. Before cross-examinations began, I routinely asked counsel for estimates of time and generally held them to their estimates. Counsel for the parties kept their cross-examinations focused, thus avoiding considerable duplication and delay. In an era in which criticism of the legal profession is common, it is heartening to be able to say that counsel at this Inquiry performed splendidly. They demonstrated a high level of competence in furthering their clients' interests while respecting the public interest by ensuring that the proceedings were thorough, expeditious, and efficient. I highly commend them.

Finally, the staff of the Inquiry put in long and often pressure-filled hours to support the hearings. Our two office staff in Walkerton, the court reporter, the court service officers, and the registrar deserve special mention for the many hours they regularly worked to ensure that the hearing proceeded in a timely way.

14.6 Public Access

All the hearings of the Walkerton Inquiry were, of course, open to the public.[49] For those unable to attend in person, the hearings in Walkerton were televised live on local cable television and rebroadcast elsewhere.[50] The broadcasts were so important that, on one occasion, we were forced to cancel a hearing day because the camera operators were snowed in. Members of the media were provided with a large room, which had a live feed from the hearing room, to assist their reporting of events, and a dedicated cadre of print and broadcast journalists served the public well in this regard.

The Commission's Web site proved very useful for making information available to the public. Among the materials accessible on the Web site were the transcripts of the hearings, lists of the Part 1 witnesses and exhibits, and all of the issue papers and submissions by the parties in Part 2. Measured by the number of visits, the Web site was a useful tool indeed.[51]

But even the Internet has its limits, and it was not feasible to post all of the materials generated for the Inquiry on our Web site. Instead, large numbers of documents were made available for public review at the Inquiry offices in Walkerton and Toronto. The documents included all the exhibits filed at the hearings, all public submissions and replies from the Inquiry, and most of the documents collected and scanned into our database.[52]

14.7 Closing Arguments

Closing arguments for Part 1 were held during eight hearing days from August 15 to 27, 2000. Specific dates and time limits were assigned for each party approximately two months in advance. Each party was afforded between

---

[49] The only exception was at the Walkerton community meetings in July 2000, as described in note 13, *supra*.

[50] I acknowledge the contribution of CPAC – the Cable Public Affairs Channel, Rogers Television, and, above all, Sautel Cable, for broadcasting the Inquiry's proceedings. Because of scheduling requirements, rebroadcasts of the hearings outside Walkerton were sometimes available only during the early hours of the morning. This generally limited access to these hearings to people who possessed (and were able to program) a video cassette recorder.

[51] The Web site, www.walkertoninquiry.com, averaged more than 200 visitors per day from August 2000 to October 2001.

[52] The public review was subject to any legal claims of privilege by the party who produced the documents and to the editing of personal information such as medical or financial information.

30 minutes and 6 hours for oral submissions, depending on the nature and scope of its interest or perspective. The order of submissions was set to begin with the two Walkerton community groups, followed by the parties whose primary interest was in Part 1A, and then those whose primary interest was in Part 1B. The final closing argument was made by counsel for the Chief Coroner.[53]

The government was given the option of delivering submissions in both Part 1A and Part 1B, in recognition of its wide-ranging role in the hearings and special interest in Part 1B. As a result, the government made submissions early in the order, and again toward the end, with the condition that it limit its second set of submissions to issues raised in Part 1B only.

The parties were required to submit written closing submissions two weeks in advance of oral argument. Copies of the submissions were then provided to each party to allow it to respond to others' written submissions during its oral presentation. Parties were also permitted to reply in writing to other parties' oral submissions. These responses were distributed, in turn, to the other parties.

Anticipating that detailed closing submissions would be very helpful to me, I recommended funding for the preparation of closing submissions for the parties with funding in Part 1. The amounts of recommended funding were for preparations ranging from 5 to 40 hours, which allowed for a review of transcripts and exhibits and other preparation. This was especially important for parties who were not present for significant portions of the hearings.

14.8 Appearances of Counsel

Commission counsel	Paul J.J. Cavalluzzo
	Brian Gover
	Freya J. Kristjanson
	Juli A. Abouchar
	Rachel Young
Concerned Walkerton Citizens	Paul Muldoon
	Theresa A. McClenaghan

---

[53] Sample closing-submission documents appear in Appendices L(i), L(ii), L(iii), and L(iv).

	Richard D. Lindgren
	Ramani Nadarajah
Walkerton Community Foundation	Richard J. Trafford
	F. Stephen Finch, Q.C.
Province of Ontario	Frank N. Marrocco, Q.C.
	Glenn A. Hainey
	K. Lynn Mahoney
	John E. Callaghan
	Peter E. Manderville
	James M. Ayres
	Keith L. Geurts
	R. Reena Lalji
	Derek A. Vanstone
Chief Coroner of Ontario	Eleanore A. Cronk
	Rochelle S. Fox
	David E. Gruber
Municipality of Brockton, David Thomson, James Bolden, and Steven D. Burns	Roderick M. McLeod, Q.C. John L. Martin J. Bruce McMeekin Kimberly T. Brand
Walkerton Public Utilities Commission and Public Utilities Commissioners	Kenneth Prehogan Kerry A. Boniface
Injured Victims Group	Scott Ritchie, Q.C.
	Denise M. Bolohan
Dr. Murray McQuigge	Earl A. Cherniak, Q.C.
	Douglas A. Grace
	Elizabeth K.P. Grace
Ontario Farm Environmental Coalition	Harold G. Elston
Environmental Coalition (CEDF Coalition)	Louis C. Sokolov
	A. Benson Cowan

Environmental Coalition (SLDF Coalition)	Douglas G. Chapman
Environmental Coalition (ALERT/ Sierra Club Coalition)	Paul G. Vogel
Allan Buckle	Gregory L. Lafontaine Paul K. Burstein
Stan Koebel	William M. Trudell Joseph Di Luca
Frank Koebel	Michael J. Epstein David Miller Hugh Griffith-Jones
Bargaining Agents Coalition (OPSEU) and James Schmidt	Ian J. Roland Donald Eady Robert Centa Timothy G.M. Hadwen
Bargaining Agents Coalition (PEGO)	Gary Hopkinson
Bargaining Agents Coalition (CUPE) and Robert McKay	Mark Wright Doug LeFaive
Association of Municipalities of Ontario	Douglas T. Hamilton Craig S. Rix
Board of Health of the Bruce-Grey-Owen Sound Health Unit	John H.E. Middlebro'
Association of Local Public Health Agencies	James A. LeNoury J. Paul Wearing
Energy Probe Research Foundation	Mark O. Mattson Craig Parry
Philip Bye	James T. Hunt

John Earl	Brian D. Barrie
Willard Page	John F. Rook, Q.C.
	Stephen Lamont
Larry Struthers	Dianne Saxe
Michelle Zillinger	Linda C. McCaffrey, Q.C.
Heather Auld and Dr. Andrea Ellis	Ian R. Dick
Robert Deakin	D. Fletcher Dawson
Brenda Elliot	Robert P. Armstrong, Q.C.
	Julia E. Holland
Environmental Commissioner of Ontario	David McRobert
Don Hamilton	Janet L. Bobechko
	Ralph Cuervo-Lorens
Goff Jenkins	Paul J. French
Dr. Richard Schabas	Julian Porter, Q.C.
Ellen Schwartzel	David Estrin
JoAnn Todd	T. Anthony Ball

14.9 Appreciation

I owe an enormous debt of gratitude to many people who helped with Part 1 of this Inquiry. It was only when I began to compile the list of those I wish to acknowledge in this Report that I realized just how many people had made significant contributions during the past 18 months. I want to formally recognize those who have been most deeply involved in the hearings and in the preparation of this report.

I start with commission counsel: Paul Cavalluzzo, Brian Gover, and Freya Kristjanson. They performed their duties with great skill, professionalism and, importantly, with the balance that is essential to the role of a commission counsel in a public inquiry. They were ably assisted by associate counsel Juli Abouchar and Rachel Young, and by a team of junior lawyers: Bay Ryley, Nimali Gamage, Niru Kumar, Michael Lunski, Rebecca Cutler, Robert Rishikof, and Moira Calderwood.

I want to express my appreciation to the Royal Canadian Mounted Police for the support the force provided to the Inquiry. Commission counsel were helped by three investigators from the RCMP: Inspector Craig Hannaford, Constable Mark Bolduc, and retired Staff Sergeant Don Glinz. Sergeant Don Clark and Corporal Ron Rimnyak of the RCMP provided important technical assistance with computer searches. The Inquiry's information system, which was crucial to processing a large number of documents, was set up and managed by Paul Coort and Grant Goldrich, and serviced by Ward Mousseau. Wayne Scott, formerly of the MOE, provided helpful assistance regarding government documents. The webmaster for the Inquiry web site was Djordje Sredojevic.

Special mention must go to Gus Van Harten, my Executive Assistant, who helped me in every way imaginable. The purpose of the Inquiry was greatly enhanced by thorough media coverage. Peter Rehak, the media consultant, was invaluable in facilitating media involvement. Ronda Bessner made an important contribution by helping me analyze the evidence and prepare the report. John Eerkes-Medrano, Brian Grebow, and Riça Night assisted with editing and formatting and did their work in a professional and timely manner.

I am grateful to those who were involved with the administration of the Inquiry: David Henderson, the Chief Administrator, and Kathleen Genore, the Financial Manager. The staff in the Walkerton office worked long hours, sometimes under enormous pressure. Nicole Caron and Deborah Harper gained the admiration of everyone associated with the Inquiry. The staff in the Toronto office – Anne MacLean, who helped set up the office, and the three secretaries who under great pressure typed the report, Pat Hall, Irene Urbanavicius, and Abbie Adelman – were thorough, careful, and very patient.

Joyce Ihamaki, the Registrar, performed her duties efficiently, keeping track of hundreds of exhibits and always helping to ensure that the parties and witnesses felt as comfortable as possible throughout the hearings. The court reporters, Wendy Warnock and Carol Geehan, the court services officers, and the television crew all contributed to enabling the hearings to proceed in a timely and effective manner.

The Government of Canada assisted the Inquiry in several respects. Health Canada, and in particular Dr. Andrea Ellis, provided expert evidence and advice to commission counsel in preparing the epidemiological evidence. Heather Auld of the Atmospheric Science Division of Environment Canada also gave evidence and was most helpful with her professional advice.

I would like to thank the various experts who were retained by the Commission and who in one way or another contributed to the work of Part 1 of the Inquiry.[54] Here I include Dr. Robert Gillham, Dr. Peter Huck, Dr. Pierre Payment, Dr. Michael Goss, Dr. Andrew Simor, Dr. Ken Howard, and Dr. Steven Hrudey. Experts called with the assistance of the Chief Coroner of Ontario, Dr. James Brunton, Dr. Lesbia Smith, and Dr. Brian Steele, also provided valuable assistance. The independent assessor, Mark Orkin, Q.C., performed his duties thoroughly and efficiently.

In planning the Inquiry, I spoke to a number of former commissioners of public inquiries, including The Honourable Rosalie Abella, The Honourable Charles Dubin, Q.C., The Honourable Fred Kaufman, Q.C., The Honourable Horace Krever, The Honourable Donald Macdonald, and The Honourable Sydney Robins, Q.C.; further, my counsel spoke with a number of former commission counsel, including Robert Armstrong, Q.C., Marlys Edwardh, Patricia Jackson, Mark Sandler, Fred von Veh, Q.C., and Douglas Worndl. The Walkerton Inquiry was greatly assisted by their advice.

Finally, I would like to thank my colleagues on the Court of Appeal for Ontario, especially Chief Justice Roy McMurtry, for their advice and support.

I have commented on the contribution of counsel for the parties and the press earlier in this chapter.

To everyone who helped out, I express my sincere appreciation and hope that they found the experience as rewarding as I did.

---

[54] I will specifically acknowledge those who assisted in the Part 2 process in the Part 2 report.

Chapter 15   Summary of Recommendations

The following is a compilation of recommendations that I have made in two chapters of this report. The recommendations are related to the findings I have reached in Part 1 of this Inquiry. Many are adopted from recommendations made by the Chief Coroner of Ontario in his closing submissions in Part 1.

In the Part 2 report, I will be making comprehensive recommendations relating to all aspects of the drinking water system in Ontario, including the protection of drinking water sources; the treatment, distribution, and monitoring of drinking water; the operation and management of water systems; and the full range of functions involved in the provincial regulatory role. The recommendations included in this report are not intended to be comprehensive and will fit into and form part of the broader framework being recommended in the Part 2 report. As such, many of the recommendations will be expanded upon in the Part 2 report.

Recommendation 1
The *Health Protection and Promotion Act* should be amended to require boards of health and the Minister of Health, acting in concert, to expeditiously fill any vacant Medical Officer of Health position with a full-time Medical Officer of Health.

Recommendation 2
Random assessments should be conducted on a regular basis by the Minister of Health, or his or her delegate, pursuant to the *Health Protection and Promotion Act*, of public health boards in Ontario to ensure their compliance with the Mandatory Health Programs and Services Guidelines of the Public Health Branch. Further, the Public Health Branch or the Minister of Health's delegate should continue to track, on an annual basis, trends in non-compliance by public health boards in Ontario, in order to assess whether altered programs and services guidelines are required and whether resourcing allocations by the Province of Ontario require adjustment to ensure full compliance.

Recommendation 3
The role of the local Medical Officers of Health and health units in relation to public health issues concerning treated and untreated municipal water systems, should be clarified and strengthened. In particular, clarification is required as to whether local Medical Officers of Health are required to

implement a proactive approach to responding to adverse drinking water sample test results upon receiving notification of those results.

Recommendation 4

Written guidance – developed in cooperation with Medical Officers of Health and the MOE – should be provided to Medical Officers of Health by the Public Health Branch. It should include steps to be taken by Medical Officers of Health upon receipt of MOE inspection reports and adverse drinking water sample test results.

Recommendation 5

Regular meetings should be scheduled between the local MOE office and local health unit personnel to discuss public health issues, including issues related to waterworks facilities as documented in MOE inspection reports. Any affected operator or laboratory should be invited to attend the meeting.

Recommendation 6

Upon the implementation by the MOE of the Integrated Divisional System (management information system), access to it should be made available to local health units and, where appropriate, to the public. This should include access to profiles of municipal water systems, and data concerning adverse drinking water quality sample test results, as included in that database.

Recommendation 7

The Public Health Branch should develop a Boil Water Protocol – a written protocol outlining the circumstances in which a boil water advisory or a boil water order could and should be issued. I will be commenting on the government's current draft proposal in the Part 2 report.

Recommendation 8

The Boil Water Protocol should be developed by the Public Health Branch in consultation with Medical Officers of Health, municipalities, and the MOE. The Boil Water Protocol should provide guidance concerning an effective communications strategy for the dissemination of a boil water advisory or order.

Recommendation 9

The MOE should develop criteria for identifying "groundwater under the direct influence of surface water."

Recommendation 10

The MOE should maintain an information data system that includes all relevant information arising from an approval application process – in particular, information relating to the quality of source water and relevant details from expert reports and tests.

Recommendation 11

The MOE should require continuous chlorine and turbidity monitors for all groundwater sources that are under the direct influence of surface water or that serve municipal populations greater than a size prescribed by the MOE.

Recommendation 12

All Certificates of Approval should be limited to a specific period of time, probably five years, and be subject to a renewal process that considers the current circumstances, including recent indicators of water quality. Conditions should be added as required.

Recommendation 13

The MOE's inspections program for municipal water systems should consist of a combination of announced and unannounced inspections. The inspector may conduct unannounced inspections when he or she deems it appropriate, and at least once every three years, taking into account such factors as work priority and planning, time constraints, and the record of the operating authority.

Recommendation 14

The MOE should develop and make available to all MOE inspectors a written direction or protocol, for both announced and unannounced inspections:

- outlining the specific matters to be reviewed by an inspector in preparing for the inspection of a water system;

- providing a checklist of matters that an inspector is required to review, as well as matters that it may be desirable to review, during an inspection of a water system; and

- providing guidance concerning those matters to be discussed with the operator of a water system during an inspection.

Recommendation 15

As a matter of policy, inspections of municipal water systems, whether announced or unannounced, should be conducted at least annually. The government's current program for annual inspections should be continued.

Recommendation 16

There should be a legal requirement that systems with significant deficiencies be inspected at least once per year. Ontario Regulation 459/00, also known as the Drinking Water Protection Regulation, should be amended to require that an inspection be conducted within one year of any inspection that discloses a deficiency as defined in the regulation. In this regard, deficiencies include any failure to comply with the treatment, monitoring, or testing requirements, or with specified performance criteria, set out in the regulation or in the accompanying drinking water standards.

Recommendation 17

The government should ensure that adequate resources are provided to ensure that these inspections are thorough and effective.

Recommendation 18

Copies of MOE inspection reports should be provided to the manager of the water system, the members of the operating authority, the owner of the water system, the local Medical Officer of Health, the MOE's local office, and the MOE's Approvals Branch.

Recommendation 19

The MOE should establish and require adherence to time lines for the preparation and delivery of inspection reports and operator responses, and for the delivery of interim status reports regarding remedial action.

Recommendation 20

The government should require all water system operators, including those who now hold certificates voluntarily obtained through the grandparenting process, to become certified through examination within two years, and to be periodically recertified.

Recommendation 21

The materials for water operator course examinations and continuing education courses should emphasize, in addition to the technical requirements necessary for performing the functions of each class of operator, the gravity of the public health risks associated with a failure to treat and/or monitor drinking water properly, the need to seek appropriate assistance when such risks are identified, and the rationale for and importance of regulatory measures designed to prevent or identify those public health risks.

Recommendation 22
The government should amend Ontario Regulation 435/93 to define "training" clearly, for the purposes of the 40 hours of annual mandatory training, with an emphasis on the subject matter described in Recommendation 21.

Recommendation 23
The government should proceed with the proposed requirement that operators undertake 36 hours of MOE-approved training every three years as a condition of certification or renewal. Such courses should include training in emerging issues in water treatment and pathogen risks, emergency and contingency planning, the gravity of the public health risks associated with a failure to treat and/or monitor drinking water properly, the need to seek appropriate assistance when such risks are identified, and the rationale for and importance of regulatory measures designed to prevent or identify those public health risks.

Recommendation 24
The MOE should inspect municipal water systems regularly for compliance with Ontario Regulation 435/93, enforce the regulation strictly, and follow up when non-compliance is found in order to ensure that operators meet certification and training standards.

Recommendation 25
The MOE should proceed expeditiously to complete the design and implementation of the management information system now under development (that is, the Integrated Development System, or IDS). That system should include the capacity for the creation and maintenance over time, in electronic form, of water system operator profiles consisting of any hydrogeological or other consultant's report relating to the water system; relevant operator chlorine residual measurements; past inspection reports; drinking water test results for a reasonable period; all operator responses to inspection reports; and all applicable Certificates of Approval, Permits

to Take Water (PTTW), Field and Director's Orders, occurrence reports, and information concerning the safety and security of public water sources and supplies.

Recommendation 26
A full needs assessment for training should be undertaken for MOE technical staff, and a component of that assessment should focus on communal drinking water.

Recommendation 27
The MOE, on the basis of the needs assessment, should develop and maintain both introductory and advanced mandatory courses for environmental officers pertaining to communal drinking water systems. These courses should emphasize science and technology, including all matters that could present a risk to public health and safety; emerging pathogen risks; existing, new, and emerging treatment technologies; the limits of particular technologies; and the proper interpretation and application of government regulations, guidelines, and policies.

Recommendation 28
The MOE should devote sufficient resources to technical training to allow the ministry to meet the challenges outlined in its "Human Resources Business Plan and Learning Plan for Fiscal Year 2000–2001."

PETER REHAK

The Inquiry hearing room Trillium Court, Walkerton.

PETER REHAK

Billboard for meetings with the Walkerton community, July 2000.

An aerial view of Well #5 and the surrounding area.

Well #5 in September 2000 after it was taken out of service.

Stan Koebel, Walkerton's water manager
in May 2000

Frank Koebel, foreman of the Walkerton
PUC in May 2000

David Thomson, Mayor of the
Municipality of Brockton, which
includes Walkerton

Michael Harris
Premier of Ontario

Dave Patterson, Assistant Director,
Public Health, Bruce-Grey-Owen Sound
Health Unit

Dr. Andrea Ellis, an epidemiologist with
Health Canada's Public Health Branch,
who heads the Federal department's
Outbreak Response and Issues
Management Section. Dr. Ellis testified at
the Inquiry and helped Inquiry staff with
the investigation of the causes of the
Walkerton outbreak.

Expert Panel: Dr. Robert Gillham, hydrogeologist; Dr. Peter Huck, water treatment engineer; and Dr. Pierre Payment, environmental microbiologist

Dr. Murray McQuigge,
Medical Officer of Health,
Bruce-Grey-Owen Sound Health Unit

Dennis R. O'Connor, Commissioner,
The Walkerton Inquiry

Paul Cavalluzzo, Lead Commission
counsel, The Walkerton Inquiry

Brian Gover, Commission counsel,
The Walkerton Inquiry

Freya Kristjanson, Commission counsel,
The Walkerton Inquiry

PETER REHAK

The media room at the Inquiry hearings in Walkerton on June 29, 2001.

PETER REHAK

While the hearings in Walkerton were under way, Commissioner O'Connor also held town hall meetings in nine Ontario municipalities. In each community he toured the water treatment facilities. Here, he is being briefed at a water treatment plant in Ottawa. The plant visits and town halls were a component of the Part Two Report which deals with the future safety of Ontario's drinking water.

During pauses in the hearings in Walkerton, Commissioner O'Connor presided over a series of public meetings with experts and parties with standing. These were aimed at the broader water safety and management issues dealt with in the Part Two report. In the photo, Gordon Miller, Ontario's Environmental Commissioner, presenting at a public hearing at Metro Hall in Toronto.

The Inquiry's town hall meeting in Thunder Bay, hosted by the Fort William First Nation, one of the nine town hall meetings held across the province.

Appendices

ORDER IN COUNCIL

APPENDIX A

Ontario
Executive Council
Conseil des ministres

Order in Council
Décret

On the recommendation of the undersigned, the Lieutenant Governor, by and with the advice and concurrence of the Executive Council, orders that:

Sur la recommandation du soussigné, le lieutenant-gouverneur, sur l'avis et avec le consentement du Conseil des ministres, décrète ce qui suit :

A number of people have died or became ill in circumstances where Escherichia coli bacteria have been found in the water supply in that part of The Corporation of the Municipality of Brockton formerly known as the Town of Walkerton.

Under the *Public Inquiries Act*, R.S.O. 1990, c. P. 41, the Lieutenant Governor in Council may, by commission, appoint one or more persons to inquire into any matter of public concern, if the inquiry is not regulated by any special law and if the Lieutenant Governor in Council considers it desirable to inquire into that matter.

The Lieutenant Governor in Council considers it desirable to inquire into the following matters of public concern. The inquiry is not regulated by any special law.

Therefore, pursuant to the *Public Inquiries Act*:

Establishment of the Commission

1. A commission shall be issued effective June 13, 2000, appointing the Honourable Dennis R. O'Connor as a commissioner.

Mandate

2. The commission shall inquire into the following matters:

    (a) the circumstances which caused hundreds of people in the Walkerton area to become ill, and several of them to die in May and June 2000, at or around the same time as Escherichia coli bacteria were found to be present in the town's water supply;

    (b) the cause of these events including the effect, if any, of government policies, procedures and practices; and

    (c) any other relevant matters that the commission considers necessary to ensure the safety of Ontario's drinking water,

    in order to make such findings and recommendations as the commission considers advisable to ensure the safety of the water supply system in Ontario.

O.C./Décret
1170/ 2000

2

3. The commission shall perform its duties without expressing any conclusion or recommendation regarding the civil or criminal liability of any person or organization. The commission, in the conduct of its inquiry, shall ensure that it does not interfere with any ongoing criminal investigation or criminal proceedings, if any, relating to these matters.

4. The commission shall complete this inquiry and deliver its final report[s] containing its findings, conclusions and recommendations to the Attorney General who shall make such report[s] available to the public.

5. The commission may make recommendations to the Attorney General regarding funding to parties who have been granted standing, to the extent of the party's interest, where in the commission's view, the party would not otherwise be able to participate in the inquiry without such funding.

6. Part III of the *Public Inquiries Act* applies to the inquiry and the commission conducting it.

Resources

7. Within an approved budget, the commission may retain such counsel, staff, investigators and expert advisers as it considers necessary in the performance of its duties. They shall be paid at rates of remuneration and reimbursement approved by Management Board of Cabinet. They shall be reimbursed for reasonable expenses incurred in connection with their duties in accordance with Management Board of Cabinet Directives and Guidelines.

8. The commission may obtain such other services and things as it considers necessary in the performance of its duties within an approved budget. The commission shall observe Management Board of Cabinet's Directives and Guidelines and other applicable government policies when it obtains services or things.

9. All ministries, Cabinet Office, the Premier's Office, and all boards, agencies and commissions of the government of Ontario shall assist the commission to the fullest extent so that the commission may carry out its duties.

Recommended _____   Concurred _____
               Attorney General   Chair of Cabinet

Approved and Ordered ___JUN 1 3 2000___   _____
                          Date   Lieutenant Governor

LIST OF PARTIES

APPENDIX B (1)

THE WALKERTON INQUIRY

Ontario

LA COMMISSION
D'ENQUÊTE WALKERTON

List of Parties in Part 1A

Party	Standing
Concerned Walkerton Citizens*	Full standing
Walkerton Community Foundation*	Full standing
Province of Ontario	Full standing
Office of the Chief Coroner	Full standing
Town of Walkerton	Full standing
Walkerton PUC/Commissioners Richard Field and Jim Kieffer*	Full standing/Limited to matters relating to their personal or official involvement
Injured Victims Group	Limited to the impact of the contamination upon them
Dr. Murray McQuigge	Limited to public health issues
OFEC*	Limited to farming and agricultural issues
Environmental Coalition - ALERT/ Sierra Club only*	Limited to environmental issues relating to farming and agriculture

David Thomson	Limited to matters relating to his personal or official involvement; shared cross-examination with Town where common interest
Party	*Standing*
James Bolden	Limited to matters relating to his personal or official involvement; shared cross-examination with Town where common interest
Steven Burns	Limited to matters relating to his performance of water-related engineering functions for the Town; shared cross-examination with Town where common interest
Allan Buckle*	Limited to his personal interests
Stan Koebel*	Limited to matters relating to his performance in his role as Manager of the PUC
Frank Koebel*	Limited to matters relating to his performance in his role as Foreman of the PUC
Bargaining Agents Coalition (OPSEU, CUPE Local 255, PEGO)	Special standing; limited to issues affecting municipal, public sector, and provincial government employees.
AMO	Special standing
Environmental Coalition (ALERT/ Sierra Club Coalition, Canadian Environmental Defence Fund/ Pollution Probe Coalition, Sierra Legal Defence Fund Coalition)	Special standing (except as noted above)

* denotes recommendation for full or partial funding

List of Parties in Part 1B

Party	*Standing*
Concerned Walkerton Citizens*	Full standing
Walkerton Community Foundation*	Full standing
Province of Ontario	Full standing
Office of the Chief Coroner	Full standing
Town of Walkerton	Full standing
Walkerton PUCommission/ Commissioners Richard Field and Jim Kieffer*	Full standing/Limited to matters relating to their personal or official involvement
AMO*	Limited to the interests of municipalities
Dr. Murray McQuigge	Limited to public health issues; shared cross-examination with Health Unit/ ALPHA where common interest
BGOSHU/ALPHA	Limited to public health issues; shared cross-examination with Dr. McQuigge where common interest
OFEC*	Limited to farming and agricultural issues
Environmental Coalition* (ALERT/ Sierra Club Coalition, Canadian Environmental Defence Fund/ Pollution Probe Coalition, Sierra Legal Defence Fund Coalition)	Full standing

Party	*Standing*
Energy Probe Research Foundation*	Limited to the issue of whether private ownership of the water system would have made a difference to what happened in Walkerton
Bargaining Agents Coalition* (OPSEU, CUPE Local 255, PEGO)	Limited to issues affecting municipal, public sector, and provincial government employees. (CUPE Local 255 and PEGO may have limited separate standing – see below)
CUPE Local 255	Separate standing where there is a conflict within the Bargaining Agents Coalition due to different perspective for the Walkerton PUC employees as opposed to provincial employees
PEGO*	Separate standing on issues of decredentialization
David Thomson	Limited to matters relating to his personal or official involvement
James Bolden	Limited to matters relating to his personal or official involvement
Steven Burns	Limited to matters relating to his performance of water-related engineering functions for the Town
Allan Buckle*	Limited to his personal interests
Stan Koebel*	Limited to matters that affect his substantial and direct personal interest
Frank Koebel*	Limited to matters that affect his substantial and direct personal interest

*denotes recommendation for full or partial funding

LIST OF WITNESSES

APPENDIX B (II)

THE WALKERTON INQUIRY **LA COMMISSION D'ENQUÊTE WALKERTON**

Ontario

List of Witnesses in Part 1

Name	*Position*	*Date Testified*
Dr. Karen Acheson	Supervising Regional Coroner for South Georgian Bay	October 31, 2000
Diana Adams	Walkerton resident	January 16, 2001
Carol Antle	Education and Training Team Leader, Provincial Planning Environmental Services Branch, Ministry of Municipal Affairs and Housing	June 19, 2001
Heather Auld	Meteorologist and Climatologist, Environment Canada	January 15, 2001
Doug Barnes	Assistant Deputy Minister of Integrated Environmental Planning Division, Ministry of the Environment	June 5, 2001
Nigel Bellchamber	Commissioner of Finance and Administration, City of London; Member of the Executive Committee and Board of Directors of Association of Municipalities of Ontario	June 4 & 6, 2001

Name	*Position*	*Date Testified*
James Bolden	Former Mayor of Walkerton (1980-1984, 1988-1998)	November 28 & 29, 2000
Michael Brodsky	Former Chief of Environmental Microbiology and Microbiological Support Services for the Ministry of Health, Laboratory Services Branch (1981 to 1999)	May 7 & 8, 2001
Daniel Brown	Golder Associates Ltd., Hydrogeologist; Former Hydrogeologist for the Ministry of the Environment (1979-1987)	July 19, 2001
Dr. James Brunton	Head, Division of Infectious Diseases, University Health Network, Mount Sinai Hospital; Member of Office of the Chief Coroner's Expert Panel	November 1, 2000
Allan Buckle	Employee, Walkerton Public Utilities Commission	December 5, 2000
Janusz Budziakowski	Specialist, Application Evaluation Section of the Water and Waste Water Unit, Environmental Assessment and Approvals Branch, Ministry of the Environment	November 8, 2000
Steve Burns	President, B.M. Ross and Associates Ltd., Engineering Consultant	November 9 & 10, 2000 January 17 & 18, 2001

Name	*Position*	*Date Testified*
Phillip Bye	District Supervisor, Owen Sound District Office, Ministry of the Environment	October 25, November 13 & 14, 2000, June 20 & July 3, 2001
Russell Calow	Vice-President, Sales and Marketing, Lakefield Research Limited	July 30, 2001
Donald Carr	Senior Program Engineer, Quality Improvement Section of Water Policy Branch, Ministry of the Environment	May 10, 2001
Andre Castel	Former Assistant Deputy Minister, Corporate Mgmt. Division, Ministry of the Environment (1987 to 1997)	May 15 & 16, 2001
Daniel Cayen	Director, Environmental Partnerships Branch, Ministry of the Environment; Manager of Policy, Policy Development Branch (Sept. 1995 to mid-1997); Liaison between Ministry of the Environment and Red Tape Commission (Sept. 1995 to Nov. 1997); Administered Provincial Water Protection Fund (from June 1998).	May 17 & June 6, 2001
Max Christie	Manager, Napanee Water & Sewage Utility; President, Ontario Municipal Water Association	June 7, 2001

Name	*Position*	*Date Testified*
Larry Clay	Director, Municipal Support Services Branch, Ministry of Municipal Affairs and Housing; Former Manager, Who Does What Secretariat, Ministry of Municipal Affairs and Housing (1996)	June 4, 2001
Stella Couban	Legal Services Branch, Ministry of the Environment, Kingston	July 4, 2001
Dr. Colin D'Cunha	Chief Medical Officer of Health of Ontario & Director of Public Health Branch, Ministry of Health	June 28, 2001
Robert Deakin	A&L Canada Laboratories East, Inc., Laboratory Manager	October 18, 2000
Dr. Helen Demshar	Former Director, Ministry of Health Laboratory Services Branch (1990-1998)	May 7 & 8, 2001
Ellen Dentinger	Secretary, Walkerton Public Public Utilities Commission	Statement of Anticipated Evidence (Ex. 249) filed February 27, 2001
Richard Dicerni	Former Deputy Minister, Ministry of the Environment (1992 to June 1995)	May 14, 2001
Brian Donaldson	Senior Policy Advisor, Ministry of Municipal Affairs and Housing	June 19, 2001

Name	*Position*	*Date Testified*
John Earl	Environmental Officer, Owen Sound District Office, Ministry of the Environment	October 30 & 31, 2000
Kent Edwards	General Manager, Windsor Utilities Commission; President and CEO, Enwin Utilities	June 5, 2001
Hon. Brenda Elliott	Minister of Intergovernmental Affairs; Former Minister of Environment & Energy (June 1995 to August 1996)	June 26, 2001
Dennis Elliott	Inspector, B. M. Ross and Associates Ltd.	January 16, 2001
Dr. Andrea Ellis	Section Head of Outbreak Response and Issue Management, Health Canada	January 11, 2001
Marc Ethier	Senior Operations Manager, Ontario Clean Water Agency	October 17, 2000, January 18 & 19, 2001
Richard Field	Former Commissioner, Walkerton Public Utilities Commission (1997 to 2000)	November 27, 2000
John Fleming	Deputy Minister of Community and Social Services; former Deputy Minister of the Environment (October 1997 to December 1998)	Statement of Anticipated Evidence (Ex. 347) filed May 29, 2001

Name	*Position*	*Date Testified*
Carmen Gauthier	Former Director of Fiscal Planning & Information, Ministry of the Environment (1997-April 2001); currently seconded to the Assistant Deputy Minister's office, Corporate Management Division, Ministry of the Environment	May 15 and 16, 2001
Brian Gildner	Human Resources Organisational Development Consultant, Ministry of the Environment; Policy Advisor to the Operator Certification Programme (1993 to 1999)	April 26 and June 7, 2001
Jack Gillespie	General Manager, CKNX radio, Wingham	January 18, 2001
Dr. Robert Gillham	Industrial Research Chair in Groundwater Remediation, University of Waterloo (May 1997 to present); Professor, Earth Sciences, University of Waterloo (July 1986 to present); Member of the Commission's Expert Panel	February 28, March 1 and July 19, 2001
Dr. Michael Goss	Chair of Land Stewardship, University of Guelph	February 27, 2001
Ian Gray	Technical Advisor for Barenco, Inc.; Former District Manager, Barrie District Office, Ministry of the Environment (1997-1999)	July 30, 2001

Name	Position	Date Testified
William Gregson	Former Manager of Certificate Approval Review Section, Environmental Assessment and Approvals Branch, Ministry of the Environment (1990-1993, 1999-2001); Former Acting Director, Approvals Branch, Ministry of the Environment (June 1998 – Sept 1999); Former Assistant Director, Approvals Branch, Ministry of the Environment (July 1993 – June 1998)	March 6 and 7, 2001
Carl Griffith	Assistant Deputy Minister, Operations Division, Ministry of the Environment; Former Assistant Deputy Minister, Corporate Management Division, Ministry of the Environment (January 1997 to January 2000)	May 15 and 16, 2001
Janice Hallahan	Secretary, Walkerton Public Utilities Commission	November 15, 2000
Kristen Hallett	Paediatrician, shared office with Dr. Ewen Porter, Owen Sound; Consultant Paediatrician at the Grey-Bruce Regional Health Centre (also referred to as Owen Sound Hospital)	January 17, 2001
Donald Hamilton	Environmental Officer, Owen Sound District Office, Ministry of the Environment	November 7 and 8, 2000

Name	*Position*	*Date Testified*
Hon. Michael Harris	Premier of Ontario (June 26, 1995 to present)	June 29, 2001
Tim Hawkins	Lineman, Walkerton Public Utilities Commission	Statement of Anticipated Evidence (Ex. 248) filed February 27, 2001
Dale Henry	Manager of Human Toxicology and Air Standards, Standards Development Branch, Ministry of the Environment; Former Manager of Drinking Water, Waste Water and Watershed Standards, Ministry of the Environment (December 1993 – June 1998); Former Manager of Drinking Water, Waste Water and Watershed Standards, Ministry of the Environment (July 1998 – July 2000)	May 10, 2001
Don Herman	Employee (Backhoe operator) Walkerton Works Department and Walkerton Public Utilities Commission	Statement of Anticipated Evidence (Ex. 247) filed February 27, 2001
Grant Hopcroft	City of London, Deputy City Solicitor; Former London City Councillor (1994-1997)	June 4, 2001
Ed Houghton	President and CEO, Collingwood Utility Services Corporation	November 28, 2000

Name	Position	Date Testified
Dr. Ken Howard	Professor of Hydrogeology, University of Toronto; University of Toronto Groundwater Research Group	October 16, 2000
Dr. Peter Huck	Professor of Civil Engineering and Chair in Water Treatment of the Natural Sciences and Engineering Research Council of Canada, University of Waterloo; Member of the Commission's Expert Panel	October 16, 2000, February 28 and March 1, 2001
Dr. Alexander Hukowich	Medical Officer of Health, Haliburton, Kawartha & Pine Ridge District Health Unit	July 4, 2001
William Hutchison	Former Environmental Officer, Owen Sound District Office, Ministry of the Environment (1975 to 1999)	November 9, 2000
Randy Jackiw	Director of Resources Management, Ontario Ministry of Agriculture, Food, and Rural Affairs	June 18 and 19, 2001
Jim Jackson	Solicitor, Legal Services Branch, Ministry of the Environment	March 6 and 7, 2001
Jim Janse	Former Director of Southwest Region, Operations Division, Ministry of the Environment (December 1994 to January 2000)	May 9, 2001

Name	*Position*	*Date Testified*
Goff Jenkins	Ontario Drinking Water Specialist, Drinking Water, Waste Water and Watershed Standards Section of the Standard Development Branch, Ministry of the Environment	May 10 and 29, July 4, 2001
Nancy Johnson	Former Investigations and Enforcement Branch investigator, Ministry of the Environment (1985 to 1998); Formerly, an active member of the Ontario Public Service Employees' Union and the Ministry Employee Relations Committee (1994 to 1998)	April 24 and 25, 2001
Chris Johnston	Employee, Spills Action Centre, Ministry of the Environment	December 6, 2000
Frances Johnston	Manager of Capital Finance, Municipal Finance Branch, Ministry of Municipal Affairs and Housing	June 6, 2001
Dr. Renu Joshi	Canadian Association for Environmental Analytical Laboratories Assessor; Group Leader, Department of Microbiology, Region of Durham	May 8, 2001
James Kieffer	Former Chair, Walkerton Public Utilities Commission (1992 to November 2000)	November 16, 2000
Frank Koebel	Foreman, Walkerton Public Utilities Commission	December 6 and 7, 2000

Name	*Position*	*Date Testified*
Stan Koebel	Manager, Walkerton Public Utilities Commission	December 18, 19 and 20, 2000
Patricia Lachmaniuk	Former Group Leader of Drinking Water Quality Program, Environmental Monitoring and Reporting Branch, Ministry of the Environment (January 1997 to October 2000)	May 10, 2001
Stein Lal	Former Deputy Minister of the Environment (March 21, 1999 to March 31, 2001); Former Deputy Minister of Consumer and Commercial Relations (1995 to March 21, 1999); Deputy Solicitor General (1998 and 1993)	Statement of Anticipated Evidence (Ex. 348) filed May 29, 2001
Kevin Lamport	Investigator, Investigations and Enforcement Branch, Ministry of the Environment, Owen Sound	July 3, 2001
Rosalyn Lawrence	Director of Electricity Policy Branch, Energy Policy Division, Ministry of Energy, Science and Technology	June 4, 2001
Dr. Charles LeBer	Senior Veterinary Consultant and Head of the Food Safety and Safe Water Unit, Disease Control Service, Public Health Branch, Ministry of Health	May 8 and 9, 2001

Name	*Position*	*Date Testified*
Tim Little	Manager, Drinking Water Regulation Implementation Team for Central Region, Ministry of the Environment (Sept. 2000 to present); Supervisor in the Assistant Director's Office, Southwest Region, Ministry of the Environment (1996 to present)	April 17 and 18, May 9, 2001
Jim Mahoney	Regional Programs Co-ordinator, Eastern Region, Ministry of the Environment; Presently seconded to Drinking Water Regulation Implementation Team	April 17 and 18, May 9, 2001
Wendy McLeod Dale	Daughter of Former Walkerton Public Utilities Commission Manager Ian McLeod	Statement of Anticipated Evidence (Ex. 251) filed February 27, 2001
Cecil Erv McIntyre	Senior Advisor to Strategic Alternatives; Former Executive Director (i.e., Assistant Deputy Minister), Ministry of the Environment (1986 to 1990) and Former Head of Approvals Branch, Ministry of the Environment (1983-1986)	March 6 and 7, 2001
Robert McKay	Employee, Walkerton Public Utilities Commission	December 4, 2000

Name	*Position*	*Date Testified*
Dr. Murray McQuigge	Medical Officer of Health, Bruce Grey Owen Sound Health Unit; Clinical Adjunct Professor, Faculty of Medicine, University of Western Ontario	January 8, 9 and 10, 2001
Jim Merritt	Former Assistant Deputy Minister of Operations, Ministry of the Environment (February 1997- December 1998); Acting Deputy Minister, Ministry of the Environment (December 1998 to March 1999)	April 12, 2001
Bev Middleton	Certified Public Health Inspector, Bruce Grey Owen Sound Health Unit	February 26, 2001
Don Moore	Administrator, Brucelea Haven Long-term Care Facility	January 16, 2001
Roger Moyer	Senior Municipal Advisor and Planner, Ministry of Municipal Affairs and Housing	June 4, 2001
Brian Nixon	Director of Land Use Policy, Ministry of the Environment; Director of Water Policy Branch, Integrated Environmental Planning Division, Ministry of the Environment	June 6, 2001
Daniel Ormerod	Employee, MDS Laboratory Services Inc.	October 23, 2000

Name	Position	Date Testified
Willard Page	Former District Manager, Owen Sound District Office, Ministry of the Environment (1974 to 1997)	November 1 and 2, 2000
Garry Palmateer	President, GAP EnviroMicrobial Services, Inc.	October 19 & 23, 2000, February 26 and 27, 2001
David Patterson	Former Assistant Director of Health Protection, Bruce Grey Owen Sound Health Unit (1989 to November 30, 2000); Certified Public Health Inspector	December 11, 13 and 14, 2000
Nicholas Paul	Manager of Direct Services, Laboratory Services Branch, Ministry of Health	May 7 and 8, 2001
Dr. Pierre Payment	Environmental Microbiologist; Member of the Commission's Expert Panel	February 28 and March 1, 2001
Percy Pletsch	Former farmer	November 8, 2000
David Powell	Supervisor, Walkerton Wastewater Treatment Plant	June 20, 2001
Richard Radford	Chief Administrative Officer, Municipality of Brockton	June 5 and 6, 2001
Catherine Marie Reich	Walkerton resident	May 29, 2001
Gordon Robertson	Investigator, Investigations and Enforcement Branch, Sarnia, Ministry of the Environment	April 24 and 25, 2001

Name	*Position*	*Date Testified*
Mary Robinson-Ramsay	Former Walkerton Councillor (One year term - 1998)	December 1, 2000
Dr. Richard Schabas	Former Chief Medical Officer of Health of Ontario & Director of Public Health Branch, Ministry of Health (1987-1997)	June 25, 2001
James Schmidt	Certified Public Health Inspector, Bruce Grey Owen Sound Health Unit (Walkerton)	December 15, 2000
Dr. Bern Schnyder	Director of Laboratory Services Branch, Ministry of the Environment	May 7, 2001
Ellen Schwartzel	Research and Resource Centre Co-ordinator, Office of the Environmental Commissioner of Ontario	May 18, 2001
Robert Shaw	Regional Director, Central Region, Operations Division, Ministry of the Environment (June 1999 to present); Project Manager of Approvals Reform (Spring 1996 to Fall 1996)	March 8, April 17, 18, 19 and 23, 2001
Dr. Andrew Simor	Head of Department of Microbiology, Sunnybrook and Women's College Health Sciences Centre; Professor, Department of Laboratory Medicine and Pathobiology at the, University of Toronto; Physician	February 26, 2001

Name	*Position*	*Date Testified*
Vivian Slater	Secretary, Walkerton Public Utilities Commission	Statement of Anticipated Evidence (Ex. 250) filed February 27, 2001
Dan Smith	Superintendent, Walkerton Jail	January 17, 2001
Dr. Lesbia Smith	Former Unit Head and Senior Medical Consultant, Environmental Health & Toxicology Unit, Public Health Branch, Ministry of Health (1990 to March 2000); Member of the Office of the Chief Coroner's Expert Panel	November 1, 2000
Dr. Brian Steele	Paediatric Nephrologist, Children's Hospital, Chedoke-McMaster, Hamilton; Dean, Post Graduate Medical Education, McMaste University; Member of the Office of the Chief Coroner's Expert Panel	November 1, 2000
Hon. Norman Sterling	Minister of Consumer and Business Services; Former Minister of Environment (August 1996 to June 1999)	June 27, 2001
Linda Stevens	Deputy Minister, OPS Restructuring and Associate Secretary of Cabinet; Former Deputy Minister, Ministry of the Environment and Energy (July 1995 to August 1997)	May 28 and 29, 2001

Name	Position	Date Testified
Larry Struthers	Environmental Officer, Owen Sound District Office, Ministry of the Environment	October 26, 2000
David Thomson	Mayor of The Municipality of Brockton	November 29 and 30, December 1, 2000
JoAnn Todd	Managing Director, Maple Court Villa, Retirement Home	January 15, 2001
Dianne Waram	Director of Patient Care, South Bruce-Grey Health Centre	January 19, 2001
Keith West	Director, Waste Management Policy Branch, Ministry of the Environment	June 20, 2001
Julian Wieder	Acting Program Manager of Investigations and Enforcement Branch, Ministry of the Environment; Implementation Team Member, Integrated Divisional System	April 24 and 25, 2001
Sheila Willis	Former Assistant Deputy Minister, Operations Division, Ministry of the Environment (May 1992 to February 1997); Former President, CEO and Chair of the Board, Ontario Clean Water Agency (June 1998 to March 2000)	Statement of Anticipated Evidence (Ex. 346) filed May 29, 2001
Dr. Richard Wilson	Director, Canadian Association for Environmental Analytical Laboratories	May 8, 2001

Name	Position	Date Testified
Dr. Mark Winfield	Special Advisor to the Pembina Institute for Appropriate Development; Former Director of Research, Canadian Institute for Environmental Law and Policy (May 1992 to March 2000)	May 28, 2001
Dr. Stephen Worthington	Hydrogeology Consultant	July 19, 2001
Michelle Zillinger	Environmental Officer, Barrie District Office, Ministry of the Environment; Former Environmental Officer, Owen Sound Area Office, Ministry of the Environment (October 1997 to September 1999)	November 6 and 7, 2000, July 3, 2001

LETTER TO THE RESIDENTS OF WALKERTON

APPENDIX C (1)

THE WALKERTON INQUIRY   **LA COMMISSION
D'ENQUÊTE WALKERTON**

Ontario

June 22, 2000

To The Residents of Walkerton:

I have been appointed as Commissioner of a public inquiry to inquire into the circumstances which caused illness and deaths of residents in the Walkerton area in May and June, 2000, at or around the same time as E. Coli bacteria were found to be present in the town's water supply. The Commission will investigate the cause of these events including the effect, if any, of government policies, procedures and practices. The terms of reference are broad and I am confident we will be able to fully explore all of the reasons that contributed to this tragedy. The Commission will also look into other matters necessary to ensure the safety of Ontario's drinking water.

The Commission considers it important that we hear from the residents in Walkerton about the impact of this tragedy on their lives and the town as a whole. One of the ways to do this is for the Commission to have a relatively informal initial community meeting with the residents. I would like to have such a meeting as early as possible. It seems to me that understanding the scope of the impact upon the residents will provide a foundation for further inquiries. However, my staff and I are concerned that we not intrude unduly on the residents at a time when they may not be ready to speak publicly about the impact of these events. If it turns out that the residents feel that it is now too early for a community meeting, we will hold it at a later date.

In the meantime, I suggest the week of July 20, 2000 for the initial community meeting. What I would like to do at the initial meeting is to hear from individual residents with respect to the impact this matter has had upon them. Individuals will be given the opportunity to come forward and speak about the impact this has had on their lives or to express their thoughts in writing.

At the more formal hearings, which will begin this Fall, the Commission will look into the causes that gave rise to the tragedy. Prior to those hearings, those wishing to apply for standing will be given an opportunity to do so. Participation in the earlier community hearing will not foreclose participation in the more formal hearings to take place this Fall.

The Commission will contact a number of local groups, including the Concerned Citizens of Walkerton, the Walkerton & District Chamber of Commerce, and the Brockton Town Council, about the proposal for a community meeting. We are interested in obtaining a broad range of views from the community. You may express your views on the desirability of and the format for a community meeting either through your connection with one of these groups or by writing the Commission at the following address:

> Commission of the Walkerton Inquiry
> The Dundas/ Edward Centre
> 180 Dundas Street West, 22nd Floor, Box 26
> Toronto, Ontario
> M5G 1Z8

The Commission hopes to announce a 1-800 phone number by next week. If you prefer you may wait to contact us by phone at that time.

In making this proposal for a community meeting, I recognize that some of the residents have sought legal advice about what has occurred. I do not want to interfere with that process in any way. However, it would be most useful to the Commission to hear from the people directly affected at the type of informal community meeting I have discussed above.

This letter is being distributed on Canada News Wire (http://www.newswire.ca) and will be published in the Walkerton Herald Times, the Owen Sound Sun Times and the London Free Press in an effort to ensure that it comes to the attention of all of the residents of Walkerton.

Yours very truly,

Dennis O'Connor

List of Walkerton Presenters

Appendix C (ii)

THE WALKERTON INQUIRY

Ontario

LA COMMISSION
D'ENQUÊTE WALKERTON

List of Presenters

Walkerton Community Meetings
Knights of Columbus Hall

Wednesday, July 26 (Public meetings)

- Pastor Beth Conroy

- Bruce Davidson, Concerned Walkerton Citizens

- Veronica Davidson, Concerned Walkerton Citizens

- Stephanie Smith, Concerned Walkerton Citizens

- Ron Leavoy, Concerned Walkerton Citizens

- Janet Glasspool, Bluewater District School Board

- Marg Becker

Thursday, July 27 (Public meetings)

- Pat Griffin

- Jane Hardwick

- Jim Zettel, Ontario English Catholic Teachers Association

- Vernon Batte, Bruce Grey Catholic District School Board

- Marilyn Maxey

- Rick Lekx, Walkerton & District Chamber of Commerce

- Gary McGregor, Walkerton & District Chamber of Commerce

- Elaine Crilly

- Arthur Jefford

- Bob White

- Pauline Gay

- Kathy McCarrel, Citizens Actively Representing Environmental Security

- Anna Errington

Thursday, July 27 (Site visits)

- Arena/ Community centre, 290 Durham W., Walkerton

- Hillside Motel, Dave and Fran Hill, 15 Maple St., Walkerton

- Residence of Jacques Gosselin, 108 Thomas Street, Walkerton

- Valumart (Mike Murphy, Manager), 1200 Yonge St. S., Walkerton

Friday, July 28 (Public meetings)

- Philip Holmes

- Betty Borth

- Lois Steffler

- Wayne Zuber

- John Finlay

- Marie Faelker

- Yvonne Carol

- Elaine Crilly (Continued)

Friday, July 28 (Private meetings*)

- A.B.

- A.C.

- A.D., A.E. and A.F.

- A.G.

- A.H. and A.I.

- A.J. and A.K.

- A.L.

- A.M.

- A.N., A.O. and A.P.

- A.Q.

- A.R.

- A.S. and A.T.

- A.U.

- A.W., A.Y., A.Z., A.X., B.A. and B.N.

- B.B. and B.C.

- B.D.

- B.E. and B.F.

- B.G.

- B.H. and B.I.

- B.J. and B.K.

- B.L. and B.M.

Saturday, July 29 (Public meetings)

- Lorraine Wells

- Adolf Stengel

- Bruce Davidson

Saturday, July 29 (Private meetings*)

- B.Q.

- B.R. and B.R.

- B.U., B.V. and B.W.

*Names have been replaced with initials to protect the identity of the participants.

RULES OF PROCEDURE AND PRACTICE

APPENDIX D (I)

THE WALKERTON INQUIRY LA COMMISSION
D'ENQUÊTE WALKERTON

Ontario

Rules of Procedure and Practice

1. Commission proceedings will be divided into two phases. Part I will focus on:

    (a) The circumstances which caused hundreds of people in the Walkerton area to become ill and several of them to die, in May and June 2000, at or around the same time as *E. coli* bacteria were found to be present in the Town's water supply; and

    (b) The cause of these events including the effect, if any, of government policies, procedures and practices.

    Part II of the Inquiry is concerned with the policy issues related to ensuring the safety of Ontario's drinking water. It will involve a review of a broad range of factors which impact on the safety of drinking water including a review of the public health, technological and management factors associated with the production, treatment and distribution of drinking water as well as the contamination of source waters, where the primary focus will be on microbial contaminants capable of causing acute threats to public health.

A.   Rules - Part I

I.   General

2. Public hearings will be convened in Walkerton to address issues related to Part I of the Inquiry.

3. All parties and their counsel shall be deemed to undertake to adhere to these Rules, which may be amended or dispensed with by the Commission as it sees fit to ensure fairness. Any party may raise any issue of non-compliance with the Commissioner.

4. Insofar as it needs to gather evidence, the Commission is committed to a process of public hearings. However, applications on some aspects of its mandate may be made to proceed *in camera* in accordance with section 4 of the *Public Inquiries Act*. Such applications should be made in writing at the earliest possible opportunity pursuant to the provisions of Section III(vi) below.

II. Standing for Part I

5. Commission counsel, who will assist the Commission throughout the Inquiry and are to ensure the orderly conduct of the Inquiry, have standing throughout the Inquiry. Commission Counsel have the primary responsibility for representing the public interest at the Inquiry, including the responsibility to ensure that all interests that bear on the public interest are brought to the Commissioner's attention. Persons or groups may be granted standing by the Commissioner if the Commissioner is satisfied that they:

(a) are directly and substantially affected by Part I of the Inquiry in which event the party may participate in accordance with section 5(1) of the *Public Inquiries Act*; or

(b) represent clearly ascertainable interests and perspectives that are essential to his mandate in Part I, which the Commissioner considers ought to be separately represented before the Inquiry, in which event the party may participate in a manner to be determined by the Commissioner.

6. The Commissioner will determine those parts of the Inquiry in which a party granted standing may participate.

7. The term "party" is used to convey the grant of standing and is not intended to convey notions of an adversarial proceedings.

8. Counsel representing witnesses called to testify before the Commission may participate during the hearing of such evidence as provided in these Rules.

III. Evidence

(i) *General*

9. In the ordinary course Commission counsel will call and question witnesses who testify at the Inquiry. Counsel for a party may apply to the Commissioner to lead a particular witness's evidence in-chief. If counsel is granted the right to do so, examination shall be confined to the normal rules governing the examination of one's own witness.

10. The Commission is entitled to receive any relevant evidence which might otherwise be inadmissible in a court of law. The strict rules of evidence will not apply to determine the admissibility of evidence.

11. Parties are encouraged to provide to Commission counsel the names and addresses of all witnesses they feel ought to be heard, and to provide to Commission counsel copies of all relevant documentation, including statements of anticipated evidence, at the earliest opportunity.

12. Commission counsel have a discretion to refuse to call or present evidence.

13. When Commission counsel indicate that they have called the witnesses whom they intend to call in relation to a particular issue, a party may then apply to the Commissioner for leave to call a witness whom the party believes has evidence relevant to that issue. If the Commissioner is satisfied that the evidence of the witness is needed, Commission counsel shall call the witness, subject to Rule 9.

(ii)   *Witnesses*

14. Anyone interviewed by or on behalf of Commission counsel is entitled, but not required, to have one personal counsel present for the interview to represent his or her interests.

15. Witnesses will give their evidence at a hearing under oath or affirmation.

16. Witnesses may request that the Commission hear evidence pursuant to a subpoena in which case a subpoena shall be issued.

17. Witnesses who are not represented by counsel for parties with standing are entitled to have their own counsel present while they testify. Counsel for a witness will have standing for the purposes of that witness' testimony to make any objections thought appropriate.

18. Witnesses may be called more than once.

(iii)   *Order of Examination*

19. The order of examination will be as follows:

    (a)   Commission counsel will adduce the evidence from the witness. Except as otherwise directed by the Commissioner, Commission counsel are entitled to adduce evidence by way of both leading and non-leading questions;

    (b)   parties granted standing to do so will then have an opportunity to cross-examine the witness to the extent of their interest. The order of cross-examination will be determined by the parties having standing and if they are unable to reach agreement, by the Commissioner;

    (c)   counsel for a witness, regardless of whether or not counsel is also representing a party, will examine last, unless he or she has adduced the evidence of that witness in-chief, in which case there will be a right to re-examine the witness; and

(d)   Commission counsel will have the right to re-examine.

20.   Except with the permission of the Commissioner, no counsel other than Commission counsel may speak to a witness about his or her evidence while the witness is giving any part of his or her evidence. Commission counsel may not speak to any witness about his or her evidence while the witness is being cross-examined by other counsel.

(iv) *Access to Evidence*

21.   All evidence shall be categorized and marked P for public sittings and, if necessary, C for sittings *in camera.*

22.   One copy of the P transcript of evidence and a list of P exhibits of the public hearings will be available to be shared by counsel for the parties. The transcript will be kept in an office outside the hearing room. A disk version of the transcript or an additional copy may be ordered by anyone prepared to pay its cost.

23.   Another copy of the P transcript of the public hearings and a copy of P exhibits will be available to be shared by the media.

24.   Only those persons authorized by the Commission, in writing, shall have access to C transcripts and exhibits.

(v)   *Documents*

25.   The Commission expects all relevant documents to be produced to the Commission by any party with standing.

26.   Originals of relevant documents are to be provided to Commission counsel upon request.

27.   Counsel to parties and witnesses will be provided with documents and information, including statements of anticipated evidence, only upon giving an undertaking that all such documents or information will be used solely for the purpose of the Inquiry and, where the Commission considers it appropriate, that its disclosure will be

further restricted. The Commission may require that documents provided, and all copies made, be returned to the Commission if not tendered in evidence. Counsel are entitled to provide such documents or information to their respective clients only on terms consistent with the undertakings given, and upon the clients entering into written undertakings to the same effect. These undertakings will be of no force regarding any document or information once it has become part of the public record. The Commission may, upon application, release any party in whole or in part from the provisions of the undertaking in respect of any particular document or other information.

28. Documents received from a party, or any other organization or individual, shall be treated as confidential by the Commission unless and until they are made part of the public record or the Commissioner otherwise declares. This does not preclude the Commission from producing a document to a proposed witness prior to the witness giving his or her testimony, as part of the investigation being conducted, or pursuant to Rule 27.

29. Subject to Rule 27 and to the greatest extent possible, Commission counsel will endeavour to provide in advance to both the witness and the parties with standing relating to issues with respect to which the witness is expected to testify, documents that will likely be referred to during the course of that witness' testimony, and a statement of anticipated evidence.

30. Parties shall at the earliest opportunity provide Commission counsel with any documents that they intend to file as exhibits or otherwise refer to during the hearings, and in any event shall provide such documents no later than the day before the document will be referred to or filed.

31. A party who believes that Commission counsel has not provided copies of relevant documents must bring this to the attention of Commission counsel at the earliest opportunity. The object of this rule is to prevent witnesses from being surprised with a relevant document that they have not had an opportunity to examine prior to their testimony. If Commission counsel decides the document is not relevant, it shall not be produced as a relevant document.

This does not preclude the document from being used in cross-examination by any of the parties. Before such a document may be used for the purposes of cross-examination, a copy must be made available to all parties by counsel intending to use it not later than the day prior to the testimony of that witness, subject to the discretion of the Commissioner.

(vi) *Confidentiality*

32. If the proceedings are televised, applications may be made for an order that the evidence of a witness not be televised or broadcast.

33. Without limiting the application of section 4 of the *Public Inquiries Act,* any witness who acquired hemolytic uremic syndrome ("HUS"), or who is related to someone who acquired HUS or died as a result of the Walkerton water contamination, shall upon application to the Commissioner be granted "Confidentiality". For the purposes of the Inquiry, Confidentiality shall include the right to have his or her identity disclosed only by way of non-identifying initials, and, if the individual so wishes, the right to testify before the Commission in private. Subject to the discretion of the Commissioner, only the Commissioner, Commission staff and counsel, counsel for parties with standing, counsel for the witness who has been granted Confidentiality and media representatives may be present during testimony being heard in private.

34. A witness who is granted Confidentiality will not be identified in the public records and transcripts of the hearing except by non-identifying initials. Any reports of the Commission using the evidence of witnesses who have been granted Confidentiality will use non-identifying initials only.

35. Media reports relating to the evidence of a witness granted Confidentiality shall avoid references that might reveal the identity of the witness. No photographic or other reproduction of the witness shall be made either during the witness' testimony or upon his or her entering and leaving the site of the Inquiry.

36. Any witness who is granted Confidentiality will reveal his or her name to the Commission and counsel participating in the Inquiry in order that the Commission and counsel can prepare to question the witness. The Commission and counsel shall maintain confidentiality of the names revealed to them. No such information shall be used for any other purpose either during or after the completion of the Commission's mandate.

37. Any witness who is granted Confidentiality may either swear an oath or affirm to tell the truth using the non-identifying initials given for the purpose of the witness's testimony.

38. All parties, their counsel and media representatives shall be deemed to undertake to adhere to the rules respecting Confidentiality. A breach of these rules by a party, counsel to a party or a media representative shall be dealt with by the Commissioner, as he see fit.

B.   Rules - Part II

I.   General

39. Because of the policy nature of the issues, Part II will not proceed by way of evidentiary hearings. Instead, in order to make its work accessible and to provide an opportunity for public participation, the Commission will proceed in three phases:

(a) It will arrrange for the preparation of papers (the "Commission Papers") from recognized experts on a broad range of relevant topics. These Commission Papers will, among other things, describe current practices in Ontario; describe current practices in other jurisdictions; identify difficulties; and review alternative solutions.

(b) Any person or group with an interest in the subject matter of Part II of the Inquiry is invited to make submissions in writing (the "Public Submissions") to the Commission about any matter relevant to Part II including the matters reviewed in the Commission Papers.

(c)   The Commission will convene public meetings (the format of which may vary) to discuss the matters raised in the Commission Papers. The participants in the public meetings may include representatives of those parties who have been granted standing in Part II of the Inquiry and, at the Commissioner's discretion, any other person or group whom the Commission concludes will contribute to the process.

(i)   *Commission Papers*

40.   The Commission has established a Research Advisory Panel (the "Panel"). The role of the Panel will be to assist the Commission in identifying the subject matters of the Commission Papers and who should be retained to prepare them. The Panel will also monitor the progress of Commission Papers and provide advice and direction to the various authors as needed.

41.   The Commission will set and publish a deadline by which all Commission Papers must be completed and the Papers will thereafter be published, in draft, on the Commission's web-site.

(ii)   *Public Submissions*

42.   Any interested person may make a Public Submission, in writing, to the Commission dealing with any matter related to Part II of the Inquiry including responses to any matter raised in the Commission Papers.

43.   The Commission will set and publish a deadline by which all Public Submissions must be received and the Public Submissions will be made available for public review either on the Commission's web-site or at the Commission's offices.

(iii) *Public Meetings*

44. Once all Public Submissions have been reviewed by the Commission, the Commission will convene a number of informal public meetings relating to the major topics comprising Part II of the Inquiry. The format of the public meetings will be tailored to the topics discussed and may vary among meetings. The public meetings may include the Commissioner, the relevant authors of Commission Papers, representatives of the parties which have been granted standing in Part II of the Inquiry, relevant members of the Panel and, based upon the contents of the Public Submissions received, other persons invited by the Commission, whom the Commissioner concludes would contribute to the discussion.

45. The public meetings shall be recorded.

II. Standing for Part II

46. Persons or groups may be granted standing by the Commissioner for Part II of the Inquiry if the Commissioner is satisfied that:

(a) They are sufficiently affected by Part II of the Inquiry; or

(b) They represent clearly ascertainable interests and perspectives that are essential to his mandate in Part II, which the Commissioner considers ought to be separately represented before the Inquiry. In order to avoid duplication, groups of similar interest are encouraged to seek joint standing.

47. Because of the different nature of the proceedings in the two phases of the Inquiry, the nature and extent of a party's participation will be different in Part II than in Part I. In addition to the ability of all members of the public to receive Commission Papers and make Public Submissions, those persons or groups who have been granted standing in Part II shall be entitled to participate directly in the public meetings.

III Access to Evidence and Documents

48. Rules 21 to 31 regarding access to evidence and documents apply to Part II of the Inquiry.

C. Funding

This information will be available on our website at www.walkertoninquiry.com the week of August 14, 2000.

Amendment to Rules
of Procedure and Practice

Appendix D (II)

THE WALKERTON INQUIRY

Ontario

**LA COMMISSION
D'ENQUÊTE WALKERTON**

October 12, 2000

Notice to Parties with Standing in Part I

Amendment to Rules of Procedure and Practice

Rules 20 and 22 of the Rules of Procedure and Practice are replaced by the following amended Rules:

20. Except with the permission of the Commissioner, no counsel other than Commission counsel may speak to a witness about the evidence that he or she has given until the evidence of such witness is complete. Commission counsel may not speak to any witness about his or her evidence while the witness is being cross-examined by other counsel.

22. Electronic copies of the P transcript of evidence will be provided to parties by the court reporter. Hard copies of the transcript may be ordered by anyone prepared to pay the cost. One copy of the P transcript and the P exhibits of the public hearings will be made available for public review.

LETTER RE: STANDING

APPENDIX D (III)

THE WALKERTON INQUIRY

Ontario

**LA COMMISSION
D'ENQUÊTE WALKERTON**

August 18, 2000

Re: Standing for Part I of the Walkerton Inquiry

In response to a number of requests, we set out below further information with respect to standing for Part 1 of the Walkerton Inquiry. The form of participation which may be granted to an applicant with Part 1 standing may vary.

Parties who obtain standing under s. 5(1) of the *Public Inquiries Act* shall be granted full standing with respect to the matters that are relevant to their interests.

It is presently contemplated that the participation of a party with full standing will include:

1. Access to documents collected by the Commission subject to the Rules of Practice and Procedure;

2. Advance notice of documents which are proposed to be introduced into evidence;

3. Advance provision of statements of anticipated evidence;

4. Seat at counsel table;

5. Opportunity to suggest witnesses to be called by Commission counsel, failing which an opportunity to apply to the Commissioner to lead the evidence of a particular witness;

6.   Right to cross-examine witnesses on matters relevant to the basis upon which standing was granted;

7.   Opportunity to review transcripts at Commission office (if you want to obtain your own copy, you must purchase it); and,

8.   Right to make closing submissions.

Parties who are granted standing on a basis other than under s. 5(1) of the *Public Inquiries Act* may be granted a form of special standing. It is presently contemplated that the participation of a party with special standing will include any or all of the following:

1.   Numbers 1, 2, 3, 5, 7 and 8 above; and

2.   Opportunity to suggest areas for examination of a certain witness by Commission counsel, failing which an opportunity to request leave to examine the witness on such areas.

Parties may be granted standing, full or special, for all or a portion of Part 1 of the Inquiry.

In your application for standing, you should indicate those areas and issues in Part 1 which you believe substantially and directly affect you, or with respect to which you have a clearly ascertainable interest or perspective and the reasons why your participation will enhance the work of the Commission.. You should also identify whether you are seeking full or special standing for all or a portion of Part 1, and the reasons supporting your request.

Please do not hesitate to call or e-mail me directly at Freya.Kristjanson@jus.gov.on.ca if you have any further questions or comments. We will continue to update our website at www.walkertoninquiry.com , and we encourage you to check the Legal Information and News Releases sections on a regular basis.

Yours truly,

Freya Kristjanson
Associate Commission Counsel
Walkerton Inquiry (416) 326-5568

PROCEDURAL GUIDELINES FOR PART IA

APPENDIX D (IV)

THE WALKERTON INQUIRY

Ontario

**LA COMMISSION
D'ENQUÊTE WALKERTON**

Outline of Procedural Guidelines for Part IA

The following is an outline of procedural guidelines, including a tentative outline of evidence and a tentative schedule, for Part IA of the Inquiry. It is intended to provide initial guidance to parties as to the format of Part IA of the Inquiry. It represents a preliminary outline and is subject to change.

I.   Participation in Part IA

A.   Standing

The following is a list of parties with standing in Part IA, limited according to their interests or perspectives with respect to the subject matter of Part IA.

List of parties with standing in Part IA

Party	Limitations on participation in Part IA
Concerned Walkerton Citizens	Full standing.
Walkerton Community Foundation	Full standing.
Government of Ontario	Full standing.
Chief Coroner of Ontario	Full standing.

Party	*Limitations on participation in Part IA*
Municipality of Brockton	Full standing.
Walkerton PUC	Full standing.
Dr. Murray McQuigge	Public health issues.
Injured Victims group	Issues relating to the impact of the contamination upon members of the group.
Ontario Farm Environmental Coalition	Issues relating to farming and agriculture.
Environmental Coalition	Environmental issues relating to farming and agriculture.
Mayor David Thomson	Matters relating to his personal or official involvement.
Former Mayor Jim Bolden	Matters relating to his personal or official involvement.
Steven Burns	Matters relating to his performance of water-related engineering functions for the Town.
Allan Buckle	Matters relating to his performance in his role as an employee of the PUC.
Stanley Koebel	Matters relating to his performance in his role as Manager of the PUC.
Frank Koebel	Matters relating to his performance in his role as Foreperson of the PUC.
Bargaining Agents Coalition	Special standing.
Environmental Coalition	Special standing (except as noted above).

Association of Municipalities   Special Standing.
of Ontario

B.   Attendance at hearings

All parties are free to attend the Inquiry hearings at any time. It is expected that parties will participate and receive funding only when the evidence comes within the scope of the issues for which they have been granted standing.

Parties granted standing under s.5(1) of the *Public Inquiries Act* are entitled to participate in the hearings to the extent that their substantial and direct interest is affected by the subject matter of the evidence to be called at any portion of the hearings.

Parties granted standing because they represent a clearly ascertainable interest or perspective which the Commissioner considers to be helpful in Part IA may participate in accordance with the Ruling on Standing and Funding. The Commissioner will exercise his discretion on the basis of whether he considers that a party's participation would be helpful with respect to the evidence that is being called at a particular time.

It is not anticipated that parties with special standing will need to participate in the Part IA hearings. As set out below, transcripts of the hearings will be made available to them. Unless the Commissioner directs otherwise, a party with special standing will not receive funding for attendance at the hearings.

C.   Outline of evidence

Attached to this letter is a tentative outline and order of the topics to be covered and the evidence to be called in Part IA. This represents a preliminary outline and order and is subject to change.

Any party who takes issue with the attached outline of evidence or the description of their standing should contact Commission counsel to attempt to kresolve the issue. If a party is not satisfied with the resolution provided by Commission counsel, the party may arrange a conference call with the Commissioner to make submissions.

In accordance with Rule 11 of the Rules of Procedure and Practice, parties may suggest to Commission counsel the names of additional witnesses to call in Part IA. In accordance with Rule 13, if Commission counsel does not call a proposed witness, the party may apply to the Commissioner for leave to call the witness. It is expected that parties will propose the names of additional witnesses to Commission counsel at or before the time that Commission counsel are calling witnesses addressing areas of the evidence to be considered by a proposed witness.

Commission counsel will write parties with limited standing under separate cover to indicate those parts of the hearings in which it is proposed they need to participate and will attempt, through discussions, to determine the extent of such participation. If a party is not satisfied with the resolution provided by Commission counsel, the party may arrange a conference call with the Commissioner to make submissions.

D.   Cross-examination

There are several parties with the same interest in each area of evidence. The enclosed outline of evidence is being circulated at an early date to enable counsel to approach the cross-examinations as efficiently as possible. It is expected that counsel for parties with standing with respect to a particular portion of Part IA will meet, where appropriate, to discuss the order and content of their cross-examinations so as to avoid repetition and delay. Where interests overlap, it is strongly suggested that one counsel take primary responsibility for the cross-examination. It is not necessary that all counsel cross-examine each witness. The Commissioner will intervene if necessary to prevent repetition.

E.   Transcripts

It is anticipated that parties will have access to non-expedited transcripts of the Part IA hearings on the Commission website. The Commission does not intend to pay the additional fee for an expedited transcript. Therefore, there will be an anticipated time delay of approximately two weeks after a hearing day before the transcript is posted. Parties may pay the additional fee to order an expedited transcript if desired. Absent special circumstances, expedited transcript fees are not included in government funding. It is noted that these guidelines amend Rule 22 of the Inquiry's Rules of Procedure and Practice.

Attached to this letter is a list of persons who made presentations during the Community Meetings held by the Inquiry in Walkerton from July 26 to 29, 2000. To protect their identity, the names of persons who participated in private meetings with the Commissioner have been replaced with initials. Copies of the transcripts of the Community Meetings, together with exhibits, are available for viewing at the Commission offices in Toronto at 180 Dundas Street West, 22nd Floor, or in Walkerton at 220 Trillium Court, Building 3, Unit 4. Copies of the transcripts may also be purchased by contacting: Brockton Reporting, P.O. Box 183, Walkerton, ON, N0G 2V0, (519) 881-1128 (tel), (519) 881-1961 (fax).

F. Funding

An independent assessor will be appointed to assess the accounts of those parties who have had applications for funding approved by the Attorney General following a recommendation by the Commissioner. Accounts should be submitted directly to the independent assessor who will forward them to the Attorney General for payment. Attached is a summary of Management Board guidelines for travel and associated expenses which counsel may refer to in making relevant claims for disbursements. Reference should also be made to the full guidelines available from the Ministry of the Attorney General. Other issues relating to funding, such as the appropriate designation of a party's counsel under the Attorney General's Hourly Fee Schedule, will be determined by the independent assessor. Contact information for the independent assessor will be posted on the Commission website after he or she has been appointed.

II. Production of documents

All parties, whether representing a party with full, limited or special standing, will receive a list of witnesses to be called, Statements of Anticipated Evidence and all documents which Commission counsel intend to put into evidence. Documents will normally be produced to parties in CD-Rom format. Parties will be responsible for printing hard copies of documents for their own purposes including for use in the hearing room. Parties are required to execute the enclosed the enclosed undertakings with respect to confidentiality before they may receive any such documents.

Statements of Anticipated Evidence and documents which Commission counsel intend to put into evidence will be produced on an ongoing basis. The Commission will endeavour to produce such documents one week before the evidence is called.

Any party will be able to view documents collected by the Commission at its offices in Toronto or in Walkerton. Interested parties should contact the appropriate office in advance to schedule an appointment.

If there are evidentiary issues which a party wishes to have addressed, counsel should speak to Commission counsel.

III. Tentative schedule

The following is a tentative schedule and is subject to change.

Tentative Schedule

Week of:	Hearing days:
October 16	Commence Part IA hearings: M-Th
October 23	M-Th
October 30	M-Th
November 6	M-Th
November 13	M-Th
November 20	Week off
November 27	M-F
December 4	M-F
December 11	M-F
December 18	M-Th (Break for Christmas)

Week of:	*Hearing days:*
December 25	Week off
January 1, 2001	Week off
January 8	M-F
January 15	M-F
January 22	If necessary, continue with Part IA until complete, then break
February 19	Commence Part IB hearings

During Part IB, the Inquiry will adjourn for March break during the weeks of March 12 and March 19.

The Commissioner proposes to sit from 10:00 a.m. to 1:00 p.m. and from 2:15 p.m. to 4:30 p.m. each day. These hours may be extended if necessary to maintain the proposed schedule for evidence. In addition, the Commissioner may decide, in order to maintain the proposed schedule, to sit on Fridays during the weeks of October 16 through November 13.

Any objections to these procedural guidelines should be raised with Commission counsel at the earliest opportunity. If a party is not satisfied with the resolution provided by Commission counsel, the party may arrange a conference call with the Commissioner to make submissions.

PROCEDURAL GUIDELINES FOR PART IB

APPENDIX D (V)

THE WALKERTON INQUIRY   **LA COMMISSION D'ENQUÊTE WALKERTON**

Ontario

Outline of Procedural Guidelines for Part IB

The following is an outline of procedural guidelines for Part IB of the Inquiry. Please find enclosed:

• an outline of evidence for Part IB,

• an updated outline of potential issues in Part IB, and

• a chart indicating anticipated participation in the Part IB hearings by parties with standing.

The enclosed documents are intended to provide guidance and to assist counsel in preparing for Part IB. They are, however, subject to change.

I.   Participation in Part IB

A.   Attendance at hearings

All parties are free to attend the Inquiry hearings at any time. It is expected that parties will participate and receive funding only when the evidence comes within the scope of the issues for which they have been granted standing.

Parties granted standing under s.5(1) of the *Public Inquiries Act* are entitled to participate in the hearings to the extent that their substantial and direct interest is affected by the subject matter of the evidence to be called at any portion of the hearings.

Parties granted standing because they represent a clearly ascertainable interest or perspective which the Commissioner considers to be helpful in Part IB may participate in accordance with the Ruling on Standing and Funding. The Commissioner will exercise his discretion on the basis of whether he considers that a party's participation would be helpful with respect to the evidence that is being called at a particular time.

The attached chart entitled "Anticipated Participation in Part IB Hearings" indicates to parties with limited standing those portions of the hearings in which it is proposed they need to participate. If a party is not satisfied with the scope of its participation as outlined in the chart, the party may raise the issue with Commission counsel. If a party is not satisfied with the resolution provided by Commission counsel, the party may arrange a conference call with the Commissioner to make submissions.

A number of parties have been designated as requiring to participate for specified witnesses only. Commission counsel intends to notify those parties in advance in circumstances where Commission counsel anticipates that the evidence of a particular witness will engage their interest or perspective. Parties will receive statements of anticipated evidence of all witnesses and will have access to the Inquiry transcripts. This should allow them to notify and discuss with Commission counsel whether they need to be present in the hearing room for a particular witness, or whether a particular witness for which the party was not present should be recalled.

B.   Cross-examination

It is expected that counsel for parties with standing with respect to a particular portion of Part IB will meet, where appropriate, to discuss the order and content of their cross-examinations so as to avoid repetition and delay. Where interests overlap, it is strongly suggested that one counsel take primary responsibility for the cross-examination. It is not necessary that all counsel cross-examine each witness. The Commissioner may suggest lead cross-examiners in appropriate circumstances and will intervene if necessary to prevent repetition.

II. Production of documents

All parties, whether representing a party with full, limited or special standing, will continue to receive statements of anticipated evidence and all documents which Commission counsel intend to put into evidence. Documents will normally be produced to parties in CD-Rom format. Parties will be responsible for printing hard copies of documents for their own purposes including for use in the hearing room.

Statements of anticipated evidence and documents which Commission counsel intend to put into evidence will be produced on an ongoing basis. The Commission will endeavour to produce such documents one week before the evidence is called.

Any party will be able to view documents collected by the Commission at its offices in Toronto or in Walkerton. Interested parties should contact the appropriate office in advance to schedule an appointment.

If there are evidentiary issues which a party wishes to have addressed, counsel should speak to Commission counsel.

III. Tentative schedule

The following is a tentative schedule for Part IB and is subject to change.

Tentative Schedule

Week of:	Hearing days:
March 5	Mon-Fri
March 12	Week off
March 19	Week off
March 26	Mon-Fri
April 2	Mon-Fri

Week of:	Hearing days:
April 9	Week off
April 16	Mon-Fri
April 23	Mon-Fri
April 30	Week off
May 7	Mon-Fri
May 14	Mon-Fri
May 21	Week off
May 28	Mon-Fri
June 4	Mon-Fri
June 11	Week off
June 18	Mon-Fri (if necessary)
June 25	Mon-Fri (if necessary)
July 2	Four weeks off
July 30	Closing submissions
August 6	Closing submissions

Any objections to these procedural guidelines should be raised with Commission counsel at the earliest opportunity. If a party is not satisfied with the resolution provided by Commission counsel, the party may arrange a conference call with the Commissioner to make submissions.

NOTICE OF STANDING HEARING

APPENDIX E (1)

THE WALKERTON INQUIRY

Ontario

LA COMMISSION D'ENQUÊTE WALKERTON

Notice of Hearing

Mr. Justice Dennis O'Connor has been appointed as the Commissioner of the Walkerton Inquiry. In Part I the Commission will inquire into the circumstances which caused hundreds of people in the Walkerton area to become ill, and several of them to die in May and June 2000, at or around the same time as *E. coli* bacteria were found to be present in the Town's water supply, and the cause of these events including the effect, if any, of government policies, procedures and practices. Part II of the Inquiry will focus on any other relevant matters that the Commission considers necessary to ensure the safety of Ontario's drinking water.

Applications by interested individuals and organizations for standing, funding, and rules governing the media in relation to both Part I and Part II of the Inquiry will be heard commencing at 10:00 a.m. on August 28, 2000 at 220 Trillium Court, Walkerton, Ontario. NO EVIDENCE WILL BE HEARD AT THIS TIME.

The criteria for standing in Part I and Part II of the Inquiry and the criteria for funding are set out in the Rules of Procedure and Practice which can be found at our website at www.walkertoninquiry.com or a copy can be obtained by contacting the Inquiry at the addresses and/or telephone numbers set out below.

Applications for standing should be made in writing and provide the following information:

(a) Whether standing is sought for Part I or Part II of the Inquiry; and

(b) A statement of how the applicant satisfies the criteria for standing set out in the Rules of Practice and Procedure.

Applications for funding should be made in writing and should provide the following information:

(a) A statement of how the applicant satisfies the criteria for funding set out in the Rules of Practice and Procedure. In demonstrating why an applicant would not otherwise be able to participate without such funding, the application may include financial statements and operating budgets and describe the number of members and membership fee structure. Applicants should also indicate whether they have contacted other groups or individuals to bring them into an amalgamated group, and the results of those contacts;

(b) A description of the purposes for which the funds are required, how the funds will be disbursed and how they will be accounted for;

(c) A statement of the extent to which the applicant will contribute its own funds and personnel to participate in the Inquiry; and

(d) The name, address, telephone number and position of the individual who will be responsible for administering the funds, and a description of the financial controls put in place to ensure that the funds are disbursed for the purposes of the Inquiry

Applications for standing and/or funding should be submitted to the Inquiry by delivering a copy either to our offices in Toronto or Walkerton at the addresses set out below or by e-mail at comments@walkertoninquiry.com by no later than 5:00 p.m. on Friday, August 23, 2000.

THE WALKERTON INQUIRY
180 Dundas Street West, 22nd Floor
Toronto, Ontario M5G 1Z8
Tel: (416) 326-4498
1-877-543-8598 (toll free)
Fax: (416) 327-8782
e-mail: comments@walkertoninquiry.com

RULING ON STANDING AND FUNDING

APPENDIX E (II)

THE WALKERTON INQUIRY

Ontario

LA COMMISSION
D'ENQUÊTE WALKERTON

Ruling on Standing and Funding

I. The Inquiry Process

I have been appointed by Order in Council 1170/2000 to conduct an inquiry into the following matters:

(a) the circumstances which caused hundreds of people in the Walkerton area to become ill, and several of them to die in May and June 2000, at or around the same time as *Esherichia coli* bacteria were found to be present in the town's water supply;

(b) the cause of these events including the effect, if any, of government policies, procedures and practices; and

(c) any other relevant matters that the commission considers necessary to ensure the safety of Ontario's drinking water.

I will be conducting the Inquiry in two parts. Part I will focus on the matters set out in paragraphs (a) and (b) of the Order in Council. Part I will be further divided into two sub-parts: Part IA and Part IB. Part IA will focus on the circumstances and causes of the *E. coli* contamination in the Walkerton water supply, other than those causes set out in paragraph (b) of the Order in Council. Part IB will address the effect, if any, of government policies, procedures and practices on the cause of these events.

I recognize that there will be some overlap in the issues to be considered in Parts IA and IB. Nevertheless, I consider the division of the Inquiry into these parts important for making my decisions on standing and funding. I will be flexible in allowing participation where the lines drawn would deny me the assistance which I consider important to a grant of standing.

In Part II of the Inquiry, I will be addressing the matters set out in paragraph (c) of the Order in Council.

A.   Part I Process

Part I will be conducted by way of public hearings to be held in Walkerton, at which witnesses will give evidence under oath or affirmation, and at which the witnesses will be examined and cross-examined. Parties with standing will make closing submissions at the end of Part I.

The Rules of Procedure and Practice which have been developed for Part I have been published on the Commission website at www.walkertoninquiry.com. These have been modelled on the rules used in other public inquiries. I thought that it would be useful to publish these Rules before the hearings on standing. However, if any party granted standing wishes to make submissions on the Rules, it should do so in writing by September 22, 2000. Any changes will be published on the Commission website. Parties granted standing should visit our website regularly for information on practical details and scheduling.

B.   Part II Process

Because of the policy nature of the issues, Part II will not proceed by formal evidentiary hearings. Instead, in order to make its work accessible and provide an opportunity for public participation, Part II will proceed in three phases. These three phases encompass Commission Papers, Public Submissions, and Public Meetings as discussed below. They will proceed concurrently with Part I.

(i)   *Commission Papers*

In the first phase, the Commission will arrange for the preparation of papers (the "Commission Papers") from recognized experts on a broad range of relevant topics. These Commission Papers will, among other things, describe current practices in Ontario, describe current practices in other jurisdictions, identify difficulties and review alternative solutions. A draft list of study topics has been published on the Commission website.

I have established a Research Advisory Panel (the "Panel"). The Panel will assist me in identifying the subject matter of the Commission Papers and who should be retained to prepare them. The Panel, under my direction, will also monitor the progress of Commission Papers and provide advice and direction to the various authors as needed. The Commission will set and publish a deadline by which all Commission Papers must be completed and the Papers will thereafter be published, in draft, on the Commission website.

(ii) *Public Submissions*

In the second phase, the Commission will invite any person or group with an interest in the subject matter of Part II of the Inquiry to make submissions in writing (the "Public Submissions") to the Commission about any matter relevant to Part II, including the matters reviewed in the Commission Papers. The Commission will set and publish a deadline by which all Public Submissions must be received. The Public Submissions will be made available for public review.

(iii) *Public Meetings*

In the final phase of Part II, I will convene a number of public meetings relating to the major topics comprising Part II of the Inquiry. The format of the public meetings will be tailored to the topics discussed and may vary among meetings.

I will preside over the public meetings. They may also include participation by the relevant authors of Commission Papers, representatives of those who have been granted standing in Part II and who in my view will make a contribution to the meeting, and selected members of the Research Advisory Panel. Based upon the Public Submissions received, I may invite other persons or groups whom I conclude would make a useful contribution to the discussions.

II. Standing and Funding

The Commission published a Notice of Hearing which invited interested parties to apply for standing. I received 47 applications for standing, some of them involving multiple individuals or organizations. The applications were heard in Walkerton from September 5 to 7, 2000.

A.   Part I Standing

There are two types of standing, full and special, in Part I. Both types may be specifically limited to those portions of the Inquiry that are relevant to the interests of the party which formed the basis for my decision to grant standing.

(i)   *Full Standing*

I have granted full standing in Part I to persons or groups who have demonstrated that they have a substantial and direct interest in the subject matter of the Inquiry pursuant to section 5(1) of the *Public Inquiries Act*, R.S.O. 1990, c.P.41 (the "Act"). In some cases I have also granted full standing, on a discretionary basis, even though the party does not have an interest under section 5(1). I have exercised this discretion on the basis of my assessment of the contribution that such a party will make to the Inquiry. In either case, I have limited full standing to those portions of the Inquiry that are relevant to the party's interests. Parties will be advised by Commission counsel when issues relevant to their interests will arise. Full standing will include:

1.   access to documents collected by the Commission subject to the Rules of Procedure and Practice;

2.   advance notice of documents which are proposed to be introduced into evidence;

3.   advance provision of statements of anticipated evidence;

4.   a seat at counsel table;

5.   the opportunity to suggest witnesses to be called by Commission counsel, failing which an opportunity to apply to me to lead the evidence of a particular witness;

6.   the opportunity to cross-examine witnesses on matters relevant to the basis upon which standing was granted;

7.   the opportunity to review transcripts at Commission offices (a copy of the transcript may be purchased from the court reporter);

8.   the opportunity to make closing submissions; and

9.   the opportunity to apply for funding to participate in Part I.

(ii) *Special Standing*

I have granted special standing in Part IA to some parties who have been granted full standing in Part IB. Even though these applicants do not have an interest in Part IA under s.5(1) of the Act, I consider that their involvement through special standing will be of assistance to me. Special standing will include:

1.   the matters listed under numbers 1, 2, 3, 5, 7, 8 and 9 above; and

2.   the opportunity to suggest areas for examination of a certain witness by Commission counsel, failing which an opportunity to request leave to examine the witness on such areas.

B.   Part II Standing

I have granted standing to persons or groups who in my view are sufficiently affected by Part II of the Inquiry or who represent clearly ascertainable interests and perspectives that I consider ought to be separately represented before the Inquiry. Standing for Part II of the Inquiry will involve:

1.   access to documents collected by the Commission which relate to Part II subject to the Rules of Procedure and Practice;

2.   the opportunity to make Public Submissions on any matter relevant to the Commission's mandate in Part II, including papers which respond to Commission Papers;

3.   the opportunity to participate directly in one or more public meetings where the Commissioner is of the view that such participation would make a contribution to the subject matter of the meeting; and

4.   the opportunity to apply for funding to participate in Part II.

C. Principles

(i) *Standing*

Before separately addressing each of the applications, I think it is useful to summarize the general principles that have guided my decisions on standing and funding.

- It is essential that the Inquiry be full and complete and that I consider all relevant information and a variety of perspectives on the issues raised in the Order in Council.

- Commission counsel will assist me throughout the Inquiry. They are to ensure the orderly conduct of the Inquiry and have standing throughout. Commission counsel have the primary responsibility for representing the public interest, including the responsibility to ensure that all interests that bear on the public interest are brought to my attention. Commission counsel do not represent any particular interest or point of view. Their role is not adversarial or partisan.

- Applicants are granted standing only for those portions of the Inquiry that are relevant to their particular interest or perspective.

- Parties may be granted special standing in Part IA, rather than full standing, in order to make the work of the Commission accessible to parties who do not have a substantial and direct interest in the subject matter of Part IA, but who nevertheless represent interests and perspectives that I consider to be helpful to my mandate. Those parties will be able to participate in the Inquiry in a meaningful way through the provision of documents, the opportunity to suggest evidence and the opportunity to make closing submissions.

- In order to avoid repetition and unnecessary delay, I have grouped certain applicants into coalitions, as discussed below. I have done this in situations where the applicants have a similar interest or perspective, where there is no apparent conflict of interest and where I am satisfied that the relevant interest or perspective will be fully and fairly represented by a single grant of standing to the parties as a group.

- In the event of a change in circumstances affecting a grant of standing, a party whose participation has been limited to a particular portion of the

Inquiry, who was granted special standing or who has been grouped into a single grant of standing, may apply for a change in its standing.

- Witnesses in Part I who are not represented by counsel for parties with standing are entitled to have their own counsel present while they testify. The witness may be represented by counsel for the purposes of his or her testimony and to make any objections thought appropriate.

I mentioned the formation of coalitions as one of the principles that has guided my decisions on standing. There are a large number of applicants with an interest or perspective that I consider important in Part I. Many of these share common interests and perspectives. In order to make Part I manageable, I have formed coalitions comprised of applicants whose interests and perspective coincide and who do not have a conflict of interest that would render a coalition unworkable.

In directing that applicants participate through a coalition I recognize that circumstances may develop that result in a coalition becoming unsuitable for a member of a coalition on one or more issues. With this in mind, I have provided for flexibility, allowing members to request separate standing should such a situation arise.

In my view the formation of flexible coalitions achieves a fair balance between the desire to have important interests and perspectives represented and the need to have an inquiry that is manageable. I am asking that the counsel and principals of applicants who have been joined in a coalition make all efforts to work within the coalition. Cooperation and reasonableness are essential. Even with coalitions, the hearings in some stages of Part I will be complex and may be protracted. In my view, the alternative of separate standing for everyone is simply not acceptable.

(ii)   Funding

The Order in Council provides that I may make recommendations to the Attorney General for funding for parties granted standing. To qualify for a funding recommendation, a party must be able to demonstrate that it would not be able to participate in the Inquiry without such funding. In addition, the party must have a satisfactory proposal as to the use it intends to make of the funds and how it will account for the funds.

In addition, I have considered the following:

- the nature of the party's interest and proposed involvement in the Inquiry;

- whether the party has an established record of concern for and a demonstrated commitment to the interest it seeks to represent;

- whether the party has special experience or expertise with respect to the Commission's mandate; and

- whether the party can reasonably be included in a group with others of similar interests.

At this time, I am not recommending payment for experts to be called by those with standing in Part I. The primary responsibility for calling experts lies with Commission counsel who will be open to suggestions from parties as to the types and names of experts to be called. Experts called by Commission counsel will be paid by the Commission.

The guidelines issued by the Attorney General for funding include the payment of counsel fees and disbursements. Disbursements for experts to assist counsel in preparing for cross-examination are not included in the guidelines.

I have decided not to make any recommendations for Part II funding at the present time although I anticipate that I will be doing so in the months to come. The Commission has published a list of proposed Commission Papers and welcomes suggestions for additions or changes. Parties with standing may suggest the names of experts to prepare papers, may offer to prepare some of the Commission Papers or may independently have papers prepared on subjects relevant to the Commission's mandate in Part II.

I anticipate that when the Commission Papers are published, parties with standing will respond with comments or criticism. At that time, I will consider applications for funding for the preparation of papers in response to Commission Papers and for attendance at public meetings. I will also consider applications for funding for counsel fees for Part II at that time. I would observe now, however, that given the nature of the Part II process, I do not foresee significant funding for legal fees.

III. Applications for Standing

I turn now to the individual applications and I address them generally in the order they were heard, although in some areas I have generally grouped the applicants according to their interests and perspectives.

A.   Walkerton Groups and Residents

There are four applicants who seek to represent the interests and perspectives of the residents of the Town of Walkerton. Each also asks that I make a recommendation for funding.

The residents of Walkerton were seriously affected by the water contamination and have a significant interest in the subject matter of Part I of the Inquiry. Given the tragedy that the residents have suffered, their interests must be represented. I have been told that many residents consider that they have different interests and perspectives than the Town and the Walkerton Public Utilities Commission (the "PUC").

All four applicants have one important interest in common. In one form or another they seek to bring before the Inquiry the nature, scope and type of impact – physical, personal and economic – experienced by the residents of the Town. The impact of the contamination is an important part of the work of the Inquiry. In recognition of this, I held informal hearings in July during which I heard directly from over 50 individuals and groups about the impact of this tragedy on their lives. I anticipate that, in Part I, Commission counsel will be calling some evidence, including expert evidence, dealing with the physical and medical problems experienced by those who were affected by the contaminated water. In Part II, one of the proposed papers will examine the economic and other long term effects of the contamination.

The residents of Walkerton also have a significant interest in the circumstances that led to the contamination and the various causes that may have contributed to it. I expect that the evidence that relates to the issues of what happened and why will form a major part of the evidence that will be called in Part I.

I have asked applicants with similar interests or perspectives to attempt to form coalitions for purposes of standing and funding. I am satisfied from the written material and the oral submissions that there is a sufficient difference in the perspective of two of the groups who have applied to represent the residents that requiring them to be represented by a single coalition would be unrealistic. The Walkerton residents have the greatest interest in Part I. Their voices must be heard even if those voices deliver somewhat different messages. As a result, I am prepared to make more than one grant of standing to represent the interests and perspectives of the residents.

The Concerned Walkerton Citizens (the "CWC") is a group comprised of over 500 residents of Walkerton and the immediate area. It was formed specifically in response to the events of May 2000. It is represented by the Canadian Environmental Law Association ("CELA") and seeks standing in Parts I and II and funding for counsel and experts in both. The CWC represents a large number of residents and importantly has demonstrated a serious, genuine and continuing concern about the issues raised by the Inquiry. I am satisfied that the CWC should be granted full standing for Parts I and II.

The Walkerton Community Foundation also seeks standing and funding for Parts I and II. This is a broadly based group comprised of the Walkerton Rotary Club, the Saugeen Masonic Lodge, the Knights of Columbus, the Knights of Columbus Auxiliary, the St. John Ambulance Society, the Walkerton Lions Club, the Walkerton Optimists Club, the Royal Canadian Legion Branch 102 and a "Community Members" group. The Foundation was also formed in response to the contamination. It is incorporated and registered as a charitable foundation. It appears that the Foundation has a different perspective than the CWC on the events that occurred in May of this year and in particular on the possible causes of the contamination of the water supply. The member organizations of the Foundation have contributed an enormous amount of time and service to the Walkerton community both before and after the tragedy. I am satisfied that the Foundation should also be granted full standing for Parts I and II.

The Walkerton District Chamber of Commerce has applied for standing in Parts I and II, specifically to examine "the existing communication mechanism for notifying of a boil water advisory and the economic implications of the absence of potable water." I am satisfied that insofar as Part I is concerned the interests of the Chamber are congruent with those of the Foundation and, in my view, the interests of the Chamber can be fully and fairly represented within the standing granted to the Foundation. In this regard, I appreciate the efforts that the Foundation and the Chamber have made to join with one another and encourage them to continue those efforts. I am not going to grant standing to the Chamber in Part I. However, if there is difficulty in arriving at a satisfactory arrangement between the two groups I may be spoken to. As to Part II, I see no need to join the two. I grant the Chamber separate standing in Part II for issues relating to the economic impact of the contamination upon the Walkerton community and issues relating to the communication of similar events by public authorities generally.

Finally, the law firm of Siskind Cromarty seeks standing in Part I for injured victims comprised of three separate groups:

- The putative plaintiffs in a proposed class action;

- parents of seriously injured children; and

- 200 individual residents of Walkerton who suffered losses as a result of the tragedy.

In its application the "Injured Victims" group says "… it is distinguishable from groups such as the Concerned Walkerton Citizen's group which represents itself as a non-partisan group seeking intervenor status at the Inquiry." The group states further that "[t]he Injured Victims of the contamination, while clearly partisan and motivated by personal interests, are, nonetheless, a critical voice to be represented at Part I of the Inquiry."

The objective of the group is to ensure that the perspective of the injured victim is brought before the Inquiry. What defines this group is their membership in a proposed class action or the fact that they have retained the same lawyers to represent them. Neither of these characteristics gives them an interest in the Inquiry. The interest that entitles them to standing arises from the fact that they are residents of Walkerton and, like many others, have suffered injury and loss from the contamination.

As I have said above, the perspective of the residents and those who have suffered must be heard. However, it is not feasible for every resident, or indeed every group of residents, who has suffered to be represented separately. Lines must be drawn. I am satisfied that the interests of the members of this group in the issues of how and why the contamination occurred can and should be represented by either of the two parties to which I have granted standing. The CWC and the Foundation have shown a genuine and ongoing interest in the issues raised by the Inquiry and between them, I believe, will fully and fairly represent the interests of all the residents.

While the impact of the contamination will undoubtedly be examined, it will not be a major focus of Part I. The relief sought by the Injured Victims in the lawsuit is something that will be addressed in a separate proceeding and involves issues that go beyond the mandate of this Inquiry. That said, I am nonetheless of the view that the Injured Victim group should be granted standing in Part IA, limited to issues relating to the impact of the contamination upon them.

In reaching this conclusion I expect that Commission counsel and counsel representing the CWC and the Foundation will be open to receiving suggestions and ideas from members of this group to ensure that their views are fully and adequately represented in those parts of the Inquiry in which they have been granted standing. If there is difficulty in this regard I may be spoken to.

I turn next to the question of funding for the residents of Walkerton. Paragraph 5 of the Order in Council provides that I may make recommendations for funding where in my view, "the party would not otherwise be able to participate in the Inquiry without such funding." CELA has agreed to represent the CWC. Counsel provided by CELA will be paid through the Ontario Legal Aid Plan. CELA will be able to act for the CWC without funding from the Attorney General. As a result, the CWC has not met the requirements of the Order in Council and I am not authorized to make a recommendation for funding of a counsel fee. However, the funding CELA receives from Legal Aid does not include disbursements. I will therefore recommend the payment of disbursements by the Attorney General. CELA has requested payment of fees for a case worker and a community worker. I understand that the Attorney General's guidelines do not include such expenses. In the circumstances, I will recommend the payment of disbursements for two counsel for CWC.

As to the request of the CWC for the payment of fees for experts to be called in Part I, I have suggested that CWC propose the names of the experts that it wishes to be called in Part I to Commission counsel.

I have granted standing to the CWC in Part II. It remains open to the CWC to make application for Part II funding.

I am satisfied that the Foundation has met all criteria for funding. I propose to recommend funding for one counsel for Part I for the Foundation.

I do not anticipate that the involvement of the "Injured Victims" will be extensive. Given the nature of the ties that bind this group I do not think it appropriate to recommend funding.

B. Government of Ontario

In light of its clear interest in the issues raised in the Order in Council, I am satisfied that the Government of Ontario meets the criteria for standing for both Parts I and II.

C. Farming and Agricultural Groups

The Commission received eight applications for standing from groups whose focus is on issues related to farming and agriculture. These groups have in common the fact that they are all interested in the potential impact of the Inquiry on issues relating to farming and agriculture. This interest encompasses an environmental perspective. Each also brings with it a different and potentially unique perspective. The groups are:

1.   the Christian Farmers Federation, an organization with more than 4,400 family farm members that approaches agricultural issues from the perspective of "the Christian value system that motivates [its] members";

2.   the Dairy Farmers Federation of Ontario, which represents approximately 6,500 dairy farmers in the Province;

3.   the Ontario Cattle Feeders Association, which represents feedlot operators who feed approximately 55 percent of the fed cattle in Ontario;

4.   the Ontario Cattlemen's Association, which represents 25,000 beef producers across Ontario;

5.   the Ontario Farm Animal Council, a coalition of groups within the livestock and processing industry, whose mandate is to provide communication and education links between livestock producers, processors and the consumer;

6.   the Ontario Federation of Agriculture, which is made up of 51 county
     and district federations representing 43,000 farm family members across
     Ontario;

7.   the Ontario Pork Producers Marketing Board, which represents 5,100
     pork producers in the Province; and

8.   the Ontario Farm Environmental Coalition ("OFEC"), which is a
     coalition of agricultural groups (including many of the organizations
     mentioned above) formed principally to advance an agricultural and
     farming position on environmental issues.

All eight groups have agreed to be represented by OFEC should standing be
granted to them in Part I of the Inquiry. However, each has applied for separate
standing in relation to Part II.

I have no difficulty in concluding that these groups represent a clearly
ascertainable interest and perspective in relation to farming and agricultural
issues, which I consider important to my mandate in Part I. I am mindful of
the fact that no individual or group which represents farming and agriculture
and has a direct interest in Part I has applied for standing. As a result, if I do
not grant standing to OFEC, the agricultural and farming perspective would
not be directly represented. In these circumstances, I exercise my discretion
and grant standing to OFEC for Part I in relation to farming and agricultural
issues.

I do not have sufficient information on the financial position of OFEC and
its members to determine whether they qualify for funding. If OFEC wishes
to pursue funding, it should submit the necessary information to me by
September 22.

In relation to Part II it is clear to me that the eight groups, taken together, have
the type of interest in this part of the Inquiry which merits standing. I am told
that the different perspectives which they represent may cause them to take
different positions on the broader policy issues which will arise in Part II and
that there may be issues in which some but not all groups wish to participate.
I accept that there is a greater possibility for such divergence in Part II and I am
prepared to grant standing separate to the extent necessary to accommodate
their different perspectives.

As noted at the outset, I am not making any decisions with respect to funding in Part II of the Inquiry at this time.

D.   Members of CUPE Local 255

CUPE Local 255 seeks standing on behalf of its members Allan Buckle, Robert McKay, Tim Hawkins, Steve Lorley, Vivian Slater and Ellen Dentinger. These are seven of the eight fulltime unionized employees of the Walkerton PUC. Mr. Frank Koebel, who is a member of CUPE Local 255, has been granted separate standing.

The Walkerton PUC bargaining unit includes employees whose duties involve both water and hydro-electric power services. Allan Buckle is the primary employee involved on the water side of the PUC and has been actively involved in maintenance and monitoring of the PUC's wells as well as water sample testing. Robert McKay, Tim Hawkins and Steve Lorley are primarily employed as hydro linespersons but from time to time have assisted employees working on the "water side" of the PUC. The other two applicants, Vivian Slater and Ellen Dentinger, are employed as clerical staff by the PUC. Their duties include sending water samples to the private sector laboratories for testing and forwarding telephone messages and faxes from the laboratories.

In my view, only Allan Buckle, who by virtue of the performance of his duties was intimately involved in the water side at the relevant time, should be granted standing personally. I grant standing to Mr. Buckle for Part I insofar as his personal interests are affected. I also recommend funding for one counsel, for Mr. Buckle, together with reasonable disbursements, but only for the purposes of representing Mr. Buckle's personal interests. If the other individual applicants are called as witnesses, they will be entitled to counsel and limited standing in accordance with Rule 17 of the Rules of Procedure and Practice. If they choose, the bargaining unit members may be represented by counsel for CUPE Local 255 at that time.

E.   The Bargaining Agents

The Commission received applications for Part I standing from CUPE Local 255, and from two provincial bargaining agents, OPSEU and PEGO. I discuss these applications together, as I am directing a coalition be formed.

CUPE Local 255 seeks standing in Part I on its own behalf, as a separate institutional entity representing the collective interests of unionized employees of the Walkerton PUC. CUPE Local 255's written submissions state that "the Local represents the collective interests of the employees in pursuing the proper, efficient and safe operation of the workplace and in ensuring that the employees are properly trained and equipped for their jobs."

The Ontario Public Service Employees' Union ("OPSEU") has applied for full standing for Parts I and II of the Inquiry. OPSEU submits that it would bring three major interests or perspectives to the Inquiry, as it is:

(a) the trade union representative for approximately 2000 employees particularly concerned with water quality and delivery issues, including Ministry of the Environment ("MOE") staff, Ontario Clean Water Agency ("OCWA") staff, employees dealing with agricultural issues, and technical and professional non-medical staff at local Health Units;

(b) the trade union for most provincial government and public sector employees, who have concerns such as funding, downsizing, alternative service delivery and privatization; and

(c) the representative of individual employees involved directly or indirectly in the events at Walkerton, including workers who work or reside in Walkerton.

Four employees of the MOE Owen Sound office for whom OPSEU acts as bargaining agent have retained other counsel. OPSEU has offered to provide legal representation to other OPSEU members at the Part I hearings, should this be necessary.

The Professional Engineers and Architects of the Ontario Public Service (PEGO) has applied for standing for Parts I and II of this Inquiry. PEGO represents those employed in the public service as engineers, including those employed by OCWA, the Ministry of the Environment and other directly involved government departments. PEGO's counsel, Mr. Fellows, noted that engineers in the public service are involved in all aspects of water regulation. They may be responsible for approval of water treatment and distribution facilities, the setting of standards, the imposition of conditions on the operation of water facilities, and policy recommendations and advice to government with respect to the operation of water facilities. Mr. Fellows stated that the issue of how the Province regulates water treatment and distribution facilities will affect the role of engineers in the public service.

There is a significant congruence of interests among CUPE Local 255, OPSEU and PEGO in Part I of the Inquiry. I believe that all three bargaining agents will assist the Commission by providing valuable perspectives with respect to the operational aspects of government policies, procedures and practices. Further, I consider the experience and expertise of the union members to be valuable in the identification of systemic issues and solutions in this area. Given the congruence of interests, the valuable perspectives which the bargaining agents will bring, and the lack of conflict except as discussed below, I make a single grant of standing in Part I to CUPE Local 255, OPSEU and PEGO. In light of OPSEU's broad representation of provincial government employees, it may be appropriate for OPSEU to take the lead in this coalition. Other than potentially providing legal representation for their members who may be called as witnesses in Part IA, I do not find an interest which warrants full standing and therefore grant special standing to OPSEU in Part IA. I grant the Bargaining Agents Coalition full standing in Part IB. The grants of standing to this coalition in both Part IA and IB are limited to those issues affecting municipal, public sector and provincial government employees.

Counsel for PEGO identified a potential conflict with both CUPE and OPSEU, bargaining agents whose members are primarily involved in front-line field work, including testing and inspections. PEGO notes the potential difference that would arise with respect to issues of decredentialization. PEGO will be addressing issues regarding functions relating to water treatment and distribution requiring the professional judgment of engineers. In this regard alone, I grant separate standing to PEGO in Part IB; otherwise their participation is to be through the Bargaining Agent Coalition. I also recognize that certain issues may result in a different perspective for the Walkerton PUC employees as opposed to provincial employees. Should this situation arise, I am prepared to grant separate standing to Local 255 in Part IB on those issues only. If other conflicts arise, then any of the three coalition partners may apply for separate standing on an issue-specific basis in Part IB.

I grant separate standing to both PEGO and OPSEU in Part II.

PEGO has also requested funding. It is not a national body, but a small organization with 410 working members. The contingency fund referred to in the annual statements filed by PEGO is in fact PEGO's strike fund. In light of the relatively small number of members employed and the lack of a national organization, I recommend funding for PEGO for one counsel limited to Part IB issues involving decredentialization only. I defer my decision on Part II funding.

OPSEU made no request for funding and I make no recommendation in this regard.

I defer CUPE Local 255's request for funding for Part IB in the hope that its national union will see fit to support the Local. I note that if CUPE Local 255 represents its member Allan Buckle, Local 255 will receive funding for its representation of the interests of Mr. Buckle. In the event that Local 255 is granted separate standing for Part IB, it may apply to me for a recommendation for separate funding with respect to those limited interests at that time.

F.   CUPE National

CUPE National has applied for standing in Part II of the Inquiry. In Ontario, CUPE represents over 40,000 municipal employees. Within many of these municipal locals, CUPE members operate and maintain water and wastewater facilities. In 1997 CUPE National identified the issue of safe, clean public water as a primary focus for its activities. It has established a "Water Watch" campaign, the objective of which is to halt the privatization of municipal water services, to identify threats to water quality, to promote access to safe water for all local residents, and to promote water conservation. I am of the view that CUPE National is in a position to assist the Commission in Part II, in light of its expertise in water and wastewater services, privatization and employment relations, as well as the front-line expertise of its members in water delivery in Ontario. I grant CUPE National standing for Part II of the Inquiry.

G.   Dr. McQuigge, Mr. Patterson and Ms. Sellars

Dr. Murray McQuigge, David Patterson and Mary Sellars have applied for standing collectively in Parts I and II. Dr. McQuigge is the Medical Officer of Health for the Bruce Grey Owen Sound Health Unit (the "Health Unit"). David Patterson is the Assistant Director of Health Protection for the Health

Unit, and a public health inspector under the *Health Protection and Promotion Act*, R.S.O. 1990, c.H.7 ("HPPA"). Mary Sellars is Dr. McQuigge's Executive Assistant. All three were involved in responding to the water contamination in Walkerton, the boil water advisory issued by the Medical Officer of Health, and the subsequent remediation efforts. Mr. Cherniak, co-counsel for the three applicants, submits that their interest is in determining the cause of the outbreak, the contributing factors and the solution to the problem. Mr. Cherniak also submits that the three applicants are substantially and directly affected, since they were in the "eye of the storm" as the contamination and its effects spread through the area served by the Health Unit.

Mr. Cherniak commented on the concurrent application of the Health Unit, which is a Local Board of Health under the HPPA and the employer of these three applicants. He noted that, pursuant to the statutory provisions of the HPPA, the role of the Medical Officer of Health is clearly separate and different from that of the Health Unit. Further, he said that Dr. McQuigge had duties placed upon him by the Ontario Drinking Water Objectives of the MOE that were not shared by the Health Unit.

Given the extensive personal involvement of Dr. McQuigge and the importance of his role as Medical Officer of Health in relation to the Walkerton contamination, I grant full standing to Dr. McQuigge on public health issues in Part I. I do not find it necessary to grant standing to Mr. Patterson or Ms. Sellars. I am also prepared to grant Dr. McQuigge standing in Part II although I would expect that his participation might usefully be joined with the Health Unit and ALPHA whose applications I discuss below. Dr. McQuigge, Mr. Patterson and Ms. Sellars have not sought funding and accordingly I make no recommendation in this regard.

H.   Bruce Grey Owen Sound Health Unit

The Health Unit has separately applied for standing in Parts I and II of the Inquiry. Mr. Middlebro', counsel for the Health Unit, noted that it is named as a defendant in a $1.3 billion civil suit relating to the Walkerton contamination. Mr. Middlebro' stated that, under the HPPA, the Health Unit is not able to direct the nature of the Medical Officer of Health's opinion, but remains responsible for his actions. Mr. Middlebro' quite properly conceded that at this point in time there is no conflict between the interests of the Health Unit and those of Dr. McQuigge, Mr. Patterson and Ms. Sellars.

I do not find that the Health Unit has a substantial and direct interest in Part I within the meaning of s.5(1) of the *Public Inquiries Act*. Dr. McQuigge has been granted standing in Part IA. I expect that the Health Unit will have the same interest and perspective in Part IA issues as Dr. McQuigge. I am not prepared to grant the Health Unit standing in Part IA. If a conflict does arise, the Health Unit may reapply.

I grant the Health Unit standing in Part IB with respect to public health issues. I find that the Health Unit shares the same interest in Part IB as the Association of Local Public Health Agencies ("ALPHA"), whose application I address below. I grant these two applicants a single standing in Part IB limited to public health issues. These two applicants will probably share the same interest on many issues with Dr. McQuigge. Where there are such common interests, only one cross-examination may be conducted. I also grant standing to the Health Unit in Part II but would encourage it to participate jointly with Dr. McQuigge and ALPHA. No application was made for funding by the Health Unit and I make no recommendation in that regard.

I.   Association of Local Public Health Agencies

The Association of Local Public Health Agencies has applied for standing and funding in respect of both Parts I and II. ALPHA is a not-for-profit organization of professional public health care providers, whose primary membership consists of Medical Officers of Health and the 37 Boards of Health of Ontario. I note that the Health Unit is a member of ALPHA, and Dr. McQuigge has served as Treasurer of ALPHA. There are also seven affiliate member associations consisting of the Association of Supervisors of Public Health Inspectors of Ontario, Association of Ontario Public Health Business Administrators, Association of Public Health Epidemiologists of Ontario, Health Promotion Ontario, Ontario Association of Public Health Dentistry, Ontario Society of Nutrition Professionals in Public Health, and Public Health Nursing Management. ALPHA's counsel noted that a primary contribution of ALPHA would be to assist the Commission in knowing expected procedures and practice in safe water delivery and protection.

I grant standing to ALPHA in Part IB jointly with the Health Unit, as described above. Given that the Health Unit has not applied for funding, I do not propose to provide funding for this group in Part I. I grant ALPHA's application for standing for Part II of the Inquiry, and will defer my decision as to funding for that part.

J. Ontario New Democratic Party

A group comprised of the Ontario New Democratic Party (the "ONDP"), the New Democratic Party Caucus of the Ontario Legislature, Howard Hampton, Leader of the Ontario New Democratic Party and Leader of the New Democratic Party Caucus, and Bud Wildman, former Minister of the Environment and Energy (the "ONDP Group") has applied for standing and funding in Parts I and II.

I recognize that the ONDP Group has demonstrated a serious and long-standing concern for environmental issues. However, I am not satisfied that it meets the criteria for standing set out in the *Public Inquiries Act* nor, for the reasons set out below, do I consider that this is a case in which I should exercise my discretion to grant standing.

In my view, the ONDP Group does not have a substantial and direct interest in the subject matter of the Inquiry as that term is used in s.5(1) of the Act. I do not anticipate that the interests of the members of this group will be substantially affected by findings or recommendations that may be made in my report.

Section 5(2) of the Act provides that no findings of misconduct can be made against any person in a report following a public inquiry unless that person has been provided reasonable notice of the alleged misconduct and is given an opportunity to participate in the inquiry. On the basis of information now available, Commission counsel do not intend to provide a s.5(2) notice to the ONDP Group.

This applicant makes two submissions in arguing that it has an interest that may be affected by findings to be made in Part I. First, it says that the Premier of Ontario has called the policies, practices and procedures of the pre-1995 ONDP government into question. In response to a question from the press, the Premier apparently said that certain changes in water testing and reporting standards had been made by the previous ONDP government. The ONDP Group suggests that this comment carried with it the innuendo that these changes contributed to what happened in Walkerton. The ONDP Group submits that it should be afforded an opportunity to participate in the Inquiry in order to deal with this allegation. I do not think that the Premier's comment gives rise to the type of interest that warrants standing under s.5 of the Act. The comment seems to have been made as part of the political process in which one politician speaks on an issue and on which an opposing politician may respond in the same forum. It is clearly open to the members of this group to respond to this comment in a forum other than this Inquiry.

I am aware that a political party was granted standing in the Houlden Inquiry. In that inquiry, however, the mandate of the Commissioner included an allegation of wrongdoing involving the political party which was granted standing. The present Inquiry is different. There is no allegation of wrongdoing against the ONDP Group in my mandate. If there are allegations of misconduct, improper behaviour, or the like directed at this group during the Inquiry, I will entertain an application for standing to answer such allegations.

The second ground upon which the ONDP Group claims an interest for which it ought to be granted standing is that the ONDP was vocal in calling for the government to establish this Inquiry. In my view, the fact that a political party or its members call for the government to establish a public inquiry, without more, does not create an interest within the meaning of s.5(1) of the Act.

Finally, I do not think that this is a case in which I should exercise my discretion to grant standing. I say this for two reasons. First, parties who have been granted standing will bring a sufficiently broad range of perspectives to enable me to fulfil my mandate. In granting standing, I have attempted to ensure that all perspectives, and in particular those such as the ones held by this applicant, which question the effect of government policies, practices and procedures, are fully represented. It is essential that there be a thorough examination of these factors in relation to the events in Walkerton. I am satisfied that this will occur.

The second reason why I am not inclined to grant this group standing is that it is, in my view, generally undesirable to use public inquiries to have political parties advance their positions or policies. There are other more appropriate arenas for them to do so. Mr. Jacobs, counsel for the ONDP Group, recognized this concern and assured me that this was not the motivation underlying the application. I accept Mr. Jacobs' assurance without reservation. Nevertheless, I think there is a danger that this applicant's participation could be viewed by the public as politicizing the Inquiry in a partisan way. To the extent possible, that result should be avoided.

Finally, I note that the considerations in granting standing to a political party differ from those which apply to a government. Governments play a different role and have different responsibilities than do political parties. Moreover, the ONDP, unlike any other applicant, will have an opportunity to participate in the subject matter of the Inquiry by responding to my report in the Legislature.

K.   The Municipality of Brockton and Related Applicants and the Public Utilities Commission

The Corporation of the Municipality of Brockton, the successor municipality to the Town of Walkerton, (referred to collectively as the "Town") has applied for standing and funding in Part I of the Inquiry, together with a number of individuals who by employment, contract or office are associated with the Town. The co-applicants are: Mayor David Thomson of Brockton ("Mayor Thomson"); Audrey Webb, Deputy Mayor; Roland Anstett, David Jacobi, Wilfred Lane, Jack Riley and Glen Tanner, the present Councillors of Brockton; the Chief Administrative Officer of Brockton, Richard Radford; former Mayor James Bolden; Don Carroll, Clayton Gutscher, David Mullen and Mary Ramsay (with the exception of one individual, the 1988 Councillors of Walkerton); and Steven Burns, a Professional Engineer with B.M. Ross and Associates Limited, in his capacity as a consultant performing the role of the Town's engineer. Mr. McLeod, counsel for the group, also proposed standing be granted to any other staff member or agent who falls within s.5(1) of the *Public Inquiries Act*, who wishes to be represented by him, and who executes a waiver and consent document and a retainer agreement. The Town and its co-applicants have applied for standing and funding in Part I of the Inquiry.

The PUC has also applied for standing and funding in Part I of the Inquiry.

Mr. McLeod has assured me that there is no conflict in his firm's representation of the Town and the individuals. He further states that he has sought and received consents and waivers with respect to the joint retainer, and has established, with the consent of his clients, a mechanism pursuant to which future conflicts may be resolved in order of priority of representation.

I turn then to the interests of the Town. The Town owns the water treatment and distribution system, which is operated by the PUC pursuant to the terms of the *Public Utilities Act*, R.S.O. 1990, c.P.52. Section 2(1) of the *Public Utilities Act* provides that:

> The corporation of a local municipality may, under and subject to the provisions of this Part, acquire, establish, maintain and operate waterworks, and may acquire by purchase or otherwise and may enter on and expropriate land, waters and water privileges and the right to divert any lake, river, pond, spring or stream of water, within or without the municipality, as may be considered necessary for waterworks purposes, or for protecting the waterworks or preserving the purity of the water supply.

Section 38 of the *Public Utilities Act* provides that:

> … the council of a municipal corporation that owns or operates works for the production, manufacture or supply of any public utility or is about to establish such works, may, by by-law passed with the assent of the municipal electors, provide for entrusting the construction of the works and the control and management of the works to a commission to be called The Public Utilities Commission….

Pursuant to section 38(6), the control and management of the works are vested in the council and the PUC ceases to exist upon the repeal of a by-law establishing a PUC.

The powers of a PUC are set out in s. 41(1) of the *Public Utilities Act*:

> Subject to subsection (4), where a commission has been established under this Part and the members thereof have been elected or where the control and management of any other public utility works are entrusted to a commission established under this Part, all the powers, rights, authorities and privileges that are by this Act conferred on a corporation shall, while the by-laws… remain in force, be exercised by the commission and not by the council of the corporation.

The *Public Utilities Act* establishes that there are to be three to five elected commissioners, including the head of council as a commissioner *ex officio*. The

PUC is required to report to council annually, providing a statement of revenue and expenditure.

Effective January 1, 1999, both the PUC and the Town of Walkerton were subject to a restructuring order by the Minister of Municipal Affairs under the *Municipal Act*, R.S.O. 1990, c.M.45 (the "Order"). Section 2(4) of the Order amalgamated the three former townships under the name "The Corporation of the Township of Brant-Greenock-Walkerton", subsequently renamed "Brockton".

Pursuant to sections 45-46 of the Order, the PUC of the Town of Walkerton was dissolved, and "The Walkerton Public Utilities Commission" was established. Section 46(2) of the Order provides that:

> The commission established under subsection 1 shall distribute and supply electrical power and produce, treat, distribute and supply water to the geographic area of the former Town of Walkerton.

Section 46(3) provides that the commission is subject to the *Public Utilities Act*. Mr. McLeod states that, since May 25, 2000, the PUC has contracted with the Ontario Clean Water Agency to operate the water treatment and distribution system.

The relationship between the Town and the PUC can be fairly summarized by saying that the PUC operates the water treatment and distribution system on behalf of the owner, the Town.

Mr. McLeod identified the interest of the Town in Part I of the Inquiry in relation to the fact that it is the owner of the water treatment and distribution system. He identified specific attributes of ownership which he asserted are relevant to the Town's interest. He noted that, as owner, the Town faces potential civil liability and is a defendant in a civil suit relating to the contamination. He also referred to the Town's exposure to regulatory initiatives of government, and specifically noted that, since at least 1997, the MOE's practice and policy has been to issue orders or enforce regulatory provisions under the *Ontario Water Resources Act*, R.S.O. 1990, c.O.40, against the Town as owner of the waterworks.

Mr. McLeod agreed that there was the possibility of some congruence of interests with the PUC with respect to events prior to May, 2000. He stated that, since the contamination, the Town and the PUC have been working together on remediation and compliance issues. He also pointed out that, under the *Public Utilities Act*, the Mayor of the Town is an *ex officio* member of the PUC.

Mr. Prehogan, counsel for the PUC submits that, since the PUC was responsible for the provision of potable water in Walkerton, and operated the water treatment and distribution system at the time of the contamination, it is substantially and directly affected by this Inquiry and its recommendations. Mr. Prehogan stated that in his view there was no conflict of interest between the PUC and the Town with respect to determining what caused the contamination. He asserted, however, that the interest of the PUC is not identical to the interest of the Town, since the PUC has its own employees and its own statutory mandate. Mr. Prehogan said that, prior to May 2000, the Town was not involved in the events giving rise to this Inquiry except through the PUC. He also said the Town has been involved in remediation efforts since late May, 2000.

I am of the view that there is a significant congruence of interest between the Town and the PUC. However, Mr. McLeod raised the prospect that a conflict could arise. Recognizing this potential for conflict, I deem it prudent to grant separate standing to the Town and the PUC. Until such a conflict arises, I expect the Town and the PUC to cooperate. There will be only one set of cross-examinations to be shared by the two parties on all issues and evidence with respect to which there is no conflict.

I turn now to the fourteen individuals and the unnamed staff members and agents for whom Mr. McLeod also seeks standing. The Mayor, David Thomson, and former Mayor, James Bolden, were both *ex officio* members of the PUC during their time in office, and were also intimately involved in responding to water-related issues raised by the MOE. Both are, to a certain extent, in the "eye of the storm," and are substantially and directly involved in the events preceding and subsequent to May, 2000. As a result, I grant both Mr. Thomson and Mr. Bolden standing in Part I of the Inquiry, limited to matters relating to their personal or official involvement.

Mr. Burns, in his capacity as a consultant performing the role of Brockton's engineer, has a long history of direct involvement in engineering aspects of the Town's wells. I consider that he has a substantial and direct interest in matters relating to his performance of water-related engineering functions for the Town. In the result, I grant him standing, limited according to his interest so described.

My comments in respect of a single set of cross-examinations for the PUC and the Town also apply to the three individuals granted standing.

I decline to grant standing to the other individual co-applicants. If they are called as witnesses, their counsel may have standing in accordance with s.17 of the Rules. I do not find that they have a substantial and direct interest.

In terms of funding, Mr. McLeod requested that I defer my decision regarding funding for the Town and the individuals represented by him. I will make my decision after Mr. McLeod has advised me of the outcome of the outstanding litigation between the Town and its insurers.

I propose to recommend funding for one counsel for the PUC.

L.   The Association of Municipalities of Ontario

The Association of Municipalities of Ontario ("AMO") is a non-profit organization, made up of several hundred Ontario municipalities serving over 98 percent of Ontario's population. Mr. Hamilton, counsel for AMO, stated that the primary interest of his client is in Part II of the Inquiry, but he also submitted that the members of AMO would be substantially and directly affected by the findings of this Inquiry in Part IB as government policies will affect other municipalities. With respect to Part IA, he stated that AMO has much less interest but suggested that AMO might help in determining systemic issues deserving a further examination. The materials filed by AMO set out AMO's extensive involvement in drinking water issues from the municipal perspective, including AMO's interest in the provincial downloading of drinking water responsibility and funding pressures posed in the area of drinking water as a result of downloading. AMO proposes to work closely with the Municipal Engineers Association and the Ontario Good Roads Association.

Mr. Hamilton has also requested funding on behalf of AMO, stating that there are no funds presently available for the Walkerton Inquiry, and that AMO has already done a cash call among its members to raise funds for the Town.

I grant standing to AMO in Part II. I also grant standing in Part IB, limited to the interests of municipalities in issues raised in Part IB. I grant special standing to AMO for Part IA, as its interests are attenuated with respect to the Walkerton-specific issues given the standing of the Town. I suggest that any issues of concern in Part IA be raised with Commission counsel.

At this time I am not recommending funding for Part I of the Inquiry. AMO is a large and well-funded organization which has the ability to raise funds from its members. If indeed they are as committed to the issues as they have stated in their materials, I would expect the organization to devote the appropriate funds to represent its interests. I also note that reference is made to the fact that in this year's budget no priority had been set for the Inquiry. As Part IB will commence after Christmas, and thus after the year-end, there should be an opportunity to re-direct priorities. If funding is not possible for reasons not presently apparent to me, AMO may reapply. I defer my decision on funding with respect to Part II.

M.   Stan Koebel

Stan Koebel was at all relevant times Manager of the PUC and his performance in this role gives him a substantial and direct interest, and therefore standing, for matters relating to his performance in this role in Part IA. Mr. Koebel also has standing in Part IB to the extent that the issues raised affect his substantial and direct personal interest. I recommend funding for one counsel for the limited interest described above.

N.   Frank Koebel

Frank Koebel was at the relevant times the Foreman of the PUC and his performance in this role gives him a substantial and direct interest, and therefore standing, for matters relating to his performance in this role in Part IA. He also has standing in Part IB to the extent that the issues raised affect his substantial and direct personal interest. I recommend funding for one counsel for the limited interests described above.

O.   Office of the Chief Coroner

The Chief Coroner of the Province of Ontario has applied for full standing in both Parts I and II. Ms. Cronk, on behalf of the Chief Coroner, indicated that given the broad mandate in the Order in Council creating the Inquiry, the

Chief Coroner considers that an inquest would involve an unnecessary duplication of effort and expense. Accordingly, the Chief Coroner does not, at present, intend to hold an inquest.

The Chief Coroner has made the results of his investigation available to Commission counsel.

I am pleased that the Chief Coroner wishes to be represented by counsel throughout the Inquiry. I appreciate the assistance the Chief Coroner has given the Inquiry to date and welcome the continued assistance of the Chief Coroner's counsel. The Chief Coroner has an interest in the work of the Inquiry and is able to contribute in a way I consider important. The Chief Coroner is therefore granted full standing in Parts I and II.

P.   The Environmental Coalitions

The Commission received applications for standing from four environmental groups including three coalitions representing a broad range of interests in environmental matters. Each of the groups has asked for full standing and for funding in Parts I and II of the Inquiry. I will deal first with the three coalitions.

(i)   *ALERT – Sierra Club Coalition*

This coalition is led by the Agricultural Livestock Expansion Response Team (ALERT) and the Sierra Club of Canada. The focus of the coalition is on the technical and regulatory issues surrounding intensive farming and manure management. Both ALERT and the Sierra Club have extensive experience with environmental concerns in the agricultural sector.

(ii)   *The Sierra Legal Defence Fund Coalition*

The Sierra Legal Defence Fund submitted an application for standing and funding on behalf of three organizations: the Canadian Association of Physicians for the Environment, whose overarching concern is children's environmental health; the Council of Canadians, a citizens' watchdog association which is focused on such issues as the safeguarding social programs, alternatives to free trade, and the commodification of fresh water; and Great Lakes United, a coalition of environmental, conservation, labour and community groups whose mission is to develop and maintain a healthy ecosystem in the Great Lakes. In both its written and oral submissions the Sierra Legal Coalition stressed the fact that it could offer the Inquiry broad national and international perspectives on the issues it would address.

(iii)   *The CEDF and Pollution Probe Coalition*

This coalition is made up of two national organizations: the Canadian Environmental Defence Fund ("CEDF"), an organization whose mandate is to intervene directly or to provide technical, legal, organizational and financial support to other organizations in relation to legal initiatives on environmental issues; and Pollution Probe, an organization focusing on a broad range of environmental issues including the enhancement of water quality. Both the CEDF and Pollution Probe have long and distinguished histories of involvement in environmental matters. They are joined in the coalition by nine other local organizations: CARD of Balsam Lake, Coalition of Concerned Citizens of Caledon, Four Corners Environmental Group, Mariposa Aquifer Protection Association, Save the Rouge Valley System, Stuart Hall Against Mismanaged Environment, Waring's Creek Improvement Association, Fort Erie Water Advocacy Group and the Attawapiskat First Nation.

(iv)   *Discussion*

On the issue of whether standing should be granted to any or all of these organizations, the three environmental coalitions in my view represent a clearly ascertainable interest and perspective which I consider important to my mandate in Part I. I do not believe that the interests of the environmental groups in Part I are accurately characterized as substantial and direct. In order to ensure that all important points of view are represented, however, I grant standing to an environmental group in Part IA to deal with environmental issues relating to farming and agriculture. I am also prepared to grant special standing with respect to the remaining issues in Part IA and full standing for Part IB. I note as well that the CWC will be represented by CELA, which brings a similar perspective to the Inquiry as this coalition. That perspective will indeed be well represented throughout Part I.

While I consider the involvement of the environmental groups in Part I to be both useful and important, I believe that the interests represented by these groups can be adequately accommodated by one grant of standing to be shared among them. In reviewing the material filed by the coalitions, it appears to me that the positions advanced by them, where they do not overlap, are at least complementary. When asked by me, none of the counsel for the groups could identify any areas of conflict among the three coalitions. Because of the special expertise in the area of agricultural and farming, I assume that the ALERT – Sierra Club Coalition will deal with environmental issues relating to farming and agriculture. When I asked them in oral argument, both Ms. Christie on behalf of the Sierra Legal Defence Fund Coalition and Mr. Sokolov on behalf of the CEDF-Pollution Probe Coalition stated that they would be able to work out a division of the remaining environmental issues among themselves. I would also recommend funding for one counsel in Part I of the Inquiry to be allocated among the three coalitions in accordance with my reasons above.

Further, the three coalitions will in my view make an important contribution to Part II. As with the agricultural groups, I am prepared to grant separate standing in Part II to the extent that, in their written submissions, they express a different interest or perspective.

On the issue of funding, it is my intention, by granting standing in Part II to each of the three coalitions, that each be entitled to provide me with a detailed application for funding setting out the nature of any papers such group intends to prepare as well as the details of the costs it expects to incur with regard to Part II.

Q.   Energy Probe Research Foundation (EPRF)

EPRF is an environmental and public policy research institute which traces its roots to Pollution Probe. I have not grouped EPRF with the other environmental groups because its focus is markedly different from the three coalitions discussed above. Specifically, EPRF advocates a drinking water system that is regulated by government, operated and managed by the private sector and in which consumers pay the full cost of the system. EPRF has applied for full standing and funding in Parts I and II of the Inquiry.

Dealing first with Part I, EPRF has a clearly ascertainable perspective which I believe will be helpful to me in fulfilling my mandate in Part IB of the Inquiry.

In my view, the unique perspective on which EPRF provides assistance is narrow. It centres on the issue of whether private ownership of the water system would have made a difference to what happened in Walkerton.

EPRF has also asked for standing in Part IA in order to ask questions of those officials in Walkerton with decision-making power over the water system. EPRF has informed me that these questions are necessary to assist in building its hypothesis about how a water utility should be structured. While I understand the reason for EPRF's request, I am of the view that its interest can be accommodated without granting it standing in Part IA. First, I understand that it is the intention of Commission counsel to call the evidence of local officials, not only in Part IA but also in Part IB. The evidence given by these officials in Part IB will focus on matters relating to government policies and procedures – the primary focus of EPRF. I therefore grant standing to EPRF in Part IB of the Inquiry for the limited perspective outlined above. I am not satisfied from the material presented that EPRF meets the funding criteria for Part IB. It is not clear to me what efforts, if any, it has made to raise funds for this Inquiry. EPRF may reapply in the future.

I am also prepared to grant standing to EPRF in Part II. As noted elsewhere in these reasons, I will defer consideration of the funding proposals for Part II.

R.   Groups Applying for Part II Standing Only

I heard from a number of groups and individuals who applied for standing only in Part II of the Inquiry. For the reasons set out below, I have granted standing to each of these applicants. As I have noted previously, I have deferred the issue of funding for the preparation and/or presentation of Public Submissions until after the Commission Papers have been published in draft. Those groups which have an interest in preparing or assisting in the preparation of Commission Papers should contact Mr. Harry Swain, the Chair of our Research Advisory Panel. I have granted standing in Part II of the Inquiry to the following applicants.

1.   *Azurix North America (Canada) Corp.*

> Azurix provides water and waste water services to more than 700 facilities in Canada and the United States, including 16 facilities in Ontario. It has offered to bring to Part II its perspective as a private operator of

water systems and I am of the view that this will assist me in the fulfill-
ment of my mandate.

2. *Indian Associations Coordinating Committee of Ontario Inc. (Chiefs of Ontario)*

The Chiefs of Ontario is an umbrella organization for all status Indian
communities in Ontario. It represents the interests of all of Ontario's 134
First Nations, comprising approximately 130,000 individuals, on a broad
range of issues. I am most appreciative of the Chiefs of Ontario's offer to
prepare a paper addressing First Nations water quality issues across the
general topics proposed for the Inquiry. I also accept the Chiefs' offer to
provide assistance on other drinking water-related issues affecting First
Nations.

3. *Conservation Ontario and Saugeen Valley Conservation Authority*

Conservation Ontario represents Ontario's 38 conservation authorities
and has applied for standing together with the Saugeen Valley Conservation Authority. The focus of these two organizations will be on the need
for a comprehensive provincial framework for sustainable water management including submissions on current provincial policies and perceived
program gaps. I note that Conservation Ontario and the Saugeen Valley
Conservation Authority have offered to share standing with the Grand
River Conservation Authority and Ducks Unlimited. While I am appreciative of the fact that this offer was made in an attempt to help shorten
the length of the Inquiry, I do not have the same concerns about an
unduly protracted process in Part II as I do in Part I. For this reason I
have granted separate standing to all three applicants. I note, however,
that when requests for funding are made, I will again be looking to avoid
any unnecessary duplication and would strongly urge these groups (and,
indeed, any groups with the same or similar interest) to find ways to
combine their efforts on any research papers which they may wish
to produce.

4. *Ducks Unlimited – Ontario*

Ducks Unlimited has a long-standing interest in the preservation and
management of Ontario's wetlands. Through its Waterfowl and Wetlands
Research Institute, Ducks Unlimited is currently preparing a report

outlining the science associated with wetlands, water quality and water management which they have kindly offered to provide to the Commisson when it is complete. I am most appreciate of this offer and look forward to further assistance from this organization.

5.   *The Grand River Conservation Authority*

The Grand River Conservation Authority works with watershed municipalities, the Province and a variety of other groups to help protect the quality of the water supply in the Grand River watershed. For the reasons noted in relation to Conservation Ontario, I have also granted standing in Part II to the Grand River Conservation Authority.

6.   *The Ontario Municipal Water Association (OMWA)*

OMWA represents more than 160 public drinking water authorities in Ontario. Its role is to lobby on behalf of its members on policy, legislative and regulatory issues related to the provision of water. OMWA offers to bring its knowledge and experience in the governance and operation of municipal public water systems to the Inquiry.

7.   *The Ontario Water Works Association (OWWA)*

The OWWA's membership includes approximately 70 large and small utilities responsible for the provision of drinking water in Ontario. While the focus of the OMWA is on the management and operation of water systems, the focus of the OWWA is on the science and technology of water treatment. The interests of the OMWA and the OWWA obviously overlap. While I have granted each of these organizations standing, I encourage them to work together on the many issues which I expect they share.

8.   *The Ontario Society of Professional Engineers (OSPE)*

The OSPE is a new organization recently spawned by the Professional Engineers – Ontario to deal with many non-regulatory concerns shared by professional engineers in Ontario. The OSPE has established a task group which will examine issues related to water quality management in Ontario from an engineering perspective. The OSPE has offered to provide input to the Commission on the following four issues: (i) the extent of engineering involvement in the production, treatment and delivery of drinking water; (ii) the gradual reduction in the extent of engineers' involvement in the drinking water process in Ontario; (iii) the value of having engineers involved in this process; and (iv) the fact that the quality of water systems is directly proportionate to the investment in such systems.

9.   *The Professional Engineers – Ontario*

The Professional Engineers – Ontario is the organization which regulates and sets standards for engineers in Ontario. It has offered to bring its vast expertise in standard setting and the regulation of engineers to the Inquiry.

10.   *The Ontario Medical Association*

The Ontario Medical Association intends to focus on the public health aspect of the Commission's mandate in Part II. Its particular interests are the roles of the Medical Officer of Health and the administrative structure and reporting requirements in the assurance of safe drinking water.

11.   *Maureen Reilly/ Sludgewatch*

Ms. Reilly is involved in public interest research and public education on the agricultural application of wastewater sewage sludge, septage and other wastes. Ms. Reilly has offered her experience in these matters to Part II of the Inquiry and I am pleased to grant her standing.

S.   Individuals

Five individuals with different experiences and backgrounds and with different points of view also sought standing. They are:

Ernest Farmer

Mary Richter

Mary-Clare Saunders

Jacqueline Schneider-Stewart (People Opposed to Ontario Pollution)

Greta Thomson

These individuals have not satisfied either of the criteria for standing. Each, however, has a point of view or experience that will be considered by Commission counsel in making decisions on what evidence should be called. I thank each of them for their interest in the Inquiry.

Summary

I have granted standing to six parties for all issues in Part I. I have also granted standing to 14 other parties, some of them coalitions, but have limited their participation because of the nature of their interest or perspective. I have granted standing to, at most, 35 applicants in Part II, some of whom I expect will form coalitions.

I have dealt with standing so as to ensure that all the relevant interests and perspectives are fully represented. My first criterion has been to ensure the Inquiry is thorough. When in doubt, I have opted in favour of inclusion. In doing so, I recognize there will be overlapping positions and a potential for duplication. I want to make two points clear about the process in Part I. I expect parties with the same interest to cooperate with one another and with Commission counsel to avoid repetition and delay. I also expect parties who have been granted standing in a limited area to stay within the permitted bounds. In light of these expectations, I will not hesitate to intervene where there is any departure from the approach I have set out above.

Finally, I want to thank the many individuals and groups who applied for standing. I appreciate your interest in the Inquiry and your willingness to help. I take great comfort from the enormous expertise that has been made available to the Inquiry through the grants of standing. I look forward to working with those granted standing on this endeavour that is so important to the people of Walkerton and the rest of Ontario.

Appendix - Appearances on behalf of applicants

- Paul Muldoon and Theresa McClenaghan, Canadian Environmental Law Association, for Concerned Citizens of Walkerton

- John Gilbert and Clayton Gutscher for the Walkerton Community Foundation

- Rick Lekx and Tom Schulz for the Walkerton & District Chamber of Commerce

- Frank Marrocco, Glenn Hainey and Lynn Mahoney for the Government of Ontario

- Paul Vrkley for the Ontario Farm Environmental Coalition

- Robert Bedggood for Christian Farmers Federation of Ontario

- Gordon Coukell for the Dairy Farmers of Ontario

- Jim Clark for the Ontario Cattle Feeders Association

- Mike McMorris for the Ontario Cattlemen's Association

- G. Michael Cooper for the Ontario Farm Animal Council

- Cecil Bradley for the Ontario Federation of Agriculture

- Larry Skinner for the Ontario Pork Producers Marketing Board

- Donald K. Eady and Timothy G.R. Hadwen for the Ontario Public Service Employees Union

- Peter T. Fallis for Mary Clare Saunders

- Greta Thompson, in person

- John H.E. Middlebro' for the Bruce Grey Owen Sound Health Unit

- Paul Wearing and James LeNoury for the Association of Local Public Health Agencies

- Earl A. Cherniak, Q.C. and Douglas Grace for Dr. Murray McQuigge, David Patterson and Mary Sellars

- David Jacobs for the Ontario New Democratic Party *et al.*

- James Caskey, Q.C. and Mark Poland for the Injured Victims

- Mr. Ernest Farmer, via telephone

- Michael Epstein for Frank Koebel

- William Trudell for Stan Koebel

- Rod McLeod, Q.C. and Bruce McMeekin for the Municipality of Brockton *et al.*

- Kenneth Prehogan for the Walkerton Public Utilities Commission

- Frank J.E. Zechner for Azurix North America (Canada) Ltd.

- Paul G. Vogel and Dawn J. Kershaw for the ALERT – Sierra Club Coalition

- E.A. Cronk for the Office of the Chief Coroner of Ontario

- Mark Mattson for Energy Probe Research Foundation

- Louis Sokolov and Benson Cowan for the Canadian Environmental Defence Fund *et al.*

- Elizabeth Christie for the Canadian Association of Physicians for the Environment *et al.*

- Jacqueline Schneider-Stewart representing People Opposed to Ontario Pollution

- Howard Goldblatt for the Canadian Union of Public Employees, Local 255, individual named members, and CUPE National

- Ian Fellows for the Professional Engineers and Architects of the Ontario Public Service

- Jonathan W. Kahn and Allison A. Thornton for the Chiefs of Ontario

- Richard Hunter for Conservation Ontario

- Jim Coffey for the Saugeen Valley Conservation Authority

- J. Anderson for Ducks Unlimited - Ontario

- Douglas B. James and Barker Willson for the Ontario Municipal Water Association

- Paul Emerson for the Grand River Conservation Authority

- Joseph Castrilli for the Ontario Water Works Association

- Robert Goodings and Joyce Rowlands for the Ontario Society of Professional Engineers

- Doug Hamilton and Craig Rix for the Association of Municipalities of Ontario

- John D. Gamble and Johnny Zuccon for the Professional Engineers of Ontario

- B.T.B. (Ted) Boadway, M.D. for the Ontario Medical Association

- Maureen Reilly for Sludgewatch (Uxbridge Conservation Authority)

- Mrs. Mary Richter, in person

The Honourable Dennis R. O'Connor,
Commissioner

SUPPLEMENTARY RULING ON STANDING AND FUNDING

APPENDIX E (III)

THE WALKERTON INQUIRY

Ontario

LA COMMISSION
D'ENQUÊTE WALKERTON

Supplementary Ruling on Standing and Funding

I have received three written requests to reconsider my Ruling of September 11.

1. The Walkerton Public Utilities Commission (the "PUC") requests that I amend my Ruling to allow the PUC to cross-examine all witnesses rather than sharing the right of cross-examination with the Town. At the standing hearing, Mr. Prehogan, for the PUC, took the position that there was no conflict of interest between the PUC and the Town with respect to the issue of what caused the contamination.

    In making the present request Mr. Prehogan now points out five circumstances which he says will make co-operation between the Town and the PUC difficult. These circumstances primarily relate to the adversity in interest between the two with regard to issues of liability for damages resulting from the contamination. The Order in Council under which I was appointed precludes me from making findings of civil liability. Nonetheless, it would be naïve to think that the positions of the two parties in civil proceedings will not affect the manner in which they approach the Inquiry. I understand why co-operation may be difficult. Accordingly, I am prepared to accede to the request and permit the PUC and the Town separate cross-examinations. In doing so, however, I note that there will likely be a congruence of interest on many issues. In those instances, I encourage counsel to agree on a single cross-examination. In any event I will insist that there be no repetition.

    The PUC also requests that I amend my recommendation for funding to include payment of a junior counsel fee. In addition to acting for the PUC, Mr. Prehogan will be acting for two of the PUC Commissioners in their personal capacities, both of whom will be called as witnesses.

In these circumstances, I am satisfied that there will be some portions of the evidence in Part IA for which a junior counsel is necessary. I therefore recommend the payment of a junior counsel fee for a maximum of 20 days during Part IA only.

2.   Stanley Koebel requests that I alter my recommendation for funding to include payment of a junior counsel fee. In my view, this request should be granted. I am limiting the recommendation for funding for a junior counsel to a maximum of 20 days.

After my Ruling, Mr. Trudell, Mr. Koebel's counsel, described certain personal circumstances of Mr. Koebel which underlie this request. These circumstances were not included as part of the original application for funding. I accept Mr. Trudell's statement that these circumstances are such that it would be difficult, if not impossible, for him to continue to act for Mr. Koebel without the assistance of junior counsel. These circumstances are tied to the central role attributed to Mr. Koebel in the events of May, 2000, the likelihood that Mr. Koebel will be compelled to testify at the Inquiry, and the anticipated positions of other parties concerning the cause of the contamination. Mr. Trudell has requested that the details of these circumstances be kept confidential because of their personal nature. I am prepared to accede to that request.

I note that no similar application has been made by Frank Koebel, and that Mr. Epstein, his counsel, has specifically indicated that he will not be seeking alteration of the funding recommendation to include payment of a junior counsel fee. Mr. Epstein has, however, supported the request made by Stanley Koebel and, in doing so, has echoed the reasons advanced by Mr. Trudell.

I therefore recommend the payment of a junior counsel fee for Stanley Koebel for 20 days during Part IA only. I would point out that under the Attorney General's guideline, when junior counsel attends hearings with senior counsel, he or she will be paid 75% of the junior counsel's hourly rate under the Attorney General's Hourly Fee Schedule.

3.   In my Ruling, I asked the Ontario Farm Environmental Coalition (OFEC) to submit additional information with respect to funding. OFEC has written to indicate that it requires funding for one counsel to represent OFEC for portions of the Inquiry hearings. OFEC indicates that it has

raised $25,000 from organizations representing commercial livestock producers and from the two general farm organizations which are members of OFEC. OFEC is reluctant to ask farm family members to contribute additional funds, beyond what they have already paid in general contributions to OFEC member organizations, in light of the particularly low crop prices and poor crops that farm families face this year.

I am satisfied that OFEC has met the criteria for funding and will recommend funding for one counsel for OFEC for those portions of the hearings that relate to farming and agricultural issues. These issues are the basis upon which I granted standing to OFEC in Part I. However, I will qualify this recommendation to fund OFEC by indicating that funding should be provided only after OFEC has exhausted the $25,000 that it has raised independently.

I note further that OFEC has indicated that it is seeking support through the Agricultural Adaption Council's Small Projects Initiative. To the extent that financial support is provided by this route, I will amend my recommendation to fund OFEC to reflect additional funding from the Agricultural Adaption Council. In particular, such additional funding should be exhausted before any funding is provided pursuant to my recommendation.

DATE RELEASED: October 3, 2000

The Honourable Dennis R. O'Connor,
Commissioner

FUNDING RECOMMENDATIONS

APPENDIX F (1)

THE WALKERTON INQUIRY LA COMMISSION D'ENQUÊTE WALKERTON

Ontario

Funding Recommendations

I. General

1. The Terms of Reference of the Walkerton Inquiry provide that:

    "The Commission may make recommendations to the Attorney General regarding funding to parties who have been granted standing, to the extent of the party's interest, where in the Commission's view, the party would not otherwise be able to participate in the Inquiry without such funding."

II. Criteria

2. To be considered for a funding recommendation an applicant must:

    (a) have obtained standing in at least one of Part I or Part II of the Inquiry;

    (b) be able to demonstrate that it does not have sufficient financial resources to enable it adequately to represent its interest; and

    (c) have a proposal as to the use it intends to make of the funds and how it will account for the funds.

3. The Commissioner will also consider other factors in making his funding recommendations, including the following:

(a)   the nature of the applicant's interest and/or proposed involvement in the Inquiry;

(b)   whether the applicant has an established record of concern for and a demonstrated commitment to the interest it seeks to represent;

(c)   whether the applicant has special experience or expertise with respect to the Commission's mandate; and

(d)   whether the applicant has attempted to form a group with others of similar interests.

4.   Further information will be provided at a later date.

FUNDING GUIDELINES – RATES

APPENDIX F (II)

Guidelines for Reimbursement
of Legal Fees and Expenses

The Ministry of the Attorney General has advised the Commission that it has determined that the appropriate rate for the reimbursement of legal fees and expenses to those who have been granted funding should be the amount paid by the Ministry for retention of private sector counsel. Those rates are:

Hourly Rates for Retention of Private Sector Lawyers

Hourly Fee Schedule (Max. 10 Hours Per Day)   *Criteria*

A.	$56 – 104	Junior Lawyer
B.	$88 – 132	Intermediate lawyer with good experience
C.	$124 – 176	Senior lawyer with extensive experience, well-recognized in area of expertise
D.	– 192	Only the most senior lawyers performing work on a significant project requiring a high degree of specialized skill

The legal fees and expenses eligible for reimbursement are those which relate to reasonable preparation for and representation at those portions of the inquiry for which standing has been accorded to the client, subject to the Commissioner's recommendations. It will not include funding related to the investigative activities of other agencies or to the investigative activities of the Commission except for attendance at interviews by Commission counsel or staff. Legal fees and related expenses accumulated prior to the signing of the Order-in-Council are also not eligible.

A lawyer accepting compensation shall not bill the client, or apply to any third party, for any additional funding for the services in question. Unless the Commission recommends otherwise, only one counsel per client is eligible for reimbursement. If the Commissioner approves a junior counsel then, if such junior counsel attends hearings with senior counsel, he or she will be paid 75% of the junior counsel's hourly rate.

Reasonable claims for travel expenses and disbursements, supported by receipts or invoices, may be claimed. Photocopying may be claimed at 10.0 cents per page.

The reimbursement of eligible legal expenses will be made on an ex gratia basis only, with no right of challenge or appeal.

In addition, the Commission proposes that all accounts for legal fees and disbursements will be referred to an independent officer who will assess the accounts on the basis of this guideline. Once approved, accounts will be forwarded to the Ministry of the Attorney General for payment.

SUMMONS TO WITNESS

APPENDIX G

THE WALKERTON INQUIRY   **LA COMMISSION D'ENQUÊTE WALKERTON**

Ontario

Summons to Witness

(Section 7)

TO:

You are hereby summoned and required to attend, [and to bring a copy of…], before the Commission of the Walkerton Inquiry at 220 Trillium Court in the Town of Walkerton, Ontario, on [Date], at the hour of 10 o'clock in the forenoon (local time) and so from day to day until the inquiry is concluded or the Commission otherwise orders, to give evidence on oath touching the matters in question in the inquiry.

Dated this   day of   A.D. 2001

The Honourable Dennis R. O'Connor
Commissioner

NOTE:

You are entitled to be paid the same personal allowances for your attendance at the hearings as are paid for attendance of a witness summoned to attend before the Ontario Superior Court of Justice.

If you fail to attend and give evidence at the inquiry at the time and place specified, without lawful excuse, you are liable to punishment by the Ontario Superior Court of Justice in the same manner as if for contempt of that Court for disobedience to a summons.

DOCUMENT REQUEST

APPENDIX H (1)

Moe Document Request # 1

Date: June 30, 2000

Definitions

"Central Agencies" refers to Management Board, the Cabinet Office, the Premier's Office and the Ministry of Finance.

"document" refers to any memorandum, data, analysis, report, minutes, briefing material, submission, correspondence, record or any other note or communication in writing in the possession, custody or control of the MOE, its agents, servants or contractors including any present or former MOE employee, Minister or exempt (political) staff, including material in off-site storage or which has been archived, and specifically including any electronic communications including e-mail both internal to the Government of Ontario, and that which has been sent to or received from external sources, in relation to the matters listed below.

"government" means the Government of Ontario, unless otherwise specified.

"MOE" means the Ministry of the Environment and predecessor Ministries, and includes agencies, boards, commissions and Crown Corporations within the responsibility of the Ministry.

"OCWA" means the Ontario Clean Water Agency.

"OWRA" means the Ontario Water Resources Act.

"PUC" means the Public Utilities Commission of or associated with the Town of Walkerton.

"Town of Walkerton" includes the Municipality of Brockton.

Time Frame: In this request, unless otherwise specified, production is requested of all documents in the period April 1, 1993 to the present time and continuing.

Document Requests

For the period April 1, 1993 to the present time and continuing, produce documents, including all copies identified as to source and where relevant, indicating the author of marginalia, which are relevant to the following matters:

1.   Since 1980, results of any inspections, tests or audits of drinking water and drinking water facilities in the Town of Walkerton including facilities operated by the PUC, including inspection reports conducted in 1991, 1995 and February, 1998, and including the inspections and audits carried out during and following the events of May, 2000.

2.   (a)   Since 1979, certificates of approval under the OWRA issued to the Town of Walkerton, including the PUC, with respect to municipal water supply and water works, and any changes to the terms and conditions, including any exemptions; and

      (b)   Since 1979, all applications for such certificates of approval changes and exemptions, together with supporting documentation.

3.   With respect to the Provincial Water Protection Fund and any other provincial loan, grant or capital programs related to water works or facilities, administered by MOE, Management Board or any other agency, board, commission, Crown Corporation or Ministry of the government, any applications, correspondence or other documents by the Town of Walkerton or any PUC related thereto, together with government response to any such applications and documents.

4.   All warnings, citations, or concerns expressed by MOE staff to the Town of Walkerton or the PUC with respect to drinking water, drinking water testing or the water works.

5.   All documents constituting communications between the MOE and the Town of Walkerton, between the MOE and any other Ministry, any of the Central Agencies, OCWA, and any other agency, board or commission, with respect to any of the matters giving rise to the Inquiry up to

the present time and continuing, including, if received, a letter from the Town of Walkerton to the Premier dated June 18, 1998 expressing concern with respect to water quality in the Town, and any attachments including any resolutions or motions by the Town Council and any reply to that letter by the Premier or any other representative of the government.

6. Documents from GAP EnviroMicrobial Services or GAP Microbial Services to MOE's Owen Sound offices, including reports and documents sent from February, 2000 and continuing, and any MOE documents relating thereto.

7. Documents from A&L Laboratories Canada East to MOE Owen Sound offices from April, 2000 and continuing, and any MOE documents related thereto.

8. Any draft Cabinet submission or internal MOE memo or document to the Minister entitled "A Cleaner Ontario" of approximately 61 pages dated on or about March 14, 2000, and all previous or subsequent drafts and documents related thereto.

9. With respect to the MOE Sewage and Water Inspection Program ("SWIP"), and all similar or predecessor programs, all documents relating to compliance and enforcement activity in or related to the Town of Walkerton, including water facilities operated by the Town of Walkerton or the PUC and the number of audits conducted under SWIP or predecessor programs in this period, by month.

10. All documents exchanged between the MOE and the Town of Walkerton including the PUC, including training materials and guidelines relating to drinking water, water works and water facilities, including testing.

11. All documents relating to the withdrawal of MOE resources from the water-related pollution control mandate of the Ministry, from drinking water labs, testing, audit and monitoring programs including documents relating to alternative service delivery strategies, risk assessment, implementation strategies, monitoring and evaluation, both prospective and actual.

12. The August 21, 1997 memorandum from the Operations Division of the MOE to the Program Development Branch of the MOE regarding

drinking water issues associated with the devolution of testing and monitoring responsibilities to the municipalities, and all draft memoranda and
documents related thereto, and all documents in response or related
thereto.

13. The November 14, 1997 "information briefing document" sent to the
MOE Drinking Water Coordinating Committee, and all documents in
preparation for, in response to, or otherwise related thereto.

14. Memoranda dated on or about January, 1997 and May, 1996 from Sheila
Willis, then ADM Operations Division of MOE, with respect to budget,
program or staff reductions and the impact thereto.

15. Documents and letters from the Canadian Institute of Public Health,
including from Ron Hartnett, including a letter dated on or about April
4, 2000, and all letters since September, 1999, with respect to the safety
of small drinking water systems in Ontario.

16. All minutes, memoranda or documents sent to or created by the MOE
Drinking Water Coordinating Committee and its members, and similar,
predecessor or successor groups or committees including Ad Hoc
Committees.

17. Draft and final memorandum and documents prepared by the MOE
Water Policy Branch entitled "Proposed Revisions to Ontario Drinking
Water Objectives (ODWO) Related to Small Systems, Alternative
Sampling and Monitoring", presented to the Drinking Water Coordi-
nating Committee, Ad Hoc Group, January 2000.

18. All correspondence from the MOE Deputy Minister or Minister to coun-
terparts at other ministries with respect to drinking water, water works,
testing, audits and drinking water enforcement/regulation.

19. With respect to the MOE's Water Management Guidelines and Procedures and all predecessor guidelines and procedures, all documents and
data with respect to the treatment requirements for drinking water and
water works, changes in those requirements, with all supporting documentation including business cases, risk assessment, implementation and
monitoring documents and variance requests by the Town of Walkerton,
including the PUC, and results of variance requests.

20. (a) With respect to the Drinking Water Surveillance Program ("DWSP"), documents relating to the prioritization and criteria for inclusion of water works in the DWSP; changes to those criteria in the period; documents relating to whether or not the Town of Walkerton, including the PUC and its municipal water works, were considered for inclusion in the DWSP, and any documents relevant to a decision thereto;

     (b) The DWSP sampling protocol and all changes thereto in this period, including documents relating to the reasons for the changes, risk assessment, implementation and monitoring, and the consideration of the effects, both prospective and retrospective;

     (c) With respect to microbiological parameters, all documents relating to the decision to discontinue sampling for microbiological parameters by the DWSP in 1996, including all documents prior to and subsequent to that decision relating to risk assessment, implementation and monitoring the impact of the decision; and

     (d) All documents relating to the DWSP Steering Committee, including minutes and reviews of the monitoring protocol and program modifications with all documents relating thereto.

21. With respect to watershed management and subwatershed projects, any requests for funding of watershed plans or subwatershed planning projects or pilot projects by the Town of Walkerton, or any PUC thereto related, and if any funding was allocated, all details of the project components.

22. A description of all devolution, partnership, franchising and privatization activities developed through the Who Does What process as it impacted on the Town of Walkerton.

23. All documents relating to provincial government consideration of, analysis and transfer, devolution, or discontinuation of provincial responsibility, funding or support for sewer and water infrastructure to municipalities, together with all funding allocations thereto, and all documents relating to Bill 107, the Water and Sewage Services Improvements Act including for all of the above:

(a) draft and final Cabinet Board submissions, Management Board submissions, Policies and Priorities Board submissions, and minutes and documents related thereto;

(b) instructions, directions and documents from the Central Agencies to MOE related thereto;

(c) documents prepared for, submitted to or received from Who Does What Committees and the Red Tape Commissions or Committees related thereto;

(d) business cases prepared by MOE; and

(e) risk assessment and implementation strategy documents including monitoring and evaluation, performance measures and documents related thereto.

24. Budgetary, human resource and program reductions: For each year, the operating budget and capital budget allocated to the MOE, together with staffing levels by Regional District, Division, Area Office, Local Offices, Branch and Section, including occupational breakdown in each of those categories in each of those years, including background documents and documents prior to and subsequent to any such budgetary, human resource and program reductions assessing the anticipated or actual impact of those reductions by functional area and occupational breakdown, including estimates and draft estimates provided to the Central Agencies or designates of Central Agencies dealing with program or expenditure reduction, and instructions from the Central Agencies to MOE related thereto.

25. The reduction in investigation and enforcement branch staff of the MOE. Number of staff positions eliminated or laid off with respect to the following matters:

- water and drinking water;

- groundwater and hydrogeology;

- watershed management; and

- waste water

by Region, District Office, Area Office, Local Office, Branch and Section, including occupational breakdown, by year.

26. All documents relating to alternative service delivery strategies for MOE staff, including <u>Summary Document for the Delivery Strategies - Draft</u>, Ministry of the Environment, April 9, 1998, together with all other drafts and any final version, and any documents related thereto.

27. A description of MOE's alternative service delivery strategies and standards relevant to drinking water, water works or drinking water facilities together with all business plans, risk assessment tools, implementation strategies, monitoring and evaluation measures.

28. All documents relating to the September, 1996 termination of the provision of drinking water testing services by the MOE and the Ministry of Health to municipalities, including all documents relating to a review of the availability, capability, capacity and costs of private sector testing and consultation with the Ministry of Health, Medical Officers of Health, District Health Councils, Local Boards of Health and municipalities relating to same, and including:

   (a) draft and final Cabinet Board submissions, Management Board submissions, Policies and Priorities Board submissions, and minutes and documents related thereto;

   (b) instructions, directions and documents from the Central Agencies to MOE related thereto;

   (c) documents prepared for, submitted to or received from Who Does What Committees and the Red Tape Commissions or Committees related thereto;

   (d) business cases prepared by MOE; and

   (e) risk assessment and implementation strategy documents including monitoring and evaluation, performance measures and documents related thereto.

29. Regarding the Ontario Drinking Water Objectives ("ODWOs"), all documents relating to the development of the parameters and changes to any

of the parameters, as well as operational guidelines and changes to operational guidelines in this period, including business cases, risk assessment, implementation, monitoring and evaluation/performance documents related thereto.

30. All documents collected or received by the MOE relating to epidemiological data or information respecting drinking water related illnesses in Ontario.

31. All reports by the Environmental Commissioner and all briefing notes and documents related to such reports.

32. All documents relating to the budget (operating and capital) of OCWA.

33. Documents relating to the Federal-Provincial Sub-Committee on Drinking Water including changes to guideline limits.

34. All relevant documents tendered to any federal/provincial forum dealing with drinking water matters, including all communiqués signed by Ontario Ministers, and Minister's briefing notes and books for federal/ provincial meetings dealing with water issues.

35. Briefing notes and House Minute Books pertaining to the contamination of the municipal water supply in the Town of Walkerton and other matters set out in the Terms of Reference of the Inquiry up to the present and on a continuing basis.

36. Issues notes prepared by the Issue Unit in the last 24 months relating to drinking water.

37. From the Regional Communications Section of the Communications Branch, all documents sent to the Area, Local or District Office responsible for the Town of Walkerton.

38. The annual performance contracts or agreements between the Deputy Minister and the Secretary of Cabinet.

39. From the Internal Audit Services Branch, audit plans and internal audit reports.

40. With respect to drinking water quality, inspection, testing and water works and facilities, all guidelines, training material, manuals, standards and performance guidelines for MOE staff and contractors in the Area, Local or District Office responsible for the Town of Walkerton.

41. Documents between MOE and the Ministry of the Attorney General regarding staffing of the MOE Legal Services Branch, and expenditures for outside counsel.

SEARCH WARRANT

APPENDIX H (II)

Search Warrant

(Public Inquiries Act, R.S.O. 1990, c. P. 41, as amended, Form 3)

TO: Inspector Craig Hannaford, Royal Canadian Mounted Police, Constable Marc Bolduc, Mr. Don Glinz, Mr. Wayne Scott, Ms. Juli Abouchar, and Ms. Rachel Young, and to such peace officers as they call upon to assist them:

WHEREAS it appears on the oath of Inspector Craig Hannaford of the City of Burlington in the Province of Ontario, a person appointed by a Commission of Inquiry to make an investigation under s.17 of the *Public Inquiries Act*, that there are reasonable grounds for believing that certain things, to wit:

See Appendix "A"

Are relevant to the subject-matter of the Commission of Inquiry issued pursuant to Order-in-Council 1170/2000 and known as the Commission of the Walkerton Inquiry and are in a certain building, receptacle or place, to wit:

The 4ᵗʰ Floor, Whitney Block, 99 Wellesley Street West,
Toronto, Ontario, M7A 1A1

(hereinafter called the "Premises");

AND WHEREAS it appears that a warrant to search for the said things should issue, notwithstanding the provisions of subsections 168(1) of the *Environmental Protection Act*, R.S.O. 1990, c. E. 19, as amended, s. 27 of the *Environmental Assessment Act*, R.S.O. 1990, c. E. 18, as amended, and the provisions of the *Freedom of Information and Protection of Privacy Act*, R.S.O. 1990, c. F. 31, as amended;

This is, therefore, to authorize and require you between the hours of 9:00 a.m. and 6:00 p.m. to enter into the said Premises on each of the following dates: January 16, 17, 18, and 19, 2001, and to search for the said things, subject to the conditions set out in Appendix "B", and to bring them before the Honourable Dennis R. O'Connor, the Commissioner conducting the said Inquiry.

GIVEN UNDER MY HAND this 12 day of January, 2001, at the Town of Milton, Ontario.

_____

The Honourable Mr. Justice Bruce Durno
Superior Court of Justice

Appendix "A"—Items to Be Searched For

Definitions

"Document" refers to any memorandum, data, analysis, report, minutes, briefing material, submission, correspondence, record or any other note or communication in writing, and specifically including any electronic communications including e-mail both internal, and that which has been sent to or received from external sources, in relation to the matters listed below.

"Government" means the Government of Ontario, unless otherwise specified.

Documents

Documents, including all copies identified as to source and where relevant, indicating the author of marginalia, which are relevant to the following matters:

1. All documents constituting communications between Management Board and the MOE, any other Ministry, any of the Central Agencies, OCWA, and any other agency, board or commission, with respect to any of the matters giving rise to the Inquiry up to the present time, and continuing.

2. All documents relating to Management Board and government analysis of the transfer, devolution, or discontinuation of provincial responsibility, funding or support for sewer and water infrastructure to municipalities, together with all funding allocations thereto, and all documents relating to exemptions from environmental laws, regulations and guidelines, and all documents relating to the *Water and Sewage Services Improvements Act, 1997*, the *Municipal Water and Sewage Transfer Act, 1997*, and *The Environmental Approvals Improvement Act, 1997* including for all of the above:

    (a) draft and final Cabinet submissions, Management Board submissions, Policies and Priorities Board submissions, and minutes and documents related thereto, including Management Board minutes;

    (b) instructions, directions and documents from Management Board or the Central Agencies to MOE or the Ministry of Municipal Affairs and Housing related thereto;

(c)   documents prepared for, submitted to or received from Who Does What Committees and the Red Tape Commissions or Committees related thereto, including minutes of sectoral tables;

(d)   business cases prepared by MOE and the Ministry of Municipal Affairs and Housing; and

(e)   budget, risk assessment and implementation strategy documents including monitoring and evaluation, performance measures and documents related thereto.

3.   All documents relating to the termination of the provision of drinking water testing services by the MOE and the MOH to municipalities, including all Management Board or Central Agency instructions, directions and analysis, all documents relating to a review of the availability, capability, capacity and costs of private sector testing and consultation with the MOH, MOE, Medical Officers of Health, District Health Councils, Local Boards of Health and municipalities relating to same, and including:

(a)   draft and final Cabinet submissions, Management Board submissions, Policies and Priorities Board submissions, and minutes and documents related thereto;

(b)   instructions, directions and documents from Management Board or the Central Agencies to MOE or the MOH related thereto;

(c)   documents prepared for, submitted to or received from Who Does What Committees and the Red Tape Commissions or Committees related thereto, including minutes of sectoral tables;

(d)   business cases prepared by MOE and the MOH; and

(e)   risk assessment and implementation strategy documents including monitoring and evaluation, performance measures and documents related thereto.

4.   All documents from Management Board to any Central Agency or Ministry including the Ministry of Agriculture, Food and Rural Affairs ("OMAFRA"), or from any Ministry or Central Agency to Management

Board relating to the *Farming and Food Production Protection Act, 1998*, intensive agricultural operations in rural Ontario, Best Management Practices, the July, 2000 proposed standards for agricultural operations in Ontario, or the effect of agricultural operations on drinking water, and including:

(a) draft and final Cabinet Board submissions, Management Board submissions, Policies and Priorities Board submissions, and minutes and documents related thereto;

(b) instructions, directions and documents from Management Board and the Central Agencies to OMAFRA related thereto;

(c) documents prepared for, submitted to or received from Who Does What Committees and the Red Tape Commissions or Committees related thereto, including minutes of sectoral tables;

(d) business cases prepared by OMAFRA; and

(e) risk assessment and implementation strategy documents including monitoring and evaluation, performance measures and documents related thereto.

5. All documents relating to the withdrawal of MOE or MOH resources from drinking water labs and drinking water related matters, testing, audit and monitoring programs including documents relating to alternate service delivery strategies, risk assessment, implementation strategies, monitoring and evaluation, both prospective and actual, and instructions, directions and documents from Management Board or the Central Agencies to MOE or MOH related thereto.

6. Budgetary, human resource and program reductions: For each year, the operating budget and capital budget allocated to the MOE, together with staffing levels, all Management Board analysis related thereto, including background documents and documents prior to and subsequent to any such budgetary, human resource and program reductions assessing the anticipated or actual impact of those reductions, including estimates and draft estimates provided by or to Management Board or to the Central Agencies or designates of Central Agencies dealing with program or expenditure reduction, and instructions from Management Board or the

Central Agencies to MOE related thereto and all minutes related thereto, including sectoral documents.

7.   A description of all devolution, partnership, franchising and privatization activities developed through the Who Does What process as it impacted on the Town of Walkerton and the PUC, including the amalgamation of municipalities.

Appendix "B"

Conditions Attaching to the Issuance and Execution of This Search Warrant

1.   This search warrant shall not be executed in a manner that interferes with any ongoing criminal investigation or proceedings.

2.   When this search warrant is executed, a copy of it shall be provided to the person apparently in charge of the premises.

3.   To the extent that original documents rather than photocopies or electronic copies are seized pursuant to this search warrant, the original documents shall be photocopied at the expense of the Commission of the Walkerton Inquiry and, as soon as is reasonably practicable, the originals shall be returned to the premises in the same condition as they had been in at the time of the seizure.

Procedures to Be Followed Where Privilege Claimed

1 (1) Definitions – In this appendix,

"Attorney General" means the Attorney General of Ontario or counsel acting on his behalf;

"custodian" means a person in whose custody a package is placed pursuant to subsection (2);

"Commissioner" means the Commissioner of the Walkerton Inquiry and includes counsel acting on his behalf;

"document" means any paper or other material on which there is recorded anything that is capable of being read or understood by a person, computer system or other device;

"Government of Ontario" includes all ministries, Cabinet office, the Premier's Office, and all agencies, boards and commissions of the Government of the Province of Ontario;

"judge" means a judge of the Superior Court of Justice for the Province of Ontario;

"officer" means a peace officer engaged in execution of this search warrant;

"privilege" means solicitor-client privilege, cabinet privilege or public interest immunity

2. **Examination or seizure of certain documents where search warrant privilege claimed** – Where an officer acting under the authority of this search warrant is about to examine, copy or seize a document in the possession of the Government of Ontario and privilege is claimed in respect of that document, the officer shall, without examining or making copies of this document,

(a) seize the document and place it in a package and suitably seal and identify the package; and

(b) place the package in the custody of the Commissioner.

3. **Application to judge** – Where a document has been seized and placed in custody under section (2), the Commissioner or the Attorney General may

(a) within sixty days from the day the document was so placed in custody apply, on two days notice of motion to all other persons entitled to make application to a judge for an order

(i) appointing a place and a day, not later than twenty-one days after the date of the order, for the determination of the question whether the document should be disclosed, and

(ii) requiring the custodian to produce the document to the judge at that time and place;

(b) serve a copy of the order on all other persons entitled to make application and on the custodian within six days of the date on which it was made; and

(c) if he has proceeded as authorized by paragraph (b), apply, at the appointed time and place, for an order determining the question.

4. **Disposition of application** – On an application under paragraph (3)(c), the judge

(a) may, if the judge considers it necessary to determine the question whether the document should be disclosed, inspect the document;

(b) where the judge is of the opinion that it would materially assist him in deciding whether or not the document is privileged, may allow the Commissioner to inspect the document;

(c) shall allow the Commissioner and the Attorney General to make representations; and

(d) shall determine the question summarily and,

(i) if he is of the opinion that the document should not be disclosed, ensure that it is repackaged and resealed and order the custodian to return the document to the Government of Ontario, or

(ii) if he is of the opinion that the document should be disclosed, order the custodian to deliver the document to the officer who seized the document or some other person designated by the Commissioner, subject to such restrictions or conditions as the judge deems appropriate;

and shall, at the same time, deliver concise reasons for the determination in which the nature of the document is described without divulging the details thereof.

5. **Privilege continues** – Where the judge determines pursuant to paragraph (4)(d) that a privilege exists in respect of a document, whether or not he has, pursuant to paragraph (4)(b), allowed the Commissioner to inspect the document, the document remains privileged and inadmissible as evidence unless the Government of Ontario consents to its admission in evidence or the privilege is otherwise lost.

6. **Order to custodian to deliver** – where a document has been seized and placed in custody under section (2) and a judge, on the application of the Commissioner, is satisfied that no application has been made under paragraph (3)(a) or that following such an application no further application has been made under paragraph (3)(c), the judge shall order the custodian to deliver the document to the officer who seized the document or to some other person designated by the Commissioner.

7. **Application to another judge** – Where the judge to whom an application has been made under paragraph (3)(c) cannot act or continue to act under this section for any reason, subsequent applications under that paragraph may be made to another judge.

8. **Prohibition** – No officer shall examine, make copies of or seize any document without affording a reasonable opportunity for a claim of privilege to be made under subsection (2).

9. **Authority to make copies** – At any time while a document is in the custody of a custodian under this section, a judge may, on an *ex parte* application of a person claiming a privilege under this appendix, authorize that person to examine the document or make a copy of it in the presence of the custodian or the judge, but any such authorization shall contain provisions to ensure that the document is repackaged and that the package is resealed without alteration or damage.

10. **Hearing in private** – An application under paragraph (3)(c) shall be heard in private.

LETTERS RE: CABINET PRIVILEGE

APPENDIX H (III)

SMITH LYONS

BARRISTERS & SOLICITORS   PATENT & TRADE-MARK AGENTS

Suite 1800, Scotia Plaza
40 King Street West
Toronto, Ontario
M5H 3Z7

Telephone: (416) 369-7200
Facsimile: (416) 369-7250

Glenn Hainey
Direct Line: (416) 369-7278
E-Mail: GAHainey@SmithLyons.ca
Web Site: www.SmithLyons.ca

November 29, 2000

Mr. Paul Cavalluzzo
The Walkerton Inquiry
22nd Floor
180 Dundas Street West
Toronto, Ontario
M5G 1Z8

Dear Mr. Cavalluzzo:

    Re: **The Government of Ontario's Claim of**
           Cabinet Privilege and Public Interest Immunity

I am writing to you to follow up on discussions that you, Ron Foerster, Frank Marrocco and I had on Monday, November 20, 2000, regarding the most appropriate procedure to deal with the Government of Ontario's claim that certain documents sought by The Walkerton Inquiry are subject to Cabinet privilege and/or public interest immunity. You indicated to us that you were considering stating a case to the Divisional Court in order to obtain a determination as to whether the Government of Ontario has waived its right to claim Cabinet privilege and/or public interest immunity in respect of any documents sought by The Walkerton Inquiry by reason of the wording of the Order in Council establishing the Commission of Inquiry on June 13, 2000.

As you know, it is our client's position that the issue as to whether claims by the Government of Ontario that certain documents are subject to Cabinet privilege or public interest immunity is a matter which ought to be dealt with under the terms of the search warrants which have been issued by The Walkerton Inquiry. The search warrants specifically contemplate that the final determination of this issue will be made by the Judge who issued the search warrants at a hearing in private, as is the normal practice prescribed by the Criminal Code of Canada. It is, accordingly, our client's strongly held view that the issue which you wish to have determined by the Divisional Court should be determined by Justice Durno in accordance with the procedure prescribed by your own search warrants.

SMITH LYONS

We discussed a number of alternative procedures and in the interests of ensuring that the Walkerton Inquiry does not become delayed by time-consuming and lengthy court applications our client is prepared to deal with this issue in the following manner:

Counsel for the Attorney General of Ontario and the Commissioner of The Walkerton Inquiry will apply to Justice Durno for an order under section 4(b) of the search warrants allowing Commission Counsel to inspect all documents for which a claim of Cabinet privilege and/or public interest immunity has been advanced. This will enable you and your legal staff to determine in an expeditious manner which, if any, of these documents you wish to enter into evidence at the Inquiry in order to fulfil the Commission of Inquiry's mandate. Justice Durno's order will make it clear (as do the terms of the search warrants) that the review of these documents by Commission Counsel does not constitute a waiver of the Government's claim for Cabinet privilege and/or public interest immunity and the document will remain privileged and inadmissible unless:

1. the Government of Ontario consents to its admission into evidence at The Walkerton Inquiry; or

2. Justice Durno, after holding a hearing as contemplated under section 3(c) of the search warrant, dismisses the claim of Cabinet privilege and/or public interest immunity and orders the document to be admitted into evidence at The Walkerton Inquiry.

As discussed, we are optimistic that in respect of those documents that Commission Counsel wishes to utilize at the Inquiry we will either agree to waive the privilege otherwise attaching to them or agree on an alternative means of introducing into evidence the information contained in the documents in a manner that does not actually waive the privilege on the document itself (e.g. through affidavit evidence or document summaries).

In the event we are unable to agree on all of the documents which you wish to introduce into evidence at the Inquiry a hearing will be held before Justice Durno to determine the issue including the "threshold issue" as to whether the Order in Council precludes the Government from making a claim for Cabinet privilege and/or public interest immunity in respect of any documents sought by the Inquiry.

Notwithstanding that your search warrants provide that the hearing before Justice Durno is to be held in private we understand that you wish to notify all parties with standing at the Inquiry of the date and place of the hearing and it will be left to Justice Durno to decide whether the hearing of the waiver issue should proceed in private or in open court.

As we have indicated to you in the past, the Government of Ontario remains committed to cooperating fully with The Walkerton Inquiry, particularly in relation to the production of documents and witnesses, however, the Government believes there is a strong public interest which requires it to protect Cabinet privilege and public interest immunity to the fullest extent possible.

Smith Lyons

Please let me know if the procedure outlined above is satisfactory to you.

Sincerely,

Glenn Hainey

GH/iw

THE WALKERTON INQUIRY   **LA COMMISSION
D'ENQUÊTE WALKERTON**

Ontario

December 4, 2000

Smith Lyons
Barristers & Solicitors
Suite 5800 Scotia Plaza
40 King Street West
Toronto, Ontario
M5H 3Z7

Attention: Mr. Glenn Hainey

Dear Sir:

RE: The Government of Ontario's Claim of Cabinet Privilege and Public Interest Immunity

Thank you for your letter of November 29, 2000 regarding the above-noted matter.

We have the following comments concerning your letter:

i)   In regard to the 1ˢᵗ paragraph on page 2, we assume that Commission Counsel including our legal staff will be permitted to inspect all documents for which a claim of Cabinet privilege and/or public interest immunity has been claimed.

ii) In respect of the hearing before Justice Durno to resolve the "threshold issue" of whether the Government is precluded from asserting Cabinet privilege and/or public interest immunity, we assume that this hearing will be in public because it raises issues of public importance. As well, we will give notice to other parties to give them an opportunity to intervene before Justice Durno.

iii)   In the event that Justice Durno is asked to resolve the privilege and/or immunity issue in the context of a particular document, notice will be given to the other parties. Justice Durno will decide whether intervenor status will be granted and whether the hearing will be in camera.

Because of the general importance of this protocol, the Commissioner will call upon the parties for their views in writing within a limited time period. We feel this is important so that the procedure is transparent and open. After receiving these submissions, Commission Counsel will be in a position to finally agree upon this protocol.

We thank you for your co-operation and creativity in attempting to resolve this difficult issue.

Yours very truly,

Paul J.J. Cavalluzzo
Commission Counsel
/nc

THE WALKERTON INQUIRY   **LA COMMISSION D'ENQUÊTE WALKERTON**

Ontario

December 20, 2000

Smith Lyons
Barristers & Solicitors
Suite 5800 Scotia Plaza
40 King Street West
Toronto, Ontario
M5H 3Z7

Attention: Mr. Glenn Hainey

Dear Sir:

RE: The Government of Ontario's Claim of Cabinet Privilege and Public Interest Immunity

Further to my letter of December 04, 2000 this is to confirm our understanding that the Commissioner will not call upon the parties for their written views in accordance with the penultimate paragraph in that letter until such time as the parties reach an impasse in regard to any document which Commission Counsel wishes to introduce into evidence. It is agreed that until such time as the Commissioner has received and reviewed these written representations, Commission Counsel will not be in a position to finally agree upon this protocol. The inspection by Commission Counsel of all documents for which a claim of Cabinet privilege and/or public interest immunity has been advanced shall not be construed in any way as an agreement to the protocol.

Finally, we agree that any application to Justice Durno to resolve any dispute between the parties in accordance with the protocol which is finally agreed upon will be deemed to be a Rule 14.01 application.

Once again, thank you for your cooperation in this matter.

Yours truly,

Paul J.J. Cavalluzzo
Commission Counsel
/nc

UNDERTAKINGS RE: CONFIDENTIALITY

APPENDIX H (IV)

THE WALKERTON INQUIRY

Ontario

LA COMMISSION
D'ENQUÊTE WALKERTON

Undertaking of Counsel to the Commission of the Walkerton Inquiry

I undertake to the Commission of the Walkerton Inquiry that any and all documents or information which are produced to me in connection with the Commission's proceedings will not be used by me for any purpose other than those proceedings. I further undertake that I will not disclose any such documents or information to anyone for whom I do not act, and to anyone for whom I act only upon the individual in question giving the written undertaking annexed hereto. In the event I act for a coalition, I will disclose such documents and information to anyone who is a member of that coalition only upon the individual in question giving the written undertaking annexed hereto.

I understand that this undertaking has no force or effect once any such document or information has become part of the public proceedings of the Commission, or to the extent that the Commissioner may release me from the undertaking with respect to any document or information. For greater certainty, a document is only part of the public proceedings once the document is made an exhibit at the Inquiry.

With respect to those documents or information which remain subject to this undertaking at the end of the Inquiry, I undertake to either destroy those documents or information, and provide a certificate of destruction to the Commission, or to return those documents to the Commission for destruction. I further undertake to collect for destruction such documents or information from anyone to whom I have disclosed any documents or information which were produced to me in connection with the Commission's proceedings.

Signature	Witness
Date	Date

THE WALKERTON INQUIRY

Ontario

LA COMMISSION
D'ENQUÊTE WALKERTON

Supplementary Undertaking of Counsel to the Commission of the Walkerton Inquiry with Respect to Experts

I undertake to the Commission of the Walkerton Inquiry that any and all documents or information which are produced to me in connection with the Commission's proceedings will not be used by me for any purpose other than those proceedings. I further undertake that I will not disclose any such documents or information to anyone for whom I do not act or who has not been retained as an expert for the purposes of the Inquiry. In respect of anyone for whom I act or any expert retained for the purposes of the Inquiry, I further undertake that I will disclose any such documents or information only upon the individual in question giving the appropriate written undertaking annexed hereto. In the event I act for a coalition, I will disclose such documents and information to anyone who is a member of that coalition only upon the individual in question giving the written undertaking annexed hereto.

I understand that this undertaking has no force or effect once any such document or information has become part of the public proceedings of the Commission, or to the extent that the Commissioner may release me from the undertaking with respect to any document or information. For greater certainty, a document is only part of the public proceedings once the document is made an exhibit at the Inquiry.

With respect to those documents or information which remain subject to this undertaking at the end of the Inquiry, I undertake to either destroy those documents or information, and provide a certificate of destruction to the Commission, or to return those documents to the Commission for destruction. I further undertake to collect for destruction such documents or information from anyone to whom I have disclosed any documents or information which were produced to me in connection with the Commission's proceedings.

_____   _____
Signature   Witness

_____   _____
Date   Date

THE WALKERTON INQUIRY

Ontario

**LA COMMISSION
D'ENQUÊTE WALKERTON**

Undertaking of Parties to the Commission of the Walkerton Inquiry

I undertake to the Commission of the Walkerton Inquiry that any and all documents or information which are produced to me in connection with the Commission's proceedings will not be used by me for any purpose other than those proceedings. I further undertake that I will not disclose any such documentation or information to anyone.

I understand that this undertaking will have no force or effect with respect to any document or information which becomes part of the public proceedings of the Commission, or to the extent that the Commissioner may release me from the undertaking with respect to any document or information. For greater certainty, a document is only part of the public proceedings once the document is made an exhibit at the Inquiry.

With respect to those documents or information which remain subject to this undertaking at the end of the Inquiry, I further understand that such documents or information will be collected from me by the person acting as my counsel who disclosed them to me.

_____
Signature

_____
Witness

_____
Date

_____
Date

THE WALKERTON INQUIRY

Ontario

LA COMMISSION
D'ENQUÊTE WALKERTON

Undertaking of Experts to the Commission of the Walkerton Inquiry

I undertake to the Commission of the Walkerton Inquiry that any and all documents or information which are produced to me in connection with the Commission's proceedings will not be used by me for any purpose other than those proceedings. I further undertake that I will not disclose any such documentation or information to anyone.

I understand that this undertaking will have no force or effect with respect to any document or information which becomes part of the public proceedings of the Commission, or to the extent that the Commissioner may release me from the undertaking with respect to any document or information. For greater certainty, a document is only part of the public proceedings once the document is made an exhibit at the Inquiry.

With respect to those documents or information which remain subject to this undertaking at the end of the Inquiry, I further understand that such documents or information will be collected from me by the person acting as counsel who disclosed them to me.

Signature	Witness
Date	Date

CERTIFICATE OF PRODUCTION

APPENDIX H (V)

Certification of Production of Documents

I .... *(full name of person)*,

of the (City, Town, *etc.*) of ....

in the (County, Regional Municipality, *etc.*) of .... ,

a .... (Deputy Minister, *etc.*)

of the .... (Ministry, Agency, *etc.*)

of the Province of Ontario, have made the necessary enquiries of others to inform myself in order to make this Certification and, to the full extent of my knowledge, information and belief, based on those enquiries, do **CERTIFY THAT**:

1. The .... (Ministry, Agency, *etc.*) received (a) document request(s) from the Walkerton Commission of Inquiry ("the Commission").

2. In accordance with the document request(s) and correspondence from the Commission dated January 24, 2001, the search for documents was restricted to documents created in the period April 1, 1993 to December 5, 2000, unless otherwise specifically directed by the Commission.

3. Staff and employees of the Ministry were directed to conduct a diligent search of the paper-based and electronically-maintained documents in the possession, custody or control of the Ministry in response to the Commission's document request(s) and any subsequent communication with the Commission which requested all documents "relevant to the subject matter of the Inquiry".

4. The process of document production was conducted as directed and I am fully satisfied that all documents requested by the Commission, as referenced in paragraph 3 above, have been produced to the Commission.

5. If I learn, before the public release of the Commissioner's final report(s) by the Attorney General, that this Certification was based on incorrect information, the Commission shall be contacted forthwith with the correct information.

Date: ....

(Signature)

SECTION 5(2) NOTICE

APPENDIX I (I)

THE WALKERTON INQUIRY   **LA COMMISSION D'ENQUÊTE WALKERTON**

Ontario

Notice of Alleged Misconduct

(Public Inquiries Act, s-s.5(2))

Pursuant to subsection 5(2) of the *Public Inquiries Act*, you are notified that in its report(s), the Commission of the Walkerton Inquiry may make a finding of misconduct by you, the substance of which alleged misconduct is set out in Schedule "A", attached.

This notice is given without prejudice to the ability of the Commission of the Walkerton Inquiry, through its counsel, to modify the particulars of the substance of the alleged misconduct as circumstances may necessitate.

Receipt of this notice entitles you full opportunity to be heard in person or through counsel with regard to those issues or areas of evidence that affect your interest.

To: [Name of recipient of Notice]   From: Paul Cavalluzzo
                                      Commission Counsel
                                      Commission of the Walkerton Inquiry

Date: October 12, 2000.

Schedule "A"

Substance of Alleged Misconduct

In his report(s), the Commissioner may find that:

[Details of substance of alleged misconduct]

LETTER OF MARCH 1, 2000 TO RECIPIENT OF SECTION 5(2) NOTICE

APPENDIX I (II)

THE WALKERTON INQUIRY **LA COMMISSION D'ENQUÊTE WALKERTON**

Ontario

March 1, 2001

Dear [Counsel to recipient of 5(2) notice]:

Re: [Name of recipient of 5(2) notice]

Thank you for your letter of February 19, 2001. I set out below responses to your inquiries.

The intention of Commission Counsel in providing your client with the Notice of February 6, 2001 was to give him notice that a finding of misconduct might be made, and to provide you with the opportunity to address such a potential finding. As a recipient of a section 5(2) notice, your client is entitled to standing limited to responding to the issues raised in the Notice. As such, he is entitled to production of all exhibits, or documents which Commission counsel intends to put into evidence, that are relevant to these issues.

You may review the transcripts of the Inquiry which are available free of charge on the Internet at www.tscript.com. Please follow the button on the left for "Transcript Repository" and, on that page, follow the button for "Walkerton Inquiry". In Part IA, XXX testified on XXX; if you go to those dates, you will find his transcript. I also note that you may find portions of the testimony of XXX relevant to issues raised in the Notice. In particular, I refer you to Mr. XXX's testimony on XXX at pages 158-60 and 166-9; and on XXX **at 15-20**, 39-40, and 136-41. I point out these references in order to provide assistance to you without suggesting that these references are exhaustive of portions of the transcripts that you might find relevant to issues raised in the Notice. You will note that there is a key-word index on the left side of the transcript, keyed into letters of the alphabet in the top left portion of the screen. All transcripts may be printed in your office.

There is a list of all witnesses, with the dates of testimony, on our main Inquiry web page at www.walkertoninquiry.com. Please follow the button on the left for "Transcripts". You will find both an index of witnesses and an index of exhibits on that page. All exhibits are available for public viewing at the Inquiry offices; you should call in advance to book should you wish to review any exhibits. Please note that documents received by the Commission, even when they are not made exhibits, may be searched electronically in our offices. If you wish to do a canvass of government policies on a particular issue, you may do an electronic database search. Again, you must book the time in advance.

Anyone is free to attend the Inquiry hearings at any time. As a recipient of a section 5(2) notice who does not otherwise have standing before the Inquiry, your client is entitled to participate in the hearings in Part IB to the extent necessary to provide him with the opportunity to respond to the issues raised in the Notice. Your client may apply to call evidence and cross-examine witnesses relating to the matters set out in the Notice. Given the nature of the testimony of Mr. XXX and Mr. XXX, and the contents of the section 5(2) notice, we do not anticipate that Mr. XXX would be engaged in the Part IB process, although you may wish to make submissions.

Commission counsel will notify you as early as possible if we anticipate that a particular witness will engage your client's interest. You will also receive copies of statements of anticipated evidence for Section III of Part IB. If you feel your client should be entitled to attend the hearings in order to cross-examine a particular witness, then you should contact Commission counsel. It is also open to you to request that Commission Counsel ask specific questions relevant to your interest. In the latter case, the decision as to whether and what to ask would be at the discretion of Commission Counsel. Finally, all of the Part IB transcripts will be available for review on the Internet.

The Part IB hearings will be commencing on March 5. The evidence will be called in approximately the order of the "Outline of Potential Issues" located on the Commission website under the "Legal Information" button.

We anticipate that time will be set aside for recipients of section 5(2) notices to apply to call additional evidence, likely at the conclusion of Part IB. You will also have the right to make closing submissions to the Commissioner relating to your client's interest. Although no date has been set, it is likely that written submissions will be due in July, 2001, with oral submissions to be heard in

August, 2001. You will also have the right to make legal submissions on the applicable criteria for the issuance, modification or amendment of section 5(2) notices.

If you choose to participate in the manner set out above, it is not necessary for you to formally apply to the Commissioner for standing. Your participation will follow from your rights under section 5(2) of the Public Inquiries Act.

You may of course apply for a formal order granting your client standing. I note, however, that written applications for standing, and the Commissioner's rulings, are public. As you know, section 5(2) notices are and will remain confidential unless you put the Notice into evidence or choose otherwise to make it public I raise this point simply to alert you as to the manner in which you might wish to approach your participation in the Inquiry generally. If you do intend to apply for a formal order granting your client standing, we would encourage you to do so at the earliest possible opportunity.

In terms of funding, the Commissioner is prepared to recommend that the Attorney General provide funding to persons who have received a section 5(2) notice. Funding would be provided in accordance with the guidelines of the Ministry of the Attorney General. If your client requires funding, you should provide a written application for funding. The Commissioner will consider such an application with reference to the criteria outlined in the "Funding" document located under "Legal Information" at www.walkertoninquiry.com.

I trust that this addresses the issues that you raised in your letter and I would like to thank you for your cooperation. Please feel free to contact me should you have any further questions.

Yours truly,

Paul Cavalluzzo
Commission Counsel

Letter of March 26, 2000 to Recipient of Section 5(2) Notice

Appendix I (III)

THE WALKERTON INQUIRY

Ontario

**LA COMMISSION
D'ENQUÊTE WALKERTON**

March 26, 2001

Dear [Counsel to recipient of 5(2) notice]:

Re: [Name of recipient of 5(2) notice]

We wish to offer further clarification about the process for you to determine whether you should participate in the Inquiry hearings in light of the issues raised in the Notice provided to your client. In addition, we have enclosed CD-Roms containing documents produced by Commission counsel to Part I parties to date; these are discussed below.

A.   Participation in hearings

As previously indicated to you, Commission counsel will endeavour to provide all summaries of anticipated evidence for witnesses in what we believe are the relevant Sections of Part IB. At present, we intend to provide you with summaries of anticipated evidence for Section III of Part IB (see the outline of issues in Part IB available on our website). In most cases you will receive these summaries, together with a list of documents we intend to enter into evidence, one week in advance.

We currently anticipate that portions of the evidence in Section III that deals with training may be relevant to your client. Evidence dealing with this issue is presently scheduled for the week of April 23 although this is subject to change. If we come to believe that other portions of the evidence are relevant to your client's interest, we will notify you at the earliest opportunity. In some cases this may be after the evidence is heard. In such cases you may apply to recall relevant witnesses.

You have access to all transcripts of the Part I hearings and this allows you to verify yourself whether portions of the evidence are relevant to your client's interest. If you feel that the evidence of a particular witness has engaged your client's interest, you may apply to recall the witness.

In summary, Commission counsel will notify you of portions of the evidence in Part IB that we believe may engage your client's interest. However we also recommend that you examine the outline of issues in Part IB, read the summaries of anticipated evidence that we provide to you, and review the transcripts of the hearings, in order to determine whether the Part I evidence is relevant to your client. In the event that you were not present for a relevant witness, you may apply to recall the witness.

You will also have the opportunity to make closing submissions on behalf of your client. Closing submissions for Part I are currently scheduled for the weeks of August 13 and 20.

Please find enclosed an updated schedule and outline of evidence for Part IB which may assist you in planning your participation in the Inquiry hearings.

B.   Production of documents

With respect to the enclosed CD-Roms, please find enclosed:

1.   Fourteen (14) CD-Roms containing seventeen (17) volumes of documents produced to Part I parties to date; and

2.   Instructions entitled How to Use SUPERText CD View and How to Print Documents and Fields using SUPERText CD View.

We are providing you with the CD-Roms to allow you to access and print hard copies of documents that may be entered into evidence at the Inquiry for portions of Part IB that engage issues raised in the Notice provided to your client. All of the required software for viewing the documents is contained on the CD-Roms. Detailed instructions for locating and printing the documents are enclosed.

You will not need to review all of the documents on the CD-Roms. Rather, you will only need to review those documents which are relevant to your client's interest. We have provided you with all 14 of the CD-Roms so that you may quickly access relevant documents when they are identified in summaries of anticipated evidence or the transcripts for relevant portions of the Inquiry hearings. In the event that a relevant document which is identified in a summary of anticipated evidence or entered into evidence in the hearing room is not contained on one of the CD-Roms produced to you, then a hard copy of the document will be made available. You may also request copies of relevant documents entered as exhibits from our Walkerton office. We also note that the CD-Roms have a search function that allows you to search for key terms relating to the issues raised in the Notice provided to your client.

The enclosed documents are being produced to you subject to undertakings concerning confidentiality executed by you. **Please do not access the CD-Roms until after you have forwarded the appropriate "undertakings re confidentiality" by counsel** which can be downloaded and printed from www.walkertoninquiry.com under "Legal Information". Documents may be further disclosed to your clients only after you have in your files appropriate undertakings concerning confidentiality executed by those persons.

As a general guide, the CD-Roms labeled "vol001" and "vol002" contain documents collected from the Government of Ontario and from GAP EnviroMicrobial Services and A&L Canada Laboratories East.

The CD-Rom labeled "vol003" contains documents collected from the Walkerton Public Utilities Commission.

The CD-Rom labeled "vol004" contains documents collected from the Municipality of Brockton, the Walkerton PUC, Robert McKay and Bell Security.

The CD-Roms labeled "vol005", "vol006", " vol007" and "vol008" contain documents collected from the Government of Ontario (Ministry of Environment).

The CD-Rom labeled "vol009" and "vol010" contains documents collected from the Government of Ontario (Ministry of the Environment), the Office of the Environmental Commissioner of Ontario, and miscellaneous documents collected by the Commission.

The CD-Roms labeled "vol0011" to "vol0017" contain documents collected from the Government of Ontario.

All documents collected by the Commission have been reviewed and filtered by Commission counsel prior to production with regard to issues of relevancy (i.e. whether the document may be put into evidence in Part I) and confidentiality (i.e. whether the document contains personal information such as Social Insurance Numbers, salary information, and marital information).

In general, documents are referred to by their Inquiry Document Number ("InqDocNo"). You can locate relevant documents on the enclosed CD-Rom using that number. You are expected to print hard copies of these documents for your own purposes including for use in the hearing room. Hard copies will not be provided to counsel at the hearings. We regret that the Commission does not have facilities for counsel to print documents in Walkerton and therefore suggest that you make alternative arrangements for local printing if necessary.

The Commission continues to obtain and review documents and expects to provide additional CD-Roms in the future. You will be able to view additional documents collected by the Commission, but not produced to you, by attending at our offices in Toronto or in Walkerton. If you wish to do so, please contact the appropriate office in advance to schedule an appointment.

Please remember, as set out in Rules 30 and 31 of the Rules of Procedure and Practice, to provide Commission counsel with any document which you intend to file as an exhibit or otherwise refer to during the hearings, and which we have not produced, at least one day before the document will be referred to or filed. The purpose of this is to enable other parties to print a hard copy of the document in advance.

I trust that this provides some further assistance and guidance in anticipation of the upcoming hearings in Part IB.

Yours very truly,

Paul Cavalluzzo
Commission Counsel

**RULINGS ON MOTIONS
RE: SECTION 5(2) NOTICES**

APPENDIX J

THE WALKERTON INQUIRY LA COMMISSION
D'ENQUÊTE WALKERTON

Ontario

RULING

On the Motion and Supplementary Motion on behalf of Michelle Zillinger

1. The *Public Inquiries Act*, R.S.O. 1990, c.P.41 ["the Act"] provides as follows:

    ....

    5(1) A commission shall accord to any person who satisfies it that the person has a substantial and direct interest in the subject-matter of its inquiry an opportunity during the inquiry to give evidence and to call and examine or to cross-examine witnesses personally or by counsel on evidence relevant to the person's interest.

    (2) No finding of misconduct on the part of any person shall be made against the person in any report of a commission after an inquiry unless that person had <u>reasonable notice of the substance of the alleged misconduct</u> and was allowed full opportunity during the inquiry to be heard in person or by counsel. [Emphasis added].

    ....

2. On February 6, 2001, Commission Counsel provided Michelle Zillinger with a Notice under s.5(2) [excerpted above]. The Notice provided:

    ....

    In his report(s) the Commissioner may find that:

As an Environmental Officer with the Ministry of the Environment, when you performed an inspection of the Walkerton water works on February 25, 1998:

> (i)   you failed to review the chlorine residual levels recorded in the daily operating logs at the three wells in other than a cursory manner, and as a result, you failed to note that the chlorine residual levels were consistently and suspiciously recorded as an almost constant .75 mg./l. or .5 mg./l. at the pump houses.

3.   On April 3, 2001, Commission Counsel provided a further Notice to Ms. Zillinger. The only change from the original Notice was the addition of specific evidentiary references relating to the substance of the Notice. Since then, Ms. Zillinger has been informed of one further piece of evidence that may relate to the Notice.

4.   On her motion, Ms. Zillinger seeks four types of relief:

a.   An order quashing the s.5(2) Notice.

b.   A declaration as to what constitutes "misconduct" within the meaning of s.5(2).

c.   An order prohibiting any further Notices under s.5(2) or amendments to the Notice.

d.   An order for disclosure should there be further allegations made against her.

The Motion to Quash

5.   Ms. McCaffrey, counsel to Ms. Zillinger, made two arguments in support of the motion to quash.

6.   The first has to do with an alleged lack of evidence to support the allegation set out in the Notice. Ms. McCaffrey variously states that there is no evidence or insufficient evidence to sustain any finding adverse to Ms. Zillinger based on the evidence introduced at the hearing. As part of this, she argues that there is no evidence to causally connect Ms. Zillinger's

conduct to the events in Walkerton. This part of her argument would have me evaluate and assess the evidence now, before final argument, and in effect screen out any possible finding of misconduct before my final report.

7.   There are two reasons why this argument fails. First, it is premature. There is no procedure under the Act or in the Rules of Procedure and Practice for this inquiry providing for a motion of this sort. I have the discretion, of course, under s.3 of the Act to determine the procedure for this inquiry. In my view, however, it is not in the best interests of the inquiry to inject a new level of decision-making of the nature proposed, prior to hearing final arguments and before the issuance of my report.

8.   Public inquiries, as this inquiry shows, can be very complex. Indeed, one of the most frequently heard criticisms of public inquiries is that they take too long and become bogged down in procedural wrangling and challenges. The public interest is served by having inquiries proceed in an efficient and timely manner.

9.   That said, it is nonetheless imperative that all parties who could potentially be adversely affected by a finding in a report be granted procedural fairness. I am satisfied that this can be done without putting in place a procedure for the screening of potential findings prior to final argument. To establish such a procedure would in my view add an unnecessary layer of complexity, expense and potential for delay.

10. I am satisfied that Ms. Zillinger has received full procedural fairness. Ms. Zillinger, like other witnesses who received a s.5(2) notice, received details of the possible allegations, full disclosure of all the evidence that could adversely affect her, the opportunity to cross-examine witnesses and to call evidence relating to the possible allegations, and, finally, she will have the opportunity to make closing submissions.

11. It must be borne in mind that this is an inquiry, not a prosecution or a civil lawsuit. In my view, the screening procedure contemplated by Ms. McCaffrey, appropriate for those types of proceedings, is neither necessary nor desirable for a public inquiry.

12. The second argument that Ms. McCaffrey makes is that her client has suffered or will suffer prejudice by the manner in which her client was

provided with the s.5(2) Notice and the way in which evidence was led. I find no merit in this argument. Ms. McCaffrey suggests that Ms. Zillinger may have testified differently if she had been forewarned that a s.5(2) Notice was in the works. The answer to this is twofold. A s.5(2) Notice was not contemplated by Commission Counsel when Ms. Zillinger testified on November 6 and 7, 2000. Moreover, Ms. Zillinger testified again yesterday and has been repeatedly offered the opportunity to testify further, if she wishes, and has declined to do so.

13.   Next, Ms. McCaffrey suggests that Ms. Zillinger only learned yesterday, when Ms. Kristjanson was testifying, what Commission Counsel intended by the Notice. I have some difficulty accepting this position. However, accepting for the sake of argument that it is the case, Ms. Zillinger has been offered the opportunity of giving evidence, cross-examining any of the witnesses who have given evidence, or calling new evidence to address what is now said to be her understanding of the content of the Notice. She has declined to do so. Further, Ms. McCaffrey does not point to any specific prejudice that has affected her client's ability to participate in the proceeding and to answer the substance of the Notice.

14.   The argument that Ms. Zillinger has or will suffer prejudice if the Notice is not quashed is without merit.

Declaration as to what constitutes "misconduct"

15.   In issuing s.5(2) notices, Commission Counsel took a broad view of the meaning of misconduct so as to afford witnesses and others who might be affected by findings in the report the fullest possible procedural protections.

16.   In her affidavit, Commission Counsel, Ms. Kristjanson, described the process as follows:

> As Commission Counsel, we will not make submissions on the evidence, and will not take any position as to findings to be made. Rather, it was our view that where the evidence might support a factual finding which, broadly construed, might be perceived as unfavourable or adverse to a person's reputation, including conduct

that might be described as careless or an oversight, it would be most fair to the person to provide a section 5(2) notice. This was so the person would be put on notice, could avail herself of procedural protections, and could respond. Upon receipt of a section 5(2) notice, a person automatically gains limited standing for the purposes of that notice. This gives certain procedural protections to the person as set out in the Commission's Rules of Procedure and Practice... as well as by the operation of the *Public Inquiries Act.*

17. Having had the benefit of these procedural protections, Ms. McCaffrey now argues that I should make a declaration that misconduct be limited to behaviour that is morally reprehensible, necessarily involving the breach of an established and definite rule of behaviour. I note in passing that Justice Cory, in *Canada (Attorney General)* v. *Canada (Commission of Inquiry on the Blood System)* (1997), 151 D.L.R. (4th) 1 (S.C.C.), did not adopt this definition. Ms. McCaffrey goes on to ask that I also declare that misconduct is not inadvertence, negligence, carelessness, or even an error in judgment.

18. These declarations, in Ms. McCaffrey's submission, tie into her first request that the s.5(2) Notice be quashed. She argues that because there is no evidence of misconduct of the more egregious type, the result is that the Notice should be quashed.

19. This argument too must fail. This is an inquiry, not a prosecution or a proceeding alleging any particular outcome; in particular, misconduct. Were it otherwise, there may be merit in defining the scope of what needs to be proved.

20. The purpose of the s.5(2) notice is to ensure that those who may be affected by a finding receive procedural fairness. It also prevents a Commission from making a finding adverse to a person when such notice and procedural fairness has not been provided.

21. Given that both notice and procedural fairness have been provided to Ms. Zillinger, I do not think it either necessary or desirable that at this stage of the proceeding I make a declaration as to what may or may not constitute misconduct. It would be inappropriate to do so in advance of hearing arguments for all the parties who may be affected by the issue; in

particular, those who may wish, in their closing arguments, to make submissions about the conduct of others and how that conduct may have contributed to the events in Walkerton.

22. In this connection, I have repeatedly made clear that if any surprise or unfairness results from submissions during closing argument, an opportunity to address concerns of unfairness will be provided.

23. In passing, Ms. McCaffrey also asks that I make a declaration that misconduct must be causally connected to the tragedy. In particular, I am asked to define the scope of causation contemplated by the Order in Council. The interpretation of the mandate in the Order in Council, and in particular what constitutes causation, will likely be the subject of submissions in closing argument. It is premature to address this issue at this stage. It would operate unfairly to others with standing and I decline to do so.

Order prohibiting further Notices and amendments;
Order for disclosure should there be further allegations

24. These requests for relief are premature. I will address the propriety of any further notices if and when they are issued and I will of course address any concerns about procedural fairness at that time.

25. The Motion and Supplementary Motion are therefore dismissed.

DATE RELEASED: July 4, 2001

THE WALKERTON INQUIRY LA COMMISSION
D'ENQUÊTE WALKERTON

Ontario

Ruling

On the Motion on behalf of John Earl

1. Mr. Earl moves to quash the Section 5(2) Notice served on him. On his behalf, Mr. Barrie makes two points.

2. First, he argues that, because the evidence discloses no morally reprehensible behaviour or other conduct that could constitute "misconduct" on the part of his client, the Notice should be withdrawn.

3. As I said in my reasons disposing of Ms. Zillinger's motion, I do not think it is necessary or desirable at this stage to address the issue of what does or does not constitute misconduct, nor do I think I should assess the evidence as it relates to any particular individual before hearing the final submissions of all the parties. At that time, Mr. Earl, through his counsel, will be given a full opportunity to make submissions and to answer the arguments of others.

4. Mr. Barrie's second argument fails for the same reason. He asks that I now define the meaning of the causal connection in the Order in Council and rule that there is no such connection between his client's conduct and the events in Walkerton. This argument is also premature.

5. I do not see any advantage in adjourning this motion until final argument. If Mr. Barrie on behalf of his client wishes to renew the matter, he will be free to do so.

6. The motion is dismissed.

DATE RELEASED: July 4, 2001

THE WALKERTON INQUIRY   **LA COMMISSION D'ENQUÊTE WALKERTON**

Ontario

Ruling

On the Motion on behalf of Larry Struthers

1. Ms. Saxe, on behalf of Larry Struthers, asks for three orders. The first, having to do with ongoing disclosure, was satisfactorily resolved on the record in the hearing room.

2. Further, Ms. Saxe seeks an order or declaration as to the meaning of the word "caused" in the Order in Council and a declaration that mere error should not be stigmatized as misconduct.

3. Ms. Saxe very fairly recognizes that I am not required to make orders of this nature but suggests that, for purposes of clarity, it would be of benefit to do so. I appreciate the spirit in which she made her submissions. However, for the reasons set out in the Rulings regarding the motions of Michelle Zillinger and John Earl, I think it would be premature to make orders of this nature at this time.

4. The motion is dismissed.

DATE RELEASED: July 4, 2001

OUTLINE OF POTENTIAL ISSUES IN PART 1B

APPENDIX K (I)

THE WALKERTON INQUIRY

Ontario

LA COMMISSION
D'ENQUÊTE WALKERTON

Outline of Potential Issues in Part IB

(Revised February 14, 2001)

Please note that this outline may change as Commission counsel proceed with their document review and other preparation for Part IB.

Section I

Certificates of Approval

1.   Framework: history and nature of Certificate of Approval ("C of A") and Permit to Take Water processes (*Ontario Water Resources Act*, R.S.O. 1990, c.O.40)

2.   Policy and practice/ Changes in policy and practice: 1975-2000

     (a)   Types of conditions attached to C of As

     (b)   Summaries of C of As and conditions in Ontario

     (c)   Changes to legislation, policies and procedures

     (d)   Water works design guidelines

3.   Granting of C of As

     (a)   Imposition of conditions

(b)   Factors considered for new sources of water

(c)   Consideration of land uses and buffer zones

4.   Tracking and updating of C of As

(a)   Provincial responses to internal and external comment

5.   Use and dissemination of C of A information to local MOE staff, owner/ operator of water works, and local Medical Officer of Health, and the public

Section II

Water Quality Standards and Testing

1.   Roles of MOE and Ministry of Health & Long Term Care (MOHLTC) laboratories: pre-1996

(a)   Funding, including shift to charging municipalities for testing services in 1994, and basis for such charges

(b)   Testing for municipal communal water systems, including reporting of both satisfactory and adverse results

(c)   Communication with local MOE offices and local Medical Officers of Health

2.   Drinking water quality standards

(a)   Ontario Drinking Water Objectives ("ODWOs")

(b)   Guidelines versus regulation

(c)   Promulgation and revisions

(d)   Roles of Ontario Drinking Water Co-ordinating Committee ("DWCC"), and federal/provincial subcommittee on drinking water, re: water quality standards

(e) Sampling and analysis requirements, protocols and procedures

(f) Reporting and notification procedures

3. Privatization of government laboratory services

(a) Historical roles of public and private laboratories in Ontario re: drinking water

(b) Cessation of routine municipal bacteriological testing and purpose of privatization

(c) Consideration of relevant issues, including:

(i) Capacity and capability of private laboratories

(ii) Certification and accreditation requirements

(iii) Communication to municipalities

(iv) Communication to local Medical Officers of Health and local MOE Environmental Officers, including guidance to client municipalities on choice of testing facilities

(v) Communication to the public

(vi) Budgetary impact on municipalities, particularly small and rural municipalities

(vii) Budgetary impact on MOE and MOHLTC

(d) Provincial responses to internal and external comment

4. Monitoring and assessment of Privatization Initiative: post-1996

(a) Responses from MOE and MOHLTC (then MOH) laboratories, local MOE offices and local Medical Officers of Health, including compliance, reporting and quality assurance concerns

    (b)   Responses from affected groups (e.g., municipalities, public health inspectors, private laboratories)

    (c)   Monitoring the accuracy and effectiveness of private laboratories

    (d)   Post-1996 reporting and notification procedures

Section III

Role of MOE in Standards, Monitoring, Compliance and Enforcement Re: Drinking Water

1.   Overview: Role of MOE in relation to MOHLTC, municipal owner/operator, and local Medical Officers of Health and Health Units, Ontario Clean Water Agency ("OCWA"), and Federal government

2.   Role of Ontario Drinking Water Co-ordinating Committee (DWCC)

    (a)   ODWOs and Bulletin 65-W-4 entitled "Chlorination of Potable Water Supplies" ("Chlorination Bulletin")

    (b)   Enforcement and implementation of ODWOs and Chlorination Bulletin.

    (c)   Minimum recommended sampling requirements program

3.   Training standards

    (a)   Training and continuing education of MOE managers and Environmental Officers

4.   Monitoring of water works

    (a)   Routine operational monitoring and reporting

        i)   nature and frequency of testing

        ii)   reporting and communication of data

iii)   record keeping

(b)   MOE inspections

i)   Inspection methodology

ii)   Dedicated inspections and follow-up

iii)   Utilization of unannounced site visits

iv)   Inspections under the Sewage and Water Inspection Program
        (SWIP)

v)   Government inspections after May 2000

vi)   Provincial responses to internal and external comment

vii)   Reporting, communication and record-keeping

(c)   Drinking Water Surveillance Program (DWSP)

(d)   Roles and responsibilities of MOE supervisors, district managers,
       regional directors, other directors (e.g. Water Resources Branch),
       and abatement officers

(e)   Annual reporting by the operator to the MOE, and follow-up

5.   MOE operational procedures

(a)   Delivery strategies and program prioritization

(b)   Work assignment and degree of specialization

(c)   Staff complement, vacancies and overtime opportunities

(d)   Record-keeping and institutional memory

(e)   Transfer of files and review of new files

(f)   Monitoring between inspections

(g)   Availability of expertise for operators and MOE staff

(h)   Consolidation and communication of policy

(i)   Relationship with local Medical Officer of Health

(j)   MOE relationship with MOHLTC and federal Departments of Health and Environment

(k)   Role of SAC

6.   Compliance and enforcement

(a)   Historical overview of compliance policies

(b)   Responses to specific non-conformance and non-compliance

(c)   Voluntary versus mandatory abatement strategies

(d)   Use of Director's Orders

7.   Environmental Commissioner/ Provincial Auditor

(a)   Impact of Environmental Bill of Rights on MOE policy re: drinking water, including exemptions

(b)   Provincial response to the Environmental Commissioner's annual reports re: drinking water

(c)   Provincial response to Provincial Auditor's reports re: drinking water

(d)   Other

8.   Changes to legal and operations regimes which may have affected Walkerton

(a)   Regulatory Reform

i)   Bill 25, *Red Tape Reduction Act*

ii)   Bill 57, *Environmental Approvals Improvement Act*

iii)   Bill 107, *Water and Sewage Improvement Act*

iv)   Bill 152, *Services Improvement Act*

v)   Bill 146, *Farming and Food Production Protection Act*

vi)   Bill 20, *Planning Act*

vii)   Provincial Water Protection Fund

(b)   Reductions in MOE budgets, personnel and resources

i)   Reductions in operating and capital budgets

ii)   Staff reductions generally

iii)   Reductions in staff responsible for water

iv)   Reductions in enforcement staff and prosecutions

v)   Deskilling and deprofessionalization

vi)   Recruitment, retention and morale of staff

vii)   Delivery Strategies and communal water

viii) Issues raised or considered by DWCC

(c)   Restructuring

i)   Withdrawal of funding for sewer and water infrastructure

ii)   Municipal amalgamations

iii)   Who Does What panel: Downloading of responsibilities to
       municipalities

iv)   Alternative Service Delivery initiatives

v)   Centralization of decision-making

vi)   Operational business changes to Ministry of Municipal Affairs & Housing ("MMAH"), MNR, MOHLTC, OMAFRA, and the MOE

vii) Provincial responses to internal and external comment

Section IV

Municipal Operation of Water Works

1. Overview: Roles of municipality, PUC, MOE, MMAH, Ministry of Agriculture, Food and Rural Affairs (OMAFRA), and OCWA

2. Governance and funding of municipal water works

    (a) Municipal government / PUC

         (i)   Overall scheme under *Public Utilities Act*, R.S.O. 1990, c.P.52

         (ii)   Municipal finance and drinking water infrastructure

         (iii) Minimum standards for municipal financing of infrastructure, maintenance and operations

         (iv)   Utility rate issues

         (v)   Relationship between the municipality and the PUC, including accountability of PUC to the municipality

    (b) Provincial grant and loan programs

    (c) Federal grant and loan programs

3. Provincial regulation of the owner/ operator

(a) Water Works and Sewage Works, O.Reg. 435/93

(b) Oversight of municipal pricing, financing and investment in infrastructure

(c) Statutory duties and responsibilities of PUC commissioners and other municipally-elected officials

(d) Orientation and continuing education of PUC commissioners

(e) Minimum operational requirements (i.e. infrastructure and technology, recordkeeping, training and supervision of staff, contingency planning)

(f) Local operator training, certification, continuing education and monitoring, and grandparenting

(g) Water Works and Sewage Works, O.Reg. 435/93 re: training standards for local operators

4. Changing municipal role and capacity re: operation of water works

(a) Effect of municipal amalgamation

(b) Effect of downloading of responsibilities, including transfer of septic inspections to municipalities (*Environmental Protection Act*, R.S.O. 1990, c.E.19)

(c) Effect of Bill 35, *Energy Competition Act*

Section V

Public Health

1. Overview: municipal communal drinking water

(a) Roles, duties and responsibilities of local Medical Officers of Health and Health Units

(b)   Roles of MOHLTC and Chief Medical Officer of Health

(c)   Roles of MOE, MMAH and OMAFRA re: safe drinking water

(d)   Role of Health Canada re: safe drinking water in Ontario

(e)   Knowledge about the health effects of *E. coli* in drinking water, and risk of pathogens generally, and timely communication of risks to operators, Health Units and local MOE inspectors

2.   Changes in the public health system re: drinking water

(a)   Impact of Who Does What process

(b)   Reductions in budgets, personnel and resources

(c)   Allocation of funding responsibilities between province and municipalities

(d)   Cessation of routine municipal bacteriological testing by Government laboratories and coordination between MOE and MOHLTC

3.   Adverse Drinking Water Results

(a)   Roles of public health inspector and local Medical Officer of Health and MOE Regional staff

(b)   Record keeping

(c)   Reporting by MOE, including inspection reports, and responses by local Medical Officer of Health

(d)   Adequacy of monitoring and enforcement (*Health Protection and Promotion Act*, R.S.O. 1990, c.H.7)

4.   Emergency planning

(a)   Adequacy of policies and procedures

(b)   Communication of information

(c)   Boil Water Advisories

(d)   Role of SAC

Section VI

Agriculture - Land Use and Groundwater Protection

1.   Overview: Roles of OMAFRA, MOE, MOHLTC, Medical Officers of Health, Ministry of Natural Resources (Conservation Authorities), the Ontario Municipal Board, Farm Practices Protection Board, and the MMAH

2.   Provincial role in groundwater protection

    (a)   Provincial groundwater quality management framework, including well head protection

    (b)   Provincial responses to internal and external comment re: monitoring of groundwater quality

3.   Municipal role in groundwater protection

4.   Environmental standards for agricultural operation

    (a)   Applicable standards and exemptions

    (b)   Best management practices, normal farm practices, and the provincial and municipal role

    (c)   Municipal by-laws, agricultural uses and safe drinking water

    (d)   Manure management standards and procedures

    (e)   Agriculturally derived pathogens and drinking water

    (f)   Aquifer vulnerability assessment and risk-based decisions on land use

(g)   *E. coli*, campylobacter, and other pathogens re: drinking water

(h)   Other tools

COMMISSIONER'S STATEMENT RE: DECISION TO CALL THE PREMIER

APPENDIX K (II)

THE WALKERTON INQUIRY

Ontario

LA COMMISSION D'ENQUÊTE WALKERTON

Commissioner's Statement

Delivered June 6, 2001 in the Inquiry hearing room in Walkerton

We are approaching the conclusion of the Inquiry's hearings relating to the events in Walkerton.

During the course of Part IB, the government policy section, we have heard from dozens of witnesses, including some from the most senior levels of the civil service. Earlier, we announced that we will be calling two former Ministers of the Environment, Brenda Elliot and Norm Sterling. They will give evidence during the week of June 25.

We are now satisfied that, in order to ensure that the work of this Inquiry is thorough and complete, it is important that we also call Premier Harris. Given that it is the Premier who is to be called, I think it is appropriate to briefly set out the reasons for our decision.

As the terms of reference make clear, the government policy section of my mandate is extremely broad. It is to look at the effect, if any, of government policies, practices and procedures on the events in Walkerton. There are many such policies which must be looked at in order to fulfill this part of the mandate. To date, we have heard a good deal of evidence during Part IB about several policies implemented through different Ministries.

There are, however, some policies and some decisions, which could be found to have a connection to Walkerton, that were not made within the Ministries or indeed even by the Ministers.

Here I refer to decisions such as the significant budget reductions in 1996 and 1997, and the program of regulatory reform, implemented around the same time. These decisions were made at the very highest level of the Government, by the Cabinet, and apparently originated within the Central Agencies and the Premier's Office.

The Premier, as the leader of the Government and the Chair of the Cabinet, is the person in the best position to answer questions about policies of this nature. For that reason, we believe it is important that the Premier testify.

That said, there are three points I want to make clear. First, the questioning of the Premier will be limited to those policies that may have some connection to the events in Walkerton. This will not be a wide-ranging examination of government policy in general. It will be focused.

Second, it is important that people keep the decision to call the Premier in proper perspective. There is a danger that some may exaggerate the significance of his testimony or even the reason he is being called.

It should be kept in mind that this is an inquiry, not a proceeding alleging wrongdoing of any sort. The Premier is being called so that he can be asked about specific policies and decisions, and their possible impacts on Walkerton, and for no other reason.

Finally, I want to make clear that the fact the Premier is being called does not mean I have concluded that the policies about which he will be questioned in fact caused or contributed to what happened in Walkerton. My conclusions will be set out in my report. It is important, however, to hear the evidence of the Premier to better enable me to reach these conclusions.

Yesterday, we informed Government counsel of our decision. We are awaiting a response as to when the Premier will be available. We have requested that he attend during the weeks of June 25 or July 2, the final weeks of the scheduled hearings, but we are of course prepared to accommodate his schedule.

CLOSING SUBMISSIONS NOTICE

APPENDIX L (I)

THE WALKERTON INQUIRY

Ontario

**LA COMMISSION
D'ENQUÊTE WALKERTON**

May 24, 2001

Notice to Parties in Part I

Closing Submissions

The Commissioner looks forward to detailed closing submissions from the parties and anticipates that they will be very helpful.

Parties should submit their closing submissions in writing no later than August 1, 2001 so that they can be distributed to all of the parties by August 8. The submissions should address the evidence in Part I regarding the cause of the water contamination in Walkerton and the effect, if any, of government policies, practices and procedures. Any submissions or proposed recommendations relating to the future safety of drinking water are more appropriately presented during the public hearings in Part II of the Inquiry.

A schedule for oral submissions in August is attached. The order of the submissions and length of time allotted to each party has been determined in light of the scope of the party's interest or perspective with respect to Part I. Parties should refer to the written submissions of other parties in the event that they wish to respond to those submissions during oral argument. Parties may also reply in writing to the oral submissions of other parties.

Parties with funding in Part IA have been allocated funding of up to 40 hours, according to the scope of their interest or perspective, for the preparation of closing submissions. Parties with funding in Part IB will be allocated funding for preparation at the close of the Part IB hearings. Parties with funding will receive funding to participate in the oral submissions for those days on which they make submissions and not for the closing submissions in their entirety.

If you have concerns regarding the above process, please let us know by May 24. You may contact Gus Van Harten at 416-325-8646 and, failing resolution of the issue, you may arrange a conference call with the Commissioner.

CLOSING SUBMISSIONS SCHEDULE

APPENDIX L (II)

Schedule – Closing Submissions

August 15 to 17
August 21 to 24
August 27

10 am to 1 pm
2 to 5:30 pm

A. Time allocations

Six hours:	Government (divided between IA and IB)
Four hours:	Chief Coroner Town + individuals
Three and a half hours:	CWC Foundation
Three hours:	PUC/ Commissioners Stanley Koebel Dr. McQuigge/ Health Unit/ ALPHA
Two hours:	AMO Environmental Coalition Bargaining Agents Coalition

One hour: OFEC
                         ALERT/ Sierra Club
                         Energy Probe Research Foundation
                         Frank Koebel
                         Phil Bye
                         Willard Page

30 minutes: Allan Buckle
                         Injured Victims
                         Michelle Zillinger
                         John Earl
                         Larry Struthers
                         James Schmidt

B. Schedule

Date	*Hours*	*Party*
Wed., August 15	3.5 hours	Foundation
	2.5 hours	CWC
Thurs., August 16	1 hour	CWC
	2 hours	Government – Part IA
	3 hours	Town + individuals
Fri., August 17	1 hour	Town + individuals
	3 hours	PUC/ Commissioners
	1 hour	ALERT/ Sierra Club
Tues., August 21	1 hour	Frank Koebel
	3 hours	Stanley Koebel
	1 hour	OFEC

Date	Hours	Party
	30 minutes	Injured Victims Group
Wed., August 22	3 hours	Dr. McQuigge/ BGOSHU/ ALPHA
	1 hour	Phil Bye
	1 hour	Willard Page
	30 minutes	Michelle Zillinger
	30 minutes	John Earl
	30 minutes	Larry Struthers
Thurs., August 23	30 minutes	James Schmidt
(Note 9:30 a.m. start)	2 hours	Bargaining Agents
	1 hour	EPRF
	2 hours	Environmental Coalition
	1 hour	AMO
Fri., August 24	1 hour	AMO
	30 minutes	Allan Buckle
	4 hours	Government – Part IB
Mon., August 27	4 hours	Chief Coroner

CLOSING SUBMISSIONS FUNDING NOTICE #1

APPENDIX L (III)

THE WALKERTON INQUIRY

Ontario

**LA COMMISSION
D'ENQUÊTE WALKERTON**

April 6, 2001

Notice to Parties with Funding in Part I

Funding for Closing Submissions

We have received a number of inquiries with respect to funding for the preparation of closing submissions.

On February 12, 2001, the Commissioner recommended that the Attorney General provide such funding to parties for whom funding has been recommended in Part I. On March 28, the Attorney General wrote to accept the Commissioner's recommendation that up to 40 hours of funding be provided to prepare closing submissions in each of Parts IA and IB. The amount allotted to each party is to be determined by the Commissioner in light of the degree of participation by a party in the respective Part.

In order to allow parties to begin to prepare their closing submissions while the evidence is fresh in their minds, the Commissioner is proposing to allot funding for closing submissions for Part IA as follows:

Walkerton Community Foundation – 40 hours

Public Utilities Commission/ PUC Commissioners – 40 hours

Stanley Koebel – 40 hours

Frank Koebel – 20 hours

Ontario Farm Environmental Coalition – 15 hours

ALERT/ Sierra Club – 15 hours

Allan Buckle – 5 hours

The Commissioner will allot funding for Part IB at or near the completion of the evidence in Part IB.

The Commissioner looks forward to detailed closing submissions from the parties and anticipates that they will be very helpful. At present the closing submissions are scheduled for the weeks of August 13 and 20 although this is subject to change.

If you have concerns about this arrangement, you should contact Gus Van Harten at 416-325-8646 by Thursday, April 12, 2001. Failing resolution with Mr. Van Harten, you may arrange a conference call with the Commissioner.

CLOSING SUBMISSIONS FUNDING NOTICE #2

APPENDIX L (IV)

THE WALKERTON INQUIRY

Ontario

**LA COMMISSION
D'ENQUÊTE WALKERTON**

June 26, 2001

Notice to Parties with Funding in Part I

Funding for Closing Submissions

On April 6, 2001, you were advised of funding allotments for the preparation of closing submissions <u>for Part IA</u> as follows:

Walkerton Community Foundation – 40 hours

Public Utilities Commission/ PUC Commissioners – 40 hours

Stanley Koebel – 40 hours

Frank Koebel – 20 hours

Ontario Farm Environmental Coalition – 15 hours

ALERT/ Sierra Club – 15 hours

Allan Buckle – 5 hours

The Commissioner proposes funding for closing submissions <u>for Part IB</u> as follows:

Walkerton Community Foundation – 40 hours

Environmental Coalition – 30 hours

Bargaining Agents Coalition – 30 hours

Public Utilities Commission/ PUC Commissioners – 30 hours

Stanley Koebel – 30 hours

Association of Municipalities of Ontario – 20 hours

Energy Probe Research Foundation – 10 hours

Ontario Farm Environmental Coalition – 10 hours

ALERT/ Sierra Club – 10 hours

Frank Koebel – 5 hours

Allan Buckle – 5 hours

In light of the scope and usefulness of their perspective, the Commissioner further proposes funding for closing submissions <u>for Part IA</u> as follows:

Environmental Coalition – 20 hours

Bargaining Agents Coalition – 20 hours

Funding for closing submissions is intended to support the preparation of thorough submissions <u>including the review of transcripts for hearing days on which a party was not present</u>. If you have any concerns about the funding allotments, you should contact Gus Van Harten at 416-325-8646 by Thursday, July 5. Failing resolution with Mr. Van Harten, you may arrange a conference call with the Commissioner.

The Commissioner looks forward to detailed closing submissions from the parties. Oral submissions will take place from August 15 to August 27 as outlined in our Notice and Schedule of May 24.

<u>We remind you that written submissions are due no later than August 1, 2001</u>. We intend to distribute the submissions to all of the parties by August 10 (rather than August 8 as previously indicated). If you foresee any serious difficulties with respect to these deadlines, please contact Mr. Van Harten at the earliest opportunity.